Trials

The International Library of Essays in Law and Society
Series Editor: Austin Sarat

Titles in the Series:

Law and Religion
Gad Barzilai

Police and Policing Law
Jeannine Bell

Law and Society Approaches to Cyberspace
Paul Schiff Berman

Law and Families
Susan B. Boyd and Helen Rhoades

Regulation and Regulatory Processes
Cary Coglianese and Robert Kagan

Rhetoric of Law
Marianne Constable and Felipe Gutterriez

Law in Social Theory
Roger Cotterrell

Ethnography and Law
Eve Darian-Smith

International Law and Society
Laura Dickinson

Legal Lives of Private Organizations
Lauren Edelman and Mark C. Suchman

Courts and Judges
Lee Epstein

Consciousness and Ideology
Patricia Ewick

Prosecutors and Prosecution
Lisa Frohmann

Intellectual Property
William T. Gallagher

Race, Law and Society
Ian Haney López

The Jury System
Valerie P. Hans

Crime and Criminal Justice
William T. Lyons, Jr.

Law and Social Movements
Michael McCann

The Role of Social Science in Law
Elizabeth Mertz

Sexuality and Identity
Leslie J. Moran

Law and Poverty
Frank Munger

Rights
Laura Beth Nielsen

Governing Risks
Pat O'Malley

Lawyers and the Legal Profession, Volumes I and II
Tanina Rostain

Capital Punishment, Volumes I and II
Austin Sarat

Legality and Democracy
Stuart A. Scheingold

The Law and Society Canon
Carroll Seron

Popular Culture and Law
Richard K. Sherwin

Law and Science, Volumes I and II
Susan Silbey

Immigration
Susan Sterett

Gender and Feminist Theory in Law and Society
Madhavi Sunder

Procedural Justice, Volumes I and II
Tom R. Tyler

Trials
Martha Merrill Umphrey

Trials

Edited by

Martha Merrill Umphrey

Amherst College, USA

ASHGATE

Wherever possible, these reprints are made from a copy of the original printing, but these can themselves be of very variable quality. Whilst the publisher has made every effort to ensure the quality of the reprint, some variability may inevitably remain.

Published by
Ashgate Publishing Limited
Gower House
Croft Road
Aldershot
Hampshire GU11 3HR
England

Ashgate Publishing Company
Suite 420
101 Cherry Street
Burlington, VT 05401-4405
USA

Ashgate website: http://www.ashgate.com

British Library Cataloguing in Publication Data
Trials. – (The international library of essays in law and society)
1. Trials
I. Umphrey, Martha Merrill
347'. 07

Library of Congress Control Number: 2007941046

ISBN 978-0-7546-2512-4

Mixed Sources
Product group from well-managed forests and other controlled sources
www.fsc.org Cert no. SGS-COC-2482
© 1996 Forest Stewardship Council
FSC

Printed and bound in Great Britain by
TJ International Ltd, Padstow, Cornwall

Contents

Acknowledgements

The editor and publishers wish to thank the following for permission to use copyright material.

Anthony G. Amsterdam and Randy Hertz for the essay: Anthony G. Amsterdam and Randy Hertz (1993), 'An Analysis of Closing Arguments to a Jury', *New York Law School Law Review*, **27**, pp. 55–122. Copyright © 1993 Anthony G. Amsterdam and Randy Hertz.

Blackwell Publishing Ltd for the essays: Austin Sarat (1993), 'Speaking of Death: Narratives of Violence in Capital Trials', *Law and Society Review*, **27**, pp. 19–58. Copyright © 1993 Blackwell Publishing Ltd; Kim Lane Scheppele (1992), 'Just the Facts, Ma'am: Sexualized Violence, Evidentiary Habits, and the Revision of Truth', *New York Law School Law Review*, **27**, pp. 123–72. Copyright © 1992 Blackwell Publishing Ltd; Stéphane Leman-Langlois (2002), 'Constructing a Common Language: The Function of Nuremberg in the Problematization of Postapartheid Justice', *Law and Social Inquiry*, **27**, pp. 79–100. Copyright © 2002 Blackwell Publishing Ltd; David Lipset (2004), '"The Trial": A Parody of the Law amid the Mockery of Men in Post-Colonial Papua New Guinea', *Journal of the Royal Anthropological Institute*, **10**, pp. 63–89. Copyright © 2004 Blackwell Publishing Ltd.

School of Law, Stanford University for the essays: Milner S. Ball (1975), 'The Play's the Thing: An Unscientific Reflection on Courts under the Rubric of Theater', *Stanford Law Review*, **28**, pp. 81–115. Copyright © 1975 Stanford Law Review; Richard K. Sherwin (1994–95), 'Law Frames: Historical Truth and Narrative Necessity in a Criminal Case', *Stanford Law Review*, **47**, pp. 39–83. Copyright © 1994 Stanford Law Review.

Shoshana Felman for the essay: Shoshana Felman (1997), 'Forms of Judicial Blindness, or the Evidence of What Cannot Be Seen: Traumatic Narratives and Legal Repetitions in the O.J. Simpson Case and in Tolstoy's *The Kreutzer Sonata*', *Critical Inquiry*, **23**, pp. 738–88. Copyright © 1997 Shoshana Felman. This article constitutes the second chapter of Shoshana Felman's book, *The Juridical Unconscious: Trials and Traumas in the Twentieth Century*, Cambridge, MA: Harvard University Press (2002), pp. 54–105.

William Finnegan for the essay: William Finnegan (1994), 'A Reporter at Large: Doubt', *The New Yorker*, 31 January, pp. 48–67. Copyright © 1994 William Finnegan. Originally published in *The New Yorker*.

Every effort has been made to trace all the copyright holders, but if any have been inadvertently overlooked the publishers will be pleased to make the necessary arrangement at the first opportunity.

Series Preface

The International Library of Essays in Law and Society is designed to provide a broad overview of this important field of interdisciplinary inquiry. Titles in the series will provide access to the best existing scholarship on a wide variety of subjects integral to the understanding of how legal institutions work in and through social arrangements. They collect and synthesize research published in the leading journals of the law and society field. Taken together, these volumes show the richness and complexity of inquiry into law's social life.

Each volume is edited by a recognized expert who has selected a range of scholarship designed to illustrate the most important questions, theoretical approaches, and methods in her/his area of expertise. Each has written an introductory essay which both outlines those questions, approaches, and methods and provides a distinctive analysis of the scholarship presented in the book. Each was asked to identify approximately 20 pieces of work for inclusion in their volume. This has necessitated hard choices since law and society inquiry is vibrant and flourishing.

The International Library of Essays in Law and Society brings together scholars representing different disciplinary traditions and working in different cultural contexts. Since law and society is itself an international field of inquiry it is appropriate that the editors of the volumes in this series come from many different nations and academic contexts. The work of the editors both charts a tradition and opens up new questions. It is my hope that this work will provide a valuable resource for longtime practitioners of law and society scholarship and newcomers to the field.

AUSTIN SARAT
William Nelson Cromwell Professor of Jurisprudence and Political Science
Amherst College

Introduction

To examine the trial as a legal form is to explore the landscape of an increasingly endangered species. If trials were ever the norm in resolving disputes in the United States, they now account for a mere fraction of the means of disposition of most legal cases, and their proportion dwindles decade after decade in favour of plea bargaining, settlement and other forms of negotiated resolution (Friedman, 2004).[1] Those more efficient and less dramatic alternative forms have quietly colonized the field of legal judgment in ways that remain remarkably invisible in public culture.[2] Yet if popular culture is in any way symptomatic of a national imagination, Americans (at least) find trials, or certain kinds of trials, utterly compelling in spite of their empirical scarcity. If our public culture appears weirdly obsessed with the tabloid world of Judge Judy, of Court TV, of O.J. Simpson and Michael Jackson, the deep fascination with which we watch these trials signals their potency and symbolic centrality as political arenas where we encounter and intimately engage the most deeply charged troubles in our national psyche (see Fox and Van Sickel, 2001; Rapping, 2003).[3]

Why invest so much meaning in the trial, an unpredictable and antic process predominantly designed to contain and salve the bitter arguments and deep wounds of individual citizens? Taken together, the essays that follow suggest that trials (particularly those in the Anglo-American adversarial tradition, which are the focus of this volume) are sites of a kind of public enchantment. The trials that occupy our attention – and if they are very few, they are nevertheless magnificent in their seeming cultural significance – draw us into a bounded space set apart from everyday life because of their rituals, their rules and their theatricality. In an almost magical way they transform bodily, material and psychological wrongs into dramatic and contested stories that are performed in court, spectacularized in popular culture

---

1 In a study commissioned by the American Bar Association Section of Litigation under the rubric of 'The Vanishing Trial', Marc Galanter (2004) has found that in 2002 only 1.8 per cent of federal civil cases were resolved by trial, down from 11.5 per cent in 1962, and only 5 per cent of federal criminal cases went to trial in 2002 compared with 15 per cent in 1962. Similar declines have occurred in both sorts of trials at the state level. These figures indicate an acceleration of a long trend away from trial as a mode of resolving legal controversy. According to Friedman (1993, p. 253), plea bargaining accounts for over 90 per cent of all convictions.

2 On current anti-adjudicative tendencies, see Resnik (1986).

3 While it is difficult to assess empirically the assertion that Americans in general are fascinated by trials, most commentators look to two factors in making such claims: the broad publication across media outlets and genres of reports on a number of sensational trials and public opinion polls gauging the public's familiarity with such trials. Fox and Van Sickel (2001, p. 2), for example, report that in the mid-1990s, more citizens could identify JonBenet Ramsay than the Vice President of the United States, and that roughly six times as many Americans knew the name of the judge presiding over O.J. Simpson's trial as knew the name of the Chief Justice of the US Supreme Court. In other words, the media saturates the public with its coverage of trials, and its interpretation of them, so that even those not specifically inclined towards trial-watching are likely to have some familiarity with notorious cases.

and received by a public both easily seduced by courtroom drama and deeply invested in its own acts of judgment. Those who follow major trials – and that by definition includes most media, to one extent or another –identify (in sometimes shifting ways) with courtroom actors, are made spellbound by emotional stories of scandal and sordid deeds, wait in suspense for the closure that comes with legal judgment and take pleasure in offering their own verdicts, not only on a defendant or a respondent but also on the law itself. Trials enthral us because they have been designed to address us both indirectly and directly as a public, staging social disorder in ways both safe and vivifying.

This volume is designed to bring into view the dialogic relation between trials and culture that enables these particular kinds of enchantment with law. Given their public nature, trials are the sites where law encounters and interacts with the culture in which it is embedded, places where legal rules exfoliate into contested stories performed before audiences both inside and outside the courtroom. Through trials, law constitutes itself via its orientation to its public; and through trials, the public comes to know its relation to legal order and judgment.[4] In collectively inquiring into the contours of that dialogic relation, the essays that follow trace the paths of cultural stories as they circulate in and through trial settings, examine how trials emerge out of particular cultural contexts and moments, and suggest ways in which trials themselves, as both singular events and generic forms, circulate and signify in culture.

The Performative Ethics and Aesthetics of Trials

The analogy of the trial to theatre is not new.[5] If in asserting it one attends inadequately to the actuality of the legal conflict's underlying social events and the very real violence undergirding legal judgment,[6] the analogy nevertheless points to a starting place in any account of the public's fascination with trials. Partly, of course, trials enchant us because of their underlying drama. They offer access to the tensions and wounds of the private sphere – the transgressions of social norms, the rule-breakings, passions, desires and alibis – all framed through the camera obscura of memory and human subjectivity. The pleasures of that access emerge from our capacity to see and hear about what has only been imaginable, or what has been utterly unimaginable. As we follow trials, whether civil or criminal, we are put in the deliciously contradictory position of the ethical peeping Tom, one who can feel the thrill of subversive watching from a sanctioned and safe position (Clover, 1998). And yet other venues offer us these kinds of pleasures – film, literature, even a keen glance at everyday life. Beyond

---

4 On dialogism, see Bakhtin (1981); see also Umphrey (1999).

5 As the analogy was drawn by Sir Edward Parry, for example, 'Even to-day when we think of a trial or a lawsuit we picture it to ourselves in terms of drama, applauding the hero or heroine, execrating the villain of the piece, chuckling at the comedian in the witness-box and expressing approval of the modest demeanour of the small-part man who walks on to the dim bench and gives the necessary cues to the great actors in the limelight. And as we read the report of a law case we recall the familiar scenery of a court house, the traditional costumes of the characters and that dramatic setting which we inwardly approve of as essential to the earliest administration of justice' (1924, pp. 7–8). See Milner Ball, Chapter 1 in this volume, for a more complex rendering of this analogy.

6 As Robert Ferguson (2007, p. 69) notes, theatricality works through a suspension of disbelief while in trials, facts and the mundane realities from which they arise are everything. On the violence of legal judgment, see Cover (1992).

substance, the very form of the trial attracts and attaches us to it. More elegant than legislative debate or public protest, more engaging than bully pulpit preaching, more dramatic than a classroom, more gripping in its realism than most imaginative culture, the trial enchants us precisely because it is a performative, dialogic and highly stylized genre of public discourse.

Trials are spaces set apart from the everyday, constituted by special rules and epistemic commitments that transform both the underlying 'reality' of any case and the audience that attends it. A trial brings the past to life in language and through stories governed by quite specific generic constraints.[7] Yet it distinguishes itself from other cultural forms that might do similar work – popular and scholarly history, historical fiction, documentary film – in its performative aspects. The performative nature of trials goes well beyond the claim that trials mimic certain dramatic conventions, and is manifest in three distinctive but interrelated ways: the trial's orientation to audience; its immediacy and contingency, or 'liveness'; and its legal conventionality, which is a product of rule-stylization and legal consequentialism. Together, these three characteristics set trials apart from other kinds of cultural forms and confer on any given trial a pointedness, an expressiveness and meaningfulness that brings law alive.

Audience Orientation

In liberal democracies most trials are at least nominally public events,[8] and in their most robust and elaborate form they interpolate multiple audiences – judges, juries and the wider public – who watch, listen and attend to evidence as each side offers it for adjudication. If spectacular trials are the most obviously theatrical in their media-driven, self-conscious histrionics (Friedman, 2004, p. 700), all trials, whether spectacular or banal, are by their very nature dialogic: attorneys and witnesses render competing versions of the past in and through language to their audiences even as they structure those renderings with reference both to the rules governing what can and cannot be said at trial and to the imagined expectations of their listeners. By its mere presence the audience triangulates the proceeding, changing what might have been a negotiated settlement (or an endless cycle of vengeance) between contending parties into an event that both demands judgment and solicits legitimation.

Within the Anglo-American trial tradition, the trial's most symbolically significant audience is the jury. It is imagined as a hybrid of the official and the popular, the crucial link between

---

7 Certain rituals and conventions must be observed for the trial's ultimate performative, the verdict, to be (in J.L. Austin's terms) a 'felicitous' speech act. Thus, for example, by violating the conventions and decorum of the courtroom, the Chicago Seven called into question the very legitimacy of their prosecution (see Lahav, 2004).

8 As Lawrence Friedman rightly reminds us, we ought not condense the entire criminal process into one imagining of a trial; historically, public justice was often done in a relatively summary manner (not unlike modes of private or quasi-public 'justice' – duelling, lynching, whitecapping and the like – common through the early part of the twentieth century in the United States). Yet however rudimentary the legal process may be, it is not carried out in secret (see, generally, Friedman, 1993). Recent policies in the United States and elsewhere have highlighted various state strategies to try 'enemy combatants' in non-public military tribunals (see, for example, Cole, 2003). Nevertheless, the US Supreme Court has ruled that federal courts retain jurisdiction over those held as 'enemy combatants', which in essence vindicates the traditional practice of public judicial review in limit cases in which the person held is not a US citizen (see *Hamdan* v. *Rumsfeld*, 126 S. Ct. 2749 (2006)).

formal institutions of legality and popular sovereignty. As such, it operates not only to check potential abuses of state power, but also to educate ordinary folk into proper citizenship. Indeed the jury trial has often been taken as a synecdoche for the workings of American democracy itself, occupying a central place in the story of the United States as a self-governing people. As Tocqueville remarked over 150 years ago, the jury is 'above all a political institution', embodying the sovereignty of the people, and the judgments produced at trial are such as to 'instill some of the habits of the judicial mind into every citizen ... the very best way of preparing a people to be free' (1988, pp. 273–74).[9] While debates about the efficacy, efficiency and fairness of the jury trial have grown as the American jury has democratized (see Adler, 1994; Abramson, 2000), those who lionize it remain convinced that it expresses 'the values and commonsense of the people in whose name the law was written' (Abramson, 2000, p. 6),[10] and it remains a significant site of democratic identification.

Those possibilities of identification make possible an easy slippage from jury-as-audience to public-as-audience, and as such it is sometimes clearly the case that legal actors project the trial outward, beyond the bounds of the courtroom. They play to a larger audience. At the extreme, states conduct trials in the manner of pedagogical events, placing a broader community at the centre rather than the periphery of the legal process. Thus in the colonial era, for example, early American trials offered what Lawrence Friedman (1993, p. 25) has called 'divine social theater' occasions for teaching the difference between good and bad, for punishing sin, and for repenting and reintegrating into the community. Justice was done openly and quickly, designed both to impress certain norms upon and into the local community and to demonstrate the power and legitimacy of the state. Show trials, staged as spectacles of justice for a broad public, are only the most overt modern manifestation of this hortatory posture (see Sklar, 1986; Hariman, 1990b; Arendt, 1994). Their self-conscious theatricality in setting and dramaturgy underscores the grand scale of adjudication in play; not only individual defendants, but politics and historical memory come to be judged as part of larger projects of nation-building and state legitimation.[11]

But even under conditions of less notoriety, trials engage, and are intended to engage, a broader public. Sometimes that engagement takes place on specifically political terms. Paul Gewirtz (1996, pp. 149–50) has argued, for example, that even as the punishments meted

---

[9] Tocqueville understood the arena of jury judgment as a critical vehicle for educating people into proper citizenship which, as he defined it in this context, consists of respect for court decisions and for the idea of right throughout all classes, a belief in equity, a tendency to take on rather than shirk responsibility and a feeling that all have a duty towards society and a share in its government. On juries, see also Abramson (2000) and Adler (1994).

[10] News coverage following findings of guilt in the corporate fraud and conspiracy charges levied against Enron executives emphasizes this view of the common-sense decision-making capacity of 'regular' Americans. Again and again in interviews jurors compared the greed and failures of highly-paid executives with their own senses of responsibility and good-faith efforts at work as public school principals, payroll managers, dairy farmers, clerks, dental hygienists and so forth (see, for example, *New York Times*, 2006; see also Burnett, 2001).

[11] In noting the theatricality of the Eichmann trial, Hannah Arendt writes that 'the show Ben-Gurion had had in mind to begin with did take place, or, rather, the "lessons" he thought should be taught to Jew and Gentiles, to Israelis and Arabs, in short, to the whole world' (1994, p. 9). For an insightful consideration of high-profile trials generally, see Ferguson (2007, Part 1).

out to individuals in trials take the public as an object of general deterrence, the public is also the active agent behind such punishments, which are said to express the morality of the community. And if the public sees trials as expressions of those community values, it also acts as a watchdog placing government power under scrutiny in the open forum of the courtroom. The public may also attend to trials for reasons that feel more psychological or moral than political: we may gain comfort from them because they impose a kind of structure on social disorder and offer a means of addressing, if not always fully resolving, large and contentious social questions (Hariman, 1990a, pp. 23–24; Gewirtz, 1996, p. 151).[12]

The moral gravitas that attends this account of the public's relation to trials is both inseparable from and complicated by the ludic quality of trial proceedings. The great medievalist Johann Huizinga has called attention to the resemblance between a lawsuit and a contest whose agonistic nature necessarily signals a domain of play, a world with a well-defined quality of action different from 'ordinary life'. A trial has many of the components of play Huizinga identifies: it is an enchanted space, set apart from the everyday by virtue of the roles and disguises humans adopt and the rules by which they act (1955, p. 13). In arguing specifically for the linking of law and play, Huizinga conceives of trials as contests that, in their earliest forms, had less to do with conceptions of right and wrong and more to do with fate, wagers and battles of both rhetorical and physical sorts – all expressions of play.[13] If modern trials contain a moral and didactic component, that component is expressed (at least in American trials) through an agonistic adversarial process that communicates social narratives about right and wrong precisely through the vehicle of play. Edification and entertainment converge as the public witnesses two parties in a case do battle over the fact and meaning of past events.[14]

Liveness

If trials are performative because they are conducted before audiences, their 'liveness' forms an essential part of their capacity to enchant (Auslander, 1999, p. 113).[15] Liveness signals

---

12 In the context of mapping new methodological strategies in cultural-legal history, Ariela Gross (2001, pp. 651–54) has suggested three ways in which treating trials as performances allows us to attend to what might loosely be understood as the cultural dimension of trials: it draws our eyes towards the actual audiences for trials and the ways in which information is presented to and consumed by them; it helps us to understand trials as public performances that exert certain kinds of moral and psychological effects on various communities; and it conceives trials as fora for the performance of certain kinds of identities, and as arenas for the representation of selves.

13 See generally Huizinga's chapter 'Play and Law' (1955).

14 Of course, we do not follow routine trials with the same attention we give to spectacular trials, a fact suggesting that their entertainment value lies in more than the pleasures of contest. Certain trials have, since the printing of murder trial narratives in the late eighteenth century, captured the public gaze. Some have concerned political corruption and rebellion; some have exposed the underbelly of the 'respectable' classes; some have dramatized conflict born of social segregation and stratification; some have laid bare the most violent and anti-normative human tendencies. On the history of gothic narratives about murder in particular, see Haltunnen (1998). On spectacular trials generally, see Hariman (1990b).

15 Auslander (1999, pp. 114–30) explores the ways in which the Confrontation Clause requires that trials be live events, and that as a result testimony is best understood as a performance of recollection.

the irreducible specificity and contingency of trials as texts for public consumption and legal adjudication. In trials, like other forms of contest, the electricity of watching a live performance comes from witnessing, from an immediate perspective, those contingencies as they come into being, without knowing the outcome ahead of time.[16] The trial is thus, in this sense, a place of 'trying' or testing of testimony and evidence, by cross-examination and audience interpretation of the results. Robert Burns emphasizes the significance of the jury's live encounter with the evidence, arguing that performance gives trials an urgency that persuades not logically but histrionically.

> The 'enactment' of the trial provides the material for a dramatic sensibility on the jury's part, a 'primitive and direct' awareness 'before predication,' as Aristotle put it, of the actions and performances displayed before it. ... The trial requires that all the evidence come before the jury in the form of performances which, in this 'primitive' but profound way, ring true or false. (Burns, 1999, pp. 139–40, footnotes omitted)

What matters, argues Burns, is not so much the deliberative nature of the jury, but the fact of live encounter with complicated, self-reflexive, competing narratives – an encounter that, in its intensity and distinctiveness, provokes a kind of intuitive response to the particular fact situation that under the best conditions produces a verdict that 'gets it right'.

Liveness gives trials an immediacy and contingency that invests them with more suspense than other narrative genres even as the gravity of trial outcomes gives them more meaning than other forms of live contest. Shifting allegiances produced by the adversarial format, surprise evidence, frustrating rulings from the bench, gaffes by attorneys, witness breakdowns – all can produce a thrilling, radical uncertainty for the trial's various audiences, that much more intensified by the trial's demand for closure and judgment. Liveness also imparts what Milner Ball (Chapter 1 in this volume) describes as an important poetic or metaphoric element to trials. '[W]hat the advocate seeks ... is', he suggests, 'the passage from the materials of fact and law (the text) by means of courtroom presentation (the performance) to a persuasive statement of what ought to be done in a given situation (the metaphor)' (p. 13).

Legal Conventionality

But if contingency gives trials a particular electricity, it rarely threatens the entire project of adjudication itself, occurring as it does within the bounds of highly stylized and authority-governed proceedings. Those same rules and structures make the trial something quite different from other kinds of events or fora that attempt to reconstruct past events or render moral judgment. In that specific sense, trials are not mirrors of or windows into the social world. Rather, in trials we see the past through a scrim, some aspects spotlighted, others banished to shadow. Procedural rules regulate what, how and when evidence can be presented to a decision-maker, often excluding information irrelevant or prejudicial that we might otherwise commonly invoke when we discuss and evaluate past events and social conflicts – gossip, general personal histories, patterns of behaviour within and between social groups, and so

[16] As Peggy Phelan has argued, 'Performance's only life is in the present. Performance cannot be saved, recorded, documented, or otherwise participate in the circulation of representations of representations: once it does so, it becomes something other than performance' (1993, p. 146).

forth. Trial rules sift through precisely that kind of evidence, excluding it on the basis of the hearsay rule, rules about character evidence, rules about statistical inference and the like.

For some, this legal formalism places the reliability and referentiality of legal proceedings in question (see, for example, Pizzi, 1999). Yet however much the rules of evidence regulate what is laid before the eyes of decision-makers, truth-production in trials is most profoundly governed by their adversarial format, which shapes the rhythm and contours of the stories lawyers tell and the evidence they present. Even when the media may offer more information to the general public than a jury can see, the binarized architecture of the trial process directs the way we understand and interpret the evidence put before us. We are forced into a way of thinking about past events as having happened either this way or not-this way, with its attendant corollaries – for example, either the evidence is directly communicative or there are significant doubts about its handling; either he is lying or he is not; either she is guilty beyond a reasonable doubt or she is not legally guilty. While shades of grey can slip though this structuring, or can be imputed, there is no formal way to articulate a middle ground at trial, only a prosecutorial narrative and its defensive undoing.[17] In other words, particularly in the United States, with its strong investment in a lawyer-driven adversarial trial structure,[18] the truth that trials produce when announcing a verdict (Latin *veredictum*, 'to speak the truth') is a *legal* truth rather than some other kind, whether historical (a best approximation of what 'really' happened), psychosociological (the mental and social causes and effects of an act or event) or sacral (moral truths concerning good and evil).

The Dialogics of the Trial

As Huizinga has suggested, staging knowledge in the form of a contest can be deeply satisfying on an aesthetic and affective level. Some have argued that the trial form may indeed be so powerful as to colour, and even structure, a national public imagination. Film scholar Carol Clover, for example, argues that the very form of the Anglo-American trial has a 'fantastic generativity' that in turn shapes an enormous amount of American popular culture, particularly in television and film. 'The narrative substructure of so much of our cinema rhymes with the narrative substructure of our trial', Clover suggests, to such an extent that even films that do not concern trials exhibit certain of their central formal properties (1998, pp. 99–100).[19] If

---

[17] Critics of trials (rather than, for example, of the jury) often focus on adversarialism as the source of most of the ills plaguing the system. They suggest that our overreliance on attorneys produces harmful excesses of advocacy and a focus on winning at any cost; that pumped-up adversarial trials are too complex, legalistic and costly to be accessible to most litigants and defendants; and that binary and oppositional presentations of facts hinder rather than encourage our capacity to determine complex truths. In addition to Pizzi (1999), see, for example, Kagan (2001, pp. 61–98) and Menkel-Meadow (1996). And yet in assuming that trials should be evaluated solely on their capacity to do justice in the narrow sense of producing a resolution to specific legal problems, these criticisms exhibit a kind of functionalism about what trials do that misses the remarkable role trials play in culture.

[18] For a comparative critique of American trial processes, see Langbein (2003); see also Pizzi (1999).

[19] Clover argues broadly that the rhythm and structure of particularly Anglo-American films place the cinematic audience in the position of a jury because they tend to be organized in a trial-like way, beginning with opening statements, followed by an evidentiary phase full of jumbled bits and pieces laid

this kind of analysis obscures some of the conventions and specificities of legal proceedings that separate the courtroom from other domains of expression, debate and truth-production, it nevertheless suggests that the trial form has become what might be called a 'floating signifier' that we take up and introject into other sectors of our cultural lives in novel, non-legalistic ways. That task is made simpler by virtue of our positioning as outside-the-jury-room spectators in the first place.

Some costs may attach to that structurally illicit but inevitable positioning. Paul Gewirtz (1996, p. 152), for one, has expressed scepticism about the kinds of generalized and unchecked judgments made beyond the structured space of the jury room, built upon an intermittent and mediated relation to the actual trial ('I feel, therefore I may judge'). The conditions that produce those kinds of judgments can turn a trial into a mass political event rather than a carefully choreographed legal exercise, skewing lawyers and judges towards the media and the public reactions its coverage engenders, to the detriment of the courtroom process itself. (O.J. Simpson's criminal trial for the murder of Nicole Simpson Brown is a paradigmatic example of just such a dynamic.) As a result, the very public nature of trials – particularly those that are spectacular and highly mediated – can undermine the public's faith in representative legal institutions (see Brummett, 1990; Sherwin, 2000; Rapping, 2003; Ferguson, 2007, Part 3).

And yet trials, whether they are undertaken in the highly formalized manner of the contemporary United States or in less formal settings elsewhere and at other times, offer a way to articulate conflict, anxiety and injury and at least promise a path beyond, traced publicly and performatively. Much as we may desire it, they may not bring a case to satisfying 'closure'; yet they may nevertheless offer one form of what anthropologist Victor Turner (1986) calls the redressive stage of 'social dramas'. Turner argues that the very performativity of trials is central to this socially redressive potential. Trials, he argues, are generative of narrative in and beyond their bounds, narrative which helps to resolve social breaches in one direction or another. These processes of redress are both reflective and reflexive – that is, they both draw us in and make us aware of the fact of their performance. They are, moreover, ultimately indeterminate insofar as their meanings issue from the gestures of *particular* performances. Turner suggests that this indeterminacy is at bottom what makes such redressive processes and performances socially valuable. Redress 'reveals that "determining" and "fixing" are indeed processes, not permanent states or givens. They proceed by assigning meanings to events and relationships in reflexive narratives.' This indeterminacy should not be regarded as the absence of social being, Turner suggests: '... it is not negation, emptiness, privation. Rather it is potentiality, the possibility of becoming' (1986, p. 77).

The Essays

The essays in this collection invite us to reflect on the ways trials pose and enact this dynamic, indeterminate, symbolically potent dialogic relation between law and culture. As such, this volume is conceived not as a defence of trials as part of a system of legal justice (though some of the essays make such a defence) so much as a foray into a rich exploration of their symbolic centrality and circulation in culture. Taken together, the authors included here conceive of

---

out in the back-and-forth rhythm of direct and cross-examination, gathered together again in opposing closing arguments, followed by the coda of a (not always satisfying) verdict.

the trial as a site of performance, a critical public space in which positive law (legal rules, principles and theory but also representational practices and epistemologies) and democratic culture (norms, representational practices, epistemologies, geographic and social locations) interact to produce a dialogized domain of legality that is responsive to and productive of both the legal and the social. As part of that project, the works here variously inquire into how trials display a distinct culture, how they take up culture and how they are taken up in culture.[20]

This volume is organized in three parts. The first, 'Trials as Sites of Performance and Narrative', focuses on the internal dynamics of trials. Milner Ball's classic 'The Play's the Thing: An Unscientific Reflection on Courts under the Rubric of Theater' (Chapter 1) moves us directly into an inquiry about the theatrical nature of trials. Taking seriously the form and format of the trial, Ball argues that their performative aspects both function as aids to judgment for decision-makers and are good in themselves insofar as they create a special world that helps to legitimize the legal process and dramatize an ideal political community. In Chapter 2, 'The Lawfulness of the American Trial', Robert Burns builds upon Ball's claims, presenting a phenomenological account of the trial as a complex, consciously structured hybrid of languages and performances. Decision-makers encounter evidence in the courtroom through the rule-guided (but not determined) performances of legal actors, and that encounter elevates the decision-making process in ways that serve the values of the rule of law.

Burns's focus on narrative and performance as essential to the truth-producing function of the trial is elaborated in the three essays that follow. Anthony G. Amsterdam and Randy Hertz's 'An Analysis of Closing Arguments to a Jury' (Chapter 3) offers a careful, theoretically informed reading of the narrative structures and techniques employed by the prosecution and defence in the closing arguments of one particular trial, a close case in which the rhetorical strategies of attorneys could determine the outcome. They attend not just to the overt thematics of each legal argument, but also to the implicit narrative and dialogic structures and microstructures each attorney uses, with relatively wide latitude, to produce a persuasive account of the trial's underlying events. In Chapter 4, 'Law Frames: Historical Truth and Narrative Necessity in a Criminal Case', Richard K. Sherwin resituates Amsterdam and Hertz's interest in narrative strategy by placing trial storytelling within the context of postmodern cultural impulses. Analysing the multiple narrative strategies taken up in Errol Morris's film *The Thin Blue Line*, Sherwin worries over the disconnect between the public's desire for linear, coherent stories and our increasing encounters with acausal, nonlinear, contingent and morally relative ways of knowing the world. He expresses hope that legal storytelling can be postmodern and yet retain a relation to knowledge that is not sceptical of the very task of truth-production. And yet his cautious optimism must be balanced, as Austin Sarat suggests, with careful attention to the political dimensions of multiple narrativity in courtrooms. Chapter 5, Sarat's 'Speaking of Death: Narratives of Violence in Capital Trials', focuses on a single capital case, analysing the ways in which attorneys represent violence linguistically, and argues that narrative processes themselves can do injustice, making physical violence vivid while muting the effects of structural and state violence. The imbalance among these three narratives of violence becomes particularly acute in racially charged cases, and

[20] 'Culture' is, of course, a highly contested term. Here I invoke it, as Naomi Mezey has suggested, as a 'set of shared signifying practices … by which meaning is produced, performed, contested, or transformed' (2003, p. 42).

Sarat's analysis of the social dimensions of trial narrativity enrich the more formal analyses of trial performance and narrative offered by Ball, Burns, Amsterdam and Hertz, and Sherwin.

The essays in Part I address what we might call the production side of meaning-making in trials, offering ways of conceiving the staging of narratives within the courtroom. Part II, 'Evidence and the Production of Truth', engages us with questions about the *relation* between the production and reception of legal meaning in and beyond the space of the trial. Kim Lane Scheppele's 'Just the Facts, Ma'am: Sexualized Violence, Evidentiary Habits, and the Revision of Truth' (Chapter 6) echoes Sarat's attentiveness to the political dimensions of trial narratives in her analysis of the gendered nature of truth-finding in sexual violence cases. Scheppele suggests that people most often believe a witness's first-told tale rather than subsequent, varying reiterations; but 'facts', she argues, are not neutral. Rather, presumptions about the credibility of evidence in cases of sexual trauma often work against women, who frequently delay talking about their abuse or change their stories over time. We ought to attend more, she suggests, to asking how socially-situated stories are rendered believable by the audience that hears them.

Questions about the nature of perception and truth-production are taken up in a somewhat different way by Jennifer Mnookin and Nancy West in Chapter 7, 'Theaters of Proof: Visual Evidence and the Law in *Call Northside 777*'. Mnookin and West offer a reading of Henry Hathaway's film, which is based upon an actual case, in order to consider the relation between the high truth-value we place on visual evidence and the role of filmic re-enactments in courtrooms. In effect, they argue, re-enactments have a strong affinity with trials insofar as both offer an account of 'what happened'; and insofar as *Northside 777* is itself a re-enactment, it can be understood as offering a popular commentary on the power of the visual in both film and law alongside a cautionary tale about audience *naïveté* concerning the truth-value and transparency of images. For Mnookin and West, visual proof is a matter, in the end, of theatre. In Chapter 8, 'Film as Witness: Screening *Nazi Concentration Camps* Before the Nuremberg Trial', Lawrence Douglas offers a similar meditation on the power of visual imagery in his examination of the role of a particular film, *Nazi Concentration Camps*, in the 1945 Nuremberg trials. In those unprecedented trials, the prosecutors used the film as a way of putting into evidence knowledge about atrocities that could not be adequately represented in words. Prosecutors framed the film with a directive narrative voice, yet it nevertheless proved a disrupted and disruptive piece of evidence at trial. In examining the film's use and reception both inside and outside the courtroom, Douglas lays bare the fragility and limits of law in adjudications of genocide. In focusing on those limits Douglas's analysis resonates on a theoretical level with William Finnegan's microhistorical *New Yorker* piece 'Doubt' (Chapter 9). Finnegan, a reporter who served on a jury and uneasily convicted a young man of robbery, moves from the receiving end of legal stories in the courtroom out into the world of journalistic investigation. Having the privilege of a double view of trials, both inside and outside, Finnegan gives us a window into the production of evidence and legal truth, and the ways in which certain trial rules ironically injure the defendants they nominally should benefit.

Finally in Part III, 'Dialogics of Law and Culture', we situate trials more broadly in their historical and cultural contexts and examine the social meaning and circulation of trials in culture. In Chapter 10, 'Story and Transcription in the Trial of John Brown', Robert Ferguson analyses the famed 1859 trial of the abolitionist in order to trace the ways in which legal stories become cultural narratives. Ferguson suggests that John Brown's trial and martyrdom resonated beyond the courtroom insofar as he was able, in his brilliant trial performance, to exploit legal rules and rituals. In doing so he cast himself as a hero of an American Romance, whose generic conventions in turn both rendered him legible and magnified his status as an American legend. He became, so to speak, the effect of a public projection. Paul Berman's 'Rats, Pigs, and Statues on Trial: The Creation of Cultural Narratives in the Prosecution of Animals and Inanimate Objects' (Chapter 11) takes up the issue of projection at an even earlier moment in time as he considers the curious late medieval practice of prosecuting animals. While they may appear nonsensical to modern eyes, the trials of rats, pigs, locusts and other vermin functioned, Berman argues, as cultural performances. 'Social dramas' in Victor Turner's parlance, these trials and their legal rituals aided in the re-ordering and reintegration of small communities after social disruption.

Stéphane Leman-Langlois's 'Constructing a Common Language: The Function of Nuremberg in the Problematization of Postapartheid Justice' (Chapter 12) moves us away from an examination of actual trial processes. Leman-Langlois's analysis of political and legal strategies at the moment of political transition in post-apartheid South Africa indicates the ways in which trials can become detached from their contexts and take on a very different set of meanings. In late 1990s South Africa, the signifier 'Nuremberg' becomes a symbol of illegitimate post-war retribution, and in that discursive role acts as a unifying myth against which the new, reconciliatory post-apartheid state defines itself. In Chapter 13, '"The Trial": A Parody of the Law amid the Mockery of Men in Post-Colonial Papua New Guinea', David Lipset suggestively expands the possible significations of trials (in general). Focusing on law's expressive dimension, Lipset offers an intriguing account of a parodic 'trial' that took place in the course of his fieldwork in Papua New Guinea. Lipset explicitly invokes the idea of dialogism to analyse the decentring of legal discourse in local culture and the ways in which law acts as a discursive medium for creative play.

We close with Shoshana Felman's 'Forms of Judicial Blindness, or the Evidence of What Cannot Be Seen: Traumatic Narratives and Legal Repetitions in the O.J. Simpson Case and in Tolstoy's *The Kreutzer Sonata*' (Chapter 14). Felman provocatively reads Tolstoy's controversial novella as a literary precursor to the 1990s trial of O.J. Simpson. Both, she contends, are narratives of trauma – in this case the trauma of domestic abuse ending in murder. Using a psychoanalytic framework, Felman reads *The Kreutzer Sonata* in relation to later legal proceedings in order to propose a way of understanding notorious trials as both sites of memory and traumatic abysses, spaces of blindness that, insofar as they signal a cultural repression, we are doomed to repeat.

Taken together, these essays argue both descriptively and normatively for the continuing centrality of trials in public imagination. However we judge any particular trial, however much as individual performances they might fail to realize themselves as ideal spaces for the doing of justice, trials continue to enchant us because of their capacity to interpolate us dramatically, even histrionically in the best sense of the word, into the very identity of law itself. We are, by virtue of this performativity, invested in the possibility of law's continual transformation.

References

Abramson, Jeffrey (2000), *We, the Jury: The Jury System and the Ideal of Democracy*, Cambridge, MA: Harvard University Press.

Adler, Stephen J. (1994), *The Jury: Disorder in the Courts*, New York: Doubleday.

Arendt, Hannah (1994), *Eichmann in Jerusalem: A Report on the Banality of Evil*, New York: Penguin.

Auslander, Philip (1999), *Liveness: Performance in a Mediatized Culture*, London: Routledge.

Bakhtin, Mikhail (1981), *The Dialogic Imagination: Four Essays*, ed. Michael Holquist, trans. Caryl Emerson and Michael Holquist, Austin: University of Texas Press.

Brummett, Barry (1990), 'Mediating the Laws: Popular Trials and the Mass Media', in Robert Hariman (ed.), *Popular Trials: Rhetoric, Mass Media, and the Law*, Tuscaloosa: University of Alabama Press, pp. 179–93.

Burnett, D. Graham (2001), *A Trial by Jury*, New York: Vintage.

Burns, Robert (1999), *A Theory of the Trial*, Princeton, NJ: Princeton University Press.

Clover, Carol J. (1998), 'Law and the Order of Popular Culture', in Austin Sarat and Thomas R. Kearns (eds), *Law in the Domains of Culture*, Ann Arbor: University of Michigan Press, pp. 97–120.

Cole, David (2003), *Enemy Aliens: Double Standards and Constitutional Freedoms in the War on Terror*, New York: The New Press.

Cover, Robert (1992), 'Violence and the Word', in Martha Minow, Michael Ryan and Austin Sarat (eds), *Narrative, Violence, and the Law*, Ann Arbor: University of Michigan Press, pp. 203–38.

Ferguson, Robert (2007), *The Trial in American Life*, Chicago: University of Chicago Press.

Fox, Richard L. and Van Sickel, Robert W. (2001), *Tabloid Justice: Criminal Justice in an Age of Media Frenzy*, Boulder, CO: Lynne Rienner.

Friedman, Lawrence M. (1993), *Crime and Punishment in American History*, New York: Basic Books.

Friedman, Lawrence M. (2004), 'The Day Before Trials Vanished', *Journal of Empirical Legal Studies*, **1**, 3, pp. 689–703.

Galanter, Marc (2004), 'The Vanishing Trial: An Examination of Trials and Related Matters in Federal and State Courts', *Journal of Empirical Legal Studies*, **1**, 3, pp. 459–570.

Gewirtz, Paul (1996), 'Victims and Voyeurs: Two Narrative Problems at the Criminal Trial', in Peter Brooks and Paul Gewirtz (eds), *Law's Stories: Narrative and Rhetoric in the Law*, New Haven: Yale University Press, pp. 149–50.

Gross, Ariela (2001), 'Beyond Black and White: Cultural Approaches to Race and Slavery', *Columbia Law Review*, **101**, April, pp. 640–90.

Haltunnen, Karen (1998), *Murder Made Foul: The Killer and the American Gothic Imagination*, Cambridge, MA: Harvard University Press.

Hariman, Robert (1990a), 'Performing the Laws: Popular Trials and Social Knowledge', in Robert Hariman (ed.), *Popular Trials: Rhetoric, Mass Media, and the Law*, Tuscaloosa: University of Alabama Press, pp. 17–30.

Hariman, Robert (ed.) (1990b), *Popular Trials: Rhetoric, Mass Media, and the Law*, Tuscaloosa: University of Alabama Press.

Huizinga, Johan (1955), *Homo Ludens: A Study of the Play Element in Culture*, Boston, MA: Beacon Press.

Kagan, Robert (2001), *Adversarial Legalism: The American Way of Law*, Cambridge, MA: Harvard University Press.

Lahav, Pnina (2004), 'Theater in the Courtroom: The Chicago Conspiracy Trial', *Cardozo Studies in Law and Literature*, 16, pp. 381–474.

Langbein, John (2003), *The Origins of the Adversary Criminal Trial*, Oxford: Oxford University Press.

Menkel-Meadow, Carrie (1996), 'The Trouble with the Adversary System in a Postmodern, Multicultural World', *William and Mary Law Review*, **38**, October, pp. 5–44.

Mezey, Naomi (2003), 'Law as Culture', in Austin Sarat and Jonathan Simon (eds), *Cultural Analysis, Cultural Studies, and the Law: Moving Beyond Legal Realism*, Durham, NC: Duke University Press, pp. 37–72.

New York Times (2006), '"I Didn't Know" Did Not Sway Houston Jury', 26 May, Section A, Column 5, p. 1.

Parry, Sir Edward (1924), *The Drama of the Law*, London: Ernst Benn.

Phelan, Peggy (1993), *Unmarked: The Politics of Performance*, London: Routledge.

Pizzi, William (1999), *Trials Without Truth: Why Our System of Criminal Trials Has Become an Expensive Failure and What We Need to Do to Rebuild It*, New York: New York University Press.

Rapping, Elayne (2003), *Law and Justice as Seen on TV*, New York: New York University Press.

Resnik, Judith (1986), 'Failing Faith: Adjudicatory Procedure in Decline', *University of Chicago Law Review*, **53**, pp. 494–558.

Sherwin, Richard K. (2000), *When Law Goes Pop: The Vanishing Line Between Law and Popular Culture*, Chicago, IL: University of Chicago Press.

Sklar, Judith (1986), *Legalism: Law, Morals, and Political Trials*, Cambridge, MA: Harvard University Press.

Tocqueville, Alexis de (1988), *Democracy in America*, ed. J.P. Mayer, trans. George Lawrence, New York: Harper Collins.

Turner, Victor (1986), *The Anthropology of Performance*, New York: PAJ Publications.

Umphrey, Martha Merrill (1999), 'The Dialogics of Legal Meaning: Spectacular Trials, the Unwritten Law, and Narratives of Criminal Responsibility', *Law and Society Review*, **33**, 2, pp. 393–423.

Part I
Trials as Sites of Performance and Narrative

[1]

The Play's the Thing: An Unscientific Reflection on Courts Under the Rubric of Theater

Milner S. Ball*

The essay form is the fit instrument for a thinker whose chief concern is to lay bare the contending claims that seek the mediation and authority of society through law, and to give some indication, at least, of how these processes of mediation in fact operate. For the essay is tentative, reflective, suggestive, contradictory, and incomplete. It mirrors the perversities and complexities of life.†

The production of plays unlike the production of goods cannot be streamlined.[1] A performance of *King Lear* requires about as much time and labor now as it did in Elizabethan England. Output per man-hour could be significantly increased in the theater only by radically transforming its quality, dynamics and nature, as, for example, by abandoning the intimate medium of live performance for the quite different mass media of television or film. Productivity gains are precluded in live performance because what the performer does is an end in itself and not the means to production of some other good. Inasmuch as it is invulnerable to greater technological efficiency through mass production or speedier processes, theater cannot reduce its costs.

The same is true of the public functions of courts. Some aspects of judicial administration are undoubtedly subject to modifications which would increase its productivity, but there is little that can be done to cut the time and labor of trials and oral arguments. Their costs can only multiply. The question, which gathers urgency as court workloads and docket congestion

---

* A.B. 1958, Princeton University; S.T.B. 1961, Harvard University; J.D. 1971, University of Georgia. Associate Professor of Law, Rutgers-Camden Law School; Member of the Presbytery of West Jersey, U.P.U.S.A.; Member of the Georgia Bar. The author wishes to express hearty thanks to those several kind people who provoked him to greater clarity of expression by their penetrating suggestions for changes in the manuscript of this essay. He has chosen to authenticate his thanks by not naming them, thus preserving them from the vagaries of a possible guilt by association.

† F. Frankfurter, Felix Frankfurter on the Supreme Court 203 (P. Kurland ed. 1970), reprinted from Frankfurter's book review of B. Cardozo, The Paradoxes of Legal Science (1928), in 77 U. Pa. L. Rev. 436 (1929).

1. *See* W. Baumol & W. Bowen, Performing Arts—The Economic Dilemma 161–72 (1966), which explores the relationship of productivity gains and the technology of live performance. The idea advanced in this opening paragraph is a pale, partial reflection of their suggestive formulation.

increase, is whether current modes of trial and oral argument based on live presentation ought to be discarded altogether.[2] If courts are viewed as producers of judgments, then conceivably other means—videotape, recordings, more exclusive use of writings—could be employed to make the same product more efficiently. Economy of this sort would constitute a radical transformation of the judicial system, however, because courts are not merely in the business of making decisions. The live presentation of cases in the courtroom, although a means to the end of judgment, is also an end in itself.[3] Trials and oral arguments are as essential to the judicial system as performance is to drama.

Certainly, judicial proceedings are a *source* of drama, as is clear from the works of playwrights from Aeschylus[4] to Shakespeare[5] to Daniel Berrigan.[6] And not infrequently the courtroom provides the *setting* for dramatic moments. This service of judicial proceedings as source and setting for drama suggests, but is not to be equated with, the allied notion that judicial proceedings are themselves a type of theater. This essay will explore that notion.

The identification of judicial proceedings as theater requiring live presentation would seem unexceptional but for the fact that the label has been rejected, as though theatrics were an expendable, intrusive embarrassment to the scientific and businesslike austerities of the courts.[7] This essay acquiesces in rather than denies the court's theatricality and it attempts to discover how much may plausibly be said about it.[8] The hope is that an examination of courtroom action as theater may help to clarify its nature and thereby make some small contribution to an understanding of the role of law in our society.[9] The only claim made for what follows is that it at-

2. The development of a "consumer perspective" among some lawyers has led them to accept certain streamlining of appellate court procedures, *e.g.*, providing full court procedures only where basic interests are at stake. *See* Weaver, *Lawyers in Favor of Court Revision*, N.Y. Times, Dec. 2, 1974, § 1, at 36, col. 3.

3. In the course of a discussion of the crime control and due process models ventured by Herbert Packer, John Griffiths noted that both models "are concerned only with the relationship of trials and pleas to the end of the process—punishment of the guilty. But if a trial can be seen as a goal in itself—a lesson in legal procedure, dignity, fairness and justice, for the public and for the accused (whether he is convicted or acquitted)—we would not want to lose its potential for good by encouraging short-circuits. Because of the constraints imposed by our ideology about criminal procedure, speculation in this direction has been almost entirely neglected." Griffiths, *Ideology in Criminal Procedure or A Third "Model" of the Criminal Process*, 79 YALE L.J. 359, 398 (1970).

4. *See* AESCHYLUS, THE EUMENIDES.

5. *See* W. SHAKESPEARE, THE MERCHANT OF VENICE, act IV, scene 1; KING LEAR, act III, scene 6.

6. *See* D. BERRIGAN, THE TRIAL OF THE CATONSVILLE NINE (1970).

7. *See* note 48 *infra* and accompanying text; Griswold, *The Standards of the Legal Profession: Canon 35 Should Not Be Surrendered*, 48 A.B.A.J. 615, 616 (1962) ("A courtroom is not a stage; and witnesses and lawyers, and judges and juries and parties, are not players. A trial is not a drama, and it is not held for public delectation, or even public information").

8. For recent, helpful commentary on the law as drama, especially with respect to its relation to religion, see H. BERMAN, THE INTERACTION OF LAW AND RELIGION 31–37, 74, 148–50 n.12 (1974).

9. It may be that appreciation of courts as theater would affect the way lawyers are trained for

tempts to avoid total enslavement to conjecture on the way to offering proposals whose improvement is sought through enticement to debate and discussion.

I. The Theatrical Elements of Courtroom Action

A. *The Elements of Form*

Clarity may be served, if at the risk of belaboring simplicities, by beginning with some preliminary comments on the theatrical elements of courtroom action: its space, audiences and format.

1. *Space.*

The courtroom is, or should be, a theatrical space, one which evokes expectations of the uncommon.[10] Unlike the proscenium arch interior of the familiar Broadway theater, the court lacks a stage, curtain and footlights, and its houselights are not darkened in signal of an imminent theatrical event. Nevertheless, the design and appointment of the courtroom, enhanced by costuming[11] and ceremony,[12] do create a dramatic aura which has even been described in hyperbolic religious terms.[13]

Theatrical effects are such dominant factors in the physical identifica-

---

and conduct trials. A view of courts as theater might also help provide content to due process analysis in the sense that courts as theater is one model of due process. Additionally, to approach judicial proceedings as theater may provide a solution to a problem presented by the Realists, who demonstrated that rules are not sufficient explanation of the way cases are decided, but left unanswered exactly how such decisions *are* made. If judicial proceedings are theater, then decisions may be viewed as a response to the larger theatrical action, of which the rules are only a part.

These issues are illustrative of the practical and jurisprudential consequences of understanding courts as theater. They are not directly addressed in this Essay, which is only a prolegomenon to discussion of these concrete possibilities.

10. Eric Bentley has observed: "To begin with, the theater is a place. This place, in all known forms, sets up such a vibration in those who frequent it that certain properties roughly suggested by the term magic are invariably attributed to the building itself. In our epoch, for example, how many journalists, and even college freshmen, have mentioned the expectant lull when the lights dim, and the thrill when the curtain rises! This, you say, may be partly a matter of audience psychology. It remains true that the paraphernalia of the theatre has of itself remarkable suggestive power. Even when no audience is present, even when the stage is bare of scenery and the brick wall at the rear is exposed, the curious machine retains an insidious attraction." E. Bentley, The Theatre of Commitment 55 (1967).

11. On the judicial robe, see J. Frank, Courts on Trial 254–61 (1950) (criticizing the robe); A.B.A. Project on Standards for Criminal Justice, Standards Relating to the Function of the Trial Judge § 1.3, at 29–30 (Approved Draft 1972).

12. There are, for example, the "Oyez" and the response of rising at the judge's entrance.

13. *See* C. Miller, The Supreme Court and the Uses of History 187 (1969); W. Murphy, Congress and the Court 1 (1962). It is possible that the aura of some courtrooms is a vestige of the ancient practice of setting apart from the ordinary world a sacred spot for the pronouncement of judgment. *See* J. Huizinga, Homo Ludens, A Study of the Play-Element in Culture 76–77 (1949). *See also* F. Cornford, From Religion to Philosophy 31–33 (1912). But many lower state courtrooms evoke profane responses; on their inadequate condition and undesirable effects, see N. Dorsen & L. Friedman, Disorder in the Court 239–40 (1973); Tigar, *The Supreme Court 1969 Term: Foreword: Waiver of Constitutional Rights: Disquiet in the Citadel*, 84 Harv. L. Rev. 1, 5–6 (1970).

tion of a courtroom that their absence may raise doubts about whether a court which lacks a properly theatrical aspect is really a court at all. For example, the absence of courtlike features from the place in which a prisoner was convicted for contempt of court was instrumental in overturning that conviction in *Thompson v. Stahl*.[14] Thompson had been arrested for public drunkenness and then taken to a booking room where his allegedly boisterous behavior drew the contempt sentence. The booking room, located beneath a jail, contained three magistrates' desks behind a steel screen at one end and, at the other, a holding cell where the prisoner was placed. The court observed that "a locked cell . . . in the United States (the 'dock' at the old Bailey notwithstanding) connotes a *jail* rather than a court."[15] Words of warning by one of the magistrates to the prisoner Thompson to be quiet "did not convert the holding cell nor the booking room into a court, nor did they set the stage for any valid exercise of contempt power."[16] Too much should not be made of a phrase, perhaps inadvertent; yet the possibility is raised that a court must appear to be a court architecturally, and that this appearance may be instructively described as the setting of a certain kind of stage.

The *type* of stage to be set, of course, must be accordant with the particular nature and demands of courtroom theater. For example, *Roberts v. State*[17] demonstrated that the staging appropriate to legitimate theater may be inappropriate to the theater of law. In that case:

> The court removed the trial from the courtroom to the theater, and stated as a reason therefor: "By reason of the insufficiency of the courtroom to seat and accommodate the people applying for admission . . . it is by the court ordered that the further trial of this cause be had at the Keith Theater," and thereupon the court was adjourned to Keith Theater, where trial proceeded.
>
> The stage was occupied by court, counsel, jury, witnesses, and officers connected with the trial. The theater proper was crowded with curious spectators. Before the trial was completed it was returned to the courtroom and concluded there. At the adjournment of court on one occasion the bailiff announced from the stage: "The regular show will be tomorrow; matinee in the afternoon and another performance at 8:30. Court is now adjourned until 7:30."[18]

A town playhouse is an inappropriate setting for court because it may lend itself to actions which belong to vaudeville or legitimate theater but not to courtroom theater. This difference between court and playhouse is one of species rather than genera, although Chief Justice Warren, concur-

14. 346 F. Supp. 401, 402, 404 (W.D.N.C. 1972).
15. *Id.* at 404.
16. *Id.*
17. 100 Neb. 199, 158 N.W. 930 (1916). The defendant's conviction of murder in the first degree was reversed because of, among other reasons, its staging.
18. 100 Neb. at 203, 158 N.W. at 931–32 (1916), *quoted in* Estes v. Texas, 381 U.S. 532, 573 (1965) (Warren, C.J., concurring).

ring in *Estes v. Texas*,[19] apparently did not perceive it as such. In that case the Court reversed the conviction of Billy Sol Estes on the ground that televising his trial had infringed the fundamental right to a fair trial. Among other things, the layout of the courtroom had been changed to permit installation of a television booth. Chief Justice Warren believed that this change ignored the importance of the courtroom. The courtroom "in Anglo-American jurisprudence," he wrote, "is more than a location with seats for a judge, jury, witnesses, defendant, prosecutor, defense counsel and public observers; the setting . . . is itself an important element in the constitutional conception of trial, contributing a dignity essential to 'the integrity of the trial process.' "[20] He found that the physical alteration of the courtroom contributed to a substantive alteration of the trial process which could divert it from the fair and reliable determination of guilt to entertainment, commercialization, or political education.[21] He referred to the lower courts' error of allowing television cameras and coverage as returning "the theater to the courtroom,"[22] and he cited the *Roberts* case to make concrete his fear of the kind of "staging of criminal proceedings" to which televising trials might lead.[23]

There is no disagreement between the position taken herein and Chief Justice Warren's assessment that the courtroom is more than a nakedly functional location, that this something more is essential to the trial process, and that the integrity of the process is to be preserved against accommodation to ulterior purposes. Disagreement arises over characterization. Televising trials should not be characterized as a return of the theater to the courtroom for two reasons. First, television is to be distinguished from live performance; they are different media. The introduction of television to trials, as to plays, is the introduction of a mass, electronic medium into an intimate, live one. Television no more returns theater to the courtroom than it does to the playhouse; rather, it represents the transformation of a medium. Second, theater cannot be returned to the courtroom since theater has never left it. What can happen is that one type of theater can be inappropriately imported into another. The correct objection to show trials, produced for commercial or political reasons, is an objection not to theater per se but to the misappropriation of one type of theater with its own purpose—trials—for some other type with different, sometimes dishonorable, purposes. Thus, if courtrooms are something more than functional locations, this something more is their theatricality—their appropriateness to the

19. 381 U.S. 532, 552 (1965).
20. *Id.* at 561 (Warren, C.J., concurring) (citation omitted). *See id.* at 572–73.
21. *Id.* at 557, 565, 573–84.
22. *Id.* at 571.
23. *Id.* at 573.

singular theatrical action of judicial proceedings. In a word, a courtroom is, following Bentham, a "judicial theatre" or "theatre of justice."[24]

2. *Audience.*

While they must provide something more, courtrooms, like any theaters, have seats for an audience. Plays can be written and read as literature or rehearsed to empty houses. But a play is only completed, only really a play, in live performance before an audience.[25] An audience is no less important to courtroom action. In court, there are potentially three audiences: spectators, jury and judge. While these participants are more specifically the subject of constitutional protection than is courtroom design, it need scarcely be said that this protection has not been tied to their character as audience whose presence is necessary to consummate a theatrical event.

The presence of spectators is subject to limitation, but a criminal trial may not ban the public altogether.[26] Constitutionally, open proceedings are viewed as a safeguard to fair trials for defendants.[27] Something of the sense in which the public may be *theatrically* necessary may underlie the observation of one court that the judicial process "does not unfold legally and normally" when it "takes place behind closed doors";[28] "participants in secret proceedings quickly tend to lose their perspective, and the quality of the proceedings suffers as a consequence."[29] The public not only monitors what happens in the courtroom but may also help the active participants keep their perspective, thereby prompting them to perform their proper roles.

Professor Gerhard Mueller detected a broader theatrical reason for public presence. After noting that criminal trials were "the theater and *spectaculum* of old rural America,"[30] he pointed out that entertainment was not the sole explanation for the popularity of trials:

> It was felt to be the business of everyone in the county to be present when in their name justice was dispensed. . . . It still is the people's trial, although they

24. J. BENTHAM, *Rationale of Judicial Evidence*, in VI WORKS OF JEREMY BENTHAM 353, 354 *passim* (J. Bowring ed. 1838–1843). Bentham referred to the courtroom as "the main theatre of justice" and the judge's chambers as the "little theatre of justice." *Id.* at 354.

25. *See, e.g.*, P. BROOK, THE EMPTY SPACE 127 (1968).

26. *In re* Oliver, 333 U.S. 257 (1948). *See* U.S. CONST. amend. VI: 6 J. WIGMORE, EVIDENCE §§ 1834–35, pp. 332–44 (1940); Annot. 49 A.L.R.3d 1007 (1973). *But cf.* Radin, *The Right to a Public Trial*, 6 TEMP. L.Q. 381 (1932). When the "public" involved are news media, then there is a constellation of problems on which there is extensive and developing case law and literature. *See, e.g.*, Sheppard v. Maxwell, 384 U.S. 333 (1966).

27. *See, e.g.*, Estes v. Texas, 381 U.S. 532, 588 (1965) (Harlan, J., concurring); *In re* Oliver, 333 U.S. 257, 270 (1948). For other grounds supporting public trials, see *In re* Oliver, 333 U.S. 257, 270 n.24 (1948); United States v. Kobli, 172 F.2d 919 (3d Cir. 1949); J. WIGMORE, *supra* note 26, § 1834.

28. Oxnard Publishing Co. v. Superior Ct., 68 Cal. Rptr. 83, 95 (2d Dist. 1968) (hearing granted in California Supreme Court was dismissed as moot due to change of venue).

29. *Id.* at 97.

30. Mueller, *Problems Posed by Publicity to Crime and Criminal Proceedings*, 110 U. PA. L. REV. 1, 6 (1961).

no longer may officially acclaim the judgment as did the *Umstand* of our Germanic past or the spectators of frontier days. Popular justice is public justice—it is play with popular emotions while doing or restoring right.[31]

The presence of the public is desirable but there is no guarantee that onlookers will exercise the right to attend. However, their absence does not mean there is no audience, for there is another, the jury. Like spectators, the jury is a subject of constitutional protection[32] and is viewed, at least in part, as a public witness which can check potential governmental oppression.[33] Unlike the right to public trial, the right to jury trial may be waived,[34] and in both criminal and civil cases there are instances in which the right to a jury trial has been held inapplicable.[35] However, when a jury is employed, it is, more decisively than a group of onlookers, a part of the trial event; as the finder of fact it is the immediate audience for whose response the case is produced in the courtroom.[36]

In the instance of nonjury proceedings, should public spectators not attend, the judge will be the only audience. The judge then performs in several capacities, including that of spectator.[37] A one-person house is minimal, but it is enough. "Can the theater exist without an audience?" Jerzy

31. *Id.* at 6–7. *See also* Tigar, *supra* note 13, at 26 n.81. *But see* Friedman, *San Benito 1890: Legal Snapshot of a County*, 27 STAN. L. REV. 687, 698 (1975), which draws a darker picture of early justice in rural America: "The newspapers seemed totally innocent of any notion of the majesty and awesomeness of law. No doubt citizens had ideas about fair trials and fair play and some pride in their legal system; at the same time, they knew it cynically as a powerful weapon of social control, a magnificent instrument for insuring power and wealth." Concludes Friedman, "Legal process was a game, a weapon, and an entertainment." *Id.* at 700.

32. U.S. CONST. art. III, § 2; amend. VI; amend. VII.

33. *See, e.g.*, Taylor v. Louisiana, 419 U.S. 522, 530; McKeiver v. Pennsylvania, 403 U.S. 528, 554–56 (1971) (Brennan, J., concurring in part, dissenting in part) (juvenile proceedings); Duncan v. Louisiana, 391 U.S. 145, 151–56 (1968); THE FEDERALIST No. 83, at 562–65 (Cooke ed. 1967) (A. Hamilton). *But see* H. KALVEN & H. ZEISEL, THE AMERICAN JURY 296 (1966).

34. *See* FED. R. CRIM. P. 23(a); FED. R. CIV. P. 38(d). *See also* Singer v. United States, 380 U.S. 24 (1965) (defendant may not waive "right" to jury trial without consent of government).

35. In criminal cases juries are not required for the trial of "petty" offenses. *See, e.g.*, Frank v. United States, 395 U.S. 147 (1969); Dyke v. Taylor Implement Mfg. Co., 391 U.S. 216 (1968); Cheff v. Schnackenberg, 384 U.S. 373 (1966). Nor are juries required in juvenile proceedings. McKeiver v. Pennsylvania, 403 U.S. 528 (1971). As a rule, juries are not utilized in equity. *See* Katchen v. Landy, 382 U.S. 323 (1966); James, *Right to a Jury Trial in Civil Actions*, 72 YALE L.J. 655 (1963); O'Neil, *Law or Equity: The Right to Trial by Jury in a Civil Action*, 35 MO. L. REV. 43 (1970). *Compare* Chesnin & Hazard, *Chancery Procedure and the Seventh Amendment: Jury Trial of Issues in Equity Cases Before 1791*, 83 YALE L.J. 999 (1974), *with* Langbein, *Fact Finding in The English Court of Chancery: A Rebuttal*, 83 YALE L.J. 1620 (1974). *See also* Note, *Congressional Provision for Nonjury Trial under the Seventh Amendment*, 83 YALE L.J. 401 (1973).

The Supreme Court is expanding those occasions when a jury may be required but contracting the size and voting requirements of the jury when it is employed. On the expansion of the jury right in criminal cases, see Bloom v. Illinois, 391 U.S. 194 (1968). On the same in civil cases, see Pernell v. Southall Realty, 416 U.S. 363 (1974); Curtis v. Loether, 415 U.S. 189 (1974); Ross v. Bernhard, 396 U.S. 531 (1970); Dairy Queen, Inc. v. Wood, 369 U.S. 469 (1962); Beacon Theaters, Inc. v. Westover, 359 U.S. 500 (1959). On the matter of nonunanimous votes, see Johnson v. Louisiana, 406 U.S. 356 (1972); Apodaca v. Oregon, 406 U.S. 404 (1972). On the issue of juries of less than 12, see Colgrove v. Battin, 413 U.S. 149 (1973); Williams v. Florida, 399 U.S. 78 (1970).

36. For a description of the historical transformation whereby jurors became triers of fact instead of witnesses, see Estes v. Texas, 381 U.S. 532, 557–58 (1965) (Warren, C.J., concurring).

37. The dominant role of the judge is that of director. *See* text accompanying note 41 *infra*. Even when a case is tried to a jury, however, the judge is also an audience.

Grotowski asked, and answered: "At least one spectator is needed to make it a performance. So we are left with the actor and the spectator. We can thus define the theatre as what takes place between spectator and actor."[38] A judge or panel of judges, the irreducible minimum, is sufficient to support a performance of judicial theater.

3. *Format.*

Besides the space and audience for theater, judicial proceedings provide the format of drama. Protagonist and antagonist confront one another,[39] present conflicting versions of the past and establish a problem to be solved. As one commentator has observed:

> The opening statement is the exposition which, by not divulging all, creates suspense. The artful order in which witnesses are called sets up crisis and climax. Conflict, the gist of any lawsuit, is developed during cross-examination and impeachment. Timing is always important; to maintain jury interest the climax should not come too soon, although, deflating as it may be for counsel's ego, it rarely seems to occur during the closing argument. Attention is given to costuming: "Be sure to wear a dark dress."
>
> If this all smacks of manipulation, it is. Like a play, a trial must be produced.[40]

At trial, the principal actors are the witnesses and the parties litigant. Overall direction of the action is the responsibility of the judge, who controls what happens.[41] Yet to a certain extent, the judge, like the jury, also performs as an actor. Similarly, attorneys perform both as directors (in producing the presentation of their clients' cases) and as actors. The dual role of judges, juries and attorneys at trial is a product of the fact that trials actually encompass two distinct plays: the small play, the advocate's pro-

---

38. J. GROTOWSKI, TOWARDS A POOR THEATRE 32 (1968).

39. An accused has the right to be "confronted with the witnesses against him." U.S. CONST. amend. VI. The dramatic potential of the right is underlined by the fact that its purpose is "to prevent depositions or *ex parte* affidavits . . . being used against the prisoner in lieu of a personal examination and cross-examination of the witness in which the accused has an opportunity, not only of testing the recollection and sifting the conscience of the witness, but of compelling him to stand face to face with the jury in order that they may look at him, and judge by his demeanor upon the stand and the manner in which he gives his testimony whether he is worthy of belief." Mattox v. United States, 156 U.S. 237, 242–43 (1895). The two-fold content of the right—both cross-examination of accusers and the observation of their demeanor by the jury—was reaffirmed in Barber v. Page, 390 U.S. 719, 725 (1968). However, more recent cases have emphasized cross-examination that can occur prior to trial, with the consequence that the dramatic possibilities are eliminated. *See* Dutton v. Evans, 400 U.S. 74 (1970); California v. Green, 399 U.S. 149 (1970); Griswold, *The Due Process Revolution and Confrontation*, 119 U. PA. L. REV. 711 (1971).

40. Simonett, *The Trial as One of the Performing Arts*, 52 A.B.A.J. 1145 (1966).

41. *See* Sheppard v. Maxwell, 384 U.S. 333 (1966) ("The carnival atmosphere at trial could easily have been avoided since the courtroom and courthouse premises are subject to the control of the court." *Id.* at 358); Dagnello v. Long Island R.R., 289 F.2d 797, 805 (2d Cir. 1961); Moore v. State, 46 Ohio App. 433, 437, 188 N.E. 881, 883 (1933) ("The test in determining whether the absence of the judge from the courtroom during the progress of the trial calls for a reversal of the judgment is whether, by his absence, he loses control of the proceedings . . . .").

duction of his client's case (played primarily to the jury or the judge), and the larger play, the trial as a whole (played before the public audience at large).[42] On appeal, attorneys are the principal actors. They take the part of their clients and, theatrically as well as legally, *represent* them.[43]

B. *The Element of Metaphor*

The case which an attorney presents for judgment in court is an admixture of fact and law. The facts are called facts because they are not, we hope, fiction. The interaction of the facts and the law is guided by a logic which may be described, following John Dewey, as an "experimental and flexible logic,"[44] or a logic "relative to consequences rather than to antecedents,"[45] a logic of prediction of probabilities rather than one of deduction of certainties. Dewey detailed the workings of this logic:

> No lawyer ever thought out the case of a client in terms of the syllogism. He begins with a conclusion which he intends to reach, favorable to his client of course, and then analyzes the facts of the situation to find material out of which to construct a favorable statement of facts, to form a minor premise. At the same time he goes over recorded cases to find rules of law employed in cases which can be presented as similar, rules which will substantiate a certain way of looking at and interpreting the facts. And as his acquaintance with rules of law judged applicable widens, he probably alters perspective and emphasis in selection of the facts which are to form his evidential data. And as he learns more of the facts of the case he may modify his selection of rules of law upon which he bases his case.[46]

---

42. It should be noted, however, that even within the small play alone, the roles of the judge and jury may shade over into participation as actors. In the judge's case, this is most likely to happen when the judge exercises his prerogative to call and question witnesses, *see* Jackson v. United States, 329 F.2d 893 (D.C. Cir. 1964), or to comment upon the evidence, *see* Patton v. United States, 281 U.S. 276, 288 (1930) (dictum); *but see* H. KALVEN & H. ZEISEL, *supra* note 33, at 420 (state courts). The jury assumes the role of actor in the small play when it renders the verdict. It may also be permitted to participate in the small play's action by asking questions. *See* Sparks v. Daniels, 343 S.W.2d 661, 667 (Mo. Ct. App. 1961); State v. Martinez, 7 Utah 2d 387, 389, 326 P.2d 102, 103 (1958). For a suggestion that the jury ought to be encouraged to assume a greater role, see Tigar, *supra* note 13, at 27. In fact, judges and counsel seldom raise the possibility of participation by the jury.

43. The French word for performance, *representation*, aptly suggests the theatrical role of appellate counsel: "A representation is the occasion when something is represented, when something from the past is shown again—something that once was, now is. For representation it is not an imitation or description of a past event, a representation denies time. It abolishes that difference between yesterday and today. It takes yesterday's action and makes it live again in every one of its aspects—including its immediacy. In other words, a representation is what it claims to be—a making present." P. BROOK, *supra* note 25, at 139.

The right to counsel applies both to criminal trials, Gideon v. Wainwright, 372 U.S. 335 (1963), and to the first appeal as of right, Douglas v. California, 373 U.S. 353 (1963), but not to discretionary appeal, Ross v. Moffit, 417 U.S. 600 (1974). For recent concern about the quality of advocacy, see Burger, *The Special Skills of Advocacy: Are Specialized Training and Certification of Advocates Essential to Our System of Justice?*, 42 FORDHAM L. REV. 227 (1973); Bazelon, *The Defective Assistance of Counsel*, 42 U. CIN. L. REV. 1 (1973); Palmer, *Implementing the Obligation of Advocacy in Review of Criminal Convictions*, 65 J. CRIM. L. & C. 267 (1974).

44. Dewey, *Logical Method and Law*, 10 CORNELL L. Q. 17, 27 (1924).

45. *Id.* at 26.

46. *Id.* at 23. *See also* J. DEWEY, ART AS EXPERIENCE 37–38 (1958).

The selection of facts and law is guided by their interaction with one another and with a third element: their potential for presentation in court. The elements of presentation—the rules of evidence, the case of the opposing side, the dynamics of the proceeding (including surprise and improvisation), the quality of evidence and witnesses, and the compellingness of the law—are considered just as carefully by an attorney as are the facts and the law. The dominant element in the presentation with which he will be concerned is the need to persuade the appropriate decisionmakers, first to a judgment that the claim is judicially cognizable, and then to a judgment favorable to the party represented.

The consequential logic, which to a degree governs the selection of facts and law, coupled with the attorney's need for a persuasive presentation, distinguishes the legal case from a scientific investigation. Dewey, for example, hastened to add to his description of the workings of experimental logic the demurrer that "I do not for a moment set up this procedure as a model of scientific investigation; it is too precommitted to the establishment of a particular and partisan conclusion to serve as such a model."[47] What distinguishes the case from scientific investigation helps to establish it as a form of dramaturgy. The case persuades histrionically. This point is neglected when the courtroom is thought of as a laboratory or a research library, with the mistaken consequence that the methods employed in the courtroom are urged to approximate "the methods of historians or physicians or geologists . . . ."[48] The methods are better understood as those of playwrights, actors and directors, and may be described as the making of metaphor.

What is meant by metaphor? In reference to the play, *The Cherry Orchard*, Francis Fergusson explained that "the larger elements of the composition—the scenes or episodes, the setting and the developing story—are composed in such a way as to make a poetry of the theater; but the 'text' as we read it literally, is not."[49] The poetry, the metaphor, is not necessarily to be found in the words of the text. Rather, it is to be found in the histrionic elements which "can only be seen in performance or by imagining a performance."[50]

About a production of the play, *Akropolis*, which he characterizes as "a poetic paraphrase of an extermination camp,"[51] Grotowski describes how, as the play begins:

> In the middle of the room stands a huge box. Metallic junk is heaped on top of it: stovepipes of various lengths and widths, a wheelbarrow, a bathtub, nails,

47. Dewey, *supra* note 44, at 23.
48. Radin, *supra* note 26, at 395.
49. F. Fergusson, The Idea of a Theater 166 (1949).
50. *Id.* at 147.
51. J. Grotowski, *supra* note 38, at 63.

> hammers. Everything is old, rusty, and looks as if it had been picked up from a junkyard. The reality of the props is rust and metal. From them, as the action progresses, the actors will build an absurd civilization; a civilization of gas chambers, advertised by stovepipes which will decorate the whole room as the actors hang them from strings or nail them to the floor. Thus one passes from fact to metaphor.[52]

The passage from fact to metaphor is what the advocate seeks. It is the passage from the materials of fact and law (the text) by means of courtroom presentation (the performance) to a persuasive statement of what ought to be done in a given situation (the metaphor).

The advocate's presentation of a case, the creation of courtroom metaphor, is marked by the coincidence of the opposites of fact and illusion. Illusion here is not falsehood but facts selected and established through artful, sometimes fortuitous, sequence. This convergence is the paradox of theater. In a recent essay on the Italian reviewer and essayist Nicola Chiaromonte, Mary McCarthy commented that "[t]he sphere of ultimate, irreducible reality which is the stage is also the licensed sphere of illusion."[53] In the course of years of reflection upon the paradox of theater, Chiaromonte had pursued the original, remarkably simple and fruitful insight that theater is "a sequence of actions performed by actors"[54] which constitutes the "repetition, re-enactment of an already accomplished fact (rather than simulation of a set of facts still in the course of happening). . . ."[55] In the playhouse, as in the courtroom, an event already completed is reenacted in a sequence which allows its meaning to be searched out. Chiaromonte concluded:

> In the theatre, the main thing is the drama, the conflict of individual situations, of ideas and passions—the clash of characters who are left, so to speak, on their own. If this is so, then the fictional element—fabulation—loses all importance. What matter are reflection and judgment. As for the plot, it plays exactly the same part as played by the corpus delicti in a law court. It has already happened and is now being re-examined, mounted on the stage for inspection—not the exterior episodes, as in a film, but the relevant and material acts, those we would turn over in our minds, in the course of reflection.[56]

At its best, the presentation of a case is a coincidence of reality and illusion, illusion not in the sense of perjury, but in the sense of theatrical metaphor—the reenactment of relevant and material elements for reflection and judgment. Although elusive, this paradoxical interplay of reality and illu-

52. *Id.* at 63–64.
53. McCarthy, *Nicola Chiaromonte and the Theatre,* N.Y. Rev. of Books, Feb. 20, 1975, at 29.
54. *Id.*
55. Chiaromonte, *On Pirandello's "Clothing the Naked,"* N.Y. Rev. of Books, Feb. 20, 1975, at 31.
56. *Id.*

sion does seem to correspond with the deeper truth of the way we experience life,[57] which is to say that it is a strength, and not a weakness or fault, in both the playhouse and the courtroom.[58]

C. *Defending the Analogy*

1. *Is courtroom action really "metaphor?"*

Several objections may legitimately be raised to viewing the courtroom as a theater. One is that it asks too much and the wrong things of the word "metaphor." A brief defense of its use here may prove useful.

Metaphor as persuasion. "Metaphor," Professor Lon Fuller has observed, "is the traditional device of persuasion. Eliminate metaphor from the law and you have reduced its power to convince and convert."[59] Certainly the law does employ metaphors. Professor Fuller illustrated his point with a consideration of the metaphor "constructive notice."[60] An additional point is sought to be made here: attorneys not only use linguistic metaphors but also produce histrionic metaphors. Constructive notice is a metaphor. A presentation which makes out a case of constructive notice is also a metaphor. Like the performance of a play, the presentation of the advocate's case seeks to persuade, and it does so openly. It is a metaphor and not a lie. Insofar as there is duplicity through selection and formulation of facts, the duplicity is open and generally accepted. Judge, jury and public expect the attorney

57. Ms. McCarthy notes, for example: "The actor, willing or unwilling, in each of us perceives his prototype on the stage, a walking shadow, the shade of a shade. . . . Now in so far as we are all actors or doers (it comes to the same, for doing, as exposed on the stage, is mere feinting, shadow play), the mask we put on is only a metaphor for the illusion we project whenever we appear among others . . . . The incomprehensible mixture of reality and unreality that we are aware of in the acts we perform is dramatically present in the situation of the actor, who consents for our pleasure to be someone both real and unreal." McCarthy, *supra* note 52, at 29.

58. Judge Frank labored to make it clear that "[t]he actual events, the real objective acts and words of [litigants], happened in the past. They do not walk into court. The court usually learns about these real, objective, past facts only through the oral testimony of fallible witnesses. Accordingly, the court, from hearing the testimony, must guess at the actual, past facts." J. FRANK, *supra* note 11, at 15–16. He saw that the proving of facts "is at the mercy of such matters as mistaken witnesses, perjured witnesses, missing or dead witnesses, mistaken judges, inattentive judges, biased judges, inattentive juries, and biased juries." *Id.* at 27. Although he rightly referred to these matters as "imperfections," *id.* at 27 n.16, there is a more fundamental mix of illusion and reality in the presentation of facts in court.

This mix is part of the human condition and is not the consequence of defaults in the way the "facts" of a case are "proved." Indeed, the impossibility of presenting literal reality in court may be due to human physiology itself. Structuralists such as Claude Levi-Strauss (anthropology), Jean Piaget (psychology), Noam Chomsky (linguistics), and Gunther Stent (biology) have contended that the reality we perceive and respond to is largely determined and confined by the structure of our nervous system. As Stent explained, "structuralism recognizes that information about the world enters the mind not as raw data but as highly abstract structures that are the result of a preconscious set of step-by-step transformations of the sensory input. Each transformation step involves the selective destruction of information according to a program that preexists in the brain. Any set of primary sense data becomes meaningful only after a series of such operations performed on it has transformed the data set into a pattern that matches a preexisting mental structure." Stent, *Cellular Communication*, SCIENTIFIC AMERICAN, Sept. 1972, at 43, 50–51. *See also* ARNHEIM, *Perceptional Abstraction and Art*, in TOWARD A PSYCHOLOGY OF ART 27 (1972).

59. L. FULLER, LEGAL FICTIONS 24 (1967).

60. *Id.* at 24–26.

to offer the construction of facts and law most favorable to the client; his purpose and point of view are apparent.

Metaphor as substitution. Like metaphor, the attorney's presentation is a mode of persuasion. Also like metaphor, the attorney's presentation proceeds by substitution. According to one popular authority, "a metaphor is a tacit comparison made by the substitution of the compared notion for the one to be illustrated."[61] The court case is a tacit comparison in which presentation of selected fact and law is substituted for the events themselves and the prior law.

There are several reasons for the substitution. The plainest is that the past cannot be reproduced exactly, so that in the nature of things some substitution cannot be avoided.[62] Another is constitutional policy, which may require deliberate exclusion of certain evidence in criminal cases.[63] A third reason arises from the task of judgment, which requires interpretation rather than a formless flow of information.[64] Finally, and most basically,

---

61. H. Fowler, A Dictionary of Modern English Usage 558 (2d ed. 1965).

62. It is arresting, but unnecessarily pejorative, to refer to the attorney's case as a "lie" simply because he must proceed by substitution. Although F.S. Cohen refers to the lawyer's presentation as "lying," he apparently intends no moral condemnation by the term: "In a certain sense, it is true that lawyers are liars. In the same sense, poets, historians, and map-makers are also liars. For it is the function of lawyers, poets, historians, and map-makers not to reproduce reality but to illumine some aspect of reality, and it always makes for deceit to pretend that what is thus illumined is the whole of reality. None of us can ever possibly tell the whole truth, though we may conscientiously will to do so and ask divine help towards that end. The ancient wisdom of our common law recognizes that men are bound to differ in their views of fact and law, not because some are honest and others dishonest, but because each of us operates in a value-charged field which gives shape and color to whatever we see. The proposition that no man should be a judge of his own cause embodies the ancient wisdom that only a many-perspectived view of the world can relieve us of the endless anarchy of one-eyed vision." Cohen, *Field Theory and Judicial Logic*, 59 Yale L.J. 238, 242 (1950).

63. *See* notes 152–57 *infra* and accompanying text.

64. In a review of Mary McCarthy's Watergate Portraits, Richard Goodwin proposed that, as distinguished from the view that truth is immanent in facts, "our tradition of criminal justice assumes we are more likely to approach correct knowledge by imposing news [*sic*—views?] about character, probability and feeling on the external evidence and on the competing logics of analysis." Goodwin, *Watergate Observed: The Mask of State*, N.Y. Times, June 30, 1974, § 7 (Book Review), at 5. Similarly, with respect to the criminal process, Packer spoke of the "tyranny of the actual" which may obscure value choices. H. Packer, The Limits of the Criminal Sanction 152 (1968).

It is for this reason that an exact recreation of or participation in the past event being judged, even if possible, would not necessarily be desirable. Counsel for defendant in *United States v. Holmes* argued that the action of Holmes in assisting to jettison passengers from an endangered lifeboat could not be fairly judged unless those who sat in judgment were "actually translated to his situation." United States v. Holmes, 26 F. Cas. 360, 364 (No. 15,383) (C.C.E.D. Pa. 1842). With this argument undoubtedly in mind, the judge, in his charge to the jury, explained that: "Whether or not 'a case of necessity' has arisen, or whether the laws under which death has been inflicted have been exercised as to hold the executioner harmless, cannot depend on his own opinion; for no man may pass upon his own conduct when it concerns the rights, and especially, when it affects the lives, of others. We have already stated to you that, by the law of the land, homicide is sometimes justifiable; and the law defines the occasions in which it is so. The transaction must, therefore, be justified to the law; and the person accused rests under obligation to satisfy those who judicially scrutinize his case that it really transcended ordinary rules. In fact, any other principle would be followed by pernicious results, and moreover, would not be practicable in application." *Id.* at 367. In the course of her reflections on the Eichmann trial, Hannah Arendt observed: "The argument that we cannot judge if we were not present and involved ourselves seems to convince everyone everywhere, although it seems obvious that if it were true, neither the administration of justice nor the writing of history would ever be possible. In contrast to these confusions, the reproach of self-righteousness raised against those who do judge is age-old; but that does not make it any the more valid. Even the judge who condemns a murderer can

the very theory of our justice system, as Justice Holmes put it, "is that the conclusions to be reached in a case will be induced only by evidence and argument in open court, and not by any outside influence . . . ."[65] This process is to be preserved even against *truthful* outside influences:

> A publication likely to reach the eyes of a jury, declaring a witness in a pending cause a perjurer, would be none the less a contempt that it was true. It would tend to obstruct the administration of justice, because even a correct conclusion is not to be reached or helped in that way, if our system of trials is to be maintained.[66]

This may or may not place truth and justice in conflict;[67] but, in any event, it does suggest that our system of trials seeks to do justice in a particular and artful manner[68]—in a metaphorical manner, it seems proper to say.

2. *Trials persuade. Does theater?*

Besides maintaining that it overloads "metaphor," another possible objection to the position adumbrated here is that, if, as has been maintained, it is the precommitment of a case to a partisan conclusion which distinguishes it from scientific investigation, then this same precommitment dis-

still say when he goes home: 'And there, but for the grace of God, go I.'" H. ARENDT, EICHMANN IN JERUSALEM: A REPORT ON THE BANALITY OF EVIL 295–96 (1965).

65. Patterson v. Colorado, 205 U.S. 454, 462 (1907).

66. *Id. Cf.* Irvin v. Dowd, 366 U.S. 717, 729–30 (1961) (Frankfurter, J., concurring); Bridges v. California, 314 U.S. 252, 283 (1941) (Frankfurter, J., dissenting).

67. Even *raising* all the questions involved in a discussion of the relationship between truth and justice would require this Essay to range far afield. But a brief word on the subject may be ventured.

It is possible to begin with the premise that "truth" and "the facts" are roughly equivalent and then proceed to different conclusions about the relation of truth and justice in trials. On the one hand, it could be argued that all the facts ought to be admitted into evidence at trials because all the truth is necessary in order for justice to be done (and the exclusionary rule, for example, therefore offends both truth and justice). On the other hand, it could be concluded that there are circumstances when all the facts should not be allowed as evidence because truth must sometimes be sacrificed to other valued ends for justice to be done (and the exclusionary rule is consequently viewed as serving justice but not truth).

A fresh approach to the relation between truth and justice at trial is made available by calling the initial premise into question. Is truth to be equated with the facts? Possibly not. For suggestive exploration of truth as something other than "optimal verbal veracity," *see* P. LEHMANN, ETHICS IN A CHRISTIAN CONTEXT 124–30 (1963); D. BONHOEFFER, ETHICS 326–34 (E. Bethage ed. 1955). If truth and facts are not readily subject to equation, then it is possible that truth may be arrived at without the consideration of all the facts. Thus, trials which do justice, notwithstanding the omission of some facts, may also arrive at truth. (The exclusionary rule could then be said to serve both truth and justice.) *See* note 69 *infra*. *See also* notes 58 and 62 *supra* and accompanying text; notes 125, 128, 152–55 *infra* and accompanying text.

68. Different views have been expressed about the relationship between trials and truth. For example, Professor Berman maintained that "[a] judicial proceeding is primarily a method of deciding what ought to be done in a given situation and only secondarily a scientific investigation of the truth. It is concerned with what happened only insofar as what happened is thought to be relevant to a possible decision, a possible outcome of the case." Berman, *Introduction* to THE TRIAL OF THE U2 at xxvii–xxviii (1960). Lord Devlin expressed a somewhat different view: "Trial by jury is not an instrument of getting at the truth; it is a process designed to make it as sure as possible that no innocent man is convicted." H. KALVEN & H. ZEISEL, *supra* note 33, at 190.

On the other hand, Justice Stewart writing for the Court in Tehan v. United States *ex rel* Shott, 382 U.S. 406, 416 (1966), said: "The basic purpose of a trial is the determination of truth . . . ." However, he went on to note that "the Fifth Amendment's privilege against self-incrimination is not an adjunct to the ascertainment of truth." *Id. See* note 67 *supra*.

tinguishes it as well from theater. In other words, judicial proceedings are not theater because theater is its own end (art for art's sake) or has some end other than that of persuading to a judgment (entertainment or cathartic excitation to pity or fear, for example).[69]

Yet, art in general and theater in particular do persuade to some conclusion. If the objective is parochial or political, then the artist's product may be, perhaps corruptly, propagandistic. If the objective is broad (for instance, a view or experience of human life) then it is contemplative. Either way there is an objective of persuasion. For example, Chekhov proposed that

> the writers whom we call eternal or simply good and who intoxicate us have one very important characteristic in common: they move in a certain direction and they summon you there too, and you feel, not with your mind alone, but with your whole being, that they have a goal, like the ghost of Hamlet's father who does not come and trouble the imagination for nothing. Some, depending on their caliber, have immediate objects: abolition of serfdom, liberation of their country, politics, beauty, or, like Denis Davydov . . . , simply vodka; others have remote objectives: God, immortality, the happiness of mankind, and so forth. The best of them are realistic, and paint life as it is, but because every line is permeated, as with sap, by the consciousness of a purpose, you are aware not only of life as it is, but life as it ought to be, and that captivates you.[70]

Of course, a play does not guide its audience, as a case guides the jury, to either an immediate decision or to a decision with immediate consequences for the life, freedom or property of another.[71] Judgments made in response to a play, other than critical ones about the play's quality, are longer range and have to do more with perceptions of life and one's own identity.[72] The question is whether this difference destroys the proposition that the case is theater or only distinguishes the theater of the courtroom from that of the playhouse. The latter alternative has been chosen here.[73]

3. *How far does the analysis carry?*

Added to the objections that the present analysis abuses both "metaphor" and the notion of theater is the further objection that the analysis is inapplicable to the methods by which some important judicial decisions are reached.

Trials, in which the greatest range of theatrics is exhibited, are a method

69. ARISTOTLE, POETICS 25 (G. Else trans. 1965); F. Fergusson, *supra* note 49, at 246; McCarthy, *supra* note 53, at 25, 28.

70. A. CHEKHOV, *Letter to Alexey S. Suvorin*, April 18, 1892, in THE PORTABLE CHEKHOV 624–25 (A. Yarmolinsky ed. 1947).

71. "In the theater our function is not to fix and assess a penalty, but to feel pity and fear—and to enjoy whatever pleasure may arise from those emotions." G. ELSE, ARISTOTLE'S POETICS: THE ARGUMENT (1957), quoted in THE MODERN THEATRE 10–11 (D. Seltzer ed. 1967).

72. *See, e.g.*, P. BROOK, *supra* note 25, at 136.

73. *See* notes 22–24 *supra* and accompanying text; note 138 *infra* and accompanying text.

for resolving only certain types of factual disputes. Professor Kenneth Culp Davis drew a useful distinction in this regard between adjudicative and legislative facts. Disputes about adjudicative facts ("facts about the parties and their activities, businesses, and properties, usually answering the questions of who did what, where, when, how, and why, with what motive or intent") are those appropriate to resolution by trial.[74] Legislative facts ("general facts which help the tribunal decide questions of law, policy, and discretion") are appropriate for oral argument and briefs, the typical procedure of appellate courts.[75]

Cases before appellate courts are governed by emphases, subject matter and methodology different from those of trials. Appellate emphasis is upon "legislative" fact, although "adjudicative" facts are neither unimportant nor without effect.[76] The subject matter is superficially the action of a lower court. The methodology places greater reliance upon argumentation and briefing and allows for extra-court development of legislative facts by the decisionmaker.[77]

The essentials of theater, however, are as clearly discernible, if less protean, in appellate as they are in trial courts. Facts and law are shaped into material which informs both a text and a histrionic presentation in a theatrical space before an audience. On appeal, the attorney's role as actor dominates that as director. Indeed, appellate attorneys are more authentically actors and more purely representative of their clients than their trial counterparts.[78] And their performance, their oral contest, is or may be critical to the outcome.[79]

To say that courtroom presentations are as essentially theatrical when they are appeals as when they are trials does not, however, address those instances in which judicial decisions are made without either trial or oral argument. The Supreme Court, for example, makes many decisions about whether or not to grant certiorari, decisions that are based upon documents. This choice of cases is of considerable importance to the Court's judicial responsibility, as the debate about a National Court of Appeals has reminded us.[80] The selection of cases and the subtle policy decisions it involves are judicial but are not the product of histrionic proceedings. They do bear upon

74. Davis, *The Requirement of a Trial-Type Hearing*, 70 HARV. L. REV. 193, 199 (1956).

75. *Id.*; *see id.* at 195. The allocation of adjudicative fact decisions to trial and of legislative facts to oral argument and briefs is not so rigid as to allow of no exceptions. *See id.* at 216.

76. *Cf.* K. LLEWELLYN, THE COMMON LAW TRADITION 121–22 (1960).

77. Davis cites the particular example of Justice Brandeis' dissent in Jay Burns Baking Co. v. Bryan, 264 U.S. 504, 517 (1924). Davis, *supra* note 74, at 193, 215 & n.82.

78. *See* notes 42–43 *supra* and accompanying text.

79. *See, e.g.*, K. LLEWELLYN, *supra* note 76, at 240 ("In oral argument lies the opportunity to catch attention and rouse interest . . . .").

80. *See, e.g.*, Black, *The National Court of Appeals: An Unwise Proposal*, 83 YALE L.J. 883, 888–90 (1974).

theater for they control which cases, which plays, will be produced. But judicial decisions which are the end product of exclusively documental occasions are not themselves theater. This limitation need not scuttle the analysis undertaken here if it be agreed that histrionic proceedings are the typical, though not exclusive, mode for reaching judicial decisions.

II. Courtroom Action as a Distinct Type of Theater

Their physical context, audiences, format and use of metaphor invite estimation of courtroom proceedings as a type of theater. Before exploring the import of the theatricality of courtroom action, it will be useful to fix more clearly, if still preliminarily, the identity of judicial theater as a distinct type.

A. *Theater of the Absurd*

One of the characteristics of judicial theater is its ordered sequences and exchanges. Disruption of the order may make it something else or may expose the fact that it has already been made into something else—perhaps theater of the absurd, a categorization suggested for the Chicago conspiracy trial.[81] The attorney's part in the specified flow of initiative and response, according to Professor Geoffrey Hazard, is "not soliloquy but—the pun is irresistible—a trialogue, a series of ordered exchanges with the judge and opposing counsel," interference with which means that "the lawyer's appearances and cues are lost or disordered and at some point his role and reason for being there simply collapse."[82] The same may be said of defendants.[83]

Superficially, it is courtroom disruption which converts judicial theater into another and incompatible type. However, it may be that attorneys and defendants abandon their preassigned roles in response to the belief that a prior transmutation has occurred and that the courts have already abandoned their own proper roles. About the Chicago trial, for example, the possibility was ventured that had the judge "consistently avoided playing it like a minstrel show, then defendants might not have played it like a

81. Lewis, *Lawyers and Civilization*, 120 U. Pa. L. Rev. 851, 862 (1972). *See generally* United States v. Dellinger, 472 F.2d 340 (7th Cir. 1972); *In re* Dellinger, 461 F.2d 389 (7th Cir. 1972); United States v. Seale, 461 F.2d 345 (7th Cir. 1972); *In re* Dellinger, 370 F. Supp. 1304 (N.D. Ill. 1973); United States *ex. rel.* Hoffman v. Dellinger, No. 69 CR 180, certificate of contempt (N.D. Ill., Feb. 14, 1970), *reprinted in In re* Dellinger, 461 F.2d 389, 404 (7th Cir. 1972); Clark, *Foreword*, & Kalven, *Introduction* to Contempt: Transcript of the Contempt Citations, Sentences, and Responses of the Chicago Conspiracy 10 (1970); Comment, *Invoking Summary Contempt Procedures—Use or Abuse?* United States v. Dellinger—*The "Chicago Seven" Contempts*, 69 Mich. L. Rev. 1549 (1971).

82. Hazard, Book Review, 80 Yale L.J. 433, 446 (1970).

83. *Cf.* Illinois v. Allen, 397 U.S. 337 (1970). Professor Berman has suggested that new rituals are necessary for trials in which defendants seek to proclaim political views, and he cites the trial of the Catonsville Nine as a case in which defendants were allowed to express their views. H. Berman, *supra* note 8, at 42. It has been suggested that "rituals will bend" to allow greater participation by criminal defendants, Tigar, *supra* note 13, at 27.

circus."[84] More broadly speaking, if the courts are perceived as instruments of oppression rather than of justice—if they are perceived to be not really courts—then notwithstanding the decorous behavior of judges, disorderly conduct may occur as an anguished protest against injustice and an appeal for justice.[85] The point sought to be made here is simply that whether disruption be immediately instigated by the parties, their counsel or the judge, it does make of the proceedings something other than the forensics of judicial theater.

B. *The Morality Play*

In addition to theater of the absurd, another type of theater from which judicial theater may be distinguished is the morality play. Especially criminal but also civil trials have been likened to morality plays.[86] The analogy fails for two reasons. First, the *dramatis personae* of morality plays were symbols or personified abstractions like Everyman, Goods, Fellowship, and Beauty.[87] Although episodes and character groupings might vary from one morality play to another, the endings were always the same.[88] In contrast, courts deal with individuals, the outcomes of whose cases have at least the potential for being neither preprogrammed, predictable nor uniform. Insofar as trials are prepackaged and routine rather than uniquely individual, it would seem that they are not really trials and might qualify as *immorality* plays.[89]

Second, morality plays featured symbols and a uniform conclusion because they were unapologetically and unrelievedly didactic—glosses on medieval Christian dogma. A trial is not the dramatization of a sermon.

84. Hazard, *supra* note 82, at 446. Hazard concludes: "The established order . . . by its own terms cannot win the struggle by the threatening mechanisms of legal prescription and penal sanction. It can win only through steadfast and unpretentious fulfillment of official roles, especially that of the judge. . . . [I]t is well to recognize that the struggles represented in political trials will not disappear until fundamental political dissension also disappears. That day may be less welcome than many might think." *Id.* at 450. A Special Committee on Courtroom Conduct of the Association of the Bar of the City of New York discovered that: "In many cases [of disruption], the judges reported that they were able to handle the disruptions simply by impressing on the defendants that they would receive a fair trial and acting to protect the defendants' rights." N. DORSEN & L. FRIEDMAN, *supra* note 13, at 6.

85. *Cf., e.g.*, Illinois v. Allen, 397 U.S. 337, 352–56 (1970) (Douglas, J., concurring). *See also* notes 164–70 *infra* and accompanying text.

86. Arnold, *The Criminal Trial as a Symbol of Public Morality*, in Y. KAMISAR, F. INBAU, & T. ARNOLD, CRIMINAL JUSTICE IN OUR TIME 137, 143–44 (1965) ("Trials are like the miracle or morality plays of ancient times. They dramatically present the conflicting moral values of a community in a way that could not be done by logical formalization. Civil trials perform this function as well as do criminal trials . . . ."); J. MORTON, THE FUNCTION OF CRIMINAL LAW IN 1962 at 30 (1962) ("It is my contention that the criminal trial is not merely suitable stuff for a play but *is itself a play*, a drama deliberately staged in furtherance of the great general end of the criminal process, that citizens should so conduct themselves as to avoid the types of behaviour which society has legally condemned. That the criminal trial is a contemporary morality play gives new meaning to the whole criminal process.")

87. *See* Anon., *The Summoning of Everyman* in THE DEVELOPMENT OF ENGLISH DRAMA 35 (G. Bentley ed. 1950).

88. *Id.*

89. *See* notes 167, 171–74 *infra* and accompanying text.

Insofar as it is made a platform for moralizing or a forum for educating, a trial is not a trial. Trials may indeed have an educative effect, but they have this effect when, instead of deliberately undertaking to teach, they treat the parties as individuals. In his concurring opinion in *Estes v. Texas*,[90] Chief Justice Warren noted that the Soviet Union's trial of U-2 pilot Francis Gary Powers sought both to determine the guilt of the individual and to provide the public with an object lesson. This divided purpose "undercut confidence in the guilt-determining aspect of the procedure and by so doing rendered the educational aspect self-defeating."[91]

C. *The Saturnalia and Play*

Quite the opposite of the morality play but equally distinct from courtroom theater is the saturnalia, an extravagant entertainment or orgy which gives vent to passion and in which all are participants.[92] The failure to distinguish between actors and audience may render saturnalia inimical to all types of theater.[93] In any event, saturnalia are incompatible with judicial proceedings. First, active participation by spectators imperils the forensic sequences no less than does disruption by attorneys and defendants. More importantly, mob scenes and the gathering and release of passion overrun reasoned deliberation and reduce the potential for protecting defendants' rights.[94]

To distinguish judicial theater from saturnalia is not to distinguish it from play, which may be understood, following Johann Huizinga, as

> a free activity standing quite consciously outside "ordinary" life as being "not serious," but at the same time absorbing the player intensely and utterly. . . . It proceeds within its own proper boundaries of time and space according to fixed rules and in an orderly manner.[95]

Orgies abandon limits and thus abandon play; court proceedings spring from play. In the course of an examination of the ancient relation between

90. 381 U.S. 532 (1965).

91. *Id.* at 575, 576. The Chief Justice's comment appears to grant that the U-2 trial was a good faith attempt to determine guilt as well as an educational lesson. Other Soviet trials may have been only a lesson whose point was not justice or the good faith determination of guilt. *See* A. SOLZHENITSYN, THE GULAG ARCHIPELAGO 299–431 (1973). According to Solzhenitsyn, the only purpose of trials was didactic, and they served as glosses on a Stalinistic sermon. They required careful management and had to be given up when they failed to keep to prearranged form. *See id.* at 419–31. *See also* notes 171–74 *infra* and accompanying text.

The potentially educative effect of trials is not to be denied. The point sought to be emphasized in the text is that this effect comes properly from the nature of the trial process as such and not from some superimposed or spurious object lesson. *Cf.* Griffiths, *supra* note 3, at 359–60. Ideally, the process should be instructive of the worth of people, which would be communicated by the respect and concern shown people in the process. *Cf.* Griffiths, *supra*, at 384–85.

92. *See* J. FRAZER, THE GOLDEN BOUGH 675–79 (Abridged ed. 1951).

93. *See* E. BENTLEY, THEATRE OF WAR 353 (1972).

94. *See* N. DORSEN & L. FRIEDMAN, *supra* note 13, at 13–15; *cf.* Moore v. Dempsey, 261 U.S. 86 (1923); Frank v. Mangum, 237 U.S. 309 (1915).

95. J. HUIZINGA, *supra* note 13, at 13.

play and law, Huizinga found that the lawsuit had originally been, in the strict sense of the word, an agon, a match or struggle, which (notwithstanding and even because of its seriousness, tension and emphasis on winning) was a form of play.[96] He discovered that an agonistic element, chiefly in the form of verbal battle, was still to be discerned in the lawsuit.[97] The engagement of adversaries in serious legal contest is agonistic but not orgiastic and is thus an expression of play.

D. *Theater of Fact*

The type of theater most obviously parallel to judicial theater is theater of fact. Theater of fact is documentary in appearance. Its scripts may consist of edited transcripts of hearings or trials. Father Berrigan, for example, simply lifted out portions of the transcript of his trial in order to make the text for a play.[98] Theater of fact is politically oriented, and its effect is generally accusatory. Hochhuth's *The Deputy*[99] does not differ greatly from a prosecutor's case, played in a theater to an audience sitting as a jury. What finally distinguishes judicial theater from theater of fact, and from other types to which it may bear similarity,[100] are the immediate judgment rendered in the courtroom and the consequences which attend it. An audience is not a jury. This distinction is only typological, however, for judicial proceedings remain theatrical in essence.[101]

III. The Functions of Judicial Theater

As a distinct type of theater, courtroom action is highlighted by ordered exchanges, nonprogrammatic individuality of outcome, and contest or play. What must now be considered are the purpose and effect of this judicial theater.

A. *Theater as a Means to Judgment*

1. *Encouraging impartiality.*

Courts may not always or even frequently do justice, but their theatrical quality does contribute to their potential for doing justice by encouraging disinterestedness in the decisionmakers. As actors, judge and jury are asked

96. *See* J. Huizinga, *supra* note 13, at 73, 76–88, 30–31, 48–53, 1–13. Huizinga's study is richly suggestive, and brief references to it must be supplemented by the acknowledgement that this essay has been much aided by it. *See also* notes 71–73 *supra* and accompanying text.

97. J. Huizinga, *supra* note 13, at 84.

98. *See* D. Berrigan, *supra* note 6.

99. *See* R. Hochhuth, The Deputy (R. & C. Winston transl. 1964). The subject of Hochhuth's controversial drama was the relationship of Pope Pius XII to the Third Reich. Specifically, the play raised questions about Pius' failure to take a public stance against the extermination of the Jews.

100. The plays of Pirandello, Ibsen and Genet are examples of other types which may be likened to judicial theater. *Cf., e.g.*, Chiaromonte, *supra* note 55 at 30; McCarthy, *supra* note 53, at 25, 29.

101. *See* notes 71–72 *supra* and accompanying text; notes 136–38 *infra* and accompanying text.

to play parts in a government of laws and not of people. They are to be those who decide according to law. Fulfillment of the roles enables judgments which rise above prejudice and which, therefore, will more likely be just. Not the least hoped for result of the theatrical trappings and conventions of judicial proceedings is to educe such performances.

Judge and jury are audience as well as actors[102] and in this capacity also may be encouraged to make unprejudiced judgments. Actors may be drawn beyond themselves by the roles they play, but they are not thereby totally absorbed in their parts for they maintain control of the characters they create on stage.[103] An equivalent mix of involvement and detachment is also possible for the audience.[104] A production which works absorbs the audience. The involvement is not total, however, for there remains a separation which arises from consciousness that what is being witnessed is a theatrical action. The separation allows the audience to make impartial judgments about what it sees.

Bertolt Brecht observed the phenomenon of audience involvement and separation and exploited it through the "alienation effect." Alienation, in this sense, "is the art of placing an action at a distance so that it can be judged objectively and so that it can be seen in relation to the world—or rather, worlds—around it."[105] Alienation stimulates conscious judgment by keeping the audience from simple identification with the characters of the play. Such alienation is encouraged by the manner in which the performers look at themselves as they perform.[106] Brecht noted of one production:

> The performer's self-observation, an artful and artistic act of self-alienation, stopped the spectator from losing himself in the character completely, i.e. to the point of giving up his own identity, and lent a splendid remoteness to the events. Yet the spectator's empathy was not entirely rejected. The audience identifies itself with the actor as being an observer, and accordingly develops his attitude of observing or looking on.[107]

This same attitude of limited identification with attorneys or parties while observing them and forming judgments about them is the attitude

102. *See* note 42 *supra* and accompanying text.

103. The complexities of acting, especially with respect to involvement and detachment are helpfully discussed by P. Brook, *supra* note 25, at 116–19. For an actress' view see Simon, *A Luminous Film Star Moves into Ibsen's "A Doll's House,"* N.Y. Times, Feb. 23, 1975, § 2, at 1, col. 1; at 7, cols. 1–6.

104. *See* McCarthy, *supra* note 53, at 25, 28–29.

105. Brook, *Introduction* to *The Persecution and Assassination of Jean Paul Marat as Performed by the Inmates of the Asylum of Charenton Under the Direction of the Marquis de Sade*, in The Modern Theatre 285, 286 (D. Seltzer ed. 1967).

106. In a discussion of the way in which the alienation effect is achieved in Chinese theater, Brecht said that the performers expressed awareness of being watched, unlike performers in the European tradition who act as though there were a fourth wall in addition to the three of the stage, thus giving the audience the feeling of being unseen spectators. The Chinese actor observes himself and "will occasionally look at the audience as if to say: isn't it just like that?" Brecht, *Alienation Effects in Chinese Acting*, in The Modern Theatre 276, 277 (D. Seltzer ed. 1967).

107. *Id.* at 278.

appropriately developed in judge and jury as audience.[108] The courtroom equivalent to alienation may arise from the way attorneys present their cases, from the comments by the judge, from bench conferences, and the like, all of which may remind the judge or jury that a decision about the action must be reached.[109] When courtroom theater is effective, then, decisionmakers are placed in roles which draw them beyond prejudice and enable them to make thinking judgments about cases.

2. *Facilitating the judgment process through live presentation.*

The case's formalization of the pertinent materials renders them amenable to judgment. Yet the construction and analysis necessary to deliver an object to judgment could be provided without histrionics. A court system can be hypothesized, for example, in which cases would be handled entirely by mail. Why is something like this not done? While the encouragement of detachment[110] may be justification enough for live presentation of cases, another connection may exist between the way cases are presented and the act of judgment in response to them which offers another rationale.

Communicating nonverbal information. It may be that live performance communicates nonverbally some of the information which the decisionmaker must take into account.[111] Demeanor evidence is an example. While it is undeniable that documents lack the capacity to convey nonverbal information, it has been contended that videotape may do so as well as live presentation.[112] Opinion on the issue will likely continue to be divided since the communication of nonverbal information is not easily made the subject of testing or verbal analysis.[113] It would seem, however, that what is true of plays is true as well of cases: "The little ritual of performance, given

108. It is tempting, but probably false, to draw an analogy between the jury and the Greek chorus. Nietzsche noted of the chorus that it was "the primary *dramatic* phenomenon: projecting oneself outside oneself and then acting as though one had really entered another body, another character. This constitutes the first step in the evolution of drama." F. NIETZSCHE, *The Birth of Tragedy* in THE BIRTH OF TRAGEDY AND THE GENEALOGY OF MORALS 55 (1956).

109. After his own service on a jury, drama critic Stanley Kauffmann wrote that "legal folk insist on being concerned with matters other than sustaining the interest of the spectators, including the jury. There are innumerable delays, recesses, readings of documents into the record and—most irritating of all—whispered conferences at the bench between judge and both counsel, out of earshot." Kauffmann, *Just Like Life, Only Different*, N.Y. Times, Feb. 27, 1966, § 2 at 1, col. 4. Kauffmann thought this side action to be "poor dramaturgy." It may well have been. But it may also have been a form of alienation effect in judicial theater, an irritant which provided distance between the jury and the witnesses and which served as a reminder that a judgment had to be formed in response to what was being presented.

110. *See* notes 102–09 *supra* and accompanying text.

111. *See* Frank, *supra* note 11, at 21.

112. *See* Note, *Video-Tape Trials: A Practical Evaluation and a Legal Analysis*, 26 STAN. L. REV. 619, 623–24 & nn.29–30 (1974).

113. *Compare id., with* Note, *Videotape Trials: Legal and Practical Implications*, 9 COL. J.L. & SOC. PROB. 363, 374 n.67, 381, 389–90 (1973). *See also* Brakel, *Videotape in Trial Proceedings: A Technological Obsession?*, 61 A.B.A.J. 956 (1975); Doret, *Trial by Videotape—Can Justice Be Seen To Be Done?*, 47 TEMP. L.Q. 228, 241–61 (1974). For judicial comment see Hendricks v. Swenson, 456 F.2d 503, 506, 507–09 (8th Cir. 1972).

just a modicum of competence, can lend to the events represented another dimension, a more urgent reality."[114]

Enlarging the mind. In addition to the communication of nonverbal information, live courtroom presentation may also correlate with the mental processes whereby judgments are formulated. Judge Joseph C. Hutcheson, Jr., explained how, in the cases not easily resolved,

> the judge may, reconciling all the testimony reconcilable, and coming to the crux of the conflict, having a full and complete picture of the scene itself furnished by the actors, re-enact the drama and as the scene unfolds with the actors each in the place assigned by his own testimony, play the piece out, watching for the joints in the armor of proof, the crevices in the structure of the case or its defense. If the first run fails, the piece may be played over and over until finally, when it seems perhaps impossible to work any consistent truth out of it, the hunch comes, the scenes and the players are rearranged in accordance with it, and lo, it works successfully and in order.[115]

The word "hunch" is loaded and, one suspects, was deliberately employed for its provocative effect. For present purposes, however, attention should be focused upon Judge Hutcheson's account of the prelude to the "hunch." The decisionmaker plays the performance over; the case is reproduced in the mind. The reproductions rearrange scenes until they work; that is, the case is played over from different points of view until it yields a consistent and satisfactory judgment.

Kant discovered that judgment is enabled by the "enlarged mind."[116] He found an enlarged mind to be indicated by the habit of reflecting upon one's own judgment from a universal standpoint which is established by shifting ground to the standpoint of others. This is not a matter of thinking like or empathizing with or being led by others. It is a matter of thinking for oneself in the position of others. According to Kant,

> we have quite got into the way of calling a man narrow (*narrow*, as opposed to being *of enlarged mind*) whose talents fall short of what is required for employment upon work of any magnitude (especially that involving intensity). But the question here is not one of the faculty of cognition, but of the *mental habit* of making a final use of it. This, however small the range and degree to which a man's natural endowments extend, still indicates a man of *enlarged mind*: if he detaches himself from the subjective personal conditions of his judgement, which cramp the minds of so many others, and reflects upon his own judgement from a *universal standpoint*.[117]

114. E. Bentley, *supra* note 10, at 207. *Cf.* F. Fergusson, *supra* note 49, at 250–55 (on the "histrionic sensibility").

115. Hutcheson, *The Judgment Intuitive: The Function of the "Hunch" in Judicial Decision*, 14 Cornell L.Q. 274, 282–83 (1929). *See* J. Frank, *supra* note 11, at 170–85.

116. I. Kant, The Critique of Judgement 150–53 (J. Meredith transl. 1957).

117. *Id.* at 153.

It may not damage Kant's insight too greatly to bring it to bear, as he did not, upon judicial decisionmaking. The courtroom presentation invites the decisionmaker to play the case over in his mind from the standpoint of the plaintiff or prosecutor, from the standpoint of the defendant, from the standpoint of judges who have decided similar cases in the past, and from the standpoint of reasonable people in general, thereby ultimately reaching a valid judgment. The courtroom presentation may act in this way as a stimulus to the enlarged mind. It may encourage the critical faculty to take account of various representations, "in order, as it were," as Kant said in a different context, "to weigh its judgment with the collective reason of mankind, and thereby avoid the illusion arising from subjective and personal conditions which could readily be taken for objective, an illusion that would exert a prejudicial influence upon its judgment."[118]

Inducing creativity. To the suggestions that it may communicate non-verbal information and may correlate with the mind's mode of making judgments, there may be added a third: Live presentation is perhaps an inducement to creativity in judgment.[119] Of the cases which come to court, one recent estimate placed at 30 to 40 percent of the total those which can be decided but one way because they clearly fall within the ambit of a clearly and authoritatively stated rule.[120] Even in these "clear" cases live presentation may promote the search for imaginative alternatives if it makes disposition less mechanical by giving force and appeal to the position of the party against whom the rule is to be applied.[121]

It is more certainly an active element in the unclear cases. In these it may give more urgent reality to the particular facts which establish distance between a given case and a general rule or which expose a given case to com-

118. *Id.* at 151.

119. Live presentation may encourage what Judge Hutcheson referred to as "hunching." *See* note 115 *supra* and accompanying text. "Hunching" is what Judge Frank would call experiencing a gestalt. FRANK, *supra* note 11, at 170–71. The word "hunch" has not been used in the present context both because it might be misleading and because it is inadequate to convey the creative nature of the phenomenon.

120. Craven, *Paean to Pragmatism*, 50 N.C.L. REV. 977, 978 (1972). Cardozo estimated 9 out of 10. B. CARDOZO, THE GROWTH OF THE LAW 60 (1924). Both estimates are based on the exercise of rule discretion. In Judge Frank's view, the exercise of fact discretion is overlooked in such accounts. He maintained that discretion in finding facts is almost boundless for trial judges. *See* J. FRANK, *supra* note 11, at 56–57. If Judge Frank is right, then it may be said that live presentation is directed to and encourages the exercise of fact discretion. The exercise of discretion and creativity may be more freely exercised by trial courts than by appellate courts in the finding and statement of fact. But the discretion exists for both, if to a lesser degree at the appellate level. It may be that there is creative interpretation of rules at the trial level in the way the facts are found and creative interpretation of facts by appellate courts in the way the rules (rather than the facts) are "found." *See generally id.* at 165–70, 316–25. In any event, the possible inducement to creativity offered by live presentation is equally applicable to trial courts, appellate courts and trial juries.

121. Live presentation may also make disposition easier. For example, it may become evident at trial that a key witness lacks credibility.

The judge's alternatives may not be as numerous as those of the jury since the latter need give no reasons for its judgments and may simply "nullify" the rule. *See* United States v. Maybury, 274 F.2d 899 (2d Cir. 1960).

peting rules.[122] Performance of cases, by thus contributing to the indeterminacy of rules, helps to bring about the conditions for creative resolution. It may also have some influence upon the creativity which is exercised in those conditions. This influence may extend no further than some potential of performance to dispose the decisionmaker to respond in kind, that is, creatively rather than routinely or with formulae. Or, live presentation of cases may have a suggestive influence upon the substance and methodology of judgment. How this might be so really requires full, separate treatment. An indication of how the analysis might proceed will have to suffice here.

In the unclear cases the rules are indeterminate and the problem is how a decision is to be made.[123] Live presentation may indicate something of the sources to which decisionmakers may turn in these cases in two ways. First, live presentation may shift attention from the rules of decision to the environment of decision.[124] That is, the human drama played out in court may in and of itself give evidence that the case takes place within a greater drama of human realities not limited to rules or abstractions.[125] Second, this greater context may bear possibilities of guidance for judgment. For example, in a

122. Cases really worth litigating will generally involve competing rules (with competing fact constructions in their support). As my colleague Professor Taylor has put the matter, "the doctrine of precedent is in most instances a theory of possibilities." Taylor, *H.L.A. Hart's Concept of Law in the Perspective of American Realism*, 35 MOD. L. REV. 606, 611 (1972).

123. *See* W. FRIEDMANN, LAW IN A CHANGING SOCIETY 53 (1972). *See generally* H.L.A. Hart, *Positivism and The Separation of Law and Morals*, 71 HARV. L. REV. 593 (1958); Fuller, *Positivism and Fidelity to Law—A Reply to Professor Hart*, 71 HARV. L. REV. 630 (1958). It may aid legal precision to distinguish between rules and principles, as Professor Dworkin does. *See* Dworkin, *The Model of Rules*, 35 U. CHI. L. REV. 14, 25–26, 36 (1967). But the distinction does not alleviate the task of judgment.

124. The distinction between the rules and the environment of decision was drawn by Professor Paul Lehmann in a discussion of ethical decisionmaking: "Obviously the kind of ethical literalism which aims at a one-to-one correlation between a specific word of Jesus and a specific action misses the point of Jesus' teaching. Decision making as the Christian understands it goes on in quite another way. For the Christian, the *environment* of decision, not the *rules* of decision, gives to behavior its ethical significance.

". . . Consequently, Christian ethics in the tradition of the Reformation seeks to provide an analysis of the environment of decision in which the principal foundations and preceptual directives of behavior are displaced by *contextual foundations* and *parabolic directives*. In a word, *the environment of decision is the context for the ethical reality of conscience*." P. LEHMANN, ETHICS IN A CHRISTIAN CONTEXT 346–47 (1963).

125. Professor Lehmann describes the context of decisionmaking in terms of God's political activity in the world "doing what it takes to make and to keep human life human in the world." *Id.* at 347; *see id.* at 74–86 *passim*. Dean Wellington displays a certain attention to the context for decisionmaking, but for him the context is one of "conventional morality." He claimed: "[W]hen dealing with legal principles a court must take a moral point of view. Yet I doubt that one would want to say that a court is entitled or required to assert *its* moral point of view. Unlike the moral philosopher, the court is required to assert ours. This requirement imposes constraints: Judicial reasoning in concrete cases must proceed from society's set of moral principles and ideals, in much the same way that the judicial interpretation of documents (contracts, statutes, constitutions—especially constitutions) must proceed from the document. And that is why we must be concerned with conventional morality, for it is there that society's set of moral principles and ideals are located." Wellington, *Common Law Rules and Constitutional Double Standards: Some Notes on Adjudication*, 83 YALE L.J. 221, 244 (1973). Yet, conventional morality, like rules and principles, is not determinative of concrete cases. And live presentation would seem to have little reference to it. The point about live presentation is that it calls into play, or may call into play, sources for judgment a good deal livelier and more dynamic than any abstraction, such as a rule, a principle, or conventional morality.

discussion of law in ancient Israel, the theologian Karl Barth said that "everything that Israel *shall* is only an imperative transcription of what Israel *is* . . . ."[126] As much in our circumstances as in those of ancient Israel, what to do may be indicated by what we as a people truly are. Hence, judgment would be sustained by correct description and understanding of the constitution of human society in general and this society in particular. Such an enterprise would not terminate questions but only assist in determining what the right questions are. Substantively, debate about right rules would be less important than debate about authentically human realities, and attention would ultimately be focussed upon preeminently theological questions[127] about history and politics.[128] Methodologically, application of rules to cases would become subordinate to apperception of how the community's reality takes shape in a given controversy.[129] All of which is to say that cases have a context and that presentation of cases to courts in live performance may make that context's resources somewhat more accessible for judgment.

It should not be concluded from the foregoing discussion that live presentation seduces courts into making undisciplined judgments. Judges may yield to bias and prejudice but not in consequence of live presentation. A legal judgment may be creative without being undisciplined.[130] In this regard it is like fine art. Although original, as Kant observed,

> there is still no fine art in which something mechanical, capable of being at once comprehended and followed in obedience to rules, and consequently something *academic* does not constitute the essential condition of the art.[131]

The formal requirement that judges, unlike artists, state reasons for what they have done offers added assurance that discipline will be exercised.[132]

126. K. Barth, 2 Church Dogmatics 572 (1957) (emphasis added). *See id.* at 562.

127. "Theological questions" are those which deal with the basis and content of human life, and are not to be confined to inquiries about the nature and existence of "God."

128. The best and most recent discussion of such questions and their relation to law is P. Lehmann, The Transfiguration of Politics 250–59 (1975). For other comment on the possible relationships between law and theology, see H. Berman, *supra* note 8; Jones, *Law and Morality in the Perspective of Legal Realism*, 61 Colum. L. Rev. 799, 801–02 (1961); Note, *The Politics of God in the Maturation of the Law*, 4 Ga. L. Rev. 555 (1970).

129. *See* P. Lehmann, *supra* note 128, at 258; Ball, *Judicial Protection of Powerless Minorities*; 59 Iowa L. Rev. 1059 (1974).

130. *See* note 115 *supra* and accompanying text; Taylor, *supra* note 122, at 614–15. *See also* J. Frank, *supra* note 11, at 183–85.

131. I. Kant, *supra* note 116, at 171–72.

132. *See, e.g.*, White, *The Evolution of Reasoned Elaboration: Jurisprudential Criticism and Social Change*, 59 Va. L. Rev. 279, 299–301 (1973). Dewey spoke of a "logic of exposition [which] is different from that of search and inquiry." Dewey, *supra* note 44, at 24. The statement of reasons for a judgment should not be confused with the act of judgment. What is decided and how the judge explains that decision have a complex interrelationship but are distinguishable. Nor is the judicial opinion to be taken as a report of the process followed by a judge in reaching a decision just as a play is not to be taken as a direct revelation of the workings of its author's mind. Rather, it is a response to and the concluding part of the courtroom event. It is the public, reasoned apologia for the correctness of what has been done. Insofar as it is a persuasive device and a substitution for (not diary of) the actual decisionmaking process, it is, like the attorney's case, a metaphor and is suggestive

B. *Theater as an End in Itself*

If the purpose of judicial proceedings is to decide cases and nothing more, then trials and oral presentations may have value as methods for producing judgments. That is, the theatricality of judicial proceedings may foster just decisions through encouraging impartiality and aiding the mental judgment process. But in the interests of economy, efficiency and productivity, other more expeditious means than live presentation might also be employed. On the other hand, if trials and oral arguments are, as much so as decisions, the "good" consumed, then they have inherent value and no adequate substitute. The validity of this latter option draws support from consideration of the dynamic functions of courts.

1. *Redirecting aggression.*

The theatrical character of lawsuits allows them to redirect aggression. Aggression, the need to fight and have revenge, is acted out[133] and is thereby ritually expressed and controlled.[134] It is in this sense that "[t]he right to sue and defend in the courts is the alternative of force."[135]

The continued capacity of lawsuits to rechannel aggression depends upon several factors, one of which is their gravity, that is, their convictive and absorptive power.[136] This power may arise from the fascination and purgation of the action itself, as was the case with the "good show" in early American courtrooms when "it was a secondary matter with the client whether he won or lost his case, so the 'pleading' was loud and long."[137] Or interest may be engaged and satisfied by the stakes. Money damages, decrees or imprisonment give to judicial theater a moment missing from that

---

of texts for future productions. Its rule cannot be set down as a precept, for, to return again to Kant and the analogy of art, "the rule [must] be gathered from the performance, i.e. from the product, which others may use to put their own talent to the test, so as to let it serve as a model, not for imitation, but for *following*." I. KANT, *supra* note 116, at 171.

133. In an intriguing analysis of the United Nations as drama, Conor Cruise O'Brien proposed that "for the preservation of peace among actual unimproved men the agonistic element remains of the greatest importance, for letting off steam, for saving face, for sanctifying retreat, for purification, and in other ways." C. O'BRIEN & F. TOPOLSKI, THE UNITED NATIONS: SACRED DRAMA 282 (1968). *See also* J. HUIZINGA, *supra* note 13, at 46–75 ("Play and Contest as Civilizing Functions").

134. Lorenz maintained that "it is particularly the drives that have arisen by ritualization which are so often called upon . . . to oppose aggression, to divert it into harmless channels, and to inhibit those of its actions that are injurious to the survival of the species." K. LORENZ, ON AGGRESSION 67 (1966). *See* C. O'BRIEN & F. TOPOLSKI, *supra* note 133, at 275–285.

135. Chambers v. Baltimore & O.R.R., 207 U.S. 142, 148 (1907). The Court went on to say that the right to sue and defend is "conservative of all other rights, and lies at the foundation of orderly government." *Id. See* Missouri v. Illinois 200 U.S. 496, 520–21 (1906). *See also* J. FRANK *supra* note 11, at 5–9, 26–27.

136. *See* J. HUIZINGA, *supra* note 13, at 49 (" 'There is something at stake'—the essence of play is contained in that phrase.")

137. J. WIGMORE, A. KALEIDOSCOPE OF JUSTICE 487 (1941), *quoted in* Estes v. Texas, 381 U.S. 532, 570 (1965) (Warren, C.J., concurring). Huizinga reports from an English newspaper the story that "a judge received a visit from a man who had lost his case on the previous day, but now said contentedly: 'I had a very bad lawyer, you know, all the same I'm glad to have had a good run for my money!' " J. HUIZINGA, *supra* note 13, at 84.

of Broadway. They do not, for all that, make it any the less play; they simply make it more serious.[138]

Besides their gravity, another, more decisive factor which maintains legal proceedings as an alternative to other forms of aggression is their fairness. The procedures and conventions of the courtroom set judicial proceedings apart from the world of common, daily affairs. Acceptance of this playworld cannot be commanded. Judges, like referees, can penalize for irregularities—dismissal of suits, contempt citations, binding and gagging defendants. But these can be no more than remedial measures. Punishment for infraction after the fact does not generate the necessary, precedent willingness to accept the special world marked off by court rules and conventions. Acceptance of judicial proceedings must be voluntary, and is consequently dependent upon the perceived fairness of the courts.[139]

If acceptance of the rules of play ultimately depends upon their fairness, acceptance of the play world they mark off depends upon that world's making good on its express and implied claims. Playgoers bring with them to the theater a "willing suspension of disbelief,"[140] a willingness not to see an actor and a bare stage when presented with Macbeth and Birnam wood come to Dunsinane. This "negative faith in the existence"[141] of the play world can be violated as a result of any of several causes: a lapse in writers' or actors' skill or a failure of artifice and craft in staging. The really serious offense for which the license granted theater is revoked is its failure to redeem the pledge to entertain or supply catharsis or mirror nature—in a word, to be theater.

Participants in judicial proceedings also bring with them a willing suspension of disbelief. It is manifested in their willingness to observe the rules and forms of the proceedings, their willingness to abide by the outcome of

138. *See* notes 95–97 *supra* and accompanying text. Stanley Kauffman has observed that while the seriousness of judicial theater is sufficient in itself to sustain audience interest, ordinary theater requires something more to achieve the same objective: "For the spectator, what holds it all together between the high points of interest is the constant realization that a live man—right there before you—will or will not have years sheared off his free life because of these proceedings. . . . In the actual courtroom, a civilized man wants primarily to see justice done. At the courtroom play [i.e. a stage drama about a trial or in a trial setting], that same civilized man wants to see blood—either the defendant's or, if he is innocent, the true culprit's. A courtroom play that merely proved the defendant's innocence and found nobody guilty would fizzle." Kauffmann, *supra* note 109, at col. 5.

139. As Huizinga concluded about the play and its rules in general, "real civilization cannot exist in the absence of a certain play-element, for civilization presupposes limitation and mastery of the self, the ability not to confuse its own tendencies with the ultimate and highest goal, but to understand that it is enclosed within certain bounds freely accepted. . . . To be a sound culture-creating force this play-element must be pure. It must not consist in the darkening or debasing of standards set up by reason, faith or humanity. It must not be a false seeming, a masking of political purposes behind the illusion of genuine play-forms. True play knows no propaganda . . . ." J. Huizinga, *supra* note 13, at 211.

140. S. Coleridge, *Biographia Literaria* in Selected Poetry and Prose 264 (D. Stauffer ed. 1951).

141. *Id.* at 349. *See also* S. Coleridge, *Lectures and Notes on Poetry, Drama, Shakespeare, and Other Critical Notes*, *id.* at 403–04.

the proceedings, and their willingness not to dismiss the legitimacy of the legal system, characterized though it may be by curious formulae, arcane rites and untoward results. Like the license granted theater, this willingness will answer for any sustained length of time only to the system's reasonable degree of success in doing what it promises, in this case justice.[142]

2. *Providing an image of legitimate political community.*

John Marshall wrote that "[i]t is emphatically the province and duty of the judicial department to say what the law is."[143] This duty involves more than the mere utterance of disembodied words. As the department charged with review, the judicial branch must be the exemplar of law. In its ceremony, its costuming, its performance, and its treatment of participants in courtrooms, it embodies the legitimate exercise of power within a given sphere.[144] Thus judicial theater is itself a continuous way of saying, in things and acts within appointed spaces, what the law is.

There is a unity between this theatrical medium and its subject—the political community. Ernest Barker noted that the state, as a sphere of legal action, may be called the scene of a legal drama played by legal actors, who are artificial persons.[145] The term "artificial persons" is not a pejorative reference but an indication of the original meaning of the word *persona*, which was a theatrical term and signified the mask worn by an actor. This sense continued to be attached to the word when it was carried over into the law. The *persona juris* is a role, just as the *dramatis persona* is. And just as *dramatis personae* are created by dramatists, *personae* in law are "juridical creations, or artifices, or fictions. . . . It is not the natural Ego which enters a court of law. It is a right-and-duty-bearing person, created by the law, which appears before the law."[146]

The *persona juris*, like the *dramatis persona*, is intended to be a humanizing rather than a repressive fixture because it is as much a means of expression *for* as it is a mask of the person, and even its masking function is protective.[147] Hannah Arendt has pointed out that the *persona* or mask worn

142. *See* notes 84–85 *supra* and accompanying text. To the degree that the theatrics of court contribute to just judgment, see notes 111–29 *supra* and accompanying text, they also contribute to the acceptance of court rules and forms as just.

143. Marbury v. Madison, 5 U.S. (1 Cranch) 137, 177 (1803).

144. A spatial significance lay behind the Greek word for law, *nomos*. Compared to the scientific notion of law, which suggests causal sequences in time, *nomos*, as F.M. Cornford observed, signified "a range or province within which power may be legitimately exercised . . . ." F. Cornford, *supra* note 13, at 30. This sense of law is not unfamiliar and is reflected in the Constitution's division between state and federal governments and the subdivision into branches, a dispensation which fixes boundaries for the exercise of power.

145. Barker, *Introduction* to O. Gierke, Natural Law and The Theory of Society lxx (E. Barker transl. 1960). *See id.* at lxxv–vi.

146. *Id.* at lxxi.

147. It is clear that the rights of the citizen are protective. But the other face of the *persona juris*, *i.e.* duties, also contributes to the vindication of the human. It does so by holding citizens responsible

by ancient actors replaced the actor's face but allowed the voice to sound through.[148] Hence, it acted also as a resonator. This double function is carried out as well by the *persona* of law. On the one hand, the *persona juris* is the means by which a member of the community has a voice in the community's affairs.[149] Those who are citizens, *i.e.*, who have *personae juris*, have purposeful roles to perform which fit them with a vehicle for being taken seriously and with a dignifying, public identity. This is the resonating function. On the other hand, the *persona juris* also has the function of hiding. The effect is less to stifle or suppress the person than to offer protection. The state may not intrude behind the mask, may not intrude upon the person beyond the rights and duties of the *persona*.

Judicial theater, then, holds up a mirror to legitimate society[150] insofar as the courtroom is the locus for trying on, trying out and proving *personae juris*. It images lawful political community. Accordingly, trial practice may serve as a measure of the out-of-court conduct of nonjudicial officials, such as the police. In *Ashcraft v. Tennessee*,[151] for instance, the Supreme Court said:

> It is inconceivable that any court of justice in the land, conducted as our courts are, open to the public, would permit prosecutors serving in relays to keep a defendant witness under continuous cross-examination for thirty-six hours without rest or sleep in an effort to extract a "voluntary" confession. Nor can we, consistently with Constitutional due process of law, hold voluntary a confession where prosecutors do the same thing away from the restraining influences of a public trial in an open court room.[152]

This image of the courtroom as standard of the stationhouse could be viewed as given effect through the exclusionary rule whereby evidence ob-

---

for actions and their consequences so that citizens may be understood and understand themselves as responsible individuals and not as automatons in the machinery of corporation or state. *Cf.* Reich, *Reflections: The Limits of Duty*, THE NEW YORKER, June 19, 1971, at 52.

148. H. ARENDT, ON REVOLUTION 102 (1965); *see id.* at 103, 296 n.42.

149. The Founding Fathers referred to the state as a stage or theater. *Cf.* G. WASHINGTON, *Address to Congress on Resigning His Commission*, Dec. 23, 1783, in 27 WRITINGS OF WASHINGTON 284, 285 (J. Fitzpatrick ed. 1938); D. MALONE, JEFFERSON AND THE RIGHTS OF MAN 274 (1951) (Jefferson); H. ARENDT, *supra* note 148, at 200 (Madison). It was the platform upon which citizens acted out public parts of importance and responsibility from local town meetings to the national congress. *Cf.* H. ARENDT, *supra*, at 111–37.

150. "[S]uit the action to the word, the word to the action; with this special observance, that you o'erstep not the modesty of nature: for anything so overdone is from the purpose of playing, whose end, both at the first and now, was and is, to hold, as 'twere, the mirror up to nature; to show virtue her own feature, scorn her own image, and the very age and body of the time his form and pressure." W. SHAKESPEARE, HAMLET, Act III, sc. 2. Bentley comments: "Hamlet spoke of the actor as holding up the mirror not to the picture people have of themselves but to nature, that is to people as they really are—a very different matter. In his use of this figure, Shakespeare was following an established tradition according to which the mirror was held up to human affairs to the end that men might be inspired by a good example or warned by a bad one. It was a normative mirror. Though art imitated life, it did not do so just for the record, but in order to improve life . . . ." E. BENTLEY, *supra* note 10, at 81.

151. 322 U.S. 143 (1944).

152. *Id.* at 154.

tained by the police in violation of the standard may be inadmissible at trial.[153] If this view was correct, then, besides effectuating the image, the exclusion of otherwise relevant evidence could also be said to preserve it, compound it, and certify its general applicability. The image of the courtroom as standard of the stationhouse rarely surfaces in judicial opinions, and one commentator has explicitly denied that the image serves as a basis for judgment about the admissibility of involuntary confessions.[154] Nevertheless, there does seem to be something of the *Ashcraft* vision in Justice Brennan's appreciation of the exclusionary rule as "enabling the judiciary to avoid the taint of partnership in official lawlessness and . . . assuring the people . . . that the government would not profit from its lawless behavior, thus minimizing the risk of seriously undermining popular trust in government."[155]

A further illustration of judicial proceedings as a normative image of legitimate society is provided by the recent case of *Goss v. Lopez*,[156] which held that public school students may not be suspended for as long as 10 days without notice of the charges against them and opportunity to be heard in response. Although such suspensions may not require "even truncated trial type procedures" but only "an informal give-and-take between student and disciplinarian," in the instance of longer or "unusual" suspensions, the Court went on to observe, more formal (or trial-like) procedures may be required.[157] In dissent, Justice Powell objected to this "constitutionalization"[158] of student-teacher relations because of, among other things, "its indiscriminate reliance upon the judiciary, and the adversary process, as the means of resolving many of the most routine problems arising in the classroom."[159]

153. Various reasons have been offered for the exclusionary rule. Justice Rehnquist, writing for the Court in *Michigan v. Tucker*, 417 U.S. 433 (1974), listed four of them: to deter unlawful police conduct, to protect the courts from unreliable evidence, to place upon government the entire load of building its case, and to recognize the imperative of judicial integrity. *Id.* at 446–50, 450 n.25. The fourth rationale was identified by Justice Rehnquist as only an assimilation of the prior three. *Id.* at 450 n.25. *See also* Kaplan, *The Limits of the Exclusionary Rule*, 26 STAN. L. REV. 1027, 1036 n.53 (1974).

154. Kamisar, *Equal Justice in the Gatehouses and Mansions of American Criminal Procedure*, in Y. KAMISAR, F. INBAU & T. ARNOLD, *supra* note 86 at 1, 11–13 (1965). *Compare* H. PACKER, *supra* note 64, at 149–246.

155. United States v. Calandra, 414 U.S. 338, 357 (1974) (Brennan, J., dissenting). The majority held that the exclusionary rule does not apply to grand jury proceedings. Grand jury proceedings would have seemed a natural circumstance for effectuation of the courtroom image through the exclusionary rule. The majority did not seize the opportunity, but neither did it explicitly reject the notion of judicial proceedings as measures of extra-court actions. It is instructive in this regard to compare Justice Powell's opinion for the majority in *Calandra* with his dissent in *Goss v. Lopez*, 419 U.S. 565, 594–95, 597 n.13 (1975) (Powell, J., dissenting). *See* notes 158–160 *infra* and accompanying text.

The author expresses indebtedness to his colleague Professor Edward Chase for instruction in the possible approaches to understanding the exclusionary rule.

156. 419 U.S. 565 (1975).

157. *Id.* at 583–84.

158. *Id.* at 597 (Powell, J., dissenting).

159. *Id.* at 594.

Apparently for Justice Powell the appropriateness of "constitutionalizing" relationships—subjecting them to the image and review of the judiciary—depends upon their characterization as "faceless" or adversarial.[160] His analysis may be related to the present one by saying that when encounters between citizens take place in depersonalized settings or involve conflicting interests, then it is fitting for courts to intervene both to supply a "face" or mask, the *persona juris*, which distinguishes and protects the individual, and to require that the actors perform roles suitable to their *personae*.[161] This intervention may be a "constitutionalization" of relationships; it also conceives them in the image of judicial theater.

Although it is not the purpose of this Essay to provide an express theory of the occasions for or the content of judicial review, a kind of standard of review can be specified. This standard combines the approaches of both the majority and minority in *Goss*[162] and may be stated as follows: "Faceless" and adversarial relationships may be judicially scrutinized. The parties will be viewed in the perspective of *persona* in judicial theater. As a relationship becomes more faceless or adversarial, the image of judicial proceedings will be brought more fully into play, and the participants will be required to approximate more closely the roles and sequences of court. Thus, in the stationhouse there is greater likelihood of facelessness and conflict of interest between police and suspects than there is in the schoolhouse between teachers and students. Correspondingly, more courtlike attitudes and procedures may be required of the police than may be required of school authorities. In both circumstances, the tendency of those in positions of power to treat those in their command as less than right-and-duty-bearing persons is countered by the insertion of a compensating requirement that elements of judicial theater be incorporated into the relationship.

The important points are that judicial proceedings may be images of the legitimate treatment of citizens by the police, by the government as a whole, and by one another in their public, social relations; and that this image is theatrical. There is not a literal correspondence between the image and the society. That is to say, the criminal process, the administration of government and the conduct of social transactions are not "judicialized"[163]

160. *See id.* at 594–95 n.13: "In many of these noneducation settings [in which due process hearings have been required] there is—for purposes of this analysis—a 'faceless' administrator dealing with an equally 'faceless' recipient of some form of government benefit or license; in others, such as the garnishment and repossession cases, there is a conflict of interest relationship."

161. *See also* note 57 *supra*.

162. The majority would seem to allow flexibility in the degree of formality in the proceedings required. *See* note 157 *supra* and accompanying text. The minority would seem to allow some flexibility in the determination of which situations require intervention. *See* note 160 *supra* and accompanying text. The combination of the two would then produce the test indicated in the text.

163. In speaking of the development of officially determined norms of the criminal process, a progression which has involved a closer and closer approximation of the "Due Process Model," Packer observed that among the principal thrusts has been the tendency "to 'judicialize' each stage of the criminal process . . . ." H. PACKER, *supra* note 64, at 239.

or "constitutionalized" or "theatricalized" by requiring that every encounter be accompanied by robing, attorneys and solemn oaths. Rather, the suggestion is that the action of the courtroom, as a type of theater, is an image of the manner in which citizens are to have parts of importance and dignity, to be taken seriously and with ceremonious, protective deference, and to have their rights and duties fairly recognized.

IV. Conclusion

This essay began with assent to the fact of the courts' theatricality and then sought to discover how much might be said, intelligibly if experimentally, about judicial theater as such. That the courtroom is theater seems clear; that it could not or should not be otherwise seems less clear. Why not pursue other modes of making judgments in the judicial system? Immemorial usage and peoples' ineluctable need for drama in some form do not necessarily preclude development of more time- and cost-efficient alternatives to judicial theater. There has been an unstated assumption in this essay's exploration of the service of judicial theater as a means to the end of judgment and as an estimable end in itself. The assumption has been that more economical alternatives to judicial theater would not only alter the essence of the courtroom, but would do so only at the excessive expense of a cherished human efficacy. A brief qualification and explanation of this assumption will serve as a conclusion to the essay.

The approbation of the theatrical character of courts which underlies the foregoing pages is qualified by acknowledgement of the vulnerability of judicial theater. The courts may fail to offer an image of the political community by turning in upon themselves, thereby either creating too great a distance from the human realities they are to mirror[164] or overemphasizing the theatrical trappings so that dress and decorum become precious objects in themselves.[165] The courts may also fail to reflect the correct image—the image not of the political community as it legitimately and really is but as it may appear at any present moment when seized by "ill

164. Some distance between the courts and the ordinary is necessary. *See* notes 105–109 *supra* and accompanying text. But this distancing does not require removal from human realities. When human realities are lost, overhaul is necessary.

165. *See* H. Berman, *supra* note 8, at 36–37; P. Lehmann, *supra* note 128, at 75–76. Lehmann found that too much and the wrong things had been made of courtroom decorum by Chief Justice Burger's address on *The Necessity for Civility*, 52 F.R.D. 211 (1971). The Chief Justice, Lehmann wrote, "chose to take moral flight above the pain and passion of mounting courtroom disorders . . . and to lecture his professional colleagues upon courtroom manners." P. Lehmann, *supra* at 75.

Lehmann claimed that, properly understood, "[i]n a genuinely civil order, civility means the pursuit of justice under law through the practice of law under justice." *Id. See* notes 139–142 *supra* and accompanying text. *See also* Weaver, *Nixon Court Gives a Conservative Ruling on the Laws of Fashion and Decorum*, N.Y. Times, Mar. 11, 1974, at 19, col. 3 (new requirement of conservative dress for attorneys appearing before Supreme Court "reportedly a reaction to dismay expressed by Chief Justice Burger when a lawyer rose to plead his case wearing a pearl-gray vest under his morning coat instead of the traditional dark one.")

humors."[166] In this latter circumstance judicial masks conceal rather than amplify grievances, and oppression is hidden from view and extended into the courtroom.[167]

Judicial proceedings must be acknowledged as vulnerable to this corruption of essence which transforms them from judicial theater as the image of legitimate society—theater of justice—into theater of cruelty or the ritualized sacrifice of scapegoats—theater of injustice. Consequently, to welcome the theatrical character of courts, as this Essay implicitly has, is not to embrace all that judicial theater may become. There is need for continual reformation. So qualified, the assumption remains that judicial theater, as it exists, is preferable to possible alternatives.

One alternative, considerably more hypothetical than real, is the complete abandonment of the present court system. From the perspective of some like the Panther 21, American trials undoubtedly appear to be political pieces adjunct to an oppressive system.[168] But a court may prove to be the scene of acquittal even for Panthers.[169] This is not to say that the just outcome of a particular trial proves the justice of the system or excuses systemic injustice.[170] It is to say that, although trials are sometimes thought to be masks for enslavement, they may yet bear some civilizing potential. Corrupt as Russian courts were under Stalin (whom Solzhenitsyn calls the "Chief Producer"),[171] control of the Soviet show trials ("these theatrical

166. The quoted phrase is that of Alexander Hamilton. THE FEDERALIST No. 78 at 527–28 (J. Cooke ed. 1961). (A. Hamilton). Hamilton argued that the independence of the courts would protect the will of the people expressed in the constitution (i.e. the legitimate or originating will) against the will of a factious majority as well as against that of factious minorities. The courts would therefore protect the constitutive will of the people against occasions when the people's will might have fallen victim to ill humors. That is to say that the judiciary would reflect the true or better will of the people.

167. This kind of oppressive masquerade is not limited to criminal law. It can occur in other areas, *e.g.*, contracts and property. But criminal law can be a fertile source for it, as plea-bargaining gives witness: " '[P]lea bargaining' is commonly practiced covertly. After the guilty plea is negotiated by the prosecutor and defense counsel and agreed to by the defendant, defendant follows the rubric of telling the court no promise has induced the plea, and while this game is played the prosecutor and defense counsel mutely corroborate the defendant's false statement. Often a court knows of the negotiations and yet plays its part in the rubric by asking the question about any promise, knowing that the answer will be false." United States v. Jackson, 390 F.2d 130, 138 (7th Cir. 1968) (Kiley, J., dissenting). Such proceedings, it has been noted, "take on the air of a solemn charade." Rosett, *The Negotiated Guilty Plea*, 374 ANNALS 70, 72, 1967). Tigar writes that "the plea is in danger of becoming a mere ritual which sanctifies a criminal process that dispenses 'justice' with only pro forma participation from an ignorant and mystified defendant." Tigar, *supra* note 13, at 23. It is the covert nature of plea-bargaining, *i.e.* its deviation from the norm of judicial proceedings in open court, which gives rise to inadequate protection of defendant's rights. *See* note 175 *infra*.

168. *See* Letter from the Panther 21 to Judge John M. Murtagh, Mar. 2, 1970: "We know very well what is meant by your statement, 'This court is responsible for maintaining proper respect for the administration of criminal justice and preventing any reflection on the image of American justice.' Properly translated, it simply means that the farce must go on. The image must remain intact."

169. *See* N.Y. Times, May 14, 1971, at 1, col. 8; Kempton, *Free at Last?*, N.Y. REV. OF BOOKS, June 17, 1971, at 30.

170. *See* M. KEMPTON, THE BRIAR PATCH 280 (1973).

171. A. SOLZHENITSYN, *supra* note 91, at 300.

productions")[172] was exacting. Unless control was constantly exercised, which was impossible, human elements broke through the prepared scripts and predetermined outcomes.[173] Consequently, as Solzhenitsyn observed, "the NKVD could never have carried out its great assignment if they had fussed about with open trials."[174]

Another alternative is to replace or supplement judicial theater in the court system with more economically efficient means for deciding cases. Pressure for greater output promotes development of tools like plea-bargaining which bypass trials and appear primarily productive in meeting quotas.[175] Such pressure fails to understand that live performances are as much the end of courts as is the disposition of cases. When courts are converted from theaters to factories, from places of play to places of fabrication, then, as the National Advisory Commission on Civil Disorders discovered, poor people find themselves dispensed "assembly-line justice,"[176] which can scarcely be called justice at all.

Judicial theater as we experience it can and should be purified; corruption and unnecessary administrative congestion are proper subjects of reformation. Purification, however, is quite a different goal than abandonment. Those who would quit judicial theater either overtly because of its injustices or covertly because of its economic inefficiencies have not reckoned its puissance: to give place to an expression of humanity wherein even the least member of the community may find "a local habitation and a name."[177] We will do well to ponder, before relinquishing it, whether this humanizing dimension of theater is not critical to the capacity of our courts for justice.

---

172. *Id.* at 419.

173. *Cf. id.* at 419–31.

174. *Id.* at 431.

175. *Cf.* Griffiths, *supra* note 3, at 396–99; note 167 *supra. See generally* Note, *The Unconstitutionality of Plea Bargaining*, 83 HARV. L. REV. 1387 (1970). One report concluded: "An example of this efficiency norm operating to the extreme and to the detriment of other principles of justice is the plea-bargaining system, which dominates, with a few exceptions, every court operation in the country." AMERICAN FRIENDS SERVICE COMMITTEE STRUGGLE FOR JUSTICE 136–37 (1971).

176. REPORT OF THE NATIONAL ADVISORY COMMISSION ON CIVIL DISORDERS 337 (Bantam ed. 1968). *See* H. PACKER, *supra* note 64, at 292. A device like plea-bargaining still makes use of some elements of theater, but these have become more rote than ritual. *See* note 167 *supra.* Consequently plea-bargaining might be salvaged by, for example, greater inquiry into the details of the plea bargain, opening it to appellate review and not insisting that the defendant acknowledge guilt, since legal guilt is properly a function of the trial process. *See, e.g.*, Tigar, *supra* note 13, at 21–25. Weinberg & Babcock, Book Review, 76 YALE L.J. 612 (1967).

177. W. SHAKESPEARE, A MIDSUMMER NIGHT'S DREAM, act V, scene 1, line 18.

[2]

THE LAWFULNESS OF THE AMERICAN TRIAL

Robert P. Burns*

Much of the recent criticism of the American trial focuses on its perceived "lawlessness."[1] Commentators have accused juries of making decisions based on emotion and prejudice, all the way up to explicit nullification.[2] Reformers have noted the low level of jury comprehension of jury instructions and propose strategies to force, or at least encourage juries to "follow the law."[3] Other commentators have compared the American trial unfavorably to its continental cousins, praising the higher level of control exercised by the European judge and his higher professional allegiance to the code he is enforcing.[4] In this Article, I argue that the American trial embodies an authentic, though complex, form of lawfulness appropriate for our time and public culture.

These criticisms of the American trial spring from a distinctive normative understanding of the trial's nature. In a recent book,[5] I argued that this traditional and powerful understanding of the American trial was deeply misconceived. Worse, the misconception impoverished our understanding of one of the great achievements of our public culture. According to that understanding, which I called "The Received View," a trial is an institutional device for realizing the Rule of Law when there are disputes of fact. In the Received View, the Rule of Law is understood as a "law of rules"[6] or a set of pre-existent commands[7] attaching

---

* Professor of Law, Northwestern University.

1. Nancy S. Marder, *The Myth of the Nullifying Jury*, 93 Nw. U. L. Rev. 877 (1999) (stating that judges often speak about jury nullification leading to "chaos" or "anarchy").

2. *Id.* at 877 n.3 (referring to the large number of journalistic criticisms of perceived nullifications in the Simpson and King cases).

3. Robert P. Charrow & Veda R. Charrow, *Making Legal Language Understandable: A Psycholinguistic Study of Jury Instructions*, 79 Colum. L. Rev. 1306 (1979); Valerie P. Hans & Neil Vidmar, Judging the Jury 121-22 (1986).

4. John H. Langbein, *The German Advantage in Civil Procedure*, 52 U. Chi. L. Rev. 823 (1985). Langbein's claims have led to a spirited debate. *Compare* Ronald J. Allen, et al., *The German Advantage in Civil Procedure: A Plea for More Details and Fewer Generalities in Comparative Scholarship*, 82 Nw. U. L. Rev. 705 (1988) (attacking Langbein's piece on various grounds), *and* John C. Reitz, *Why We Probably Cannot Adopt the German Advantage in Civil Procedure*, 75 Iowa L. Rev. 987 (1990) (arguing in favor of the American adversarial system), *with* John H. Langbein, *Trashing the German Advantage*, 82 Nw. U. L. Rev. 763 (1988) (defending his hypotheses, research methods, and conclusions on the German system). *See generally* Michael Bohlander, *The German Advantage Revisited: An Inside View of German Civil Procedure in the Nineties*, 13 Tul. Eur. & Civ. L.F. 25 (1998) (discussing the German system from the viewpoint of a German judge.).

5. Robert P. Burns, A Theory of the Trial (1999).

6. Antonin Scalia, *The Rule of Law as a Law of Rules*, 56 U. Chi. L. Rev. 1175, 1187 (1989) (arguing that "the totality of the circumstances" standard is to be avoided whenever possible, relying instead upon legal determinations that reflect a general rule).

consequences to determinate categories of events. Most basically, the devices of the trial allow the trier[8] to "find facts," that is, to determine a single value-free narrative of events and then engage in an act of "fair categorization" by which the trier determines whether such a value-free narrative falls within the categories announced in the rules, and, in jury trials, communicated to the jury in the instructions. The Received View explains a whole range of the most distinctive features of the American trial: judicial decisions about when to hold trials rather than employ more summary dispositions, the rules of evidence and trial procedure, several of the most important of the trial's linguistic practices,[9] the availability of motions for judgment as a matter of law, and the use of jury instructions. Because the Rule of Law as the law of rules is an ideal (among others) to which legislatures, judges, and juries are actually committed, it has come to structure many of the most important of the trial's features. It is an ideal that is also a cause.

There are, however, features of the American trial that are deeply discontinuous with the Received View. Liberal rules of pleading make it relatively easy to "get a jury."[10] Trial lawyers may, and perhaps must,[11] choose that theory of the case most likely to realize the client's goals.[12] That means concretely that the theory and theme embedded in each lawyer's opening statement, his or her claim as to what is true, is designed to achieve a purpose. Facts are already partisan purposes. And so the trier's choice is between clients' narratively embedded purposes.[13] The permissible devices of trial rhetoric, particularly the opening statement, in which

7. Brian Leiter, *Positivism, Formalism, Realism*, 99 COLUM. L. REV. 1138, 1141-45 (1999) (reviewing ANTHONY SEBOK, LEGAL POSITIVISM IN AMERICAN JURISPRUDENCE (1998)) (discussing the place of the "command theory of law" in classical and contemporary positivism).

8. I will usually use the term "trier" for bench or jury. In A THEORY OF THE TRIAL, I referred to the trier throughout as "the jury" solely for ease of reference. I want to use the broader terms here to remind the reader that the trial is fundamentally the same whether to the bench or to a jury. *See* HARRY KALVEN, JR. & HANS ZEISEL, THE AMERICAN JURY 55-65 (1966) (discussing the convergence of decision-making between judges and juries).

9. Notably the fundamental preference for testimony is the language of perception.

10. *Compare* Conley v. Gibson, 355 U.S. 495 (1957) (stating all that is required of plaintiffs is a short and plain statement of the claim which gives the defendant fair notice of the plaintiff's claim), *with* Richard L. Marcus, *The Revival of Fact Pleading under the Federal Rules of Civil Procedure*, 86 COLUM. L. REV. 433, 439 (1986) (arguing that more formal and specific pleading would better serve the judicial system).

11. MODEL RULES OF PROF'L CONDUCT 1.2(a) (client sets the goals of the representation).

12. Bernard Jackson calls this the "narrativization of pragmatics," the embedding of appeals for particular course of action into storytelling that appears merely to recount "what happened." BERNARD S. JACKSON, LAW, FACT, AND NARRATIVE COHERENCE (1988).

13. This control over the process of proof by lawyers is one of the points most often criticized by partisans of continental modes of trial. *See* Langbein, *The German Advantage in Civil Procedure*, *supra* note 4. That lawyers *must* embed purposes into narrative is part of the process by which claims of desire or need must be translated into claims of entitlement and the process by which individual claims are submitted to public norms. *See* BURNS, *supra* note 5. In many complex ways, claims are limited by the forms of truth that we have decided politically to allow to emerge at trial. The choice at trial, then, is between two "mediations" of the client's needs and desires with norms that may be moral, legal, or political. The ethical rules requiring some level of candor to the tribunal serve to create some continuity between those norms and what actually happened in this case. The evidentiary rules maintain continuity between the latter occurrences and the legal norms. *Id.* at 73-102.

an advocate may tell a "natural"[14] story structured by a whole range of common sense moral norms,[15] which may or may not be reflected in the jury instructions, suggest that the evidentiary base to which the trier of fact responds[16] is woven with moral sources that stretch beyond the rules embodied in the instructions.[17] The general verdict and rules limiting the impeachment of verdicts insulate the determinations of juries from scrutiny designed to prevent reliance on such moral sources.[18] Standards for judicial rejection of jury verdicts, both at trial and on appeal, are extremely deferential.[19] Doctrines of harmless error now insulate even significant misstatements of law in the jury instructions, the inner sanctum of the legal rules.[20] Finally, the strong drift toward admissibility in the law of evidence over the last quarter century places before the trier of fact a range of factual detail which inevitably invoke moral and political norms enormously broader than those elevated by the instructions.[21]

Thus even the trial's legal substructure, where we ought to find a high level of fidelity to the ideal of the Received View, hints at our acceptance of a very different notion of decision-making at trial. Because this acceptance is pervasive in the ways I described above, the legitimacy of such an alternative ideal has achieved the status of one of our "considered judgments of justice,"[22] an institutionalized judgment made under favorable conditions and in which we have a high level of confidence. Finding one's way around that ideal requires a synthetic grasp of how

---

14. On narrative as a "natural" mode of comprehending human action, see BURNS, *supra* note 5, at 159 (discussing JEROME BRUNER, ACTS OF MEANING (1990)).

15. On "ordinary morality" as a coherent system of norms, see ALAN DONAGAN, A THEORY OF MORALITY (1977). On common sense morality as reflecting the ethos of a "life world" somewhat distinct from the "systems" world through which we organize economic life, see JURGEN HABERMAS, BETWEEN FACTS AND NORMS: CONTRIBUTIONS TO A DISCOURSE THEORY OF LAW AND DEMOCRACY (William Rehg trans., 1996).

16. The social science literature consistently concludes that "the discipline of the evidence" is the most important factor explaining jury decision-making. *See* BURNS, *supra* note 5, at 143-45. A human practice, including the practice of legal judgment, is an intelligent performance, to use Peter Steinberger's happy phrase. PETER STEINBERGER, THE CONCEPT OF POLITICAL JUDGMENT 240-43 (1993). That judgment, like all such performances, is usually an "unreflective reaction to the meaningfulness of the situation in which one is engrossed." Dennis M. Patterson, *Law's Pragmatism: Law as Practice and Narrative*, 76 VA. L. REV. 937, 939 (1990).

17. On the notion of a "moral source," see CHARLES TAYLOR, SOURCES OF THE SELF (1989); Robert Cover, *Nomos and Narrative*, 97 HARV. L. REV. 4 (1983).

18. BURNS, *supra* note 5, at 26-27.

19. *Id.* at 28-29.

20. *See, e.g.*, Yates v. Evatt, 500 U.S. 391, 402 (1991) (harmless error analysis applicable to burden-shifting instruction); Carela v. California, 491 U.S. 263, 266 (1989) (mandatory presumption instruction).

21. A distinguished critic put it this way:

> A sentence always means more. Even a single word, within the weave of incommensurable connotation, can, and usually does . . . . No formalization is of an order adequate to the semantic mass and motion of a culture, to the wealth of denotation, connotation, implicit reference, elision and tonal register which envelop saying what one means, meaning what one says, or neither . . . ."

GEORGE STEINER, REAL PREFERENCES 82-83 (1989).

22. JOHN RAWLS, A THEORY OF JUSTICE 47 (1971).

all the rules and linguistic practices of the trial, its "consciously structured hybrid of languages,"[23] function together to provide the meaningful context in which the trier is engrossed and to which he or she responds. This is the true "discipline of the evidence" which the social science investigators consistently find to be the most important factor in trial decision-making.[24] Understanding the distinctive lawfulness of the trial requires "a continuous dialectical tacking between the most local of local detail and the most global of global structures in such a way as to bring both into view simultaneously."[25] Then we can "think what we do," as Hannah Arendt liked to put it, to achieve a rational reconstruction of the trial and the kind of lawfulness of which it is capable.

My task in *A Theory of the Trial* was to provide the elements for this kind of grasp. I will not rehearse that detailed description here except as it bears directly on the question of the trial's lawfulness. The first part of this Article provides this focused and compressed account of my conception of the American trial. The second part inquires specifically into the significance of those conclusions for the ideal of the Rule of Law. I conclude that an appreciation of the trial's distinctive languages and performance cannot but enrich, though quite often changes, standard understandings of "what law is."

I. A THEORY OF THE TRIAL

A. *A Phenomenology of Trial Practice*

The truth that emerges at trial is a grasp of a factual and normative reality implicit in often harsh tensions of opposites. The trial's consciously structured hybrid of languages and performances creates these tensions. They are supported by the scaffolding of the Rules of Evidence and of Professional Responsibility.[26] The former keep the trial focused on a limited range of issues, while the latter combine principles of energy in advocacy and respect for simple fact. There are tensions between the competing narratives of opening statement, each urging the relative importance of the norm, the "theme," as trial lawyers put it, around which the story is told and the appropriateness of the mode of social ordering[27] the advocate urges. The mere doubling of the narratives relativizes each and begins the process by which the trier is forced to look through the competing narratives and toward a truth beyond storytelling. The mere fact that there are *two* stories dramatizes gaps between the real story and the telling of it. There is a tension

23. BURNS, *supra* note 5, at 3.

24. JEFFREY ABRAMSON, WE, THE JURY: THE JURY SYSTEM AND THE IDEAL OF DEMOCRACY 143-78 (1994).

25. Clifford Geertz, *From the Native's Point of View: On the Nature of Anthropological Understanding*, *in* INTERPRETIVE SOCIAL SCIENCE: A READER 239 (Paul Rabinow & William M. Sullivan eds., 1979). On the importance of situated ideals, see TAYLOR, *supra* note 17, at 531-71.

26. BURNS, *supra* note 5, at 73-102.

27. *Id.* at 103-23.

between the natural, fully characterized, and quite partisan storytelling of opening statement and the bare, stripped-down, highly constrained narratives of direct examination, controlled both by the oath and by the ethical prohibitions on presenting false evidence. Opening statements easily reflect the practical truths embedded in the "life world" and good lawyers know how to speak that kind of truth. Direct examination may contain a more particular truth, more personal perhaps, that fits only imperfectly even into the best conceived theory of the case, that is hard to "subsume" under *either* the trier's "common sense and experiences in life" *or* the rules found in the instructions. There are tensions between the narratives of direct examination and the deconstruction of those narratives on cross-examination.[28] There are tensions between what a witness wants to say and what he can defensibly and admissibly say. There are tensions among the roles of lawyer and witness, and, in jury trials, between the roles of judge and jury.

These linguistic performances occur within aspects of the trial that are so familiar that we easily can lose a feel for their importance. "Those aspects of things that are most important for us are hidden because of their simplicity and familiarity. One is unable to notice something—because it is always before one's eyes. . . . [W]e fail to be struck by what, once seen, is most striking and most powerful."[29] Those aspects contribute to the distinctive normative context for trial decision-making. First, trial presentation focuses on the concrete, the factual, and the multiple.[30] The rules surrounding opening statement and direct examination force the attention of the trier of fact into an almost obsessive concern as to *precisely* what took place. Practice under those rules implicitly says to the trier of fact that the details of what occurred are *important* for the judgment to be made. That practice empowers the trier, implicitly saying that the kinds of language and the kinds of events with which the trier is intimately familiar from daily life are sufficient for the task the trier has been given. This inquiry drives the mind downward and away from easy generalization: "no ideas but in things."[31] Witnesses are permitted only to recount facts and are precluded from using the full range of speech acts: they may not make promises (not to do it again, for example) or make predictions or advise the trier of fact as to the best course of action. This sustained focus on the past is quite extraordinary and discontinuous with mediative, political, and bureaucratic modes of social ordering. Lawyers have a right to answers to all proper questions, and so have the ability to force into a forum of power truths that are unpopular and discontinuous with social conformity or

28. I describe the range of cross examination devices at BURNS, *supra* note 5, at 59-67.

29. LUDWIG WITTGENSTEIN, PHILOSOPHICAL INVESTIGATIONS *129 at 50 (G.E.M. Anscombe trans., 1953).

30. In mediation, concern with the past usually is considered a form of preliminary "venting" before the real business of rebuilding a relationship begins. The primacy of narrative of past events is what limits the political nature of the trial, turns the trier's attention away from the future, and so from expediency. Ordinary language and the implicit moral judgments that are embedded in it place a brake on bureaucratic transvaluations of values, always preceded by linguistic transvaluations, in the interests of the goals or organized power.

31. WILLIAM CARLOS WILLIAMS, PATTERSON 14 (1951).

political power. There will not be One Big Story. As the trial proceeds through time, each bit of evidence becomes for a moment the privileged lens through which all the evidence can be understood, multiplying the possible normative perspectives on that evidence. In contrast with the rich and extended narrative structure of the trial itself, "the law" comes to the jury in the instructions stripped down to the barest of formulaic pronouncements, and so likely to be only a secondary source of norms.

Other devices of the trial intensify the struggle over the *meaning* of events. In contrast to the continental trial, where the inquiry literally evolves until the judge concludes no further inquiry is warranted, the American trial, especially jury trial, occurs over an extremely compressed time period. This elevates the effectiveness of thematic, factual, and normative unities, the trial lawyer's "theory and theme." Temporal compression allows for more "holistic"[32] approaches to the evidence by removing the obstacles of fading memory to the vast web of interpenetrating mutual implication of all the evidence. It allows the lawyers to show what cannot easily be said[33] and fosters the tacit grasp of "the cumulations of probabilities . . . too fine to avail separately, too subtle and circuitous to be convertible into syllogisms."[34] Each side has considerable control over what to make an issue of, what aspects of the evidence to contest. Almost as important as the theory of the case, the initial cut into the evidence, are the innumerable choices in the course of the trial as to which gambits to accept and which issues to join.[35] The goal of each lawyer will be to focus on his strongest (most "significant") evidence again and again as the trial progresses, but each will be forced into engaging his opponent's strengths. These contrary rhetorical exigencies tend to focus the trial, as it winds down, on just the most significant points.

Still other aspects of the trial work to suspend judgment, to keep the trier of fact's mind just open *enough*.[36] There is a taut balance at trial between speaking continuously and being interrupted. The trial begins with two opposed opening statements. Then the party with the burden of proof presents his evidence continuously.[37] This presentation is interrupted by cross-examination, which implicitly asks the trier of fact to consider other modes of interpreting the events to

---

32. WILLIAM TWINING, RETHINKING EVIDENCE: EXPLORATORY ESSAYS 238-42 (1990).

33. *See* JAMES BOYD WHITE, FROM EXPECTATION TO EXPERIENCE: ESSAYS ON LAW & LEGAL EDUCATION 54-56 (1999).

34. JOHN HENRY NEWMAN, AN ESSAY IN AID OF A GRAMMAR ASSENT 288 (Longmans, Green & Co. ed., 1930).

35. Lon L. Fuller, *The Adversary System*, *in* TALKS ON AMERICAN LAW 35, 36-37 (Harold J. Berman ed., 1972) (the lawyer's task is to present the case "as it appears to interested eyes, in the aspect it assumes when viewed from that corner of life into which fate has cast his client").

36. *See* Lon Fuller, *The Forms and Limits of Adjudication*, 92 HARV. L. REV. 353, 383 (1978) (discussing the importance of institutional devices that suspend the adjudicator's judgment).

37. Many jurisdictions prohibit the defense from presenting any evidence during the cross-examination of the plaintiff's or prosecution's witnesses. *See* FED. R. EVID. 106 (1997) (allowing for the presentation of evidence which ought in fairness to be considered at the same time as a writing offered by the opponent is the exception that proves the rule).

which a witness testifies or to entertain doubts about that witness's credibility. There follows the presentation of the defense case, similarly interrupted by the plaintiff or prosecution. During this time, jurors are not to discuss the case, and thus not to express a premature opinion, or even implicitly to commit themselves to a position in the way that asking a question in public often does. The devices of the trial allow the trier to grasp the entire case offered by each advocate and so the significance of its parts, while being reminded continuously that there is another way of understanding both the whole and the parts.

Finally the trial provides a dramatic event. The courtroom drama provides a lens on the evidence while the conduct of lawyers and witnesses at trial offers a metaphor by which to understand what is essential in the underlying events. The parties and other important actors in the case are usually witnesses; their truthfulness or untruthfulness, at many levels and in many subtle ways, reveals the moral dimension of the underlying case. A good case will *allow* a lawyer to be fairer to all of the evidence, including the evidence provided by an opponent, in a way that reveals how the case fits into the whole range of public norms. The trial's aural medium, the simple fact that it is spoken and heard, provides for a momentary identification with almost all witnesses. The physical distance from which witnesses speak and are observed within the formality of the courtroom provide for a distancing of the jury from the perspective of each witness. In short, the trial provides for the preconditions for good judgment, sympathy, and detachment.[38] Performance allows for the integration of broad public norms and very specific situations[39] while giving "more urgent reality to the particular acts that establish distance between a given case and general rule or that expose a given case to competing rules. Performance of cases, by thus contributing to indeterminacy, helps to bring about the conditions for creative resolution."[40] The clash of witnesses, and of witnesses with lawyers, serves to reveal the core issue in the case. By engaging the full range of human feeling, the dramatic nature of the trial creates the conditions for good judgment[41] and assures that all the evidence comes before the jury in the form of performances that may in a "primitive" but profound way ring true or false.

The social science investigators have noticed the effects of just those trial devices.[42] Juries bring an elevated intelligence to their work and the conclusions they reach in individual cases generally cannot be predicted by broad demographic

38. RONALD BEINER, POLITICAL JUDGMENT 158-62 (1983).

39. *See* Bernard Hibbits, *Coming to Our Sense: Communication and Legal Expression in Performance Cultures*, 41 EMORY L.J. 873, 957 (1992) (discussing the value of performance in the law).

40. MILNER BALL, THE PROMISE OF AMERICAN LAW 61 (1981).

41. MARTHA C. NUSSBAUM, THE FRAGILITY OF GOODNESS: LUCK AND ETHICS IN GREEK TRAGEDY AND PHILOSOPHY 390 (1986).

42. I am summarizing in a few sentences a vast literature and emphasizing only those conclusions which I regard as the most important and which investigators using different methods agree on. *See* BURNS, *supra* note 5, at 141-54 (discussing what emerges most clearly from empirical studies of trials).

categories, such as race or class. The jury instructions play a subordinate role in the jury decision-making, but the norms implicit in the language practices of the trial are of central importance. Juries understand the public significance or political dimension of their work. Deliberation is of less importance than is the encounter of the individual juror with the evidence, which is intense and absorbing. The trial's the thing.[43]

B. The Significance of the Trial's Linguistic Practices: Thinking What We Do

The centrality of narrative at trial allows the trier of fact to organize vast amounts of evidence around the significance of a human action.[44] Telling a story requires a simplifying judgment that inevitably assigns a meaning to a human action, a meaning that is inevitably rooted in the highly contextual common sense morality of the life world.[45] Narrative structure resists bureaucratization and the obfuscation of technical language and preserves a "strong truth-bearing everyday language, not marred or corrupted by technical discourse or scientific codes . . . of which we are in need as citizens, and as moral agents."[46] Stories are told when there has been a disruption of habitual patterns; they explain this deviance by invoking a stock of beliefs that explain the sources of deviance and thus provide coherence to the community's threatened moral experience.[47] Because story structure is built around a sequence of legitimate status quo, a disruption of that status quo, and its restoration, it precisely mirrors the pattern of corrective justice,[48] the erasing of the effects of a wrong done to a just distribution. More importantly, it places the trier *within* the story, because it is the action urged on the court that will correct the alleged injustice. This assures that the trier will take a position internal to the legal order and serves to reinforce his or her practical or moral role. The devices of the trial serve to remind the jury that it is surely not "the finder of fact" in the sense of the dispassionate creator of a value-free account of events that have occurred in the past simply for their theoretical, historical, or journalistic interest.

Of course, there is not one opening statement, but two. The doubling of opening statements serves a number of functions. It allows each advocate to urge *in narrative form* what is most important in the facts, what "this case is about." Each opening will provide a normatively charged interpretive design by which to

---

43. *Id.* at 154.

44. W. LANCE BENNETT & MARTHA S. FELDMAN, RECONSTRUCTING REALITY IN THE COURTROOM: JUSTICE AND JUDGMENT IN AMERICAN CULTURE 5 (1981).

45. BURNS, *supra* note 5, at 171-72 (discussing narrative and the moral point of view).

46. IRIS MURDOCH, METAPHYSICS AS A GUIDE TO MORALS 162 (1992).

47. "The function of the story is to find an intentional state that mitigates or at least makes comprehensible a deviation from a canonical cultural pattern." JEROME BRUNER, ACTS OF MEANING 49-50 (1990).

48. ARISTOTLE, NICHOMACHEAN ETHICS, Book V (discussing actions with which justice is concerned, what sort of mean justice is, and between what extremes the just act is intermediate).

understand the usually ambiguous evidence presented at trial. If "every fact has two faces," as trial lawyers like to say, each opening suggests that it is more reasonable, more important, to interpret all the fact in the way suggested. Since the part is understood in light of the whole, and the whole in light of the parts,[49] the facts of the case simply cannot be compared to the theories of the case embedded in the openings[50] to determine which is better supported by "the weight of the evidence." For what the facts are, even how the circumstantial evidence for those facts should best be described, will be determined in part by the theory of the case that is more persuasive, for all the reasons, factual and narrative, that one story may be more persuasive than another. And, of course, the fact that there are *two* openings invites the jury to look through both openings, and so dramatizes "the gaps between what is told and the telling of it."[51]

One or another of these normatively laden narratives is likely to be more persuasive than the other, for reasons that are only partially "factual."[52] To be sure, one theory may tell a factual story that is more consistent with what we may call the empirical generalizations that constitute one aspect of the jury's common sense. But common sense is much more than a set of purely empirical generalizations with a determinate range of application.[53] All narratives, even historical narratives, reflect moral judgment. Storytelling "is a demand . . . for moral meaning, a demand that sequences of events be assessed as to their significance as elements of a moral drama."[54]

> Social action is intelligent because we compare what we see with a stock of socially transmitted models, each one of them accompanied by a particular social evaluation. The one which most resembles that which we observe renders our observation intelligible in a cognitive sense; *it also provides an evaluation of it.*[55]

---

49. HANS-GEORG GADAMER, TRUTH AND METHOD 167, 235, 258 (1975).

50. Thomas S. Kuhn, *Objectivity, Value Judgment, and Theory Choice*, *in* THE ESSENTIAL TENSION: SELECTED STUDIES IN SCIENTIFIC TRADITION AND CHANGE 47 (1977). Kuhn notes that the proponents of the scientific theories often "talk by each other" in a way that makes a decisive experiment impossible. For the meaning of the facts that emerge from experiment will be interpreted differently by each theory.

51. MIKHAIL BAKHTIN, THE DIALOGIC IMAGINATION xxix (Caryl Emerson trans. & Michael Holquist ed., 1990).

52. On the other hand, the narrative is heavily *constrained*. First, it is constrained by the ethical prohibition on making a statement that will not be supported by admissible evidence. MODEL RULES OF PROF'L CONDUCT 3.4(e). More importantly, it is constrained by the performance aspect of an opening statement which *promises* to produce evidence for each of its claims.

53. One of the reasons why probabilistic identification evidence is suspect is that its generalizations *do* come with assigned probabilities, and so are very difficult to integrate into the more holistic style of reasoning that a trier must employ. *See* ROBERT P. BURNS & STEVEN LUBET, PROBLEMS AND MATERIALS IN EVIDENCE AND TRIAL ADVOCACY: TEACHER'S MANUAL 40 (1994).

54. *See* Hayden White, *The Value of Narrativity in the Representation of Reality*, *in* ON NARRATIVE 1 (W.J.T. Mitchell ed., 1981).

55. JACKSON, *supra* note 12, at 99 (1988) (emphasis added) (discussing the difference between the modern, abstract legal rule and ancient, narrative model).

This evaluation is not, however, simply a moral judgment. It is also a political act in that it serves to reconstitute the public identity of the community. "Stories tell us how each one finds or loses his just place in relation to others in the world. And the communication of the story is confirmed when justice has been recognized."[56] Narrative is one means by which the jury's political self-consciousness is realized: "By obliging men to turn their attention to other affairs than their own, it rubs off that private selfishness which is the rust of society."[57]

Of course, the trial is not over after opening statements end. The essential tension at trial is between the broader, more public meanings, moral and political, embedded in the opening statements and the more particular accounts given by the witnesses. This creates an almost unbearable tension between the narrative assimilation of a problematic situation to prevailing moral and political norms embedded in the opening statements and other demanding values. Witnesses are rarely public people. They do not speak diplomatically and the full significance of their accounts often cannot be subsumed by the more public meanings around which theories of the case are spun. By giving particularity and empirical truth their due, the trial disciplines and clarifies the norms and purposes embedded in the opening statements. It resists the bureaucratic assimilation, too easy in the saying, and often awful in the doing, of the truth of an individual situation to a few overgeneralized norms. The devices of the trial described above make it hard for the decision in the individual case to flow too easily from the "sort" of case presented. They create a "justice that is strife" by creating a fair contest between real values where the appropriate balance can only be fought out.[58] A system where there is relatively little internal strife among languages, and so values, will be one with correspondingly little justice, for it is "only by entertaining multiple and mutually limiting points of view, building up a composite picture, can we approach the real richness of the world."[59]

The devices of the trial create a situation where there are no fixed anchors. Even on the most "basic" questions of how the circumstantial evidence itself should be described, there are likely to be fierce contests. The *meaning* of that evidence, which bare factual narrative it suggests,[60] can be even more contested, depending as it does on empirical generalizations whose applicability in *this particular case* are always open to honest debate. At the next level, the level at which opening statements are given, the trier must decide which is the *fairer* way of describing events, which narrative invokes more *important* values, which narrative integrates

56. Melvyn A. Hill, *The Fictions of Mankind and the Stories of Men*, *in* HANNAH ARENDT: THE RECOVERY OF THE PUBLIC WORLD 289-90 (Melvin A. Hill ed., 1979).

57. 1 ALEXIS DE TOCQUEVILLE, DEMOCRACY IN AMERICA 295 (Henry Reeve trans., 1945).

58. *See* STUART HAMPSHIRE, JUSTICE IS CONFLICT (2000).

59. Richard Rhodes, *The Philosopher Physicist*, N.Y. TIMES, Jan. 26, 1992, at sec. 7 (reviewing ABRAHAM PAIS, NIELS BOHR'S TIMES: IN PHYSICS, PHILOSOPHY AND POLITY).

60. Of course, that is the simplest and most abstract sense of "meaning."

those values with the facts in the case in a way that "rings true." All those judgments are, of course, normative. Some may be intrinsically contestable, in the sense that a truth never can be demonstrated, is always dependent on judgment.[61] The trial is designed to force the mind to *move* over the consciously structured hybrid of languages, and so over the norms and the facts embedded in them. The decision reached is much less a deduction and much more a practically oriented *integration* of incommensurable norms.[62]

This "integrative" mode of thought is suited to the kind of practical situation into which the trier is placed. Any purely factual narrative a trier might settle on would be deeply woven with different sorts of uncertainty and ambiguity. More significantly, the trier never actually creates such a value-free account of the facts before moving to the process of evaluation. By the end of the trial, by the time the jury instructions are read, a rich factual and normative context has been created, but it is hardly a screenplay of past events. It contains different sorts of narratives, deconstructed through different sorts of argument, dramatic encounters of different sorts among different sorts of trial performers—lawyers, witnesses, and judge. It is this pattern to which the trier responds in a practical way. By the end of the trial there survives no one simple set of "findings of fact" to which legal norms may be "applied." Any such set of findings of fact would have precisely the character of the factual narratives that inhabit appellate decisions—constructions designed to justify a decision. The modes of decision-making that occur at trial realize human capacities that are richer and more subtle than those suggested by the usual version of mechanical jurisprudence. I have portrayed the levels of integration performed at trial in the chart on the following page.

Any such graphic depiction cannot fairly portray the practical dimension of what occurs at trial. The trier ultimately grasps not a mental screenplay of past events, to which it then applies legal categories to decide the case, but an indescribable synthesis of events, norms, and possibilities for action. This grasp, and the judgment that accompanies it, is the jury's own "intelligent performance." It is a practical response to the performances of all the participants in the trial: lawyers, witnesses, and the judge. The latter create for the trier's imagination the most demanding sort of tension of incommensurables, ultimately incommensurable values to be resolved not by a theoretical account, but by practical judgment and action.[63] My claim was that this set of linguistic and performative tensions

61. The notions of "reflective judgment" and "interpretive understanding" are philosophical attempts to articulate the intelligibility, or reasonableness, of those processes. BURNS, *supra* note 5, at 212-19 (explaining reflective judgment and interpretive understanding and how they fit into the trial).

62. The post-empiricist philosophy of science suggests that this is a feature of all human understanding, just as the hermeneutical tradition has always maintained. *See* Kuhn, *supra* note 50. On the centrality of integrative judgment in legal practice, see WHITE, *supra* note 33, at 61.

63. On justice as a tension of opposites, see STUART HAMPSHIRE, PUBLIC AND PRIVATE MORALITY 39 (1978); HAMPSHIRE, *supra* note 58; *see also* NUSSBAUM, *supra* note 41, at 69.

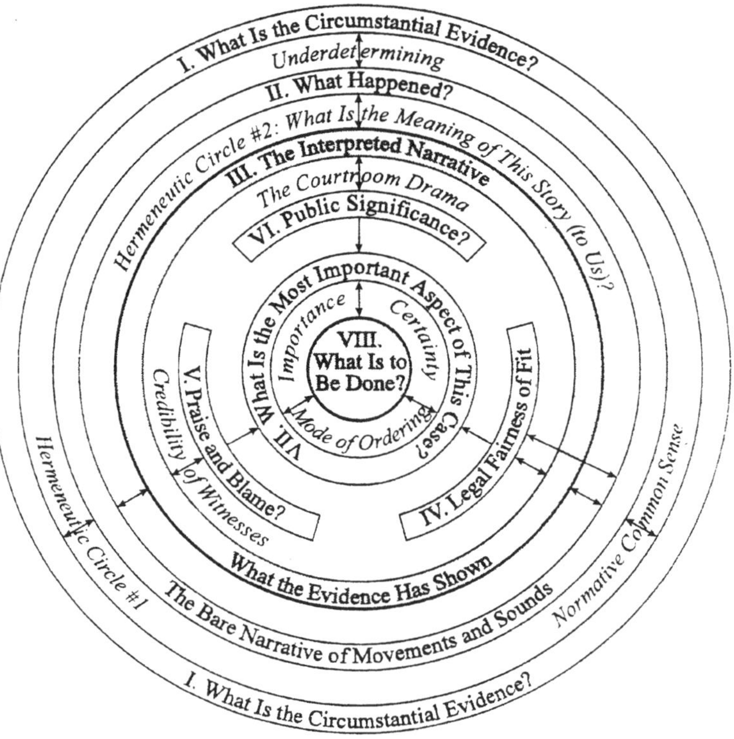

reflect broader modes of social organization, "forms of life." Most triable cases[64] *are* the conflicts between distinct principles—fraternity, efficiency, respect for decency, stability, honoring rights—that find their natural homes in different forms of social life—family life, economic organization, civil interaction, executing plans of life that require time and stability to realize—but which cannot remain vital without qualification by principles that animate other spheres. This weaving into each area principles that are primary in other spheres allows the spheres of social life to "redeem" each other, again to use Arendt's phrase.[65] They require the trier of fact to determine—really, not theoretically—the just tension among those

64. A triable case is a case some aspect of which is fairly disputable. Even the simplest cases, where the dispute is "purely factual"—identity in a murder case, for example—present normative questions. For example, "do we have a level of certainty that would justify imprisoning this defendant in order to achieve general deterrence, individual deterrence, or retribution?" Or, at the other end of the spectrum, "Will rewarding this kind of police behavior with a conviction have a more destructive effect on our community than releasing someone whom we believe beyond a reasonable doubt to have committed a murder?"

65. Our contemporary political task is "less to create constantly new forms of life than to creatively renew actual forms by taking advantage of their internal multiplicity and tensions and their friction with one another." DAVID KOLB, THE CRITIQUE OF PURE MODERNITY: HEGEL, HEIDEGGER AND AFTER 259 (1986).

values in the particular context of the case. Justice is strife. The extreme attention to particular detail that the devices of the trial impose disciplines what would otherwise be lazy overgeneralized principles. At another level the tension is between meaningfulness, what Bennett and Feldman call "the more powerful norm,"[66] and truth, between what is more significant *in general* and what is true in light of "the brutally elemental data"[67] of this particular case. The "truth of what is" emerges through a dramatization of the real tensions that exist in our forms of life. The truth of verdicts is a practical truth about what is to be done in a concrete situation in light of the relative importance of the moral, legal, and political aspects of the case.

I have described in an extremely compressed way the consciously structured hybrid of languages that is the trial to provide the reader with a sense of the density and the power of the trial's linguistic practices and performances. Such a sense is the precondition for understanding the kind of lawfulness that the trial reflects.

II. THE LAWFULNESS OF THE TRIAL

The lawfulness of the American trial depends ultimately on the constitutional place of the jury trial in the American legal order and the place of the ordinary morality and public identity of the jury within that order. I will address those questions shortly. I have emphasized the *complexity* of trial languages and of the values they represent, and the way in which the tensions among those languages and values elevates the quality of trial decision-making. Within that complexity, there is an important role played by legal rules, and so for the rule of law as the law of rules at trial.

A. The Place and Functions of Rules at the Trial

There can be no doubt that the law of rules functions to screen out, through dispositive motions, those civil cases where success under the stated rules is not even arguable. This provides a device for assuring that the just resolution of individual cases does not intolerably threaten the politically imposed basic structure of society. The latter, embedded primarily in constitutional law, statutory enactment, and common law is thus *somewhat* insulated from fully contextual reexamination by local democratic juries. Dispositive motions keep contextual judgment within the bounds established by larger, overtly political fora, which have established inevitably very general rules. Some of these rules protect rights defined more expansively and rigidly than the contextual decision-making that occurs at trial. Some of these rules protect what is perceived as the incentive

---

66. BENNETT & FELDMAN, *supra* note 44 (1981).

67. HANNAH ARENDT, *Truth and Politics*, *in* BETWEEN PAST AND FUTURE: EIGHT EXERCISES IN POLITICAL THOUGHT 227, 239 (1954).

structure of one or another market and serve, in the view of a prevailing public philosophy, instrumental functions that would be compromised by the kind of contextual thinking that the trial employs. What pretrial devices accomplish is to screen out of trial a subset of cases that pose the most serious threats to the basic structure, judgments that are of such basic universal, structural, or "constitutional" significance that they may not be overwhelmed by the normative exigencies implicit in the narratives and drama of the particular case.[68] Although this is not an argument I can make in detail here, it seems that this identifies much more reliably those cases that are screened out than does the claim that there do not exist substantial issues of material fact.

But the law of rules also reaches into the conduct of the trial of those cases which survive dispositive motions. It is true that the low level of comprehension of jury instructions means that the latter are unlikely to be a major determinant of jury decision-making. Likewise, the importance of the first vote taken by juries[69] suggests, though it does not compel, the conclusion that the instructions are unlikely to be decisive. The law of rules does, however, significantly structure the meaningful context in which the trier is engrossed and to which its intelligent performance is a practical response. All of the trial's linguistic performances are highly *constrained*, and it is often true that, in one way or another, the law of rules provides those constraints. It is the burden of the next section to explain the ways in which this occurs.

B. The Law of the Trial Is Not a Bipolar Relationship Between Rule and Fact

The simplest version[70] of the Received View involves a sequential three-step process. First, the trier understands the evidence, direct and circumstantial; then he infers a narrative of what occurred; then he applies the law to decide the case. In the strictest versions of the Received View,[71] this latter decision is limited to a determination concerning the fair meaning of the words in the legal rule and whether the narrative of what occurred falls within or without that legal rule. This last crucial determination is bipolar: the trier of fact moves back and forth between

68. *See* Robert P. Burns, *The History and Philosophy of the American Jury*, 83 CAL. L. REV. 1477, 1486-89 (1995) (discussing theories regarding the jury's authority over law).

69. *See* BURNS, *supra* note 5, at 145 (stating that the most reliable predictor of a jury verdict is the first ballot).

70. This is the schema I identified at *id.* at 24. A somewhat more complex version of fundamentally the same schema is provided by Nancy Pennington & Reid Hastie, *The Story Model for Juror Decisionmaking*, *in* INSIDE THE JUROR: THE PSYCHOLOGY OF JUROR DECISION MAKING 192 (Reid Hastie ed., 1993).

71. This strictness may stem from positivist views of law whether of the right or of the left. *Compare* Frank H. Easterbrook, *Statutes' Domains*, 50 U. CHI. L. REV. 533, 540-41, 547 (1983) (noting statutory interpretation to effect a statute's purpose is otiose since statutes mark only the negotiated equilibrium between interest group pressure), *with* ROBERTO UNGER, PASSION: AN ESSAY ON PERSONALITY 47 (1984) (describing a conception of legal rules as the unstable "truce lines in a brutal and amoral conflict").

the value-free[72] narrative of what occurred and the meanings of the key terms in the jury instructions to reach a decision.

A somewhat more subtle understanding of trial decision-making grants that the trier's task, like that of an appellate court, is inevitably interpretive. Any plausible account of legal interpretation concedes a circular movement between the meaning of the legal categories and the facts of the case. Neither side of this bipolar relationship is absolutely fixed. The meaning of the legal terms may be refined as they are brought to bear on the particular facts of the case. The characterization of the facts (and so the facts "themselves") may change as their significance under the legal rules is appreciated.[73] The terms of this relationship between fact and norm are no longer conceived as fixed. Thus the trier cannot simply compare a determinate factual narrative with an equally determinate set of legally defined norm categories to reach an either-or decision on inclusion or exclusion. However, the relationship between fact and norm is still bipolar. The trier moves around only one hermeneutic circle.

The naturalness to American lawyers of the notion that a trier decides a case by applying law to facts may be an artifact of the structure of appellate opinions. The rhetoric of appellate opinions is designed, in part, to reflect the conception of the Rule of Law that is expressed in the Received View.[74] Only hypothetical facts, or facts that are "found" by a court, lose the morally significant uncertainty and the normative multivalence surrounding virtually all "facts" in the trial court, and, I might add, in the world. The temptation to recount such "facts," by choices of characterization and inclusion with the legal norms and the preferred outcome in mind is almost irresistible. The expected unity of the opinion demands it. And so it is no surprise that lawyers, even appellate lawyers, often believe that the account of the facts provided by appellate courts is deeply unfair.[75] The significant point here is that, unlike the world of the appellate opinion, there are no "preexisting" ultimate facts to which the legal rules can be "applied." In the language I used above, the one "fully characterized narrative" need not ever – and, I believe, rarely is – actually accepted by the trier in order to reach its decision. The opening statements that contain such narratives are merely ladders, usually kicked away by the end of the trial, that are helpful, very helpful, in allowing the jury to grasp the

72. It must be value-free in these strict positivist perspectives because the *only* norms allowed to have effect in the trial are the norms in the jury instructions. On how the devices of the trial support such a perspective, see BURNS, *supra* note 5, at 19-23.

73. GADAMER, *supra* note 49, at 36-38, 289-94. Gadamer argues that law "application" has exemplary significance for hermeneutics as a whole. There is some empirical evidence that the jury does engage in this kind of "cycling" between facts and norms. Deanna Kuhn, et al., *How Well Do Jurors Reason? Competence Dimensions of Individual Variation in a Juror Reasoning Task*, 5 PSYCHOLOGICAL SCIENCE 289-96 (1994).

74. It is significant that appellate opinions in casebooks remain the primary source of the notion of rule of law that is absorbed by lawyers being socialized into the profession in American law schools.

75. Anthony D'Amato, *The Ultimate Injustice: When a Court Misstates the Facts*, 11 CARDOZO L. REV. 1313 (1990) (arguing misstatement of facts in *Branion v. Gramly*).

events, norms, and possibilities for action necessary to resolve the case. In the trial court, events, norms, and possibilities for action are determined together in an act of practical judgment. In such an environment, rules function much more importantly in helping to shape the evidence than in providing the norms by which preexisting facts are evaluated.

Thus the bipolar notion of law application, in either the basic or more sophisticated version, is not so much wrong as altogether too simple, and really quite impoverished, a notion of the trial. It vastly underestimates the full interpretive reality of the trial. The "factual" side of the trier's judgment is never fixed before the normative issues are brought to bear. Again, the very nature of the circumstantial evidence, including the simplest sounds and movements, is often crucial, debatable, *and* fiercely contested.[76] Even if the precise physical movements are uncontested, their significance may be ambiguous. Every fact has two faces.[77] The nature of individual bits of circumstantial evidence is codetermined with the plausibility of the kind of highly characterized stories that are told in opening statements. That plausibility derives from their moral and political *meaning*, as well as their conformity to purely empirical common sense generalizations. The whole determined in light of the parts and the parts in light of the whole. Those stories are constructed and told to *exhibit* the most powerful norms underlying the case.[78] Those norms are derived from the common sense morality of the "life world" and the public identity of the trier. They will be only incompletely congruent with the norms embedded in the jury instructions.[79]

This account of choice between two normatively charged narratives suggests a coherent notion of truth at trial and is *itself* partial. The doubling of narratives at trial itself serves to disrupt and relativize what can be a coherent, "aesthetic" assimilation of events to the more general moral and political norms embedded in

---

76. In *Lozano v. State*, 584 So.2d 19 (Fla. Dist. Ct. App. 1991), a widely reported case which became part of Miami racial politics, a policeman claiming to be in fear for his life shot a motorcyclist, resulting in the deaths of the driver and a passenger. Much of the trial was fought out on questions such as the following: "How fast was the motorcyclist traveling?" "How far was the motorcycle from the officer when he fired?" "Was the police car so positioned that the officer could not step out of the way of the oncoming cycle?"

77. I provided the following examples:

> [I]n a murder case, the fact that the defendant was drinking before a shooting may suggest that his self-control was reduced. On the other hand, it may suggest that he could not have the coordination to aim and to fire the lethal shot. Anger may provide a motive to kill or it may be a symptom of a serious psychological disorder that may provide a defense. A witness's high level of certainty may enhance credibility or may be evidence of bias. Assume a defamation action. The fact that a wealthy homeowner had previously lectured a maid about eavesdropping may provide evidence that he had no reason to expect that his subsequent criticism of another maid would be overheard, or good reason to believe that it would be overheard . . . .

BURNS, *supra* note 5, at 91 n.58.

78. A narrative may, obviously, be more or less persuasive before any evidence is presented. *See id.* at 155-75.

79. *See* PAUL H. ROBINSON & JOHN M. DARLEY, JUSTICE, LIABILITY, AND BLAME: COMMUNITY VIEWS AND THE CRIMINAL LAW (1995).

the narratives of opening. Cross-examination and closing argument can deconstruct the narratives of opening statements, as can the more concrete witness narratives of direct examination. These devices assure that the trier's course around the hermeneutic circle between specific fact and general norms will not be a smooth one. Once again, the trial, as it progresses, creates an almost unbearable tension between the narrative assimilation of a problematic situation to prevailing moral and political norms and other demanding values.[80] The latter surround the respect due an individual litigant expressed in careful attention to the specifics of his situation, and the refusal to turn his concrete plight into a purely symbolic instance of a more general principle. This tension serves to refine and elevate the common sense judgment in which the trier engages[81] and largely explains the intensity and feeling of substance of what occurs at trial. This circular process of refinement is more important to the decision than is the mutual adjustment of rule and fact. It is at the heart of the trial. It is the legal rule, as rule, that is secondary, though still important. If a trial is law's self-critique, as David Luban has put it, it is even more the self-critique of common sense morality and public identity.

It is not, then, that the reality dramatized, literally brought to life, by the trial's hybrid of languages and performances, and the moral and political values implicitly invoked by them, serves as a kind of background context within which the rule of law as the law of rules functions. It does not serve merely to provide a hint of the sort of equitable considerations that may soften slightly the real business of rule application by the trial. That structured hybrid of languages provides an independent source of norms. The general point is once again that the trier's decision is an intelligent performance, a practical resolution of the issue presented by the compelling situation in which the jury is engrossed. The primary importance of the legal rules is the way that they serve to structure this situation, not as they are announced in the instructions.

As my figure illustrates, there are three circular movements at work at the explicitly evaluative level at trial. One is the familiar one between legal rule and fact. A second is between full moral evaluation and the richly characterized narrative usually found in opening statements. The third is between public identity and this same characterized narrative. This narrative is, as we have seen, itself the result of the mutual codetermination of the whole story and its inevitably circumstantial evidentiary support. We do not have a hermeneutical circle, but circles within circles. The evaluative pole of each circle consists of norms that are incommensurable with the norms that dominate the other circles. And so, in the

80. *See* BURNS, *supra* note 5, at 176-81.

81. "It is only when we are confronted by the demands of action *in context of a particular set of circumstances* that we get a true understanding of what our ends really are, and reassess those ends in relationship to a new understanding of our life as a whole. Action in the particular circumstances of life is a continuing dialogue between what we think out life is about, and the particularities of moral and practical exigency." RONALD BEINER, POLITICAL JUDGMENT 24 (1979).

course of a trial, the trier will feel the moral force of factual plausibility, legal stability, moral decency, social identity, and political purpose in ways that dramatize and sharpen the tensions among those values. To resolve the case justly, the trier must understand "a juxtaposed rather than an integrated cluster of changing elements that resist reduction to a common denominator, essential core, or generative first principle."[82] We are capable of performances that manifest just that kind of understanding.[83] Because there is no easy summing of these legal, moral, and political values along one single continuum, the final step in trial decision-making must be a judgment of relative importance. The trier must decide what is most important about the case and which of the ways of interpreting the evidence reflects "a more powerful norm." This will vary from case to case. Thus, in some cases that invoke very little of the common morality of the "life world" (e.g., certain commercial cases), that do not involve redefinition of our public identity, or where the parties have relied heavily on the precise meanings of the legal terms, the trier may put great emphasis on the "fairness of fit" of the legal categories. More often the legal rules will function primarily not as explicit criteria of decision-making, but as guidelines for the judge and the attorneys, for the structuring of the case. Of course, in a democratic society, there is every reason to think that there will be substantial overlap, varying from area to area of the law, between the norms to be found in the instructions and those of a "narrative morality." To the extent that this is true, concern about whether the trier "follows the law" will be academic. Practically, the *source* of the norms will make little difference in the outcome of a case. And regardless of source, the trial's linguistic practices will serve to refine their significance for the case at hand.

C. *The Actual Function of Legal Rules in the Trial*

Only those cases that meet a certain threshold will get to trial at all. This is, again, a major means for protecting the consciously over-generalized rules that function as the "basic structure"[84] of society. It is at least as important that the law of rules also affects the rich context within which the jury is immersed. It need not await the jury instructions to have its effects felt. The evidentiary doctrine of materiality mandates that each bit of evidence presented have at least an arguable connection to one of the official norms. The legal rules may, in the vast majority of situations where they approximate those norms, serve as the ancillary considerations, providing some clarity, often some relevant distinctions, for the norms implicit in the devices of the trial. In this same majority of situations, they also

---

82. RICHARD J. BERNSTEIN, THE NEW CONSTELLATION: THE ETHICAL-POLITICAL HORIZONS OF MODERNITY/POSTMODERNITY 201 (1991) (quoting MARTIN JAY, ADORNO 14 (1984)).

83. BURNS, *supra* note 5, at 204-19.

84. RAWLS, *supra* note 22, at 7-11.

provide the judge with a touchstone for his or her determinations of materiality.[85] They allow the judge to keep the evidence arrayed around the central norms in the case so as to heighten precisely the normative tensions that elevate the quality of trial decision-making.[86] That is how they *actually* function. Even potential evidence that meets the requirements of materiality still may be excluded if it too strongly invokes norms that are discontinuous with those in the instructions and which suggest a contrary outcome. The mere ritual of objection followed by ruling provides a liturgical endorsement of the notion that the trial's purposes are limited. The whole range of normative judgments about people as well as about actions[87] simply does not belong here.

Additionally, lawyers will, throughout the trial, have to be concerned about the possibility of a motion for judgment as a matter of law and will have to orient a significant amount[88] of their evidence to satisfy the trial judge and the appellate court of that account. And so there will be at least available to the trier of fact a significant amount of evidence that connects up with the norms embedded in the instructions. Opening statements cannot be given if they promise evidence that the law of evidence, dominated by the requirement of materiality, prohibits. Closing arguments that explicitly urge grounds for decision-making discontinuous with the official norms are objectionable. Cross-examination is controlled by legally defined notions of impeachment that are designed to limit the introduction of "character" evidence other than that directly related to credibility. Direct examination does prevent a witness from offering his testimony in language that is heavily charged or normative and from giving advice on how the case is to be resolved. The law of rules will be well represented in the event to which the jury responds.

D. Two Jurisprudential Questions: What Is Adjudication and What Is Law?

1. The Nature of Adjudication

The account of trial decision-making summarized above does not fall neatly within any one of the major understandings of adjudication dominant in the American jurisprudential tradition. It has some obvious affinities with the accounts of adjudication – mainly appellate adjudication – offered by the principal Legal

85. Unfortunately, they also allow a trial judge to distort the presentation of evidence so as to destroy the discipline of the evidence.

86. The alternative would not produce "the discipline of the evidence" but sentimental invocation of "hot button" prejudices and emotions that define sophistry, whether of the ancient rhetoricians or contemporary political consultants.

87. See ALAN DONAGAN, A THEORY OF MORALITY 75-142 (1977) (making the distinction between first order and second order moral precepts, the first controlling the evaluations of actions and the second the evaluations of persons).

88. I referred to a trial lawyer's creation of a "double helix" of norms for his case – one strand dictated by the legal rules and the other by whatever is the most powerful norm that the narratives or the trial invoke. BURNS, *supra* note 5, at 36.

Realists.[89] On the other hand, its insistence that the trial be understood "from within" and in a language that is self-consciously normative connects up with a tradition represented most recently by Lon Fuller and Ronald Dworkin. It shares with the Realists the view "that doctrine obscured more than it explained about why a court decided as it did,"[90] a conviction implicit in my criticism of the Received View of the trial. Put positively, the major realists, in one way or another, urged that "judges react primarily to the underlying facts of the case, rather than to applicable legal rules and reasons (the latter figuring primarily as ways of providing post-hoc rationales for decisions reached on other grounds.)"[91] It also has *one* kind of affinity with what Brian Leiter has called the "Sociological Wing" of Realism,[92] in that it looks for an understanding of trial decision-making in socially constituted aspects of the trier's "situation sense." But it differs from what I take to be the major thrust of Sociological Realism, in that it has no interest in providing a social scientific account of that sense, as a "psycho-social fact[]"[93] "explained," at least in aspiration,[94] by social scientific covering of laws[95] which

89. See Leiter, *supra* note 7, at 1138 (arguing persuasively that it is possible to generalize on the points discussed in the text about the core convictions of the major realists, Karl Llewellyn, Jerome Frank, Max Radin, Underhill Moore, Hessel Yntema, Felix Cohen, Herman Oliphant, Leon Green, and Joseph Hutcheson).

90. L.A. Powe, Jr., *Justice Douglas After Fifty Years: The First Amendment, McCarthyism and Rights*, 6 CONST. COMM. 267, 271 (1989).

91. Leiter, *supra* note 7, at 1148 (paraphrasing Herman Oliphant, *A Return to Stare Decisis*, 14 A.B.A. J. 71, 75 (1928)). Jerome Frank invoked Chancellor Kent's admission that "[h]e first made himself 'master of the facts.' Then (he wrote) 'I saw where justice lay, and the moral sense decided the court half the time; I then sat down to search the authorities . . . but I almost always found principles suited to my view of the case . . . .'" Brian Leiter, *Rethinking Legal Realism: Toward a Naturalized Jurisprudence*, 76 TEX. L. REV. 267, 276 (1997) [hereinafter Leiter, *Rethinking Legal Realism*] (quoting JEROME FRANK, LAW AND THE MODERN MIND 104 n.* (1930)).

92. Leiter, *supra* note 7, at 1148.

93. Leiter, *Rethinking Legal Realism*, *supra* note 91, at 277.

94. In "aspiration," because this kind of explanation usually remains just a "program," which seldom succeeds in practice. On the limited, though still important and useful, range of social scientific generalization, see ALASDAIR MACINTYRE, AFTER VIRTUE 88-108 (2d ed. 1984).

95. The Realist aspiration to science raises the large philosophical question concerning the compatibility of scientific explanation, on the one hand, and normative justification of the human actions "explained," on the other. In this context, what would the predictability of trial decision-making mean for the enterprise of providing a normative justification of those decisions? If the "causes" or "independent variables" in the scientific account are capable of normative redescription such that they can be recognized as "justifications" then there is no incompatibility. The two languages may peacefully coexist. On the other hand, if they are incapable of that kind of redescription, then there is an apparent conflict. Practically, such a conflict would call for reformist efforts at institutional change so that decisions followed from reasons, not from "irrational" aspects of our psychosocial make-up, our "nature," as understood by a naturalistic empirical science. If those scientifically identified determinates could not be blunted by institutional meaures, if "political" action could not free us from "nature" (as Arendt might put it) then the theoretical question addressed most systematically by the Kantian tradition would be posed: does deterministic explanation entail the absence of free, and so morally significant, human action? Here the issues are very subtle, and well beyond my scope here. Suffice it to say that there are a number of philosophically defensible perspectives from which it is possible to affirm both social scientific explanation and what we might call normative integrity.

Even those Realist attempts to create a "science" of law based on types of situations present a picture of the law that is partial by virtue of its general focus on appellate cases. The statement of facts in an appellate case is composed after the fact, and cannot help but, even in the determination of what was and was not the case, be

allow prediction of the results in future cases. It also has a different emphasis than do less scientifically ambitious versions of Realism. The latter seek predictive power in the "situation types" of the cases, the recurrent factual aspects of cases to which doctrine is not sensitive, but which the "intuitive sense of justice"[96] of the trier finds to be consistently dispositive. There is nothing in the account that I have given which suggests that such situation types do not exist and cannot be dispositive for normative ("sense of justice") reasons. My emphasis is, however, on the ways in which all generalizations, including the generalizations of common sense "intuitive" morality are subjected to both refinement and critique by the devices of the trial. That emphasis does not, however, suggest a nominalism that would claim that there are no recurrent, normatively salient, situations that find their way to trial and that do not "survive" the trial's devices to remain dispositive. Similar cases *are* similarly decided, for fully individual aspects of cases are ineffable,[97] incapable of expression in the inevitably discursive or general predicates of human language. And so they are *insignificant or* meaningless as well, incapable of providing a basis for judgment. Still, a case may be so complex, in factually and normatively significant ways, that it resists reduction to a few preannounced norms or rules.[98] Yet the more interesting probability is that the consciously structured hybrid of practices and languages in the trial creates a honeycomb of incommensurable considerations that causes that appearance of a truly *significant* individuality, just as the unspeakable complexity of the brain seems to cause the appearance of a unique human personality. This significant

influenced by the decision in the case that already has occurred. It is not only that the judge decides for ten reasons and gives one, it is that the one that he gives involves a "finding" that already was made to justify a decision. Such findings are particularly suspect when, as a normative matter, they serve to justify the decision made. In jury cases, where there is usually only a transcript and a general verdict, appellate courts are relatively free to narrate the "facts" based on their own selection and characterization of the evidence. In trials to the court, the findings of fact of the trial judge inevitably are influenced by the trial judge's interest in protecting a determination against reversal, and so likely to be constructed to produce a judgment that is adequate "as a matter of law."

These skeptical considerations simply point out the limitations of what I happily concede to be quite successful attempts to identify "the law" based on recurrent patterns of facts. In commercial law, for example, an academic investigator's discovery that promises not to compete were enforced when made by a person selling a business to another, but not by an employee, may well identify a factual aspect of the case that has sufficient normative salience to justify *and* to cause the result. Such an aspect of the case is all the more reliable to the extent that it was not, on factual grounds, subject to serious dispute at trial. On the other hand, to the extent to which such a normatively salient fact was subject to dispute at trial, its serving both the "explanation" of the decision, and the criterion for predicting future decisions will be weakened, for such a finding may be the result of a determination reached on other grounds rather than the cause of that determination.

96. DOUGLAS LAYCOCK, THE DEATH OF THE IRREPARABLE INJURY RULE ix (1998).

97. "Individuum est ineffabile" was a scholastic precept.

98. Kalven and Zeisel concluded that there was a significant limitation on modes of social scientific analysis of real cases that seek to isolate independent variables in the trial stemming from the vastness of potentially significant variables in most trials, a conclusion they found to be "flattering to law." KALVEN & ZEISEL, *supra* note 8, at 91.

individuality of the case may be *shown* by the operation of all the trial's devices, but may resist articulation in purely propositional terms.[99]

The broad point is that the account I have given of trial level decision-making suggests that the law may be something that is much more closely woven into the particulars of a given case than a single generalization, whether or not it tracks the legal doctrine, will suggest. But this does not mean that a decision of the trial court is indeterminate or that it is the exercise of "arbitrary" discretion. Indeed, my argument is quite the reverse. It is the dense combination of the consciously structured hybrid of languages at trial to *converge* on a uniquely appropriate outcome, leaving much less to arbitrary decision-making than would decision-by-rule-alone. It is the trial's complexity and multiplicity of languages and performances, its ability to invoke the entire range of common sense factual and normative resources, and then to criticize them, that makes the *best* course apparent. Those languages and performances determine the rights of the parties in a way similar to the sense in which Dworkin describes the one uniquely best way, "'best' from the standpoint of political morality."[100] If that account is correct, as I believe it is, the trial would produce outcomes that were far from arbitrary, even though they were likely to be unpredictable by either doctrinal or the usual social scientific means.

Now, of course, the trier of fact is, at least theoretically and sometimes practically, capable of steeling himself against the combined power of the consciously structured hybrid of languages that is the trial, though this is difficult. The trial, given a modicum of competence of the participants, is a powerful experience. The aural medium, enormously more prominent at trial than on appeal, functions to take the listener out of himself and "into" the trial.[101] A decision-maker who claims to be following a rule in the quiet of his or her office is a good deal "freer" from the common norms powerfully deployed by the trial's practices, and, thus, more likely to be "arbitrary." It is not necessary to accept the extreme claims of global indeterminacy of legal language to appreciate the force of the argument made by Realists and Critical Legal Theorists on this account. Those arguments have additional force when legal decisions are in the hands of career officials, individuals who suffer under an institutional temptation to see new cases as old cases. Moral density occurs much more at trial than on appeal.

The Realist account of adjudication usually is opposed to a formalist account. Leiter has summarized legal formalism as committed to three theses: (1) law is rationally determinate in that the class of legal reasons justifies one and only one

---

99. For a critique of the exclusively propositional notion of truth dominant in the legal academy, see WHITE, *supra* note 33, at 52-56.

100. Leiter, *supra* note 7, at 1158.

101. *See* Bernard Hibbits, *Making Sense of Metaphors: Visuality, Aurality, and the Reconfiguration of American Legal Discourse*, 16 CARDOZO L. REV. 229, 342-43 (describing the ability of sound to create a "sense of intimate involvement" in the listener).

outcome to a legal dispute; (2) judging is mechanical in that judges exercise no discretion and that they do not render decisions by reasoning in ways that are not sanctioned by legal reasons or reach judgments that legal reasons do not justify; and, as corollary to (1), (3) legal "reasoning" is autonomous in that legal reasons determine a unique result without recourse to non-legal reasons.[102] He recognizes that the last condition is question-begging, in that, for a given theorist, Dworkin, for example, moral reasons are "part of the law." Surprisingly, decision-making at trial meets two of the three elements in the formalist understanding of adjudication.

I argue that the languages and performances of the trial converge on a uniquely appropriate resolution of a case at trial. They leave little real discretion, in the sense of freedom from public norms. (Again, a given trier may ignore "the discipline of the evidence" and decide the case for idiosyncratic reasons, but that is a possibility that the most committed formalist would concede for the work of any given judge as well). On the other hand, the modes of thought that the trier employs are not deductive, or "mechanical." They are integrative or interpretive. So the account is formalist in one sense, in the sense that the trier does not, after a well-tried case, possess "discretion," and not in another, in that the operative cognitive processes are not "mechanical." The uniquely correct resolution of the case is the judgment that best integrates the competing moral, political, and strictly legal aspects of the case in the precise factual context of the situation. This is, of course, something very close to what Llewellyn meant by "situation sense,"[103] a perception that is necessarily oriented toward inevitably determinate practical resolution of a problematic situation.

Finally, it is worth repeating here that these normative considerations embedded in the trial's consciously structured hybrid of languages and performances cannot be reduced to rules or completely reproduced in language "about" the trial. In the same way that drama and other art allows us to see aspects of a situation that we cannot see any other way,[104] that even the best criticism fails fully to capture, so any theoretical account of the trial will not be adequate to what it routinely accomplishes.

2. *The Nature of Law*

Trial decision-making under the description I give may properly be called "legal" under either positivist or natural law philosophies of law. Whereas formalism and realism are theories of adjudication, positivism and natural law, including "interpretivist" styles of jurisprudence such as Dworkin's, divide on the

---

102. Leiter, *supra* note 7, at 1145-46.

103. KARL LLEWELLYN, THE COMMON LAW TRADITION: DECIDING APPEALS 403 (1960).

104. And so, once again, we often simply cannot "compare" for accuracy the trial's rendering with what is "already-out-there-now-real."

nature of law.[105] The account of the trial given above is much closer to Dworkin's than to that of positivists such as Hart, since it does not seek to provide a purely descriptive account of this particular legal institution, the trial,[106] but rather an interpretive understanding from "within" the normative world that the American trial constitutes. Hart himself recently recognized this distinction:

> Legal theory conceived in this [Hart's own] manner as both descriptive and general is a radically different enterprise from Dworkin's conception of legal theory (or "jurisprudence" as he often terms it) as in part evaluative and justificatory and as "addressed to a particular legal culture," which is usually the theorist's own and in Dworkin's case is that of Anglo-American law. The central task of legal theory so conceived is termed by Dworkin "interpretive" and is partly evaluative, since it consists in the identification of the principles which both best "fit" or cohere with the settled law *and legal practices* of a legal system and also provide the best moral justification for them, thus showing the law "in its best light." For Dworkin the principles thus identified are not only parts of a theory of law but are also implicit parts of the law itself.[107]

My account of the trial is different from Dworkin's account of (largely appellate) law in that it locates the moral aspect of the law less in "principles" that stand "above" and provide the purpose for more narrowly legal provisions and more in the narrative, argumentative, and dramatic resources embedded in the trial. It is more Hegelian, less Kantian. The trial does have an ideal element, an ability to move beyond a positivistic notion of the jurors' preexistent opinions, a "plebiscitary"[108] notion of its common sense, and the narrow meaning of legal texts. That element, which "principles" play in Dworkin's account, is created by the tensions among all the trial's resources.

But the languages and practices of the trial define "law" within either a positivist or a Dworkinian perspective. For a positivist like Hart, whether or not a given norm is "law" is a matter of social *fact,* a "Rule of Recognition" by which the relevant officials[109] decide cases and claim to be justified in so doing. The norms that the rules and practices of the trial allow and encourage, it seems, now fall within such a Rule of Recognition. That they are "moral" and "political" does not prevent them from meeting the requirements of such a rule, understood as

105. Leiter, *supra* note 7, at 1140.

106. H.L.A. HART, THE CONCEPT OF LAW 239-41 (2d ed. 1994) (postscript to the 2d edition).

107. *Id.* at 240-41 (emphasis added).

108. PETER J. STEINBERGER, THE CONCEPT OF POLITICAL JUDGMENT 230 (1993)

109. It is somewhat difficult to determine the significance of Hart's "officials" in the context of the jury trial. It seems that officials are both jurors insofar as they actually do decide cases a certain way, and claim to be justified in so deciding. It would more obviously include judges who do not disturb jury verdicts which appear to be decided in a way discontinuous with the Received View. I summarize the most reliable conclusions of the social science literature on how jurors actually do decide at BURNS, *supra* note 5, at 141-54.

"patterns of convergent behavior in accord with the rule."[110] Indeed, my polemic against the adequacy of the Received View is precisely that it no longer adequately captures the patterns of convergent behavior at many levels of legal practice.[111]

I maintain, as well, a sense that what law is and what it ought to be are different questions, the second core principle of positivism. Triers decide a case based on the narratively rooted common sense and political self-understanding of the community. The devices of the trial serve to elevate and refine that common sense and self-understanding. The trial serves as a moral critique of both. But there is a moral level beyond which the devices of the trial cannot go: if the common sense of the trier is entwined with systematic injustice, the law that the trial makes will be unjust. In an area where either the common sense of the community or substantive legal norms are corrupt, only languages other than the language spoken at trial may allow us to articulate that injustice.

The natural lawyer may respond that it is then not "true law." For example, Dworkin may respond, in the "interpretist" version, that the trier has not made "true law" because the judgment rendered is not the *best* integration of the moral, political, and strictly legal values that are at play in the trial. A positivist may respond, in turn, that the jury has made law, just bad law. Bad law or no law? I believe that is an important question, but that it turns on much broader philosophical, indeed metaphysical, commitments about the best way to understand human institutions and practices, and about the inevitability of a normative element in social explanation.[112]

Finally, the integrative, as opposed to the mechanical, nature of the cognitive operations at trial surely does not preclude the norms employed from being understood as "true law." Cass Sunstein has pointed out[113] that uncontroversially "legal" provisions, such as a statute or administrative rule, are often framed in terms of "factors" rather than rules.[114] Where a legal provision is framed in terms of factors:

> There is no rule because the factors are not described exhaustively and precisely in advance, and because their weight has not been fully specified. Hence the decision-maker cannot rely simply on "finding the facts" and "applying the law." The content of the law is not given; part of it must be found. There is a degree of *ex post* allocation of entitlements.[115]

Thus, the mere fact that the cognitive operations that occur at trial require the

---

110. Leiter, *supra* note 7, at 1143.

111. BURNS, *supra* note 5, at 26-33.

112. *See* Kenneth I. Winston, *The Ideal Element in a Definition of Law*, 5 LAW & PHIL. 89 (1986) (discussing the relationship between definitions of law and broader understandings of the place of ideal elements in social understanding).

113. Cass R. Sunstein, *Problems with Rules*, 83 CAL. L. REV. 956 (1995).

114. *Id.* at 963-64.

115. *Id.* at 964.

integration of incommensurable values does not itself disqualify trial decision-making from being properly understood as "legal" decision-making. Second, many other uncontroversially "legal" decisions require the application of norms that are better characterized as "standards" than "rules." "A ban on 'excessive' speeds on the highway is familiarly thought to involve a standard; so too with a requirement that pilots be 'competent,' or that behavior in the classroom be 'reasonable.'"[116] Because of the high burden of interpretation in concrete situations to discern the meaning of standards, it is likewise often difficult to identify in advance what the significance of the standard in a particular situation will be. Rule application does not have a monopoly on uncontroversially legal decision-making.

Both Realist and Formalist traditions have contributions to make to the understanding of the nature of trial adjudication. Both positivist and natural law perspectives can understand trial decision-making as "true law," although whether a given decision is best described as "bad law" or "no law" turns on much broader intellectual commitments concerning the nature of social explanation.

E. Process or Constitutional Understandings of the Jury's Role

There remains the question of the legitimacy of the *source* of the norms that are evoked and elevated by the devices of the trial. I have suggested that those devices actualize implicit moral and political self-understandings of the jury. Of course, institutions such as the trial are not "inert conduits directing human energies . . . toward certain desirable end-states,"[117] but are, rather, "active thing[s], projecting themselves into a field of interacting forces, reshaping those forces in diverse ways and in varying degrees."[118] Second, though law certainly creates rules, law is not the same thing as the rules it creates. Just as Fuller subordinated the rules that emerged from the processes of common law adjudication to that process itself, so the trial's processes are no less law for being other than rule-like. Indeed, since they concern concrete cases, they could not be rule-like. Fuller also insisted that the process of adjudication is a process of lawmaking, and that it was a moral enterprise, largely dependent upon the forms of the life of the relevant portion of society, an "ethics already realized."

The lawfulness of the trial depends ultimately on the place of the trial, notably the jury trial, within our legal order. To the extent that the trial is a genuine lawmaking practice, and that practice is legitimate within our Constitutional order, the lawfulness of the trial will be consistent with the law of the land. This assertion raises questions that ripple out quickly into the fundamental issues of constitu-

---

116. *Id.* at 964-65.

117. LON L. FULLER, *Means and Ends*, *in* THE PRINCIPLES OF SOCIAL ORDER 47, 58 (Kenneth I. Winston ed., 1981).

118. *Id.* at 54, *quoted in* Robert G. Bone, *Lon Fuller's Theory of Adjudication and the False Dichotomy Between Dispute Resolution and Public Law Models of Litigation*, 75 B.U. L. REV. 1273, 1287 (1995).

tional interpretation. Is the legitimate place of the jury in our constitutional order to be determined by the original intent of the Congress that approved the Bill of Rights,[119] or the state legislatures that ratified them, or the Congress that passed or the state legislatures that ratified the Fourteenth Amendment or the efforts of the Court to interpret a living constitution or some "higher law" that the constitution reflects?[120] More broadly still, there are philosophical questions concerning the extent to which it is appropriate to invoke the actual rules and practices of existing institutions in normative argument.[121] In what follows, I will be assuming a position not far from Rawls's: that the actual practices of existing institutions in which we have confidence, considered in their historical context, and the more overtly philosophical considerations both have weight and must be considered together. Ultimately, judgments concerning the trial's role in our legal order must be justified "by the mutual support of many considerations, of everything fitting together into one coherent view."[122] There is no need to go beyond this very general proposition for my purposes here.

Commentators have begun to develop an understanding of the jury trial's place in our constitutional order that is consistent with the theory of the trial described above. Professor Nancy Marder recently has set out what she calls a "process" view of the jury.[123] She first describes the many interpretive functions that we assign to the jury that cannot be assimilated into what I have called the Received View. Juries engage in broad-gauged interpretation in vast areas of the law, including determinations of negligence and every application of an undefined "reasonable doubt" standard.[124] Patterns of jury determinations have been crucial in establishing a changed "legal regime." "[J]uries, by declining to find contributory negligence, essentially created a regime of comparative negligence long before the legislature and judges had eliminated contributory negligence as a

---

119. The Constitution of 1787 provided for jury trials in federal criminal cases, but was silent as to civil cases and it was not until after the Fifth, Sixth, and Fourteenth Amendments that the Court imposed trial by jury in criminal cases on the states. The Seventh Amendment has yet to be incorporated into the Fourteenth Amendment, but similar state constitutional provisions provide a right to trial by jury in many civil cases.

120. Edward Corwin, *The "Higher Law" Background of American Constitutional Law*, 48 HARV. L. REV. 149 (1928).

121. The range among theorists is great. For Bentham, existing institutions not justified by the principle of utility are likely to be an amalgam of force and superstition, "nonsense on stilts." *See generally* DANIEL BOORSTIN, THE MYSTERIOUS SCIENCE OF THE LAW (1941). The middle position is occupied by Rawls, whose theory of justice is justified by a circular movement between existing institutions in which we have great confidence and broad philosophical principles justified by other means. JOHN RAWLS, A THEORY OF JUSTICE (1971). Farther along the continuum, one finds Hegel's elevation of *Sittlichkeit*, the highly situated ideals of a civilization, over *Moralitat*, a ethic of abstract principle. HEGEL'S PHILOSOPHY OF RIGHT 75-155 (T.M. Knox trans., 1952). Farther along yet, there are more conservative views that oppose virtually any place of universal principle in legal or political discourse.

122. RAWLS, *supra* note 121, at 579.

123. Marder, *supra* note 1, at 907-26.

124. *Id.*

defense."[125] Likewise, patterns of jury verdicts in the law of product safety, wrongful discharge, and in the imposition of punitive damages have altered significantly the "basic structure" of our legal order.[126] The same probably is occurring today in the tobacco litigation.

Marder supports this process understanding of the trial from both history and a political understanding of institutional checks and balances. The majority view among legal historians is that the jury and the trial occupied a much larger role in the American legal order until the middle of the nineteenth century than they do today.[127] There are many reasons for this development, but some, at least, cannot serve as *justifications* for the rise of the judiciary at the jury's expense.[128] From an institutional viewpoint, Marder argues that jurors acting after trial have positive characteristics that legislatures lack. Jurors are not beholden to interest groups; they are not made up of professionals and not removed from "the experiences and common sense of ordinary citizens."[129] Especially in light of the consciously structured hybrid of languages employed at trial, jurors are likely to focus on the "subtleties revealed throughout trial" through "the discipline of the evidence." This process will most usually involve genuine interpretation and only rarely true nullification. The lay jury's focus on the particular facts of the case, even if eventually producing a politically significant pattern, places it in an institutionally legitimate "dialogue" with the executive and legislative branches.[130]

Now the trial makes law only for the case before it. That is a conscious limitation on this form of decision-making consistent with the depth with which the trial's devices illuminate the complexities of the individual case. Because the linguistic practices at trial are so *constrained*, and constrained by broad notions of procedural and substantive justice imbedded in rules, and the trial event itself is so *structured* by similarly universal notions, the decision at trial is hardly devoid of the influence of the deepest commitments of the society, including its qualified commitment to the rule of law as the law of rules. But because that commitment is heavily qualified, and we recognize, in our institutions, both the vast range of *significant* differences from case to case and the importance of respecting those differences, we recognize as well the limited value of trial decisions as precedent, for the exact constellation of significant facts and norms actualized by the trial's rules and practices cannot be translated into a form that could be useful as

---

125. *Id.* at 910 (citing Stephen C. Yeazell, *The New Jury and the Ancient Jury Conflict*, 1990 U. CHI. LEGAL F. 87, 113).

126. Marder, *supra* note 1, at 910.

127. *See, e.g.*, ABRAMSON, *supra* note 24, at 57-95; WILLIAM E. NELSON, AMERICANIZATION OF THE COMMON LAW: THE IMPACT OF LEGAL CHANGE ON MASSACHUSETTS SOCIETY, 1760-1830 (1975); Mark DeWolfe Howe, *Juries as Judges of Criminal Law*, 52 HARV. L. REV. 582 (1939); Drew L. Kershen, *Vincinage*, 30 OKLA. L. REV. 3 (1977).

128. Howe, *supra* note 127, at 161.

129. Marder, *supra* note 1, at 918.

130. *Id.* at 925.

precedent. The closest analogue to that precedent is the sensibility of the "wise and strong trial court"[131] judge. The judge is, however, so much a creature of "officialdom" and his temptation, after the dulling effect of case after case after case over a long career, to stop really seeing what is new and significant is so great, that our institutions err on the side of the densely particular judgment of the jury. As Abe Fortas put it:

> [J]udges do become case-hardened. Judges do sometimes tend, after many years, to take a somewhat jaundiced view of defendants. Many trial judges tend to come a bit prosecution minded. That's the basic justification for a jury.[132]

Marder's view of the jury ultimately rests on a notion of jury legitimacy that reaches back to a source of authority that lies beyond legislative enactment. Professor Akhil Reed Amar recently has provided such a source in the Bill of Rights, at whose "heart" lies the jury.[133]

> If we seek a paradigmatic image underlying the original Bill of Rights, we cannot go far wrong in picking the jury. Not only was it featured in three separate amendments (the Fifth, Sixth, and Seventh), but its absence strongly influenced the judge-restricting doctrines underlying three other amendments (the First, Fourth, and Eighth).[134]

Amar recounts the centrality of the jury during the founding period and the pervasive understanding that it was to serve a self-consciously political function, as an ultimate source of norms unaffected by the corruptible "magistrates" in the legislature and judiciary. Amar's account is consistent with Gordon Wood's seminal treatment of Federalist constitutional theory.[135] Wood's argument was that the Federalist philosophical innovation was to locate sovereignty directly in the people, not in the legislature, and certainly not in the judiciary. Even legislators could be "magistrates," government officials with designs inconsistent with the common good. This notion of sovereignty had a plausibility to a generation that had directly experienced the people's own constitution-making and lawmaking power. One of the "remnants of the Founders' vision"[136] of the constitutional authority of the people survives, Amar argues:

> [I]n rules [that] prevent judges from directing verdicts of guilt or requiring special verdicts in criminal cases; barring trial judges from reversing, and

---

131. Michelson v. United States, 335 U.S. 469, 485-86 (1948).

132. Alan W. Scheflin, *Jury Nullification: The Right to Say No*, 45 S. CAL. L. REV. 168, 213 (1972). *See also* G.K. CHESTERTON, TREMENDOUS TRIFLES 64-65 (1920).

133. AKHIL REED AMAR, THE BILL OF RIGHTS: CREATION AND RECONSTRUCTION 83 (1998).

134. *Id.* at 96.

135. GORDON WOOD, THE CREATION OF THE AMERICAN REPUBLIC, 1776-1789 (1970).

136. AMAR, *supra* note 133, at 103.

> appellate courts from reviewing, criminal jury acquittals; allowing criminal defendants to escape government efforts to use collateral estoppel offensively; and preventing challenges to inconsistent criminal jury verdicts.[137]

Amar argues that the jury is one place where this "pre-legislative" sovereignty continues to be exercised. One element of this sovereignty is the authority to adjudicate the constitutionality of legislative enactments and common law doctrines that come before it. Amar's own scholarly ambivalence about this authority[138] roughly parallels the constrained way in which juries actually do exercise this ultimate authority. For the law of rules is well represented before and at trial, in the structuring of the engrossing event to which the jury responds. Democratically enacted law is unlikely to be far distant from commonsense moral and political norms. True nullification is rare. All the constraints that surround trial decision-making create a continuum, differing from criminal to civil cases and within those categories as well, from highly contextual decision-making to true nullification. I have tried to show how that context, the consciously structured hybrid of languages at trial, realizes the sovereignty of the people in the best sense.

F. The Trial and the Values Behind the Rule of Law

Before concluding, it is worth discussing briefly whether and how the American trial serves the values that lie behind the Rule of Law. The latter is not, of course, an end in itself and the lawfulness of the trial can only fully be assessed in light of those underlying purposes.

1. Control of Officialdom

I have argued that the trial's consciously structured hybrid of languages and performances converge on a normatively best outcome, leaving little indeterminate. The engaging and constraining nature of its devices makes it difficult for the trier to decide the case other than through "the discipline of the evidence," evidence that is largely structured by the law of rules and the values underlying them. The jury trial takes the decision out of the hands of officials who may lose interest in attending to the factual details of the case. In all these ways, the languages and performances of the trial protect against the arbitrariness of government actors, a key basic value underlying the rule of law. The devices of the trial are designed to thwart the bureaucratic language that almost always precedes Orwellian nightmares. They maintain a simple, clear language that is a prerequisite to decency, a "strong truth-bearing everyday language, not marred or corrupted by

137. *Id.* at 104.

138. "In setting forth the strong arguments for jury review, I do not mean to suggest that I am wholly convinced. But the mere fact of their strong plausibility shows how strikingly powerful the jury might have become had post-1800 history unfolded differently." *Id.* at 103.

technical discourse or scientific codes . . . of which we are in need as citizens, and as moral agents.[139] The jury trial has, of course, always been viewed as a principal antidote to the tyranny of officialdom, a proposition that was repeated over and over during the founding:

> Judges, unincumbered by juries, have been ever found much better friends to government than to the people. Such judges will always be more desirable than juries to [would-be tyrants,] upon the same principle that a large standing army . . . is ever desirable to those who wish to enslave the people.[140]

2. *Justice as Regularity*

The element of the Rule of Law that demands that similar cases be treated similarly also is honored by the trial. The norm of consistency will be offended by (1) subsuming cases that have normatively dispositive differences under the same rule or (2) failing to subsume cases with normatively dispositive similarities under the same rule. Of course, what needs interpretation in each case is whether the inevitable similarities and differences *are* normatively dispositive. The trial's devices are designed to assess just that. The aspects of the case that honor norms that have large reach, that are likely to be normatively dispositive in a large number of cases, stem from the structuring effect of the substantive legal norms discussed above and the relative stability of the common sense morality of the community from which judge and jurors come. Conversely, the extreme, even obsessive, attention to the factual details of the individual case assures that the cases are not too easily assimilated to a single, over-generalized norm. The latter would fail to take full advantage of the complexity of a community's moral sensibilities. This aspect of the trial assures that *dis*similar cases are not similarly decided. It is the trial's aspiration to the ideal combination of what we may call more universal and more specific norms generated by all of its devices that work against "the subtle distortion of prejudices and bias as these effectively discriminate against certain groups in the judicial process."[141]

3. *Predictability*

It is possible to consider the "predictability" of trial outcomes from two perspectives. The first perspective, that of a lawyer contemplating the settlement of

---

139. MURDOCH, *supra* note 46, at 162.

140. *An Old Whig* (VIII), *reprinted in* 3 THE COMPLETE ANTI-FEDERALIST 46, 49 (Herbert Storing ed., 1981), *quoted in* AMAR, *supra* note 133, at 84.

141. RAWLS, *supra* note 121, at 235. Recall that in the civil context only those cases that have undergone a pretrial screening to determine, in effect, whether there is a legal norm that disposes of the case regardless of *any other possible* normatively significant aspect of the case (no "substantive issue of material fact") will go to trial. Thus the class of cases goes to trial where there has been a prior determination that the more particular aspects of the case are normatively significant.

a case, does not directly implicate Rule of Law values, though it is important in assessing the likelihood of settlement and the efficiency of the legal system because the action of the client already has led to litigation. The predictability of the outcome of a trial at that stage, when there is significantly more information available than there was to the client deciding how to act, does not increase that freedom that comes from knowing the exact location of the line the crossing of which will trigger the exercise of adverse state power. As I discuss below, it is certainly possible to design rules that will result in an extremely high level of predictability, such as "Plaintiff always wins a forcible detainer action" or "A person whose act causes the death of another shall be guilty of murder." It is likewise relatively easy to design summary proceedings of one kind or another to enforce those rules, the results of which can be predicted with a high level of certainty. But as the rules are refined to capture a larger range of the normative considerations that our moral, and sometimes constitutional, commitments demand and begin to look like the rules we actually have in many areas, the arguably relevant factual base continues to expand in a way that inevitably invokes a larger and larger web of norms. Once that occurs, it is not at all clear that summary proceedings become more predictable to lawyers than are trials.

We have learned from both Realists and Critical Legal Scholars that little can be deduced from most legal rules in the kinds of cases that actually are litigated. It seems to me that, in those cases where there truly are *arguably* "substantial issues of material fact," it is not easier to predict the decision of a judge ruling on a summary judgment motion than it is to predict the result at trial. In those cases, it seems that the judge faced with an arguable summary judgment motion has more *true* discretion than does a judge or jury at trial. That is because the record on summary judgment tends to be more abstract, less articulated in a way that triggers the "discipline of the evidence," that which makes a case intellectual and morally "compelling." A trial lawyer considering a trial, "playing it out" in his or her own mind may be able to predict the result to a higher level of probability than the resolution of the same case under more summary procedures.

More directly implicating the Rule of Law is the question of whether the complexity, I would say depth, of the normative considerations that the trial brings to bear on a human action renders it impossible for a citizen to predict the outcome of a possible trial at the time he takes action that may subject him to legal sanctions.[142] For another aspect of the Rule of Law, "closely related to liberty," is the liberal notion that a citizen ought to know the reach of his legal obligations[143] before taking such action. One response is to focus on the inevitable tension

142. H.L.A. HART, PUNISHMENT AND RESPONSIBILITY: ESSAYS IN THE PHILOSOPHY OF LAW (1968).

143. There exists a spirited debate as to whether it is optimal, from fairness and efficiency perspectives, that a citizen know precisely what his legal obligations are before acting. *See* Stephen McG. Bundy & Einer Elhauge, *Knowledge About Legal Sanctions*, 92 MICH. L. REV. 261 (1993); Meir Dan-Cohen, *Decision Rules and Conduct Rules: On Acoustic Separation in Criminal Law*, 97 HARV. L. REV. 625 (1984).

between predictability in this sense and what we may call substantive justice. It is always possible to increase predictability by impoverishing judgment and it is often true that the price of predictability is too high.[144] Second, it is not always true that a sharp and precise estimate of the likely results of enforcement efforts always furthers the purposes of the law.[145] Additionally, the unimpeachably "legal" norms that are enacted by statutes that rely on "factors" and "standards" also reduce the level of predictability. For in both of those cases, "interpreters have to do a great deal of work in order to generate the necessary content for a legal provision" and so "it is not possible to know what we have in advance."[146] Sunstein has argued persuasively that in many contexts we make the judgment between rules and rulenessness on pragmatic grounds, and are more likely to have recourse to norms expressed other than through rules under a number of recurring circumstances: when the cost of error in specific cases are unacceptably high, when the legislator must act in the absence of reliable information, when circumstances are changing rapidly, and so on.[147] Even were we to employ rules, discretion in their application is unavoidable, if only to eliminate obviously unjust or absurd results (and then, in *every* case to determine *whether* the result of decision-by-rule application is unjust or absurd). One may regard the trial as a particularly sophisticated way in which this inevitable casuistry is conducted, in those cases where summary resolution is inappropriate or constitutionally prohibited.[148]

A legislature or an appellate court has a very limited ability to screen out the moral context within which law functions while still preserving a refined and subtle inquiry into the events leading up to the lawsuit. It *is* possible to create rules for decision-making that generate "factual" inquiries so limited and abstract that they can be adjudicated using summary methods. But note what is being sacrificed here. The sphere of human interaction that such procedures govern must be stripped of their natural relations to the narrative bearers of our moral life and appropriate devices for criticizing those narratives. Summary judgments and, to a somewhat lesser extent, appellate decisions based on a review of trial transcripts

---

144. Fuller made a similar point in support of common law modes of adjudication:

> A statute that reveals itself as a patent misfit for situations of fact that later come to court—situations plainly covered by the language of the statute, but obviously misunderstood or not foreseen by the draftman—such a law certainly has no special claim to praise simply because it is clear in meaning and announced in advance. The virtue of the common law is that, proceeding case by case, it can fit and refit its prescriptions to the configurations of life as they reveal themselves in litigation. What the common law lacks in the way of clear advance formulation, it may more than make up for by its capacity to reshape and reword its rules in the light of the actual situations that offer themselves for decision.

Lon L. Fuller, *Human Interaction and the Law*, *in* PRINCIPLES OF SOCIAL ORDER 236-37 (Kenneth I. Winston ed., 1981).

145. *See id.*

146. Sunstein, *supra* note 113, at 965.

147. *Id.* at 1014-16.

148. *Id.*

are deprived of many of these aspects of what the consciously structured hybrid of trial languages and performances offers. Since these trial languages and performances do not simply play off one another, but rather function together to reveal morally, legally, and politically significant aspects of the situation, these summary or appellate decisions are in a sense impoverished.[149] It is not that judges deciding summary judgments have different or better ways of mediating the full significance of a set of legal principle in a particular case. Summary judgment is a decision that we have insufficient reason to believe that the moral and factual sources that only a trial can reveal are of importance in this case.

What remains is the question of when such impoverished decision-making is appropriate. Put bluntly, that occurs when we are convinced that one aspect of a situation is of such overriding significance that we basically say, "That is all I need to know." Note the characteristics that such an aspect of a situation must have in order to enable us to engage in summary adjudication. Historical judgment and so historical knowledge always involve normative commitments of the kind that narrative requires. Any account of human action that avoids the full range of evaluation that is implicit in narrative and its critique will be accepting the "disjointed parts of some possible narrative." This suggests a persistent problem for policy makers. Let us assume, putting aside questions of proof, that a certain legal rule discontinuous with common sense suggests itself on substantive moral, political, fairness, or efficiency grounds. It may even be possible to specify the rule with great precision. However, if the rule as promulgated requires "fact finding" concerning human actions, especially, though not exclusively, with regard to human motive, intention, purpose, or knowledge, it will be very difficult to assure that the rule can actually be applied in American trial-type hearings.

For the richness of the trial's devices have not evolved without reason. I have argued that they build on "natural" modes of understanding human actions and are adapted in a refined way to the needs of our public culture. In their absence we are

---

149. It was this danger of impoverishment that Judge Patricia Wald identified in the overuse of summary judgment in the federal courts:

> And one must at least think about the implications of the new regime, in which law is mostly made on the basis of undisputed facts "pleaded," "stipulated," or "inferred" rather than on fuller trial records that may more accurately represent the complexity and ambiguity of life. Will our law be less sensitive to the multivalenced and perspectival qualities of human events? Will our jurisprudence craft rules and principles and hand them down fully formed from the netherworld of law school hypotheticals, instead of forging them in the heat of pitched battle and hammering them in shape on the anvil of trials, witnesses, cross-examinations, and live evidence evaluated by ordinary lay persons?
>
> *****
>
> If Oliver Wendell Holmes was right when he said that "[t]he life of the law has not been logic: it has been experience," then the decoupling of law from experience could strike a mortal blow to its integrity; our law would not disappear, but it could become lifeless, like a whale washed up on the beach.

Patricia Wald, *Summary Judgment at Sixty*, 76 TEX. L. REV. 1897, 1942, 1944 (1998).

likely to have highly ideological judging masquerading as a concern for the "law itself." Real discretion is at work here—hidden in findings of fact (or decisions about the lack of disputed issues of material fact). Here result-orientation, based on very abstract features of the case, may embody the kinds of willfulness that really offend the Rule of Law.

There are many contexts, then, in which predictability, and the liberal values that surround it, are balanced against other considerations.[150] Common law adjudication, for example, is inherently less predictable than some forms of bureaucratic decision-making. My argument throughout has been that it is impossible to identify that reality that is actualized by the trial except through the devices of the trial. But that does not mean that trial outcomes are wholly unpredictable. Clients are well-served by counselors at law who have both a developed common sense and also a developed imagination for how a course of action under consideration "is going to look to a jury." There is, at the trial level, a lower level of prediction based on broad "types" than there is based on the lawyer's imaginative projection of the way the case will "play out" under the demanding constraints of the trial courtroom. The difference is the enormously greater level of normatively significant factual detail leading to literally infinite possible factual and normative inferences, the tacit knowledge about "character"[151] that comes from live witness presentation, and the significance of "enactment." A lawyer who has interviewed his client carefully and done a responsible amount of additional investigation is in a position to reduce the unpredictability of trial outcomes. And, of course, that clients routinely seek out such counselors suggests that a fair level of predictability is routinely achieved.

III. CONCLUSION

The trial is "the central institution of law as we know it."[152] Its lawfulness is a densely complex matter, respecting both the law of rules and moral and political sources that are more fundamental than any written enactments.

---

150. *See, e.g.*, Steven Smith, *Believing Like a Lawyer*, 40 B.C. L. REV. 1041 (1999) (describing the retroactive application of newly "declared" legal rules, supported by the notion that the rule declared was "found" and so always existed).

151. This "character" evidence often is translated into the formally legitimate language of "witness credibility." The trial judge's finding that a witness was not credible, or the possibility that a jury could have found a witness "not credible" is usually immune from appellate review.

152. WHITE, *supra* note 33, at 108.

[3]

AN ANALYSIS OF CLOSING ARGUMENTS TO A JURY

ANTHONY G. AMSTERDAM*
RANDY HERTZ**

This article examines the lawyers' closing arguments to the jury in a single criminal case: a 1991 homicide prosecution in New York City.[1] The defendant was a twenty-two-year-old man whom we will call David Jones.[2] He was socially acquainted with the victim, twenty-year-old Mary Smith, and with her two friends, Susan Stone and Nancy Gregg.

Late one evening in 1987, Smith, Stone, and Gregg were seated in Gregg's parked car talking with other young people on the sidewalk. Stone and Gregg were in the front seat, Smith in the rear. A friend of Stone's came by and Stone got out of the car to talk with him. At about this time, Jones came over to the car. Jones began to argue with Gregg and then with Smith. He accused them of spreading stories that he had engaged in oral sex with women. After a few minutes, Gregg left the car to talk to some friends. Jones got into the rear of the car, closing the door behind him, and sat beside Smith. He and Smith continued to argue inside the car.

Stone and Gregg remained nearby, talking with their acquaintances. They heard Jones and Smith yelling at one another. Stone heard Smith call out: "David, no!" Stone saw Smith grab at Jones's jacket, then heard a gunshot.

Just before the shot, Gregg saw the right rear car door open and Jones back out. She saw Jones pop a link chain off Smith's neck. Gregg heard

---

* Edward Weinfeld Professor of Law and Director of the Lawyering Program, New York University Law School.

** Professor of Law, New York University Law School.

1. Earlier versions of the article were presented at the Lawyering Theory Conference at New York Law School and in sessions of the Lawyering Theory Colloquium at New York University Law School. We are grateful for the criticisms of the participants and for much aid and inspiration by Jerry Bruner, Peggy Davis, Kim Hawkins, Florian Miedel, Richard Sherwin, and David Soskin. [For purposes of clarity and understanding, the style used in this article departs at times from the 15th edition of *The Bluebook: A Uniform System of Citation* (Ed.).]

2. We have assigned fictitious names to everyone involved: the defendant, victim, witnesses, and lawyers. A reporter's transcript of the closing arguments is on file with the *New York Law School Law Review*. In quoting from the transcript, we sometimes italicize words or phrases to emphasize specific language; all such emphases are ours. An asterisk between quotations indicates that they are taken from separated passages of the transcript.

the shot and saw Jones put a handgun in his pocket. Jones was standing bent over, partly outside the car, with his head still inside. Other young people urged him to take off before the cops came. He did and was not apprehended for more than three years.

Stone and Gregg drove Smith to the hospital, where she died. The cause of death was a single bullet entering her chest and penetrating her heart, liver, stomach, and pancreas before lodging in her back.

The sole issue at trial was whether Jones was guilty of second-degree murder or of manslaughter. Under New York law, murder requires a specific intent to kill. Killing by a reckless act is only manslaughter. Thus, the question for the jury was whether, when Jones shot Smith in the chest at close range, he intended to cause her death.[3] That question had to be decided on the testimony of the prosecution's witnesses, principally Stone and Gregg. Jones did not testify or present evidence.

In our experience, this is the kind of case in which a jury can go either way. During times of media clamor about violent crime, it would probably be listed at two-to-one odds for a murder verdict in the weekly D.A.'s and P.D.'s office pools. In less frenzied times it would be an even-money case. Savvy lawyers in both offices would bet both sides at both sets of odds.

After the verdict was in, the second-guessers in both offices would have a lot to say about why the case was won or lost. The backgrounds of the jurors, the prosecutor's or defense counsel's eloquence or maladroitness, this or that witness's emotionality or dispassion, whether juror number three was looking at the judge when the left judicial eyebrow rose in that practiced arc of skepticism—all these topics and others would be fully canvassed in the controversies of the *cognoscenti* at the coffee machines.

---

3. The judge charged the jury:

> "Section 125.25 of the Penal Law . . . reads as follows: A person is guilty of murder in the second degree when[,] with intent to cause the death of another person, he causes the death of such person.
>
> "Now, for you to find the defendant guilty of this crime, the People are required to prove from all the evidence in the case beyond a reasonable doubt . . . that the defendant shot Mary Smith with the intent to cause her death."

The judge defined intent as "a person's conscious aim or objective," then added:

> "Now the element of intent is obviously a subjective element, certainly can't look into a person's mind to see what he was thinking at the time of the incident. Intent is the secret operation of the mind. But the law permits you to infer intent from a person's actions, leading up to, surrounding and following the incident. That is, you are permitted to infer but need not that a person intends that which is the natural and necessary and probable consequences of the acts done by him."

Without disparaging the importance of each of these factors, we think the *Jones* case is a useful setting in which to study particularly the lawyers' closing arguments. For it is in this kind of case—where the evidence, being subject to divergent interpretations, frames the jury's decision but does not compel it—that the lawyers' arguments can make a crucial difference.[4] What do the lawyers say to the jury in such a case, and how?[5]

Our first examination of the arguments produced no surprises. Both lawyers used the same time-tested pattern. They praised the jury for approaching the case in a proper frame of mind. They summarized the testimony. They stated the issue that the jury must decide. They analyzed the evidence or the lack of evidence bearing on that issue. They explained how it supported their own position. They summarized their opponent's argument and criticized its logic. They expressed confidence in the jurors' good judgment, which would assure the verdict sought. This was all very

---

4. *Cf.* W. LANCE BENNETT & MARTHA S. FELDMAN, RECONSTRUCTING REALITY IN THE COURTROOM: JUSTICE AND JUDGMENT IN AMERICAN CULTURE 89-90 (1981):

> "[T]he structure of stories becomes crucial to judgment in cases in which a collection of facts or evidence is subject to competing interpretations. In such cases, it may not be the evidence that sways final judgment; judgment hinges on the structure of interpretation that provides the best fit for the evidence."

5. Closing argument is, of course, only one of the means through which a lawyer speaks to the jury. S/he may address the jurors directly in opening argument and, in some courts, by questioning them personally on voir dire during jury selection. Where the latter practice is not permitted, s/he may communicate indirectly with the jurors by submitting questions for the judge to ask on voir dire. S/he may submit requests for instructions to be included in the judge's charge to the jury.

In examining witnesses, the lawyer speaks both directly through the phrasing of questions and indirectly through the answers, which are often shaped by meticulous pretrial preparation. The lawyer's choice of witnesses may itself be a communication: a witness may symbolize or convey by his or her appearance more than the content of the testimony s/he gives. A lawyer may offer physical evidence and may prepare and offer visual aids as exhibits. S/he may make objections and arguments on objections that communicate a part of the message constituting his or her case. The way s/he interacts with his or her client at counsel table may send another part of that message.

And so forth.

By isolating closing argument for study in this article, we do not ignore or disparage the importance of these other means of making presentations to the jury. Rather, by concentrating on a single form of presentation, we hope to contribute to efforts to understand others as well. Analyses of lawyers' courtroom storytelling can be found in JANICE SCHUETZ & KATHRYN HOLMES SNEDAKER, COMMUNICATION AND LITIGATION: CASE STUDIES OF FAMOUS TRIALS (1988); BENNETT & FELDMAN, *op. cit. supra* note 4; BERNARD S. JACKSON, LAW, FACT AND NARRATIVE COHERENCE (1988); W. Lance Bennett, *Storytelling in Criminal Trials: A Model of Social Judgment*, 64 Q.J. SPEECH 1 (1978).

straightforward and obvious. We discuss it in somewhat more detail in Parts I and II.

However, below the surface, complex things were going on. These are the subjects of Parts III through V. Two broad generalizations emerge:

First, a trial lawyer has great latitude in choosing what story s/he will tell and how s/he will tell it even when s/he is arguing a relatively uncomplicated case. Although the lawyer's range of choice is circumscribed by the evidence, by the substantive law, by procedural rules, and by the stock scripts that shape everybody's notions of what a closing argument should look like, lawyers nonetheless retain the power to construct widely diverse tales beneath a superficial semblance of sameness and conventionality. In the *Jones* case, the prosecution and defense arguments ostensibly analyze an identical set of events within an identical logical framework, using an almost identical terminology. However, they tell entirely different stories. The prosecutor's story is about what happened on a New York City street in 1987. Defense counsel's story is about what is happening at the trial itself in 1991.

Second, the story that is told and the manner of the telling are inseparable. The lawyer's power to create his or her chosen tale is exercised, and its exercises can be detected, largely in terms of language structuring. Much of what a jury argument says is conveyed by implicit narrative and dialogic structure and by linguistic microstructure.

I. A First Take: Forensic Technique

From beginning to end, the lawyers' closing arguments in *Jones* are textbook models of the recommended content and style of a jury argument.

Both lawyers started with the conventional gambit of lauding traits that the jurors had demonstrated on voir dire and would now be called upon to demonstrate once more in deciding the case. They referred to the principles which the jurors had accepted in undertaking their responsibilities (to decide the case solely on the evidence presented, to hold the government to its burden of proof, and so forth) and to the characteristics which enable jurors to adhere to these principles and fulfil these responsibilities. Defense counsel (who, under New York practice, argues first[6]) extolled dispassion and fidelity to the principle of proof beyond a reasonable doubt; the prosecutor extolled intelligence and common sense. As treatises on closing argument explain, this kind of preamble simultaneously reinforces the attitudes to which each lawyer will appeal and establishes *rapport* between the lawyer and the jurors.[7]

---

6. N.Y. Crim. Proc. Law §§ 260.30(8)-(9), 320.20(3)(c) (McKinney 1982). In a case such as *Jones*, each lawyer argues once; there is no rebuttal argument.

7. *See, e.g.*, Henry Rothblatt, Successful Techniques in the Trial of

Both lawyers then reviewed the evidence, focusing upon the testimony of Susan Stone and Nancy Gregg, which established (as the prosecutor emphasized) and established only (as defense counsel emphasized) that David Jones shot Mary Smith in the chest at close range during a quarrel. They specified the question posed for the jury's decision upon this evidence: whether Jones intended to bring about Smith's death. They pointed to the particular factual circumstances that, in their view, did or did not support a finding of intent to kill. Defense counsel emphasized that the prosecution had presented no proof that Jones aimed specifically at Smith's chest and no proof that Jones said anything signifying an intention to take Smith's life. He conceded that Jones's pulling out a gun while engaged at close quarters in an altercation was an act of complete and culpable indifference to human life (the state of mind required for a manslaughter conviction), but denied that it proved a conscious purpose to kill. The prosecutor urged the jury to infer an intent to kill from the firing of a single, close-range shot directly into Smith's heart and from the defendant's coolness in walking away immediately after he fired that shot, unconcernedly leaving Smith to die. Each lawyer paraphrased and rebutted his or her opponent's reasoning (or anticipated reasoning) from the facts.

Once again, all of this conforms to the canons. The lawyers do—and do well—exactly what the treatises recommend doing. Each lawyer identifies the issues that are and are not in controversy.[8] Each marshals the facts, law, and logic supporting his or her position.[9] Each dissects the evidence, highlighting favorable details and explaining away problematic features.[10] Each rehearses or anticipates and refutes the other side's arguments.[11]

Both lawyers' perorations reflect the received wisdom that a jury argument should end with an appeal to the higher interests at stake.[12]

CRIMINAL CASES 107 (1961); LAWRENCE SMITH, ART OF ADVOCACY—SUMMATION § 1.12, 1-B.12 (1982); CHARLES W. TESSMER, CRIMINAL TRIAL STRATEGY 120 (1968); 3 ANTHONY G. AMSTERDAM, TRIAL MANUAL 5 FOR THE DEFENSE OF CRIMINAL CASES § 337, at 44-45 (1989); Joseph T. Karcher, *The Closing Argument*, 15 PRAC. LAW., No. 3, at 49, 67 (1969); G. Arthur Martin, *Closing Argument to the Jury for the Defense in Criminal Cases*, 58 J. CRIM. L., CRIMINOLOGY & POL. SCI. 2, 5 (1967).

8. *See, e.g.*, THOMAS A. MAUET, FUNDAMENTALS OF TRIAL TECHNIQUES 288-89 (3d ed. 1992); 3 AMSTERDAM, *op. cit. supra* note 7, § 446(C) at 264.

9. *See, e.g.*, ROTHBLATT, *op. cit. supra* note 7, at 115-19.

10. *See, e.g.*, *id.* at 119, 123, 128, 163; SMITH, *op. cit. supra* note 7, § 1.22; TESSMER, *op. cit. supra* note 7, at 121-22.

11. *See, e.g.*, MAUET, *op. cit. supra* note 8, at 298; ROTHBLATT, *op. cit. supra* note 7, at 123-24, 128, 163; TESSMER, *op. cit. supra* note 7, at 129-32.

12. *See, e.g.*, ROTHBLATT, *op. cit. supra* note 7, at 168-69; SMITH, *op. cit. supra* note 7, § 1.26.

Using the approach favored in primers for defense attorneys,[13] defense counsel reminded the jurors of the responsibility that rests upon their shoulders as the ultimate adjudicators of the defendant's guilt or innocence. The prosecutor used a similarly well-worn prosecutorial coda,[14] appealing to the jury to deliver its verdict in accordance with the interests of justice.

II. A SECOND TAKE: RHETORICAL STRUCTURE

Let us now examine the fit between the arguments and classic rhetorical models. Both lawyers start by referring to the last time they spoke with the jurors, when the jury was selected on voir dire. We have just noted that this standard technique is designed to recall the amicable relationship established between counsel and the jurors at the beginning of the trial and to remind the jurors that they were accepted by counsel and the court because they exhibited the qualities necessary to be *good* jurors. Counsel can then go on to define those qualities in terms of values that favor his or her case.

Notice that this stock beginning is nothing less—although, as we shall soon see, defense counsel makes it a great deal more—than an Aristotelian Proem. In Aristotle's formal model for a rhetorical presentation, the Proem serves to secure the good will of the audience by making the speaker appear to be a worthy person (for, as Aristotle puts it, "good character always commands more attention") and, at the same time, by appealing to values that the audience and the speaker share (sounding, as Aristotle puts it, a "note of praise [that] includes [the audience]").[15]

---

13. *See, e.g.*, CRIMINAL JUSTICE TRAINING COMMISSION, STRATEGIES AND TECHNIQUES IN CRIMINAL DEFENSE 242 (2d ed. 1983); TESSMER, *op. cit. supra* note 7, at 133.

14. *See, e.g.*, John F. Keenan, *Thoughts on Summations, in* BUREAU OF PROSECUTION SERVICES & DIVISION OF CRIMINAL JUSTICE SERVICES, CRIMINAL LAWYER'S SUMMATION MANUAL 14, 22 (1987).

15. ARISTOTLE, THE RHETORIC OF ARISTOTLE, bk. 3, ch. 14, at 224-25 (Lane Cooper trans., 1960); *see also* I CICERO, DE ORATORE, bk. I, ch. XXXI, at 99 (E.W. Sutton trans., 1942) ("[B]efore speaking on the issue, we must first secure the goodwill of our audience."); II QUINTILIAN, THE INSTITUTIO ORATORIA OF QUINTILIAN, bk. IV, ch. 1, at 9 (H. Butler trans., 1921) (The "sole purpose of the *exordium* [or Proem] is to prepare our audience . . . by making the audience well-disposed" and "secur[ing]" their "good-will" so as to "gain admission to the mind of the judge in order to penetrate still further."); *cf.* KENNETH BURKE, A RHETORIC OF MOTIVES 55 (1969) ("If, in the opinion of a given audience, a certain kind of conduct is admirable, then a speaker might persuade the audience by using ideas and images that identify his cause with that kind of conduct.").

Thereafter, the prosecutor's argument continues to track the Aristotelian structure for a speech.[16] From the Proem it proceeds to a Statement, in which the prosecutor relates the defendant's shooting of the victim in vivid detail. The prosecutor does a good job of aligning this rhetorical structure[17] with a strong narrative sequence by the device of purporting to tell the jury what is *not* in issue between the parties, much as Shakespeare's Antony resolutely insists that he has not come to praise Caesar. Thus, says the prosecutor:

> "You don't have to decide whether the defendant was the one who pulled the trigger of that gun and who caused that bullet to penetrate Mary's heart and her liver and eventually lodge in her back and eventually cause her to bleed to death in Harlem Hospital. You don't have to decide who did that. We know it was . . . the defendant."

After relating the case in this manner, as a series of historical acts that indisputably occurred and leave only the actor's motivation to be considered, the prosecutor passes on to the Aristotelian Argument proper, first specifying the nature of the dispute between the parties, then erecting the prosecution's case, then stating and refuting each of defense counsel's contentions with the logic of historical fact. For example:

---

16. *See* ARISTOTLE, *op. cit. supra* note 15, bk. 3, ch. 13, at 220 (explaining that a speech generally consists of four stages: the "Proem, Statement, Argument, and Epilogue").

17. The classical rhetoricians viewed the selection of an appropriate argument structure as a critical part of the art of persuasion. *See, e.g.*, I CICERO, *op. cit. supra* note 15, bk. I, ch. XXXI, at 99; III QUINTILIAN, *op. cit. supra* note 15, bk. VII, ch. 10, at 165. Quintilian compared the orator's arrangement of the parts of an argument to a wartime general's "distribut[ion of] his forces for battle." *See id.* at 170-71. Modern rhetoricians have found other analogies in the arts, comparing the construction of an argument to the process of "composing an essay," EDWARD P.J. CORBETT, CLASSICAL RHETORIC FOR THE MODERN STUDENT 274 (1965), and comparing the "set stages in the strucure [sic] of an oration" to the "formal . . . movements of a symphony," BURKE, *op. cit. supra* note 15, at 69. In these very different contexts, the identification of a "natural" or inherently "appropriate" arrangement of the parts, III QUINTILIAN, *op. cit. supra* note 15, bk. VII, ch. 10, at 165, is said to produce an essential "'quality of organic wholeness,'" CORBETT, *op. cit. supra*, at 274-75 (quoting RONALD S. CRANE, THE LANGUAGE OF CRITICISM AND THE STRUCTURE OF POETRY (1951-1952)). *Compare* MONROE C. BEARDSLEY, THE POSSIBILITY OF CRITICISM 58-59 (1970) (A "whole poem can be thought of as a single act, made up of several: the compound illocutionary act of its fictional speaker.").

> "Do [the defendant's] . . . actions after committing this crime comport with the actions of someone who just committed a terrible accident? [Defense counsel] argues to you that he was just cool and calm and just didn't care what . . . he . . . did. That's right, he didn't care. He had just killed a person he intended to kill in front of people to show he was a big . . . man . . . and he walked away . . . . I mean he wasn't saying, 'Oh, call the ambulance, let's get her to a hospital.'"

Consequently, in the Aristotelian Epilogue, the prosecutor can argue that a trial is a search for the truth, that justice is a verdict based on the evidence, and that the only verdict based on the evidence is guilty of second-degree murder.

Defense counsel's argument, by contrast, does not follow any standard rhetorical sequence. Nor does it have any intelligible narrative structure as a story with the defendant and the victim as the principal characters. It contains ten separate capsule descriptions of the shooting:

— first, in the form of a chronological recitation of the testimony of Susan Stone;

— second, in the form of a chronological recitation of the testimony of Nancy Gregg;

— third, in a shorthand, nontemporal inventory of the salient circumstances of the shooting;

— fourth, in a nontemporal review of the defendant's words and actions at the outset of the encounter that led to the shooting;

— fifth, in a shorthand, nontemporal inventory of the salient characteristics of the defendant's character as revealed by the shooting;

— sixth, in a brief summary of the physical motions of the defendant and victim at the moment of the shooting;

— seventh, in a condensed, chronological version of the "worst gloss" that the jury can put on the shooting;

— eighth, in a nontemporal review of the defendant's actions after the shooting;

— ninth, in a review of the victim's words and actions just prior to the shooting; and

— tenth, in a series of one-sentence "hypotheses" as to how the shooting might have happened without any intent to kill on the defendant's part.

With the exception of the recitations of the testimonies of the two prosecution witnesses—which defense counsel fills with reminders that the witnesses are speaking from their individual perceptual standpoints and cannot be telling the complete story[18]—none of these mini-stories is sustained for long enough to build up an engrossing narrative momentum. They are vignettes, not tales. And again with the exception of the two witnesses' accounts, they have neither the familiar form of narratives ("patterns of events occurring over time"[19]) nor the Aristotelian benchmarks of a narrative (a beginning, a middle, and an end) nor the structure that has been found to characterize even short and humble narratives.[20] Nor do these mini-stories build upon each other to compose a narrative whole.[21] They appear and disappear with no regard for any sequential, durational, plot-like development of the argument as a whole. So, if the defense argument is about what happened to the victim at the hands of the defendant, it is either a very poor and patchwork narrative or no narrative at all.

18. There are more than a dozen such reminders, ranging from statements (made in the course of conceding the witnesses' credibility) that the witnesses "testified as best they could" (or "as best they recalled") to statements (made in the course of summarizing their testimony) that "[s]he couldn't remember the exact words" or "[i]t appeared to Nancy that there was an argument in the car."

19. Jerome Bruner, *The Narrative Construction of Reality*, 18 CRITICAL INQUIRY 1, 6 (1991); *see also* PAUL RICOEUR, HERMENEUTICS & THE HUMAN SCIENCES 277 (John B. Thompson trans., 1981) (describing narrative as "a sequence of actions and experiences of . . . characters . . . represented in situations which change or to the changes of which they react . . . giving rise to a new predicament which calls for thought or action or both"); MIEKE BAL, NARRATOLOGY: INTRODUCTION TO THE THEORY OF NARRATIVE 8 (Christine van Boheemen trans., 1985); CLAUDE BREMOND, LOGIQUE DU RECIT 131, 332 (1973).

20. For example: orientation, complication, evaluation, resolution, and coda. *See* William Labov & Joshua Waletzky, *Narrative Analysis: Oral Versions of Personal Experience*, *in* ESSAYS ON THE VERBAL AND VISUAL ARTS 431-40 (June Helm ed.) (Proceedings of the 1966 Annual Spring Meeting of the American Ethnological Society).

21. *Cf.* VLADIMIR PROPP, MORPHOLOGY OF THE FOLK TALE 92-96 (Laurence Scott trans., 1968); BAL, *op. cit. supra* note 19, at 143-49; *see also* ROLAND BARTHES, *Introduction to the Structural Analysis of Narratives*, *in* THE SEMIOTIC CHALLENGE 95, 111-17, 128-33 (Richard Howard trans., 1988).

III. A THIRD TAKE: NARRATIVE STRUCTURE

But if the defense argument is viewed as a tale with *the jury* as protagonist and the courtroom as its setting, it has not only a coherent overall narrative structure but an almost classic narrative theme:

First, the Hero is set on stage. Defense counsel's opening sentences depict the voir dire process through which the jury is constituted.

Second, the virtues of the Hero are extolled. Defense counsel describes the "concepts" and "values" that make for valorous jurors, for duteous jurors, and he attributes them to this jury.

Third, the temptations that may sway the Hero from obedience to duty are described: the understandable temptations of the jury to despise the defendant, to convict him for his evil nature without demanding proof of his criminal guilt, or to demand that he prove his innocence by evidence. Forewarned of these temptations, the jury swears a sacred oath (several times recounted) to resist them. "How easy," defense counsel exclaims and repeats, "how easy would it be" to break those sacred oaths! But if the jury can uphold its oaths and do its duty, "then you deserve our great admiration and I hope you can do it."

Fourth, with its vows sworn, the Hero is called to its Task. There is a break in scene (not unlike the traditional transportation of the Hero to the Kingdom where the Quest must be pursued[22]); the prosecution's witnesses are introduced; their testimonies are recounted. In this scene, the prosecutor first appears, as Questioner of the Witnesses. Under questioning, the witnesses present testimony that confronts the Hero with a Riddle. The witnesses' testimony, while certainly not "an exact match of the story," appears to be basically truthful. "There is a problem, though. Does anyone in that testimony actually tell you how specifically the shooting occurred?" The Riddle, which the Hero must solve, is whether to accept the prosecutor's version of the facts (in which the defendant intended to kill the victim) or to conclude that "in no way can you be satisfied that the evidence proves beyond a reasonable doubt that my client shot . . . [the victim] with the conscious . . . objective of causing her death."

Fifth, the Hero struggles to solve the Riddle. Where is the evidence of intent to kill? Can intent to kill be inferred from the defendant's words? (These are reviewed.) From his actions at the time of the shooting? (They are reviewed.) From the consequences of those actions? (They, too, are reviewed.) From his behavior after the shooting? (It is reviewed.) From his character or motives? (These are reviewed.) From the victim's outcry? (It is set in context and thereby made ambiguous.) From any other evidence? (The dregs are searched.) No. "[I]f you just look at the

22. *See* PROPP, *op. cit. supra* note 21, at 50-51.

evidence, the lack of evidence and don't make any irrational leaps or bounds . . . [,] you can't find proof beyond a reasonable doubt that my client intended to cause the death. The ambiguity remains." Hence does the Hero, puzzled, arrive at the predicted temptation. It is driven to demand that defense counsel "tell us how a woman is shot in the chest at close range if it's not intentional murder?" And defense counsel can offer no answer. "I don't know." All that counsel can offer is a set of "hypotheses"—a series of alternative possible visions flashed across the screen like the successive acts of Kurosawa's *Rashomon*—which may or may not be true. So the Riddle appears unanswerable.

But, sixth, the Hero finds the Answer. The Answer lies in keeping faith with the sacred oath that the Hero swore before beginning this Quest, "the promise that you made to not make me prove to you in any way how . . . [the killing] may have occurred." Thus does the Hero perform the Difficult Task and achieve Apotheosis:

> "So what I'm really asking you to do is to do what I think will probably be one of the hardest things that you have ever been required to do in public, which is to stand up and at some point look over at David Jones and while looking at him vote not guilty of charges brought against him. Thank you."

The Quest of the Hero theme is unmistakable.[23]

---

23. "The myth of the hero" has been characterized as "the most common and the best known myth in the world." Joseph L. Henderson, *Ancient Myths and Modern Man*, *in* MAN AND HIS SYMBOLS 101, 101 (Carl G. Jung ed., Laurel 1968); *see id.* at 101-19. A few of the epic versions are the stories of Inanna (later Ishtar, Isis, Aphrodite, and Venus), Gilgamesh, Odysseus, Theseus, the Argonauts, Hercules, Psyche, Beowulf, Cuchulainn, the Grail Hero, Shen I, Hare (and Red Horn), Budak Yoid Intoie, Paul Bunyan and—more recently—J.R.R. Tolkien's *The Lord of the Rings*, Stephen Donaldson's *Chronicles of Thomas Covenant the Unbeliever*, Gordon Dickson's *Childe Cycle*, Janny Wurts' *Cycle of Fire*, Gene Wolfe's *Book of the New Sun*, Katherine Kurtz's *Deryni Chronicles*, Terry Brooks' *Shannara* and *Magic Kingdom* cycles, and Robert Jordan's *Wheel of Time* cycle. Hierophantic versions are found in the traditions of many religious creeds. The structure of the common folktale versions is the subject of Propp's great formalist classic cited in note 21 *supra*. "Popular tales represent the heroic action as physical; the higher religions show the deed to be moral; nevertheless, there will be found astonishingly little variation in the morphology of the adventure, the character roles involved, the victories gained." JOSEPH CAMPBELL, THE HERO WITH A THOUSAND FACES 38 (1968). Campbell's book is the best general survey of these subjects of which we are aware. Aspects are illuminated in, *e.g.*, GEORGES DUMEZIL, THE DESTINY OF THE WARRIOR 111-38 (A. Hiltebeitel trans., 1970); NORTHROP FRYE, *Archetypal Criticism: Theory of Myths*, *in* ANATOMY OF CRITICISM: FOUR ESSAYS 131, 186-206 (1957); DOROTHY NORMAN, THE HERO: MYTH/IMAGE/SYMBOL (1969); CAROL PEARSON & KATHERINE POPE, THE FEMALE HERO IN AMERICAN AND BRITISH

This particular story line has a distinct advantage for defense counsel. It permits the defendant's activity in killing the victim—an activity that defense counsel is not denying and can hardly tuck under the rug—to be fitted into the narrative without becoming the dominant action of the tale. For it is a commonplace of narrative structure that, in addition to the protagonist or "subject" of a *fabula*,[24] at least one other active agent plays an accepted role. This is the role which Greimas called the *destinateur*

LITERATURE (1981); LORD RAGLAN, THE HERO: A STUDY IN TRADITION, MYTH AND DRAMA 58-72, 120-209, 267-275 (1949); JESSIE L. WESTON, FROM RITUAL TO ROMANCE (Doubleday Anchor 1957).

More specifically, the version of the Quest of the Hero embodied in defense counsel's argument parallels the common oriental form of Quest narrative that has the World Savior as its Hero. This is no accident. Like defense counsel's argument, that version in particular undertakes the ultimate, difficult task of persuading the listener to accept No Answer as the Answer to the riddle of existence. It is the special task of this narrative to lead the listener to nirvana—to the void—by endowing him or her with the strength to bear the terrors of a cosmic disorder without succumbing to the illusion of order. Here the Quest assaults the Hero in the Hero's home territory, and the Hero must and does remain unmoved before the onslaught of the most powerful positive and negative forces of persuasion:

First, the Hero takes his position—for example, Gautama Shakyamuni (the Buddha-to-be) on the eastern side of the Bodhi Tree; Lord Parshva (of the Jain teaching of Mahavira) standing naked in the dismissing-the-body posture.

Second, the virtues of the Hero are recalled—the life or lives that led to this position at the midpoint of the universe.

Third, the Hero swears that he will not be moved from his seat until he has attained ultimate wisdom.

Fourth, the Lord of Life Illusion appears and assaults Gautama first with appeals to the duty of his caste and rank, then with an army of hideous, misshapen demons; Meghamalin assaults Parshva with tigers, elephants, scorpions, darkness, and a cyclone.

Fifth, the Hero remains unmoved, ignoring all of these alluring and frightening illusions. The Adversary ravens and steps up the attack, sending new hordes against the Hero.

And, sixth, a voice utters from the sky to protect Gautama, dispersing the Adversary's hordes with a few words; or, from beneath the earth, the king and queen of serpents arise to shield and protect Parshva; whereupon, the Hero is illuminated, and a rain of flowers descends.

See EDWARD THOMAS, THE LIFE OF BUDDHA AS LEGEND AND HISTORY 227-32 (3d ed. 1949); E.H. BREWSTER, THE LIFE OF GOTAMA THE BUDDHA (from the Pali Canon) 75-76, 77-78, 135 (1926); 2 JOSEPH CAMPBELL, THE MASKS OF GOD [ORIENTAL MYTHOLOGY] 218-19 (Penguin Books 1976).

24. We use *fabula* in the traditional formalist sense of "a series of logically and chronologically related events that are caused or experienced by actors," BAL, *op. cit. supra* note 19, at 5, as distinct from the *sjužet*, which is a "*fabula* that is presented in a certain manner," *id.* We sometimes use "story" as a synonym of *sjužet* and use "story line" as a synonym of *fabula*.

("sender")—an actor or a force that enables the protagonist to achieve his or her objective or prevents the protagonist from achieving it.[25] The *destinateur*'s role in the *fabula* requires a high level of activity,[26] which nonetheless remains functionally subordinate to the protagonist's and does not overshadow it. Thus the defendant can kill the victim without that action becoming the center of attention if the story line goes: *The jurors, faithful to their oath, acquitted the defendant although he sorely tempted them to do otherwise by killing the victim in a dastardly fashion.*

The trick is to do at a semantic level what this italicized sentence does at a grammatical level: to put the activity of killing into a dependent clause and to create a narratively convincing independent clause having the jury as its subject and acquittal as its outcome. Defense counsel does this by a number of structural devices:

In the opening sentences of the defense argument, the subject is defense counsel, but the verbs are all about *talk*[27] and immediately make apparent that counsel's role is simply that of Wollflin's *Sprecher*—one who points verbally to the central action that is taking place. This action—the jury's assumption of its Task—is described in sentences in which the jurors or their intentional states and emotions are consistently the subject. The defendant has no active role in these sentences. He appears not as an agentive subject, but as the object of the jury's actions[28]

25. A.-J. GREIMAS, SEMANTIQUE STRUCTURALE: RECHERCHE DE METHODE 128-34, 172-91 (1986); in the English translation: A.-J. GREIMAS, STRUCTURAL SEMANTICS: AN ATTEMPT AT A METHOD 146-52, 197-221 (Daniele McDowell, Ronald Schleifer, & Alan Velie trans., 1984).

26. *See* BAL, *op. cit. supra* note 19, at 28: "In principle, the subject [the protagonist] and the power [the *destinateur*] predominate more, or are more active in a grammatical sense . . . because they are the agent, or the (grammatical) subject, either of the function of intention/evasion or of giving/receiving."

27. *E.g.*,

> "When I spoke to you all about a week ago I tried to emphasize with you all what I thought were two critical concepts . . . ." * "And I'm going to assume now that I was right in thinking that these two values permeated this jury, because if I'm wrong then I fear that my summation will fall on deaf ears." * "What are the two concepts or values that I tried to speak about in voir dire?" * "Why do I say it's important that you have a feeling or a notion that however you feel towards the defendant won't influence you in the decision you make?"

28. *E.g.*,

> "And that you would not assign blame to him [the defendant] unless specific blame worthiness had been proved to you beyond a reasonable doubt." * "Because each and every one of you has a right to despise the man who I represent."

or attitudes.[29] The first clauses of the defense argument in which the defendant takes the place of subject are dependent members of compound sentences or their equivalent.[30] Sometimes the jury is the subject of the independent clauses;[31] sometimes it is not (as when the independent clause is some form of the statement: "A witness testified")[32]; in either case, the

---

29. *E.g.*,

"One concept was that whatever passion you felt or didn't feel towards the Defendant, no matter what attitude you may have toward the Defendant David Jones, that no way would that interfere with the verdict that you would bring in this case." * "Why do I say it's important that you have a . . . notion that however you feel towards the defendant won't influence you in the decision you make?"

30. *E.g.*,

"You all said . . . that you can still apply the laws to him, a man who is obviously responsible for the death of Mary Smith." * "And if at the end you decided that something was not clarified for you, if you decided that ambiguities in the evidence still remain, that you would in no way hold us responsible for clarifying these ambiguities for you and you would in no way expect us, me or Mr. Jones or Mr. Bell, to make up for the lack of clarity . . . ."

The very first passage of the defense argument in which the defendant is the subject of a verb is this:

"Whatever he did in a legal sense or an illegal sense, whatever his state of mind may have been at the time, that man had a loaded gun in his hand during an argument in a car and he pulled the trigger and he killed a young woman. Yet you all tell me that you can still apply the law to him, a man who created such a perilous situation."

See note 33 *infra*.

31. *E.g.*,

"How easy it would be for each of you to say, 'Why should we care about what crime is actually proved against him when he in so cavalier a manner apparently pulled a gun and ended up killing another humanbeing [sic]?'" * "If it's not proved by the People's evidence that he had an intent to kill, then you would just find him not guilty of that charge."

See also the first example in note 30 *supra*.

32. *E.g.*,

"Well Susan Stone testifies that everybody knew each other. That Dave came down, Dave being my client. That he had an argument with Nancy Gregg. That Dave got into the car. . . ." * "Another question from Ms. Brooks, 'Let me take you back. You said that after Mary said something to the effect of "No, Dave, don't." That is when you said he shot her?' Susan Stone's answer, 'Yeah, I was looking, it's like she was holding onto his jacket or something and then he shot her. It's like he backed out of the car and he spun around like . . . .'" Or "evidence" or "testimony" may be the subject of the independent clause: *e.g.*, "Ms. Brooks will argue that in context that testimony shows that my client shot Mary Smith with intent to kill . . . ."

relegation of the defendant's activity to a structurally subordinated plane keeps it from invading the narrative mainstream.[33] At every pivot of the argument, whenever a new perspective is introduced, the same sort of compound sentence structure is used (although with wide stylistic variation) to subordinate the active verbs whose subject is the defendant.[34]

The *fabula* develops in three large movements: the jury undertakes its duty; the jury is tempted to abandon its duty; the jury perseveres and does its duty. Only in the second movement, and after that movement has been both foreshadowed[35] and framed[36] by locutions that consign the defendant's

---

33. This is striking even at the level of grammatical analysis. Throughout the initial three-fifths of the defense argument there is only a single sentence in which the defendant is the subject of a verb found in a simple sentence or independent clause. The one exception is quoted at the end of note 30 *supra*: it is an instance in which the defendant's activity, while grammatically coordinate (at least in the reporter's transcript) is syntactically subordinate to the jury's activity. Concerning subordination, see BREMOND, *op. cit. supra* note 19, at 320-21.

34. *E.g.*,

> "Yet you all tell me that you can still apply the law to him, a man who created such a perilous situation." * "I mean how easy would it be for each of you to say, 'Why should we show any serious regard for a man who showed so little regard for the life of another?'" * "If it's not proved beyond a reasonable doubt that Mr. Jones is guilty of intentional murder, then it's just not proved." * "You all said basically that you would not say at this point, '. . . Let him get up and tell us what really occurred if it's not a murder that he committed . . . .'" * "You cannot fail to acquit because Jones or myself have not adequately explained to you what occurred in the car." * "Nancy testifies that she sees Dave come down. . . . [S]he says that my client says to Mary . . . ." * "And I will argue that it's not shown, that in no way can you be satisfied that that evidence proves to you beyond a reasonable doubt that my client shot Mary with the conscious aim or objective of causing her death." * "Is there any proof before you that shows that my client actually aimed the gun at Mary? There is none. Is there any evidence before you that shows that my client actually pointed the gun at Mary? There is none." * "Well what should you do then . . . ? Just figure that some reason must have made him decide to kill Mary?" * "But where is the proof presented to you that he aimed there?" * "She says stuff, he grabs at her neck and she grabs at his jacket and assume that he knowingly and voluntarily and consciously fires a bullet into a car . . . ."

See also the first and third examples in note 32 *supra*.

35. The foreshadowing occurs in two passages early in the defense argument, one quoted in part in the last examples in each of notes 28 and 30 (indented) *supra*, the other quoted in part in the first example in note 31 *supra* and in the second example in note 34 *supra*.

36. After summarizing the testimony of the prosecution witnesses, defense counsel begins his analysis of that testimony with the following framing passage:

action in killing the victim to the status of a subplot (one of the jury's temptations)[37] do there occur simple declarative sentences or independent clauses in which the defendant is the subject.[38] In the first movement, he appears almost always in prepositional phrases, as the object of "to" or "toward";[39] in the last movement, he emerges as the object of the jury's activity of acquitting.[40] By contrast, in the prosecutor's argument, the defendant's actions are usually recounted either in simple sentences[41] or in dependent clauses joined to independent clauses that contain no competing narrative to subordinate the story line "David shot Mary in the chest": Most commonly, they are variants of "There is no question that . . . "[42] or "You know that . . . "[43]

A subtler signature of the difference between the stories being told in the defense and prosecution arguments is their differing focalizations. *Focalization* has to do with the perspective, the vantage point, from which a narrated event is seen.[44] The *focalizor* is not necessarily the *narrator*:

> "Look, the issue here is not so mysterious. Ms. Brooks will argue that . . . that testimony shows beyond a reasonable doubt that . . . [the defendant's] intent was to kill that woman. And I will argue that it's not shown, that in no way can you be satisfied that that evidence proves to you beyond a reasonable doubt that my client shot Mary with the conscious aim or objective of causing her death."

37. The passages referenced in note 35 *supra* and those quoted in text and footnote at note 82 *infra* exemplify the temptation motif.

38. *E.g.*,

> "Did he say during the shooting, 'Die.' Did he say, 'I want you . . . dead.' Did he say, 'I'm going to kill you.'?" * "Is he angry? Yes. Does he have a gun? Absolutely. Does he fire a shot in a small confined space? No doubt." * "I mean look at the evidence in a really bad light. My client's mad. She says stuff, he grabs at her neck. He has no specific conscious objective. He shoots . . . ."

See also the passage quoted in text at note 75 *infra*.

39. *E.g.*, the examples in note 29 *supra* and the first example in each of notes 30 and 34 *supra*.

40. *See* defense counsel's peroration, the last passage quoted on page 65 *supra*.

41. *See, e.g.*, the last example in note 53 *infra*.

42. *E.g.*,

> "There is no question as to who pulled the trigger[,] who fired the shot into Mary Smith's chest causing her death." * "[T]here is no question that the defendant felt insulted and I'm sure you all know that people have been killed for less."

43. *E.g.*,

> "[Y]ou know that he was angry and you know that he was insulted by remarks that Nancy or that Mary had been spreading around about him."

44. The concept of focalization originated with Genette, *see* GERARD GENETTE,

"narrator" refers to the voice that is recounting an event; "focalizor," to the lens or eye—the epistemological intake scoop—through which the event is perceived.[45] In narrative analysis, it is often instructive to disentangle the two.[46]

When this is done to the predicative statements in the *Jones* arguments in which defense counsel and the prosecutor recount the actions of David and Mary in 1987, the result is revealing. The statements fall into five general categories. Category one consists of recountings of acts performed by David or Mary from the standpoint of *what the evidence does or does not tend to show.*[47] Defense counsel makes thirteen such statements; the prosecutor, nine. This is quite an even distribution, since defense counsel's overall argument is slightly less than half again as long as the prosecutor's. Category two consists of recountings of acts performed by David or Mary from the standpoint of *what has or has not been proved.*[48] Defense counsel makes seven such statements; the prosecutor, one.

FIGURES III (1972), and has been most usefully elaborated by Bal, *see* BAL, *op. cit. supra* note 19, at 100-17, 130-32; MIEKE BAL, NARRATOLOGIE: ESSAIS SUR LA SIGNIFICATION NARRATIVE DANS QUATRE ROMANS MODERNES (1984); Mieke Bal, *On Meanings and Descriptions, in* 6 STUDIES IN TWENTIETH CENTURY LITERATURE 100, 134-42 (Nomi Tamir-Ghez ed., 1981); *cf.* Lubomír Doležel, *Truth and Authenticity in Narrative*, 1 POETICS TODAY, no. 3, at 7, 15-24 (1980).

45. BAL, *op. cit. supra* note 19, at 100-01, articulates the distinction as being "between, on the one hand, the vision through which the elements are presented and, on the other, the identity of the voice that is verbalizing that vision. To put it more simply: . . . a distinction between *those who see* and *those who speak.*" Thus, when the *Jones* prosecutor argues: "I submit to you that he had just shot her in the chest," the *narrator* is the prosecutor herself—the lawyer who is doing the submitting; the *focalizor* is an *omniscient* or *external* focalizor—commonly called an "EF" by narratologists, *see* BAL, *op. cit. supra* note 19, at 105.

46. Bal's 1984 *Essais*, cited in note 44 *supra*, develop a number of powerful insights through this analytic technique. In his 1981 article, cited in the same note, he illustrates the use of the technique to unravel an aspect of Emma's character in Flaubert's *Madame Bovary*. *See id.* at 134-37.

47. Common frames for this focalizor are, *e.g.*:

> "No, you don't have any evidence of the defendant getting in that car and saying to Mary, 'I'm going to kill you.'" * "[W]hat you do have is evidence of the defendant getting out of that car with a smoking gun right after that shot is fired." * "Is there any evidence that shows him reaching back and getting a mark on her so he can be sure to shoot in a specific place?"

48. Common frames for this focalizor are, *e.g.*:

> "Ms. Brooks will argue that in context that testimony shows that my client shot Mary Smith with intent to kill . . . ." * "[That] doesn't show that [at] the time when she was killed that he intended to cause her death." * "If it's not proved by the People's evidence that he had an intent to kill, then you would just find him not guilty of that charge."

Category-two focalization, like category-one focalization, is, of course, traditional closing-argument jargon for both prosecutors and defense lawyers; it differs from category one principally in that the perspective of the jury is slightly more engaged than in category one.[49]

Category three consists of recountings of acts performed by David or Mary from the standpoint of *what the jury finds, thinks, believes, infers,* and so forth.[50] Defense counsel makes fifty-six such statements; the prosecutor, twenty. Category four consists of recountings of acts performed by David or Mary from the standpoint of *what a witness perceived or what an attorney conceived.*[51] Defense counsel makes seventy-eight such statements; the prosecutor, seven. Category five consists of recountings of acts performed by David or Mary from the standpoint of an EF—an external focalizor[52]—statements, that is, about

---

49. "We have proved *X*" or "they have not proved *Y*" implicates the jury's perspective as factfinder somewhat more than "the evidence shows *X*" or "there is no evidence showing *Y*" or "where is there any evidence of *Z*?"

50. Common frames for this focalizor are, *e.g.*:

> "You know what, give this case and this scenario really the worse gloss that I think you can. I mean look at the evidence in a really bad light. My client's mad. She says stuff, he grabs at her neck . . . ." * "[E]ven if he's a man who you think is capable of killing because he carries a gun . . . ." * "[D]oesn't that make you question whether or not Mr. Jones had the intent to kill?" * "[B]y the woman's plea, by her statement, 'Dave, no[,]' . . . [i]s she really saying to us Dave was pointing the gun at my chest and I am begging for my life . . . ." Standard-form rhetorical questions are also a subspecies of this category.

51. Common frames for this focalizor are, *e.g.*:

> "[Reading from the transcript of testimony of Nancy Gregg:] Question, 'When was the first time that you looked over in the direction of the defendant and Mary? . . .' Answer, 'After the car door opened and he stepped out of the car.' 'And as he was stepping out of the car, what did you see him do if anything?' 'She had a link chain on her neck and he popped it off.'" * "According to Nancy[,] he's actually the one who brings it up. He's the one who goes over to a car and within the hearing of other people says, 'Why are you saying that I like to suck pussy?'" * "[T]here is no question in there [sic] minds that he was the one that shot her. And that in fact they did see the gun in his hand as he was walking away." * "I can put foward another [hypothesis], that he has a gun and he's taking it out to scare her, that she grabs at his coat and in the struggle he accidentally pulls the trigger."

52. *See* note 45 *supra*.

what happened.[53] Defense counsel makes nineteen such statements; the prosecutor, sixty.

Plainly, the prosecutor is telling a tale about how David shot Mary in 1987 and is asking the jury to accept that tale as true in 1991. Equally plainly, defense counsel is telling a tale about how the jurors in 1991 are deciding where the truth lies after listening to the testimony of witnesses and the arguments of lawyers anent an intriguing but intangible murder mystery set in 1987—a play within a play, and one in which Gonzago's poisoning is of considerably lesser consequence than the catching of Claudius's conscience.[54]

On the compositional level, it is particularly interesting to compare how the two lawyers talk about the central issue that the jury must decide: whether David Jones's killing of Mary Smith was intentional. Now and again each lawyer uses most of the grammatical parts of speech through which the concept of intentionality is commonly expressed in English: verbs (such as whether Jones "intended to kill" Smith), adverbs (such as whether Jones "intentionally killed" Smith), nouns (such as whether Jones "had an intent to kill" Smith or whether Jones shot Smith "with an intent to kill"), and adjectives (such as whether this was "an intentional killing"). These four parts of speech are essentially interchangeable from a denotative standpoint. But they are not interchangeable from a narrative standpoint. Verb formulations fit seamlessly into a story about what David Jones did to Mary Smith in 1987; they intrude awkwardly into a story about the trial in 1991 because they do not predicate any plot action that can occur in 1991.[55] Noun formulations fit smoothly into both stories and can serve to mediate between them—Jones's "intent" being, on the one hand, something that he did or did not have in 1987 and, on the other

---

53. Common frames for this focalizor are, *e.g.*:

> "Is he angry? Yes. Does he have a gun? Absolutely. Does he fire a shot in a small confined space? No doubt." * "That's right, he didn't care. He had just killed a person he intended to kill in front of people to show that he was a big, you know, he was a big man, wasn't going to take any insults from Mary or anybody else and he walked away."

54. Of course the different focalizations of the defense and prosecution arguments have not only syntagmatic but paradigmatic—specifically, epistemological—implications. We will return to the latter, particularly in note 127 *infra*.

55. Thus, expressions of intentionality in verb form tend to look backward to the events of 1987 even when the defendant is not the subject of the verb. Consider, for example, the prosecutor's argument:

> "[I]t's only through speculation and hypothesizing that you can find anything other than that the defendant in this case when he pulled the trigger and fired that shot into Mary's heart that he intended to kill her.
>
> "You don't point a loaded . . . gun at someone and . . . pull the trigger when you don't intend to kill them."

hand, something that the jury searches for and does or does not find in 1991.[56] Adverb formulations are primarily grounded in the story of the 1987 killing but connect it to the story of the 1991 trial by emphasizing that the way in which Jones did what he did in 1987 depends upon the way in which the jury does its interpretive job in 1991.[57] Adjective formulations highlight even more strongly the jury's interpretive role.[58]

Thus, the frequency with which the lawyers use the various parts of speech reveals—and at the same time shapes—the stories that they choose to tell. The prosecutor overwhelmingly favors verb formulations, using relatively few nouns, very few adjectives, and no adverbs at all. Defense counsel favors noun formulations over verb formulations; he also uses significant numbers of adjectives and adverbs.[59] While the prosecutor

---

56. Consider, for example, defense counsel's argument:

> "Were any words heard before, during or after that my client uttered that shows an intent to kill? . . . Is there any of that shown in the evidence that you have before you to prove to you an intent to kill?"

57. When a description of the quality of an action is embedded in a verb, its dependence on interpretation is less obvious than when it is isolated in an adverb. This is why Gérard Genette was obliged to make his well-known demonstration that verbs *are* to some extent descriptive; "Even a verb can be more or less descriptive in the precision it gives to the spectacle of the action. It suffices to compare 'seized a knife' with 'took a knife'; consequently no verb is totally free of descriptive implication." Gérard Genette, *Boundaries of Narrative*, *in* 8 NEW LITERARY HISTORY 1, 5-6 (Ann Levonas trans., 1976). Far from concealing their descriptive thrust, adverbs advertise it and thereby call attention to the necessity for a separate narrative to motivate an interpreter/describer. *Cf.* Evelyn Cobley, *Description in Realist Discourse: The War Novel*, 20 STYLE, No. 3, at 393, 404 (1986) ("A new arrival appears because a description of the devastated landscape requires his presence. Although the narrative succession might persuade us that the new arrival generates the description, the causal relationship is in fact the reverse."); *see also* MICHAEL RIFFATERRE, TEXT PRODUCTION 24 (Terese Lyons trans., 1983). Thus, defense counsel's turn to adverbs to express intentionality spotlights the jury's fact-finding quest. Consider, for example, his argument:

> "I mean[,] look at the evidence in a really bad light. My client's mad. She says stuff, he grabs at her neck and she grabs at his jacket[,] and assume that he knowingly and voluntarily and consciously fires a bullet into a car, a small place[,] knowing a human is there, knowing that a bullet may well strike another and he just doesn't care."

58. Consider, for example, defense counsel's argument:

> "Then what then, what[,] Mr. Lee, you tell us[,] I can hear you all saying, you tell us how a woman is shot in the chest at close range if it's not intentional murder."

59. The prosecutor uses the verbs *intend*, *mean*, *try*, and *want* 19 times in connection with the defendant's or a suppositious killer's mental state at the time of the killing. She says four times that the defendant "knew" something, once that he "perceived" something, four times that he "didn't care," and once that he "wasn't

recounts an historical chronicle, defense counsel incants a narrative of rediscovery.

IV. A Fourth Take: Dialogic Structure

Yet, more than storytelling is going on here. Because the subject of the prosecutor's argument is the killing in 1987, its form of narrative is the History. Because the subject of defense counsel's argument is the trial in 1991, its form of narrative is the Drama. Both lawyers use their particular forms of narrative to embody an epistemology.[60]

The defense epistemology, as befits Drama, is performative and constructivist. Its organon is dialogue. By contrast, the prosecutor wants no part of dialogue. For, to engage in dialogue is to participate in the creation of meaning. Defense counsel strives mightily to draw the jurors into this kind of constitutive conversation. The prosecutor strives as mightily to keep them out of it.

Both strategies make sense. Consider that in the *Jones* trial the prosecutor has presented all the evidence; the defense, none. So long as meaning, reality, truth are conceived as immutable, inherent properties of "the facts," to be found in the evidence and not constructed out of it, the prosecutor has a big advantage. Moreover, the first impression created by the prosecution's evidence fits a folk-cultural script for intentional killing. If the jury takes the evidence at face value, a murder verdict is assured. Imaginative pursuit of alternative meanings is required to derail that train.

---

concerned." She says twice that he "was [*or* is] angry" and twice that he "was [*or* felt] insulted." Once she uses a purposive infinitive to describe his motivation ("he had just killed a person . . . to show that he was a big . . . man . . ."). By contrast with these 34 verb formulations, she uses 10 noun formulations ("intent" six times, "conscious desire" once, and "accident" three times), two adjective formulations ("intentional shooting" and "intentional murder"), and no adverb formulations.

Defense counsel uses the verbs *intend* and *want* seven times—*try* and *mean* not at all—in this connection. He uses the verb phrase "make sure" four times and he uses "decide" once. He says thrice that the defendant "knew" something, once that the defendant "doesn't care," once that the defendant "[i]s . . . unconcerned," and once that the defendant "showed . . . little regard" for the victim. He speaks three times of the defendant's being embarrassed, shamed, or ashamed, and twice of the defendant's being angry or mad. Once defense counsel uses a purposive infinitive to describe the defendant's motivation ("he has a gun and he's taking it out to scare her"). By contrast with these 24 verb formulations, defense counsel uses 30 noun formulations ("intent" 17 times, "aim" or "objective" or both five times, "reason" twice, "state of mind" once, "depraved and damnable mind" once, "depravity" once, "complete indifference to human life" once, and "callous disregard" twice), four adjective formulations, and four adverb formulations.

60. *Cf.* Jackson, *op. cit. supra* note 5, at 33-36.

Defense counsel wants to stimulate the pursuit; the prosecutor wants to suppress it.

But defense counsel cannot explicitly invite the jury to be imaginative, for at least three reasons.

First, the judge will charge the jury that it is not permitted to "speculate," so defense counsel cannot allow what he is doing to be perceived as asking the jury to speculate.

Second, the common image of defense counsel in a criminal case includes the con-artist (smoke-and-mirrors) stereotype and the "Officer Krupke" stereotype. Defense counsel must avoid the appearances of being either a trickster or a peddler of psychological soft stuff.[61]

Third, the judge will charge the jury that the prosecution bears the burden of proving every element of the crime beyond a reasonable doubt. Defense counsel cannot afford to forfeit the benefit that this standard of proof, as applied to the elusive element of intent to kill, confers on the defense.

For all of these reasons, defense counsel must *implicitly* draw the jurors into an imaginative dialogue while *explicitly* insisting that they "stick to the facts." He must embed in the structure of his argument the notion that the jury has an active role to play in the creation of facts. And he must embed this notion in his argument too deeply and too subtly to be extracted and criticized because, as we shall mention in a moment, the notion is at war with powerful legal and folk-cultural conceptions of "facts" as objective realities. To counter those conceptions, defense counsel must proceed by immersing the jury in a different and more compelling reality—the reality of the trial in which they are actors, the reality of the dialogic process, which assigns meaning to events.

For her part, the prosecutor can explicitly urge the jurors to be unimaginative—and can do so without demeaning their intelligence and independence—only to the extent that she can identify imaginativeness with "speculation." She wants to ask them to restrict their thinking to conventional patterns because two conventional patterns of considerable force favor her position.

The first is the legal canon, which the judge will charge the jury, that the defendant can be found to have intended the natural and probable consequences of his acts.[62]

The second is the canon of folk psychology that "[c]omplex human actions are assumed to be voluntary unless something indicates otherwise. A voluntary action is one in which someone did something to accomplish some goal."[63]

---

61. We return to this subject at pages 106-10 *infra*.

62. *See* note 3 *supra*. The prosecutor explicitly tells the jury that the judge will so instruct them.

63. Roy D'Andrade, *A Folk Model of the Mind*, *in* CULTURAL MODELS IN

The two conventions authorize a line of reasoning that gives the prosecutor her best hope of satisfying the jury, beyond a reasonable doubt, that the defendant intended to kill. Lawyers and logicians would call this kind of reasoning a permissive inference. But the prosecutor does not want the jury to think about it as permissive or as an inference. She wants them to view it rather as a connection that is innate in the facts of the case. She would much prefer that the jury not think about the reasoning involved at all, but just *do* it, since thinking about it may detrack it.

The prosecutor faces the problem that if she emphasizes the strength of her evidence concerning the physical acts and events surrounding the killing—which she wants to do because she possesses a monopoly of such evidence and it paints a picture of the defendant as a wanton killer—the very strength of this evidence may call the jury's attention to the comparative weakness of her evidence concerning the defendant's mental state, which is the rubber issue (in every sense) in the case. She can overcome this problem if she can keep the jury from focusing on the epistemological differences between physical acts and mental states.[64] In this she is aided by another and deeper convention of folk psychology: that mental states and physical acts are interconnected parts of an objective chain of events, a true story, something that happens in the world, something that is *real* and, being real, is knowable—something, in short, that a jury can *find* from *evidence*. She will want to root her argument in this convention.

LANGUAGE AND THOUGHT 112, 120 (Dorothy Holland & Naomi Quinn eds., 1987). The prosecutor repeatedly argues that "you don't fire a shot into someone's chest from a handgun without intending to kill them, without that being your conscious desire."

64. One way in which the prosecutor does this is to embed the physical details in the narrative flow of her argument at every point, thereby avoiding transitions that would flag the question of their epistemological status. *See* Bal, *supra* note 44, at 109-10 (discussing the technique of description in which a "character carries out an action with an object. The description is . . . [thus] made fully narrative." *Id.* at 109.). *See generally* PHILIPPE HAMON, INTRODUCTION A L'ANALYSE DU DESCRIPTIF 180-223 (1981). The most striking example of this technique is the prosecutor's repeated narration of the defendant's action as "shooting a person in the chest." Virtually every time the prosecutor talks about "shooting" or "firing," she follows the verb with the phrase "in the chest" or "in the heart," as though *shoot in the chest* was an indissoluble predicative unit. By contrast, defense counsel talks about the chest shot only when he wants to focus the jury precisely on the question whether the location of the wound will support an inference that the defendant intended to kill: "In no way am I telling you to ignore the fact that she was shot in the chest where her heart was. . . . But where is the proof presented to you that he aimed there?"

A. *Macrostructure*

The macrostructure of the lawyers' arguments reflects their respective strategies.

1. The Defense Argument

Defense counsel's opening words portray him as engaged in a dialogue with the jury:

> "When I spoke to you all about a week ago I tried to summarize with you all what I thought were two critical concepts [or values] that I thought were necessary in a jury that was going to hear the evidence in this case."

The dialogue is partly verbal and partly empathic:

> "[E]ven though I didn't talk to each and every one of you, I sensed from most of you or from the collective that was here an awareness of those values and an assuredness that you would apply these two values to the evidence in the case."
>
> "[Counsel's argument will] assume . . . that I was right in thinking that these two values permeated this jury, because if I'm wrong then I fear that my summation *will fall on deaf ears*."

But the jury will have to do more than listen; it will have to continue the dialogue after counsel has finished speaking. Counsel calls on those jurors who appreciate the two concepts to "talk to the other members of the jury and explain to them" the importance of these concepts.[65]

Counsel proceeds to cast the jury for its part in the dialogue by describing the two concepts "that I tried to speak about in voir dire."

The first concept is that the jurors would set aside their natural repugnance for the defendant as someone who has killed a young woman by a wanton act of violence and would hold him accountable only for the specific crimes "proved to you beyond a reasonable doubt." This concept is enacted performatively in a pair of explicit dialogues between counsel and the jury in which the jury is depicted as speaking out repeatedly:

> "Yet *you all tell me* that you can still apply the laws to him, a man who created such a perilous situation.

65. *See* the first indented passage quoted on page 92 *infra*.

> "*You all said or said to me* that you can still apply the laws to him . . . . *You said* you would still apply the laws to him . . . ."
>
> "I mean, how easy would it be for *each of you to say*, 'Why should we show any serious regard for a man who showed so little regard for the life of another?' How easy it would be for *each of you to say*, 'Why should we care about what crime is proved against him when he in so cavalier a manner apparently pulled a gun and ended up killing another humanbeing[sic]?'"

The second concept is that if facts were not proved, the jury would treat them as unproved and would not expect the defense to present evidence about them. This concept, too, is developed in the form of an active dialogue between the jury and defense counsel and the defendant:

> "*You all said* basically that *you would not say* at this point, 'Well, wait a second, there were two people in that car, . . . [the defendant] and . . . [the victim]. . . . [T]hey are the two who really knew what happened. She obviously can't speak, *let him speak*. Let him get up and *tell us* what really occurred . . . . [I]f it wasn't a shooting with intent to kill, then you . . . [the defendant] get up and *you tell the jury* what occurred.'
>
> "Well, *you promised him and you promised me* that you understood that the law does not give you a right to demand or *ask* that of . . . [the defendant]. *You cannot ask him to speak* and most importantly you cannot in any way use his silence against him."

Defense counsel then summarizes the testimony of the witnesses, states that the issue that the jury must resolve is whether the defendant had an intent to kill, and argues that there is insufficient evidence to allow the jury to find an intent to kill. His argument ends with a final dialogue, a fully enacted dramatic dialogue, between himself and the defendant and the jury, in which defense counsel asks the jury to "stand up," to "look over at" the defendant, and "while looking at him[,] vote not guilty."[66]

2. The Prosecution Argument

The prosecutor also begins by describing her argument as a "discussion" with the jury, but she does so in a perfunctory, conventional style and immediately signals that her conception of "discussion" is non-dialogic:

---

66. *See* the last passage quoted on page 65 *supra*.

> "This is the last opportunity I'll have *to talk with you* concerning the evidence in this case. I am going to take this opportunity *to discuss with you* how the evidence proves the defendant's guilt beyond a reasonable doubt. You may find my argument to be persuasive and you may not.
>
> ". . . [Defense counsel's] arguments are not evidence and my arguments are not evidence and I'm relying on the common sense and your own intelligence and innate abilities to determine the facts in this case."

Thus, no interchange of ideas appears to be contemplated. The prosecutor will offer the jury her arguments on a take-it-or-leave-it basis. Moreover, the arguments are not evidence, and the jury's real job is to get right down to the work of determining the facts of the case on the basis of the evidence.

Of course, the statement that counsels' arguments are not evidence is a boilerplate item that has a number of traditional functions and may be virtually obligatory in some prosecutors' offices. Technically, it helps to insulate the prosecutor from reversible error if she inadvertently misstates the record; rhetorically, it reminds the jury of her dominant position when, as is ordinary, the prosecution's evidence was bulkier than the defendant's; and in cases where, as in the present one, the defendant has presented no evidence at all, it permits the prosecutor to call the jury's attention to that omission without risking a rebuke for commenting on the defendant's exercise of the privilege against self-incrimination. Here, the arguments-are-not-evidence statement lays the groundwork for the prosecutor's premier theme to come: that defense counsel has offered nothing but irresponsible speculation to support a finding of unintentional homicide. But the interjection of the statement at the outset reinforces the tendency of that theme to project the prosecutor's relationship with the jury as non-dialogic: When one's claim is that the evidence said it all, there is little left to converse about.

The prosecutor proceeds immediately to offer a rather different account than defense counsel of the virtues for which the jurors "were chosen": these were "common sense, . . . fairness and . . . what we perceived to be in you the ability to judge the evidence in this case."[67]

---

67. Thus, the prosecutor defines the jury's role as bringing common sense to the task of judging evidence, *see* note 87 *infra*, whereas defense counsel (in the opening set out at pages 78-79 *supra*) defines the jury's role as exercising self-discipline in the critical scrutiny of evidence, *see* note 80 *infra*.

Note another difference between the lawyers' openings. Both undertake to establish an empathetic relationship between counsel and the jury in the traditional way: by adverting to the previous interchange between counsel and the jury during voir dire. But

Hearing, rather than speaking, discernment rather than discourse, seem to be their chief features:

> "Now there are certain things which aren't in issue . . . [,] certain things which are not being disputed in this case as I'm sure you just *heard* [during the defense argument] and as you probably *perceived* during the course of this trial."

The prosecutor dwells for some time on these things, which permit her to talk about the fact of the killing "over four years ago," its "violent and senseless" nature, its concrete anatomical details, the defendant's identity as the killer, the fact that the killing occurred in the course of a quarrel between the defendant and the victim, and (simultaneously) the credibility of the prosecution's witnesses — all to a double drum roll of epistemological certainty:

> "I mean there is no question that . . . ."
> "There is no question that . . . ."
> "There is no question . . . ."
> "There is no issue apparently . . . ."
> "[T]here is no issue that . . . ."
> "[T]here is no question about . . . ."
> "[T]here is no question . . . ."
> "Those things aren't in issue . . . ."

And:

> "We all know that."
> "You know they were telling the truth."
> "You know they didn't tailor their testimony."
> "You know that . . . ."
> "You know that . . . ."
> "You know that . . . ."
> "[Y]ou know . . . "
> "[Y]ou know . . . "
> "We know it was . . . the defendant."[68]

---

defense counsel's portrayal of the relationship is dialogic: counsel "*sensed* from most of you or from the collective that was here an awareness of . . . [certain] values and an *assuredness* that you would *apply these . . . values to the evidence.*" Defense counsel *receives* from the jurors a sense that they will be *active* in upholding *values* of a particular sort. The prosecutor *perceives* in the jurors certain attributes bearing on their *ability* to *judge*, and she (together with the judge and defense counsel), *chose* the jurors for those attributes. Here there is a less active interplay between counsel and the jurors, less activity of any sort on the jurors' part.

68. These "there is no question" and "you know" formulations will recur later in

With this firm substructure of indisputable facts established—not by dialogue or reasoning, but because "there is no question" about any of it and the jury "know[s]" it all from the evidence—the prosecutor next states "[t]he thing that is in issue": "[T]he only question for you is what did . . . [the defendant] intend . . . ." The way the jury is to decide that question is immediately stated:

> ". . . I'm not going to ask you to speculate on things that aren't in evidence. I'm not going to ask you to hypothesize about other theories of this case.
>
> ". . . The Judge will tell you that you're not to speculate on things that aren't in evidence. So what I am going to discuss with you is what the evidence shows in this case."

There follow a dozen pages (about fifteen minutes) of interwoven arguments of three sorts:

a. "The defense would have you believe that in this case and in fact in any case unless . . . the defendant walks up to another person[,] declares his intent to kill that person, pulls the trigger, aims the gun at a chest or head, says 'Gee[,] I'm glad I did that, I really meant to kill you' . . . [a]nd walks away, that it's impossible to prove a person's intent beyond a reasonable doubt." But "I'm sure you all know that simply isn't true."[69]

b. Rather, the jury needs only use its "common sense"[70] to put together the physical facts of the case (which "you know") and certain principles of human conduct (which, also, "you know") in order to conclude that the defendant intended to kill the victim. For example, "[y]ou don't point a loaded gun at someone . . . and pull the trigger when you don't intend to kill them"; also, the defendant's "callous disregard" for someone he had just shot in the chest "shows that this wasn't an accident."[71]

c. "It would be pure speculation and pure imagination on your part" to accept defense counsel's hypothetical scenarios of unintended killing, because "[t]here is no evidence in this case that anything other than and

---

the argument as well. *See* note 127 *infra*.

69. This point is elaborated at some length, with variations on the theme, in three separate passages in the middle and at the end of the argument.

70. *See* text and note at note 87 *infra*.

71. This point is elaborated recurrently and extensively, with variations on the theme, from the middle through the end of the argument.

[sic] intentional murder took place,"[72] and "it's only through speculation and hypothesizing that you can find anything other than that the defendant in this case when he pulled the trigger and fired that shot into . . . [the victim's] heart that he intended to kill her."[73]

The prosecutor's peroration picks up the theme that "I'm not going to ask you to hypothesize, to use your imaginations. I'm simply going to ask you to use your common sense to evaluate the evidence that you heard and to base your verdict on that evidence." "What's being sought in this courtroom . . . is . . . justice[,] and justice is a verdict based on the evidence." "Justice cries out for a conviction in this case."

B. *Microstructure*

By contrasting defense counsel's argument with the prosecutor's, we have seen that the defense argument has three interrelated properties. It tells the story of the trial, not the killing. It tells that story as Drama. The Drama is performed by drawing the jury into dialogue.

So far we have examined these properties primarily as functions of macrostructure. We now focus on microstructure.

1. Defense counsel's use of verb tense is a powerful instrument for focusing the jury on the present rather than the past. The events surrounding the killing are, for the most part, described in the *present tense*. The play of tense throughout the defense argument is remarkable:

— The form for describing the witnesses' testimony is mostly "she testifie*s*" that "X happened," but sometimes counsel even paraphrases testimony in the present tense.

— *Analysis* of the evidence is mostly but not entirely in the present tense: "Where does she see all this from?" "Where does she position herself?"

— *Tension* ("difference") in the evidence is described in the present tense. The jury is asked to wrestle in the present with the present (or eternal present) state of evidence about what happened in the past tense: "[Y]ou must find in his actions something that proves to you what was in his mind." * "But if ther [sic] is no adequate motive that

---

72. This point is made, with variations, a half-dozen times within four pages.

73. This point is made, with variations, in three passages of some length within four pages.

has been presented to you, doesn't that make you question whether or not Mr. Jones had the intent to kill?"

— *Lack* of evidence is almost always described in terms of present-tense ignorance about past-tense happenings. "But where is the proof presented to you that he aimed there?" When there is an unclarity in the story, it is (suddenly) because this all "happened four years ago."

— The facts that the prosecutor and defense counsel are portrayed as arguing or as having to prove are described in the past tense. "Ms. Brooks will argue that . . . that testimony shows my client shot Mary Smith with intent to kill . . . . "

— But direct accounts of the "reality" of what happened on the street are virtually all in the present tense.[74] For example:

> "Is an intent to kill established by his cold manner in which he walks away from the scene? He spins around and puts the gun away and walks away. I mean he knew this woman. They're all friends of some sort. He killed her. Is he unconcerned? Likely, he leaves a woman dying, he's a bad guy. Is he in shock when he walks away? Maybe. We don't know. Everyone says split, someone says to him go up the street and he goes. He gets out of the scene. . . ."[75]

The prosecutor, on the other hand, tells the story of the killing wholly in the past tense.[76] For the most part, even the testimony of the witnesses is recounted with the introduction "she testifi*ed*" or "she sa*id*."

---

74. *See, e.g.*, the last two examples in note 38 *supra*. (The first example in that footnote shows the use of the past tense in a lack-of-evidence statement.)

75. Notice that the two past-tense verbs in this passage function syntactically as past perfect statements. Sometimes counsel's persistence in using the present tense to describe the happenings on the street produces extraordinary verbal gymnastics. Once, for example, counsel interpolates a single sentence of his own into a lengthy recitation of witness testimony; all of the testimony is in the past tense but counsel's interpolation is in the present tense. In another passage, within a few lines counsel shifts from a past-tense lack-of-evidence statement to a present-tense narration of events: "But where is the proof presented to you that he aimed there? . . . [H]ere we have people in a car, in motion, in movement. He's aiming at what? Is he aiming at anything at all?" Elsewhere, within a single sentence he shifts from a past-tense statement of what the prosecutor has to prove to a present-tense statement of what the facts are.

76. There are only two exceptions in the prosecutor's 15-page argument, and one appears in a sentence that contains a past perfect tense in another clause.

2. The prosecutor uses several additional, connected devices to give her story the solidity of an authoritative history:

— She keeps her prefatory remarks short, states matter-of-factly that "certain things . . . aren't in issue," and—within twenty-five lines of greeting the jury—begins her tale. It starts: "I mean there is no question that on February 10, 1987 over four years ago Mary Smith, a 20 year old woman was the victim of a violent and senseless death."

— Her discussion of the killing itself has a physical quality—an iconicity—that is almost totally lacking in the defense argument. We have given one example of this in footnote sixty-four: Defense counsel talks about Mary's being shot in the chest only when he is explicitly debating whether the location of the entry wound proves an intent to kill; the prosecutor repeatedly refers to a chest shot whenever she talks about shooting, whether or not the location of the wound is logically relevant in context. The point is made more generally by the following chart, which shows the frequency with which the two lawyers use various phrases to describe the act of killing:

phrase	*defense counsel*	*prosecutor*
created a perilous situation	1	-
killed her	6	2
shot [*intransitive*]	2	-
shot her [or Mary or a person]	6	3
fired	3	7
pulled the trigger	2	6
caused a shot to go into her side	-	1
caused the bullet to penetrate her heart and liver	-	1[77]

— The prosecutor also gives concrete solidity to the historical events of the killing by making frequent use of an object metaphor to describe

77. That this pattern is not the result of a higher level of abstraction in the defense argument as a whole is indicated by the respective lawyers' uses of the following phrases in discussing the defendant's actions before and after the killing:

phrase	*defense counsel*	*prosecutor*
had a gun	7	3
pulled the gun	5	-
pointed the gun	3	1
aimed the gun	6	2
put the gun [back] in his pocket	5	-

facts or evidence or testimony about the killing as *things* that the jury *has*.

> "[W]e *have* . . . [the victim] and the defendant inside a car." * "What other evidence *do we have* of the defendant's intent . . . " * "No, *you don't have* any evidence of the defendant . . . saying . . . 'I'm going to kill you.' But *what you do have* is a continuing argument . . . where the defendant is angry and the defendant has a gun and *what you do have* is a shot being fired and *what you do have* is evidence of the defendant . . . with a smoking gun . . . ."[78]

3. Defense counsel's means for transmuting the process of factfinding into a Drama with the jury as protagonist are complex:

a. As noted above, counsel begins his argument by describing the way in which the jurors should go about deciding the case. He frames this description in terms of certain *virtues* that the jurors will bring to the task of decision making—namely, two basic "concepts" or "values" concerning a juror's proper role in a criminal trial, which the jurors "have" and will "apply." These concepts and values are described as being in tension with other, negative emotions that the jury may entertain toward the defendant—passions, feelings, and attitudes[79] that each juror "has the right" to have but which the jurors have promised on voir dire that they would put aside. Thus, the jury's decision making is portrayed as a process which begins with the jurors' own mental activity, involves a conflict between the jurors' feelings and duties, and requires the exercise of *will* to resolve that conflict.

So the Drama in which the jury is cast as the Hero is a psychological drama. Externally, the jury's Difficult Task is to answer the riddle of the evidence. Psychologically, it is to overcome the temptation to answer the riddle in a manner that is inconsistent with the Hero's Duty. The Duty is portrayed as that of disciplined inquiry.[80] The temptation is repeatedly

78. In all, the prosecutor uses this object metaphor nine times. Defense counsel uses it only twice.

79. Defense counsel's language is: "whatever passion you felt or didn't feel towards the Defendant" * "no matter what attitude you may have towards the Defendant" * "however you feel towards the defendant."

80. The jury is not to "assign blame" to the defendant "unless specific blame worthiness had been proved to you beyond a reasonable doubt." Although the defendant cavalierly did a perilous act that killed another human being (defense counsel twice concedes), "you all tell me that you can still apply the laws to him" (a formula that

described in terms of undisciplined passions and feelings that are at war with this duty:[81]

> "Is it horrible? Is it proof of a depraved and damnable mind? Yes. But even if you think that[,] you must acquit.[82]
> "The law is specific that you have agreed to uphold. . . ."
>
> "Then what then, what[,] Mr. Lee [defense counsel], you tell us[,] I can hear you all saying, you tell us how a woman is shot in the chest at close range if it's not intentional murder. If there was no intent to kill, what's the scenario[,] how did it happen. I don't know. And I'm not going to play detective and it's not my job and I'm going to just hold you to the promise that you made to not make me prove to you in any way how it may have occurred."[83]

---

defense counsel repeats thrice). "The law is specific that you have agreed to uphold": it requires the prosecutor to prove that the defendant had a conscious intent to kill. The jury cannot convict the defendant even if it is persuaded that he has a "depraved and damnable mind." The jury must put aside such impressions and "apply the law in a cool rational way," "in a cool dispassionate way." "[I]f you can do that . . . ," says counsel "then you deserve our great admiration and I hope you can do it."

81. *See, e.g.*, the second indented passage quoted on page 79 *supra*; the first indented passage quoted on page 90 *infra*; the first indented passage quoted in paragraph d on page 91 *infra*. This point is reiterated in a half-dozen passages in addition to the examples given in the text.

82. The defendant's conceded blameworthiness undergoes a significant transmogrification in the course of the defense argument. It starts out as something that the jury will feel because of what the defendant did—because of the killing that he committed and for which he is on trial. But then the defendant's blameworthiness is recast in the present tense and in personal terms, as in the quoted passage or, *e.g.*, "Is he blameworthy? Absolutely." Thus, it will be "one of the hardest things that you have ever been required to do in public . . . to . . . look over at David Jones and while looking at him vote not guilty." Progressively, blameworthiness becomes something that attaches to the defendant *not* because of the evil acts for which he is on trial but because of some (unspecified) evil aura that hangs about him. Consequently, while it is natural for the jury to detest the defendant, it is not cool to do so; this kind of emotionality must be recognized as human but resolutely controlled.

83. And:

> "You all said basically that you would not say at this point, 'Well, wait a second[,] there were two people in that car, . . . [the defendant and the victim]. . . . [T]hey are the two who really know what happened, She obviously can't speak, let him speak. Let him get up and tell us what really occurred if it's not a murder that he committed . . . .'
> "Well, you promised him and you promised the judge that you understood that the law does not give you a right to demand or ask that of . . . [the

The prosecutor, on the other hand, does not depict the jury as internally conflicted. Like defense counsel, the prosecutor emphasizes the importance of the jury's own attitudes and natural reasoning processes. And like defense counsel, the prosecutor acknowledges that these may be of two kinds. First, the jurors have "imaginations." The prosecutor several times identifies "imaginations" with "hypothesizing" and with "speculating,"[84] and she warns the jurors that the judge will tell them not to speculate.[85] But this prohibition is not couched in such a way as to generate tension: hypothesizing and speculating are not temptations that have much allure for sensible people to begin with.[86] Second, the prosecutor tells the jurors that they have "common sense." Common sense is a good and attractive quality, and the prosecutor repeatedly invites the jury to use its "common sense."[87] To the extent that there is any

---

defendant]. You cannot ask him to speak and most importantly you cannot in any way use his silence against him."

"Well what should you do then, just assume he's crazy? . . . You can't speculate in that way. You need proof presented to you before you make that decision."

84. The following passage is representative:

"I'm not going to ask you *to speculate* on things that aren't in evidence. I'm not going to ask you *to hypothesize* about other theories of this case.

I'm not going to ask you to use your *imaginations* . . . because that is not your job."

85. *See* the indented passage quoted on page 82 *supra*.

86. Defense counsel's argument had also told the jurors that they "can't speculate." Both attorneys were anticipating that the judge's boilerplate charge would admonish the jury not to speculate, as indeed it did.

87. Thus:

"I'm relying on the common sense and your own intelligence and innate abilities to determine the facts in this case.

"You were chosen because of that common sense, because of that fairness and what we perceived to be in you the ability to judge the evidence in the case."

"Common sense" is the repeated keynote. The prosecutor uses the phrase a half-dozen times and reinforces it with cognate phraseology (for example, asking the jury to make "a reasonable assumption"). A variant is the "you [*or* we] all know that" appeal to common sense, which the prosecutor uses again and again. *See* note 127 *infra*.

Note the absence of words of analysis and intellection in the prosecutor's description of the jury's role: the jury will intuit truth directly and comfortably. The prosecutor's final paragraph begins: "I know that when your service is over here you want to look back on your jury service and *feel* that you did the right thing, you want to *feel* that you returned the just and appropriate verdict in this case and that is a verdict based on the evidence . . . ." Similarly, the evaluation of the credibility of testimony appears to be linked to intuition rather than analysis: "You heard the witnesses testify[,] you heard with compelling emotions how they told you of Mary's death four years ago."

possibility of conflict between the appealing quality of common sense and the unappealing quality of hypothesizing or speculating, the prosecutor defuses it by a double move. She employs an object metaphor (THOUGHTS ARE OBJECTS) to *externalize* both qualities—making "imaginations" and "common sense" *objective instruments*[88]—and she then asks the jurors to *use* the fitter instrument:[89]

> "I'm not going to ask you to *use your imaginations* . . . because that is not your job."
>
> "I'm relying on you as I said in the beginning to *use your own common sense* in deciding what it was the defendant intended to do."
>
> "I'm not going to ask you hypothesize, to *use your imaginations* . . . . I'm simply going to ask you to *use your common sense* to evaluate the evidence that you heard and to base your verdict on that evidence."

b. Defense counsel, having by contrast cast the jury as a Hero torn between desire and duty, calls upon it to resolve this conflict in the classic heroic mode: by an exercise of will.[90] He consistently uses verbs of volition to describe what the jury must do and to remind the jurors of the responsibilities that they have taken on themselves:

---

88. The prosecutor's argument does not attribute emotions of any sort to the jury. She uses the verb *feel* with the jury as the subject only twice, in a single passage, describing how the jurors will want to feel at a later day, after their jury service is finished. This passage (which is set out in footnote 87 *supra*) harmonizes rather than opposing feeling and duty.

89. Defense counsel never makes the jurors' internal states the object of the verb *use*. When the jury is the subject of this verb in the defense argument, the object is something other than the jurors' own mentation:

> "You cannot ask him to speak and . . . *you cannot in any way use* his silence against him."

90. In a very subtle move, defense counsel praises the prosecution's star witnesses, Susan Stone and Nancy Gregg, as models of dispassion. "[T]hey testified as best they could." * "[T]hey were both recounting as they described, as best they could, as best they recalled the death of a close friend." * "[T]hey actually testified pretty much free of any bias they have a right to hold or have against the defendant." Surely, counsel insinuates but avoids saying overtly, the jury can do as well. After all, Nancy Gregg is a criminal who had to be caught and put behind bars before she came to "understand that she has a real obligation to the Criminal Justice System" to tell the truth. Maybe she "is really proof that in some way our much maligned criminal justice system actually works." Inspired by such paragons of discipline, the jury is called to make the system work.

> "One concept [mentioned on voir dire] was that whatever passion you felt or didn't feel towards the Defendant, no matter what attitude you may have towards the Defendant . . . that no way *would* that interfere with the verdict that you *would bring* in this case."[91]
>
> "[Y]ou *would not assign* blame to him unless specific blame worthiness had been proved to you beyond a reasonable doubt . . . ."
>
> "[Y]ou *would not in anyway expect* us . . . to prove or to disprove anything . . . ."
>
> "[Y]ou *would in no way hold us responsible* for clarifying these ambiguities for you and you *would in no way expect* us . . . to make up for the lack of clarity . . ."[92]

The prosecutor, by contrast, never uses forms of the verb "will" with the jury as the subject.

c. Another way in which defense counsel plays the same theme is by the use of phrases that conjoin volition and emotion: "show . . . regard for"; "care about"; "desire to analyze"; "be concerned."[93] Phrases of this sort mark an exception to the ordinary tenet of folk psychology that "[f]eelings, like perceptions, are not considered to be under one's direct control."[94] They reflect a belief, or at least an aspiration, that one can

---

91. *See also, e.g.*, the last indented passage quoted on page 79 *supra* and the first indented passage quoted in paragraph d on page 91 *infra*.

92. And:

> "[T]he second concept I thought was critical was if *you would be willing* at the end of the case to say if certain matters aren't proved beyond a reasonable doubt that there[sic] just not proved."
>
> "If it's not proved by the People's evidence that he had an intent to kill, then *you would just find him not guilty* of that charge."

See also paragraph e *infra*.

93. *See* the second indented passage quoted on page 79 *supra* and the first indented passage quoted in paragraph d on page 91 *infra*.

94. D'Andrade, *supra* note 63, at 119. D'Andrade explains that:

> "One may be able to modify one's feelings by thinking of one thing rather than another, or by engaging in various activities, but according to the folk model, one cannot will oneself to hate or not to hate, to love or not to love someone, or even to enjoy something (but one can try)."

Id. The last parenthetical suggests that D'Andrade is aware of some tension on this point in folk psychology. And the exhortations commonly heard in American discourse to "care" and to "be concerned" do appear to reflect a belief that at least certain aspects of one's feelings are subject to a measure of volitional control. It is particularly noteworthy in the *Jones* arguments that words that touch upon these aspects—words such

direct one's feelings by an act of will. The prosecutor uses no such language in connection with the jury.

d. A key passage in the defense argument summarizes the jury's moral dilemma and the need for the jurors to make a deliberate choice between the paths of natural temptation and higher duty:

> "I hope I make clear to you why I still believe . . . [that the concepts and values which the jurors accepted on voir dire] are critical to your ability and maybe even more to your desire to analyze this case.
>
> "Why do I say that it's important that you have a feeling or a notion that however you feel towards the defendant won't influence you in the decision you make? Why is that critical in this case? Because each and every one of you has the right to despise the man who I represent.
>
> "Whatever he did in a legal sense or an illegal sense, whatever his state of mind may have been at the time, that man had a loaded gun in his hand during an argument in a car and he pulled the trigger and he killed a young woman. Yet you all tell me that you can still apply the laws to him, a man who created such a perilous situation.
>
> "You all said or said to me that you can still apply the laws to him, a man who is obviously responsible for the death of Mary Smith. You said *you would still apply the laws to him, still be concerned and still only convict him for what is really proven against him.*"

By contrast, the prosecutor describes the jurors' "innate abilities" as given, requiring no act of will to exercise, and harmonious with the paths of law and logic which lead naturally to conviction:

> "I'm relying on *the common sense and your own intelligence and innate abilities* to determine the facts in this case."

> "You were chosen because of that *common sense*, because of that fairness and because of what we perceived to be in you *the ability to judge* the evidence in this case."

The following parallel passages epitomize the contrast:

---

as "expect" and "ignore"—are found exclusively in defense counsel's summation, never in the prosecutor's.

Defense counsel: "[S]ome of you do have these values and understand these concepts [referring to the same values and concepts mentioned in the immediately preceding excerpt from the defense argument] and I'm going to rely on those of you who do have these concepts to talk to the other members of the jury and explain to them why these concepts or values are so critical in evaluating the evidence . . . ."

The prosecutor: "And I'm going to rely on your common sense and your ability to determine the facts in this case in making a decision as to whether the defendant in fact intended the natural consequences of his actions."[95]

e. The way in which the respective lawyers use the deontic forms *must*, *need*, *have to*, and *should* in relation to the jury are particularly revealing. With one exception,[96] defense counsel always invokes these forms in the positive voice, as commands of duty:

> "[I]f proof is lacking then you *must* acquit."
> "But you *must* find before you convict him of Murder a specific intent to kill and you *must* find in his actions something that proves to you what was in his mind."
> "But even if you think that[,] you *must* acquit."[97]

Conversely, in the prosecutor's arguments, the same forms are invariably negative or dismissive, stating an absence of command:

> "You don't *need* to consider whether it [the motive] might be enough for a reasonable person."[98]

---

95. *See also* the second and third indented passages quoted on page 89 *supra*.

96. "Is there something presented to you that proves an intent to kill so that *you don't have to speculate* to draw that conclusion?"

97. And:

> "You *need to be—has to be* proven to you that . . . [the defendant's] conscious aim . . . was to cause her death . . . ."
>
> "[H]ow easy would it be for each of you to say, 'Why *should* we show any serious regard for a man who showed so little regard for the life of another?' How easy it would be for each of you to say, 'Why *should* we care about what crime is actually proved against him . . . ?'"
>
> "Well what *should* you do then, just assume he's crazy? You can't speculate in that way. You *need* proof presented to you before you make that decision."

98. And:

"You don't *have to* put yourself in the defendant's mind and decide whether[,] you know[,] you think it's reasonable that that was enough of an insults [sic]."

"All you *have to* do in this case is to make a reasonable assumption about the defendant's intent based on his conduct . . . ."

f. The verbs of action that the lawyers attribute to the jury in their respective arguments are also significant. Defense counsel uses the verb *do* in connection with the jury nine times, thrice in his closing sentence asking the jury to vote his client not guilty. With two possible exceptions,[99] all of these uses are affirmative and empowering.[100] The prosecutor uses the verb *do* in connection with the jury four times. With one exception,[101] each of these uses is negative or restrictive.[102]

"I said you may infer. You *need not*, but one of the ways that you can tell what somebody means to do is what they eventually do."

"You don't *have to* decide whether the defendant was the one who pulled the trigger of that gun. . . . You don't *have to* decide who did that. We know it was, the defendant."

99. "Well *what should you do* then, just assume he's crazy? . . . You can't speculate in that way. You need proof presented to you before you make that decision."

See also note 96 *supra*.

100. "If you *can do that*, if you *can do that* in a cool dispassionate way, then *do* it."

"[I]f you can put that aside, if you can apply the law in a cool rational way, then you deserve our great admiration and I hope that you *can do* it."

"So what *I'm really asking you to do* is *to do what* I think will probably be one of the hardest things that you have ever been *required to do* in public, which is to stand up and at some point look over at . . . [the defendant] and while looking at him vote not guilty of charges brought against him."

101. "[W]hen your service is over here you want to look back on your jury service and feel that *you did the right thing* . . . ."

(The full passage is set out in the first indented passage quoted on page 94 *infra*.) Notice that the temporal perspective, looking backward from the future, blunts the active quality of the verb *did*.

102. "You don't have to put yourself in the defendant's mind and decide whether[,] you know[,] you think it's reasonable that that was enough of an insults [sic] . . . . *No one is asking you to do* that."

"[Y]ou can't go into the defendant's mind and decide what exactly was going through it . . . . *Nobody can do* that . . . ."

"*All you have to do* in this case is to make a reasonable assumption about the defendant's intent."

Defense counsel often refers to the ultimate act that the jury will perform in the case, using verbs of action: "convict," "acquit," "vote not guilty." The prosecutor never uses such action verbs. Even in her peroration, the prosecutor uses a remarkable combination of devices—a relatively abstract verb phrase (*return a verdict*),[103] a muted future perfect tense,[104] and a compound sentence ending in two successive copulas—to mitigate the action that she is asking the jury to take:

> "I know that when your service is over here you want to look back on your jury service and feel that you did the right thing, you want to feel that *you returned the just and appropriate verdict* in this case and that is a verdict based on the evidence and I submit to you that the only verdict based on the evidence in this case is guilty of Murder in the Second Degree."

This peroration contrasts starkly with defense counsel's, in which the jury is asked to "stand up," to "look over at" the defendant, and "while looking at him," to "vote not guilty."[105] And the contrast is plainly strategic. For in the passage immediately preceding her peroration, the prosecutor is at pains to portray the jury's verdict as something other than an engine of the jury's agentivity—or, indeed, of any human agency. Not human will or human purpose, but transcendent "Justice" will speak in the verdict:

> "Ladies and Gentlemen, we are not—the People are not seeking vengeance in this case. . . . [The victim's] family is not seeking vengeance in this case. I mean a trial is a search for truth. I mean it's not an excuse to find doubts. I'm not going to ask you to hypothesize, to use your imaginations, I'm simply going to ask you to use your common sense to evaluate the evidence that you heard and to base your verdict on the evidence.
>
> "What's being sought in this courtroom[106] as I said is not vengeance but it's justice and justice is a verdict based on the evidence. Justice cries out for a conviction in this case, Ladies and Gentlemen."

---

103. The *most* abstract term that defense counsel uses to describe the jury's final action in the case (to *bring in* a verdict) is less abstract than this. And it occurs only once, early in the defense argument.

104. *See* note 101 *supra*.

105. *See* the last passage quoted on page 65 *supra*.

106. Note the depersonalizing shift to a passive form.

In defense counsel's philosophy, on the other hand, it is "law" rather than "justice" that is the transcendent value; and "law" is not a self-moving force but a canon that the jury must *apply*.[107]

> "[I]f you can put . . . [aversion to the defendant] aside, if you can *apply* the law in a cool rational way, then you deserve our great admiration and I hope that you can do it."[108]

g. Defense counsel tends to use metaphors that depict the jury's thinking processes as physical and active:

— He makes extensive use of the metaphor THINKING IS SPEAKING. When referring to the mental operations of the jury, defense counsel consistently describes the jurors as *talking*:

> "[H]ow easy would it be for each of you to *say*, 'Why should we show any serious regard . . . .'"
>
> "[H]ow easy would it be for each of you to *say*, 'Why should we care . . . .'"
>
> "[T]he second concept I thought was critical was if you would be willing at the end of the case to *say* if certain matters aren't proved beyond a reasonable doubt that there [sic] just not proved."
>
> "[On voir dire:] You all said basically that you would not *say* [meaning "think"] at this point, 'Well, wait a second . . . .'"
>
> "Can you go from assuming that . . . [particular fact] to leaping and *saying* therefore when the gun went off he intended to kill?"
>
> "I can hear you all *saying*, ..."[109]

107. *See* the first indented passage quoted in paragraph d at page 91 *supra*.

108. Also:

> "I sensed from most of you or from the collective that was here an awareness of these two values and an assuredness that you would *apply* these two values to the evidence in the case."

The prosecutor never speaks of the jury as applying the law. In the prosecutor's argument, the jury's job is "to determine the facts" and to "judge the evidence." *See* pages 97-98 & note 114 *infra*. Thus, on the one occasion when the prosecutor speaks of the jury "applying" anything, it is "common sense principals [sic] you all *apply* every day."

109. The prosecutor uses the THINKING IS SPEAKING metaphor in connection with the jury only three times; in two of these, the activity of the verb is diluted by non-declarative and dismissive formulations:

This metaphor is consistent with two defense strategies: (a) to depict the trial as an exercise in dialogue, in which the lawyers and the jury are engaged in an exchange and in which the jury's role is an active, not merely a passive one, and (b) to support the defense argument that because David Jones never *spoke* a single *word* expressing an intent to kill, the evidence of intent to kill is fatally ambiguous.[110] Of course, defense counsel neither states the THINKING IS SPEAKING metaphor overtly nor connects it explicitly with the issue of the defendant's intent. If he did so, he'd get chopped to pieces. What he does do is to establish the metaphor *performatively*[111] and then reason implicitly from its entailments.[112]

— Defense counsel uses the metaphor LOOKING IS ATTENDING TO in the same way:

> "*Look*, the issue here is not so mysterious."
> "*Look*, in no way am I telling you to ignore the result."
> "*Look* at the evidence in a really bad light."
> "If you just *look* at the evidence, the lack of evidence . . . ."

Then, in the peroration of defense counsel's argument, the verb "look" is used literally to dramatize the jury's agentivity and responsibility: Defense counsel asks the jury to "stand up and . . . *look over at David Jones* and *while looking at him* vote not guilty."[113]

> "Does it make sense to *say*, 'Oh, well[,] maybe he just meant to hurt her.' . . . He wasn't twenty feet away on a sidewalk firing aimlessly at someone, 'Well, *maybe you can say* he didn't mean to kill the person . . . .'"

Indeed, only once in the prosecutor's argument does she use the verb *say* with the jury as its explicit subject. *See* note 121 *infra*.

110.
> "Were any words heard before, during or after that my client uttered that shows an intent to kill? Did he say during the shooting 'Die.' Did he say, 'I want you . . . dead.' Did he say, 'I'm going to kill you.'? Is there any of that shown in the evidence that you have before you to prove an intent to kill?"

The same point is also made in another passage.

111. The art of "definition by performance," JAMES BOYD WHITE, HERACLES' BOW 144 (1985), is explicated in *id.* at 146-47, 148, 153-55, 158, 162-64, 180, 238; *see also* Victor Turner, *Social Dramas and Stories About Them, in* ON NARRATIVE 137, 155, 157, 162 (W.J.T. Mitchell ed., 1981).

112. *Cf.* GEORGE LAKOFF & MARK JOHNSON, METAPHORS WE LIVE BY 52-54 (1980); PAUL RICOEUR, THE RULE OF METAPHOR 235-38, 243-46, 302 (Robert Czerny trans., 1981).

113. *See* the last passage quoted on page 65 *supra*. The prosecutor only twice uses the verb "look" with the jury as the subject. One use is literal and unremarkable ("[The medical examiner] described the path of the wound and you can *look* at the chart if

h. Defense counsel occasionally uses classic heroic verbs with the jury as the subject:

> "[I]f proof is lacking then you must acquit. You cannot *fail* to acquit . . . ."
> "The law is specific that you have agreed to *uphold* . . . ."

The prosecutor uses no such verbs. The prosecutor's verbs to describe the jury's function in the trial stress *judgment*;[114] defense counsel's stress *action* and the Heroic Quest. Consider the comparison in the following chart:

---

necessary"); the other involves no present activity by the jury but portrays the jurors in the future remembering ("look[ing] back") on their jury service (quoted in the first indented passage on page 94 *supra*).

114. This is one aspect of the prosecutor's more general tendency to cast the jury in the roles of disengaged observer and arbiter. For example:

(1) With the jury as the subject, the prosecutor uses the verb *hear* five times and *perceive* once. Defense counsel uses the verb *hear* once and *perceive* never. Defense counsel does makes one indirect reference to the jury *hearing*—a reference in which *hearing* is portrayed as neither passive nor disengaged. He says that unless the jury holds the two basic concepts or values that are the virtues of good jurors, his "summation will fall on deaf ears." Notably, both of the defense references to *hearing* occur in the opening moments of the argument, when counsel is describing what an idealized jury should be or do. Once defense counsel begins to discuss the actual activity of this jury, the verb *hear* is never used. By contrast, defense counsel twice uses the active verb *listen* with the jury as the subject; the prosecutor never does.

(2) The prosecutor makes scant use of the verbs *have* and *be* in connection with the jurors. These are the verbs most commonly used in English to round out personality by endowing people with attributes. For example, in defense counsel's argument, the jurors "have", *inter alia*, "values," "concepts," "attitude[s]," "a feeling or a notion," and a "right" to feel in a certain way. The prosecutor uses the verb *have* to give the jurors only "evidence" (several times), "testimony" (a couple of times), and facts (*e.g.*, "what you do *have* is a continuing argument in a car where the defendant is angry and the defendant has a gun and what you do *have* is a shot being fired") (a couple of times)—plus, on one occasion, the attribute of good imaginations, *see* pages 88-89 *supra*. In this "imaginations" passage, the prosecutor appears rather to be taking off on defense counsel than independently imbuing the jury with a characteristic of personality; in any event, the characteristic is unequivocally disparaged:

> "I'm not going to ask you to use your imaginations, although I'm sure you all *have* good ones[,] and try to figure out some scenario of how this could have occurred, because that is not your job."

And while defense counsel uses the verb *be* to attribute a number of intentional states to the jury—states in which the jurors are "concerned," "willing" to act, and "satisfied" or not satisfied that they have a basis for action—the prosecutor never once uses the verb *be* with the jurors as the subject.

VERB	NUMBER OF USES WITH JURY AS SUBJECT	
	prosecutor	*defense counsel*
judge	1	0
decide (or *make a decision*)	6	4
tell (in the sense of *discern*)	1	0
determine	2	0
conclude (or *draw a conclusion*)	1	1
base a verdict on evidence	1	0
infer	1	0
figure (or *figure out*)	1	1
evaluate	1	1
analyze	0	1
ADD IT ALL TOGETHER	0	1
APPLY THE LAW	0	4
ASSIGN BLAME	0	1
FIND	2	4
BE SATISFIED	0	1

i. Another way in which defense counsel creates an heroic role for the jury is apparent in his use of the verb *can* with the jury as its subject. Both lawyers' arguments are full of statements that the jury "can" or "cannot" do certain things—draw inferences, reach conclusions, take a certain view of the evidence, etc. However, in the defense argument, more than half of these passages refer to positive or negative constraints of duty—obligations that the jury has undertaken or must observe to keep faith with the law:

> "If you *can* do that, if you *can* do that in a cool dispassionate way, then do it."[115]

115. *See also* the first indented passage quoted in paragraph d on page 91 *supra* and the first indented passage quoted on page 95 *supra*. And:

> "[Y]ou promised him and you promised the Judge that you understood that the law does not give you a right to demand or ask that . . . [the defendant testify and explain what really happened]. *You cannot ask* him to speak and . . . *you cannot* in any way use his silence against him."
>
> "[I]f proof is lacking then you must acquit. You *cannot* fail to acquit because . . . [the defendant] or myself have not adequately explained to you what occurred."
>
> "You *can't* speculate in that way. You need proof presented to you before you make that decision."

The residue refer to things that the jury can or cannot do as a matter of logic.[116]

In the prosecution's argument, by contrast, almost all of the *can* and *cannot* passages have to do with what is physically or logically possible[117] rather than with what is legally or morally permissible.[118]

4. Defense counsel uses a variety of means to carry out the project of engaging the jury in a dialogue.

a. His argument is full of rhetorical questions. Whole paragraphs are nothing but series of questions and answers:

> "Were any words heard before, during or after that my client uttered that shows an intent to kill? Did he say during the shooting 'Die.' Did he say, 'I want you . . . dead.' Did he say, 'I'm going to kill you.' Is there any of that shown in the evidence that you have before you to prove an intent to kill? Is there any proof before you that shows that my client actually aimed the gun at . . . [the victim]? There is none. Is there any evidence before you that shows that my client actually pointed the gun at . . . [the victim]? There is none. Is there any evidence that he held it out in a grip so that he could make sure he killed her? There is none. Is there any evidence that shows him . . . getting a [bead] . . . on her . . . . There is none. Is there something presented to you that proves an intent to kill so you don't have to speculate to draw that conclusion?
>
> "Is he angry? Yes. Does he have a gun? Absolutely. Does he fire a shot in a small confined space? No doubt. Is he blame worthy? Absolutely."

---

116. *E.g.*,
"[G]ive this case . . . really the worse [sic] gloss that I think you *can*." * "You know you *cannot* assume that we intend all the consequences of our actions."

117. *E.g.*,
"[Y]ou may infer. You need not, but one of the ways that you *can* tell what somebody means to do is what they eventually do." * "[The medical examiner] described the path of the wound and you *can* look at the chart if necessary." * "You *can't* put yourself in the defendant's mind."

118. Two of the prosecutor's *can* passages do involve legal permissibility:
"[I]t's only through speculation and hypothesizing that you *can* find anything other than that the defendant . . . intended to kill . . . ." * "[T]he Judge will tell you you *can* presume from the defendant's actions what his intent was."

Defense counsel asks a total of sixty-five rhetorical questions in a twenty-one-page argument. By contrast, the prosecutor asks five rhetorical questions in a fifteen-page argument.

b. Defense counsel repeatedly describes himself as engaged in conversation with the jury. The defense argument contains eleven sentences that portray defense counsel as "speaking" or "talking" to the jury, "saying" or "telling" something.[119] By contrast, the prosecutor's argument contains four sentences that portray the prosecutor as speaking to the jury.[120] Defense counsel's peroration begins with the phrase: "[W]hat I'm really asking you to do." The prosecutor's argument contains six sentences in which she is the subject of the verb "ask" and the jury is the indirect object. Five are negative: "I'm not going to ask you to speculate . . . ." * "I'm not going to ask you to hypothesize . . . ." * "I'm not going to ask you to use, your imaginations . . . ." * "I'm not asking you to rely completely on that evidence but its [sic] very compelling." * "I'm not going to ask you to hypothesize, to use your imaginations . . . ." (*Cf.*: "No one is asking you to do that.")

c. When defense counsel talks about facts being proved, he repeatedly uses the formulation "proved to you" (the jury); when he talks about evidence that was presented, it was "presented to you." There are twenty-three formulations of this sort; much less often does defense counsel say simply that facts were "proved" or evidence "presented." The prosecutor's argument contains five statements in the form: "[a witness] told you," or "[a witness] testified . . . in front of you," or "we will prove to you"; more frequently she says simply "we have proved," or "the evidence proves," or "there is no question," or "no issue" about certain facts, or "[t]here is no evidence" of facts to support the defense position; or she talks about "what the evidence shows in this case."

d. In the defense argument, the jurors are frequently portrayed as speaking.

— As noted at pages 95-96 above, defense counsel consistently uses "say" to mean "think" when he describes the mental operations of the jury.[121]

---

119. It contains one sentence that portrays the prosecutor as "telling" the jury something. It also contains one sentence saying that the prosecutor "will argue" something and one sentence saying that defense counsel "will argue" something.

120. It contains three sentences that portray defense counsel as speaking to the jury. The prosecutor says once that she "suggests" some point to the jury; she says six times, "I submit to you." Defense counsel never uses these nontalky formulations.

121. Only once in her argument does the prosecutor use the verb "say" with jurors

— The jurors' commitments on voir dire are described as having been spoken to counsel:

> "you all *tell* me," or "you all *said or said to me.*"[122]

— Defense counsel sometimes puts specific words in the jury's mouth.

> "You all said [on voir dire] basically that you would not *say* at this point, '*Well, wait a second* there were two people in that car, . . . [the defendant] and . . . [the victim]. . . . She obviously can't speak. *Let him get up and tell us what really occurred. . . .*'" * "[Y]ou tell us[,] I can hear you all saying, you tell us *how a woman is shot in the chest if it's not intentional murder? If there was no intent to kill, what's the scenario[,] how did it happen?*"

— Or defense counsel poses questions as though the jury were asking them of him and then proceeds to answer them.

> "Is he capable of scaring someone with a gun? Yes. Is he a bully? Absolutely[,] and most bullys [sic] are just that, they're bullys [sic]."

---

as the subject: "Now you may *say*[,] where is the evidence that he pointed the gun . . . ." (On another occasion the verb "say" is associated with a transcendent reasoner who is held out as a model to the jury, but the verb here is not in the active mode: "Does it make sense to *say*, 'Oh, well[,] maybe he just meant to hurt her.' . . . He wasn't twenty feet away on a sidewalk firing aimlessly at someone, 'Well, maybe you can *say* he didn't mean to kill the person . . . .'")

122. Also:

> "[Y]ou *promised* him [the defendant] and you *promised* the Judge that you understood that the law does not give you a right to demand or ask that of David Jones. You cannot ask him to speak . . . ."
>
> "I'm going to just hold you to the *promise* that you made to not make me prove to you in any way how it may have occurred . . . ."

The prosecutor never uses the words "say," "tell" or "promise" to describe the jurors' commitments on voir dire. When she refers to those commitments, her formulation is "you all *agreed* that we don't have to prove a motive." (Defense counsel once uses the same formulation: "The law is specific that you have *agreed* to uphold.") The prosecutor's only uses of "say" in connection with the jury are collected in note 121 *supra*. She uses the verb "tell" with jurors as the subject only once: "[O]ne of the ways that you can *tell* what somebody means to do is what they eventually do." She never uses the verb "promise" with jurors as the subject.

— The defense argument portrays the jurors as wanting to ask questions; defense counsel reminds them that there are some questions that they are not allowed to ask[123] but he encourages others.[124] He describes the jurors as continuing the dialogue in the jury room.[125]

5. By contrast, the prosecutor's argument employs several related strategies:

The jury is discouraged from taking any active role in the construction of the facts on which its verdict will rest. The facts are something that happened four years ago. The jury's job is to discern those facts by observing their fossils in the evidence. (Concededly, the prosecution bears the burden of proof of the defendant's intent and must prove it by circumstantial evidence. But fossils are the most powerful species of circumstantial evidence.)

Resolving the issue of the defendant's intent is simply a matter of perceiving a reality which certain facts inherently possess and which their fossilized remains in the evidence therefore "prove." Reality does not need to be created. It is already out there, in events.[126] It is knowable.

---

123. *See* the first passage quoted in note 122 *supra*.

124. "But if ther [sic] is no adequate motive . . . , doesn't that make you *question* whether or not . . . [the defendant] had the intent to kill?"
The prosecutor never uses the verbs "ask," "demand" or "question" with jurors as the subject. When she does use the word "question" in connection with the jury, it is as a noun: "the only *question* for you is what did he intend . . . ." This usage comes in a passage that has established "question" as synonymous with "issue"; the two words are used interchangeably and imply no active inquiry by the jury. *See also* the set of indented passages in the middle of page 81 *supra*.

125. *See* the first indented passage quoted on page 92 *supra*, in which defense counsel says that he will rely on those jurors who value the rule of law and other basic concepts to "talk to" the other members of the jury and "explain to them" why these concepts are so important. The prosecutor never uses the verbs "talk" or "explain" with jurors as the subject.

126. The prosecutor repeatedly uses the phrases "in fact" and "the fact that." Defense counsel never uses the phrase "in fact" and he only once uses the phrase "the fact that":

> "I cross-examined her about the fact that she didn't tell the police officers or at least wasn't in the written statement her allegation that Mary had stated, 'No, Dave, don't.' Maybe she did tell the police, maybe she didn't. Maybe that was there, it appears that it was."

Defense counsel's frequent uses of "maybe," "may be," "apparently," and "seems" occur most often when he is discussing the killing and the events and mental states surrounding it. By contrast, the prosecutor's single use of any of these epistemological hedges in connection with the killing scene is a parody of the defense argument: "Does

Indeed, having heard the prosecution's evidence and being capable of using common sense, the jury already "knows" the relevant reality.[127]

---

it make sense to say, 'Oh, well[,] maybe he just meant to hurt her.'" The prosecutor's other uses of such hedges include, for example: "[t]here are certain things which are not being disputed in this case as I'm sure you just heard and as you probably perceived during the . . . trial," and "[t]here is no issue apparently about the credibility of the witnesses."

127. *E.g.*:

> "*We all know that* [*i.e.*, that there is no question of the defendant's identity as the killer]."
>
> "*You know* they [the prosecution witnesses] were telling the truth. *You know* they didn't tailor their testimony.
>
> "*You know* that . . . they were there with . . . [the victim]. *You know* that . . . [the victim] had some argument with the defendant. . . . *You know* that they were both in a position to see what they saw. *There is no question* about whether they might have been mistaken about[,] *you know*, seeing the defendant with the gun. . . .
>
> "I mean *you know* they saw what they saw. . . ."
>
> "You don't have to decide who did that [killed the victim]. *We know* it was . . . the defendant."
>
> "You can't put yourself in the defendant's mind. But whatever it was[,] the insult . . . or however the defendant perceived that, *you know* that he was angry and *you know* he was insulted . . . ."
>
> "No, there is no medical or scientific evidence . . . which proves conclusively how far the defendant was from . . . [the victim] when he fired the shot. But *you know* it was within the confines of a small car. *You know* must [sic] have been from a few feet away and you also know that in order to hit her in the chest he must have aimed to a certain extent."
>
> "You *recall* how . . . [the victim] and the defendant were seated . . . ."

In all, the prosecutor's argument contains 23 uses of the verb *know* with the jury as its subject. (This contrasts with four such uses in the defense argument, as noted *infra*.) Four of the prosecutor's uses are filled pauses. Four are statements of generic truths. (*E.g.*, "I mean[,] that only happens in the movies. Doesn't happen in real life. I'm sure *you all know* that.") Fifteen are statements of historical fact. (*E.g.*, "*You know* and he [the defendant] knows that he had just finished shooting a person in the chest in front of a whole lot of people and he just didn't care, he just walked away.")

For his part, defense counsel never speaks of the events surrounding the shooting as the subject of knowledge. His only uses of the verb "know" in connection with those events are: "Well, who knows?" * "We don't know." * "I don't know." * "I don't know," and four quotations of the testimony of prosecution witnesses that they "don't know" something. He also quotes the witnesses as saying that they couldn't remember, didn't recall, and didn't see aspects of the events, even though he says several times that he is not contesting their credibility. Indeed, he phrases a general concession of their credibility in terms that turn it into a pronouncement of the ultimate unknowability of facts:

> "I want to talk to you all about what I see as really a non-issue in this case. And that non-issue is the credibility of Susan Stone and Nancy Gregg.

Defense counsel is perversely trying to distract the jury from that reality—to make it abandon the "search for the truth"—by luring it into an imaginative dialogue which is "an excuse to find doubts." This kind of imaginative exercise is synonymous with "hypothesis" and "speculation"; the law forbids the jury to hypothesize or speculate. Thus, defense counsel and the jury really have nothing to talk to one another about. Lawyers' arguments are not evidence and the defense presented no evidence. The prosecutor, who did present evidence, can talk *to* the jury authoritatively about "what the evidence shows in this case" and "how the evidence proves the defendant's guilt beyond a reasonable doubt."

6. The prosecutor explicitly criticizes defense counsel for resting his argument on a scenario that "only happens in the movies. Doesn't happen in real life." This is a two-pronged attack, contemning both the defense attorney's tale and the tale teller.[128] The prosecutor dismisses defense

---

> My position is that they both testified *as best as they could*. . . . That indeed they were both recounting as they described, *as best they could, as best they recalled* the death of a close friend.
>
> ". . . We didn't know if they would come in and exaggerate or add details or consciously lie. Well *it appears* that they didn't.
>
> ". . . [T]hus she [Nancy] spoke the truth *as best she could* to all of us."

And later:

> "And is it an exact match *the story, not the story, the rendition* of what occurred? Of course not, it happened four years ago.
>
> "If it was an exact match between the two versions then certainly people would believe that there was fabrication or that they had gotten together. Is it exactly what occurred? *I guess not. I guess memory has it's [sic] failures after four years, but it sounds pretty close.*
>
> "Is there a difference between them in who hears what? Yes. Is there a difference in the sequence, the specific sequence of events? Yeah. There is something different about . . . [facts recited by one witness and the other]. So what. There is a problem, though. Does anyone in that testimony actually tell you how specifically the shooting occurred?"

All told, defense counsel uses the verb *know* with the jury as its subject only four times. Two of these uses are filled pauses; the object of the others is logical or generic truth rather than historical fact:

> "You *know* you cannot go [*i.e.*, reason] backwards."
>
> "You *know* you cannot assume that we intend all the consequences of our actions."

128. As Erving Goffman has noted:

> "Fabrications . . . are subject to a special kind of discrediting. When the . . . party [whom the fabrication is designed to take in] discovers what is up, what was real for him a moment ago is now seen as a deception and is totally destroyed. It collapses. Here 'real,' as James suggested, consists of that understanding of what is going on that drives out, that 'dominates', all other understandings."

counsel's scenario of an intentional killing—a killer with a motive, a carefully aimed weapon, a statement manifesting intent to kill—as the kind of story that could only come out of the Hollywood dream factory; she simultaneously disparages the defense attorney for trying to pass off this celluloid fantasy as legitimate argument.

The prosecutor is right that defense counsel has tapped into a story line immortalized in movies and television shows: the cold-blooded killer who kills for some identifiable motive (hatred, revenge, to eliminate a witness to a previous crime), taking careful aim before firing and preceding or punctuating the killing with some dramatic remark.[129] The effectiveness of devices like the rhetorical questions with which defense counsel develops his theme of the cold-blooded murderer commonly depends upon predicting accurately and playing to the stereotypical assumptions of one's audience.[130] Motion pictures and other sources of popular culture (television, best-selling novels, and so forth) offer a window into the stock scripts that are familiar to our culture.[131] By taking

---

ERVING GOFFMAN, FRAME ANALYSIS: AN ESSAY ON THE ORGANIZATION OF EXPERIENCE 84-85 (1974). And the fabricator as well as the fabrication is attainted:

> "The discrediting that occurs may retrospectively and prospectively undermine a linked series of prior occasions and anticipated ones. . . . Indeed, in the United States, the so-called Stalin Trials tend to be seen as a collective whole, a use of a nation's basic legal institutions for the sole purpose of staging a show, a systematic translation of a judicial process into a political display, and this whole is read as discrediting evidence regarding an entire political system."

Id. at 121.

129. *E.g.*, PATRIOT GAMES (Paramount 1992); CAPE FEAR (Universal 1991 & 1962); RICOCHET (HBO 1991); SOMEONE TO WATCH OVER ME (Columbia 1987).

130. *See, e.g.*, CORBETT, *op. cit. supra* note 17, at 63 (to use enthymemes, an orator "who seeks to persuade a select audience must apprise himself of the generally held opinions of that group"); James C. Raymond, *Enthymemes, Examples, and Rhetorical Method, in* ESSAYS ON CLASSICAL RHETORIC AND MODERN DISCOURSE 140, 142 (Robert J. Connors, Lisa S. Ede, & Andrea A. Lunsford eds., 1984) ("[T]he major premise in an ethymeme may be implied rather than expressed because the audience is presumed to know it . . . [and it] may be unproved (or even unprovable) if the audience believes in it."). Although this observation is usually made about enthymemes, it is equally true of rhetorical questions. *See* note 132 *infra*.

131. *See, e.g.*, JOSEPH W. REED, AMERICAN SCENARIOS: THE USES OF FILM GENRE 5-6 (1989) ("[H]ow we see ourselves, what we think of us, what we think our world is like, how we think it works, all come from the movies (and now from television as well)."); JAMES W. CAREY, *Taking Culture Seriously*, *in* MEDIA, MYTHS, AND NARRATIVES: TELEVISION AND THE PRESS 8, 14 (1988) ("[T]he popular arts . . . [are], by definition, close to the hard surfaces of life . . . and a relatively direct apprehension of the world of their makers and users."); *see also* note 135 *infra*. For further discussion of stock scripts and their workings, *see* note 146 *infra*.

these stock scripts into account, an advocate can prompt his or her audience to supply the "right" answers to the syllogisms that s/he sets up.[132]

Thus, it is not surprising that the prosecutor, after faulting defense counsel for relying on a movie script, taps into two such scripts herself. First, she counters defense counsel's arguments about the absence of any proof of motive by drawing on the story, commonly featured in news reports as well as motion pictures, of the killer so disdainful of human life that s/he will kill for the slightest provocation or imagined slight.[133] "What we have proved," the prosecutor says, "through the insulting conversation that was overheard by Nancy and Susan, . . . is a motive[; it] may not be a motive that you would act on, may not be a motive that a reasonable person would act on, but it was a motive that the defendant acted on." And again:

> "[W]hether you understand the nature of that insult or not really isn't at issue here. But there is no question that the defendant felt insulted and I'm sure you all know that people have been killed for less."

Second, the prosecutor alludes to the oft-told story of the "mad dog killer,"[134] portraying the defendant as having "killed a person he intended to kill in front of people to show that he was a big, you know, he was a big man."

Like her attack on defense counsel's tale, the prosecutor's attack on the teller evokes stock scripts. By characterizing defense counsel's arguments as not just wrong but Hollywood hype, the prosecutor

---

132. As rhetoricians have explained, the deductive logic of an enthymeme must draw upon "a body of accepted opinions . . . [or] 'truths' which have never really been demonstrated but in which the people have faith, almost to the point of accepting them as self-evident." CORBETT, *op. cit. supra* note 17, at 63; *see also* note 130 *supra*. By the same token, a rhetorical question cannot serve its intended function—of "inducing the audience to make the appropriate response," *id.* at 445—unless it rests upon a logic and a way of thinking about the world that the audience will find compelling. *Cf.* RICHARD RIEKE & RANDALL K. STUTMAN, COMMUNICATION IN LEGAL ADVOCACY 211-12 (1990) (describing empirical studies that indicate that rhetorical questions are more effective than affirmative statements when used to present a "persuasive message" but that the opposite may be true when rhetorical questions are used to present "weak" messages).

133. *E.g.*, James C. McKinley, Jr., *Queens Youth Fatally Shot in Fight over Moped: Are Youngsters in High Crime Areas Losing Respect for Life?*, N.Y. TIMES, Aug. 3, 1990, at B1; BOYZ 'N THE HOOD (Columbia 1991); COLORS (Orion 1988).

134. *E.g.*, SCARFACE (Universal 1983 & Howard Hughes 1932); THE PUBLIC ENEMY (Warner Brothers 1931). *See generally* CARLOS CLARENS, CRIME MOVIES: FROM GRIFFITH TO THE GODFATHER AND BEYOND (1980).

implicitly asks the jury to view her opponent through the stock script of the amoral, opportunistic defense attorney who will stop at nothing to "get the client off."[135] In this, she acts upon the insight of the classical rhetoricians that a speaker's credibility depends upon the audience viewing him or her as a person of "good will" and "good character."[136] Once defense counsel has been cast in the role of the con artist, the jury is more likely to view his arguments skeptically; what might otherwise have seemed deft argumentation may be transformed into unfair manipulation.[137]

The most effective way for defense counsel to avoid being cast in this role is to persuade the jury to apply a different, more favorable stock

---

135. *E.g.*, TRUE BELIEVER (Columbia 1989); ANATOMY OF A MURDER (Columbia 1959); THE MOUTHPIECE (Warner Brothers 1932); *see also* Anthony Chase, *Lawyers and Popular Culture: A Review of Mass Media Portrayals of American Attorneys*, 1986 AMER. B. FOUND. RES. J. 281, 287 (describing the "characterization [in some films and television shows] of the defense attorney as [some]one who dangerously subjects the community to grave risk (by getting thugs and crazies 'off')"). In recent years, legal commentators have begun to pay closer attention to portrayals of lawyers in movies, television shows, best sellers, and other sources of popular culture, *see, e.g.*, *id.*; Lawrence Friedman, *Law, Lawyers and Popular Culture*, 98 YALE L.J. 1579 (1989); Stephen Gillers, *Taking* L.A. Law *More Seriously*, 98 YALE L.J. 1607 (1989); Stewart Macaulay, *Images of Law in Everyday Life: The Lessons of School, Entertainment, and Spectator Sports*, 21 LAW & SOC'Y REV. 185 (1987); Richard A. Posner, *The Depiction of Law in* The Bonfire of the Vanities, 98 YALE L.J. 1653 (1989); Steven D. Stark, *Perry Mason Meets Sonny Crockett: The History of Lawyers and the Police as Television Heroes*, 42 U. MIAMI L. REV. 229 (1987), as well as in literature, *see generally* Robert Weisberg, *The Law Literature Enterprise*, 1 YALE J. L. & HUMAN. 1 (1988). Commentators disagree as to what such portrayals of lawyers can teach us. While some maintain that popular depictions of lawyers and the legal system influence public perceptions and attitudes, *see e.g.*, Gillers, *supra*, at 1622; Macaulay, *supra*, at 185-86; Stark, *supra*, at 230, others suggest that they merely "reflect rather than . . . influence the popular understanding," Posner, *supra*, at 1660; *see also* Friedman, *supra*, at 1598. Regardless of which view is correct—or whether literary and popular depictions of lawyers and the legal system both reflect and affect cultural attitudes—such depictions are valuable resources for the practicing lawyer and for those who study and teach the art of lawyering.

136. *E.g.*, ARISTOTLE, *op. cit. supra* note 15, bk. 2, ch. 1, at 91-92 (explaining that speakers must "give the right impression of . . . [themselves and] evince a certain character," for otherwise they will be regarded as "untrustworthy in what they say or advise"); I CICERO, *op. cit. supra* note 15, bk. II, ch. XLIII, at 329 (advising speakers to employ "particular types of thought and diction . . . [and] delivery . . . [that will make them] appear upright, well-bred and virtuous men"); *see also* note 15 *supra* and accompanying text.

137. *See* GOFFMAN, *op. cit. supra* note 128, at 121:

> "When a mark tumbles to what has been happening in the Big Con and sees things for what they are, he sees that a whole sequence of . . . [actions by the Con artist] involve a concerted fabrication."

script.[138] There are screen images that portray defense lawyers in a better light. The earliest and most enduring image is the one popularized by Erle Stanley Gardner's "Perry Mason": the crusader who fights nobly on behalf of an innocent client (or at least a client whom s/he reasonably believes to be innocent).[139] Also admirable is the image of the defender as paladin: the defense attorney who, although a "hired gun," achieves a higher nobility and morality by performing his or her professional duty in a scrupulously conscientious manner.[140]

Often, a defense attorney's task is to navigate successfully among these stock scripts, encouraging the jury to think in terms of either the Perry Mason or the paladin script and avoiding the image of the con artist.

---

138. *See* GOFFMAN, *op. cit. supra* note 128, at 159:

> "[B]ecause a keying [that gives rise to a particular interpretation of an activity] is already a mock-up of untransformed activity . . . , the *retransformation* of this result into a rekeying . . . would seem to require less work than that entailed in the original transformation. Whatever it is that makes untransformed activity vulnerable to transformation makes transformations even more vulnerable to retransformations . . . ."

139. The character of "Perry Mason" is of course best known because of the popular T.V. series (which aired in first-run episodes from 1957 to 1966) and more recent television movies. The character had a loyal following even before the T.V. series, as a result of Gardner's "Perry Mason" books (the first of which was published in 1933) and a radio series that ran from 1943 to 1955. *See* BRIAN KELLEHER & DIANA MERRILL, THE PERRY MASON TV SHOW BOOK (1987). Other portrayals of the defender as noble crusader can be found in movies such as SUSPECT (Tri-Star 1987), LEGAL EAGLES (Universal 1986), TO KILL A MOCKINGBIRD (Universal 1962), and WITNESS FOR THE PROSECUTION (United Artists 1957), and television series such as *L.A. Law* (NBC 1986-present), *Judd for the Defense* (ABC 1967-1969), and *The Defenders* (CBS 1961-1965); *see also* Chase, note 135 *supra*, at 282-83. For our present purposes, it matters little whether the client is actually innocent (as in the classic Perry Mason story) or is someone whom the lawyer reasonably believed to be innocent (as in *Witness for the Prosecution*); under either scenario, the defense lawyer emerges as a person of noble character, rightfully concerned with protecting the innocent. Of course, the former script has additional implications for a juror's willingness to believe in the defendant's innocence; but as we point out in note 142 *infra*, *Jones* was not a case in which defense counsel tried or could have tried to depict his client as innocent in the Perry Mason sense.

140. *E.g.*, PRESUMED INNOCENT (Warner Brothers 1990); BREAKER MORANT (South Australian Film Corp. 1980); THE CAINE MUTINY (Columbia 1954); *L.A. Law* (NBC 1986-present); *see also* Chase, note 135 *supra*, at 282-83. For typical portrayals of the paladin in his or her usual incarnation as mercenary warrior, see, e.g., THE SEVEN SAMURAI (Toho 1954); THE MAGNIFICENT SEVEN (United Artists 1960); STAR WARS (20th Century Fox 1977); and the television series *Have Gun, Will Travel* (CBS 1957-1963); *see also* FRANK MCCONNELL, STORYTELLING AND MYTHMAKING: IMAGES FROM FILM AND LITERATURE 142-43 (1979) (discussing the archetype of the "gunfighter . . . [who] tries to sustain the personal ethics of his professional knight-errantry").

In *Jones*, several aspects of the defense argument which we have already mentioned have the effect of placing defense counsel squarely within the stock script of the paladin. First, counsel uses the Aristotelian Proem to establish himself in the jurors' eyes as a professional who is committed to follow the rule of law. Second, counsel's heavy reliance on rhetorical questions helps to refute the negative con-artist script. Con artists are notorious for their manipulative use of speech ("fast-talk," "doubletalk," "sweettalk"). By asking questions instead of making assertions, counsel fosters the impression that he wants the jurors to think through the issues on their own and to use their independent judgment. Third, by repeatedly conceding that his client's conduct—even under the defense theory of the facts—was reprehensible, defense counsel demonstrates that he is neither a bleeding-heart apologist for his client's misdeeds nor a trickster trying to conceal unpalatable facts with smoke and mirrors. ("Look, in no way am I telling you to ignore the result. In no way am I telling you to ignore the fact that she was shot in the chest where her heart was.") He is able, as a result, to cast himself in the role of legal technician, required by the law to focus on a very narrow question of mens rea and performing that task in an appropriately professional manner. Fourth, counsel takes pains to read directly and extensively from the trial transcript of the testimony of the prosecution witnesses. Six or seven minutes of his argument is devoted to straightforward reading. How, then, can it be doubted that his facts and he are straightforward?[141] Finally, defense counsel presents the myth of the Hero performatively, implicitly encouraging the jurors to view themselves in that role rather than explicitly exhorting them to play the role. Counsel thereby limits the risk that the jurors will perceive him (or that the prosecutor will be able to portray him) as trying to manipulate the jury.

In addition to using the stock script of the paladin defensively to guard against a prosecutorial attack, counsel uses it affirmatively. The same story line that enables him to assume the *persona* of the paladin also

141. Like other strategies, this one serves more than one function. Because the witnesses were prevented by the personal knowledge rule from testifying to anything explicitly relating to the defendant's mental state, counsel's direct quotation of their testimonies as the means for presenting "the evidence that I think exists in this case" enables him to describe the evidence without a single word referring to mentation. His argument before and after this review of the evidence is full of words about intent, *see* pages 73-75 *supra* and accompanying notes; yet not one word about intent appears from beginning to end of his description of the testimony. It is as though he was saying: *The prosecutor and I will have a lot to say to you about intent, and you will have to concern yourselves with intent as the central issue in this trial, but the evidence shows absolutely nothing on the subject of the defendant's intent.* Like other powerful messages conveyed by the structure of counsel's argument, this one remains unstated and therefore invulnerable to the raking-over it would get if stated.

enables him to cast the jurors in the role of the Quest Hero. Disciplined obedience to duty is the soul of it.[142]

V. Concluding Observations

Please recall again the factual issue framed for the jury's decision by the law of New York in the *Jones* trial: whether David Jones intended to kill Mary Smith. Recall also the evidence and the posture of the parties regarding the evidence. All of the testimony indicated that Jones had fired one shot from a handgun during a loud argument with Smith in the back seat of a parked car; this shot entered Smith's chest, pierced her heart, and killed her; Jones fled. Defense counsel did not dispute that these events were proved; the prosecutor did not assert that any additional relevant events were shown.

In this state of the record, the prosecutor could be expected to argue that people do not shoot others in the heart at close range unless they intend to kill them. She so argued. Defense counsel could be expected to argue that the possibility of other unexcluded but evidentially unidentified explanations for the shooting left a reasonable doubt. He so argued. At the logical level, these two arguments were pretty much everything the lawyers said in closing. Logically, there was little more for them to say.

But their closings also drew upon resources other than logic. Notwithstanding their complete agreement about the events before, during, and after the shooting of Mary Smith, the lawyers told completely different stories, with completely different plots, completely different themes, completely different narrative structures. They evoked different stock scripts. They used different metaphors and different grammars. Despite their acceptance of the same legal and logical canons—or perhaps because of it—they created different worlds that gave those canons different meanings.

142. By casting the jury in the role of paladin, counsel also averts the risk that the jury might apply a very different (and, from his perspective, problematic) stock script. One of the few current stock scripts for *jurors* is that of TWELVE ANGRY MEN (United Artists 1957) and SUSPECT (Tri-Star 1987): the crusading juror, fighting to exonerate a falsely accused defendant. (There are not many alternative images because courtroom dramas usually treat jurors as ciphers, moving them off-stage at the very moment when they would naturally have a speaking part—during the jury deliberations. This is also largely true of literature, although there are a few notable exceptions. *See* Emily Stipes Watts, *From American Literature, in* THE JURY SYSTEM IN AMERICA: A CRITICAL OVERVIEW 161 (Rita James Simon ed., 1975).) In a case like *Jones*, where the defendant obviously was not "innocent," defense counsel could not afford to allow the jurors to approach the case with a crusader mentality. Jones's only hope lay in the jurors curbing their zeal and dispassionately applying the reasonable doubt principle. Thus, counsel had to persuade the jurors to see themselves in the role of paladin rather than crusading juror.

The recognition of this phenomenon raises interesting questions. One wonders, most immediately and practically, whether the creation of these different worlds in closing arguments has any effect upon the jury's reactions to a case. If so, what effects, and under what conditions? These are subjects that would lend themselves to study through empirical research techniques like those developed to examine other aspects of jurors' thinking;[143] but, so far as we are aware, little such study has yet been done.[144]

---

143. These include interviews of actual jurors in the tradition pioneered by Harry Kalven and Hans Zeisel in the Chicago Jury Study, *see, e.g.*, HARRY KALVEN, JR. & HANS ZEISEL, THE AMERICAN JURY (1966); William S. Geimer & Jonathan Amsterdam, *Why Jurors Vote Life or Death: Operative Factors in Ten Florida Death Penalty Cases*, 15 AM. J. CRIM. L. 1 (1987-1988); John M. Conley & William M. O'Barr, *The Power of Language: Presentational Style in the Courtroom*, 1978 DUKE L.J. 1375, and trial simulations, *see, e.g.*, INSIDE THE JUROR: THE PSYCHOLOGY OF JUROR DECISION MAKING (Reid Hastie ed., 1993); REID HASTIE, STEVEN D. PENROD, & NANCY PENNINGTON, INSIDE THE JURY (1983); Claudia L. Cowan, William C. Thompson, & Phoebe C. Ellsworth, *The Effects of Death Qualification on Jurors' Predisposition to Convict and on the Quality of Deliberation*, 8 LAW & HUM. BEHAV. 53 (1984); William C. Thompson, Claudia L. Cowan, Phoebe C. Ellsworth, & Joan C. Harrington, *Death Penalty Attitudes and Conviction Proneness: The Translation of Attitudes into Verdicts*, 8 LAW & HUM. BEHAV. 95 (1984); Neil Vidmar, *Effects of Decision Alternatives on the Verdicts and Social Perceptions of Simulated Jurors*, 22 J. PERSONALITY & SOC. PSYCHOL. 211 (1972). Hans Zeisel, the dean of all jury studies, was still developing innovative approaches to both of these techniques at the time of his death in 1992; he reported (in personal communications) finding judges increasingly willing to permit the interviewing of actual trial jurors; and he noted that the expanding practice of videotaping "real" trials has created new possibilities for studying both "real" jurors' reactions to a case and the reactions of experimental jurors to realistic and controlled trial simulations. If we follow his ideas along this line—for which, among many other things, we are deeply indebted to him—we can project experimental designs in which substantial numbers of simulated jurors attend trials that are identical in all respects other than the closing arguments (using a single videotape of the pre-argument trial proceedings and the judge's instructions, together with a common voir dire for the experimental subjects), while the closing arguments are systematically varied to isolate the aspects that one wants to study.

144. Although there have been a few efforts to study the effects of lawyers' arguments on jurors, *see, e.g.*, Michael G. Parkinson, *Verbal Behavior and Courtroom Success*, 30 COMM. EDUC. 22 (1981), very little is yet known about the subject, *see, e.g.*, RIEKE & STUTMAN, *op. cit. supra* note 132, at 203 (noting that empirical "research findings in the area [of closing arguments] are thin"); RONALD J. MATLON, OPENING STATEMENTS AND CLOSING ARGUMENTS: A RESEARCH REVIEW 65-68 (Oct. 10-13, 1991) (paper presented at the convention of the American Society of Trial Consultants, San Francisco, CA) (on file with the *New York Law School Law Review*) (concluding that empirical research on opening statements and closing arguments has been "scanty," *id.* at 67, and that "much remains to be done," *id.* at 3); WALTER F. ABBOTT, FLORA

A second level of questions has to do with the nature of the processes through which the lawyer's closing arguments might affect the jurors' reactions. If the kinds of stories, tropes, and linguistic devices that we have found exemplified in the *Jones* arguments influence jurors' cognition, *how* does this happen? A considerable body of theoretical work from a number of disciplines is potentially relevant here. The ways in which narratives and myths shape people's interpretations of experience have been the subject of varied, richly polyphonous theorizing.[145] So have the

---

HALL, & ELIZABETH LINVILLE, JURY RESEARCH: A REVIEW AND BIBLIOGRAPHY 180-201 (1993). The most ambitious and thoughtful analysis of lawyer's courtroom storytelling that we have found focuses upon the presentation of evidence and contains nothing about jurors' reactions to lawyers' arguments. *See* BENNETT & FELDMAN, *op. cit. supra* note 4. *See also* JACKSON, *op. cit. supra* note 5, at 61-88 (discussing Bennett's & Feldman's theories of courtroom storytelling).

145. Louis Mink observes that "narrative is a primary cognitive instrument—an instrument rivaled, in fact, only by theory and by metaphor as irreducible ways of making the flux of experience comprehensible." Louis Mink, *Narrative Form as a Cognitive Instrument, in* THE WRITING OF HISTORY: LITERARY FORM AND HISTORICAL UNDERSTANDING 129, 131 (Robert H. Canary & Henry Kozicki eds., 1978). He notes that "story-telling is the most ubiquitous of human activities, and in any culture it is the form of complex discourse that is earliest accessible to children and by which they are largely acculturated." *Id.* at 133. Jerome Bruner develops both of these points with characteristic penetration and learning in JEROME BRUNER, ACTUAL MINDS, POSSIBLE WORLDS (1986) and JEROME BRUNER, ACTS OF MEANING (1990). Bruner documents the extent to which young children are literally swaddled in narratives told by their caretakers. *See id.* at 83-84. He suggests that "[n]arrative structure is . . . inherent in the praxis of social interaction before it achieves linguistic expression . . . [and that] it is a 'push' to construct narrative that determines the order of priority in which grammatical forms are mastered by the young child." *Id.* at 77; *see also id.* at 68-80, 90. "[A] protolinguistic grasp of folk psychology is well in place as a feature of *praxis* before the child is able to express or comprehend the same matters by language." *Id.* at 74; *see also id.* at 79, 89-94. By "folk psychology," Bruner refers to "a system by which people organize their experience in, knowledge about, and transactions with the social world." *Id.* at 35. "[I]ts organizing principle is narrative rather than conceptual." *Id.* Bruner speaks with particular pertinence to our present subject when he theorizes that, "while a culture must contain a set of norms, it must also contain a set of interpretive procedures for rendering departures from those norms meaningful in terms of established patterns of belief. It is narrative and narrative interpretation upon which folk psychology depends for achieving this kind of meaning. Stories achieve their meanings by explicating deviations from the ordinary in a comprehensible form . . . ." *Id.* at 47; *see also id.* at 39-40, 67, 81-86, 95-97. "*The function of the story is to find an intentional state that mitigates or at least makes comprehensible a deviation from a canonical cultural pattern.*" *Id.* at 49-50. *Cf.* Nancy Pennington & Reid Hastie, *The Story Model for Juror Decision Making, in* HASTIE, *op. cit. supra* note 143, at 192.

Bruner's ideas are paralleled by those of Victor Turner, who sees the "social drama" as "the social ground of many types of 'narrative.'" Turner, *supra* note 111, at

141. The social drama is "a spontaneous unit of social process and a fact of everyone's experience in every human society." *Id.* at 145; *see also id.* at 154, 163-64. It has "four phases[:] . . . breach, crisis, redress, and *either* reintegration *or* recognition of schism." *Id.* at 145. The social drama grounds not only narrative but also ritual and the elaborations of ritual that constitute a culture's ceremonies (including theater and religion) and its redressive or reconciliative processes (including adjudication). *See id.* at 146-47, 151-54; *see also* VICTOR TURNER, DRAMAS, FIELDS, AND METAPHORS: SYMBOLIC ACTION IN HUMAN SOCIETY (1974); VICTOR TURNER, FROM RITUAL TO THEATRE: THE HUMAN SERIOUSNESS OF PLAY 9-15, 24-30, 61-87, 106-12 (1982). Turner thus deepens and broadens Malinowski's insights into primitive myth,

> "which is not an explanation in satisfaction of a scientific interest, but a narrative resurrection of a primeval reality, told in satisfaction of deep religious wants, moral cravings, social submissions, assertions, even practical requirements. Myth fulfills in primitive culture an indispensable function: it expresses, enhances and codifies belief; it safeguards and enforces morality; it vouches for the efficiency of ritual and contains practical rules for the guidance of man."

BRONISLAW MALINOKSKI, *Myth in Primitive Psychology*, *in* MAGIC, SCIENCE AND RELIGION, AND OTHER ESSAYS 101 (Doubleday Anchor 1955).

The connectedness of myth and language is a central thesis in the work of Ernst Cassirer. *See* ERNST CASSIRER, THE PHILOSOPHY OF SYMBOLIC FORMS (Ralph Manheim trans., 1955); ERNST CASSIRER, LANGUAGE AND MYTH (Susanne K. Langer trans., 1946). Cassirer argued that

> "[w]hat holds these two kinds of conception, the linguistic and the mythical, together in one category, and opposes both of them to the form of logical thought, is the fact that they both seem to reveal the same sort of intellectual apprehension, which runs counter to that of our theoretical thought processes. The aim of theoretical thinking . . . is primarily to deliver the contents of sensory or intuitive experience from the isolation in which they originally occur. . . . Mythical thinking . . . comes to rest in the immediate experience; the sensible present is so great that everything else dwindles before it."

Id. at 31-32; *see also id.* at 57-58, 88. Mircea Eliade takes a narrower view of myth but also emphasizes the immediacy of mythical experience. In archaic societies, he writes,

> "one 'lives' the myth, in the sense that one is seized by the sacred, exalting power of the events recollected or reenacted.
>
> . . . [O]ne ceases to exist in the everyday world and enters a transfigured, auroral world impregnated with the Supernaturals' presence. What is involved is not a commemoration of mythical events but a reiteration of them."

MIRCEA ELIADE, MYTH AND REALITY 19 (Willard R. Trask trans., 1963). Through this reiteration, human beings understand what they are and how they came to be that way. "Myths . . . narrate not only the origin of the World . . . but also all the primordial events in consequence of which man became what he is today—mortal, sexed, organized in a society, obliged to work in order to live, and working in accordance with certain rules." *Id.* at 11. *See also* Mircea Eliade, *Myths and Mythical Thought*, *in* ALEXANDER ELIOT, THE UNIVERSAL MYTHS 14, 28 (Meridian 1990), describing an Osage postnatal ritual whose function is to "validate . . . [the newborn child's] existence by announcing

ways in which stock scripts and other prototypes organize thinking.[146] So

---

that it conforms with the mythical paradigms."

> "Myth assures man that what he is about to do *has already been done*, in other words, it helps him to overcome doubts as to the result of his undertaking. There is no reason to hesitate before setting out on a sea voyage, because the mythical Hero has already made it in a fabulous Time. All that is needed is to follow his example."

ELIADE, MYTH AND REALITY *op. cit. supra*, at 141. Although Eliade insists upon the difference between the experience of life in archaic societies and in modern societies pervaded by "desacralization," *see* MIRCEA ELIADE, THE SACRED AND THE PROFANE: THE NATURE OF RELIGION 13 (Willard R. Trask trans., 1959), he acknowledges that "[s]ome forms of 'mythical behavior' still survive in our day," ELIADE, MYTH AND REALITY *op. cit. supra*, at 181; *see also* MIRCEA ELIADE, IMAGES AND SYMBOLS 10-21 (Philip Mairet trans., Princeton Paperback 1991), and he gives as an example the experience of a reader of the detective novel (*see* ELIADE, MYTH AND REALITY, *op. cit. supra*, at 185):

> "On the one hand, the reader witnesses the exemplary struggle between Good and Evil, between the Hero (=the Detective) and the criminal (the modern incarnation of the Demon). On the other, through an unconscious process of projection and identification, he takes part in the mystery and the drama and has the feeling that he is personally involved in a paradigmatic—that is, a dangerous, 'heroic'—action."

There is, of course, a broad range of other conceptions of the means through which narratives and myths may "operate in men's minds without their being aware of the fact," 1 CLAUDE LÉVI-STRAUSS, MYTHOLOGIQUES [THE RAW AND THE COOKED] 12 (John Weightman & Doreen Weightman trans., 1983), from Lévi-Strauss's "constraining structures," *id.* at 10, through Carl Jung's "archetypes," *see, e.g.*, CARL G. JUNG, *Approaching the Unconscious*, *in* JUNG, *op. cit. supra* note 23, at 56-94, and Joseph Campell's version of the archetype: the "inherited image," *see* 1 JOSEPH CAMPBELL, THE MASKS OF GOD [PRIMITIVE MYTHOLOGY] 30-49 (Penguin Books 1976), and so forth.

146. In the terminology of Schank and Abelson, a *script* is a stereotyped sequence of events which is familiar to the individual in a culture and guides his or her interpretation of experience. *See* ROGER C. SCHANK & ROBERT P. ABELSON, SCRIPTS, PLANS, GOALS, AND UNDERSTANDING: AN INQUIRY INTO HUMAN KNOWLEDGE STRUCTURES (1977); Roger C. Schank, *Language and Memory*, 4 COGNITIVE SCI. 243 (1980). A range of cognate concepts—*prototypes*, *frames*, *schema*, *cultural models*, etc.—are elaborated in the essays collected in HOLLAND & QUINN, *op. cit. supra* note 63, and are surveyed in the book's introductory chapter, *see* Naomi Quinn & Dorothy Holland, *Culture and Cognition*, *in id.* at 3, 20:

> "The papers in this volume illustrate how our knowledge is organized in culturally standardized and hence familiar event sequences that tell, for example, how marriage goes . . . ; or how anger is engendered, experienced, and expressed . . . ; or what to expect in a relationship between two young adults of opposite gender . . . ; or that wishes give rise to intentions and intentions to actions . . . . These 'stories' include prototypical events, prototypical roles for actors, prototypical entities, and more. They invoke, in effect, whole worlds in which things work, actors perform, and events unfold

> in a simplified and wholly expectable manner. These events are chained together by shared assumptions about causality, both physical and psychological, as Abelson's characterization of scripts suggests."

For example, Geoffrey White observes that "[n]arrative comprehension frequently proceeds by using existing knowledge structures to process new information and draw inferences about the social and moral implications of what is said; in other words, to get the point." Geoffrey M. White, *Proverbs and Cultural Models: An American Psychology of Problem Solving*, *in* HOLLAND & QUINN *op. cit. supra* note 63, at 151, 152.

> "Proverbs are . . . used to pick out and communicate salient aspects of a social situation in terms of prior knowledge about similar situations. As in the use of metaphor generally, uncertain or ambiguous events can thus be understood and evaluated in terms of existing models of social experience.
>
> . . .
>
> Proverbs function as effective communicative devices because they set up the listener to draw . . . practical inferences by expressing one or more key propositions embedded in a cultural model with known entailments. By instantiating certain elements of an existing model, other, related propositions are invoked through inference."

Id. at 154-55; *see also id.* at 161-69.

Erving Goffman has suggested that it is not merely the interpretation but what is interpreted that is "shot through with various framings and their various realms." GOFFMAN, *op. cit. supra* note 128, at 561.

> "[I]n many cases, what the individual does in . . . life, he does in relationship to cultural standards established for the doing and for the social role that is built up out of such doings. . . . The associated lore itself draws from the moral traditions of the community as found in folk tales, characters in novels, advertisements, myth, movie stars and their famous roles, the Bible, and other sources of exemplary representation."

Id. at 562.

Coming at the matter from a semiotic perspective, Roland Barthes made a similar point in several important essays:

> "[T]he closed logic which structures a sequence is indissolubly linked to its name: any function which inaugurates a *seduction*, say, prescribes upon its appearance, in the name which it produces, the whole process of seduction that we have learned from all the narratives which have formed in us the language of the narrative."

BARTHES, *op cit. supra* note 21, at 115; *see also* ROLAND BARTHES, *The Sequences of Action*, *in* THE SEMIOTIC CHALLENGE 136, 140-42 (Richard Howard trans., 1988):

> "We must further know how we can constitute these sequences, how we decide that an action belongs to one sequence and not to another. As a matter of fact, this constitution of the sequence is closely linked to its nomination; and, conversely, its analysis is linked to the unfolding of the name which has been found for it: it is because I can spontaneously subsume various actions such as *leaving, traveling, arriving, remaining* under the general name *Journey*, that the sequence assumes consistency and is individualized (sets itself in opposition to other sequences, other names); conversely, it is because a certain practical experience convinces me that under the term *Appointment* is

have the workings of metaphor.[147] And so, lately, have the semiotic codes

---

> arranged ordinarily a series of actions such as *proposing, accepting, honoring* that, this term having been in one way or another suggested to me by the text, I am entitled to observe, specifically, its sequential schema; to release the sequences (from the signifying mass of the text, whose heteroclite character we have mentioned) is to classify actions under a generic name (*Appointment, Journey, Excursion, Murder,* etc.); to analyze these sequences is to unfold this generic name into its component parts. . . .
>
> "[T]o read a narrative is in effect (by the rushing rhythm of reading) to organize it in fragments of structures, it is to tend toward names which 'summarize' more or less the profuse sequence of notations, it is to proceed within oneself, at the very moment when one 'devours' the story, to nominal adjustments, it is constantly to tame the novelty of what one is reading by known names, proceeding from the vast anterior code of reading; it is because in myself, very rapidly, certain indices produce the name *Murder* that my reception of the tale is effectively a *reading*, and not the simple perception of phrases whose linguistic meaning I would understand, but not the narrative meaning . . . ."

Cf. MICHAEL RIFFATERRE, FICTIONAL TRUTH 3-4 (1990):

> "[The indicators of coherent motivation] reflect the . . . prevailing ideology or ideologies that may be mobilized in assessing a situation or individual behavior. These mental frames of reference, however, are not just habits of thought; they constitute potential ministories, ready to unfold when needed and ready for reference when alluded to. The action *having a drink* or just the idea of a drink, in any narrative or indeed any conceptualization, depends on the availability of a verbal sequence: ordering and obtaining the drink . . . [etc.] Parallel to this narrative unit are valorizations with their own ready-made sequences, such as conviviality, including the option of the bartender as conscience-director, versus solitary soaking-up, etc., etc."

Bruner speaks of the processes through which "[t]he illusion . . . [is] created by skillful narrative that . . . a story 'is as it is' and needs no intepretation." Bruner, *supra* note 19, at 9. One of these is what he calls "'narrative banalization.' That is, we can take a narrative as so socially conventional, so well known, so in keeping with the canon, that we can assign it to some well-rehearsed and virtually automatic interpretive routine." *Id.* "Breaches of the canonical, like the scripts breached, are often highly conventional and are strongly influenced by narrative traditions. Such breaches are readily recognizable as familiar human plights–the betrayed wife, the cuckolded husband, the fleeced innocent, and so on." *Id.* at 12. "[A] story that requires a 'betrayal' as one of its constituent functions can convert an ordinarily mundane event into something that seems compellingly like a betrayal." *Id.* at 13-14.

147. Paul Ricoeur reviews earlier theories and expounds his own in his classic treatise, RICOEUR, *op. cit. supra* note 112. *See also* SHELDON SACKS, ON METAPHOR (1979). A powerful new illumination has been cast on the subject by the works of George Lakoff with Mark Johnson and others. LAKOFF & JOHNSON, *op. cit. supra* note 112; GEORGE LAKOFF, WOMEN, FIRE, AND DANGEROUS THINGS: WHAT CATEGORIES REVEAL ABOUT THE MIND (1987); GEORGE LAKOFF & MARK TURNER, MORE THAN COOL REASON: A FIELD GUIDE TO POETIC METAPHOR (1989). They emphasize that

that, in the telling of a story, create "a grammatical framework engineered to ensure proper interpretation."[148]

A third level of questions has to do with the nature of the processes through which the lawyers themselves *produce* the sort of argumentation that we have detected in *Jones*: thickly textured tales in which the lawyer's explicit logical reasoning is backed by the implicit sending of additional messages, strikingly harmonious, mediated by the multiple devices of narration, allusion and linguistic coding. It is hardly plausible to suppose that all of these communicative strategies are employed deliberatively, or even deliberately. The defense lawyer in *Jones* may or may not have consciously chosen to structure his argument as a prototypical Hero's Quest; it is much less likely that he consciously chose to use his SPEAKING IS THINKING metaphor; it is almost inconceivable that he consciously chose to use each of implicit focalizations, dialogic speech acts, dependent and independent sentence constructions, verb tenses, and so forth that he put together with such remarkable consistency and mutually reinforcing interplay. As Claude Lévi-Strauss has pointed out, "It is the same with myths as with language: the individual who conscientiously applied phonological and grammatical laws in his speech, supposing he possessed the necessary knowledge and virtuosity to do so, would . . . lose the thread of his ideas almost immediately."[149]

So how did he do it? Is the process involved akin to the workings of a computer program: once the lawyer chose the overall message that he

---

> "many aspects of our experience cannot be clearly delineated in terms of the naturally emergent dimensions of our experience. This is typically the case for human emotions, abstract concepts, mental activity, time, work, human institutions, social practices, etc., and even for physical objects that have no inherent boundaries or orientations. Though most of these can be *experienced* directly, none of them can be fully comprehended on their own terms. Instead, we must understand them in terms of other entities and experiences, typically other *kinds* of entities and experiences.
>
> ". . . [M]ost of our indirect understanding involves understanding *one kind* of entity or experience in terms of *another kind*—that is, understanding via metaphor."

LAKOFF & JOHNSON, *op. cit. supra* note 112, at 177-178.

148. RIFFATERRE, *op. cit. supra* note 146, at 12.

"Instead of looking for the rules that govern narrative structures," Riffaterre's approach is to "look for the rules that govern their textual actualization and, consequently, those rules that govern the way literary discourse functions as communication. . . . [Those rules] alone can explain how the text guides the reader toward a correct interpretation." RIFFATERRE, *op. cit. supra* note 57, at 158-159; *cf.* MICHAEL S. TOOLAN, NARRATIVE: A CRITICAL LINGUISTIC INTRODUCTION 33-39 (1988).

149. 1 LÉVI-STRAUSS, *op. cit. supra* note 145, at 11.

wanted to send to the jury, all of the subroutines for sending that he had evolved throughout the course of his professional and personal life went "on line" and sent accordingly? Is there something here akin to the wisdom of the Zen masters who, after the most intensive preparation and discipline, are enabled to pass beyond a conscious concentration on technique and achieve the spontaneity of oneness with their art?[150]

We do not know the answers to these questions. We are thinking about them, and we hope this article may intrigue others to think about them also and to share their thoughts with us. That has been its primary objective.

Such thinking is work for scholars who are interested in understanding the complicated processes through which trials construct the reality which they are authorized by law to announce. It is also, we think, work for practicing lawyers and for those who educate lawyers for practice. To be sure, we have just said that we doubt any lawyer's ability to consciously mobilize all of the linguistic strategies that we found exemplified in the *Jones* arguments—themselves a small sample of the vast range of linguistic strategies that the lawyers might have used. But this is not to say that conscious attention to the nature of these strategies is impractical.

While perhaps not conscious, many of the strategies would seem to be at least preconscious: they are susceptible to being thought about and thereby modified. Let us close with a single example from the *Jones* trial.

As we have seen, the prosecutor's argument—like defense counsel's—was remarkably self-consistent. There was, however, one quite striking exception. Despite the prosecutor's mobilization of all of the resources of language to portray David Jones's mental state as an activity

---

150. *See* EUGEN HERRIGEL, ZEN IN THE ART OF ARCHERY 38-41 (R.F.C. Hull trans., Vintage 1989):

> "[I]f he is to fit himself self-effacingly into the creative process, the practice of the art must have the way smoothed for it. For if, in his self-immersion, he saw himself faced with a situation into which he could not leap instinctively, he would first have to bring it to consciousness. He would then enter again into all the relationships from which he had detached himself; he would be like one wakened, who considers his program for the day, but not like an Awakened One who lives and works in the primordial state.
>
> ". . . [This is] why the technically learnable part of . . . [archery] must be practiced to the point of repletion. If everything depends on the archer's becoming purposeless and effacing himself in the event, then its outward realization must occur automatically, in no further need of the controlling or reflecting intelligence.
>
> ". . . The pupil . . . discover[s] in the course of years that forms which he perfectly masters no longer oppress but liberate."

See also id. at 71-78; D.T. Suzuki, *Lectures on Zen Buddhism, in* ERICH FROMM, D.T. SUZUKI, & RICHARD DE MARTINO, ZEN BUDDHISM & PSYCHOANALYSIS 1, 19-22 (1960).

that was simply part of the whole historical sequence of activities leading to the violent death of Mary Smith, the prosecutor somehow got herself into (to mix a metaphor) a *container* metaphor for mind. She repeatedly says things like:

> "[T]hey [the prosecution witnesses] told you about something which frankly they probably would rather put *out* of their minds . . . ."
>
> "[T]here is no question *in* there [sic] minds that he was the one that shot her."
>
> "You don't have to put yourself *in* the defendant's mind and decide . . . ."
>
> "You can't put yourself *in* the defendant's mind."
>
> "[Y]ou can't go *into* the defendant's mind and decide what exactly was going *through* it at the time he fired that shot."
>
> "[S]cience hasn't invented the instrument which can look *into* someone's head and tell us all what they mean or what their intent is."

This was understandable, certainly. In the first place, the MIND IS A CONTAINER metaphor is such a common structuring metaphor for English speakers[151] that it would have come naturally to anyone's lips. In the second place, the trial judge's instructions to the jury, which the prosecutor may have anticipated, used the metaphor.[152] Lawyers in closing

---

151. The ubiquitousness of the metaphor is evident:
What do you have *in* mind?
You are *out* of your mind.
She is *full* of ideas.
He flipped his *lid*.
They were *brimming* with ideas.
My mind is *dry*.
He is an *empty*-headed fool.
It is one of a wide range of container metaphors, *see* LAKOFF & JOHNSON, *op. cit. supra* note 112, at 29-32, 58, which, in turn, are but an example of the human tendency to "conceptualize the nonphysical *in terms of* the physical—that is, we conceptualize the less clearly delineated in terms of the more clearly delineated," *id.* at 59. The MIND IS A CONTAINER metaphor is consistent with the conduit metaphor for language, in which LINGUISTIC EXPRESSIONS ARE CONTAINERS and communication is sending. *Id.* at 10-13. Because it is often invisible to the user and exerts a powerful force in structuring the user's thought and discourse, it can raise hob with legal argumentation. See Steve Winter's criticism of Stanley Fish in Steven L. Winter, *Bull Durham and the Uses of Theory*, 42 STAN. L. REV. 639, 649-64 (1990).

152. *See* note 3 *supra* ("certainly can't look *into* a person's mind to see what he was thinking"). We cannot determine from the trial transcript whether, at the time of her

argument often do well to encapsulate phrases that they know the judge will charge, either to obtain the support of the judge's authority for their own reasoning if the phrase is helpful or to set unhelpful phrases in the least hurtful context for damage-control purposes.[153]

However, it seems to us that this particular metaphor was just about the worst way that the prosecutor could have talked about mental states generally and the defendant's intent particularly. To the extent that the jury's deliberations were modeled as an effort to peer into a container (the mind) from the outside and discern a solid object (the specific intent to kill) inside, the defendant had every advantage. The walls of the container are notoriously opaque (a point that defense counsel emphasized by repeated use of a KNOWLEDGE-IS-LIGHT/IGNORANCE-IS-DARK metaphor)[154] and the criterion for satisfactory discernment is the daunting beyond-a-reasonable-doubt rule (which defense counsel belabored).

We would guess that the prosecutor fell into this trap simply for want of attending to the metaphoric quality of language. The prosecutor probably never realized that phrases like "in the defendant's mind" *are* only metaphors, that there are other metaphors for mind, and that it would have been to her advantage either to seek one or to avoid metaphors entirely in this connection.

Once these things are realized—once the trap is seen—a bit of additional thought is necessary to avoid it. One says: "There must be alternative metaphors available to a prosecutor; the job is to rev up one's mind to think about them. Or is it 'tool up one's mind'?" *Hmmmm.* What *about* the MIND IS A MACHINE metaphor?

> I can't get my mind to WORK right this morning.
> He has a SCREW loose.
> That really started my WHEELS spinning.
> His mind went into high GEAR.
> She has a HIGH POWERED mind.

---

argument, the prosecutor knew the exact language that the judge planned to use in charging the jury. This portion of the judge's charge deviated from the New York pattern jury instructions, *see* note 158 *infra*, but may have been in the judge's personal charge book. It was not discussed between the lawyers and the judge in any recorded colloquy settling the instructions.

153. *See, e.g.*, 3 AMSTERDAM, *op. cit. supra* note 7, § 447, at 266.

154. *E.g.*:

> "And if at the end you decided that something was not clarified for you, if you decided that ambiguities in the evidence still remain, that you would in no way hold us responsible for clarifying these ambiguities for you and you would in no way expect us . . . to make up for the lack of clarity which could still exist at the end of this case."

He had a mental BREAKDOWN.
They kept CRANKING OUT ideas.

The MIND IS A MACHINE metaphor is consistent with the familiar IDEAS ARE PRODUCTS metaphor.[155] It offered a viable alternative to the prosecutor in *Jones*, since it is about as commonplace as the MIND IS A CONTAINER metaphor[156] and has very different entailments.[157] Also, the MACHINE metaphor, like the CONTAINER metaphor, was reflected in the judge's instructions.[158]

As soon as one begins to fish for alternative conceptualizations, of course, additional ideas will start to swim into one's mind. So, what *about* the MIND IS A FLUID metaphor?

That's a mind-*curdling* thought.
I *sank* into a reverie.
Her mind *runs deep*; she's a *profound* thinker.
She is *level*-headed—*cool, calm*, and collected.
My mind *froze*.
Let's wait until our thinking *gels*.
She is *clear*-headed; her ideas are not *muddy*.

---

155. *See* LAKOFF & JOHNSON, *op. cit. supra* note 112, at 47.

156. *See* D'Andrade, *supra* note 63, at 116:

"[T]he folk model has two different ways of regarding the mind—as a collection of 'internal states' versus a set of 'internal processes.' . . . Thus, the mind is treated both as a *container* that is in various states and conditions, thereby having large number [sic] of potentialities simultaneously, and also as a *processor* engaged in carrying out certain operations, thereby limited to a small number of concurrent actions."

157. *See* LAKOFF & JOHNSON, *op. cit. supra* note 112, at 28: "The MACHINE metaphor gives us a conception of the mind as having an on-off state, a level of efficiency, a productive capacity, an internal mechanism, a source of energy, and an operating condition."

158. *See* note 3 *supra* ("[i]ntent is the secret *operation* of the mind"). The New York pattern jury instructions use this metaphor twice and do not use the container metaphor:

"What a defendant intends is of course an *operation* of the mind. A jury, even if present at the time of the commission of the crime, cannot examine the invisible *operation* of a person's mind."

1 COMMITTEE ON CRIMINAL JURY INSTRUCTIONS, CRIMINAL JURY INSTRUCTIONS—NEW YORK, at CJI 9.31 (1983) (emphasis added). We cannot know whether, if the prosecutor had attempted to get the judge to give this pattern instruction instead of the one he did give, he would have been amenable.

The MIND IS A FLUID metaphor has particular potential here because it can be conjoined with useful FLUID metaphors for emotion—"he shot her in cold blood"—that play well for the prosecution.

There are other metaphors for mind but our circuits are becoming overloaded, so we'll stop with these. The point is not that the prosecutor should have used any one of them, but that a bit of brainstorming about the various ways in which one can talk about the mind might prove useful to you if you are a prosecutor in a similar situation. Exploring a range of ideas can sometimes get us out of a rut. It can expand our mental horizons, as it were. It can make our minds more fertile, sprout the seeds of new ideas, make them grow. It can help to break the chains that too often bind our thinking as well as its expression. It can enable us to spin out different lines of thought, perhaps even whole new webs of ideas.[159]

---

159. We are not suggesting that the only way in which the prosecutor might have avoided using the MIND IS A CONTAINER metaphor is to use others. She might instead have framed her argument in straightforward subject/verb/object sentences of action in which the concept of intentionality was conveyed by adverbs: "The issue is whether, when the defendant killed Mary Smith, he did it intentionally or unintentionally." This or that "shows that he deliberately killed her" or "purposely shot her to death." She might have used subject/verb/object sentences of mentation in which the concept of intentionality was conveyed by the verbs themselves: "The issue is whether he intended to kill her." This or that "shows that he wanted her dead" or "intended to take her life." She might have used verbal copulas to connect "intent" with the specific intent that had to be proved: "The issue is whether his intent was to kill her or just to shoot a gun at her at close range without killing her." This or that "shows that his intent was to kill her." We have noted at pages 73-75 *supra* that the use of noun formulations was, in general, less consistent with the prosecutor's overall argument than verb formulations. However, the kinds of noun formulations described here have the virtue of implicitly predicating that the defendant had *some* intention while asking the jury to consider only *what* that intention was. They are thus consistent with the fundamental tenets of a folk psychology that is "about human agents doing things on the basis of their beliefs and desires, striving for goals, meeting obstacles which they best or which best them, all of this extended over time." JEROME BRUNER, ACTS OF MEANING 42-43 (1990). And such a folk psychology was, of course, the prosecutor's pigeon in *Jones*. *See* note 87 *supra* and accompanying text.

[4]

Law Frames: Historical Truth and Narrative Necessity in a Criminal Case

Richard K. Sherwin*

Postmodern storytellers can fashion narratives that convey many different, yet equally convincing, visions of reality. Although these stories replicate our experience of the quick-cut image sequences that define contemporary popular culture, they can have only limited persuasive force in the legal arena when they prevent their audience from reaching articulable, justifiable conclusions. Faced with such important tasks as ascertaining truth and promoting justice, this audience will favor storylines that offer meaningful resolution. In this article, Richard K. Sherwin examines the interplay of a traditional linear story with a discursive postmodern story in Errol Morris' film The Thin Blue Line. *Professor Sherwin concludes that Morris' linear tale effectively eclipses the uncertainties introduced by its acausal counterplot, and he attributes the failure of this second story to the more general epistemological failure of skeptical postmodernism. As an alternative to orthodox linear narratives, which reach closure only by concealing or denying inconsistent details, and to skeptical postmodern narratives, which never reach closure or even attempt to make sense of their details, Professor Sherwin urges lawyers and legal scholars to engage in "affirmative postmodern" storytelling. Affirmative postmodern tales embrace the multiplicity and complexity of details, but they orient their audience within a shared cultural storyline—a popular myth, a stock metaphor, a familiar character type—that allows one to create meaning out of the mass of information presented. Because they respect the complexity of reality and yet facilitate meaningful decisionmaking, Professor Sherwin argues, affirmative postmodern narratives offer an alternative way for the law to define truth and justice.*

> "You reasoned it out beautifully," [Dr. Watson] exclaimed in unfeigned admiration. "It is so long a chain, and yet every link rings true."
>
> *The Adventures of Sherlock Holmes*[1]

* Professor of Law, New York Law School. I wish to thank Professor Natalie Zemon Davis for the opportunity to present my ideas on legal storytelling at her colloquium on "Proof and Persuasion" at Princeton University. I benefited greatly from the insights of Professor Davis and the colloquium members. I also wish to thank Professor Steve Ellmann and members of the Clinical Theory Workshop at the New York Law School, as well as those who provided helpful comments at the 1993 annual meeting of the Law & Society Association. For their critical comments on early drafts, I am indebted to Neal Feigenson, Ruti Teitel, Robert Blecker, Michael Perlin, and Michael Sinclair. Laura Colatrella and Charles Hellman provided invaluable help at the final stage of this essay's preparation. Finally, I wish to express my gratitude to Charlie Musser for his early assistance in this project.

1. Arthur Conan Doyle, *The Red-Headed League*, *in* 1 The Annotated Sherlock Holmes 418, 438 (William S. Baring-Gould ed., 1976) (1891-1892).

> The matter of interest seems to be the configuration formed by chance events in the moment of observation, and not at all the hypothetical reasons that seemingly account for the coincidence.
>
> C.G. Jung, Foreword to *The I Ching*[2]

I. Introduction: Legal Realities, Legal Fictions

> We must keep up the boundaries of actions, otherwise we shall introduce the utmost confusion.
>
> Lord Raymond[3]

People prefer stories neat. Recognizable characters, familiar motives, and recurring scenarios of conflict and resolution are typical elements of our workaday narrative world. Legal narratives are no different.[4] And trial lawyers, especially prosecutors and defense attorneys, are only too glad to indulge a preferred image or storyline if it will help win a case.

The trouble with having one's stories neat, however, is that they tend to leave things out—the things that make a story messy, hard to keep in mind. Of course, such infelicitous details can be dealt with. That's what recurring storylines, familiar genres and plots, and typical characters, conflicts and resolutions are for.[5] They keep the mess out. It simply won't do to be telling a

2. C.J. Jung, *Foreword* to The I Ching i, xxiii (Richard Wilhelm trans., 1961).

3. Scott v. Shepherd, 96 Eng. Rep. 525 (1773), *reprinted in* Richard Epstein, Cases and Materials on Torts 76 (5th ed. 1990) (quoting Lord Raymond).

4. *See, e.g.*, Michael E. Tigar, Examining Witnesses 5 (1993) ("People, including judges and jurors, understand and restate events in terms of stories. They take the available evidence and weave it into a coherent whole. If pieces are missing, they will fill in the gaps based on intuition, probability, or prejudgment. . . ."); Albert J. Moore, *Trial by Schema: Cognitive Filters in the Courtroom*, 37 UCLA L. Rev. 273, 277 (1989) ("In an actual case there will be many potential frames of reference which *could be* recalled by jurors from their schematic databases and contribute to assessments of similarity. However . . . cognitive biases and limitations cause jurors to filter out many of these potential frames of reference."). *See generally* Reid Hastie, Steven D. Penrod & Nancy Pennington, Inside the Jury 22-23 (1983) (describing the hypothesis that jurors impose a narrative structure on trial information based on case-specific facts, knowledge of similar events, and generic expectations provided by traditional storylines.); Anthony G. Amsterdam & Randy Hertz, *An Analysis of Closing Arguments to a Jury*, 37 N.Y. L. Sch. L. Rev. 55 (1992) (examining the impact of metaphors on jurors' responses to closing arguments).

5. For example, according to Nisbett and Ross:

> Few, if any, stimuli are approached for the first time by the adult. Instead, they are processed through preexisting systems of schematized and abstracted knowledge—beliefs, theories, propositions, and schemas. These knowledge structures label and categorize objects and events quickly and, for the most part, accurately. They also define a set of expectations about objects and events and suggest appropriate responses to them. A price is paid for this mental economy, however. The knowledge structures themselves are not infallible guides to the nature of physical or social reality.

Richard Nisbett & Lee Ross, Human Inference: Strategies and Shortcomings of Social Judgment 7 (1980); *see also* Jerome Bruner, Acts of Meaning 20-22 (1990); Roger C. Schank & Robert P. Abelson, Scripts, Plans, Goals and Understanding: An Inquiry into Human Knowledge Structures 36-38 (1977). *See generally* Howard Gardner, Frames of Mind: The Theory of Multiple Intelligences 299-327 (1983) (discussing the socialization of human intelligences through symbols); George Lakoff, Women, Fire, and Dangerous Things: What Categories Reveal About the Mind 5-7 (1987) (describing categorization as the primary way people make sense of their experiences); Richard K. Sherwin, *Lawyering Theory: An Overview—What We Talk About When We*

story and have it trail off, or break up, or have another story poke its nose in. When you tell a story, you make a choice. That's the story you're telling. It could have been otherwise, but it isn't. The story told, in order to be told, represses other possibilities.

Since stories are supposed to make sense, and since the sense they make is supposed to be believable, it helps if the recounted events, actions, characters, and backgrounds involved seem necessary. If it were otherwise, if it seemed that other stories could just as easily be told, perhaps with equal truth (or incredibility), who'd want to accept the offered version as true? When making meaning happen, it helps to suppress chance and multiplicity. That, at least, is the lesson of narrative necessity.

This essay is about the murder of a Dallas police officer named Robert Wood and the different kinds of stories that were subsequently told about that crime. First there was the story told at trial, which led to the conviction of Randall Dale Adams and his sentence of death by the electric chair.[6] Then there was the story told by filmmaker Errol Morris in *The Thin Blue Line*.[7] Morris' story made so many people disbelieve the trial story that the courts eventually reexamined the case. That reexamination led to Randall Adams' release from prison. Adams had served twelve years inside, a good part of it on death row. Morris' film was credited as the catalyst that righted a wrong and set the Dallas criminal justice system straight.[8]

How did these different stories achieve what they achieved? By what craft? And what are we to think when a legal reality, freedom for a supposed cop killer, follows hard upon the heels of a cinematic "docudrama"? It is this mingling of forms, art on the one hand, legal reality on the other, this shifting back and forth between ways of making meaning in narrative and the ways people see and make judgments about reality, that drives this inquiry.

In this article, I explore how it happens that law's demand for truth and justice can clash with the modern mind's demand for closure and certainty. When truth defies certainty and becomes complex, justice requires difficult decisions on the basis of that doubt. The struggle between shifting cognitive needs and legal duty is commonplace, and without a way to question how a given narrative shapes and informs our desire for certain and tidy justice, that desire, and competing ones, cannot be adequately understood. As a result, the kind of justice operating in a particular case at a given cultural juncture may remain confused or hidden from view. The emergence in our time of a postmodern narrative of justice, one that is spontaneous, contingent, and irre-

Talk About Law, 37 N.Y. L. Sch. L. Rev. 9, 18 & n.23 (1992) (explaining how a narrative approach may be developed to tap into various cognitive models).

6. *See* discussion in Part II *infra*.

7. The Thin Blue Line (Third Floor Prods. 1988) (transcr.) [hereinafter Transcript].

8. Philip Gourevitch, *Interviewing the Universe*, N.Y. Times, Aug. 9, 1992 (Magazine), at 18 (identifying Errol Morris as the man "whose film 'The Thin Blue Line' saved a man from death row"). Movie critic Clarke Taylor opened his review with this hook: "Will a new movie succeed in getting convicted murderer Randall Dale Adams freed from prison? Director Errol Morris and Miramax, the distributor of 'The Thin Blue Line,' frankly acknowledge that they hope the answer is yes." Clarke Taylor, *Thin Blue Line: Advocate for a Killer*, L.A. Times, Aug. 28, 1988, at 28.

pressibly messy, provides a case in point. The challenge is to tap the salient cultural storylines, both familiar and newly emerging, that give meaning and coherence to uncertainty, so that when a case demands, we can feel sure enough in our reasonable doubt.

In some of what follows, I shall be arguing uphill, in favor of complexity, insinuating ambivalence about the kind of order legal stories typically create. I shall approach the disorder that lurks beyond the bounds of these well-told tales. Perhaps more unforgivable, I shall question whether the specific tale of Randall Dale Adams might be less tidy than we'd prefer. What if the modernist penchant for dichotomies that produces starkly polar choices like guilt/innocence, frameup/frameup undone, injustice/injustice corrected—the very mindset that gives us such satisfaction in seeing justice's scales finally balanced—were part of the problem? I want to suggest that the simplicity of these polarities, and the calm they induce, are at least partly responsible for making us leave things out. The messy things. The things that leave a sense of disorder and lack of control, the unsettling things we refuse to see or discuss. These are the things that make it hard to make legal decisions, decisions that can have irrevocable effects upon the body and soul of a person: prison, prison life, perhaps even death. No less grave, they are decisions that could lead to erroneous acquittal and the recurrence of violence by the liberated defendant. It is precisely because the stakes are so high that I want to examine how we might guard against facile resolutions without getting mired in indecision and meaninglessness. In particular, I want to explore a form of postmodern legal storytelling that can serve a sustainable sense of justice as well as order. But to follow this path we must learn to question our own complicity in making truth appear overly neat and coherent. Thus, rather than share in the triumph of having seen the system set straight, we must ask ourselves whether we are not accomplices in a form of realitymaking that let the Adams frameup occur in the first place and that could let similar frameups occur in the future.

Uncontrollable disorder within the criminal justice system is an admittedly disturbing topic, and I don't enjoy dwelling on it any more than you do. But surely it is a good thing to increase our awareness of how we deal with the omnipresent possibility of disorder, as well as the possibility that conflicting legal stories may simultaneously be true.[9] This sort of knowledge helps us

---

9. *See, e.g.*, JAMES CLIFFORD, THE PREDICAMENT OF CULTURE: TWENTIETH CENTURY ETHNOGRAPHY, LITERATURE, AND ART 277-346 (1988) (analyzing in the context of a land claim filed by the Mashpee Native-American group the different meanings attributed to the terms "tribe" and "community" by the Mashpee, local residents, ethnographic experts, and Clifford himself); Kim Lane Scheppele, *Just the Facts, Ma'am: Sexualized Violence, Evidentiary Habits, and the Revision of Truth*, 37 N.Y. L. SCH. L. REV. 123 (1992) (analyzing several common sense notions about truth and lying that operated in the Anita Hill/Clarence Thomas hearings and that arise in cases involving delayed reports by sexual harassment victims).

Also notable in this context is a disturbing essay by Anton Kaes, *Holocaust and the End of History: Postmodern Historiography in Cinema*, *in* PROBING THE LIMITS OF REPRESENTATION: NAZISM AND THE FINAL SOLUTION 206 (Saul Friedlander ed., 1992). Discussing Hans Jürgen Syberberg's film, *Hitler—A Film from Germany* (1978), Kaes analyzes Syberberg's multiple accounts of Hitler (Romantic, aestheticized, dehistoricized) in connection with the rise of Nazism. The danger of these accounts, accord-

guard against deception by others, and by ourselves,[10] and better enables us to distinguish credible from incredible narratives. In criminal law, where lives hang in the balance of a tale, this ability is critical.

Ironically, my effort to pursue the topics of order and disorder in legal storytelling risks the same fate as the film I set out to describe. *The Thin Blue Line* has become a cultural symbol. It is, after all, Morris' story that helped free a man from the corrupt grip of an ugly frameup. But Morris' film is not simply an exposé of injustice. It also confronts the complexity of seeking the truth and the multiplicity of its forms. Like the film, whatever is simple in these pages, or what can be made by popular preference to seem so, will most likely eclipse what is not. Each of us is well equipped to deny complexity, particularly when it threatens to destabilize what we want or need to believe about ourselves, others, and the world around us.

But to beat that temptation I had better get on with my story and tell you more about the event that spawned so many stories, including this one, which is also a story about legal storytelling in criminal cases.

II. The Event: Murder in Dallas

> We still haven't reached any consensus on the specifics of the crime: the number of gunmen, the number of shots . . . the list goes on and on. Beyond this confusion of data, people have developed a sense that history has been secretly manipulated . . . . I think we've developed a much more deeply unsettled feeling about our grip on reality.
>
> Don DeLillo[11]

I begin this way, but it could be otherwise:[12]

On Thanksgiving night, November 25, 1976, Randall Dale Adams and his brother arrived in Dallas, Texas. The two were heading to California from their home in Ohio. Meantime, they took up residence in a Dallas motel. The day after their arrival, Adams landed a job at an abandoned airport near Fort Worth.

On that same day, Friday, November 26, 1976, a month after his sixteenth birthday, David Harris decided to run away from home. That afternoon, he broke into a neighbor's home and stole some money. Later that evening, Harris also stole his neighbor's 1972 blue Mercury Comet. He packed some clothes, a 12-gauge shotgun, and his father's .22-caliber nine-shot pistol. Harris put the

ing to Kaes, lies in their apocalyptic longing, a theme that insulates Syberberg's film from the contamination of (and perhaps the responsibility for) the historical event of Nazism. *Id.* at 222.

10. *See* Ruth Morse, Truth and Convention in the Middle Ages: Rhetoric, Representation and Reality 56-57 (1991) ("The only defense against the manipulation of the listener's emotions was an alert ear trained to discriminate not only good from bad arguments, but successful from unsuccessful ploys. . . . [W]e may pity the speaker, or be seduced by her, but we are meant to think and to resist.").

11. Anthony DeCurtis, *"An Outsider in This Society": An Interview With Don Delillo,* S. Atlantic Q. 281, 286 (1990).

12. I have assembled the following "facts" from a number of sources: Randall Adams, Adams v. Texas (1990); Transcript, *supra* note 7; local newspaper articles about the case; and the entire corpus of legal papers, the trial transcript, and official statements made by Adams, Harris, and Police Officer Turko. *See* notes 20-28 & 34 *infra.*

fully loaded pistol and a plastic box of .22-caliber ammunition underneath the driver's seat of the Comet and then left his hometown of Vidor, Texas.

Harris drove late into the night, finally stopping in the northern outskirts of Houston where, parked in a department store lot, he slept. When he awoke, it was daylight. Harris proceeded to Dallas, arriving sometime Saturday afternoon. It was his first time in the city.

After purchasing brake fluid and gasoline, Harris picked up a hitchhiker. The twenty-eight-year-old man who entered Harris' car, wearing blue jeans and a dark jacket and sporting bushy brown hair and a drooping mustache, was Randall Dale Adams. Adams, whose car had run out of gas, thanked Harris for the lift.

The boy and the man proceeded to find a gas station and returned to fill Adams' car. Adams then drove his car, with Harris following, to the Dallas motel where Adams and his brother were staying.

Adams and Harris went in. Adams' brother was watching TV. Adams changed his shirt and left with Harris in Harris' car. Adams brought some stereo equipment and three 8-track tapes. Harris had some electrician's tools in the car. They drove to several pawn shops in an effort to get money for the things they had with them. Along the way, Harris showed Adams the loaded handgun under the driver's seat. They did not pawn the gun; either Harris told Adams that it was not for sale[13] or he asked Adams to pawn it, and Adams refused.[14]

With the pawn money in hand, Adams and Harris hung out together for the rest of the day and evening. They drove to the airport where Adams worked, smoked some marijuana, drank some beer. They went back to town, to the Bronco Bowl, to have some lunch, some beer, and perhaps to play some pool. After, they went to a store to buy more beer, wandered around a shopping mall, drank the beer. Adams asked Harris if he would like to see a film. They went to a drive-in. *The Swinging Cheerleaders* was playing—soft porn. Maybe Harris chose the film, or maybe Adams did. They drank beer, smoked more pot. The next film, *The Student Body*, came on, and they watched that one too.

Adams wanted to go. It was close to midnight now, or maybe it was only 10:00 p.m. They left the drive-in.

Then, according to Harris:

Adams drives the Comet down Inwood Road. Soon, a police car, lights flashing, appears behind them. Adams pulls over, tells Harris to get down. A policeman approaches the driver. Adams rolls down the window, reaches beneath the seat for the pistol and, as the officer comes up to the car, fires five or six shots. Adams and Harris drive off, returning to the motel. Adams asks Harris if he needs a place to sleep. Harris says he does. Adams goes in to get the okay from his brother. Once Adams is inside, Harris slides behind the wheel and drives off.

According to Adams, it happened like this:

13. *See* Transcript, *supra* note 7, at 67 (statement of David Harris).

14. Adams, *supra* note 12, at 22.

They leave the drive-in and head back to the motel. Adams picks up some cigarettes and a newspaper at the convenience store next to the motel. Maybe Harris asks Adams if he can stay at the motel with him. Maybe Adams says no.[15] Adams says he will see if he can get Harris a job at the place where he works. They arrange to meet on Monday morning. Adams goes in. His brother is asleep with the TV on. It's the end of *The Carol Burnett Show*.

Later, while in police custody, Adams will say in an illegally obtained statement that he drove that evening onto Inwood Road, the site of the murder. Adams will say in the statement that he remembers nothing more until he turned left onto Fort Worth Avenue.

Years later, while on death row for a different murder, David Harris will tell an interviewer that he was alone in the car when Officer Wood was shot and that he held the gun when the five bullets were fired.

III. The Trial: Conviction and Appeal

> Many techniques of the effective advocate . . . involve the undermining of rational argument rather than its promotion: they include techniques for keeping relevant information out, for trapping or confusing witnesses, for "laundering" the facts, for diverting attention or interrupting the flow of argument, and for exploiting means of non-rational persuasion.
>
> William Twining[16]

Initially, the trial sets up a swearing contest: David Harris' word against Randall Dale Adams'. Each accuses the other of the shooting. The Adams defense is fairly confident. Adams has no prior criminal record, and there appear to be no eyewitnesses to the shooting. The slain police officer's partner cannot describe the lone occupant of the car that they stopped that night for driving without headlights. The sole witness against Adams is David Harris, who at sixteen already has a criminal record that includes three burglaries. After returning to Vidor, Harris was also involved in yet another series of crimes, including burglary and armed robbery. And it was Harris himself who led the police to the murder weapon, and to his own arrest.

After the shooting of Officer Wood, Harris had given the pistol to his friend Alvin "Hooty" Nelson. Nelson and his brother Frank say Harris claimed at the time to have shot the Dallas officer, but they figured he was just joking around.[17] Alvin and Frank Nelson's father subsequently found the gun in the house and dumped it in a swamp after his sons told him it had been used to shoot a policeman.

In the meantime, Harris' father reported his gun stolen. Someone else reported to police that David Harris had been bragging about killing a cop in

15. Adams recounts this part of the exchange in his book, *id.* at 25, but his description of these events in the film omits it. *See* Transcript, *supra* note 7, at 13-14.

16. William Twining, Rethinking Evidence: Exploratory Essays 22 (1990).

17. Dennis Johnson and Randy Hayes, classmates of Harris at Vidor High School, also heard Harris' claim that he killed a police officer. They testified for the defense. *See* Adams, *supra* note 12, at 88.

Dallas. The Vidor police visited Harris, and he told them that he gave the gun to the Nelsons. The police then convinced Charles Nelson to take them to the swamp where he dumped the gun.

With this information in hand, the defense feels it has a decent chance of creating a reasonable doubt about Adams' guilt in the minds of the jurors. It is a matter of discrediting Harris and the three polygraph tests reportedly showing that Adams lied when he denied shooting the officer and denied that Harris told the truth when he claimed Adams was responsible. But then the trial took a different turn.

Contrary to defense requests, the trial judge refuses to admit evidence of Harris' prior criminal convictions or of the postshooting offenses then pending in the courts.[18] The Vidor sheriff's office claims it cannot locate any of the Nelsons, so the defense subpoena for their testimony remains unexecuted. Then the prosecution introduces three surprise rebuttal witnesses. Suddenly, there they are in the courtroom, ready to be sworn in.

Each of the new witnesses claims to have been driving by the scene of the murder just as the shooting took place. Each identifies Adams in court as the man who shot Officer Wood. The defense seeks to discredit the alleged eyewitnesses on cross-examination. But Adams' attorneys have nothing with which to impeach their testimony—the District Attorney has unlawfully withheld the witnesses' prior written statements.[19] It is not until the recess before closing arguments that one statement is finally turned over and another is read to the defense over the telephone. According to the written statement, one eyewitness had described the gunman to police as a Mexican or a light-skinned black man. The only possible gunmen, however, were Harris and Adams, both white. The statement received by telephone casts doubt on another eyewitness. Yet when Adams' attorney seeks to confront these two witnesses with their prior inconsistent statements,[20] the trial judge accepts the prosecutor's argument that the statements are consistent and refuses to admit them for impeachment.[21]

The legally admissible evidence is now in: The attorneys' closing arguments end. The jurors leave to deliberate. When they return, they read their verdict: Randall Dale Adams is guilty of capital murder.

The state requests the death sentence. The jury now hears from two psychiatrists, Dr. John Holbrook and Dr. James Grigson, both of whom interviewed

18. *See* Adams v. State, 577 S.W.2d 717, 720-21 (Tex. Crim. App. 1979) (en banc) (upholding the trial court's exclusion of Harris' prior criminal record).

19. *See* Zanders v. State, 480 S.W.2d 708 (Tex. Crim. App. 1972) (holding that it is reversible error to deny defendant the opportunity to inspect prior written statements of a state witness and have such statements present in the appellate record for purposes of showing injury); Gaskin v. State, 172 Tex. Crim. 7, 353 S.W.2d 467 (Tex. Crim. App. 1961) (holding that when a timely request is made, defendant is entitled to use prior written statements by a state witness for cross-examination); *see also* Brady v. Maryland, 373 U.S. 83 (1963) (finding that prosecutorial suppression of evidence favorable to an accused, after a request for such evidence has been made, violates the due process rights of a criminal defendant); United States v. Bagley, 473 U.S. 667 (1985) (defining "materiality" of state-suppressed *Brady* material in terms of whether disclosure would have altered the outcome of the trial).

20. Record at 1162-68, State v. Adams, No. F-77-1286-I (Tex. Crim. App. 1979).

21. *Id.*

Adams in prison. Dr. Grigson, known as "Dr. Death" for his repeat performances in capital sentencing cases, gives his standard testimony: Randall Dale Adams is a killer who, if released into the community, will almost certainly kill again. In a similar vein, Dr. Holbrook tells the jury that Adams is a sociopath, a predator without conscience. The jury has all it needs. Randall Dale Adams is sentenced to death for the murder of Dallas Police Officer Robert Wood.

Several months after sentencing, the defense team files a motion for retrial. They have uncovered evidence indicating that the three alleged eyewitnesses committed perjury in court. But the information comes too late; as a matter of state law, this kind of impeachment evidence must be presented within thirty days after sentencing to warrant a new trial.[22] Adams waits on death row as his appeals continue, moving first through the state judicial system, where he loses,[23] then through the federal system.[24]

On June 25, 1980, three and a half years after Adams' arrest in Dallas, the United States Supreme Court declares unconstitutional the Texas death penalty statute under which Adams was sentenced.[25] The state now has the option of trying Adams for capital murder a second time under a corrected sentencing procedure.[26] Instead, the Dallas District Attorney, the trial judge who presided over Adams' trial, and the Dallas Sheriff petition the Governor for a commutation of Adams' sentence to life imprisonment.[27] On July 11, 1980, the Governor complies.[28] And that proclamation of commutation removes the only legal taint remaining in Adams' case. All the irregularities and potential due process violations at trial have been dismissed. Adams' legal remedies have run out.

---

22. *See* Tex. Code Crim. Proc. Ann. art. 31(a)(1) (West Supp. 1994); *see also* Herrera v. Collins, 113 S. Ct. 853, 860 (1993) (holding that a claim of factual innocence based on newly discovered evidence is not grounds for reversal on collateral review).

23. *Adams*, 577 S.W.2d at 717.

24. Adams v. Texas, 448 U.S. 38 (1980) (reversing the imposition of the death penalty and remanding to the Texas Court of Criminal Appeals).

25. *Id.* at 49-50. The Supreme Court's decision surprised defense attorneys working on the *Adams* case. Interview with Joel Berger, Attorney for Adams' Federal Appeal, in New York, N.Y. (Feb. 12, 1993). It now appears that the *Adams* appeal affected the fate of numerous other prisoners on death row—each of whom had been sentenced under similarly flawed, and thus unconstitutional, state sentencing statutes. *Id.*

26. The sentencing procedure declared unconstitutional had required a prospective juror to state "under oath that the mandatory penalty of death or imprisonment for life [would] not affect his deliberations." Tex. Penal Code § 12.31(b) (Vernon 1974). The statute was amended to eliminate this requirement. Tex. Penal Code § 12.31(b) (Vernon Supp. 1994).

27. Letter from Henry Wade, Criminal District Attorney, Dallas County, Don Metcalfe, Judge, Criminal District No. 2 & Carl Thomas, Sheriff, Dallas County, to Connie Jackson, Chairman, Board of Pardons and Paroles (July 9, 1980) (on file with the *Stanford Law Review*). The Board of Pardons and Paroles proceeded to recommend commutation to the governor. Letter from Connie L. Jackson, Chairman, Ruben M. Torres, Vice Chairman & George C. Killinger, Member, Board of Pardons and Paroles, to Bill Clements, Governor of Texas (July 11, 1980) (on file with the *Stanford Law Review*).

This decision resulted from the bifurcated structure of the trial. In the first phase of a capital trial, the jury determines guilt or innocence. If there is a conviction, the jury must determine the sentence to impose in a second phase. The Supreme Court decision only addressed the sentencing portion of the trial and did not affect the guilty verdict.

28. Proclamation by the Governor of the State of Texas, No. 80-6242 (July 11, 1980) (on file with the *Stanford Law Review*).

And there the story would end, but for a strange and serendipitous event. In the course of making a film about the infamous "Dr. Death," Errol Morris hears the story of an inmate named Randall Dale Adams.[29] Intrigued, he decides to change the focus of his film. The film Morris makes and releases narrates the frameup of Randall Adams. It is this story that ignites the public's attention, but the film also takes up a larger theme. According to Morris, the film is also about the contingency of truth and the manifold ways in which truth may be constructed.[30] It is to this process of meaningmaking that we now turn.

IV. Framing the Frameup—the Detection and the Mystery: Conventions and Complicity

> [The detective] reassures us of an ultimate rationality, "a benevolent and knowable universe," "a world that can be interpreted by human reason, embodied in the superior intellect of the detective." . . .
>
> . . . The detective's skill is precisely the ability to code "seemingly unrelated data into a coherent system of signs, a text identifying the malefactor." . . .
>
> . . . [T]o the degree the crime novel puts the signification process into doubt or even exploits the gap between socially accepted signification and ultimate reality, it subverts the reassurances of the detective novel.
>
> Tony Hilfer[31]

The prosecutors at the trial of Randall Dale Adams told a convincing story about a hitchhiker, a drifter up to no good, who smoked marijuana and drank no mean amount of beer with a sixteen-year-old kid, took the kid to a soft-porn drive-in and then to his motel. They described a guy whose luck ran out late that night when he happened to be seen by five local Texans, including the young David Harris and the slain officer's partner,[32] each of whom either saw Adams shoot Officer Wood or could place him at the scene of the murder. Adams denied his guilt, but there were no witnesses to support his claims at trial.

Now, according to the popular media, and in the minds of many who saw it, *The Thin Blue Line* correctly resolved a murder case.[33] Perhaps it did, and perhaps it didn't. From the point of view of the legal system, of course, it did

29. *See* Lawrence Van Gelder, *Movie Is Its Own Murder Probe*, Chi. Trib., Sept. 1, 1988, at 11J; Press Release by American Playhouse Television, *Errol Morris, 'The Thin Blue Line' Filmmaker, Says Movie has Taken Control of his Life* (1988).

30. Peter Bates, *Truth Not Guaranteed: An Interview with Errol Morris*, 17 Cineaste 16, 17 (1989) (" '*The Thin Blue Line* is a story about how easy it is to deceive ourselves into thinking that we have some privileged access to the truth' " (quoting Morris)); *see also* Gourevitch, *supra* note 8, at 53 (citing Morris' characterization of another of his "miscarriage of justice" films as concerning "how we piece together a picture of the world").

31. Tony Hilfer, The Crime Novel: A Deviant Genre 7 (1990) (footnotes omitted).

32. Officer Turko, the partner, told the jury that from where she was standing at the rear of the car, she thought that the driver had brown bushy hair like Adams'. Transcript, *supra* note 7, at 26 (paraphrasing Randall Adams' account of Turko's statements). That testimony differed significantly from her statement immediately following the shooting but before her "internal review" process with the Dallas police force. *Id.*

33. *See* note 8 *supra* and accompanying text.

just that. The film triggered an official inquiry into the case that culminated in Adams' release from prison[34]—an innocent man scapegoated by a corrupt D.A. and a biased judge. But I believe there is more to it than that. The film tells us a good deal about how people—lawyers, jurors, judges, witnesses, police officers, criminal defendants—typically make sense of guilt and innocence in a criminal case.[35] But it also presents a way of making meaning that we tend to reject. In fact, I believe the film elucidates my contention that our habits of making meaning are so entrenched when it comes to matters like determining guilt or innocence that to oppose them becomes a highly subversive act—assuming that we allow such opposition to register at all.

Before proceeding to that argument, however, a word is due on the different ways in which people "make meaning" in the legal culture.

A. *The Construction of Meaning*

According to recent studies in cognitive and cultural psychology and anthropology, making sense of things involves applying a good deal of everyday cultural knowledge.[36] The way we organize experience—how we interpret what happens around us and arrive at judgments concerning truth and justice—depends on many components of such knowledge. The components of cultural knowledge are the products of numerous influences, including our everyday interactions with family members, neighbors, merchants, colleagues, and professionals. Cultural knowledge also derives from a host of other common experiences, ranging from films, television, theater, and literature, to gossip,

34. In 1988, the year of its release, *The Thin Blue Line* generated sufficient public interest to pressure Dallas authorities into investigating the need for a new trial. After a hearing on the matter, Judge Larry W. Baraka, who succeeded District Judge Don Metcalfe in 1984, recommended granting Adams' motion for a new trial. State v. Adams, No. W-77-1286-I (Nov. 30, 1988) (ruling on motion). Following this recommendation, the Court of Criminal Appeals vacated Adams' conviction and ordered a new trial. *Ex parte* Adams, 768 S.W.2d 281 (Tex. Crim. App. 1989). The court found that: (1) the state illegally suppressed witness Emily Miller's prior inconsistent statement, (2) the prosecutor failed to correct Mrs. Miller's perjured testimony that she had identified Adams in a lineup, and (3) the improper police coaching of Miller and failure to disclose problems with her testimony deprived Adams of a fair trial. *Id.* at 291-92.

Following the reversal of his conviction, Adams said: "Without the facts that came from the movie, no, I wouldn't be here in this courtroom today." David Denby, *The Wrong Man?*, N.Y. MAG., Sept. 5, 1988, at 62, 70 (quoting Adams). Adams' attorney, Randy Schaffer, echoed that sentiment: "No, if Errol had not decided on his own that this story was a story worth telling, Randall Adams would have been buried forever." *Id.* (quoting Schaffer).

35. Errol Morris has said: "The scary part is that our desire to seek the truth is a lot weaker than our desire to tell ourselves what we want to hear, to perpetuate our own beliefs." Bates, *supra* note 30, at 17. Elsewhere, reflecting on what he calls "truth by convenience" and "the enormous gulf between belief and reality," Morris recalls the scene from the film "where a police officer is heard saying about Harris, 'I didn't want him to tell us what he thought; I wanted him to tell us what we knew.' " Alvin Klein, *Film Dissects Murder and Justice*, N.Y. TIMES, Oct. 23, 1988, at 14 (quoting Morris).

36. *See* BRUNER, *supra* note 5, at 11-14; Sherwin, *supra* note 5, at 18, 34-36 & n.69; *see also* RICHARD A. SHWEDER, THINKING THROUGH CULTURES 8 (1991) (noting that "traditions not only obscure but also illuminate"); *cf.* HAYDEN WHITE, TROPICS OF DISCOURSE: ESSAYS IN CULTURAL CRITICISM 1 (1978) ("[W]e never say precisely what we wish to say or mean precisely what we say. Our discourse always tends to slip away from our data towards the structures of consciousness with which we are trying to grasp them . . . .").

newspapers, and other written and "paratextual"[37] sources. These sources of knowledge help construct our understanding of many things, including our own personal, professional, and social identity; how to behave in particular situations; and how we make sense of one another's speech and actions. In the context of the law and legal judgments, the internalized frameworks that we draw upon to organize and interpret events, experiences, and actions are necessary to the most basic acts of separating out the believable from that which is false, incredible, or simply unacceptable.

One example of such an organizing framework is the "schema." This knowledge structure facilitates understanding by generating appropriate inferences. Charles Nuckolls illustrates this process with the following two sentences: "John went to a party. The next morning he woke up with a headache."[38] It is common knowledge that people who go to parties often drink too much and wake up the next morning with a hangover. The point here is that this causal explanation "goes considerably beyond the information given."[39] The schema acts like a familiar story that we carry around in our heads asking for completion. By calling upon such schemata, we infer what should happen next.[40]

A related knowledge structure that enables us to make sense of things is a "script." "Scripts represent knowledge about events that are widely known and shared, like eating in a restaurant and visiting a doctor's office. A script for such events consists, in part, of the ordered sequence of actions, its standard characters and subjects."[41] So, for example, entering a restaurant triggers behavior that follows the appropriate script: being shown a table, receiving a menu, discussing the food, and ordering. A kind of script hierarchy operates here. The master script, "a visit to a restaurant," breaks down further into superordinate actions or "scenes," such as "eating" and "ordering." Each of these actions is taken for granted. It is simply "what everyone does." Indeed, someone who enters a restaurant and fails to behave "restaurant-like" is likely to cause other diners to search for a set of meanings that will explain such deviant behavior.[42] In short, any violation of the commonly known rules governing ordinary speech and social situations demands interpretation. We must make sense of an interference with the script.

Scripts tend to organize information in a particular order or sequence. For example, one study has shown that when people were presented with popular stories with their plot sequences out of order, they would nevertheless recount

37. A "paratext" is an electronic recording produced by technologies that record the images and sounds of persons, places, and events. *See* Ronald K.L. Collins & David M. Skover, *Paratexts,* 44 STAN. L. REV. 509, 510 (1992).

38. Charles W. Nuckolls, *Culture and Causal Thinking: Diagnosis and Prediction in a South Indian Fishing Village,* 19 ETHOS 3, 4 (1991) (discussing theories of knowledge construction).

39. *Id.* at 4-5; *cf.* Nancy Pennington & Reid Hastie, *A Cognitive Theory of Juror Decision Making: The Story Model,* 13 CARDOZO L. REV. 519, 528 (1991) ("A story is plausible to the extent that it corresponds to the decision maker's knowledge about what typically happens in the world and does not contradict that knowledge.").

40. Nuckolls, *supra* note 38, at 5.

41. *Id.* at 9-11 (discussing SCHANK & ABELSON, *supra* note 5, at 36-37).

42. BRUNER, *supra* note 5, at 48.

the stories with the actions shifted toward their proper sequence.[43] In other words, we tend to distort things in the direction of the familiar, with scripts acting as templates toward which we tailor the unfamiliar. Similarly, another study has shown that people have much more trouble determining the proper order of two actions that generally occur in sequence if the actions are presented as temporally distant.[44] This finding suggests that a temporal order is also embedded in our mental representations of events and that temporal memory, like scripts themselves, influences the way we make sense of things.[45]

Other mental representations, aside from schemata and scripts, also help us organize information in such a way as to give it meaning. They include metaphors, stereotypes, narrative genres, and recurrent plot lines. These cultural artifacts enable us to construct and deploy (often without reflection) the knowledge we have about ourselves, others, and the world.[46] An understanding of these epistemological devices is crucial to an appreciation of the power of legal narrative. By studying how knowledge is organized and made operational in specific legal contexts, we can better understand how people make decisions and judgments. For example, an analysis of our common sense knowledge, by helping to discern under what circumstances a particular framework for making meaning is used, and by whom,[47] opens up to critical reflection the means people use to test, evaluate, and negotiate the explanations or accounts they have constructed.[48]

---

43. Nuckolls, *supra* note 38, at 9 (citing Gordon H. Bower, John B. Black & Terrence J. Turner, *Scripts in Memory for Text*, 11 COGNITIVE PSYCHOL. 177 (1979)); *see also* Sherwin, *supra* note 5, at 18 ("[M]uch of the order we perceive is there only because we put it there.").

44. *Id.* at 10 (citing James A. Galambos & Lance J. Ripps, *Memory for Routines*, 21 J. VERBAL LEARNING & VERBAL BEHAV. 260, 277 (1982)); *cf.* NISBETT & ROSS, *supra* note 5, at 23-28, 43-61, 113-37 (discussing perceptual and cognitive deceptions and mistakes); Dorothy Holland & Naomi Quinn, *Cultural Cognition, in* CULTURAL MODELS IN LANGUAGE AND THOUGHT 3, 33 (Dorothy Holland & Naomi Quinn eds., 1987) (discussing "causal chainings" by which people simplify the world into predictable sequences of events).

45. *See* Nuckolls, *supra* note 38, at 9-10; *cf.* TEUN A. VAN DIJK, PREJUDICE IN DISCOURSE 25 (1984) (noting that when people recall a text or event, instead of simply reactivating actual representations of it, they conjure a more general model of the situation from which they will infer what has probably taken place).

46. They may also be described as heuristic processes. *See, e.g.*, John A. Robinson & Linda Hawpe, *Narrative Thinking as a Heuristic Process, in* NARRATIVE PSYCHOLOGY: THE STORIED NATURE OF HUMAN CONDUCT 111 (Theodore R. Sarbin ed., 1986).

47. *See* Jerome Bruner, *The Narrative Construction of Reality*, 18 CRITICAL INQUIRY 1 (1991) (discussing how we organize our experience and memory); Richard A. Shweder & Maria A. Sullivan, *Cultural Psychology: Who Needs It?*, 44 ANN. REV. PSYCHOL. 497, 507-17 (1993) (discussing some processes by which meanings inhere in different contexts).

48. Consider, for example, how film director Lawrence Kasdan uses latent stereotypes from popular culture. In an opening scene from his film *Grand Canyon*, a white male in a late model Lexus sedan chats on his car phone while driving through a poor neighborhood of Los Angeles. Several young black males in a new BMW pass in the other direction. They exchange glances. Minutes later the Lexus begins to lose power. The BMW passes by again, its occupants staring at the Lexus and its driver. The Lexus driver glances nervously back at the BMW. GRAND CANYON (Twentieth Century Fox 1992). Without having presented a single explicit image of violence, Kasdan infuses the scene with a sense of foreboding by triggering images already inside the viewer's mind. In other words, Kasdan manages to tell part of his story, and to provoke the participation of a significant number of viewers, by drawing upon latent stereotypical imagery of contemporary urban violence.

These unspoken inferences represent bits of sociocultural knowledge within the common stock of things people generally know, or think they know, about themselves and the world. One might say that

B. *A Tale of Two Tales*

I propose to test the potential helpfulness of this cognitive and cultural approach to meaningmaking within the legal system by using it in a detailed analysis of both the Adams case and Morris' film about it. This analysis will parallel the two contemporaneous but opposing plot lines that make up Morris' film: the story as told in a classically linear fashion (beginning, development, conclusion) and the provocative yet unresolved nonlinear narrative.

First I will examine the operation of knowledge constructs within the context of a classic linear storyline. This narrative style is perhaps best exemplified by the familiar genre of the detective story wherein the detective-hero, by identifying and combining significant clues, resolves a disturbing mystery.[49] In Morris' film, the audience as detective/juror traces the clues that point to a sinister plot by state officials to frame Randall Dale Adams. The clues fit neatly into a story that ends when the mystery of the frameup is revealed and solved. Once revealed, the plot is obvious and familiar: Lies, corruption, and abuse of power made Adams a scapegoat for a crime that he did not commit.

Next I will examine how knowledge constructs operate within the context of a less familiar, nonlinear (arguably postmodern) form of storytelling. Rather than offering closure, this form leaves a disquieting sense of inadequate resolution and residual mystery.[50] Was Harris the gunman? If he was, is that all there is to the story? What about the loose ends? Where was Adams at the time of the murder? What were the two of them up to that day? Does it take a serendipitous interview with an artful filmmaker to save a prisoner from a life in jail or a death by execution? What if the plotting of chance or fate[51] actually played a larger part in the criminal justice system? Surely such uncontrollability of events and human actions dissipates, in rather short order, the complacent

Kasdan stimulates his viewer to supply the suppressed premise (violence) for the visual enthymeme that the scene creates. *See* ARISTOTLE, ON RHETORIC 31-33 (George A. Kennedy trans., 1991) (describing a similar inferential process triggered by what Aristotle calls the "enthymeme," a syllogism with a suppressed premise); JEROME BRUNER, ACTUAL MINDS, POSSIBLE WORLDS 7 (1986) ("[T]he story is not by itself the model. It is, so to speak, an instantiation of models we carry in our own minds."); *cf.* Amsterdam & Hertz, *supra* note 4, at 86 (describing defense counsel's strategic transformation of juror factfinding into "a Drama with the jury as protagonist").

49. *See* HILFER, *supra* note 31, at 2-4 ("The function of the detective hero is to guarantee the reader's absolution from guilt. This is basic to the genre's form of wish fulfillment . . . . What matters is the detective's revelation, not the murderer's punishment, for in this myth of rationality truth takes priority over justice. (footnote omitted)); *cf.* WALTER J. ONG, ORALITY AND LITERACY 149 (1982) (describing the classic detective story's relentless ascension to an unbearable tension, followed by climactic recognition and release as details fall into place and the mystery is solved).

50. In this sense it emulates the crime novel rather than the classically linear detective story. Again, consider Hilfer: *"[T]he central and defining feature of the crime novel is that in it self and world, guilt and innocence are problematic.* The world of the crime novel is *constituted* by what is problematic in it." HILFER, *supra* note 31, at 2. A crime novel maneuvers its reader into various forms of complicity, managing to subvert the reassurances of the detective novel by "put[ting] the signification process into doubt or even exploit[ing] the gap between socially accepted signification and ultimate reality." *Id.* at 3, 7.

51. *See* WILLIAM CHASE GREENE, MOIRA: FATE, GOOD AND EVIL IN GREEK THOUGHT 8 (1944) (distinguishing fate, the due portion or moral share assigned to a person, from chance, the unforeseeable forces that affect life but have little or no moral quality).

"all's right with the world because truth and justice will out in the end" attitude that the linear story would have us believe.[52]

In short, there are two tales here, and one subverts the other. When framed as a causal-linear documentary and detective story, Morris' film employs conventional wisdom (including schemata, scripts, and stereotypes) about lying, madness, official corruption, local prejudice, and psychological trauma to take us along a straight path of meaning: from mystery (why is this man in jail?) to resolution (because he was framed!). Within this frame, we know that human nature and the world operate according to causal-linear principles.[53] Things make sense, and judgments are not difficult. When the film is framed as a nonlinear composite of symbols, however, we find ourselves in a universe of fate and fortune, circularity and irresolution. The nonlinear story about the murder of Officer Wood suggests that our conventional knowledge about causation and meaning may not be sufficient. It suggests that while the conventional mystery genre often shapes and informs the way lawyers tell their clients' tales, it may not do justice to what is going on in the world. As distasteful as it may be, it suggests that it may not be possible for us to wholly account for truth and justice within a conventional, causally sequenced storyline. Perhaps the mythic narratives of ancient Western (and even some current non-Western) cultures, most notably the classical culture of Sophocles and Aeschylus, with their vast interjaculating array of nonhuman forces, are also (perhaps have always been) shaping our world. If so, coming to grips with disruptive forces like deceit, corruption, and pathology is not enough—not enough if chance and necessity must also be reckoned with when assessing individual accountability.

But if more than one story about Officer Wood's murder is believable, which one do we choose as a matter of law? Surely the legal system, which enforces official decisions about truth and justice with the power of the state, can be expected to resist judgments that take root in shifting standards of style and taste. Little wonder, then, that after vacillating between linear resolution and nonlinear complexity, so many will succumb to the pull of the familiar, the

52. One of only a handful of film reviewers who discerned the complex structure of Morris' film commented:

> "The Thin Blue Line" is more than just a sterling investigative documentary about a miscarriage of justice; in expanding into a uniquely perceptive film about the limits and distortions of perception, "The Thin Blue Line" is one of film's few works of epistemological reach. It's not only a brilliant detective story, but an even more brilliant evocation of the ultimate tension between chaos and order tugging at every atom in the universe.

Jay Carr, *More than a riveting whodunit*, BOSTON GLOBE, Sept. 22, 1988, at 81, 83. Janet Maslin also remarked on the film's complexity: "[E]ach interview invariably creates more questions than it answers. And the more maps, diagrams and key details the director assembles, the more frighteningly the truth slips away." Janet Maslin, *Anatomy of a Murder: A Real-Life Whodunit*, N.Y. TIMES, Aug. 26, 1988, at C6. Errol Morris' comments about the film support this interpretation: "On one level, it's the story of a miscarriage of justice. On another level—at least I like to think of it as such—it's a story about self-delusion and fantasy." David Sterritt, *Film focuses on possible mishandling of criminal case*, CHRISTIAN SCI. MONITOR, Aug. 26, 1988, at 21 (quoting Morris). Elsewhere, Morris hits the note more severely: "Truth isn't guaranteed by style or expression. It isn't guaranteed by anything." Bates, *supra* note 30, at 17.

53. *See, e.g.*, Denby, *supra* note 34, at 62 ("In Morris' film the truth is knowable.").

path of least dissonance, with a preferred sense of resolute justice, or redress, or right outcome. For here we witness the actualization of deep modern beliefs about what justice is and how it gets done in the world. Yet, at the same time, these beliefs operate so deeply that the way they shape our understanding and our practical judgments remains largely hidden from view. Perhaps this is so because we deal here with things that could not be otherwise.[54] The beliefs at stake may be so necessary to a particular culture's or community's collective sense of order and coherence that, like gravity or causality, once they are questioned the universe seams irrevocably disturbed.[55] Perhaps that is why we do not let them be questioned.[56] In law, as elsewhere, radical change rarely comes without resistance.

It is the hypothesis of this essay that familiar mental constructs not only help shape the outcome of criminal cases and predispose us to play out certain scripts, schemata, and stereotypes, but that they also demand those narrative genres that best reflect a preferred sense of truth and justice. I apply this hypothesis to *The Thin Blue Line* precisely because the film enacts but also refutes the classic modern narrative of straight-arrow truth and constant justice. Morris activates this polarity by directly implicating the viewer (as juror) in the frameup of reality. Unlike some of its more distant forebears in classical tragedy, however, *The Thin Blue Line* offers no transcendent resolution. The gods do not intervene when meaning fails.[57] In this respect, the film's existential credentials might appear impeccable. Yet such a comparison misses the mark. It is the existential hero who anchors our faith in the human will to meaning.[58] But here, no such hero can be found.

---

54. Wittgenstein suggests that it may be impossible for humans to escape inherited paradigms:

> [W]hen someone says: "If you follow the *rule*, it *must* be like this," he has not any *clear* concept of what experience would correspond to the opposite.
>
> Or again: he has not any clear concept of what it would be like for it to be otherwise. . . .
>
> . . . What compels us to proceed according to a rule . . . ? What compels us to talk to ourselves in the forms of the languages we have learnt?
>
> For the word "must" surely expresses our inability to depart from *this* concept.

LUDWIG WITTGENSTEIN, REMARKS ON THE FOUNDATIONS OF MATHEMATICS 121e (G.H. von Wright, R. Rhees & G.E.M. Anscombe eds. & G.E.M. Anscombe trans., 1964).

55. *See id.; see also* Dennis Patterson, *The Metaphysics of Legal Formalism*, 77 IOWA L. REV. 741, 761 (1992) (discussing the implausibility of doubting or questioning everything).

56. One may recall here Nietzsche's quip: "[M]an would sooner have the void for his purpose than be void of purpose." FRIEDRICH NIETZSCHE, THE GENEALOGY OF MORALS 299 (Francis Golffing trans., 1956) (1887); *see also* Don Oldenburg, *Typing a Cast of Character*, WASH. POST, July 4, 1988, at D5 (" 'People love to get marching orders . . . . [They] would rather have guiding fictions than ambiguities.' " (quoting Auke Tellegen, professor of psychology at the University of Minnesota)).

57. *The Thin Blue Line* has some precedent in the ancient world. Consider Euripides' *Hecuba*. EURIPEDES, HECUBA (Christopher Collard trans., 1991); *see* MARTHA CRAVEN NUSSBAUM, THE FRAGILITY OF GOODNESS: LUCK AND ETHICS IN GREEK TRAGEDY AND PHILOSOPHY 397, 400 (1986) (discussing Hecuba's contention that no higher moral authority existed beyond human convention: "Deep human agreements (or practices) concerning value are the ultimate authority for moral norms. If 'convention' is wiped out, there is no higher tribunal to which we can appeal.").

58. *E.g.*, FYODOR DOSTOEVSKY, CRIME AND PUNISHMENT (Richard Pevear & Larissa Volokhonsky trans., 1991) (1866); *see* Jean-Paul Sartre, *Existentialism*, *in* A CASEBOOK ON EXISTENTIALISM 275, 288 (William V. Spanos ed., 1966).

No, Morris does not chant with Sartre: God is dead—long live humanity![59] Rather, he moves us closer to the postmodern world of Beckett: We go on, yes, but not because we understand why.[60] In this view, there is no longer a straight path to truth and justice, no longer the autonomous will to meaning. More than one frame for meaning now lies before us, and while surely it is up to us to decide which frame to believe in, the task of choosing which to accept grows increasingly difficult: Standards are clouded, meaning's possibilities proliferate, while human agency itself seems close to dissolution.

In the arena of criminal law, this indeterminacy of meaning can be fatal to judgment. Even the criminal defense attorney, who deliberately sets out to activate uncertainty in order to establish that the state has failed to carry its burden of proving guilt beyond a reasonable doubt, may go too far. For uncertainty, without more, is highly volatile. It is a state that cannot be maintained. Jurors in its grip will seek relief elsewhere, in any respite of meaning, grasping for a way to tolerate the difficult responsibility of deciding whether to acquit or condemn.[61]

Uncertainty alone, under the onerous strictures of the law, will not do. The defense must buttress any uncertainty it induces with something stable, or risk sending the jurors scurrying for any scrap of certainty the prosecution offers. And to be sure, the prosecution will be offering certainty. After all, it is the prosecution's task to provide a smooth and easy ride on the currents of historical truth and legal necessity.[62]

In what follows, I will draw upon the Randall Adams case to support what I have so far only asserted. I believe that the epistemological difficulties that the film presents offer important insights for lawyers and legal scholars. I suggest that the key lies in more self-reflective discernment of the multiple worlds of meaning and mental representations (or structures of knowledge) by which the law plays out: whether through the causal-linear (the realm of historical truth and legal necessity), the rhetorical (the realm of factual probabilities and legal persuasion), or the poetic (the realm of narrative necessity and the willing suspension of disbelief).

---

59. Sartre, *supra* note 58, at 297.

60. *See, e.g.*, SAMUEL BECKETT, *The Unnamable*, *in* THREE NOVELS BY SAMUEL BECKETT 291, 414 (Samuel Beckett trans., 1958) ("[P]erhaps they have carried me to the end of my story . . . I don't know, I'll never know, in the silence you don't know, you must go on, I can't go on, I'll go on."); *see also* Katherine Dieckmann, *Private Eye*, AM. FILM, Jan.-Feb. 1988, at 38 (" 'Why did this happen? The answer is, I don't know. Maybe it happened for no good reason, except that evil things happen to people.' " (quoting Morris)); Mark Singer, *Profiles: Predilections*, NEW YORKER, Feb. 6, 1989, at 38, 46 (" 'One of the things that have always fascinated me about abnormal behavior is that we can't really explain it to our satisfaction. . . . Almost everything I do now in my work is about epistemic concerns: how do we come by certain kinds of knowledge?' " (quoting Morris)).

61. *See* TIGAR, *supra* note 4, at 20.

62. *See id.* at 5-6.

1. *The causal-linear frame: a documentary exposé.*

> [I] did not get my picture of the world by satisfying myself of its correctness; nor do I have it because I am satisfied of its correctness. No: it is the inherited background against which I distinguish between true and false.
>
> Ludwig Wittgenstein[63]

Just because the framework for our beliefs is invisible, that does not mean it is not actively shaping the way we see and understand ourselves, others, and the world around us. So it is with common sense. And so it is with common sense that Errol Morris molds our perception of the official frameup that landed Randall Dale Adams in prison. Morris makes deceit and corruption look simple; each of the characters' motives fits the archetypal plot of a frameup.

Consider first official corruption. Everyone knows that unchecked power breeds corruption and oppression. And everyone knows what oppression looks like. We recognize it in the film's opening image: Randall Adams sitting incommunicado in police custody, a false confession placed before him, the barrel of an officer's revolver held inches from Adams' face. Yes, that's what oppression looks like. And when Adams talks about a nightmare from which he cannot awake,[64] we tend to agree: Yes, that's what oppression must feel like. It's Kafkaesque.[65]

So, too, do we recognize the confident, smiling face of the interviewing officer when he smugly describes the same interrogation scene as a "casual friendly conversation"[66]—yes, this is what one would expect an oppressor to look like. And when the officer can't see through his own bias, but we can, when an accused's protestation of innocence is only taken to signify a lack of conscience, we are persuaded. Adams had it right when he said, "They did not want to believe me."[67]

Everyone knows consistency bespeaks truth, and contradiction lying. What Adams says about his situation is consistent with what we are shown—a gun, a false confession, threats. Thus we are inclined to believe him. In contrast, the police officer's words reflect contradiction: There was nothing friendly about that initial encounter between them. But what can you expect? Oppressors lie. It makes sense. Adams is in the hands of oppressive liars. The frameup has begun.

Knowing what we know so early on in the film, we are not surprised to learn later that the District Attorney got David Harris to lie about the exchange of immunity for his testimony against Adams,[68] or that the D.A. "reminded"

63. LUDWIG WITTGENSTEIN, ON CERTAINTY ¶ 94 (G.E.M. Anscombe & G.H. von Wright eds. & Denis Paul & G.E.M. Anscombe trans., 1969).

64. TRANSCRIPT, *supra* note 7, at 39.

65. Kafkaesque refers to the terrible and absurd power of nameless, inscrutable bureaucracies. *See, e.g.*, FRANZ KAFKA, THE TRIAL 174 (Willa Muir & Edwin Muir trans., 1992) ("A detached observer might sometimes fancy that the whole case had been forgotten .... No one really acquainted with the Court would think such a thing. No document is ever lost, the Court never forgets anything.").

66. TRANSCRIPT, *supra* note 7, at 3 (statement of Officer Gus Rose).

67. *Id.* (statement of Adams).

68. *Id.* at 49.

Harris of the chronology of events leading up to the murder.[69] That's what official corruption is like. And when Adams describes what it's like to be caught up in such a mechanism, that it's like living in a "Hell on Earth"[70]—yes, that's the right image for oppression. That's true. Adams is telling the truth.

Power corrupts, everyone knows that. Now consider greed. Greed, too, corrupts. And like oppression, greed has familiar guises. Consider Mr. Miller, one of the eyewitnesses that got Adams convicted. Mr. Miller was heard to have said that for enough money, he would testify to anything.[71] Yes, that's what a greedy and corrupt person would say. We also discover that Mr. Miller and his wife only decided to testify against Adams after they had already been in police custody following three days of domestic violence. They'd been booked for disorderly conduct and drunkenness. Besides, their cooperation got their daughter out of some robbery charges that could've landed her a life sentence.[72] These folks are indeed the sort who would lie for money. Greed, deceit, corruption: They fit the image and they fit the script.

As does that other eyewitness, Michael Randall. As a black man in Dallas, he knows the score: "The D.A. will put something in your mouth if he wants too. That's why they call it the 'Hall of Justice'—the scales are not balanced. The scales are in the hall and they go up and down."[73] Randall's behavior is consistent with his experience of the world, and his experience has been awash in corruption and deceit. And again, the persuasive image of a quid pro quo. Randall, too, lied to get what was his for the taking—his share of the reward money.

Greed and power corrupt. But there is also madness, which needs no reward. And anyone with eyes in her head could see that Mrs. Miller, the third eyewitness, is mad. She sees crimes happening all around her: "[I]t's always happening to me, everywhere I go, you know. Lots of times there's killings or anything, even around my house."[74] And it's Miller who wants to solve the crime, quicker than the cops.[75] Anyone can recognize such blatant pathology. Even her husband, whom she once had arrested for carrying fantasized drugs in the trunk of his car, said: "[O]h man, she's . . . ."[76] Though he chuckles without finishing the sentence, it's not hard for us to fill in the blank: Yeah, she's crazy.

Almost all the main players in the frameup are before us now, the corrupt officials—from Dallas cops to the District Attorney—as well as the greedy, self-interested, or delusional eyewitnesses. The only characters that remain are

69. *Id.* at 46-47.

70. *See id.* at 53 (Adams describing his mother's first impression of Dallas).

71. *Id.* at 32 (statement of Elba Carr).

72. *Id.* at 40.

73. *Id.* at 49 (statement of Randall).

74. *Id.* at 27 (statement of Mrs. Miller).

75. Mrs. Miller proudly declares, "I'm always trying to decide who's lying, or who killed who before the police do; see if I can beat them." *Id.*

76. *Id.* at 30 (statement of Mr. Miller).

the trial judge and David Harris himself. And common sense, Morris shows, has no trouble placing them in the thick of the plot.

Everyone knows that arbitrary justice is no justice at all. When a person can be sentenced to death simply because he's an unwanted outsider, and his sacrifice will save the neck of a local boy, common sense stirs our outrage. And outrage at local prejudice could hardly find a better catalyst than in the person of Judge Metcalfe.

Metcalfe knows who the good guys are. He's known since childhood, for he's been taught the greatest respect for law enforcement. You see, his dad was a G-man in the days of gangsters like Baby Face Nelson and John Dillinger. Judge Metcalfe has a personal understanding of what it's like to risk life and limb in service to law and order. He learned it from his dad. We are not surprised that he choked up during the D.A.'s summation.[77] We know what side Metcalfe is on.

And who is Randall Dale Adams, anyway? As Metcalfe puts it, he is just a drifter.[78] Not worth blotting the perfect win record of a legendary D.A. Besides, it's a matter of local justice. Consider Metcalfe's response to the United States Supreme Court's reversal of the death sentence he'd imposed: "[I]n Austin, in our State Appeals Court, I was nine [votes] to nothing correct and in Washington I was one to eight incorrect. If you tally all those votes, I come out ten to eight, and yet the case was reversed."[79] For Metcalfe, it's as if the Civil War went the other way. The federal Constitution remains on par with state law. It is what you'd expect of an old boy network: Insiders count more. And when Randall Dale Adams, with his bushy hair and drooping mustache, stops off in Dallas on his way to California, a better outsider would be hard to imagine.

Last but not least, there's David Harris, the local boy from Vidor. Common sense tells us he committed the murder. Morris even gets Harris to say that Adams is innocent. Harris says he's the one who should know. And we believe him. After all, hasn't he been straight with *us*? Hasn't he come clean about the deceitful way that he played into the hands of the authorities in the Adams case?[80] We understand Harris. His behavior makes sense. Everyone knows that a terrible trauma at a tender age can lay down a pattern of aggressive behavior for the rest of one's life. And just look what happened to him when he was a little kid. His older brother drowned in a neighbor's pool when Harris was only three years old. His father, who was supposed to be watching them, never dealt with the guilt. And when a new child took the deceased sibling's place, Harris never could gain his father's acceptance.[81] As Harris says, "There you go."[82] The pattern was laid down. Harris became the kind of

77. *Id.* at 35 (statement of Judge Don Metcalfe).

78. According to Adams' defense attorney, Judge Metcalfe once inquired of someone interested in the case, "Well, what do you care? He's only a drifter." *Id.* at 22 (statement of Edith Jones).

79. *Id.* at 43 (statement of Judge Metcalfe).

80. *See id.* at 46-48.

81. *See id.* at 55.

82. *Id.* at 56 (statement of Harris).

person who would beat up his commanding officer[83] or shoot a cop. Uncontrolled aggression against authority figures. It was like he was acting out his hatred toward his father and then punishing himself by making sure he got caught. It doesn't take Freud. Common sense tells you Harris is the kind of person who would shoot a cop.

It's common sense. In a world of official corruption, greed, cynical self-interest, madness, local prejudice, and profound psychological trauma, these things happen. Innocent outsiders get framed, and local sociopaths go free. It makes sense. Randall Dale Adams should never have been in prison at all. The film sets the record straight. Justice miscarried, but truth will out in the end. The causal-linear metaphysics of common sense triumphs. Morris' exposé allows us to rest easy: Error can be corrected, order can be reimposed, and, above all, our belief in the ultimate triumph of justice can be confirmed.

The persuasive force of Morris' techniques within the documentary frame of the film is strong. We want to believe Adams is innocent; he fits our image of a likely victim of official abuse. Similarly, it is easy for us to distrust the people who participate in the frameup; they fit the script for the corrupt and deceitful. Nevertheless, Morris' linear exposé frame is not without fissures and unanswered questions. Even this narrative, which offers certainty, does not banish doubt. In a film about the different forms of deception, Morris leaves room to realize that certainty often demands self-deception.

Consider, for example, the following factual ambiguities: Two local officials,[84] Officer Turko (the slain officer's partner),[85] David Harris,[86] and Harris' friend Dennis Johnson[87]—all claimed that there were two people in the car when the shooting occurred. And Adams, who conceded that the statement he made while in custody was "basically what I liked,"[88] seems to admit at one point that he was driving when he and Harris drove onto Inwood Road, the scene of the murder.[89] Why did Adams have nothing to say about the period of time after he turned onto Inwood Road until he got back to his motel room ten minutes later? Did he really forget? Was Adams with Harris at the time of the shooting? Why did so many different people say there were two people in the car? In one account, Harris says he and Adams returned to the motel and Adams went in to ask his brother if Harris could stay with them that night. According to Harris, the brother "[didn't] like to do that."[90] So Harris left. In another version offered by Harris, he drove off without waiting for the brother's word.[91]

83. *See id.* at 46.
84. *See id.* at 5 & 10.
85. *Id.* at 26.
86. *Id.* at 11.
87. *Id.* at 9.
88. *Id.* at 14.
89. *Id.* (statement of police official Jackie Johnson).
90. *Id.* at 11.
91. *Id.* at 14 (statement of Harris).

But why didn't Adams' brother confirm Adams' story or at least verify one of Harris' versions of events at the trial?[92] If Harris made it all up, why such detail? The climax of the movie comes when Harris mysteriously proclaims that Adams might only be in jail because "he didn't have no place for somebody to stay that helped him that night . . . . That might be the only, total reason why he's where he's at today."[93] Consider the ambiguity of this statement. It might mean that had Adams' brother agreed to let Harris stay over, the shooting would not have occurred. It might mean that had Harris stayed over, Adams would not have found himself on Inwood Road that night with David Harris. It might mean that there would have been no grudge, no basis to pin the murder on Adams.

But why would Adams drive off at night with David Harris? Perhaps the answer comes in response to a broader question: What was twenty-eight-year-old Adams doing spending the day with sixteen-year-old Harris, drinking and smoking dope, going to a soft-porn drive-in movie? The sexual connotations fit the schema we have for such things, that sort of thing of which Adams' brother disapproved. Why were the car's lights off that night on Inwood Road?[94] Some connection between a tryst that night along a dark road and the shooting of the police officer cannot be ruled out. It may be the sort of thing neither Harris nor Adams would care to own up to. We do not know. But the film invites this sort of speculation and does not resolve it.

So was Randall Dale Adams in the car at the time of the shooting? Even if he did not pull the trigger, was he an accomplice in the murder of Officer Wood? Even within the linear framework of Morris' documentary, these uncertainties remain, defying the reassuring conclusiveness of the genre. Such doubt invites us to confront our desire to be taken in by the metaphysics of linear resolution, our desire to suppress all of the messy and disturbing details. Is it more important to have a simple frameup, with its concomitant certainty about truth and justice, than to wind up with a set of mysteries?

If a certain amount of denial—framing out unpleasant, dissonant details for the sake of a neat and reaffirming ending—attends even the linear exposé frame of the film, it should come as little surprise that the film's nonlinear, antidocumentary frame may be met with denial on an even grander scale. Is it seen at all? Yet, there it is: An acausal theme, presented both discursively and stylistically, pervades this work.

To appreciate Morris' acausal counterplot we must leave the ordered world of the detective for the mystery of the crime novel. We must abandon the causal thinking that has long dominated common sense. But if this antidocumentary frame isn't commonsensical, then what is it? What must one believe in order for Morris' counterplot to make sense? To address this question we must explore the metaphysics of acausality. This analysis will sweep us into Morris' antidocumentary frame.

92. *See id.* at 25.

93. *Id.* at 57 (statement of Harris).

94. *See id.* at 4.

2. *The acausal/nonlinear frame: fateful reversions.*

The heavens themselves, the planets, and this centre
Observe degree, priority, and place,
Take but degree away, untune that string,
And, hark! what discord follows . . .
Force should be right; or rather, right and wrong—
Between whose endless jar justice resides—
Should lose their names, and so should justice too.

William Shakespeare[95]

As a paradigm of how we make sense of social reality, the Adams case draws our attention not only to how we recognize truth and justice, but also to those underlying shared beliefs that allow us to agree upon a particular interpretation or meaning of an event. The discrete mental representations that constitute our social knowledge, our common sense, tell us why Harris is guilty and Adams innocent. A deep belief in the straight path of truth and justice convinces us that the mystery of the Adams frameup has finally been solved.

But the Sherlock Holmes world of linear logic is not the only one that Morris puts before us. He also has us ponder: What if rationality, rather than being a triumphant force in the world, turned out to be the loser? What if chance (coincidence) or fate (necessity) were instead the dominant forces? Then human agency would be greatly diminished, and human responsibility along with it. Things would "just happen" to us.[96] This vision is one of the emplotting threads that runs through *The Thin Blue Line*. It is a vision that leads us into a peculiarly nonlinear, antidocumentary frame.

If Morris had wanted to tell a purely linear tale, he certainly would have proceeded differently. Consider, for example, the film's failure to provide captions identifying who is speaking. Why this blatant defiance of the conventional documentary style? Instead of telling us how to take the words of the speaker in terms of his or her social or legal status, we are left with the words themselves, and perhaps also with the felt need to know the speaker's status in order to know how to take what he or she is saying. This technique of nondisclosure provokes a feeling of disorientation.[97] And this disorientation is only the beginning. Morris goes much further to knock us out of the standard causal-linear cognitive loop.

Consider how fate and chance are introduced early on in the film and maintained discursively throughout. At the very outset we have the classic image of endless possibility in America: Like so many others before them, Randall Ad-

95. William Shakespeare, *Troilus and Cressida*, *in* The Complete Works of William Shakespeare 667, 672 (W.J. Craig ed., 1959).

96. As Odo Marquard notes: "Fateful accidents are the reality of our life, because as human beings we are always 'entangled in stories.'" Odo Marquard, In Defense of the Accidental 120 (Robert M. Wallace trans., 1991) (quoting William Schapp).

97. As Morris attests, "All my interviews are staged for the camera with the same lighting and poses." Bates, *supra* note 30, at 17. This compilation of visual and auditory data in Morris' film has been described as "an apt parallel to the randomness of evidence." Luc Sante, *Murder In the Raw*, Interview, Sept. 1988, at 152, 152.

ams and his brother are making their way across the country.[98] Possibility—or destiny? Destiny—or chance? The main characters in the film, Harris and Adams, play up both the necessity and the fortuity of the circumstances. For example, Adams muses at the beginning: "I'm not in town a half a day and I've got a job. It['s] just . . . everything clicked. It's as if I was meant to be [in Dallas]."[99] Adams' gloss on fate is immediately followed in the film's opening sequence by Harris: "[T]his all started when David was running away from home. And he takes . . . I took a pistol from my dad's, a shotgun . . . . Ended up coming to Dallas."[100] Thus, a strange pattern is set. At times the dominant operative force for both Adams and Harris seems to be fate as necessity; at other times it seems to be fate as chance. But the upshot remains the same: Both Adams and Harris appear to suffer events rather than cause them to happen. Things are simply playing themselves out. As Adams says: "[W]hy did I meet this kid? I don't know. Why did I run out of gas at that time? I don't know. But it happened. It happened."[101]

For Harris, fate is the dominant force in the universe. At one point he states, "Everybody's life's going to take some kind of path regardless of what happens."[102] He seems to be saying that whether his violent behavior was an effort to "get back at [his father] for the way he treated me"[103] or was "nothing but hurting myself,"[104] he had no choice in the matter. It's as if he'd been born into a life predestined to unfold as it did. And it's not just Harris' life that's dominated by fate rather than reason. Harris says, "There's probably been thousands of innocent people convicted and there will probably be thousands more. Why? Who knows."[105]

Who knows? Things just happen. The only problem is that in a universe run by fate, truth or justice may be impossible. Truth requires a reasonable basis for certainty, and justice requires a reasonable basis for assigning responsibility. In their own discursive accounts, Harris and Adams question the possibility of both individual responsibility and certainty.[106] Moreover, the film's stylistic techniques in what I call its nonlinear antidocumentary frame do much to reinforce this theme.

Morris conveys the film's nonlinearity through recurring metaphors of reversion. We keep seeing the endlessly circling red police light; we keep returning to the scene of the shooting—obviously fictional but replayed again and again as if seeing it one more time would tell us something new.[107] The film offers other breaks from representational reality. For example, Morris

98. TRANSCRIPT, *supra* note 7, at 1.
99. *Id.*
100. *Id.*
101. *Id.* at 2.
102. *Id.* at 55.
103. *Id.* (statement of Harris).
104. *Id.*
105. *Id.* at 56.
106. *See, e.g., id.* at 26, 38, 46, 50, 55-57.
107. "[E]ven the causal order does not escape parodic circularity, which is somehow the revenge of the reversible order." JEAN BAUDRILLARD, FATAL STRATEGIES 84 (Jim Fleming ed. & Philip Beitchman & W.G.J. Niesluchowski trans., 1990).

splices in black and white clips of Hollywood detective movies from the 1940s,[108] a Tinseltown landscape of crimesolving offered to illustrate the mental reality that Mrs. Miller inhabited. Or consider the G-man and gangster images offered to convey the trial judge's mental construction of the world. And permeating the film is that reversionary score by composer Philip Glass in which chords melt into one another like floating arabesques in an opium dream.

These pervasive figures of reversion do not tell us anything specific about the events themselves. Rather, they are metaphysical tropes that tell us something about how reality is framed in both life and art. Part of this story, they tell us, is about storytelling itself. The film offers not just one frameup, the causal-linear frameup of Randall Dale Adams, but perpetual, repeat frameups, indifferent to narrative logic and linear time. Sometimes these frames conflict, leading us to wonder: What world are we in? What sense does it make?

In sum, *The Thin Blue Line*, in its antidocumentary, antidetective frame, implicates not just a few deranged or corrupt folks around Dallas, the kind we like to condemn in the service of our own dedication to truth and justice in a causal-linear world. The film implicates all of us in our complacency about how easily we employ ready-made notions of truth and justice to save ourselves from the anxiety and doubt that might otherwise plague our judgments.[109] By exposing some of the epistemological devices that we all use to make meaning out of chaotic life, the film makes it more difficult to laugh contentedly at Mrs. Miller's pathetic inner world of Hollywood gangsters and her delusions about her own ace detective skills. Such laughter is a defense, a way to distance ourselves from other people's seemingly bizarre internal scripts and views of the world. Surely, no ill-conceived constructs filter our view of reality, no odd cultural artifacts interfere with our discernment of who's who and what's what.

Informed by the film's acausal, nonlinear frame, we come to see that the same common sense wisdom that allowed us to solve a mystery now breaks reality into fragments that we cannot neatly reassemble. The discrete elements of the Adams case, each rotating on its own axis of impersonal truth and necessity, may invite too many stories, each of whose meanings are too overdetermined, potent, and varied for any confidence in the overarching order of things to survive. The nonlinear frame leaves us uncertain, mystified. What really happened, and why? What might it mean? Who can we blame?

Faced with radically different ways in which to see and make sense of the world—the causal-logical system of the documentary genre on the one hand,

108. TRANSCRIPT, *supra* note 7, at 27.

109. All of us inherit prejudices; they make judgment possible. *See* Richard A. Shweder, *The Authority of Voice*, 37 N.Y. L. SCH. L. REV. 251, 257 (1992) ("Almost everyone in the academy these days has heard of the continental dictum that it is our prejudices that makes it possible for us to see, which means that in thinking, as in life, if you do not fix a starting point you'll never get started."). Shweder also cites a relevant quip from the literary critic Anatole Broyard: " 'Hang on to your prejudices, they are the only taste you have got.' " *Id.* *See generally* HANS-GEORG GADAMER, TRUTH AND METHOD 270, 276-77 (Joel Weinsheimer & Donald G. Marshall trans., 1989) (1960) ("[P]rejudice certainly does not necessarily mean a false judgment, but part of the idea is that it can have either a positive or a negative value. . . . [T]he prejudices of the individual, far more than his judgments, constitute the historical reality of his being . . . .").

and the acausal-reversionary system of the antidocumentary on the other—we are left to wonder which frame to choose. To be able to ask this question confirms the artistic triumph and social importance of Morris' film. *The Thin Blue Line* is undoubtedly important as an exposé of injustice and official corruption in the Dallas criminal justice system. But on an allegorical level, the film depicts a battle that rages back and forth, moment by moment, across a thin blue line of representational order. It is a battle against chaos, fate, and deception, forces that could easily destroy human agency and make individual responsibility impossible. Metaphorically, the film asks a fundamental and daring question: Who (or what) polices meaning?

It is a daring question that Morris does not quite see through. For in the end, the counterplot does not take hold. Having raised the specter of unaccountability, of the unknowability (or perhaps the untellability) of truth, the film ultimately reverts back into linear certainty and resolution. After all, we know Randall Adams was framed.[110]

By describing the critical storytelling failures that occur within *The Thin Blue Line*, I hope to elucidate important lessons for lawyers and legal scholars about the art of persuasion in legal storytelling. It is, one hopes, a truism to say that law does not operate in a cultural vacuum. Yet strangely enough, few have explored the implications of culture generally, and cultural postmodernity specifically, for law and lawyering. Overcommunication, a surplus of images, a popular culture with more signs than referents,[111] and an increasingly mass-mediated reality are cultural phenomena that lawyers and legal scholars cannot ignore.[112] This is all the more true in light of the salience of media images of

110. Perhaps part of our experience of a reversion to linearity stems from Morris' decision to end the film with a "moment of truth," namely, David Harris' tape-recorded "confession," in which he very nearly admits to shooting Officer Wood. *See* note 127 *infra* and accompanying text; *cf.* ONG, *supra* note 49, at 142-43 (linking climactic linear plotting to literate and typographic cultures).

111. *See, e.g.*, BAUDRILLARD, *supra* note 107, at 52 ("Illusion is not false, for it doesn't use false signs; it uses senseless signs, signs that point nowhere. This is why it deceives and disappoints our demand for meaning, but it does so enchantingly."); JAMES B. TWITCHELL, CARNIVAL CULTURE: THE TRASHING OF TASTE IN AMERICA 51 (1992) ("What characterizes the condition of culture since World War II is . . . that now we have more signs than referrents [sic], more images than meanings that can be attached to them. The machinery of communication often communicates little except itself—signs just refer to each other, creating a 'simulacra' [sic] of reality.").

112. Actually, legal scholars ignore these phenomena more than do practitioners. *See* Philip N. Meyer, *"Desperate for Love": Cinematic Influences Upon a Defendant's Closing Argument to a Jury*, 18 VT. L. REV. 721, 740-45 (1994) (describing criminal defense attorney Jeremiah Donovan's use of cinematic stylizations in litigation). Considering their audience, it may not be surprising that trial practitioners can ill afford not to keep a close eye on the public. As for what the public is eyeing, consider for example June 17, 1994, when most major television networks suspended their prime-time programming to broadcast images of a phalanx of police cars in pursuit of a white Ford Bronco driving down a Los Angeles freeway. Inside the Bronco, football icon O.J. Simpson allegedly sat with a gun to his head. These images captivated the public. *See, e.g.*, Tom Bierbaum, *ABC in Court Beats NBC's Hardcourt*, DAILY VARIETY, June 29, 1994, at 6 (noting that Nielsen ratings generated by one network's coverage of the O.J. Simpson case overshadowed even the ratings for the national basketball championships).

Especially striking in the O.J. Simpson case are the complex interpenetration of media and reality and the near impossibility of telling one apart from the other. Consider again the infamous "chase" scene: It is the media that created the allure of Simpson's initial celebrity; it is the media that established the prototype of the car chase sequence; and it is the media that helped to generate a state of public fascination simply by interrupting the familiar feel of viewers' everyday lives with prolonged, live national news coverage, an event reminiscent of the aftermath of the John F. Kennedy assassination.

the law.[113] As the advertising experts caution: "To be successful today, you must touch base with reality. And the reality that really counts is what's already in the prospect's mind."[114] Likewise, the only reality that counts for a trial lawyer is the one in the jury's mind. And we have a fairly decent idea of what's there—a barrage of television images:[115] quick cuts, multiple-montage, slow dissolve, animation, computer graphics, magnified close-ups, wild angles, rock stars, starving children, catastrophes, Patriot missiles, Nike tennis shoes. Electronic images of the commercial and the political flow together in one puls-

---

See, e.g., Jack Mathews, *The Chase Scene in the Twilight Zone*, NEWSDAY, June 26, 1994, at 4 (describing the Simpson chase scene as "one of the most riveting moments in television since the Kennedy assassination"). Noteworthy as well is the media's notoriously self-referential representation of reality. *See, e.g.*, Noel Holston, *Shockmaster Howard Stern is Not Just Heard, But Seen—on Cable Show*, STAR TRIBUNE, June 21, 1994, at 3E (describing the Simpson chase scene as an "impromptu remake of *The Fugitive*"); Matthews, *supra*, at 4 (comparing the chase scene to Oliver Stone's film *Natural Born Killers*).

More ominously, media image control today has become more pervasive and subtle. For example, was what the public saw on June 17, 1994, really, as most commentators called it, a chase scene? Or was it a neatly orchestrated image of self-restraint deliberately intended by the L.A.P.D. to displace another, starkly contrasting, media image of recent vintage—a group of out-of-control Los Angeles police officers beating Rodney King?

113.

> Almost one-third of all prime time entertainment shows since 1958 have concerned law enforcement and crime, and nearly a third of the characters on prime time television are involved in either the enforcement or violation of the law. In a normal week, the average television viewer sees approximately thirty police officers, seven lawyers, and three judges in prime time, a figure that does not even include the large number of lawyers featured on popular daytime soap operas and syndicated courtroom dramas, such as *Divorce Court, The People's Court*, and *Miller's Court*.

Steven D. Stark, *Perry Mason Meets Sonny Crockett: The History of Lawyers and Police as Television Heroes*, 42 U. MIAMI L. REV. 229, 230-31 (1987) (footnote omitted).

The accumulation of media portrayals of the law has had a similar blurring effect on reality. *Id.* at 231-32 (noting that children have been particularly affected by television's depictions of the legal system, and that, according to a recent poll, 73% of the children surveyed "could not cite any difference between judges depicted on television shows and those in real life"); *see also* TWITCHELL, *supra* note 111, at 238 (observing that the attraction of reality-based television crime shows "depends on blurring the line between street action and street theatre"). Consider the prosecutor's examination of an uneducated and naive defendant, a farmer accused of murdering his brother in the recent documentary *Brother's Keeper*. The prosecutor must test his witness' ability to understand a preconfession waiver of rights: Do you watch television? What do you watch? Perhaps *Hunter, Mayberry RFD?* In this questioning, the sequence of life and art reverses such that, in court, a legal reality follows the televised one. BROTHER'S KEEPER (Orion 1992); *see also* Debra Seagal, *Tales from the Cutting Room Floor: The reality of reality-based television*, HARPER'S MAG., Nov. 1993, at 50 (offering a story analyst's account of how producers of the reality-based cop show *American Detective* molded and embellished real-life videos, using the same formulas as the famous, old cop shows, such as *Dragnet, The Mod Squad*, and *The Rookies*, to fulfill viewers' expectations).

114. AL RIES & JACK TROUT, POSITIONING: THE BATTLE FOR YOUR MIND 5 (1981). The authors suggest that advertising, like any narrative, must fight the overaccumulation of meaningless signs and follow cognitive scripts: "The mind, as a defense against the volume of today's communications, screens and rejects much of the information offered it. In general, the mind accepts only that which matches prior knowledge or experience." *Id.* at 6.

115. Over 95% of households in the country have at least one television set, which "is on more than six hours a day." TWITCHELL, *supra* note 111, at 195. That is the equivalent of a full day per week of watching television. *Id.* In addition, more than 55% of American households are wired for cable, a service that costs viewers a total of over $14 billion each year. *Id.* at 214. And, according to one estimate, Americans own 224 million remote control units for commanding the show. Anthony Ramirez, *When the New Remotes Zap, Everything Listens*, N.Y. TIMES, June 24, 1993, at C2.

ing mosaic.[116] There's no mistaking it: Postmodernism is an everyday si(gh)t(e).[117] And so it is to postmodernism and its relevance to legal storytelling that we shall now turn.

V. Historical Truth and Narrative Necessity: Skeptical and Affirmative Postmodernism for Lawyers

> With all due respect, Justice Brennan's proposed ending to this lawsuit is as unsatisfying as the conclusion of a bad mystery novel: we learn on the last page that the victim has been done in by a suspect heretofore unknown, for reasons unrevealed.
>
> Justice Byron S. White[118]

> There is no inside story; there are only images.
>
> James B. Twitchell[119]

Law and lawyering are inescapably part of postmodern culture. Yet postmodern ideas about the demise of the author and of authority in general,[120] the dissolution of the autonomous, rational subject, the end of linear time and causation, the erasure of difference between truth and error, reality and fiction, and the abandonment of stability to the contingency of truth and justice, seem to have limited appeal and dubious utility for persuasive legal storytelling.[121]

116. *See* Twitchell, *supra* note 111, at 267.

117.

> A central fact about the present seems to me to be that both of these—the perception of reality, and fiction increasingly take on a semifictive character, and thus tend to converge with each other. That is why it is so easy, nowadays, to ignore really terrible things . . . , and almost easier, even, to believe in imagined terrible things and to be blind to really positive ones—in other words, to accept what suits one and to suppress what does not.

Marquard, *supra* note 96, at 80; *see also* Richard A. Lanham, The Electronic Word: Democracy, Technology, and the Arts 5 (1993) (noting that the "textual surface has become permanently bistable" in the sense that "[w]e are always looking first AT and then THROUGH it").

The image-inundated techniques of MTV are beginning to appear in literature as well as television. *See, e.g.*, Mark Leyner, I Smell Esther Williams and Other Stories (1983) (emulating the techniques of MTV by telling a story in staccato, fast-moving image bites); William Grimes, *Providing in Prose the Eerie Voice of Madness*, N.Y. Times, June 15, 1993, at C13 (describing Irish novelist Patrick McCabe's addiction to the television series *Miami Vice* and his "appetite for lurid colors and nonstop action, a sneaking fondness for the cheap thrill, the instant gratification of modern advertising and consumer packaging. He is attuned to the poetry of the advertising slogan. He understands the iconic power of a candy bar wrapper." (reviewing Patrick McCabe, The Butcher Boy (1992)).

118. The quotation is taken from a memo written by Justice White, regarding a recent civil rights case, and discovered among Justice Marshall's papers. David Johnston, *Marshall Papers Reveal Court Behind the Scenes*, N.Y. Times, May 24, 1993, at A10.

119. Twitchell, *supra* note 111, at 236.

120. *See* Pauline Marie Rosenau, Post-Modernism and the Social Sciences: Insights, Inroads and Intrusions 28-32 (1992) (tracing the "death of the author" phenomenon in postmodernism).

121. *See, e.g.*, Daniel A. Farber & Suzanna Sherry, *Telling Stories Out of School: An Essay on Legal Narratives*, 45 Stan. L. Rev. 807, 845 (1993) (asserting that "to the extent that fictional or fictionalized accounts purport to be scholarship, they jeopardize the credibility of legal scholarship"); Daniel A. Farber & Suzanna Sherry, *The 200,000 Cards of Dimitri Yurasov: Further Reflections on Scholarship and Truth*, 46 Stan. L. Rev. 647, 655-60 (1994) (discussing the difficulty of incorporating postmodernist philosophical insights into legal scholarship); *see also* Paul D. Carrington, *Of Law and the River*, 34 J. Legal Educ. 222, 226-28 (1984) (arguing that legal nihilism, as represented by the critical legal studies movement, is inconsistent with the role of law schools in training professionals).

This may be due to the law's natural conservativism, its affinity for stable meanings and clearly delineated rules. Moreover, on the law's field of violence and death,[122] the postmodernist's playful irony and obsessive deconstruction seem misplaced.[123] In law, we are less eager to forgo the aspiration to find shared normative ideals. While intellectuals may view such ideals as illusory universals whose meanings are inherently suspect,[124] within the legal culture it may be that shared ideals are vital. For at stake are the values and beliefs that make stories of guilt and innocence cohere. And these are the stories that make judgment possible.

None of this implies that textual meaning is secure or free from postmodern subversion, or even that such subversion is suspect or wrong. Nor should non-linear, image-steeped meanings be rooted out of the legal culture. Indeed, given the mass mediation of most aspects of life, any expectation that one might rely exclusively upon stable, textual, causal-linear meanings is simply a pipedream. Atextual, nonlinear, image literacy is an inescapable part of contemporary culture and deeply informs the way people make sense of their lives and the world. The question for lawyers and legal scholars, then, is not whether to postmodernize, but rather what kind of postmodernity we shall enact.

Conventional wisdom dictates that although criminal defense lawyers may pursue a variety of different trial tactics, three reliable strategies stand out: "[I]f you've got the facts on your side, argue the facts to the jury. If you've got the law on your side, argue the law to the judge. If you've got neither, confuse the issue with other parties."[125] The first strategy is that of the good historian: Defense counsel reconstructs the past and shows the jurors that the defendant "didn't do it" and must be found innocent. Or she establishes the fact of an-

---

For a recent critical response to Farber and Sherry, see Jane B. Baron, *Resistance to Stories,* 67 S. CAL. L. REV. 255, 256-67 (1994) (criticizing Farber and Sherry for premising their argument on unexamined assumptions about truth, reason, and analysis). For earlier, similarly aligned views, see Alan Hunt, *The Big Fear: Law Confronts Postmodernism,* 35 MCGILL L.J. 507, 514 (1990) (arguing against the false dichotomy between truth and relativism); Allan C. Hutchinson, *Inessentially Speaking (Is There Politics After Postmodernism?),* 89 MICH. L. REV. 1549, 1550 (1991) (noting the anguish and fear that has accompanied postmodernist scholarly assertions about the end of modernism); Joseph William Singer, *The Player and the Cards: Nihilism and Legal Theory,* 94 YALE L.J. 1, 6, 51 (1984) (discussing the charge of nihilism that traditional legal theorists have directed at scholars who question the rational, objective, and apolitical foundation of the legal system).

122. *See* Robert M. Cover, *The Supreme Court, 1982 Term, Foreword:* NOMOS *and Narrative,* 97 HARV. L. REV. 4, 7 (1983).

123. Richard Shweder has noted this possibility, but without fully developing its implications for law:

> Of course, special problems may arise in the study of "lawyering," which do not arise in the study of "sciencing," "philosophizing," or "internationalizing theory." Other things are at stake in legal settings besides simply binding you to a reality. A higher-order goal seems to be operating, which is to bind judges or juries to a reality such that someone gets nailed or someone gets off the hook.

Shweder, *supra* note 109, at 258.

124. *See, e.g.,* BARBARA HERRNSTEIN SMITH, CONTINGENCIES OF VALUE: ALTERNATIVE PERSPECTIVES FOR CRITICAL THEORY 181-83 (1988) (advising wariness toward normative ideals).

125. *Nomination of Clarence Thomas to be Associate Justice of the Supreme Court: Hearings before the Senate Committee on the Judiciary,* 102d Cong., 1st Sess., pt. 4, at 241 (1991) (statement of Senator Heflin).

other's guilt. The defense thus battles the prosecution on the prosecution's own turf: the playing field of historical truth and legal necessity. This is the site of the imperative, linear story frame, for here a particular historical truth mandates a particular legal outcome.

The third strategy of "confusing the issue" is consistent with an acausal, nonlinear frame and often employs postmodern tactics. The defense attempts to attack the prosecutor's history, impeach the credibility of the state's witnesses, and deconstruct the linear narrative that the prosecutor offers, breaking it up until it is transformed into a nonsensical, incredible tale too full of inconsistencies and loose ends to withstand the onslaught of reasonable doubt.[126] Unlike historical narration, the most important time frame for historical deconstruction is the present, not the past. A good historical narrative account is temporally closed off and can simply be accepted. ("Makes sense to me. That must've been the way it happened.") A good deconstruction, by introducing hesitation, emphasizes and dilates the present moment of doubt. ("Hey, wait a minute. First he said it was 10 p.m., then he said midnight. He must be lying.") The believable history is what already happened; the deconstructed history is what happens in the courtroom.

In *The Thin Blue Line*, Morris adopts the first and third defense tactics I have described. With the film's viewer cast as juror, Morris not only deconstructs the state's causal-linear history ("Those witnesses are lying! They didn't see Adams shoot anyone that night."), but he also substitutes a linear, prosecutorial history of his own, pointing to someone else. ("It's Harris, not Adams, who shot Police Officer Wood.") The film's linear plot shows us why the witnesses lied (greed, delusion) and why the frameup was set in motion in the first place (the only suspect old enough to electrocute was Adams). At the film's close, the historical truth of David Harris' guilt is sealed with Harris' own words: Morris: "[W]hat do you think about whether or not he's innocent?" Harris: "I'm sure he is . . . . 'Cause I'm the one that knows."[127]

It is partly due to the strength of Morris' linear plot that his counterplot fails. When I say it fails, I mean that it does not stimulate us sufficiently to question the certainty that the linear plot induces; without such stimulation, the audience is borne along with much the same ease that created the frameup in the first place.[128] Ironically, by simply stranding the viewer in a domain of echoing reversions and uncertainty, the practical effect of the film's nonlinear techniques is to reinforce its linear plot—strengthening our willingness to blame Harris and exonerate the long-suffering Adams. These techniques fail to take us in when they are in plain view as servants of radical subversion. Put differently, the counterplot does not hold our imaginations because its techniques are those of a skeptical, rather than affirmative, postmodernism.

126. *See, e.g.*, Amsterdam & Hertz, *supra* note 4, at 62-63 (describing how a defense summation attempted to subvert the coherence of the prosecution's linear narrative by proffering 10 incommensurable accounts which made the crime in question).

127. TRANSCRIPT, *supra* note 7, at 56.

128. *See* note 110 *supra*.

A. *Skeptical Postmodernism*

As an example of the kind of postmodernism I have in mind here, consider contemporary sociologist Jean Baudrillard's assertion that in the current media age, conventional dialogue has become too slow: "Looking is much faster; it is the medium of the media . . . . Everything must come into play instantaneously. We never communicate. In the to-and-fro of communication, the instantaneity of looking, light and seduction is already lost."[129] In Baudrillard's view, our culture is rapidly slipping from communication with content, into "simulation," what he calls the "ecstasy of the real."[130] According to Baudrillard, this state of ecstasy is a state of empty form; it is reality aesthetically heightened to the point that it is stripped of all meaning and becomes pure seduction. Like pornography. Like fashion. When the ecstatic form absorbs all the energy of its opposite, that which gives it meaning, the result is sheer simulation. The commercial media best embody this absorption.[131]

The cultural vision shared by writers like Baudrillard may be called "skeptical postmodernism."[132] Skeptical postmodernism manifests a cultural preference for contingency, for the surface play of images, for the sensual jolt of unexpected juxtapositions—the flattening out of meaning.[133] In short, the skeptical postmodern denies the possibility of truth, authority, and history. Reality and human agency are viewed as illusory; objective representation is deceptive. Yet without intentionality and causation, or the means with which to reliably narrate human activity, individuals can no longer be held accountable

129. Baudrillard, *supra* note 107, at 8; *see also* Ong, *supra* note 49, at 175-76 (contrasting communicative exchange and the media's "pipeline transfer" of information).

130. Baudrillard, *supra* note 107, at 9.

131. *Id.* at 8-10; *see also* Fredric Jameson, *Diva and French Socialism*, *in* Signatures of the Visible 55, 60 (1990) (remarking on the media's "new gratification in surfaces" as well as their "new ground tone," which inverts high modernism into "a strange new exhilaration").

A scene from Oliver Stone's television program *Wild Palms* exemplifies this ecstatic accumulation of self-referential images. We see a room where a television is on, and on that television (which is on *our* television) we see Oliver Stone playing Oliver Stone being interviewed. He is asked what it is like to have been vindicated in his conspiracy theory of the JFK assassination, now that the unsealed Kennedy papers have undercut the credibility of the Warren report. Here is a conflation of images whose meanings keep circling back on themselves: We watch a television show about a television interview of a filmmaker, who is also the show's producer, discussing his film about JFK, in which he uses both historical film footage of the actual shooting as well as fake footage made to look real. JFK (Warner Bros. 1992). Is this an instance of poetic license or poetic justice?

132. *See* Rosenau, *supra* note 120, at 14-17.

133. While not a necessary component of the skeptical view, the role of chance in human affairs is a recurrent theme of many postmodernist artists because it aptly captures an other-than-rational, not-in-control, "desubjectivized" sense of people and events. *See, e.g.*, Paul Auster, The Music of Chance 1 (1990) ("It was one of those random, accidental encounters that seem to materialize out of thin air—a twig that breaks off in the wind and suddenly lands at your feet."); Michel Foucault, The Archaeology of Knowledge 230-31 (A.M. Sheridan Smith trans., 1972) ("The fundamental notions now imposed upon us are no longer those of consciousness and continuity . . . nor are they those of sign and structure . . . . We must accept the introduction of chance as a category in the production of events."). This fascination with chance events and serendipitous juxtapositions is evident in the music of John Cage, the paintings of Jackson Pollock, the novels of William Burroughs, the films of Robert Altman, as well as in the work of the artists who staged "happenings" at Black Mountain College, to mention only a few. *Cf.* Stephen Holden, *Films From New Directors Taking Literary License*, N.Y. Times, Mar. 19, 1993, at C24 (describing a new theme that pulsed through the 1993 New Directors/New Films series as the lack of control characters have in relation to events).

for having "authored" or caused an event to happen.[134] Consequently, the skeptical postmodern is left only with endless irony and play. It is to the extent that Errol Morris' acausal, nonlinear counterplot in *The Thin Blue Line* embodies such a vision that it fails. Indeed, the counterplot fails in the same way that skeptical postmodernism is likely to fail in law and lawyering generally. In a legal context, the reality that it portrays is aesthetically and psychologically untenable. In matters of life and death, whether it be the execution of the accused or the possibility of his killing again, we instinctively reject the message of skeptical postmodernism. Human traits like prejudice, deceit, greed, abuse of power, and the reality of a deliberate frameup are things we can understand. But mystification, time's circularity, fate, and coincidence defeat the practical demands of human judgment.

In *The Thin Blue Line*, Morris employs bizarre imaging techniques to persuade viewers that Adams was framed. We see the cartoonish cops-and-robbers clip that accompanies Mrs. Miller's account of the Dallas shooting, the Chicago gangster shootout scene that overlays Judge Metcalfe's wistful reflections on law and order and his dad's golden days. These images engage the viewer in an act of deconstruction. We see why the defense case for Adams makes sense: The judge and Mrs. Miller cannot be trusted; police and prosecutorial corruption fueled the state's frameup of Adams.

But now consider the equally obvious and deliberately cartoonish reenactment of the shooting, the chocolate malt flying slo-mo and oozing like blood on the ground,[135] the single-framed revolver flame lighting up the night, the slam of the gun echoing off the butt-littered interrogation room table, the lonely echo of cowboy boots in the early morning hours of Randall Adams' ordeal.[136] Yet these parodic, postmodern, self-conscious images are eventually overwhelmed by the linear detective plot. The viewer resists the invitation to find problems in the film's linear plot. We refuse to entertain the possibility that the purported "documentary" nature of the film is itself merely another dramatic reenactment. We reject the parody and prefer to play it straight.

The counterplot fails both aesthetically and psychologically to make us question our craving for certainty and the ease with which we embrace it. Aesthetically, the causal-linear frame of the detective story is familiar and easy to

134. *See* ROSENAU, *supra* note 120, at 32-33 (discussing the demise of causality and responsibility in skeptical postmodernism).

135. Morris uses this image as a visual trope for deceit; it reminds the viewer of Officer Turko's questionable account of her whereabouts when her partner was shot. According to Turko's testimony, she had exited the squad car and taken up a position right behind the Comet while her partner approached the driver. But some investigating officers speculated that Officer Turko had actually remained inside the squad car drinking her chocolate malt while Officer Wood approached the Comet driver. TRANSCRIPT, *supra* note 7, at 7 (statement of Dale Holt). Morris invokes the latter account by focusing on the malt as it flies out the squad car window—presumably thrown by Officer Turko the moment she heard shots fired. Later in the film, Morris uses the image of Officer Turko drinking a malt to play up the inconsistent accounts of her whereabouts.

136. Morris exaggerates these sounds in the film. Take, for instance, the hallucinated echo of the pen that drops, in slow motion, onto the purportedly fake confession papers that Adams is asked to sign. This is as it would sound in a dream or a nightmare from which, as Adams himself puts it, he could not wake up. TRANSCRIPT, *supra* note 7, at 38-39.

follow; it is built from and produces conventional, contextualized, graspable meanings.[137] In contrast, the counterplot operates within the strange and mystifying domain of the criminal novel.[138] It is a world that appears to be dominated by chance and fate. It is a place where events are difficult, if not impossible, to explain—causal reasoning fails; things just happen. Such a place offers no outcomes, no closure; the only constant is uncertainty.

Such unresolved mystery points to a second ground for the failure of Morris' counterplot—a psychological one. Psychologically, we crave meaning. Meaning lends order and control.[139] Chaos is disorienting and unpleasant, especially in matters of life and death. Decisions of such consequence are no time for epistemological conundrums or aesthetic musings. Thus, once nestled in the sobering frame of a criminal trial, storytelling fictions such as Morris' self-consciously cartoonish images and their playful interference with the linear documentary have a boomerang effect. These caricatures of reality only send us running back to a "truer" reality, the reality that the linear plot alone is able to provide.[140] Faced with untenable disorder on the one hand, and a meaningful drama on the other, there is no choice. There is no meaning in a story in which Adams just happens to meet Harris on the side of a Dallas highway; in which Harris happens to act out the rage of a father's rejection; in which a filmmaker happens to hear a story that culminates in a movie that happens to get a convicted murderer out of prison. Such acausal "happenings" take and leave us nowhere. They conjure a world robbed of personality, motivation, intentionality, and a story robbed of a structure that allows the listener to make sense of human actions and interactions.[141] Such psychological fatality is intolerable to those—judges, jurors, lawyers, victims, suspects, spectators, the media—who face the law's demand for public judgment. Without coherent stories, judgment becomes impossible.[142]

The Thin Blue Line's aesthetic and psychological failures offer a cautionary lesson about the art of persuasive legal storytelling: The law has little use for the kind of skeptical, radically subversive postmodernism that has been featured of late in some legal and much nonlegal scholarship.[143]

---

137. *See* Bruner, *supra* note 47, at 6-20 (describing the elements of successful narrative).

138. *See* note 50 *supra.*

139. *See, e.g.,* BRUNER, *supra* note 48, at 153 ("The transcendent is an unshakable, axiomatic acceptance of 'meaningfulness,' like Descartes' axiom that God will not falsify our perceptions of the world or Einstein's that He will not play dice with us."); FRIEDRICH NIETZSCHE, TWILIGHT OF THE IDOLS, OR, HOW ONE PHILOSOPHIZES WITH A HAMMER, *reprinted in* THE PORTABLE NIETZSCHE 463, 497 (Walter Kaufmann ed., 1954) (1889) ("First principle: any explanation is better than none.").

140. *See* Daniel S. Bailis & Deborah A. Prentice, Biased Assimilation of Fictional and Factual Information 1-3 (June 25, 1993) (unpublished manuscript, on file with the *Stanford Law Review*) (demonstrating that people's prior attitudes have a greater effect on their processing of fictional information than of factual information).

141. *See* BRUNER, *supra* note 48, at 20-21, 27-28 (discussing how story structure enables readers to understand and interpret the text).

142. *See* Pennington & Hastie, *supra* note 39, at 527-28 (discussing how coherence influences jurors' acceptance of a story).

143. *E.g.,* Peter Gabel & Duncan Kennedy, *Roll Over Beethoven,* 36 STAN. L. REV. 1, 23 (1984) ("I want paradox and unconsciousness. Paradox and unconsciousness allow one experientially, existentially, to exist outside of the contradiction-space of separateness and unity."); *see also* BAUDRILLARD,

B. *Affirmative Postmodernism*

The Thin Blue Line, however, offers a second lesson about a form of postmodern legal storytelling that can succeed in practice and that may represent an increasingly popular style of legal persuasion for today's television-bred lawyers and juries. This genre of storytelling may be called "affirmative postmodernism."[144] Affirmative postmodernism employs postmodern storytelling techniques, but unlike its skeptical cousin, it either closes around a coherent meaning or at least points to one.[145] Thus, while it is postmodern in its use of popular cultural images and symbols, it does not employ these images and symbols in an insular or solely self-referential manner.[146] While the affirmative postmodern concedes the demise of the autonomous modern subject, s/he still finds meaning through the distributed self: an identity made up of discrete cultural and social constructs shared by others.[147]

Like skeptical postmodernism, affirmative postmodernism also recognizes the irreducibility of truth and justice to any abstract meta-narrative (e.g., system based on axiomatic principles such as fairness, liberty, or some felicific calculus). But the affirmative postmodern still sees truth and justice as coher-

supra note 107, at 11-13, 74; ROBERT SCHOLES, PROTOCOLS OF READING 56 (1989) (asserting that "[s]ince there is no Truth there is no error either, and all beliefs are equal"); Klaus Scherpe, *Dramatization and Dedramatization of "The End": The Apocalyptic Consciousness of Modernity and Post-Modernity*, CULTURAL CRITIQUE, Winter 1986-1987, at 95 (describing the meaninglessness and hopelessness of the present and the sense of waiting for catastrophe); Pierre Schlag, *Fish v. Zapp: The Case of the Relatively Autonomous Self*, 76 GEO. L.J. 37, 55 (1987) (maintaining that there is no reason to believe in interpretive communities or in the relatively autonomous self); Gianni Vattimo, *Myth and the Destiny of Secularization*, SOC. RES., Summer 1985, at 347, 360 (asserting that "[w]e have to keep on dreaming, while being conscious of the fact that all is a dream").

144. *See* ROSENAU, *supra* note 120, at 14-17.

145. Of course, the image seized upon may not always fit the bill. Recall how the investment firm Merrill Lynch floundered with one of its advertising campaigns, "Bullish on America," after it botched the applicable myth by presenting a herd of bulls, rather than the lone, rugged one who braves the odds and follows his own instinct instead of the herd's. The image of the lone bull provides a better fit with the classic American profile, and the firm ultimately featured it in a subsequent commercial, "A Breed Apart." Oldenburg, *supra* note 56, at D5. For a discussion of another cinematic use of this symbol of individualism, see FRANK MCCONNELL, STORYTELLING AND MYTHMAKING: IMAGES FROM FILM AND LITERATURE 98-100 (1979).

146. That is, an image is not used merely for the quick-fix zap of gratification that characterizes the world of MTV or the image surfing of the remote control.

147. *See* BRUNER, *supra* note 5, at 107-09; ROSENAU, *supra* note 120, at 42-44, 52-61.

While the archetypal modernist discovers the self by systematically cutting off sensory stimulation in search of universal reason within, the archetypal postmodernist takes the reverse course—seeking massive sensory stimulation along superhighways of informational input. *Compare* RENE DESCARTES, MEDITATIONS CONCERNING FIRST PHILOSOPHY 90-91 (Laurence J. Lafleur trans., 1960) (1641) (describing the modern, thinking self that follows from systematic sensory closure) *with* JAY DAVID BOLTER, WRITING SPACE: THE COMPUTER, HYPERTEXT, AND THE HISTORY OF WRITING 213-14 (1991) (describing the destabilized, mutable self that is presented by electronic technology) *and* MARK POSTER, THE MODE OF INFORMATION: POSTSTRUCTURALISM AND SOCIAL CONTEXT 14-15 (1990) (describing how electronic technology alters the modern self). *See generally* ANTHONY SMITH, BOOKS TO BYTES: KNOWLEDGE AND INFORMATION IN THE POSTMODERN ERA 126-27 (1993) ("In passing from analogue signal to digital we seem to be passing also from the objective view of knowledge . . . to the relativistic, endlessly interpretative view of knowledge.").

The dissolution of the modern self appears less threatening when one realizes its cultural and historical contingency. As Walter Ong has shown, oral cultures have always lacked an abstract sense of self. ONG, *supra* note 49, at 54-55 (citing A.B. LURIA, COGNITIVE DEVELOPMENT: ITS CULTURAL AND SOCIAL FOUNDATIONS (Michael Cole ed. & Martin Lopez-Morillas & Lynn Solotaroff trans., 1976)).

ent. Abstraction may give way to particularity, contextuality, multiplicity; judgment may turn toward individual voices and localized accounts.[148] But for the affirmative postmodern such localization and contextualization is not fatal to meaning. In addition, while acknowledging the distortions inherent in representation and linear causation, the affirmative postmodern also finds meaning in the contingency, unpredictability, and spontaneity of concepts like truth and justice.[149] The postmodern subject responds to the demand for judgment with culturally specific pragmatism, drawing meaning from known storytelling genres, familiar social stereotypes, and deeply rooted cultural myths. And like myths—or dreams or film—the meanings affirmative postmodernism narrates also lack classic linear form. Persuasiveness here comes from the sudden power of an isolated phrase or image or type[150] or from novel juxtapositions of familiar mental representations. Such meanings are irreducible to, though they may not be wholly cut off from, traditional forms of deductive and inductive reasoning.[151] Thus, unlike the skeptical postmodern montage of ever-shifting impersonal surfaces, here there is a human depth. In the affirmative postmodern world, internal forces (like motivation and intention) rather than wholly external forces (like chance or fate) can still accout for events and provide a basis for narrative coherence and individual accountability.[152]

---

148. *See* Smith, *supra* note 124, at 183 (explicating the contingency of relativism in terms of a particular systems interacting at "particular time and place"); Gianni Vattimo, The Transparent Society 4-5 (David Webb, trans., 1992) (noting the decisive role of mass media in the birth of postmodern society, which has been accompanied by a giddy proliferation of communication as increasing numbers of subcultures have their say); *see also* Rosenau, *supra* note 120, at 66-67, 82-85 (noting the importance of genealogies, studies of local cultures, ordinary life and ordinary people, and of community-based narratives as substitutes for truth and theory).

149. Rosenau, *supra* note 120, at 32-33, 92-105; *see also* Bolter, *supra* note 147, at 3, 7-9, 31, 35 (correlating modes of human thought and representation with technological developments and noting the shift from print-based linearity, stability, and authority to the unstable, deplotted, and deauthored intertextuality of electronic writing spaces); Smith, *supra* note 124, at 30-32, 43, 54 (noting the constructed and radically contingent nature of value and beliefs); *cf.* Ong, *supra* note 49, at 142-45 (remarking that oral narratives typically do not follow a linear path or strict temporal sequence, but instead mimic the way ordinary memory operates).

150. *See, e.g.*, Ong, *supra* note 49, at 151 (noting that in oral cultures the "type character" serves both to organize a storyline and to manage its nonnarrative elements); *see also* note 163 *infra*.

151. *See, e.g.*, Ernst Cassirer, Language and Myth 18 (Susanne K. Langer trans., 1946) (describing mythological consciousness as "instantaneous, a fleeting, emerging and vanishing mental content, whose objectification and outward discharge produces the image of the 'momentary deity' "). According to Cassirer, the symbols of myth, art, language, and science are not mere figures representing reality but "forces" that produce and posit worlds of their own. *Id.* at 8; *see also* Roland Barthes, Mythologies 109 (Annette Lavers trans., 1972) (describing myth as a type of speech); Yvette Biró, Profane Mythology: The Savage Mind of the Cinema 42-43 (Imre Goldstein trans., 1982) (noting that consciousness contains "a whole gallery of visual images," and that even a fragment or tiny detail can evoke a whole experience, as when hearing a rattling wagon induces seeing the wagon, and vice versa). Following Barthes, Biró states: "[M]yth is defined by the way it makes use of certain messages, social or otherwise. Myth uses material already processed—beliefs, views, concepts already formed—which it then retransmits in its own language." *Id.* at 104-05.

152. Affirmative interpretations of events build on the projected mental scripts from which our common sense of things is constructed. Eliade, for example, identifies the salience of one familiar narrative:

> On the one hand, the reader [of a detective novel] witnesses the exemplary struggle between Good and Evil, between the Hero (=the Detective) and the criminal (the modern incarnation of the Demon). On the other, through an unconscious process of projection and identification, he

To sense the efficacy of an affirmative postmodern account, consider the story told at an actual homicide trial by a criminal defense attorney who framed reasonable doubt within a meaningful myth-based narrative.[153] After having thoroughly deconstructed the linear history of the crime,[154] the defense attorney went on to provide the jury with a meaningful exit from the chaos and unremitting uncertainty that such an attack might leave behind. The proffered exit would lead the jury into a drama of compelling significance—a drama enacted in the real time of trial. Playing upon the deep, persistent cultural myth of the hero called to the difficult task of solving the riddle of the evidence,[155] defense counsel sought to seduce the jury away from the prosecution's straightforward narrative about what happened before trial into the present performance of the heroic courtroom drama.[156] As the defense put it at the end of closing argument:

> So what I'm really asking you to do is to do what I think will probably be one of the hardest things that you have ever been required to do in public, which is to stand up and at some point look over at [the defendant] and while looking at him vote not guilty of charges brought against him. Thank you.[157]

In this contemporaneously enacted drama, the challenge for the jurors, as for the quest hero of the myth, is to resist the temptation to summarily convict—despite the passions the crime may arouse and the sense of justice a conviction may inspire—and to stay true to their heroic and sworn duty to convict only in the absence of reasonable doubt.[158] Notably, this mythic counterframe is mobilized and sustained by unreflective associations to popular cultural images of the heroic quest, images that derive from classical as well as contemporary sources.[159]

This is an example of affirmative postmodern storytelling. The defense employed mythic images that resonated deeply to pull the jury into the dramatic tension of a personal drama that operates according to its own narrative logic and necessity. This differs from conventional lawyerly recourse to text-based

---

> takes part in the mystery and the drama and has the feeling that he is personally involved in a paradigmatic—that is, a dangerous, "heroic"—action.

MIRCEA ELIADE, MYTH AND REALITY 185 (Willard R. Trask trans., 1963); *see also* Amsterdam & Hertz, *supra* note 4, at 112 n.145 (showing how narrative and storytelling serve as basic instruments for understanding and interpreting human experience).

153. This discussion is based on an actual criminal case argued in 1991, in New York City. *See* Amsterdam & Hertz, *supra* note 4, at 55 & n.2.

154. *Id.* at 61-63.

155. *Id.* at 64-65.

156. *Id.* at 58.

157. *Id.* at 65; *see* VICTOR TURNER, THE ANTHROPOLOGY OF PERFORMANCE 101 (1986). Turner highlights the significance of such courtroom performance:

> Most cultural performances belong to culture's "subjunctive" mood. "Subjunctive" is defined by Webster as "that mood of a verb used to express supposition, desire, hypothesis, possibility, etc., rather than to state an actual fact, as the mood of *were,* in if I were you." Ritual, carnival, festival, theatre, film and similar performative genres clearly possess many of these attributes.

Id.; *see also* BRUNER, *supra* note 48, at 26 (noting that the use of the subjunctive mode in discourse "traffic[s] in human possibilities rather than in settled certainties" and thereby tends to "recruit presuppositions" to fill gaps or uncertainties in the narrative).

158. Amsterdam & Hertz, *supra* note 4, at 58, 64-65.

159. *See id.* at 65 & n.23, 108 & n.139.

linear logic.[160] There are no explicit syllogisms or analogies at work here. Instead, seeking to induce the jury to believe that the defendant lacked the requisite intent to murder, the defense challenges the jurors to act out, then and there in the courtroom, the role of quest hero.

In *The Thin Blue Line*, Morris' use of gangster filmstrips and cops-and-robbers clips attempts to create a similar dramatic tension. He draws upon popular images of caricatured reality to communicate the absurdity of the prosecution's case against Randall Adams. Such associative, nonlinear storytelling techniques may be persuasive in the context of law, if they are used in the service of a discrete and coherent storyline. Thus, Morris' postmodern storytelling succeeds when it serves the film's causal-linear plot but fails when it is used in the service of the film's radically subversive, what I have called skeptical postmodern, counterplot. One wonders how the film's destabilizing counterplot might have fared had it tracked a more affirmative postmodern narrative form.

C. *Errol Morris' Revisions Revisited*

Although the more subversive techniques of Morris' film fail to affect the linear storyline of the frameup, one could imagine a different counterplot, one made of the same material but fashioned to fit the affirmative postmodernist frame that I have described above. Imagine the same techniques of the nonlinear counterplot harnessed to reach the opposite outcome—a defense of Harris. Around what tropes or myths would the film's images now curve?

The character trope of the trickster fits Harris well: the playful prankster, the shadowmaster and shapeshifter,[161] always in control, always mocking, especially of those invested with authority (like police officers and documentary filmmakers). The film could easily portray Harris as acting out a drama of almost-confessions for the sake of spiteful playfulness, for the pure thrill of manipulation. With this in mind, consider the following *possible* sequence from Morris' film:

> [Adams:] "The kid scares me. Kid scares me."
> [Cut to Harris, in dirty saffron prison garb. He's smiling, inscrutably.]
> [Harris:] "Everybody's life's going to take some kind of path regardless of what happens . . . ."
> [Morris:] "Is he innocent?"
> [Harris:] "Did you ask him?"
> [Morris:] "Well he's always said he's been innocent."
> [Harris:] "Didn't believe him, huh? Criminals always lie."[162]

160. *See* Sherwin, *supra* note 5, at 17-18 (describing texts invoked to provide mutually acceptable resolutions to conflict).

161. Christopher Vogler describes the shapeshifter as the one who seeks to seduce or entrap the hero. For example, "[t]he wicked Queen in Snow White assume[d] the form of an old crone to trick the hero into eating a poisoned apple." Christopher Vogler, The Writer's Journey: Mythic Structures for Screenwriters and Storytellers 80 (1992).

162. Transcript, *supra* note 7, at 53-56.

Cut to a film clip as Harris speaks: a sequence in which we see an arch trickster, W.C. Fields or perhaps Bugs Bunny, foil the hapless aggressor.[163] Watching from such an affirmative postmodern frame, do we really believe that Harris, the trickster-sociopath,[164] suddenly tells the truth on film but not at trial?[165] Has Harris really seen the light? Has he experienced, as one of his self-serving monologues suggests, self-transformative psychological insight?[166] Might this be remorse? Is this introspective voice Harris' "true" voice, or just another prank?

We could also imagine a retelling in defense of Harris that tracks the prosecution's causal-linear style. This argument might emulate defense lawyer Barry Slotnick's strategy in his successful defense of Bernhard Goetz, the man who shot four black youths who he claimed were about to rob him on a New York subway.[167] The argument, which attempts to discredit the defendant's own incriminating statements, might run something like this:

> Ladies and gentlemen of the jury, you cannot trust this man, speaking to you on tape from prison. In fact, David Harris is his own worst witness. What we know of him establishes that what he says is of questionable reliability. Consider the previous lies; the desperate need to get people's attention; the pitiful show of bravado. It makes sense that he'd try to claim yet another macho, anti-authoritarian act. There was a reason his friends didn't believe him when he bragged about killing the cop: He had a lot of hot air but no guts. Harris would say anything. Even if we were to rely on Harris' account of these events, what do we really know? All of Harris' ambiguous statements care-

163. Compare Joseph Campbell's Nigerian story, recounted by Vogler, of the trickster god Edshu who walks down a road in a hat that's red on one side and blue on the other. Fights ensue between people who traveled on opposite sides of the road about whether the man they passed had been wearing a red or blue hat. The god takes credit for the trouble, saying "[s]preading strife is my greatest joy." *Id.* at 91.

164. Notably, Officer Sam Kittrell remarks on David Harris' trickster quality: "Just anything he could do to make a joke and cut up out there. He was just really having a good time." TRANSCRIPT, *supra* note 7, at 52.

165. Harris' confessions on film could easily be as unreliable as his defense at trial. Morris himself attested to the difficulty of interviewing Harris, recounting that once Harris missed an interview "because he was off killing someone." Eileen Daspin, *The Plot Thickens: Erroll Morris Finds There's a Thin Line Between Art and Obsession,* ROLLING STONE, Aug. 25, 1988, at 23, 23 (quoting Morris). But did Harris tell Morris this? And if so, how does Morris know Harris told the truth? *See* Dieckmann, *supra* note 60, at 38 ("By gradually winning Harris' trust, and by a canny use of reverse psychology, Morris eventually prodded Harris to give a confession that is *The Thin Blue Line*'s chilling denouement . . . .").

166. *See* TRANSCRIPT, *supra* note 7, at 55.

167. In this attempted homicide case, Goetz told police on videotape that he deliberately shot four teenagers who he thought were about to mug him on a New York City subway car. In his account, Goetz stated that after he shot each of the four teenagers once, he walked up to his fourth victim and said, "You seem to be doing alright; here's another." GEORGE P. FLETCHER, A CRIME OF SELF-DEFENSE: BERNHARD GOETZ AND THE LAW ON TRIAL 117 (1988). That statement, carefully released to the public by the prosecutor after the first grand jury's refusal to indict on any offense more serious than illegal gun possession, contributed to a turn in the public mood against the subway gunman. *Id.* at 1, 4-5. For a discussion of other factors contributing to the turn of public opinion against Goetz, see Jimmy Breslin, *The Gunner Grows Smaller as the Facts Mount,* DAILY NEWS (New York), Jan. 3, 1985, at 6.

At Goetz's trial, defense attorney Slotnick sought to show through eyewitness accounts that Goetz fired all the shots in rapid succession, leaving no time for the pause, the inspection, and the infamous, self-condemning words that Goetz (in his mind, ladies and gentlemen, in his mind) thought he had uttered. FLETCHER, *supra,* at 122.

fully stop short of actual confession, and Adams' denial of guilt is obviously self-serving. On what basis can we confidently conclude that Harris rather than Adams committed the crime?

In the face of either the linear or nonlinear counterplot, could we walk away as content in the knowledge that the mystery had been conclusively solved? Is it possible that Harris didn't do it after all? Could it be that our desire for firm resolution is powerful enough to let a film (rather than the Dallas D.A.) create a frameup? Only *this* frameup gives us a different scapegoat. The "young sociopath" David Harris steps in for the "long suffering" Adams. Can we cling heroically to our legal duty, content to convict neither Harris or Adams, as long as a reasonable doubt remains in our minds? Or should we convict both?[168]

Fortunately for us, we need not decide this case one way or the other. My point here is simply this: Set within an affirmative postmodern frame, *The Thin Blue Line*'s counterplot might have induced more uncertainty than its unsuccessful skeptical postmodern frame. For the affirmative postmodern story to work, however, there must be a coherent storyline to cling to. There must be something to make us feel, if not heroic, at least gratified and confident that justice in some form has been done. And it is precisely the demands of that unavoidable judgment that make even an unbelievable truth (Adams'? Harris'? Morris'? mine?) coupled with a believable myth (hero? scapegoat? trickster?) preferable to no coherent story at all.

D. *A Working Hypothesis*

By way of summary, let me offer the following hypothesis: The array of deeply ingrained, culturally inherited, and socially instilled storylines that we carry, often subconsciously, in our heads recapitulate an equally deep sense of how truth and justice operate in the world. We believe truth travels a straight line and deceit curves. We believe justice will out in the end because the law's machinery, once set in motion, ensures that it must, and because the narrative demands of the story promise that it will. Yet we can also tolerate a nonlinear tale, as long as it appears to be serving truth's straightforward ends. Just as we can tolerate the justice in factual ambiguity, in reasonable doubt, as long as we locate it in a tale that lets us feel certain about something—even if it is only the certainty that we are heroic in resisting the temptation to yield to a false certainty.

If people's judgments about truth and justice reproduce deep social, cultural, and psychological frames of meaning, then there are important practical

168. Morris' film omits references to the trips that Harris and Adams made together to Dallas pawnshops. *See* Voluntary Statement of Randall Dale Adams, State v. Adams (No. F-77-1286-I 1979). Perhaps the suggestion that the two shared an interest in thievery, in addition to beer and marijuana, might have tainted the film's well-crafted image of Adams as an innocent scapegoat.

Morris also seems to have played a role in shaping the interviews that went beyond the obvious demands for directorial selection and editing. *See, e.g.*, Dieckmann, *supra* note 60, at 38 (" 'Finally, we get [Adams] to talk, and as soon as he gets to . . . David Harris' name, he stops. . . . And I want him to keep going. I was telling him, "Look, I really believe you're innocent, this is your only chance!" ' " (quoting Morris)).

lessons that attorneys should attend to. For example, we may begin to see that regardless of content, the form of one legal story may give it significantly more credibility than another story whose form fails to trigger any of the applicable tropes, narrative genres, and familiar storylines that are in our minds.[169] More generally, one might say that for a lawyer to persuasively convey an idea, it must be expressed in a way that comports with how the relevant audience typically makes sense of such an idea.

This suggests that the conventional wisdom about successful legal storytelling in criminal cases should be enlarged. The lawyer's goal is not simply to argue the facts and play the good historian for the jury when the facts look good, or to argue the law to the court when the facts may hurt, or to distract the jurors by pointing to another when all else fails. While these are important strategies, attorneys need to pay close attention to the uses of narrative framing. A knowledgeable attorney's deliberate choice of appropriate meaningmaking tools[170] presupposes a familiarity with at least some of the cognitive structures and mental representations—the popular myths, narrative genres, familiar metaphors, schemata, and so on—through which an advocate can persuasively frame particular topics within a given context. While this practical knowledge of the way meanings get triggered involves storytelling skills that may be intuitively grasped and developed by the naturally gifted, they are skills that lawyers can study and reflectively cultivate.[171]

Finally, as a cultural phenomenon, legal storytelling must also keep current with changing culture. The stories that lawyers tell, and the frames within which they tell them, must reflect the changing narrative conventions and meaningmaking structures that resonate with one's audience. In this respect, culturally attuned lawyers probably have an edge over those who are not. But culture comes in a variety of forms. Films such as Spielberg's *E.T.*[172] and Lucas' *Star Wars*[173] stand alongside classical textual sources like the Bible, Homer, and Shakespeare as sources of enduring myths. And the nonlinear plot, reflected by TV image-surfing or MTV montage, must assume its narrative place alongside the causal-linear form. As litigators are increasingly realiz-

169. *See* text accompanying notes 36-48 *supra.*

170. *See* BRUNER, *supra* note 5, at 11 (discussing the "symbolic systems" that individuals use to construct meaning and how deeply entrenched they are in culture and language).

171. Amsterdam & Hertz, *supra* note 4, at 118 (commenting that although they "doubt any lawyer's ability to consciously mobilize all of the linguistic strategies . . . , this is not to say that conscious attention to the nature of these strategies is impractical").

172. E.T. (Universal 1982).

173. STAR WARS (Twentieth Century Fox 1977).

ing,[174] in legal storytelling, as in other cultural narratives, life imitates art, and vice versa.[175] The question to pursue is, how so? What frame when?

Although I have focused on the meaning of one criminal case, the capital murder case against Randall Dale Adams, far more is at stake here. The modernist view, dominant in our culture since the Enlightenment, has taught us to discard rhetoric as mere window dressing, that which obscures reality. This bias against rhetoric distracts us from the rational, scientific rhetoric that champions of the Enlightenment have used so effectively. According to the modernist, correct storytelling proceeds on the basis of a causal-linear frame of meaning. Anything else is fiction, myth, or just plain nonsense. As a result, the sciences have long dominated our legal reasoning and our beliefs about truth. The postmodern age allows us to see that the causal bias of scientific modernism is but one among many rhetorical strategies. In today's complex culture, the challenge has become to articulate the appropriate limits and contexts within which to use the multiple forms of narrative meaningmaking at our disposal.[176] The challenge may be greater than before, but this is, after all, the price to be paid, if we are willing, for the responsible exercise of enhanced freedom in the creation of meaning.

In both mainstream and legal culture, fear and uncertainty have accompanied an awareness of the multiplicity of narrative frames. The temptation is to lock ourselves within a familiar world of parochial meanings. But a world of forced certainty is a dangerous one. As I have attempted to show in the case of Randall Adams, popular local notions of truth and justice may unwittingly coincide with prejudice, deceit, and corruption. Exposing such injustices to popu-

174. For example, consider the video that plaintiff's counsel used as part of the closing argument in a suit against the accounting firm Price Waterhouse. Standard Chartered PLC v. Price Waterhouse, No. 88-34414 (Ariz. Super. Ct. 1988). Dubbed *The Titanic*, the 18-minute documentary-style tape interspersed scenes from a British movie about the sinking of the Titanic, A NIGHT TO REMEMBER (J. Arthur Rank 1958), with information and graphics about how a faulty Price Waterhouse audit of United Bank caused the investment bank Standard Chartered PLC to suffer huge financial losses. The plaintiffs won a stunning $338 million verdict for negligence and an additional $3.8 million for securities fraud. Rorie Sherman, *And Now the Power of Tape: Videos are being used to argue the case and not just demonstrate the "facts,"* NAT'L L.J., Feb. 8, 1993, at 1, 30 (noting that the general counsel of the accounting firm Ernst & Young was so impressed with the video that he held four in-house screenings of it for his legal staff); *see also* Robert F. Seltzer, *Improving Trial Efficiency with Visual Communication*, LEADER'S LEGAL TECH. NEWSL. (Litigation Science Inc., Culver City, Cal.), Sept. 1991, at 2 ("Studies have shown that, after 72 hours, people remember as little as 10 percent of the information presented to them orally, yet they are likely to retain as much as 85 percent of what is presented both orally and visually.").

175. At a recent meeting of the Los Angeles County Lawyers Association, a writer for the television series *L.A. Law* recounted how practicing trial attorneys had emulated some of the characters from the show. His message to the lawyers was, in essence, "Lighten up, folks, it's just a TV show." But one could sense the response: "If it's good enough for the Nielsens, it's good enough for us."

176. Witness the modern/postmodern war over authoritative canons and cultures that has spread from the academy to popular culture. For example, the television miniseries *Wild Palms* passionately reenacts Allan Bloom's defense of the traditional classical or modernist curriculum against the challenges it sustains from those who call for "multiculturalism" and the eradication of "cultural hegemony." *Wild Palms* (ABC television broadcast, May 16-19, 1993). *Compare* ALLAN BLOOM, THE CLOSING OF THE AMERICAN MIND (1987) (urging universities to stop stifling their intellectual freedom with concern over society's problems) *with* STANLEY ARONOWITZ, ROLL OVER BEETHOVEN (1993) (defending the value of contemporary cultural studies in the United States and Great Britain).

lar scrutiny does not guarantee its cure. There is no guarantee, but cautionary steps may be taken. We must learn to discern and guard against the more repugnant forms of narrative manipulation. For ordinarily, only our own prejudices—our ingrained perceptions, understandings, and beliefs—stand between narratives of truth and justice and the exercise of power over the criminal defendant. Sometimes, perhaps, all that stands between such narratives and a person's death is fate. For this reason, we must carefully examine how decisions are being made under the color of law.

VI. Conclusion: Proof and Persuasion in Legal Storytelling

> What has been well called the long conversation of mankind may be growing so cacophonous that ordered thought of any sort, much less the turning of local forms of legal sensibility into reciprocal commentaries, mutually deepening, may become impossible. But however that may be, there is . . . no choice. The primary question, for any cultural institution anywhere . . . is whether human beings are going to continue to be able . . . to imagine principled lives they can practicably lead.
>
> Clifford Geertz[177]

Forces beyond our reckoning and control—forces like chance, fate, or even illusion—seem to have no place in the legal system.[178] For how could we judge in a universe that does not recognize human agency? What could judgment mean in a world without motivation and intentionality, in a world where things just happen? Without order and certainty about the past (historical truth) and the present (narrative necessity) there is no place for us. Fear of human obsolescence and chaos may thus make even the lie a haven.[179] At least there, there is a place to be in, and a place from which judgments can be made.

The ancient Greeks wondered whether it was fate or chance that ruled our lives and dictated justice.[180] Others in the Judeo-Christian tradition have wondered whether the secular order allows for revelatory insights into justice.[181] Or, if prophecy fails, does justice then depend on individual virtue and heroic

177. Clifford Geertz, Local Knowledge: Further Essays in Interpretive Anthropology 234 (1983).

178. *See* Marquard, *supra* note 96, at 80 ("[W]e need a confidence that resists being undermined by . . . experience [of overwhelming, incomprehensible complexity]. If necessary, the guarantees of this confidence are invented . . . in the form of postulates of practical reason.").

179. Caveat deconstructor: In the domain of legal storytelling, a repugnant truth, perhaps even an unbelievable one, is often preferable to none at all. The question is not whether, but *how*, truth can be framed.

180. *See, e.g.*, Aeschylus, Oresteia 3 (David Grene & Wendy Doniger O'Flaherty trans., 1989) (depicting necessary retribution passing from one generation to the next by the messengers of fate, the Furies, until they are tamed by civil law).

181. *See* Robert M. Cover, *The Folktales of Justice: Tales of Jurisdiction*, 14 Cap. U. L. Rev. 179, 183 (1985) (suggesting that "there are sacred narratives of jurisdiction that might constitute the texts to ground judicial commitments"); Richard K. Sherwin, *Law, Violence, and Illiberal Belief*, 78 Geo. L.J. 1785, 1807-11 (1990) (critiquing Cover's argument that law can provide a bridge of redemption, bringing the Messiah); *cf.* Walter Benjamin, *Theses on the Philosophy of History*, *in* Illuminations 255, 264-66 (Hannah Arendt ed. & Harry Zohn trans., 1968) (comparing materialist historiography with conceptions of Messianic time).

imagination? Or is justice simply another futile fiction in a world governed by chance?[182]

Errol Morris' film about the capital murder case of Randall Dale Adams provokes these sorts of musings. By offering us two opposing narrative frameworks for the organization of meaning, the causal-linear detective story and the acausal tale of irresolvable mystery, Morris invites us to see how reality can be fashioned in very different ways. He also depicts the lapses and manipulations that plague each of these framings. In the comforting form of linear narrative, all the clues add up. Its narrative necessity assures us that truth and justice will triumph in the end. Adams is innocent. He was framed. End of story. We want so much for it to be so, that we forget or ignore the details that get in the way. Especially in a case of capital murder, we prefer causality, closure, and factual resolution over the discomfort of unending mystery.

I have argued that this desire for order effectively buries the nonlinear and mystifying aspects of Morris' film. I advocate a far less comforting complexity. The Adams case *should* make us uneasy. To leave unchallenged our belief that "truth and justice will out in the end" ignores the tapestry of interwoven yet opposing frameworks that Morris skillfully invites us to contemplate. As Morris suggests, that tapestry, its acausal threads no less than the causal, is a product of the mind.

Yet in law, unlike in academia or in film, official decisionmakers get to have their meanings enforced by the police. What responsibility must be shouldered, then, for the framing of reality that the law and human judgment often require?

As an important part of our obligations, we must increase our knowledge of cultural and cognitive tools and tendencies—the preconceptions and mental pictures that enable us to frame reality through the legal narratives we use. The Adams "frameup" highlights the need to scrutinize more closely the different ways in which we perceive and assess events and others' actions. It is simply not enough to see and judge. If we are to guard against our unwitting participation in convenient and comforting frameups of reality, we must be better acquainted with the filters through which we see and judge. How do we hear another's story? How do we translate it into terms consonant with our own experience, desires, and preferences? What do we tend to omit or distort in an effort to tell a smoother tale—a tale whose prototype waits in the mind to be triggered?

Lawyers and legal scholars can learn to assess more candidly their own and others' meaningmaking habits. This includes evaluating omissions, inconsistencies, and plotlines that flow from deep (usually hidden) beliefs and assumptions about what truth and justice are and how they operate in the world. These beliefs in turn often stem from subconsciously assimilated story forms, myths, and popular images. If this is so, we need to recognize and assess the effect of these ingrained preferences on how we tell stories as well as on how we hear

182. Consider the way in which David Mamet's film *Homicide* makes the case for empty coincidence rather than order imposed by human agency. HOMICIDE (Triumph 1991).

them, being particularly alert to the exploitation of instinctive preferences for narrative techniques like causal linearity, story closure, and tantalizing scripts and stereotypes.[183]

This heightened sociocultural and psychological knowledge may also enable us to expand our meaningmaking capacities,[184] adding new resources, cognitive tools, and mental representations to the narrative repertoire. For example, we may be able to better appreciate how someone who lives outside the range of our ordinary experience makes sense of a particular situation. Such an enhanced capacity for localized seeing and understanding can also expand our ability to translate from one cultural context to another, perhaps cultivating more widely shared notions of individual dignity and equal justice under law. Without such knowledge, I do not believe we can take adequate responsibility for the judgments we make nor for the concrete consequences that our narratives of truth and justice produce.

If better training in the possibilities of narrative meaningmaking leaves lawyers and judges more sensitive to the multiple forms of legal proof and persuasion, it will also provoke increased critical reflection in the profession upon those forms of proof and persuasion that look like unacceptable manipulation, triggers for judgmental error. Lawyers, judges, scholars, and the lay public may thus more readily recognize unacceptable stereotypes (e.g., Harris as the good old local boy, Adams as just a drifter), false closure based on a denial of uncertainty, and unsupported assumptions about what truth and justice look like.

This cultural and cognitive approach to legal meaningmaking offers no guarantee of certainty. It does, however, alter our impression that meaning is something that we passively receive; rather, we come to see how we all actively construct meaning both culturally and psychologically. Because any frameup of legal reality implicates us all, we must accept greater responsibility for the legal realities we help to establish when we tell or accept one legal story rather than another.

Aristotle reminds us of the enormous creativity and responsibility in the human act of making meaning: Midway between the unintelligible and the commonplace, it is a metaphor which most produces knowledge.[185] Classical or postmodern, it is the metaphor—the mental image, the deeply rooted mythic tale, the resonant story form—by which we take account of others' and our own actions. These judgments, these accounts, may become most truly ours when we knowingly claim them as ours. Yet to do this we must understand the mechanisms by which we judge: What cognitive tools, what stock narratives,

183. *See, e.g.*, Vicki L. Smith, *When Prior Knowledge and Law Collide: Helping Jurors Use the Law*, 17 LAW & HUM. BEHAV. 507, 509 (1993) (describing the conflict between jurors' naive mental representations of crimes and judicial instructions and discussing ways to improve decisional accuracy); *see also* note 46-48 *supra* and accompanying text.

184. We may also learn to live within our epistemological means—identifying what we can know as well as what we may not be able to know with certainty. *See* MARQUARD, *supra* note 96, at 113-14.

185. ARISTOTLE, *supra* note 48, at 244 ("Metaphor most brings about learning; for when Homer calls old age 'stubble,' he creates understanding and knowledge . . . ." (footnote omitted)).

what assumptions about truth and justice make up the legal stories that capture belief?

VII. Epilogue

Although I was continually inspired by his historic achievements, I have perhaps been most personally affected by Justice Marshall as raconteur.

. . .

. . . [Once] he told me about the time he and his mentor, Charles Hamilton Houston, the vice-dean at Howard Law School, traveled to Loudoun County, Virginia, to help a man on trial for his life. The man, George Crawford, had been indicted by an all-white Grand Jury of murdering a white woman from a well-to-do Virginia family, as well as her white maid. Despite their defense challenge to the exclusion of African Americans from the jury, Crawford was convicted of murder by an all-white jury, and sentenced to life. "You know something is wrong with the government's case," Justice Marshall told me, "when a Negro only gets life for murdering a white woman."

After the trial, Justice Marshall said, the media asked if Crawford planned an appeal based on the exclusion of African Americans from the jury. "Crawford said, 'Mr. Houston, if I have another trial, and I got life this time, could they kill me the next time?' Charlie told him yes. So Crawford told Charlie: 'Tell them the defendant rests.' "

Justice Sandra Day O'Connor, Summer 1992[186]

[F]ederal habeas courts sit to ensure that individuals are not imprisoned in violation of the Constitution—not to correct errors of fact.

Chief Justice William Rehnquist, writing for the majority in *Herrera v. Collins*.[187]

Justice O'Connor concurred in the opinion, Winter 1993.[188]

186. Sandra Day O'Connor, *Thurgood Marshall: The Influence of a Raconteur*, 44 Stan. L. Rev. 1217, 1217-20 (1992).

187. 113 S. Ct. 853, 860 (1993) (holding that claims of factual innocence based on newly discovered evidence do not in themselves entitle a prisoner facing execution to have those claims considered by a federal court).

188. *Id.* at 870.

[5]

Speaking of Death: Narratives of Violence in Capital Trials

Austin Sarat

How are violence and pain put into legal discourse? How does law distinguish its violence—capital punishment—from other kinds of violence? Do the strategies used to differentiate legal and extralegal violence alleviate anxiety about law and the uses to which law's violence is put? This article addresses these questions through an analysis of a capital trial in which an African-American man is being retried for the murder of a young white woman. It examines the social and cultural resources used to speak about violence and to differentiate legal and extralegal violence, and it suggests that the juxtaposition of narratives about violence in capital trials arouses rather than alleviates anxiety.

At 8:30 A.M. on 15 July 1977, William Brooks accosted Janine Galloway at gunpoint and forced her to drive to a wooded area behind a neighborhood school. There Brooks raped her and shot her to death. Eventually Brooks was arrested, tried, and convicted of kidnapping, robbery, rape and murder; he received a death sentence and two life terms in prison plus 20 years. On appeal the murder conviction and death sentence were overturned though his other convictions and punishments were unaffected.

In January 1991 I traveled to Madison, Georgia, a small town about 60 miles northeast of Atlanta, to attend the retrial of William Brooks. The sole object of this retrial was to reinstate both his murder conviction and death sentence. This trial provides one vehicle through which to consider the complex relationship of law and violence and one opportunity to observe what Robert Cover (1986b:1601) called the "field of pain

I am grateful for the helpful comments of Robert Burt, Marianne Constable, Lawrence Douglas, Tom Dumm, Joel Handler, and Stephanie Sandler. Address correspondence to Austin Sarat, Department of Law, Jurisprudence and Social Thought, Amherst College, Amherst, MA 01002.

and death" on which law acts. In that trial and others like it, violence is put into discourse, and distinctions between the violence of law and violence outside the law are richly marked. As a result, capital trials, though rare, are enormously important moments in the life of the law (Cover 1986b:1622–23).

Violence, as both a linguistic and physical phenomena, as fact and metaphor (Cornell 1990:1689),[1] is integral to the constitution of modern law (Hobbes 1986; Kelsen 1945; Bobbio 1965; Benjamin 1978). As Cover argues (1986b:1613), "[L]egal interpretation is a practice incomplete without violence. . . . [I]t depends upon the social practice of violence for its efficacy."[2] Modern law is built on representations of aggression, force, and disruption (Sarat & Kearns 1991b), of aggressive acts like the rape and murder of Janine Galloway. And, once built, law traffics in violence every day, using its own force to deter and punish acts it brands illegal. The proximity of law to, and its dependence on, violence raises a nagging question and a persistent doubt about whether law can ever be more than violence or whether law's violence is truly different from and preferable to what lurks beyond its boundaries (see Benjamin 1978; Derrida 1990). To answer that question and to quiet that doubt is for law a continuing necessity. It is achieved, to the extent it is achieved at all, in the representational practices and discursive modes deployed to speak about violence inside and outside law, to distinguish capital punishment from murder in the situated moments—capital trials—when both are spoken about at once.

As pervasive as is the relationship of law and violence (see Held 1989; Minow 1990; Navreson 1991; Wellman 1991), it is, nonetheless, difficult to speak about that relationship or to know precisely what one is talking about when one speaks about law's violence (see Dworkin 1977:15; Sarat & Kearns 1991b:211).[3] This difficulty arises because law is violent in

[1] Cornell (1990:1689) suggests that the violent "foundation" of law is allegorical rather than metaphorical; "the Law of Law is only 'present' in its absolute absence. The 'never has been' of an unrecoverable past is understood as the lack of origin 'presentable' only as allegory. The Law of Law, in other words, is the figure of an initial fragmentation, the loss of the Good. But this allegory is inescapable because the lack of origin is the fundamental truth."

[2] Cover (1986a:818–19) insisted, even at the price of doing linguistic violence, that "the violence . . . [of law] is utterly real—in need of no interpretation, no critic to reveal it—a naive but immediate reality. Take a short trip to your local prison and see." The coercive character of law is central to law, systematic, and quite unlike the "psychoanalytic violence of literature or the metaphorical characterization of literary critics and philosophers." Cover thus invited us to imagine and construct a jurisprudence of violence, and to theorize about law by attending to its pain-imposing, death-dealing acts.

[3] As Ronald Dworkin (1977:15) argues:

> Day in and day out we send people to jail, or take money away from them, or make them do things they do not want to do, under coercion of force, and we justify all this by speaking of such persons as having broken the law or having

many ways—in the ways it uses language and in its representational practices (MacKinnon 1987; Armstrong & Tenenhouse 1989), in the silencing of perspectives and the denial of experience (Minow 1989; Scott 1991:773; de Lauretis 1989), and in its objectifying epistemology (West 1991). It arises from the fact that its linguistic, representational violence (as seen in capital trials) is inseparable from its literal, physical violence (capital punishment). As Peter Fitzpatrick suggests (1991:1; also Wolff 1971b:5):

> In its narrow, perhaps popular sense, violence is equated with unrestrained physical violence. . . . A standard history of the West would connect a decline in violence with an increase in civility. Others would see civility itself as a transformed violence, as a constraining even if not immediately coercive discipline. . . . The dissipation of simple meaning is heightened in recent sensibilities where violence is discerned in the denial of the uniqueness or even existence of the "other". . . . These expansions of the idea of violence import a transcendent ordering—an organizing, shaping force coming to bear on situations from outside of them and essentially unaffected by them.

The difficulty of talking about violence is, however, a difficulty not just for scholars seeking to understand the constitution of modern law. It is, in addition, a continuing problem for law itself. Legal discourse, like all discursive forms, confronts the limits of language and representation when it speaks, as it must in capital trials, about physical violence and physical pain. However, the limits confronted in representing violence would seem, at first glance, to be the opposite of those confronted in representing pain. Violence is visible and vivid. It speaks loudly, arouses indignation, and, as a result, its representation threatens to overwhelm reason. Thus the problem of representing violence would seem to be one of taming and disciplining its representations.

Pain, on the other hand, is invisible. As Elaine Scarry argues (1985:3):

> failed to meet their legal obligations. . . . Even in clear cases . . ., when we are confident that someone had a legal obligation and broke it, we are not able to give a satisfactory account of what that means or why it entitles the state to punish or coerce him. We may feel confident that what we are doing is proper, but until we can identify the principles we are following we cannot be sure they are sufficient. . . . In less clear cases, . . . the pitch of these nagging questions rises, and our responsibility to find answers deepens."

Another version of this difficulty is described by Samuel Weber (1990:2). As he says, "To render impure, literally; to 'touch with' (something foreign, alien), is also to violate. And to violate something is to do violence to it. Inversely, it is difficult to conceive of violence without violation, so much so that the latter might well be a criterion of the former: no violence without violation, hence, no violence without a certain contamination."

> Physical pain has no voice. . . . When one hears about another person's physical pain, the events happening within the interior of that person's body may seem to have the remote character of some deep subterranean fact, belonging to an invisible geography that, however portentous, has no reality because it has not yet manifested itself on the visible surface of the earth.

Pain is, according to Scarry (p. 4),

> [v]aguely alarming yet unreal, laden with consequence yet evaporating before the mind because not available to sensory confirmation, unseeable classes of objects such as subterranean plates, Seyfert galaxies, and the pains occurring in other people's bodies flicker before the mind, then disappear. . . . [Pain] achieves . . . its aversiveness in part by bringing about, even within the radius of several feet, this absolute split between one's sense of one's own reality and the reality of other persons. . . . Whatever pain achieves, it achieves in part through its unsharability, and it ensures this unsharability through its resistance to language.

Yet violence and its linguistic representation is inseparable from pain and its representation. We know its full measure only through the pain it inflicts; the indignation which we experience in the presence of violence is, in large part, a function of our imaginings of the hurt it engenders. In this sense, the problem of putting violence and pain into discourse is one problem rather than two.

It is the business of law in general and capital trials in particular to know violence and pain, and to find the means of overcoming their resistances to language and representation. Scarry herself suggests (1985:10) that the courtroom and the discourse of the trial provide one particularly important site to observe the way violence and pain "enter language." In that discourse the problem of putting violence and pain into language is compounded by the fact that

> it is not immediately apparent in exactly what way the verbal act of expressing pain . . . helps to eliminate the physical fact of the pain. Furthermore, built into the very structure of the case is a dispute about the correspondence between language and material reality: the accuracy of the descriptions of suffering given by the plaintiff's lawyer may be contested by the defendant's lawyer. . . . For the moment it is enough to simply notice that, whatever else is true . . . [a trial] provides a situation that once again requires that the impediments to expressing pain be overcome. Under the pressure of this requirement, the lawyer too, becomes an inventor of language, one who speaks on behalf of another person . . . and attempts to communicate the reality of that person's physical pain to people who are not themselves in pain (the jurors). (Scarry 1985:10; emphasis omitted)

Scarry invites us to consider trials as occasions for lawyers to "invent" languages of violence and pain (for an important examination of these processes see Bumiller 1991). However, Scarry suggests (1985:13) that in law, as elsewhere, the languages which can be invented are quite limited. "As physical pain is monolithically consistent in its assault on language," Scarry writes, "so the verbal strategies for overcoming that assault are very small in number and reappear consistently as one looks at the words of patient, physician, Amnesty worker, lawyer, artist. . . . " Those verbal strategies "revolve [first] around the verbal sign of the weapon." We know violence and pain, in the first instance, through its instrumentalities. Second, we know them through their effects. Here violence and pain are represented in the "wound," that is, "the bodily damage that is pictured as accompanying pain" (p. 15).

As violence and pain are put into language, we may be tempted to forget that their metaphorical representation as weapons and wounds cannot truly capture the meaning of violence and pain themselves (ibid.). And, in the process of putting those things into language, some kinds of violence and pain, those engendered by particular weapons and those which leave visible marks on the body, may be more easily available to us (see Bumiller 1991; Cobb 1992), whereas more diffuse, systemic violence which leaves no visible marks or scars—the violence of racism, poverty, and despair—will be less easily represented and understood as violence and pain. "A great deal is at stake," Scarry herself suggests (p. 6), "in the attempt to invent linguistic structures that will reach and accommodate this area of experience normally so inaccessible to language."

My analysis of the Brooks case focuses on the representation of violence in capital trials and the ways lawyers use linguistic structures to represent different kinds of violence. How does law overcome the resistance of violence and pain to language? How is the direct, physical violence done by William Brooks to Janine Galloway, the violence of kidnapping, rape, and murder, the violence that extinguished a life put into discourse? How is the more diffuse violence that pervaded Brooks's life from childhood onwards known and understood?

But the discourse of capital trials involves more than the representation of violence beyond law's boundaries. In such trials the specter of law's own violence is real and immediate. It too must be put into language, and it must be put into language in a way that reassures us that law's violence is different from and preferable to the violence it is used to punish and deter. As Cover suggests (1986b:1622–23):

> Because in capital punishment the action or deed is extreme and irrevocable, there is pressure placed on the word—the interpretation that establishes the legal justification for the act. At the same time, the fact that capital punishment consti-

> tutes the most plain, the most deliberate, and the most thoughtful manifestation of legal interpretation as violence makes the imposition of the sentence an especially powerful test of the faith and commitment of the interpreters. . . . Capital cases, thus, disclose far more of the structure of judicial interpretation than do other cases. (Footnote and emphasis omitted)

In this article I describe the ways law's own violence is brought into discourse and how, in that discourse, boundaries are constructed between it and the other forms of violence (e.g. murder and abuse) with which it traffics.[4] In capital trials, law seeks to distinguish the killings which it opposes and avenges from the force which expresses its opposition and through which its avenging work is done. In such trials violence of the kind done to Janine Galloway is juxtaposed to the "legitimate force" the state seeks to apply to her killer.

Here I will pay particular attention to the way law's violence is linguistically transformed into such "legitimate force" (Sarat & Kearns 1991b) and distinguished from "the violence that one always deems unjust" (Derrida 1990:927; Friedenberg 1971: 43).[5] In this way law denies the violence of its origins (Derrida 1990:983–84) as well as the continuing disorder engendered by its own violent ordering and peace-making efforts (Wolff 1971b; Waldenfels 1991; Weber 1954; Hay 1975). As Robert Paul Wolff argues (1971b:59), violence is, in the eyes of the law, "*the illegitimate or unauthorized use of force to effect decisions against the will or desire of others*. Thus, murder is an act of violence, but capital punishment by a *legitimate* state is not" (emphasis in original).[6]

In capital trials the violence of law is inscribed in struggles

[4] Some (see, e.g., Camus, 1957) suggest that there is no real difference between capital punishment and murder. Others (Nietzsche, 1956:214–15) note that the law's reliance on violence erodes its capacity to transform or reform those who disobey its commands. "[W]e must not underestimate the extent to which the criminal is prevented, by the very witnessing of the legal process, from regarding his deed as intrinsically evil. He sees the very same actions performed in the service of justice with perfectly clear conscience and general approbation: . . . the cold blooded legal practices of despoiling, insulting, torturing, murdering the victim."

[5] Friedenberg (1971:43) argues: "If by violence one means injurious attacks on persons or destruction of valuable inanimate objects . . . then nearly all the violence done in the world is done by legitimate authority, or at least by the agents of legitimate authority engaged in official business. . . . Yet their actions are not deemed to be violence." Legitimacy is thus one way of charting the boundaries of law's violence. It is also the minimal answer to skeptical questions about the ways law's violence differs from the turmoil and disorder law is allegedly brought into being to conquer (Wolff 1971b).

[6] Friedenberg (1971:43) contends: "The police often slay; but they are seldom socially defined as murderers. Students who block the entrances to buildings or occupy a vacant lot and attempt to build a park in it are defined as not merely being disorderly but violent; the law enforcement officials who gas and club them into submission are perceived as restorers of order, as, indeed, they are of the *status quo ante* which was orderly by definition." As Fitzpatrick (1991:15) puts it, "[T]his association of law with order, security and regularity rapidly became general and obvious, the violence associ-

to put violence into discourse and to control its discursive representation. Here the language of law becomes, at one and the same time, the medium of law's violent expression and of its reassuring restraint. That language seeks to do a double deed. First, it strains to instantiate and vividly portray the violence that exists just beyond law's boundary—the killing of Janine Galloway—that brings pain to the innocent, that merits condemnation. Second, it works to mute other kinds of violence, the violence of racial injustice, poverty, and abuse, as well as the violence of law itself. This is done in the hope of affirming the social value of law, of reassuring citizens that its use of violence is somehow different from and better than illegal violence,[7] of alleviating anxiety about law by identifying a more terrifying other (Dumm 1990),[8] and, in so doing, of overcoming inhibitions against the conscious, willful use of violence and infliction of pain as an instrument of law itself.

In capital trials those two linguistic gestures coexist, but their coexistence is, I argue, an uneasy one. It is uneasy because, in the Brooks trial and others like it, both gestures are replete with racial symbols.[9] The narratives of violence and victimization that appear in capital trials frequently are racially charged (for a similar argument in another context see Bumiller 1991); they chart the boundaries between law and nonlaw along a racial divide of us versus them, order versus disorder, reason against the mob (Peller 1987:28; Butler 1993).

Because Galloway was a young white woman from a respectable Christian family and Brooks was an unemployed, drug-using, young black male, the Brooks trial (re)enacted a familiar story of race and law (Williams 1991; Lawrence 1987; Carter 1988) in which legal violence is authorized as a response to imagined racial savagery (Fitzpatrick 1991; Omolade 1991; Butler 1993).[10] The juxtaposition of the images of Galloway

---

ated with the establishment of law and order assuming insignificance in the immeasurability of the violence and disorder of savagery."

7 As Weisberg argues (1984:385), "The criminal trial is . . . a representational medium that . . . serves as a grammar of social symbols. . . . The criminal trial is a 'miracle play' of government in which we carry out our inarticulate beliefs about crime and criminals within the reassuring formal structure of disinterested due process."

8 As Dumm (1990:54) puts it, "In the face of the law that makes people persons, people need to fear. Yet people also need law to protect them. . . . Hence fear is a political value that is valuable because it is critical of value, a way of establishing difference that enables uncertainty in the face of danger."

9 In addition to my observation of the Brooks trial, I read the trial transcripts of 12 other capital cases that reached the penalty phase. The themes of race, law, and violence that are so vividly exemplified in the Brooks trial are found in most of those other trials as well. One important difference was the quality of Brooks' defense team. In many death penalty cases defendants have inexperienced, underqualified lawyers (see Coyle et al. 1990). Brooks's lawyers, in contrast, were highly regarded death penalty specialists. Throughout this article I refer to the lead counsel as Brooks's lawyer.

10 Fitzpatrick (1991:14–15) argues that in the construction of modern law, "Law and order were constantly combined not just in opposition to but as a means of subdu-

and Brooks told a story of lost innocence and racial danger. Thus even as we are reassured about the legitimacy of law's violence and its difference from violence outside the law, the racialization of that difference arouses other fears which themselves motivate an acceptance, if not a warm embrace, of law's violence as a necessary tool in a struggle between "us" and "them" (Omolade 1991:16).[11]

In this article I use the Brooks trial to examine the representational practices through which violence and pain are put into legal discourse. I examine the explicit and implicit ways law draws distinctions among the various kinds of violence with which it traffics—the violence done to the victim, the violence which allegedly shaped the life of her killer, and the violence of law itself. Throughout, I show the racial content of the different images of violence and pain that appear in the Brooks case, and illustrate how race provides a way of interpreting the relationship of law and violence.

I. Putting Violence into Discourse in the Trial of William Brooks: The Life and Death of Janine Galloway

An Innocent Life: Racial Purity and the Attack on Innocence

Perhaps not surprisingly, the Brooks trial revealed few details about the life of the victim, Janine Galloway. She, after all, was not on trial. At the center of the first, or guilt, phase of the trial was, instead, a narrative about the lawless violence that Brooks perpetrated and that Galloway endured. Indeed as the trial unfolded, Janine's white, female body and the attack on it became a symbol for what the prosecutor called "the body of mankind." The violence unleashed against her body was, at the same time, unleashed against a body that was not her own, the disembodied body of "everyone." Her death became a trope in a Hobbesian tale of anomic violence against a supposedly universal body (Hobbes 1986).

Yet the displacement of Janine and her life story could not be and was not complete. That story was the story of a special

ing the 'disordered and riotous' savages in their state of lawless 'anarchy'. . . . [T]his association of law with order, security and regularity rapidly became general and obvious, the violence associated with the establishment of law and order assuming insignificance in the immeasurability of the violence and disorder of savagery."

According to Omolade (1991:6), "For the West, the mythic power of skin color determines good and evil, guilt and innocence, ignorance and knowledge in the real lives of black and white people."

11 Here, of course, the first trial of the police officers who beat Rodney King provides a vivid example of the way law's violence is portrayed as an acceptable tool in a racial struggle. See Dumm 1993; also Williams 1992.

life, a life of innocence, purity, and virtue.[12] Throughout the trial it was the innocence of Janine's body that provided the context for the discursive representation of the violence and pain which she suffered. Her innocence became the true measure of her worth and of the horror of her body's violation. It was the white, good Janine who was slain by the black, evil Brooks; it was good assaulted and sullied by evil. Although the prosecutor denied the significance of race ("This isn't black versus white . . ."), the imagery on which he consistently relied was a racial imagery.[13] Sometimes the imagery was overt, as in his repeated references to the fact that Brooks had led his life in "dark places"; sometimes it was more indirect, as in the contrast between those, like Janine, who embrace the "American way, play by the rules, and work hard" and those, like Brooks, who are "mean and lazy." For the prosecutor, and he hoped for the jury, the trial was an opportunity to vindicate, if not restore, Janine's fallen innocence, to assert the value of white life against the devaluing acts of black men (for similar arguments in other contexts see Carter 1988; Omolade 1991:16). As Brooks's defense lawyer said to me in an interview after the case was completed, "It was a classic sort of race case with the young white woman, a virgin according to the newspapers, who was taken from her home by a black man. Your classic southern death penalty case is the rape of a white woman by a young, black man."

The image of Janine's innocence and of the value of her white life was constructed by calling attention to particular facets of her life and emphasizing certain of her attributes, the first of which involved her place as the "child" in a loving family, the second her virginity. In 1977, she was a 23-year-old piano teacher at a local music store and engaged to be married to Harold "Bob" Murray, though she still lived at home with her parents, Earl and Heddie. On the day of Janine's death, Heddie, who worked for an optometrist, was home on vacation. Janine went out the door at 8:30 A.M. to meet her friend, Ann Overton, for breakfast. As Heddie put it in her testimony:

H: Janine went out to the carport. I was beginning to relax after breakfast, and I put the chain on the door because I was alone in the house. I looked out the window and saw Janine's car with the door to the driver's side open. . . .

Q: At that time did you see anyone?

[12] Unlike the rape trial that Bumiller (1990) described, in the Brooks trial the defense did not contest or call into question the victim's innocence.

[13] "The law in its majestic neutrality takes no official note of the race of the victim. . . . Yet our public insistence that race be divorced from debate over crime does not match the activities of our institutions. At the level of private fears, private categorizations, the link between race and crime is an intimate one." See Carter 1988:440.

H: No. I didn't see anyone. I opened the kitchen door and went outside. I called to her, but no one answered. So I went back into the house to see if she was there. And then I walked back out to the carport. That's when I heard her say 'I'm in here.' Her voice came from the utility room.
Q: Where is this?
H: The utility room is just off to the left of the kitchen door. I heard a voice say "I'm in here." And I said, "What are you doing in there?" She said, "I'm just looking for something." She said, "Go back in the house. When I find what I'm looking for I'll let you know." So I went in the house and called my neighbor. I knew something was wrong, but nobody answered. Then I went outside again. The door to the utility room was closed. I started to go back in the house again and the phone rang. I picked it up and it was Ann Overton wanting to know where Janine was and whether she was coming to breakfast. I told her that someone had her in the utility room and I said she should come over here fast. As soon as we hung up I tried my neighbor again. Then I heard the car start up and I ran to the door.
Q: What did you see?
H: I saw her in her car with a black man on the passenger side. I'd never seen him before. I looked inside the car and I got very close to it. She began to back down the driveway. I walked along as she backed out, and I kept my eyes on him. I called out to her to "Please wait." "No," she said, "I'll be back. Don't worry."

There is something nightmarish and terrifying in this testimony of the mother's witnessing of Janine's kidnapping and her excruciating inability to stop it. Both prefigure and foretell the murder to come. It is as if the violence done to Janine was already present, symbolically displaced, and expressed in Heddie's disbelief of Janine's reassurances. Heddie is here depicted as if in a terrible dream in which she is forced to look at the living corpse of her daughter.

In Heddie's testimony race makes a prominent appearance. What is noticed and recounted is the race of the man in the car next to Janine. The danger that first appears as a disruption of domestic routine is thus a racial danger. At an early stage in the trial, in the voice of the victim's mother, a portrait of the violence on the other side of law's boundary and of its association with race begins to emerge.

Lawless violence invades the unworried, safe space of home

and family. Yet that space is a bit less unworried than it might first appear. Even where there has been, as yet, no invasion, the specter of violence is already present. Mrs. Galloway's testimony contained a stark reminder of our collective anxieties about violence. She was herself sufficiently aware of its possibility and its presence that she chained the door to protect herself. Hers was a diffuse anxiety about the particular vulnerability of the woman alone. Her response was to lock the world out so she could "relax."

In addition, the awareness of and anxiety about criminal violence was sufficiently part of Janine's life that, according to the testimony of her fiance, she "went to seminars about what to do if you are raped." For Janine lawless violence could not be locked out; hers was a life in which neither law nor locks could provide security or certainty. Yet in her world of innocence, preparation to meet such lawless violence seemed to some to be nearly incomprehensible. As Bob Murray, her fiance, explained to the court, "I couldn't understand why she went [to the seminars on rape]. I treated it lightly."

Beyond law's boundaries is a violence so bold and powerful that no preparation is adequate. It is so bold and powerful that it takes the innocent daughter literally right out from under her mother's eyes. Thus Heddie watched helplessly as Janine drove away with an unidentifiable "black man" beside her, and as a nightmare of racial victimization was played out before her eyes.[14] Implicit in the testimony about this nightmare is a contrast between the description of domestic routine and the known, but unspoken, soon-to-be-realized fate of Janine Galloway.[15]

Not only was Janine's innocence that of a dutiful daughter, it was, in addition, a virginal innocence. The fact of Janine's virginity was admitted into evidence over the strenuous objection of the defense which contended that it was irrelevant and inadmissible, that it went to no material issue in the case. The prosecution responded that the fact of her virginity went to the issue of nonconsent; it showed that there "was no consent to the crime of intercourse."

Once admitted, Janine's virginity would quickly became quite an important fact in the discursive representation of the

14 "The black male suspect's guilt or innocence of raping the white woman . . . can not be accurately assessed within a society of believers in racial mythologies and who thirst for hanging black flesh. . . . If the men are innocent of the rape, then they have been guilty of the crime of being black and male which takes precedence over legal innocence. If they are guilty of rape who can separate the guilt associated with their race and gender from their guilt for the crime. . . . [B]lack men are always guilty of raping white women because of who they are" (Omolade 1991:15–16).

15 But the testimony is equally potent in conveying an image of Janine's effort to distance her mother from danger and to calm her, "I'll be back. Don't worry." The daughter, in her own moment of danger, heroically becomes the mother to her mother.

violence done to her. It became an essential part of the story of the "wounds" which the prosecutor would use to bring Brooks's violence and Janine's pain into discourse. Once admitted, virginity helped to racialize the narrative of Janine's rape. It became the quite unsubtle symbol of her innocence and worth, and Brooks's crime became the paradigm of the racial attack on white womanhood.[16]

In a statement given to the police at the time of his arrest, Brooks said that after he had intercourse with Janine he asked her, "Was it your first time?" and that she had responded that it was. On Brooks's own account, "I didn't believe her." Against his disbelief the trial provided the occasion for an affirmation of the truth of what she had uttered as if her virginity were itself on trial.[17]

The Violence that Knows No Law

If the story of Janine's life was a rather linear narrative of a racial innocence and a gendered purity, the story of her violation was quite complex. From the beginning of the trial the prosecution painted a picture of the violence committed against Janine Galloway as gruesome, wanton, cruel, and unnecessary. In the words of the prosecutor, "Janine died a horrible death. . . . She did nothing to deserve to die."

With these words the prosecutor presented an implicit contrast between the violence outside the law that is visited upon the deserving and the undeserving alike, and respects neither innocence nor virtue, and law's own violence which is reserved for those who by virtue of their guilty acts deserve it (Morris 1970). Unlike the indiscriminate use of violence against the innocent Janine, law provides elaborate procedures (in Brooks's case, a trial, an extended process of review and appeal, and now a retrial) to insure that its violence is visited only on the guilty. What is unspoken here is that unlike Janine, Brooks has done something to deserve death, and that the death to which Brooks might be subject at the hands of the law will be neither wanton, nor cruel, nor unnecessary.

Throughout the trial the prosecutor referred to the irrationality of the crime committed against Janine Galloway and tried to describe the full measure of the pain which she endured. He returned again and again to the issue of her blamelessness. "What did she do?" he asked repeatedly. "She just went outside her home. She was not running around in skimpy

[16] For a vivid exemplification of the fear of such an attack see *McQuirter v. State* (1953).

[17] That affirmation came in the testimony of the medical examiner who had conducted the autopsy on Janine. It was his testimony that Janine "was a virgin prior to the attack."

clothes, and she was taken from her home." In his effort to describe the senseless horror of Brooks's crime, the prosecutor used the behavior of other rape victims whose dress, he seems to suggest, invites the crime as a foil to highlight Janine's innocence (Bumiller 1990). Thus Janine's virtue became a standard against which the flaws of other women, less pure and innocent than she, could be measured.

In his opening statement the prosecutor told the jury that Janine was

> accosted by the defendant at gunpoint. She was forced to drive with him to the woods behind Dawson school. There she was forced at gunpoint to disrobe. She was raped. And then she was shot in the neck at a downward angle. Some time later she died from the gunshot and the fact that she received no medical attention. . . . Behind the school at gunpoint the defendant had Janine strip and then he raped her. She was begging "Let me go." But he taunted her about her virginity. And then he shot her in the neck because she was screaming and she wouldn't shut up.

With these words, the prosecutor sought to make violence and pain speak (Scarry 1985), though he acknowledges to the jury that "it is not easy for us to appreciate the horror" of Janine's suffering. "Shot in the neck at a downward angle," and "begging 'let me go' " suggest that Janine was on her knees when she was shot. The violence unleashed by the shot was designed to silence its victim who was by then so degraded and desperate that she could only beg for a mercy that was not forthcoming.

The violence that Brooks inflicted on Janine Galloway was, in the prosecutor's description,

> done in the course of rape, in the course of armed robbery, in the course of kidnapping with injury. Kidnapping is horrible but this involved an injury to the breast and vaginal area. This was a crime of torture. The defendant wasn't content with just the physical act. He taunted her with his cruel question about her lack of sexual experience.

The prosecutor told the jury that Janine had been shot at close range and that the medical examiner had "found that she had been raped and had been torn up in her private parts. Her panties were very bloody, and on her breast were bite marks. She bled to death over an extended period of time." Violence and pain are put into discourse as a description of wounds and their aftermath.

In the effort to bring violence into discourse and to represent pain as wounds on the body, Janine's body was partialized, objectified, and marked in discrete ways (Bumiller 1991); Brooks's lawless violence is attached to particular parts of her body. It is inscribed as a hole in the neck, bite marks on the breast, blood from "her private parts." As Bumiller argues (1991:5) about rape trials: "The harm to the victim is verified by making visible pain and pleasure; the 'truth' of the women's violation is located in its visibility."

But it is not vision and visibility that dominate in the recreation of the lawless violence done to Janine Galloway. It is speech that carries the burden of representing violence. Three speech acts were central to the narrative of Janine's suffering. First is the statement of Brooks himself given to the police at the time of his arrest. Second is Janine's speech as well as her silence. Third is the testimony of the medical examiner, Dr. Weber.

Brooks's statement became the interpretable text on which much of the narrative of Janine's suffering was written. While he did not testify in his own defense, it was his statement that set the scene and the action of the crime.

> We drove down the dirt road by the Dawson School into the woods. When we got there I told her to stop the car and get out. She asked me to let her go, but I told her to take her clothes off. Then I had sex with her. When we got done I told her to get dressed. I asked her if it was her first time, and she said yes. I told her that I didn't believe her, and she started to scream. I pointed the gun at her and told her to be quiet. I cocked the gun and it went off. She fell. She was still screaming but I couldn't hear her.

On this account Janine's own movement from silence to speech occasioned the violence of her death. She was unable or unwilling to silently endure, to acquiesce in Brooks's demand for silence in the face of his disbelief in her lost innocence. She spoke in the only way she could, first in an audible then in a quickly silenced scream.

Her silence was, throughout the trial, treated as a kind of heroism, even as its end marked the end of her life. As the prosecutor put it,

> the defendant came up to her, but she didn't scream. She was scared to death but she didn't scream. She had taken a course, but she didn't scream. The defendant hid Janine when her mother came outside looking for her. She wanted to say "Momma save me," but she didn't because she knew what would happen. She didn't scream when she was forced to strip naked as a baby or when she was forced to lay down in the woods or when she was penetrated and her body was torn. Still she didn't scream. Then he taunted her about her virginity. It was only then, only when she saw her death in his eyes that she screamed. And then he killed her.

A third speech act played an important, if unusual role, in representing the lawless violence of William Brooks and in giving a language to Janine's pain by describing the wounds on her body. This was the testimony of the deceased Dr. Weber, the medical examiner who had testified at Brooks's first trial. In a strange reenactment of that testimony a member of the prosecution team took the stand equipped with the transcript of the first trial. As if from beyond the grave, Weber became an embodied speaker. Another prosecutor asked the same questions that had been asked in the first trial, and Weber's answers were read verbatim. Those answers suggested that Janine's death had been caused by a bullet fired from short range that entered the base of the neck, "tore away the trachea, hit a rib and the spinal column, lacerated a lung and exited between the third and fourth rib."

Weber stated that Galloway had not died quickly; in his opinion she lived for between one-half hour and two hours after being shot. During this time, he suggested, she had endured a great deal of suffering. In addition, Weber indicated that he found "teeth marks on the left nipple, injuries to the vagina including a lacerated hymen . . . and hemorrhaging around the pelvis." He noted that Janine was a virgin prior to the assault and that her injuries were "associated with violent sexual activity." In his account virginity becomes the context for understanding the overt marks of violence and pain. Here again violence and pain speak, as Scarry (1985) argues they must, through their visible effects—lacerations and hemorrhaging.

The context of a capital trial insures that the difficulty of putting violence and pain into discourse is compounded because at every turn, "the accuracy of the descriptions of suffering" given by one lawyer will be "contested" by the other (Scarry 1985:10). This is exemplified in the way the defense reacted to the testimony of Dr. Weber and his representations of Janine's pain. The response was, in fact, to call another medical examiner as an expert witness to contest those representations.

That witness put the words of Dr. Weber on trial; he called particular attention to the language of Weber's autopsy report and his testimony. "Dr. Weber," the expert contended, "used words in his report that I would never use and that I've never seen before. He didn't use the standard scientific terms to describe what he was seeing. He talked about rips and tears. As a result, I don't know what he actually saw. . . . And while he described the hymen as virginal, you can't ever tell that."

On cross-examination, this witness persisted for a time in his analysis of Weber's language.

Q: Have you ever found rape in a murder victim?

ME: I prefer to call it sexual battery not rape. The presence of sperm in and of itself doesn't equal rape.

Q: What is the difference between sexual battery and rape?

ME: Well, a stick or a finger would do injury, and sexual battery takes all this into account.
Q: The defendant said he raped her. Are you arguing with that?
ME: No. But Weber's testimony said more than he said in his report. Sometimes medical examiners say more than they should in order to help prosecutors. Anyway his testimony and his report are inconsistent.

While there would be no argument about Brooks's self-incriminating words, Weber's words could be doubted and argued about. Quickly, however, the prosecutor turned his attention to the language of the expert himself.

Q: Are you saying Janine wasn't raped?
ME: No. But you can be raped without being injured. There is still plenty of evidence to indicate that she was raped.
Q: Does the blood on her panties indicate the trauma associated with this rape?
ME: Yes.
Q: Does it suggest the presence of brute force?
ME: No. What we know is that someone had intercourse with her, caused a laceration, and it bled. Many people are, in fact, raped gently.
Q: Was Janine raped gently?
ME: The bruise on her nipple may or may not have come from a bite. Other than the gunshot wound and the small tear in her vagina there is no evidence she was beaten or choked. There is evidence she was raped but not beaten up.
Q: She was kidnapped and forced to strip at gunpoint, then raped . . .
ME: The defendant said he had sex with her.
Q: The girl said she was a virgin?
ME: Yes.
Q: Was this a pleasant situation to lose her virginity?
ME: No.
Q: Is this the way virgins choose to lose their virginity?
ME: Some might. She did not.
Q: Would this have been painful?
ME: Yes.

In this sequence of questions and answers Weber's speech is put aside and the focus is on the expert's use of the phrase "gentle rape." His introduction of this absurd idea rendered oxymoronic the very idea of rape itself, and it provided the prosecutor a chance to remind the jury again of Janine's violated innocence, the wounds she had suffered, and the pain spoken through those wounds.

The question of language and its adequacy in describing violence was critical throughout the trial. Brooks's defense insisted that his statement should be taken literally, that it be treated as an honest, full, and precise account of the events surrounding Janine Galloway's death, that the agent of her pain was the gun that "went off" on its own.[18] The prosecutor, in contrast, suggested that the words of that statement, especially the words "it went off" not be taken literally. As the prosecutor explained to the jury, "That's just how he happened to say it. That's just what his lawyer picked up on." Against the literalism of the defense was juxtaposed a theory of linguistic accident, of happenings rather than intentions, of words given meaning only by interpreters with purposes quite foreign to those of the original speaker.[19]

For the prosecutor, what was not said in Brooks's statement was as revealing as what was said in it. "I want you to think about committing crimes and if you were telling the truth when you got to the part about the shooting you'd speak pages. 'I didn't mean to. I was going to let her go.' But none of that was ever said."

The defense responded that the statement was accurate and complete, and it appealed to a rather conventional idea of what makes a persuasive narrative (see Booth 1983).

> The first thing to look at is the statement itself. . . . It is long and detailed. It tells about everything that happened. It said that she was made to get into a car with a gun. The defendant didn't make things up. The statement tells about the crimes he committed in great detail. Those details are, in addition, corroborated by other evidence. Those details are the kind of things that no other person could have known. And every detail paints as bad a picture of the defendant as could be. Everything says it is true. And the prosecution wants you to believe everything but one sentence. Well they can't have it both ways. The whole statement is truthful.

---

[18] Brooks's defense lawyer told me:

> I think one of the classic mistakes that people make is to try to keep denying the statement or challenging the voluntariness of it even when it is clear that it is coming in. When they had Brooks admitting to the rape and the robbery and admitting to every other evil, criminal thing that he did and then they wanted to say he was just trying to explain it away. As you know, my argument was that if we accepted everything else we should credit the statement in its entirety. Lawyers should find ways to turn statements like the one Brooks gave to their own advantage. That is what we were trying to do.

[19] The defense accused the prosecution of rhetorical excess, of making a terrible thing seem needlessly worse than it was. "Part of this process is integrity. Things are bad enough. Some of these things were embellished. Things are bad enough. They don't need to be embellished."

Taking the statement literally would mean that the gun would become the personified agent of death. "The gun went off." Here agency is attributed to the weapon itself.[20]

The literal reading of the defendant's statement with its attribution of agency to the gun was bolstered by the testimony of a firearms expert.

Q: Is it possible for a gun to go off by itself?
FE: Yes.
Q: Is it possible for a 357 Charter Arms to discharge inadvertently?
FE: Yes.
Q: How can a revolver discharge accidently?
FE: It depends on the condition of the revolver and whether the safeties are operative. If the weapon is in poor condition the trigger pull might be much too tight so that when a person doesn't intend it, it might fire. You might pull back the trigger accidently after having the hammer back.
Q: Could the shooting in this case have been accidental?
FE: Yes. There was one shot from close range. And the statement of the defendant that the hammer had been pulled back and that it went off. These things are all consistent with the conclusion that the gun in this case could have gone off accidently.

While the defense treated the gun as the agent of death in a killing which Brooks himself did not control or intend, the prosecution presented another version of the weapon and of the agency of violence which was visited on Janine Galloway.

> Guns are dangerous, but they have their place. We all know that they don't just sit there looking to go off. The gun that snuffed out her life didn't really do it. That defendant did it. He pulled the trigger. The mouth that marked her breast is that mouth there. The sex organ that penetrated her is on that man right there. The hand that fired the fatal bullet is on that man.

"Mouth," "sex organ," "hand," each a weapon used against Janine Galloway; each an agent of the violence done to her, each a sign of the pain unjustifiably imposed on her (Scarry 1985). As Cobb puts it (1992:11–12), "The weapons take on the attributes of the pain and require that the 'violated' position themselves as victims of the weapons. . . . Pain and its objectification is accompanied by a loss of self, a loss of voice

---

[20] As Cobb (1992:11) explains, "[P]ain is a manifestation of violence; but since there can be no description of violence that transcends subjectivity . . . we must understand pain by the way it is objectified via . . . 'the language of agency.' Pain is objectified, that is it is presented as located in that which inflicts pain, i.e. the weapon."

that both signals the disintegration of the world of the person and confers the attributes of pain on the object of the pain—and, in the process, pain is read as power." "Mouth," "sex organ," "hand," these are the significations of a power brutally abused, a power able to silence Janine Galloway, to render her screams unhearable. But they also signify the dismemberment of Brooks's own body, a symbolic dismemberment in which each part of his body is linked with a discrete injury to his victim.

While the violence of Janine's death was, in the words of the defense, a tragic and accidental violence which knew no logic and for which no one could be held responsible, the prosecution portrayed the violence which took the life of Janine Galloway as the painful, humiliating violence of torture and slow death. But most of all, it was an unnecessary violence. "If he wanted her to shut up he could have hit her with a big hand. When she woke up he would have been gone." This violence was, moreover, the willful, immoral, predatory gesture of an evil will transgressing against innocence itself. "One thing keeps coming back. It was all so unnecessary. If one person hadn't decided to use another for his lust she would still be alive. This is not the age of disposable people."

"It was all so unnecessary . . ." and using another "for his lust . . ." bring together two different narrative strands in the prosecution argument. The first is the portrait of violence outside the law with its implicit comparison to law's own violence, and the second is the story of race. With regard to the first, the violence outside law is senseless, random, almost inexplicable. Why did Brooks pick Galloway as his victim? Why that woman at that time? As the prosecutor put it, "We don't know whether he had staked out the Galloway house or whether he was just looking for anybody to rob." Thus the horrifying quality of Janine Galloway's murder was that it was a

> chance encounter between strangers, in which what . . . [was] casually exchanged happens to be death. . . . The radical disjunction, or discontinuity, between the immeasurably great value of what is being destroyed . . . and the minuscule, trivial, "perceived gain" that prompted the murder . . . leaves . . . a palpable, profound and almost physical need to reestablish sense and meaning in the universe. (West 1990:10–11)

Galloway's murder, as described by the prosecution, was an instance of what Robin West has called "post-modern murders" (p. 11) Such murders, West argues,

> strip the natural world of its hierarchy of values—life, love, nurture, work, care, play, sorrow, grief—and they do so for no reason, not even to satisfy the misguided pseudo-Nietzschean desire of a Loeb or Leopold to effectuate precisely

that deconstruction. They are meaningless murders. (Emphasis omitted)

If there is meaning in Galloway's death, it is found only in a racial narrative in which "animal" passions of the young black male lead him to use another person to satisfy his "lust" (Omolade 1991:16). "How," the prosecutor asked, "did the defendant treat Janine—like some mother's baby, some daddy's little girl, or like something disposable?" The invitation in this question is to recover meaning by assigning responsibility and by asserting the difference between a violence which knows no law and a violence necessary to control or deter it, between the animal inability of black men to control their "lust" and respect the sanctity of human life and the human need for self-respect and self-control.

Garfinkel (1956:422), in his famous discussion of the "conditions of successful degradation ceremonies," gives us a way of seeing how William Brooks and his heinous act can be accommodated to a general scheme of preferences and values. Both Brooks and his act are treated as instances of a "type." The prosecutor's denunciation of Brooks as the type who would use another human being for his pleasure and then dispose of her invites the jury to identify with a "dialectical counterpart" (ibid.). It is only, as Garfinkel argues (p. 423), by the reference "it bears to its opposite" that the "profanity of an occurrence . . . is clarified."[21] As between meaninglessness and a racially coded meaning, the invitation is to reject the former and embrace the latter (West 1990:12)[22] and to see Brooks and his act as "inexplicably alien, horrendous and inhuman" (p. 15). The jurors in the Brooks case accepted that invitation and rejected what the prosecutor had disparagingly called the "I didn't mean to" version of the death of Janine Galloway. As a result, they convicted Brooks of malice murder, and the trial moved into the second or sentencing phase.

[21] Indeed Garfinkel (1956:423) makes explicit reference to murder trials as examples of degradation ceremonies. "The features of the mad dog murderer," he argues, "reverse the features of the peaceful citizen."

[22] West (1990:12) argues that such narratives

> create a palpable need to reassert responsibility and human agency for a momentous act and momentous deprivation; so that we can again feel in control of our destiny. They create a need to assign responsibility, not just liability and not just guilty. The defendant's ultimate responsibility for the murder is, in a nutshell, essential to the coherence of those stories as human stories, and the coherence of these stories is essential to the meaningfulness of our lives.

II. Putting Violence into Discourse in the Trial of William Brooks: The Life and Death of William Brooks

The story of Janine Galloway's murder exemplifies one way in which violence is brought into legal discourse and suggests one set of comparisons between law's violence and its lawless counterpart. That story embodies what Stephen Carter calls (1988:421) "bilateral individualism." In such a conception the status of victim is accorded to

> someone who loses something—property, physical safety—because of the predation of someone else. Victimization, then, is the result of concrete, individual acts by identifiable transgressors . . . [B]ilateral individualism . . . invents a reality in which the only victims [of crime] are those who have suffered at the hands of transgressors. (Ibid.)

In the penalty phase of Brooks's trial we see another way in which violence is put into legal discourse and a story about a different kind of violence. In this phase it was a narrative about violence that the defendant himself had endured that took center stage. Here again, a racial narrative was constructed, only this time by the defense, a narrative of racial pain and racial victimization in which the rage of the young black male is portrayed as an understandable, if not justifiable, response to the constitutive violence of a world beyond his making.

In contrast to the direct, personal, decontextualized violence that Janine suffered at Brooks hands, the violence that was part of the defendant's life story was more diffuse, spread out over a longer period of time, and more systemic. In contrast to the violence that took Janine's life, the violence that Brooks had endured made his life what it is. In this alternative conception of violence and victimization, both become matters "of the sweep of history, not the actions of individual transgressors. . . . In this vision of victimhood, the criminal behavior of so many black males is itself a mark of victimhood, a victimhood virtually determined from birth"[23] (Carter 1988: 426–27).

If in the first phase of the trial the narrative of violence and death was thick and the narrative of life thin, just the opposite would be the case in the penalty phase. In this phase, Brooks's life became the central object of inquiry while the violence that

[23] The construction of this narrative is made all the more complex when, as in the Brooks case, the defense lawyer resists "bilateral individualism" and argues that the defendant did not do what he is accused of doing [malice murder] in the guilt-innocence phase of the trial, and then, in the penalty phase, shifts the frame to the alternative conception of violence and victimization in order to explain *why* the defendant did what the jury found him guilty of doing.

might take his life was, as Foucault (1977) would have suggested, left virtually invisible.

Seeing the Tragic Life behind the Tragic Event: From Predator to Victim

In the penalty phase of the capital trial "[t]he overall goal of the defense is to present a human narrative, an explanation of the defendant's apparently malignant violence as in some way rooted in understandable aspects of the human condition" (Weisberg 1984:361). Thus Brooks's lawyer began his opening argument in the penalty phase by saying,

> It is hard to get up in front of you. You reached a verdict on Saturday that is not what we had hoped, but I accept it. To this point, however, all you've heard about is one terrible incident. Now you must consider the larger picture of William Brooks's life as you decide about the most extraordinary and extreme punishments—life in prison and being electrocuted by the state. The fact of his conviction for murder is not enough. The state must prove particular aggravating circumstances in this case. And even if those circumstances are established you still have to consider whether this person is so beyond redemption that he should be eliminated from the human community. To do that you must look at his whole life—good and bad. . . . We are going to tell the story of a life. In court we usually talk about just one incident. . . . Now we are going to talk about a life.

The invitation in this argument is to consider the person behind the crime, to put the crime in context.[24] Through his rhetorical insistence that it is a "life" that must be talked about, Brooks's lawyer reminds the jury of the reality of law's violence; he reminds them that there is now another life at stake, a life that can be extinguished through a legal gesture and a legal judgment with as much crushing finality as the life-destroying gesture of Brooks himself. Brooks's lawyer names that gesture "electrocution" and, in so doing, makes the violence of law at least momentarily visible by identifying its instrumentality. He urges each juror to take full responsibility for a life-or-death decision that is now unavoidable. "Each of you," he says, "is the Supreme Court today. It is your decision whether he lives or dies."

This is an anxiety-producing exhortation which is fraught with its own anxieties. As Scarry (1985:10) suggests, the effort to invent a language to represent violence and pain is shaped by the awareness of the jury's capacity to accept particular linguistic representations. In the narration of the violence in

[24] On the role of blameworthiness in criminal sentencing see Wheeler et al. (1988). Another way of thinking about the penalty phase would be to see it as an instance of the "expansion" of a dispute. See Mather & Yngvesson 1980–81.

Brooks's life and in the description of the context against which his crime might be judged, the defense has the difficult task of explaining that that narrative does not undo, or diminish, the seriousness of the murder itself. If it fails, or suggests that context overdetermines crime,[25] it invites the jury to reaffirm the correctness of its judgment of guilt by imposing the death penalty (West 1990:11).[26] What must be provided, then, is a narrative of violence and pain and a context for understanding both that explains but does not excuse, "that could respond to the need to assign responsibility . . . to the defendant, society, or history" (ibid., p. 14), and that helps the jury understand the sources and origins of the lawless violence perpetrated by William Brooks without suggesting that they should forgive that violence or recant their judgment.

> The defendant has hurt people and sinned against man and God. What you need to consider is what forces pushed him in that direction. But will any of this excuse what happened? Nothing excuses or justifies his crime. . . . Let me remind you what is not before you. This isn't about whether the defendant will be excused. There is no excuse for what William Brooks did. When you consider mitigating evidence it isn't to excuse or justify. He is responsible for what he did. That's why we are here, why we are at this point. That's been decided. . . . Mitigating evidence is offered to help you understand what he did and why, not to excuse or justify it.

Instead of excusing the crime, the narrative of Brooks's life is presented as a reason for showing mercy (see Davis 1987; Murphy & Hampton 1988). Brooks's lawyer appealed to the jury to be better than the killer who showed no mercy to Janine Galloway, to follow "feelings of mercy and sympathy that flow from the evidence." "As Christians," he argued,

> we learn about the place of mercy and compassion. Here the law makes room for mercy and compassion. We are proud of our law because it allows us to show mercy. If you find mitigation that can be a reason to give life—anything about William Brooks's life and background, or about his life in prison that makes him worthy of not being killed. If anything you think merits mercy whether I've told you or not, you can vote for life.

This appeal to mercy suggests that law's violence can and should be different from the violence Brooks used against Janine Galloway, and that law can and should show compassionate concern for even the undeserving. It suggests that the question of whether law's violence, in the end, will be different rests in the hands of the jury. To establish its difference and to

[25] For an example of a case in which the defense argument suggested that crime was overdetermined see *State v. Sikora* (1965).

[26] And to reaffirm, as West (1990:11) notes, "meaning and value in a world deconstructed by random violence."

legitimate law's violence, the jury must show the very restraint which Brooks himself did not show; it must hear the call of mercy in ways that Brooks himself did not hear when Janine Galloway begged for her life. In making this argument, Brooks's defense gave the state "its moral victory by acknowledging his crime" while at the same time trying to "persuade the jury that it can accommodate the crime into the assumptions of [a] social order it wants to reaffirm" (Weisberg 1984:362). At the center of those assumptions is the view that law must be different and better than those over whom it exercises the power of life.

The story of Brooks's life that might merit mercy was one of abuse, cruelty, and victimization. This story itself is a reminder not of law's victories but of its defeats, not of its capacity to protect but of its frustrating limits. Brooks was the object of a lawless violence that showed no mercy. In contrast to the untroubled innocence of Janine Galloway's life, "the defendant's life," his lawyer contended, "was one nightmare after another." His family was torn apart by violence and abuse, violence first directed at his mother by an alcoholic father who was himself ultimately murdered on the streets of Columbus, Georgia, and then against Brooks by his stepfather.

In this narrative of violence and victimization directed against the perpetrator of violence, the defense faced the same task of representing pain, of putting pain into language, that the prosecution faced in its own efforts to speak about the pain of Janine Galloway. Here again the appeal was to wounds and weapons as the medium of pain's representation (Scarry 1985). As the defense lawyer put it,

> The defendant carries scars on his back from the beatings he received from his stepfather who would take him in a room, lock the door and whip him on his back with a belt buckle. Gwen [Brooks's sister] used to come home and hear William screaming. When the beating was done William would come out of the room, his back bloody from the beatings. Such beatings were a daily event.

The story of the violence done to Brooks was played against a domestic and familial life quite different from that of Janine Galloway. While home for her was a fortress against lawless violence, for Brooks it was the continuous scene of such violence. Whereas Janine's mother was called to the stand to speak about lost innocence, the disruption of domestic tranquility, and her singular, tragic inability to rescue her child from harm, Brooks's mother was called to testify to her continuous inability to do so.

Q: What happened after you moved to Columbus?
M: My husband began to drink heavily. And then he would try to hit me and we would have fights. He'd hit me and we would tussle. William saw all of this. He saw everything and he'd get very upset. Once [my husband] broke my nose and I had to go to the hospital. Another time he hit me and I began to beat him with the heel of my shoe. All the kids were there.
Q: Did you ever inflict injuries on your husband?
M: Well, once I scalded him with hot coffee . . . when we had a fight. And the children they saw it. They were all at the table.
Q: How frequent were the fights?
M: Every weekend. Pretty soon I had to leave every weekend and take the kids to my parent's house. . . . Later my father bought me a shot gun and told me to use it if he tried to beat me again. . . . Once my oldest daughter took the gun and shot him in the hand.

Three of William Brooks's sisters also testified about the violence he and they had experienced as they grew up. Brooks's sister Gwen provided the most vivid portrait of William's victimization.

Q: What was life like with your stepfather?
G: It was a kind of holy terror. He was abusive and when he wasn't being abusive he made us feel unwanted. He'd curse us and made us feel out of place in our own home. He'd always have a house full of young men drinking, smoking and being fresh. He could get away with all that being abusive because my mother was at work.
Q: How did he treat William?
G: He really hated him. He beat him all the time with his belt buckle or with an extension chord. He was always hitting him and pushing him against the wall. More than once I'd heard my brother screaming when I came home. Once I pushed against the door in the room where the screams were coming from. My brother was lying on the mattress and there was blood all over the walls. William begged me to make him stop, but he threw me out of the room and started beating William again.

There is no lost innocence, no fall from grace, in this story because there was never an innocence to be lost. The violence directed against Brooks has its own particular instrumentalities—the "belt buckle" and the "extension chord." It was brutal, continuous, and inescapable. Like many young black men, Brooks lived in a kind of state of nature close to home, a state of nature made real in the pains imposed on him and the inscriptions on his body. What is made visible in this story is the specter of violence generating violence in which law is complicit by its inability to provide protection or defense.

But the discourse of law could neither fully contain nor explain the lawless violence to which the defendant was subject and the impact of that violence in precipitating or explaining what he did to Janine Galloway. For such an explanation the defense turned to an expert, a social worker experienced in issues of child development and in child abuse and neglect. As she put it,

> William Brooks was subject to persistent and brutal abuse throughout his childhood. He saw explosive tempers all around him, and they became for him a model of how to behave. . . . To say the least, he grew up in the absence of a nurturing environment. . . . The abuse and neglect which he suffered caused fear, anxiety and anger. He was left alone to deal with these things. He needed but did not get professional help. Through no fault of his own the very volatile feelings inside him were left to fester. . . . He did not develop internal controls or mechanisms for dealing with his anger. He never found a place to put it.

The introduction of this testimony turned the penalty phase of the Brooks trial into a high culture/scientific expertise versus low culture/commonsense contest in which what was contested was the extent to which violence constituted Brooks as a subject, the extent to which it shaped him and contributed to his own violent acts. The high culture/scientific discourse implied that the explanation for Brooks's behavior was complex and hard to disentangle from the violence which made him what he was. The low culture/commonsense rendering searched for a more parsimonious explanation. Thus in the midst of his cross-examination of the social worker, the prosecutor asked:

Q: Do you believe in the Christian principle of free moral agency? Do you believe that God gave us the capacity to choose right from wrong?

SW: Yes, that can happen if one has a nurturing environment that would support that capacity and allow it to be used.

Q: Do you believe that Almighty God gave us the capacity to know right from wrong?

SW: Almighty God gave us the potential. . . .

Q: How do you explain why some people who come from bad homes do well in life?

SW: We all have different innate endowments and ability to tolerate frustration. One can't just look at people and know who will turn out good and who will turn out bad. You have to look carefully at the environment and especially at family dynamics.
Q: Are you saying that people are not responsible for what they do?
SW: What William Brooks did was the product of interaction between himself and his environment.
Q: Can a child be spoiled?
SW: Yes.
Q: Can someone be just plain mean?
SW: No, not without reason. Children aren't born mean. Children are responsive to their environment.

In this denunciation of Brooks and counterexplanation of his actions, the prosecutor seeks to identify with what Garfinkel (1956:423) calls the "dignity of the supra-personal values of the tribe," of a community of persons committed to the theological principle of free choice. "Just plain mean" is presented as the community's commonsense response to a "scientific" discourse that seemed to make the explanation for violence disappear or to locate it outside the acting subject. For the prosecution what was at stake was the location of the responsibility for violence in a freely acting subject, what was at stake was the very idea of responsibility itself. As the cross-examination continued this theme reappeared.

Q: Was the defendant a time bomb? Was violence inevitable?
SW: He had no way of expressing what was happening to him. His feelings were just festering inside him. He could have learned to channel those feelings and the violence if he'd gotten help.
Q: Suppose he confronted a young woman in her yard, twenty-three years old, a small woman, and he heard her mother coming. Would he be able to transport his victim to a place of seclusion so as to be able to continue his criminal enterprise?
SW: One could not have predicted how he would act out. His anger was there. How it would be expressed could not be predicted.

. . .

Q: Whose fault was it that Brooks kidnapped Janine?
SW: He would have to take responsibility for that.
Q: And for all his other voluntary acts?

SW: He would be responsible.

. . .

Q: Isn't it true that heaven helps those who help themselves?
SW: That capacity, like any other human capacity, needs to be activated by outside sources.
Q: Not even God could help him. It would take counseling.
SW: The counselor would be an instrument of God.

. . .

Q: Aren't you saying that he wasn't responsible?
SW: I'm not saying that. I'm not saying that he wasn't responsible for what he did. I am saying that things in his childhood caused problems and that he needed professional help that he never received.

The language of responsibility again provided the medium through which the prosecutor could construct a narrative about violence, about the life of William Brooks and his violent acts. Those acts have to be assigned individuated agency for law's response to have any pretense of efficacy. The narrative of violence begetting violence, of an abused person enacting his abuse, was characterized by the prosecution as a "Devil made me do it" defense. Such a defense "had" to be rejected (see *State v. Sikora* 1965:202). Ironically, perhaps, the language of compulsion is used to authorize/require the idea of responsible choice which the prosecution sought to defend. "We *have* to believe that God gave everybody the ability to know right from wrong, good from evil. . . . It is the American way to play by the rules, work hard. That's what he rejected. . . . The defendant, by his own volition, selected to live his life in dark places."

The prosecution denied that there was anything special about Brooks's life. He was a subjectivity constituted not by the violence of its origins and influences but by the violence engendered by its willed choices (Dan-Cohen 1992). Brooks had to be judged and punished in the same way as anyone who made such choices should be judged and punished. For the defense, however, the story of Brooks's life was a story of difference not similarity. It was a life entirely contained by violence, a life unlike those imaginatively denoted by appeals to God's will or the American way.

> People aren't all the same [Brooks's defense lawyer argued]. Free will, yes, but we are not all the same. . . . Some people grow up in good ground, but William Brooks's seed was sown among the thorns. Yes, some sown among the thorns will grow up well. Some will survive, but even they aren't like those that are planted in the field. This little seed tried to struggle through the thorns. And the fact that some make it,

> well, that's life. You've got to look at where his seed was sown. "Just plain mean"—some people are just plain mean. When we see new babies do we see anyone who is just plain mean? When kids are two or five are they just plain mean? Do they exercise free will in deciding whether they are going to turn out to kill people? . . . People who are abused and neglected, it isn't surprising that they get in trouble. We know there's a road to that even though it doesn't make it okay. . . . It doesn't make it okay. . . . We are not saying if you are abused you can kill.

The narrative of Brooks's life was itself a narrative of violence and pain. The appeal to understand his suffering was, in turn, an appeal to see in it pain acting in a world known only as a source of pain. It was an appeal not to privilege and power but to the recognition of the ways that powerlessness and racial deprivations act out their powerful rage. The appeal here is to a shared, though not equally shared, responsibility for Janine Galloway's death. It suggests "an alternative understanding of societal responsibility" that challenges the prosecutor's "bi-lateral individualism" (Carter 1988:42). Brooks, after all, was not "Ted Bundy. He didn't go to law school. He isn't somebody who had all that smarts. You've got to ask yourself, is this some poor kid who had never been taught values? You punish those people differently." In the discourse of law, punishment is the measure of all things. In this discourse the recognition of a different, of a violated, life required a different, less violent punishment.

Naming Law's Violence

In the penalty phase of a capital trial, law's own violence is put, as it always must be, precariously into discourse, and the disposition and use of law's ultimate power over life and death is made the subject of contention. In this moment the legitimation of that power is the most pressing because law enlists ordinary citizens and asks them to exercise its power over life and death. In so doing law seeks to make its violence our violence.

Yet even at this moment it is striking that so little is actually said about the nature of that violence. In contrast to the detailed presentation of the violence outside the law by both prosecution and defense, neither presented a similarly detailed narrative of the prospective violence to which the jury is being asked to commit William Brooks. This is, of course, not surprising as a tactic of the prosecution; one would expect him to foreground the violence done to the victim and the pain which she endured and to tread lightly on the terrain of law's own violence (see Weisberg 1984; West 1990). It is, however, not what one would have expected, at least initially, from the defense until one confronts the fact that in all death cases the defense confronts a "death-qualified" jury, that is, a group of persons who as a condition of their service in a capital case must have already attested to their ability and willingness to impose the death penalty.[27] Given such an audience with its known dispositions, to attack frontally and repeatedly the death penalty, to highlight its gruesome violence, would be to undertake the burden of conversion.

Nonetheless, while neither prosecution or defense undertakes a detailed explication of the nature of law's violence, the question before the jury in the penalty phase of a capital trial like that of William Brooks is what kind of violence are they being asked to do? And how does that violence differ from the violence to which it is opposed? The prosecution in the Brooks case consistently called that violence "the death penalty" as if there were no means or mechanisms of violence that would necessarily be deployed to bring about death. The instrumentality, the weapon, the objectification of the pain of the violence imposed, found no expression.

The defense, not surprisingly, both named the weapon and the act. What the prosecution called the "death penalty" the defense called the "most extreme and extraordinary punishment." Brooks's lawyer insisted that what was at stake was the "elimination of life by 2200 volts of electricity." What was at stake was not a penalty abstractly called death but whether law would "kill" William Brooks. The insistence that law's violence is a killing violence effectively blurs the distinction between the

[27] I arrived in Georgia in time to watch the jury being selected for the Brooks trial. Immediately the specter of law's violence took center stage as the presiding judge, Judge Lawson, a stout, balding, serious-looking man, conducted voir dire. Lawson provided each potential juror with a brief overview of the procedure to be followed in the case. "The defendant," he said,

> is charged with one count of malice murder and if he is convicted the state will seek the death penalty. This trial will take place in two stages. In the first phase guilt and innocence is the only question. If the defendant is found guilty there will be a second stage or sentencing hearing. At the conclusion of the sentencing hearing the jury decides between life and death. The jury's decision is final. In this state the death penalty is authorized in particularly aggravated circumstances. The death penalty can be imposed on more serious, more severe murders. Aggravating circumstances mean more than being guilty of murder. But if the jury finds aggravating circumstances it is not required to impose the death penalty. Imposition of the death penalty is never mandatory. The defense is permitted to present mitigating circumstances, that is, anything in mercy and fairness having to do with the defendant or his background. Imposition of the death penalty is never mandatory. Finally, I would instruct you that you are to draw no inferences about the guilt or innocence of the defendant from the fact I have given you these instructions.

These instructions introduce potential jurors to the prospect of imposing a death sentence before they have been empaneled and heard any evidence. Because the death penalty is never mandatory, each of the potential jurors at the outset would have to face the question whether they could, should circumstances warrant, impose death as a punishment. As part of what is called the process of "death qualification" Lawson asked each of the jurors, "Are you conscientiously opposed to the death penalty?" "If the state seeks the death penalty and you felt the death penalty was justified would you be able to vote to impose it?"

act of the criminal and the act of law itself (Camus 1957). And it suggests that the legitimation of law's violence cannot rest securely in any sanitized renaming of the death-doing, life-destroying instrumentalities of law itself.

The prosecution addressed the question of the legitimacy of law's violence by making explicit what had earlier in the trial been left unspoken. Here the violence on law's side of the boundary is overtly labeled purposive, measured, and necessary. "We have a right," the prosecutor claimed, "to be vindicated and protected." "We" is both an inclusive and a violent naming, a naming fraught with racial meaning. Who is included in the "we"? While this "we" reaches from this world to the next as a remembrance of and identification with Janine, at the same time, it makes the black Brooks an outsider in a community that needs protection from people like him. It excludes him by claiming law as an entitlement against him. Law's violence is necessary both to vindicate and protect "us" from him.

By speaking the language of "we" the prosecutor seeks to invest himself with authority to speak for the jury and the community it represents as well as to speak to it. He reminds the jury that the trial which has brought them to the point of considering a capital sentence "has been conducted according to the rule of law." He identifies himself with the jury and the community while distancing himself and them from the defendant who he denounces. As Garfinkel (1956:423) puts it, in a successful degradation ceremony "the denounced person must be ritually separated from a place in the legitimate order. . . . He must be placed 'outside,' he must be made 'strange.' "[28] In this case law's violence could, the prosecutor claimed, properly be used to vindicate Janine's lost innocence and to protect those who, like her, lead innocent lives from those like Brooks who live in "dark places" and have "forfeited their place in the human community."

And the prosecutor argued that this vindication and protection would be, again engaging the project of legitimating law's violence by differentiating it from violence of the kind that Brooks visited on Janine Galloway, a proportionate response to a horrible and horrifying violence:

> It fits the crime. Janine was taunted and tortured. It wasn't like TV. When it was all over she didn't get up and walk away. . . . When the defense says "mercy," think of what the defendant did to Janine. . . . Go back behind Dawson School when Janine was screaming, begging for her life and the de-

[28] As Garfinkel (1956:423) puts it, "The denouncer must arrange to be invested with the right to speak in the name of those ultimate values. . . . The denouncer must get himself so defined by the witnesses that they locate him as a supporter of those values. Not only must the denouncer fix his own distance from the person being denounced, but the witnesses must be made to experience their distance from him also."

> fendant shot her and she was screaming and no scream came out. I want you to hear that silent scream when you hear him [the defense lawyer] say "mercy and mitigation."

But in the end, the most powerful authorization and the most unquestionable legitimation of law's violence rests with those to whom it would be applied (Morris 1970). Unlike Janine who did nothing to precipitate the violence that was done to her, Brooks had, by his own choice and acts, put himself in harm's way. "Some," the prosecutor argued, "by their own acts forfeit the right to breathe the air we breathe. If he had left Janine alone none of this would have happened. Mr. Brooks showed in what he did to her that he believes in the death penalty."

Juxtaposed to this argument was the defense's contention that the death penalty would be neither necessary nor rational *in this case*. To apply it would expose law's violence as excessive; to apply it would be, in essence, to reduce law's violence to the level of the violence which by their earlier verdict the jury had, in essence, condemned. Killing Brooks would be a vindictive desecration of someone who was already leading a life on the other side of a line that separates the incarcerated from the free, those in law's custody from those allegedly beyond its confinement. In some sense Brooks was already dead (Scheppele 1990:49). The defense continued:

> What's at stake in this case isn't life as we know it. We are not talking about someone who can go home and play with his kids. We are talking about life lived inside a prison. I know the defendant is here because I hear the chains rattling. A life in chains and in prison, that is already an extreme and harsh punishment. . . . This is not about not being punished. You are choosing between two punishments. And you should remember that society has ways of punishing without killing people.

This questioning of the necessity of another killing dominated a defense argument that suggested that a violence dispensed excessively, unnecessarily, is a violence no different from the violence used against Janine Galloway. For law's own violence to be different and better it has to meet the test of necessity and, in so doing, live with its own restraint. According to the defense this was a threshold that had not been; and could not be, met in the Brooks case.

> We don't need to kill this defendant. The law doesn't require us to do so. There may be times when we need to but this isn't one. . . . No case requires the death penalty. There is no automatic capital punishment. There was no death penalty for the people who murdered those young, black children in Atlanta, or for the man who killed Dr. King or Medgar Evers. . . . No case has to bring the death penalty. . . . Society can be protected without killing William Brooks. . . . You don't have to kill. . . . Brooks's crimes were terrible, evil, and

> vile. But Janine Galloway's life can't be brought back. If we could bring Janine back I would electrocute William Brooks myself. . . . For everything there is a season. This is a time to punish, but not to kill.

While "You don't have to kill William Brooks" was the repeated refrain in the defense's argument against "electrocution," Brooks's lawyer's statement that "If I could bring Janine back I would electrocute William Brooks myself" was quite extraordinary in marking the nature of law's violence. It served to identify the defense lawyer with the jurors; like them, he suggests he has no conscientious objection to the death penalty. Rather than seeking to turn them against the death penalty, this lawyer suggests that law's violence must be used in measured ways to achieve purposes which can be achieved by no other means. In this case, his statement serves to drive home the point that each use of law's violence must be justified on its own terms. In this case, he challenged the jury to maintain the legitimacy of law's violence by exercising restraint and by insuring that it is not used where it is unnecessary.

For William Brooks this was a persuasive appeal.[29] For him, January 1991, in fact, turned out to be a time to be punished, but not to be killed, a time to receive yet another life sentence rather to be killed by electrocution.

III. Conclusion

Capital trials remind us that law's violent constitution does not end with the establishment of legal order. The law constituted, in part, in response to metaphorical violence traffics with literal violence (see Friedenberg 1971:43; see also Fitzpatrick 1991:15; Todorov 1984). In capital trials, we see the ways different kinds of violence first are made part of legal discourse and then are differentiated from one another.

First, of course, is the death of the victim. In constructing a narrative of violence and pain and in telling this story, prosecutors, like the prosecutor in the Brooks case, construct a sociologically simple world of good and evil and a morally clear world of responsibility and desert (Weisberg 1984:361; see also Dan-Cohen 1992). The prosecution seeks to create a binary opposition between the "angelic" character of the victim, who did not deserve to die (Bumiller 1990) and the "evil" character of

29 When I later asked Brooks's defense lawyer to explain the verdict he suggested:

> No jury is just going to let a guy walk away free when he's responsible for another person dying. . . . But this is the kind of thing that would cause a jury to compromise upon a penalty verdict. I don't think they were sure that he (Brooks) really maliciously intended this, but they could go and convict him of murder and then give him a life sentence as a compromise.

the perpetrator who does not deserve to live. This is the dominant cultural motif for representing violence and victimization.

The second kind of violence and pain whose "reality" is put into discourse in capital trials is the violence done, in their childhood and throughout their life, to defendants like Brooks, the violence of an abusive home and family, the violence that crafts a life and a way of living. Inventing a language to accommodate and express this kind of violence and pain involves contesting the dominant cultural conception of violence and victimization (Carter 1988). Defending a murderer like Brooks requires the construction of a more complex narrative of causation and accident, of mixed lives and mixed motives (Weisberg 1984:361).

The third kind of violence that is put into discourse in capital trials is the violence of law itself. While the other kinds of violence are presented as weapons and wounds and described in vivid, concrete, gory detail, law's violence is hardly presented at all. It is named, when it is named, in the most general, abstract, and impersonal ways. As Foucault argues (1977:9):

> Punishment . . . [has] become the most hidden part of the penal process. This has several consequences: it leaves the domain of more or less everyday perception and enters that of abstract consciousness; its effectiveness is seen as resulting from its inevitability, not from its visible intensity; it is the certainty of being punished and not the horrifying spectacle of public punishment that must discourage crime. . . . As a result, justice no longer takes public responsibility for the violence that is bound up with its practice.

In this process, capital punishment in particular becomes, at best, a hidden reality. It is a violence known by indirection.[30] What we know about the way law does death comes in the most highly mediated way as a rumor, a report, an account of the voiceless expression of the body of the condemned rather than in a detailed recounting in the narratives of capital trials. However, even such highly mediated accounts convey the ferocity of

---

[30] Silencing the condemned and limiting the visibility of lawfully imposed death is part of the modern bureaucratization of capital punishment and part of the strategy for transforming execution from an arousing public spectacle of vengeance to a soothing matter of mere administration (Foucault 1977:ch. 1). The association of law and violence though rendered invisible in the bureaucratization of capital punishment is sometimes made visible elsewhere, for example, in the use of lethal force by police. It is, moreover, linguistically present in the ease and comfort with which we speak about enforcing the law. "Applicability, 'enforceability,' is not," as Derrida (1990:925) puts it,

> an exterior or secondary possibility that may or may not be added as a supplement to law. . . . The word "enforceability" reminds us that there is no such thing as law that doesn't imply in itself, *a priori*, . . . the possibility of being "enforced," applied by force. There are, to be sure, laws that are not enforced, but there is no law without enforceability, and no applicability or enforceability of the law without force, whether this force be direct or indirect, physical or symbolic."

death at the hands of the law and, in so doing, arouse anxiety and fear.[31]

The events those accounts describe suggest that law's violence bears substantial traces of the violence it is designed to deter and punish. In Foucault's words (1977:9), "it . . . [was] as if this rite that 'concluded the crime' was suspected of being in some undesirable way linked with it. It was as if the punishment was thought to equal, if not to exceed, in savagery the crime itself . . . to make the executioner resemble a criminal, judges murderers." The bloodletting which such acts signal strains against and ultimately disrupts all efforts to normalize them, routinize them, and cover their tracks. While execution itself is effectively hidden from public view, the spectacle of law's dealings in death may be (re)located and made visible, if it is made visible at all, in capital trials like that of William Brooks. Under the force of this relocation we focus on the case rather than the body of the "condemned" (Foucault 1977:9). As Foucault puts it (ibid.), "publicity has shifted to the trial, and to the sentence; the execution itself is like an additional shame that justice is ashamed to impose on the condemned man."

The Brooks trial, and others like it, expresses and embodies a deeply felt anxiety about the proper relationship of law and these three forms of violence. This anxiety is reflected in the scrupulousness with which capital trials are themselves organized, regulated, and reviewed. It is also reflected in the enormous efforts put into the rationalization and justification of the apparatus of punishment, efforts which serve to efface the violence of law by renaming it. As Robert Weisberg recently observed (1992:175–76):

> Anglo-American law has traditionally suffered a serious identity crisis over its awkward relation to violence. . . . Our system assumes that law is to hold a monopoly on violence, but this is a monopoly viewed as both necessary and discomforting. It is necessary because it is viewed as the alternative to something worse—unrestrained private vengeance—and it is discomforting because those who make and enforce the law would like us to believe that, though they may be required to use force, force is somehow categorically distinguishable from violence. . . . [T]he efforts of modern jurisprudence to finesse or deny the role of violence have not ceased.

In all capital trials the juxtaposition of narratives about violence is disquieting if not destabilizing. This is especially true of the juxtaposition of the narratives of violence outside law with the linguistic representation of law's own violence. In

31 A recent story about the execution of Robert Alton Harris reported that "According to several witnesses Mr. Harris appeared to lose consciousness after about one and one-half minutes although his body continued a series of convulsive movements and his head jerked backward several times" (Bishop 1992; see also Sarat & Vidmar 1976; Johnson 1990).

these moments putting law's violence into discourse threatens to expose law as essentially similar to the antisocial violence it is supposed to deter and punish.[32] Benjamin (1978:286) argues that "in the exercise of violence over life and death more than in any other legal act, law reaffirms itself. But," he continues, "in this very violence something rotten in law is revealed, above all to a finer sensibility, because the latter knows itself to be infinitely remote from conditions in which fate might imperiously have shown itself in such a sentence." The violence of law itself threatens to expose the facade of law's dispassionate reason, of its necessity and restraint, as just that—a facade (Sarat & Kearns 1991b:269) and to destabilize law by forcing choices between the normative aspirations of law and the need to maintain social order through force (see *McCleskey v. Kemp* 1987; Cover 1975).[33] Violence threatens to swallow up law and leave nothing but a social world of forces arrayed in aggressive opposition (LaCapra 1990:1065). Where violence is present, can there be anything other than violence? This question puts enormous pressures on events like the capital trial to demonstrate and affirm the difference between the violence of law and the violence that law condemns.

Here, then, is the site of the most intense efforts to finesse and deny the role of violence in law, to mark the differences between violence beyond law's control and that which law itself dispenses, and to transform law's violence into legitimate force. Capital trials are occasions for overcoming doubt and regaining stability. The cultural resources for doing so are both internal and external to law itself. Random, unnecessary, irrational violence is vividly portrayed. While the violence outside the law is unnecessary, irrational, indiscriminate, gruesome, and useless, law's violence, the violence of the death penalty, is described as rational, purposive, and controlled through values, norms, and procedures external to violence itself. In capital trials, the force of law is represented as serving common purposes and aims against the anomic savagery lurking just be-

---

[32] See also Camus (1957). The imperatives of violence may be so overwhelming as to distort and destroy prevailing normative commitments. Two powerful examples are provided by Justice Powell in *McCleskey v. Kemp* (1987:1756) (holding that statistical evidence of racial discrimination may not be used to establish *prima facie* case of discrimination in death penalty cases), and by Justice Rehnquist in *Payne v. Tennessee* (1991) (devising new understanding of the bindingness of precedent to overturn two decisions forbidding the use of victim impact information in death penalty litigation).

Unfortunately, except in the utopian imagination, there is no symmetry in the relation of law and violence. Law never similarly threatens violence. Even when we realize the way law itself often exaggerates the threat of violence *outside* law, we can never ourselves imagine that law could ever finally conquer and undo force, coercion, and disorder; its best promise is a promise to substitute one kind of force—legitimate force—for another.

[33] "Force is disdainful of reason; it pushes it aside; it takes over completely. Reason and force have no way to share control of human agency" (Sarat & Kearns 1991b:269).

yond law's boundaries (Jacoby 1983; Rieder 1984).[34] Elaborate rituals and procedures, "super due process," give evidence of the care and concern with which law traffics in violence. The case of the condemned is treated with a seriousness equal to, if not greater than, any other in law. Thus the procedures and purposes of law are emphasized while its instrumentalities and wounding effects are kept in the background.

Externally, law draws upon cultural symbols of race and danger. Law's violence is, thus, "our" violence against "them" (Higginbotham 1978). As Justice Powell reminded us in *McCleskey* (1987:1778), the racialization of capital punishment and its disproportionate use against black men and especially those who kill white victims is not sufficiently disturbing in this culture to be "constitutionally significant." It is the allegedly civilizing violence of white order against savage disorder. Thus in the Brooks trial and in others like it, the price paid for such efforts to alleviate anxiety is very great. In addition to the actual violence which is all too often unleashed and the linguistic violence done in the ritual naming and in the process of rendering law's violence abstract, racialized social conventions—as well as flat narratives of purity and danger, responsibility and excuse, and innocence and guilt—are regularly reaffirmed.

Yet the anxiety which surrounds the violence of law is not put to rest. Capital trials place several narratives of violence side by side, one a narrative of violence which has already taken life, one a narrative of abuse and poverty which has shaped another life, and one the story of a prospective killing. While the first is intended to justify and strengthen the last, the last stands as an internal reminder of the artifice and artificiality of the very distinctions on which law's anxiety-alleviating legitimacy depends. Each narrative of lawless violence—whether of the kind that Brooks did or the kind that he suffered—is a reminder of the failure of law's own violence to guarantee security. Each narrative of lawless violence reminds us that law's violence constitutes us as anxious, fearful subjects (Dumm 1990) caught between a fearful aversion to the former and a fearful embrace of the latter.

References

Armstrong, Nancy, & Leonard Tenenhouse, eds. (1989) *The Violence of Representation: Literature and the History of Violence.* London: Routledge.

Benjamin, Walter (1978) "Critique of Violence," in P. Demetz, ed., *Reflections*, trans. E. Jephcott. New York: Harcourt, Brace.

[34] As Justice Stewart put it in his concurring opinion in *Furman v. Georgia*, (1972:309), "The instinct for retribution is part of the nature of man and channelling that instinct in the administration of criminal justice serves an important purpose in promoting the stability of a society governed by law."

56 Narratives of Violence in Capital Trials

Bishop, Katherine (1992) "After Night of Court Battles, a California Execution," *New York Times*, 22 April, sec. A, p. 1, col. 2.

Bobbio, Noberto (1965) "Law and Force," 49 *Monist* 321.

Booth, Wayne C. (1983) *The Rhetoric of Fiction.* 2d ed. Chicago: Univ. of Chicago Press.

Brady, J. B., & N. Garver, eds. (1991) *Justice, Law, and Violence*. Philadelphia: Temple Univ. Press.

Bumiller, Kristin (1990) "Fallen Angels: The Representation of Violence against Women in Legal Culture," 18 *International J. of the Sociology of Law* 125.

——— (1991) "Real Violence/Body Fictions." Presented at Law and Society Association and Research Committee on the Sociology of Law of the International Sociological Association meetings, Amsterdam.

Butler, Judith (1993) "Endangered/Endangering: Schematic Racism and White Paranoia," in Gooding-Williams 1993.

Camus, Albert (1957) "Reflexions sur la Guillotine," in A. Camus & A. Koestler, *Reflexions sur la peine capitale*. Paris: Calmann-Levy.

Carter, Stephen (1988) "When Victims Happen to Be Black," 97 *Yale Law J.* 420.

Cobb, Sara (1992) "The Domestication of Violence in Mediation: The Social Construction of Disciplinary Power in Law." Presented at the Amherst Legal Seminar, Amherst College.

Cornell, Drucilla (1990) "From the Lighthouse: The Promise of Redemption and the Possibility of Legal Interpretation," 11 *Cardozo Law Rev.* 1687.

Cover, Robert H. (1975) *Justice Accused: Antislavery and the Judicial Process*. New Haven, CT: Yale Univ. Press.

——— (1986a) "The Bonds of Constitutional Interpretation: Of the Word, the Deed, and the Role," 20 *Georgia Law Rev.* 815.

——— (1986b) "Violence and the Word," 95 *Yale Law J.* 1601.

Coyle, Marcia, Fred Strasser, & Marianne Lavelle (1990) "Fatal Defense: Trial and Error in the Nation's Death Belt," *National Law J.*, p. 30 (11 June).

Dan-Cohen, Meir (1992) "Responsibility and the Boundaries of the Self," 105 *Harvard Law Rev.* 959.

Davis, Natalie Zemon (1987) *Fiction in the Archives: Pardon Tales and Their Tellers in Sixteenth-Century France.* Stanford, CA: Stanford Univ. Press.

De Lauretis, Teresa (1989) "The Violence of Rhetoric: Considerations on Representation and Gender," in Armstrong & Tenenhouse 1989.

Derrida, Jacques (1990) "Force of Law: The 'Mystical Foundation of Authority,'' 11 *Cardozo Law Rev.* 921.

Dumm, Thomas L. (1990) "Fear of Law" 10 *Studies in Law, Politics & Society* 29.

——— (1992) "The New Enclosures: Racism in the Normalized Community.", in Gooding-Williams 1993.

Dworkin, Ronald (1977) *Taking Rights Seriously.* Cambridge, MA: Harvard Univ. Press.

Fitzpatrick, Peter (1991) "Violence and Legal Subjection." Unpublished, Univ. of Kent.

Foucault, Michel (1977) *Discipline and Punish: The Birth of the Prison*, trans. A. Sheridan. New York: Random House.

Friedenberg, Edgar (1971) "The Side Effects of the Legal Process," in Wolff 1971a.

Garfinkel, Harold (1956) "Conditions of Successful Degradation Ceremonies," 61 *American J. of Sociology* 420.

Gooding-Williams, Robert, ed. (1993) *Reading Rodney King/Reading Urban Uprising.* New York: Routledge.

Hay, Douglas (1975) "Property, Authority and the Criminal Law," in Doug-

las Hay et al., *Albion's Fatal Tree: Crime and Society in Eighteenth-Century England*. New York: Pantheon Books.
Held, Virginia (1989) "Violence, Terrorism, and Moral Inquiry," in D. T. Goldberg, ed., *Ethical Theory and Social Issues: Historical Texts and Contemporary Readings*. New York: Holt, Rinehart.
Higginbotham, A. Leon, Jr. (1978) *In the Matter of Color: Race in the American Legal Process* New York: Oxford Univ. Press.
Hobbes, Thomas (1986) *Leviathan*, ed. C. B. MacPherson. New York: Penguin Books.
Jacoby, Susan (1983) *Wild Justice: The Evolution of Revenge*. New York: Harper & Row.
Johnson, Robert (1990) *Death Work: A Study of the Modern Execution Process*. Pacific Grove, CA: Brooks/Cole.
Kelsen, Hans (1945) *General Theory of Law and State*, trans. A. Wedberg. New York: Russell & Russell.
LaCapra, Dominick (1990) "Violence, Justice, and the Force of Law," 11 *Cardozo Law Rev.* 1065.
Lawrence, Charles R., III (1987) "The Id, the Ego, and Equal Protection: Reckoning with Unconscious Racism," 39 *Stanford Law Rev.* 317.
MacKinnon, Catharine A. (1987) *Feminism Unmodified: Discourses on Life and Law*. Cambridge, MA: Harvard Univ. Press.
Mather, Lynn, & Barbara Yngvesson (1980–81) "Language, Audience, and the Transformation of Disputes," 15 *Law & Society Rev.* 775.
Minow, Martha (1989) *Making All the Difference: Inclusion, Exclusion, and American Law*. Ithaca, NY: Cornell Univ. Press.
——— (1990) "Words and the Door to the Land of Change: Law, Language, and Family Violence." Law School, Harvard Univ.
Morris, Herbert (1970) "Persons and Punishment," in A. I. Melden, ed., *Human Rights*. Belmont, CA: Wadsworth.
Murphy, Jeffrie G., & Jean Hampton (1988) *Forgiveness and Mercy*. Cambridge: Cambridge Univ. Press.
Navreson, Jan (1991) "Force, Violence, and Law," in Brady & Garver 1991.
Nietzsche, Friedrich (1956) *The Birth of Tragedy and the Genealogy of Morals*, trans. F. Golffing. Garden City, NY: Doubleday.
Olivecrona, Karl (1939) *Law as Fact*. Copenhagen: Einar Munksgaard.
Omolade, Barbara (1991) "Black Codes: Then and Now: The Central Park Jogger Case and Multiple Representations." Unpublished, City Univ. of New York.
Peller, Gary (1987) "Reason and the Mob in the Politics of Representation," *Tikkun*, p. 28 (July/Aug).
Rieder, Jonathan (1984) "The Social Organization of Vengeance," in D. Black, ed., 1 *Toward a General Theory of Social Control*. New York: Academic Press.
Sarat, Austin, & Thomas R. Kearns, eds. (1991a) *The Fate of Law*. Ann Arbor: Univ. of Michigan Press.
——— (1991b) "A Journey through Forgetting: Toward a Jurisprudence of Violence," in Sarat & Kearns 1991a.
———, eds. (1992a) *Law's Violence*. Ann Arbor: Univ. of Michigan Press.
——— (1992b) "Making Peace with Violence: Robert Cover on Law and Legal Theory," in Sarat & Kearns 1992a.
Sarat, Austin, & Neil Vidmar (1976) "Public Opinion, the Death Penalty, and the Eighth Amendment: Testing the Marshall Hypothesis," 1976 *Wisconsin Law Rev.* 171.
Scarry, Elaine (1985) *The Body in Pain: The Making and Unmaking of the World*. New York: Oxford Univ. Press.
Scheppele, Kim Lane (1990) "Facing Facts in Legal Interpretation," 30 *Representations* 42.

Scott, Joan W. (1991) "The Evidence of Experience," 17 *Critical Inquiry* 773.
Todorov, Tzvetan (1984) *The Conquest of America: The Question of the Other*, trans. R. Howard. New York: Harper & Row.
Waldenfels, Bernhard (1991) "The Limits of Legitimation and the Question of Violence," in Brady & Garver 1991.
Weber, Max (1954) *Max Weber on Law in Economy and Society*, ed. M. Rheinstein. Cambridge, MA: Harvard Univ. Press.
Weber, Samuel (1990) "Deconstruction before the Name: Some [Very] Preliminary Remarks on Deconstruction and Violence." Unpublished, U.C.L.A.
Weisberg, Robert (1984) "Deregulating Death," 1983 *Supreme Court Rev.* 305. Chicago: Univ. of Chicago Press.
——— (1992) "Private Violence as Moral Action: The Law as Inspiration and Example," in Sarat & Kearns 1992a.
Wellman, Carl (1991) "Violence, Law, and Basic Rights," in Brady & Garver 1991.
West, Robin (1990) "Narrative, Responsibility and Death: A Comment on the Death Penalty Cases from the 1989 Term," 1 *Maryland J. of Contemporary Legal Issues* 1.
——— (1991) "Disciplines, Subjectivity, and Law," in Sarat & Kearns 1991a.
Wheeler, Stanton, Kenneth Mann, & Austin Sarat (1988) *Sitting in Judgment: Sentencing White Collar Criminals*. New Haven, CT: Yale Univ. Press.
Williams, Patricia J. (1991) *The Alchemy of Race and Rights*. Cambridge, MA: Harvard Univ. Press.
——— (1992) "The Rules of the Game," *Village Voice*, p. 32 (12 May).
Wolff, Robert Paul, ed. (1971a) *The Rule of Law*. New York: Simon & Schuster.
——— (1971b) "Violence and the Law," in Wolff 1971a.

Cases Cited

Furman v. Georgia, 408 U.S. 238 (1972).
Godfrey v. Georgia, 446 U.S. 420 (1980).
Gregg v. Georgia, 428 U.S. 153 (1976).
Maynard v. Cartwright, 486 U.S. 356 (1988).
McCleskey v. Kemp, 481 U.S. 279 (1987).
McQuirter v. State, 63 So. 2d 388 (1953).
Payne v. Tennessee, 111 S.Ct. 2597 (1991).
Proffitt v. Florida, 428 U.S. 242 (1976).
State v. Sikora, 210 A.2d 193, 44 N.J. 453 (1965).
Woodson v. North Carolina, 428 U.S. 280 (1976).

Part II
Evidence and the Production of Truth

[6]

JUST THE FACTS, MA'AM: SEXUALIZED VIOLENCE, EVIDENTIARY HABITS, AND THE REVISION OF TRUTH

KIM LANE SCHEPPELE*

I. MATTERS OF FACT

Sergeant Joe Friday, a no-nonsense kind of detective on the old television series *Dragnet*, used to confront distraught women with the clipped injunction: "Just the facts, ma'am." Everyone knew what he meant. These "hysterical" women, privileging the expression of emotion over the recitation of relevant detail, were not being good witnesses. They confused what an event felt like with what it was; they wandered off the point into a tangle of irrelevancies. They did not crisply present the sort of evidence that would allow a conscientious detective like Sergeant Friday to catch the criminal. In short, these women were not helpful to the law.

Though Sergeant Friday no longer barks commands at weeping women on television, except in reruns, women's evidence is often still suspect in law. The stories women tell in court, particularly in cases of sexualized violence like rape, sexual harassment, incest, and woman battering, are vulnerable to attack as unbelievable. Cases of sexualized violence often evolve into a "he said, she said" battle of competing narratives in which the "he," who is the defendant, wins by default simply because the evidence is contested. Default rules about the burden of proof

---

* Arthur F. Thurnau Associate Professor of Political Science and Public Policy and Adjunct Associate Professor of Law, University of Michigan. I would like to thank Jane Bennett, Jerome Bruner, Sally Burns, Fernando Coronil, Peggy Davis, John Kitsuse, Rick Lempert, Jack Meiland, Francois Rochat, Roger Rouse, Ted Sarbin, David Scobey, Peter Seidman, Richard Sherwin, Julie Skurski, and Scott Styles as well as seminar participants at the New York Law School, the New York University Law School Clinic, the Michigan Institute for the Humanities, the Stanford Humanities Center, and the Chicago-Kent College of Law for making more comments of a more fundamental nature than I could possibly have taken into account in writing this paper. The first version of these ideas was presented at the annual meetings of the American Political Science Association in August 1991, another version was written for social psychologists as Kim Lane Scheppele, *Practices of Truth-Finding in a Court of Law*, *in* CONSTRUCTING THE SOCIAL (Theodore Sarbin & John Kitsuse eds., forthcoming 1993), and this represents yet another rethinking of those ideas. Those of you who have seen the earlier versions will have to judge for yourselves whether to believe this revised version, which may not yet be the end.

and the benefit of the doubt resolve all divergent accounts in favor of the accused when there are merely contested stories with no "hard" evidence to compel choice between them. Though laws on the books look more woman-friendly on issues of sexualized violence than they used to, women do not always find that helpful laws produce victories for women.[1] The worst of the overt sexism of the law may have been dismantled: gone, for the most part, are corroboration requirements[2] and the unrestrained admissibility of the woman's sexual history in rape trials;[3] the exemption in rape law that says rape cannot happen within marriage;[4] legal

---

1. Susan Estrich argues that the rape reform statutes did not accomplish as much as feminists thought they would. Instead, acquaintance rape still is hard to prosecute. *See* SUSAN ESTRICH, REAL RAPE 13, 80-81 (1987); *see also* Kim Lane Scheppele, *The Re-Vision of Rape Law*, 54 U. CHI. L. REV. 1095, 1097-98, 1102 (1987). In sexual-harassment cases, judges have repeatedly found that the particular instances of alleged abuse were not serious enough to warrant a successful claim of employment discrimination. *See, e.g.*, Rabidue v. Osceola Ref. Co., 805 F.2d 611 (6th Cir. 1986) (finding that the woman could not succeed in her sexual-harassment claim, despite vigorous dissent arguing for a "reasonable woman" standard). In Britain, Parliament passed a statute explicitly intended to allow women to get temporary restraining orders (TROs) against their battering husbands, only to find that the courts interpreted men's common-law rights of property in their homes as narrowing the effective range of cases in which such TROs were obtainable to only those cases in which the woman alone owned the house. *See* WILLIAM TWINING & DAVID MIERS, HOW TO DO THINGS WITH RULES: A PRIMER OF INTERPRETATION 356-73 (3d ed. 1991).

2. Although the Model Penal Code draft of 1980 incorporated a corroboration requirement, *see* MODEL PENAL CODE § 213.6(5) (Official Draft and Revised Comments 1980), 35 states had already eliminated their corroboration requirements, and eight others had limited the requirement. *See* Note, *The Rape Corroboration Requirement: Repeal Not Reform*, 81 YALE L.J. 1365, 1367-68 & nn.16-18 (1972).

3. Forty-nine states and the federal government have enacted rape-shield laws that limit the admissibility of evidence about a victim's prior sexual history. *See* James A. Vaught & Margaret Henning, *Admissibility of a Rape Victim's Prior Sexual Conduct in Texas: A Contemporary Review and Analysis*, 23 ST. MARY'S L.J. 893, 895 & nn.9-10 (1992); *see also* Harriett R. Galvin, *Shielding Rape Victims in the State and Federal Courts: A Proposal for the Second Decade*, 70 MINN. L. REV. 763, 765-66 (1986) (examining how different states approach rape-shield legislation and proposing an alternative legislative solution that preserves the underlying rationale of rape-shield laws as well as the defendant's constitutional rights); Andrew Z. Soshnick, *The Rape Shield Paradox: Complainant Protection amidst Oscillating Trends of State Judicial Interpretation*, 78 J. CRIM. L. & CRIMINOLOGY 644, 644-45 & nn.1-3 (1987) (noting that 40 states enacted rape-shield laws through statute, nine states used evidentiary rules to accomplish the protection, and Arizona provided protection through judicial opinion). The federal rape-shield rule has been codified in FED. R. EVID. 412. For a brief history and discussion of Rule 412, see 23 CHARLES A. WRIGHT & KENNETH W. GRAHAM, JR., FEDERAL PRACTICE AND PROCEDURE §§ 5381-5393 (1980).

4. For an overview of recent developments, see Anne L. Buckborough, *Family Law:*

permission for husbands to beat their wives in the name of proper discipline;[5] the view that children's complaints of sexual abuse are primarily fantasy;[6] and approval of sexual harassment as an implied condition of work for women.[7] But these apparent victories are superficial. More persistent aspects of sexism have been merely pushed underground.

In this article, I argue that the law is still sexist, but now in the name of fact rather than doctrine. Courts have continued to use woman-unfriendly habits of evaluating what counts as legal evidence. Representatives of the law still want "just the facts, ma'am." But these particular facts are hardly neutral or natural. Facts must be constructed and interpreted just as laws must be,[8] and the production of facts as an accomplishment of legal practitioners is only now beginning to be examined.[9] When we begin to focus on the way in which facts are

---

Recent Developments in the Law of Marital Rape, 1989 ANN. SURV. AM. L. 343, 343 (1990) (stating that "most states recognize some legal limitation on a husband's 'right' to have sex with his wife, but no consensus exists as to the extent of that limitation").

5. Such legal permission is customarily traced to William Blackstone. *See* 1 WILLIAM BLACKSTONE, COMMENTARIES ON THE LAW OF ENGLAND 444 (Univ. of Chicago Press, 1979) (1765-1769).

6. The view that complaints by children about sexual abuse were most likely fantasy was forwarded most famously, and perhaps most powerfully, by Sigmund Freud. *See* SIGMUND FREUD, INTRODUCTORY LECTURES ON PSYCHOANALYSIS 126-35 (James Strachey ed. & trans., 1977). This view has since been widely discredited for children's complaints in general. *See, e.g.*, JEFFREY HAUGAARD & N. DICKON REPUCCI, THE SEXUAL ABUSE OF CHILDREN 149-50 (1988). It has also been discredited even about Freud's own cases. *See* JEFFREY M. MASSON, THE ASSAULT ON TRUTH: FREUD'S SUPPRESSION OF THE SEDUCTION THEORY 50 (1984); Suzanne Gearhart, *The Scene of Psychoanalysis*, *in* IN DORA'S CASE: FREUD-HYSTERIA-FEMINISM 106-07 (Charles Bernheimer & Claire Kahane eds., 2d ed. 1990).

7. *See* Meritor Sav. Bank v. Vinson, 477 U.S. 57, 66 (1986) (concluding that sexual harassment is actionable as a form of sexual discrimination).

8. *See* KIM LANE SCHEPPELE, LEGAL SECRETS: EQUALITY AND EFFICIENCY IN THE COMMON LAW 86-108 (1988) (providing an account of the way in which the interpretation of law and the interpretation of fact go on simultaneously in the processes of lawyering and judging).

9. *See generally* Kim Lane Scheppele, *Facing Facts in Legal Interpretation*, 30 REPRESENTATIONS 42 (1990) (arguing that legal interpretation necessarily constructs accounts of law and fact simultaneously and discussing whether the flexibility judges have in interpreting facts undermines the legitimacy of legal institutions) [hereinafter Scheppele, *Facing Facts*]; Kim Lane Scheppele, *Foreword: Telling Stories*, 87 MICH. L. REV. 2073 (1989) (discussing evidentiary habits in the construction of stories from evidence) [hereinafter Scheppele, *Telling Stories*]. For other accounts of the practices of

presented as natural and interpreted as truth, we see that much misogynistic work is done in the construction of "reality."

This article focuses on one of many elements in the construction of facts that works to the disadvantage of women. Women who delay in telling their stories of abuse at the hands of men or who appear to change their stories over time about such abuse are particularly likely to be discredited as liars. The very fact of delay or change is used as evidence that the delayed or changed stories cannot possibly be true.[10] But abused women frequently have exactly this response: they repress what happened;[11] they cannot speak;[12] they hesitate, waver, and procrastinate;[13] they hope the abuse will go away;[14] they cover up for

---

fact-interpretation in law, see W. LANCE BENNETT & MARTHA S. FELDMAN, RECONSTRUCTING REALITY IN THE COURTROOM: JUSTICE AND JUDGMENT IN AMERICAN CULTURE 41-65 (1981); JEROME FRANK, COURTS ON TRIAL: MYTH AND REALITY IN AMERICAN JUSTICE 14-36, 80-102 (1949); BERNARD S. JACKSON, LAW, FACT AND NARRATIVE COHERENCE (1988); WILLIAM TWINING, THEORIES OF EVIDENCE: BENTHAM AND WIGMORE (1985); *see also* NARRATIVE AND THE LEGAL DISCOURSE: A READER IN STORYTELLING AND THE LAW (David R. Papke ed., 1992) (collection on the uses of narrative in legal reasoning). *See generally* Symposium, *Legal Storytelling*, 87 MICH. L. REV. 2073 (1989) (special issue on the uses of narrative in the law).

10. *See* Morrison Torrey, *When Will We Be Believed? Rape Myths and the Idea of a Fair Trial in Rape Prosecutions*, 24 U.C. DAVIS L. REV. 1013, 1041-43 (1991); *see also* People v. Brown, 524 N.E.2d 742, 747 (Ill. App. Ct. 1988) (finding that "evidence of the victim's prompt complaint should be admissible to overcome the adverse inference which would otherwise arise from her silence"); Dawn M. DuBois, *A Matter of Time: Evidence of a Victim's Prompt Complaint in New York*, 53 BROOK. L. REV. 1088 (1988) (stating that the prompt-complaint doctrine is based on "antiquated perceptions of how women respond to rape" and suggesting an alternative to the doctrine). *But see* MODEL PENAL CODE § 213.6(4) (Official Draft and Revised Comments 1980). The Model Penal Code proposed placing strict time limits on those making rape complaints: "No prosecution may be instituted or maintained under this Article unless the alleged offense was brought to the notice of Public authorities within three (3) months of its occurrence." *Id.*

11. Many rape victims suffer from short-term memory loss, which may result from an attempt to escape from a fear-inducing situation. Lois G. Veronen et al., *Treating Fear and Anxiety in Rape Victims: Implications for the Criminal Justice System*, *in* PERSPECTIVES ON VICTIMOLOGY 150 (William H. Parsonage ed., 1979).

12. "During my last semester of law school, a friend tried to rape me in my apartment in Cambridge, Massachusetts. I lived alone. While it was happening, I felt disembodied and I lost my voice." Terry N. Steinberg, *Rape on College Campuses: Reform Through Title IX*, 18 J.C. & U.L. 39, 39 (1991) (describing the author's personal experience as the victim of a violent rape).

13. Most women do not report sexualized threats and sexualized violence against them at all. In one survey conducted in San Francisco, only 9.5% of the women reported

their abusers;[15] they try harder to be "good girls";[16] and they take the blame for the abuse upon themselves.[17] Such actions produce delayed or altered stories over time,[18] which are then disbelieved for the very reason that they have been revised.[19]

The disbelief of delayed or revised stories reflects a view that the truth is singular, immediately apparent, and permanent—a view not unique to law. As this article shows, the construction of facts in law is not based only, or even primarily, on the special expertise of lawyers or on detailed knowledge of the law. Of course, lawyers have a great deal of influence in shaping the facts as they appear at trial. But lawyers, at least successful

---

their rapes. DIANA E.H. RUSSELL, SEXUAL EXPLOITATION: RAPE, CHILD SEXUAL ABUSE, AND WORKPLACE HARASSMENT 31 (1984). Estimates on the number of rapes which are actually reported range from 5 to 30%. MENACHEM AMIR, PATTERNS IN FORCIBLE RAPE 27-28 (1971); *see also* Scheppele, *supra* note 1, at 1096 (stating that approximately half of all victims fail to report rapes or rape attempts and that acquaintance rapes are largely unreported). Of those who do report, many delay before calling the police. One New York study found that most victims wait two to seven days before reporting a rape, while a Massachusetts study reported that half of the rape victims waited before reporting. Torrey, *supra* note 10, at 1016 n.10 (citing studies that illustrate that only about half of rape victims report what has happened to them). Apparently, women tend to wait even longer if they know their assailant. SEDELLE KATZ & MARY A. MAZUR, UNDERSTANDING THE RAPE VICTIM: A SYNTHESIS OF RESEARCH FINDINGS 188-90 (1979); *see also* Kimberly A. Mango, *Students versus Professors: Combatting Sexual Harassment Under Title IX of the Education Amendments of 1972*, 23 CONN. L. REV. 355, 359 n.13 (1991) (citing a study of sexual-harassment victims at Cornell University that found that less than one percent of the victims actually filed complaints); Kathleen Waits, *The Criminal Justice System's Response to Battering: Understanding the Problem, Forging the Solutions*, 60 WASH. L. REV. 267, 275 (1985) (stating that experts agree that statistics underestimate the extent of woman-battering because of the victim's reluctance to report the crimes).

14. In one government study, 52% of the female victims of sexual harassment ignored the harassing conduct and did nothing about it. *See* U.S. MERIT SYS. PROTECTION BD., SEXUAL HARASSMENT IN THE FEDERAL GOVERNMENT: AN UPDATE 24 (1988).

15. Battered women often refuse to tell anyone that they are being beaten. *See* LENORE WALKER, THE BATTERED WOMAN 74 (1979).

16. Experience of sexual harassment caused Anita Hill to keep notes on all the work she did to show what a model employee she was. *See infra* text accompanying notes 30-31.

17. *See* Kim Lane Scheppele & Pauline Bart, *Through Women's Eyes: Defining Danger in the Wake of Sexual Assault*, 39 J. SOC. ISSUES 63, 79 (1983).

18. *See* JUDITH LEWIS HERMAN, TRAUMA AND RECOVERY 179-80 (1992).

19. *See* Torrey, *supra* note 10, at 1044.

lawyers, do not just mobilize their legal expertise to achieve these ends. They must also mobilize ordinary storytelling practices that are present outside legal settings, in which credibility, coherence, and plausibility are all judged against a background of common knowledge, itself shot through with unthinking assumptions.

II. BELIEVING ANITA HILL[20]

During a riveting weekend in October 1991, many Americans tuned their television sets to the Supreme Court Confirmation Hearings of Judge Clarence Thomas. These hearings had turned to the question of sexual-harassment allegations made against Judge Thomas by his former close aide, Professor Anita Hill. The Republican members of the Senate Judiciary Committee, unfettered by technical rules of evidence that would operate in a court of law, were able to show in stark form just how such a witness could be discredited. They used every strategy they could think of to undermine Professor Hill's testimony. Prominent among the strategies was their focus on: (1) her delay in reporting the harassment; and (2) the change in her accounts of what the harassment involved as she went through successive retellings of the story. In the space opened up by Professor Hill's silences and versions, Republican senators attempted to insert various stock stories[21] about the scorned woman, the woman who

20. At this point, this is hardly a controversial proposition. A survey of state and federal judges, taken around the time of the initial testimony, revealed that two-thirds of them believed Anita Hill. *See Hearings Turn off Judges; NLJ Survey Finds They Don't Want Top Spot*, NAT'L L. J., Oct. 28, 1991, at 1. At the time of the hearings, a poll showed that more Americans believed Clarence Thomas than believed Anita Hill. The figures stood at 40% for Thomas and only 24% for Hill. *See* Jill Smolowe, *Anita Hill's Legacy: A Year After the Clarence Thomas Hearings, Women Wonder if the Consciousness-Raising Made Enough of a Difference*, TIME, Oct. 19, 1992, at 56. A year later, however, several surveys revealed that more people believed Anita Hill than believed Clarence Thomas. A *Wall Street Journal*/NBC News survey reported that 44% of registered voters believed Hill while only 34% believed Thomas. *Id.* A *U.S. News and World Report* poll reported a 38% to 38% deadlock in credibility ratings one year after the hearings, while polls at the time registered 60% to 20% in favor of Thomas. Gloria Borger et al., *The Untold Story*, U.S. NEWS & WORLD REP., Oct. 12, 1992, at 28. It is significant to note that the percentage of people who thought Hill had been treated unfairly rose from 8% at the time of the hearings to 39% a year later. *Id.*

21. On stock stories, see ROGER C. SCHANK, TELL ME A STORY: A NEW LOOK AT REAL AND ARTIFICIAL MEMORY (1990); Gerald P. Lopez, *Lay Lawyering*, 32 UCLA L. REV. 1 (1984).

had lost touch with reality, and the woman motivated by political animus who was making a bid for attention.

Although the Senate Judiciary Committee members who held the hearings repeatedly emphasized that the proceedings were not a trial, legalistic conceptions of "burden of proof" and "presumption of innocence" were used throughout the three days of marathon sessions.[22] But there the legal formality ended. Evidence was introduced without supporting witnesses;[23] insinuations were made about Professor Hill's motivation and credibility that had no basis in evidence;[24] people without any expertise in evaluating psychiatric claims were asked for their opinions of Professor Hill's personality and sanity;[25] questioning was limited by the unwillingness of then-Judge Clarence Thomas to answer questions outside the scope that he deemed fit for inquiry,[26] even though much of what he refused to talk about would have been thought relevant had this been a proper trial; and witnesses who had relevant evidence to introduce were kept dangling and ultimately not asked for the information they had as part of the hearings.[27] Whatever the Senate hearings might have been designed to accomplish, they left innuendo and unsubstantiated stories in their wake.

These stories reveal some popular, common-sense biases in the evaluation of historical accounts, particularly when women are making claims that they have been the target of abuse. To see how popular conceptions of truth can be mobilized to discredit a witness, it helps to look first at the themes that politicians believe both will work to undermine a claim and be understandable to the public. Then we can see how these same strategies are used in more formal legal settings in muted form. To begin, let us look at how those defending Judge Thomas repeatedly emphasized that Professor Hill had delayed making her accusations in the first place and had changed her story once she did.

---

22. *See Nomination of Clarence Thomas to Associate Justice of the Supreme Court of the United States: Hearings of the Senate Judiciary Committee*, 102d Cong., 2d Sess., Federal News Service, Oct. 11, 1991, *available in* LEXIS, Nexis Library, Fednew File [hereinafter *Hearings*].

23. *See id.*

24. *See id.*

25. *See id.*

26. *See id.*

27. *See id.*

A. *Silences*

Professor Hill's initial delay in reporting the harassment—and her public silence until the last moment before the confirmation vote was to occur—was particularly salient to the senators. Senator Strom Thurmond raised the issue in his opening statement, before Anita Hill had even testified:

> The alleged harassment she describes took place some ten years ago. During that time, she continued to initiate contact with Judge Thomas in an apparently friendly manner. In addition, Professor Hill chose to publicize her allegations the day before the full Senate would have voted to confirm Judge Thomas. While I fully intend to maintain an open mind during today's testimony, I must say that the timing of these statements raises a tremendous number of questions which must be dealt with, and I can assure all the witnesses that we shall be unstinting in our effort to ascertain the truth.[28]

In other words, why didn't Professor Hill come forward at the time with her accounts of sexual harassment? Given that she remained silent and continued on as if nothing had happened, Senator Thurmond strongly suspected that the initial silence and its revelation at the moment of the confirmation hearings spoke for itself: the message was that the harassing conduct never occurred.

Judge Thomas himself emphasized Professor Hill's initial silence in his account of events:

> I find it particularly troubling that she never raised any hint that she was uncomfortable with me. She did not raise or mention it when considering moving with me to EEOC [Equal Employment Opportunity Commission] from the Department of Education, and she'd never raised it with me when she left EEOC and was moving on in her life. And, to my fullest knowledge, she did not speak to any other women working with or around me who would feel comfortable enough to raise it with me, especially Diane Holt [Thomas's secretary], to whom she seemed closest on my

28. *Id.*

> personal staff. Nor did she raise it with mutual friends such as Linda Jackson or Gil Hardy.[29]

Senator Arlen Specter pressed Professor Hill on her initial silence, focusing on her lack of contemporaneous notes about the harassing behavior:

> As an experienced attorney and as someone who was in the field of handling sexual harassment cases, didn't it cross your mind that if you needed to defend yourself from what you anticipated he might do, that your evidentiary position would be much stronger if you had made some notes?[30]

Professor Hill indicated that she kept detailed records of her assignments and work products while the harassment was going on because she wanted documentation of her professional performance in the event Judge Thomas tried to fire her for refusing his solicitations. But only contemporaneous records of the harassment itself would have demonstrated to Senator Specter that it had actually happened.

Talk of the "eleventh hour charges" and of Professor Hill's puzzling silence pervaded the hearings, as if the timing of her statement to the committee alone was evidence of its falseness. A number of senators believed that her only motivation for coming forward at that time was political and that politics and truth-telling were mutually exclusive motivations. So, the initial silence hung over the proceedings as evidence that political revenge was the true story.

Trying to put her initial silence in some context, Professor Hill explained how she reacted to Judge Thomas's conduct at the time:

> My reaction to these conversations was to avoid them by eliminating opportunities for us to engage in extended conversations. This was difficult because at the time I was his only assistant at the Office of Education—or Office for Civil Rights. . . . When Judge Thomas was made chair of the EEOC, I needed to face the question of whether to go with him. I was asked to do so, and I did. The work itself was interesting, and at that time it appeared that the sexual overtures which had so

29. *Id.*

30. *Id.*

> troubled me had ended. I also faced the realistic fact that I had no alternative job. While I might have gone back to private practice, perhaps in my old firm or at another, I was dedicated to civil rights work, and my first choice was to be in that field. Moreover, the Department of Education itself was a dubious venture. President Reagan was seeking to abolish the entire department.[31]

Pressing Professor Hill on her failure to say anything at the time, Senator Leahy asked what the mechanisms for reporting complaints within the EEOC would have been then. Professor Hill responded by saying that she believed she would have had to go to the Congressional oversight committee. Asked what she believed would have happened had she done so, Professor Hill replied: "Well, I can speculate that it might have been difficult. I can speculate that had I come forward immediately after I left the EEOC, I can speculate that I would have lost my job at Oral Roberts" University, where she taught law.[32] Professor Hill did testify that she talked to close friends about the harassment, but she did not speak to anyone at work. When asked how she could have allowed this "reprehensible conduct to go on right in the headquarters" of the agency charged with enforcing sexual-harassment laws,[33] Professor Hill replied:

> Well, it was a very trying and difficult decision for me not to say anything further. I can only say that when I made the decision to just withdraw from the situation and not press a claim or charge against him, that I may have shirked a duty, a responsibility that I had. And to that extent I confess that I am very sorry that I did not do something or say something, but at the time that was my best judgment. Maybe it was a poor judgment but it wasn't a dishonest [one], and it wasn't a completely unreasonable choice that I made given the circumstances.[34]

Some of the people to whom she originally confided the sexual-harassment allegations testified on her behalf. Four friends and colleagues of Professor Hill testified to versions of the harassment story that

31. *Id.*

32. *Id.*

33. *Id.*

34. *Id.*

Professor Hill had told them either at the time that it occurred (witnesses Ellen Wells, Susan Hoerchner, and John Carr) or when she was applying for jobs and had to explain why she had left the Equal Employment Opportunity Commission where she worked with Clarence Thomas (witness John Paul).[35] Each of the four witnesses had contacted Professor Hill after they heard of her allegations, offering to testify that she had told them these stories earlier. None of the four witnesses had met any of the other corroborating witnesses prior to appearing in Washington to testify at the Senate hearings. But none of them were able to reproduce in detail just what had occurred between Thomas and Hill, because Professor Hill's accounts to each of them had been quite nonspecific, general, and brief. Although the combined testimony of the four witnesses indicated that Professor Hill had confided in each of them at or near the time when the incidents were alleged to have occurred, the lack of detailed corroboration led the Republican Senators on to their next problem with Professor Hill's testimony.

B. *Revisions*

Many versions of events were presented during the course of the hearings. Once her allegations became known to the Senate Judiciary Committee, Professor Hill had three opportunities to narrate what had happened: once, to the FBI agents who arrived at her house one evening after work to interview her; again, to the Senate Committee staffers who were trying to work out what she would say if called as a witness; and yet again, to the whole world as it watched her testimony live on television before the Senate Judiciary Committee. In the televised account, new details emerged that had not been present in the earlier versions, though none of the new details conflicted with earlier, more general stories. But the very fact of the growing detail was used as evidence that Professor Hill was lying. Senator Orrin Hatch described her stories as "[t]hree different versions, each expansive, each successively expansive."[36] Constancy of stories over time was presented as the crucial marker of truth. Lack of constancy meant a lack of truth.

35. *See Nomination of Clarence Thomas to Associate Justice of the Supreme Court of the United States: Hearings of the Senate Judiciary Committee*, 102d Cong., 2d Sess., Federal News Service, Oct. 13, 1991, *available in* LEXIS, Nexis Library, Fednew File.

36. *Hearings*, *supra* note 22.

Even Judge Thomas used Professor Hill's increasing detail as evidence of the falsity of the charges:

> The facts keep changing, Senator. When the FBI visited me, the statements to this committee and the questions were one thing. The FBI's subsequent questions were another thing, and the statements today as I received summaries of them were another thing. It is not my fault that the facts changed. What I have said to you is categorical; that any allegations that I engaged in any conduct involving sexual activity, pornographic movies, attempted to date her, any allegations, I deny. It is not true. So, the facts can change, but my denial does not.[37]

Judge Thomas invoked the popular idea that statements that remain the same over time appear more reliable than statements that appear to change. He was asserting that his categorical denials were more true than Professor Hill's "changing" facts precisely because his denials had never been subject to revision.

That Professor Hill's story appeared to change over time received much attention during Senator Specter's questioning. He tried to establish crucial inconsistencies and additions, markers of falsehood of the whole account, by taking each individual fact she had stated and holding it up against prior individual facts she had described. Picking apart the stories required *denarrativizing* the accounts or, in the words of Andrew Ross, engaging in "the fetishizing of detail."[38] One statement, surgically cut from its context, was compared to another, similarly surgically cut. Professor Hill, sensing that her story was getting lost in the false concreteness of specificity, told Senator Specter:

> Well, I think if you start to look at each individual problem with the statement, then you're not going to be satisfied that it's true. But I think the statement has to be taken as a whole. There is nothing in this statement that—or nothing in my background, nothing in my statement—there is no motivation that would show that I would make up something like this. And I guess one really

37. *Id.*

38. Andrew Ross, *The Private Parts of Justice*, *in* RACE-ING JUSTICE, EN-GENDERING POWER: ESSAYS ON ANITA HILL, CLARENCE THOMAS, AND THE CONSTRUCTION OF SOCIAL REALITY 40, 56 (Toni Morrison ed., 1992).

> does have to understand something about the nature of sexual harassment. It is very difficult for people to come forward with these things—these kinds of things. And it wasn't as though I rushed forward with this information. I can only tell you what happened and, to the best of my recollection, what occurred and ask you to take that into account. Now, you have to make your own judgment about it from there on, but I do want you to take into account the whole thing.[39]

The *whole* story, Professor Hill argued, was more than the sum of its parts.

Why didn't she tell the FBI about Coke can incident, Senator Specter asked? Why did she omit a vivid description of the specific acts Judge Thomas had told her he enjoyed when watching pornographic movies? The FBI report contained "no reference to any mention of Judge Thomas's private parts or sexual prowess or size, et cetera,"[40] noted Senator Specter. Professor Hill responded to these questions by saying, "the FBI agent made clear that if I were embarrassed about talking about something, that I could decline to discuss things that were too embarrassing but that I could provide as much information as I felt comfortable with at that time."[41] Though she later said, "I never declined to answer a question because it was too embarrassing," she also said, "I told them the nature of the comments and did not tell them more specifics." She added, "I was very uncomfortable talking to the agent about that, these incidents. I am very uncomfortable now. But I feel that it is necessary. The FBI agent told me that it was regular procedure to come back and ask for more specifics if it was necessary. And so at that time, I did not provide all the specifics that I could have."[42]

C. *Counterstories*

On the other side, Judge Thomas denied Professor Hill's allegation and substituted in part his own narrative of what had happened—that he was the true victim in the proceedings. He could present himself in this way because he called on the stock story of a man betrayed by a woman

39. *Hearings*, *supra* note 22.

40. *Id.*

41. *Id.*

42. *Id.*

he had trusted. He had always treated his whole staff professionally, cordially, and without the interjection of personal distractions, he said. Most memorably, however, he imposed another strong narrative pattern on the proceedings:

> Senator, in the 1970s, I became very interested in the issue of lynching, and if you want to track through this country in the 19th and 20th century the lynchings of black men, you will see that there is invariably or in many instances a relationship with sex and an accusation that that person cannot shake off. That is the point that I'm trying to make, and that is the point that I was making last night, that this is a high-tech lynching. I cannot shake off these accusations because they play to the worst stereotypes we have about black men in this country.[43]

And so Judge Thomas, who had tried in his first round of confirmation hearings to epitomize "racelessness," as Toni Morrison has described it,[44] found himself invoking race as his ultimate defense.[45] As Senator Hatch led him through a series of questions concerning specific stereotypes about black men and their sexual prowess that were invoked by Professor Hill's charges, Judge Thomas confirmed in detail just which allegations partook of stereotyping and which ones did not.

Supplementing the historical race narrative, Judge Thomas added personal and political narratives. The personal narrative featured a man from Pin Point, Georgia, who had grown up to be offered the greatest opportunity in the world, only to have it snatched away from him by the demeaning politics of race. But he would survive it:

> This has been an enormously difficult experience, but I don't think that that's the worst of it. I'm 43 years old, and if I'm not confirmed, I'm still the youngest member of the U.S. Court of Appeals for the D.C. Circuit. I'll go on. I'll go back to my life of talking to my neighbors, and cutting my grass, and getting a

---

43. *Id.*

44. Toni Morrison, *Introduction: Friday on the Potomac*, *in* RACE-ING JUSTICE, EN-GENDERING POWER: ESSAYS ON ANITA HILL, CLARENCE THOMAS, AND THE CONSTRUCTION OF SOCIAL REALITY at vii, xxi (Toni Morrison ed., 1992).

45. *See Hearings*, *supra* note 22.

> Big Mac at McDonald's, and driving my car, [and] seeing my kid play football. I'll live. I'll have my life back.[46]

But, in Thomas's view, the country would not do as well:

> I think the country has been hurt by this process. I think we are destroying our country, we are destroying our institutions, and I think it's a sad day when the U.S. Senate can be used by interest groups and hate mongers and people who are interested in digging up dirt to destroy other people, and who will stop at no tactics when they can use our great institutions for their own political ends. We are gone far beyond McCarthyism. This is far more dangerous than McCarthyism. At least McCarthy was elected.[47]

Presenting himself as the man victimized by malicious uses of his race to discredit him, Judge Thomas allied himself with the image of the United States, which had been victimized as well.

D. *Filling in Silences and Revising Revisions*

Multiple versions from Hill's own accounting, a blanket denial and counternarratives from Thomas, as well as many other versions from various witnesses, left the Senate Judiciary Committee with a lot to pick apart. And much of the strategy of those who won by getting Judge Thomas through the confirmation process and onto the Supreme Court depended on presenting Clarence Thomas as the real victim and Anita Hill as the true aggressor. This reversal was accomplished in large measure by presenting Anita Hill's story as a revised account, growing out of a suspicious silence.

In the gap created within the initial account and in the spaces chipped out of the apparent inconsistencies in Professor Hill's multiple versions, many alternative narratives about Professor Hill were presented as plausible. Witnesses supporting Judge Thomas presented alternative stories that would explain Anita Hill's charges of sexual harassment, ranging from Professor Hill's alleged grandiosity and ambition (witness J.C. Alvarez), to Professor Hill's status as a "scorned woman" (witness Phyllis

---

46. *Id.*
47. *Id.*

Berry), to her alleged flights of fantasy (witness John Doggett).[48] Other witnesses for Judge Thomas expressed disbelief that he could do the acts alleged (witnesses Nancy Fitch and Diane Holt),[49] opening up more opportunities to recast Professor Hill's story as the story of a woman bent on revenge, a woman given to fantasy, a calculating politica,[50] a decontextualized woman lost in space.

The Hill/Thomas hearings were not a judicial forum. But the tactics used in an attempt to discredit Hill's testimony borrow both from the courtroom and from daily life. Stories that emerge from silence or that are revised over time—elaborated, altered in tone, emerging in public out of a silence that went before—are presented as suspect *precisely because* they are delayed or revised. With the polls showing that the tactic worked to make Judge Thomas's counter-stories more believable (or at least no less credible) than Professor Hill's harassment narrative and with Senators apparently believing the same, Clarence Thomas was confirmed.

III. SILENCES AND REVISIONS

Anita Hill is not the only woman to have remained silent about sexual harassment. In fact, most women do not immediately talk about the details of sexual harassment in ways that are likely to make prosecuting the offenders straightforward in a court of law.[51] Women who experience rape, domestic abuse, incest, and other forms of sexualized threats and sexualized violence often have the same reaction.[52] Many women do not talk about the events with anyone at the time, and even those women willing to talk at the time do not report the threats and violence against them to the police or other officials who can mobilize the law.[53] When women first talk about the unspeakable to others, they often present initial accounts that try to make things normal again. They try to smooth out social relations by minimizing the harm of the abuse, engaging in self-

48. *See id.*

49. *See id.*

50. What else should we call a female politico?

51. *See* CATHARINE A. MACKINNON, SEXUAL HARASSMENT OF WORKING WOMEN 28 (1979).

52. *See id.*; *see also* Torrey, *supra* note 10, at 1044-45 (stating that "a significant number of women who are raped do not report the rape for several days or may even experience a 'silent reaction' and not tell anyone of the assault").

53. *See supra* notes 13-15 and accompanying text.

blame, telling stories that offer alternative explanations of events so that the full consequences of the abuse do not have to be dealt with at the time, and disguising the brutality through descriptive distortions of events.[54]

In psychological terms, women who have been sexually assaulted, whether through rape, incest, domestic brutality, workplace harassment, or extended periods of "domestic captivity,"[55] often show signs of post-traumatic stress disorder.[56] Survivors of extraordinary brutality often literally cannot say what they have seen or put into words the terror that they have felt.[57] Picking through the shards of a former life, survivors can no longer put the pieces into relation with each other to tell a coherent and compelling narrative about how things disintegrated. As therapists who have worked with traumatized patients have noted, "[t]he survivor's initial account of the event may be repetitious, stereotyped, and emotionless. . . . It does not develop or progress in time, and it does not reveal the storyteller's feelings or interpretations of events."[58] As women's sense of safety in the world has been shattered, so too has their sense of narrative coherence.[59]

---

54. *See supra* notes 11-12, 16-19 and accompanying text.

55. Herman, *supra* note 18, at 74.

56. *See id.* at 76-80.

57. Post-traumatic stress syndrome, as Herman's book makes clear, is not confined to women. Combat veterans often have the same symptoms, as do Holocaust survivors, political prisoners, and disaster victims, regardless of gender. *See id.* at 74-75, 181-82, 188. In the realm of criminal law, however, the vast majority of people suffering from this psychological response are women whose brutalities generally come in the name of common crimes. *See id.* at 175-87.

58. *Id.* at 175.

59. In our research on recovery from the trauma of rape, we discovered that women who were attacked when they thought they were safe had more severe reactions than women who were attacked when they believed that they were taking risks or were otherwise in danger, controlling for the severity of violence in the assault. *See* Scheppele & Bart, *supra* note 17, at 76-78. For the women with the most disoriented reactions, narrative consistency was disturbed, but so was any sense of associative logic. *See id.* One woman who had been attacked in a cornfield near her childhood home (where she felt safe) developed a terror of urban elevators. *Id.* at 69. A woman attacked at 10 A.M. coming back from the grocery store felt terrified to drive. *See id.* at 77. In one of the most severe reactions, a woman who was attacked at a party given by friends was subsequently placed in a mental institution for several years. *Id.* at 70-71. All of these women had trouble explaining why their fear spread the way it did from situations like the one in which they were attacked to other situations, apparently unrelated to the outside observer, in which the woman had previously felt safe as well. Nothing "made sense" in conscious terms.

Later, however, often through working in therapy, becoming overtly feminist, or getting enough emotional distance on the events to begin to deal with them, brutalized women revise their stories. Women who were silent begin to speak out for the first time. Women who were silent about the violence, who at the time said that nothing happened, or who took the blame themselves for anything that did happen, begin to tell stories of abuse. As these stories are told with more confidence, they "may change as missing pieces are recovered. This is particularly true in situations where [the survivor] has experienced significant gaps in memory."[60] What the survivor is trying to do at this point is to figure out a story that makes sense of her memories. The process of making coherence out of previously fragmented knowledge results in adjustments in the details that are recalled or in the way the details are put together.[61] One sign of *recovery* from the abuse is that women's stories change over time.[62]

Though the influence of extreme trauma on narrative consistency over time is quite pronounced, lesser traumas may produce something of the same effect. Women who have experienced sexual harassment at work also report many of the same symptoms as women who have suffered more extreme forms of physical abuse.[63] Women who have been "merely hassled" also show signs of extreme stress.[64] Even Anita Hill, who

60. HERMAN, *supra* note 18, at 179-80.

61. *See id.* at 176-81.

62. *See id.*

63. The woman who has been sexually harassed may experience "severe physical effects, including irritability, nausea, headaches, loss of concentration, dizzy spells, stomach aches, fatigue, muscle spasms, hypertension and psychogenic pain." *See* Tina Kirstein-Ezzell, *Eradicating Title VII Sexual Harassment by Recognizing an Employer's Duty to Prohibit Sexual Harassment*, 33 ARIZ. L. REV. 383, 386 (1991) (footnote omitted); *see also* Robinson v. Jacksonville Shipyards, Inc., 760 F. Supp. 1486, 1519 (M.D. Fla. 1991) (explaining that women who had been sexually harassed at work reported sleep disturbances and other signs of trauma).

64. My suspicion is that many women who experience sexual harassment as students drop out of school or otherwise significantly change their career plans to avoid the men who harass them. Because most studies of sexual harassment in schools involve women who have remained at the school, those who left are not included. Based on discussions with many undergraduate and graduate students, I can say that being "hassled" by a male teacher or by male students has led quite a few female students to lose sleep, to go into therapy, to start doing badly in their coursework, and, eventually, to leave the university. One woman student I spoke with had been the victim of a particularly cruel joke at a fraternity party. This woman was unable to attend classes without snickering men from that fraternity teasing her and reminding her of the event. She had difficulty eating and sleeping, and eventually withdrew from school. The men who did this to her have

stayed on the job and tried to ignore the harassment she later publicly described, "was hospitalized on an emergency basis for five days for acute stomach pain which [she] attributed to stress on the job."[65] Eventually, the accounts of what produced the stress may change as the details emerge from a traumatized memory and as the world feels a safer place in which to tell complete stories.[66] Or, as Anita Hill explained, she was asked a direct question ten years later and could not lie about what had happened.[67]

But we should not see this problem of shifting stories as being only a psychological response to individualized events. Larger forces are in play that provide a social and cultural context in which shifting stories appear as a response to sexualized threats and sexualized violence—and in which the threats and the violence are themselves displaced and denied through the fact of delayed accounts. Psychological explanations may be able to tell us how the individually experienced events are cognitively managed, but we need to understand more about the historical and cultural setting to understand why those cognitive strategies are necessary in the first place.

My suspicion is that stories that shift in their focus, detail, or attribution of blame over time are a response to violence when violence is normatively unexpected. Such violence may be very common, but it may be culturally disguised as the rare deviation from generally accepted norms. Despite estimates that as many as fifty percent of all women will be victims of domestic violence at some point in their lives,[68] and that nearly one in three women will be raped,[69] woman-battering and rape are

---

graduated, but the woman has never returned to school. Another student, sexually harassed by a male faculty member, quit school in mid-semester. Years later, she returned to try to complete the courses she abruptly left, wiser about the effects of sexual harassment, but with a large gap in her resume that needs to be explained when she applies for a job.

65. *Hearings*, *supra* note 22.

66. *See* HERMAN, *supra* note 18, at 183.

67. *See Hearings*, *supra* note 22.

68. *See* Martha R. Mahoney, *Legal Images of Battered Women: Redefining the Issue of Separation*, 90 MICH. L. REV. 1, 10 (1991) (citing LENORE WALKER, THE BATTERED WOMAN 19 (1979)).

69. This figure is contested. *Compare* Allan G. Johnson, *On the Prevalence of Rape in the United States*, 6 SIGNS 136, 144-45 (1980) (using FBI statistics and very conservative assumptions to estimate that 20-30% of women between the ages of 12 and 70 will experience a rape attack in their lifetimes) *and* Diana E.H. Russell & Nancy

still portrayed as unusual occurrences that need special explanation in the individual case. The "normal" case is constructed as the nonviolent marriage or the unraped woman, and the battered or raped woman stands out against this picture of normality as an exception. Because exceptions are generally explained by models that emphasize deviance, the women subjected to "deviant" practices come under the spotlight as participants, perhaps even willing participants, in deviant conduct. The woman is examined to see if she is to blame. For women, if violence is "not supposed to happen" or is "not supposed to happen to me," then it may be hard to narrate the violence credibly because she must first explain to herself why this particular "I" was singled out for the violence that was not supposed to happen and why this particular "him" did this. To construct such a story, a woman must narrate into some powerful cultural headwinds, forces of opposition that appear natural, unless she can cast her experience in the light of an obvious, socially comprehensible narrative.[70]

The culturally available narratives about sexualized violence are stories of provocation,[71] passion,[72] or deranged character or insanity,[73]

Howell, *The Prevalence of Rape in the United States Revisited*, 8 SIGNS 688, 694-95 (1983) (using somewhat less conservative assumptions to estimate that 46% of women will be victims of a rape attack during their lifetimes) *with* Douglas Laycock, *Vicious Stereotypes in Polite Society*, 8 CONST. COMMENTARY 395, 403-04 (1991) (using data from a 1985 Department of Justice National Crime Survey to estimate that 15% of women between the ages of 12 and 80 will experience a rape, attempted rape, or verbal threat of rape in their lifetimes).

70. We might interpret Susan Estrich's account of a "real rape" as a sexual assault that fits nicely within a culturally available story. After Estrich, who is white, was raped by a stranger, who was black and who also stole her car, police considered her a credible victim and treated her with sympathy. When women are raped by men of the same social category as their own and in a "friendly" setting, however, their stories do not fit the typical rape model and, therefore, are not readily believed. *See* ESTRICH, *supra* note 1, at 3.

71. Many people believe that most rapes would not happen if women did not provoke them. Nineteen percent of Anglo men, 25% of Anglo women, 73% of Black men, 23% of Black women, 32% of Mexican-American men and 70% of Mexican-American women believe this to be true. JOYCE E. WILLIAMS & KAREN A. HOLMES, THE SECOND ASSAULT: RAPE AND PUBLIC ATTITUDES 135 tbl.17 (1981).

72. James Check and Neil Malamuth report that up to 40% of both men and women indicate that it is acceptable for a man to force a woman to have sex with him if she "gets the man sexually excited, is stoned or drunk, or has had intercourse with other men." James V.P. Check & Neil M. Malamuth, *An Empirical Assessment of Some Feminist Hypotheses About Rape*, 8 INT'L J. WOMEN'S STUD. 414, 416 (1985).

73. When asked whether rapists were mentally ill, Williams and Holmes report that

told against the backdrop of the assumed rationality of all conduct. People do things for reasons, we learn to believe. In criminal law, as in detective stories, we solve the crime by finding the motive,[74] and to find the motive, we find the reason. If a man is violent, then he must have had a reason. Perhaps he was provoked and it is really the woman's fault. Or perhaps it was a sign of passion and then perhaps the woman brought it on. Or perhaps it is a "character issue" and the accused is a sexual deviant, a pervert, or a criminal type. Or perhaps he did not have a reason, in which case, he is crazy.

Faced with the evident social competencies of many men who harass, beat, rape, or assault women,[75] the narrative routes that emphasize insanity or serious character defects often seem blocked. Only "real rapes," those committed by strangers, often with weapons, against random women,[76] are arguably good candidates for the insanity narrative. That leaves passion or provocation as available, believable narrative strategies for the routine daily violence that women often experience. But passion narratives contradict the methodical, systematic form that abuse often takes over time. Women who are subjected to repeated, deliberate, personally targeted harassment by men have a hard time seeing passion as the cause when the conduct seems quite calculated. Provocation narratives put the blame back on the woman, silencing her when she tries to make sense of what it was she did that could have produced this attack.

Suppose the woman believes the provocation story—that she is to blame after all. Women often tell stories of self-blame and complicity, if they say anything at all, at the time that sexualized violence occurs.[77]

91% of Anglo men, 92% of Anglo women, 83% of Black men, 98% of Black women, 87% of Mexican-American men, and 63% of Mexican-American women believed that this was the case. *See* WILLIAMS & HOLMES, *supra* note 71, at 136 tbl.18.

74. Technically, evidence of motive is not required for criminal prosecutions. WAYNE R. LAFAVE, MODERN CRIMINAL LAW: CASES, COMMENTS AND QUESTIONS 105 (2d ed. 1988). But it is hard to convince a jury that the defendant actually did the crime he is accused of unless there is a motive.

75. *See* Check & Malamuth, *supra* note 72, at 415 (noting that "[d]espite . . . numerous efforts to identify ways in which rapists are abnormal, the results have generally indicated very few differences between rapists and nonrapists which would justify any conclusion that rapists are grossly abnormal"). In a study of "normal" male college students, about 35% reported some proclivity to rape women and 20% reported a strong proclivity. *See* Neil M. Malamuth, *Rape Proclivity among Males*, 37 J. SOC. ISSUES 138, 140 (1981).

76. The term is taken from Susan Estrich. *See* ESTRICH, *supra* note 1, at 3.

77. In a study of rape victims, we discovered that many women engaged in self-

Such self-blame often comes through in a feeling of *shame*, a feeling that would only make sense if the victim were taking the blame for the actions of the perpetrator.[78] But shame may be produced by the recognition both that her own story of abuse requires, as a matter of cultural legibility, a prominent role for herself as the reason for the abuser's conduct and also a knowing judgment of what such a role would mean about herself in the eyes of others. If the victim eventually recasts her story, the story initially told from a perspective of self-blame may eventually be replaced by a story with another narrative organization—one that allows a subaltern cultural frame to be the organizing feature of such a narrative. Perhaps, just perhaps, the sexualized violence a woman has experienced is actually common enough to be believed without the requirement that she act the provocateur. Perhaps this violence is the statistical norm and not the freak exception. And perhaps the sexualized violence women experience is the result of women's disadvantaged and sexualized position in the larger society. Perhaps it is not her personal and individual fault.

These later *revised* stories, replacing either silence or an alternative version of events, lose their social authority as a statement of truth precisely because they are generally late in arriving. They also lose their legal power for the same reason. Revised stories present problems in the law because one of the implicit rules juries and judges use for finding stories to be true is the same rule that the Senate Judiciary Committee invoked in the Hill/Thomas hearings:[79] to be believable, stories must be told immediately and must stay the same over time.[80] Truth is supposed to be fixed and stable. Real truth doesn't shift with time. Victims of abuse

---

blame as a way of recovering from brutal rape attacks. By telling herself that she can avoid rape in the future if only she does not walk home at night alone, if only she does not go into the park by herself, or if only she does not get into elevators with strange men, a woman can make the world seem manageable again. This enables her to recover from the assault more quickly than other women who do not tell themselves these self-blaming accounts. *See* Scheppele & Bart, *supra* note 17, at 79.

78. Feelings of shame have been common among survivors of Nazi concentration camps. *See* PRIMO LEVI, THE DROWNED AND THE SAVED 70 (Raymond Rosenthal trans., Summit Books 1988). The shame comes from one's memory of imagined complicity with the oppressor and of interpreting the horrors one has suffered as a judgment of one's self. "Coming out of the darkness," Levi writes, "one suffered because of the reacquired consciousness of having been diminished." *Id.* at 75.

79. *See Hearings*, *supra* note 22.

80. *See id.*

may tell one story at the time of the trauma and another story later. But these later stories are rarely believed.

IV. Erasing Sexualized Violence in Court

If these presumptions in favor of immediate and coherent narratives are embedded in the culture of facticity outside of formal law, then we would expect to see delayed and revised stories being attacked as false when women press claims of sexualized violence in court. And this is exactly what happens.

A. *Unreliable Women*

In *Reed v. Shepard*,[81] for example, JoAnn Reed worked as a "civilian jailer" in the Vandenburgh County, Indiana Sheriff's Department, beginning in mid-1979.[82] The civilian jailer program employed people to take care of prisoners—guarding, feeding, transporting, and processing them—as less costly substitutes for the more expensive deputy sheriffs.[83] In 1984, Reed was fired, without a hearing, for alleged misconduct in her job.[84] Reed charged, under section 1983 of the United States Code,[85] that she had been denied due process. The district court[86] and the court of appeals[87] found that, as an at-will employee, she was not entitled to have a hearing before her employment was terminated but that the allegations of misconduct were serious enough to justify her termination in any event.[88] She had sued on multiple counts, however, also charging that her employer had engaged in sexual discrimination and that she had been sexually harassed on the job in violation of Title VII of the Civil Rights Act.[89] The story she told about

81. 939 F.2d 484 (7th Cir. 1991).

82. *Id.* at 485.

83. *Id.*

84. *Id.*

85. *See* 42 U.S.C. § 1983 (1988).

86. Reed v. Shepard, No. EV85-21-C (S.D. Ind. May 25, 1990) (unpublished opinion of Chief Judge Gene E. Brooks).

87. *Reed*, 939 F.2d at 484.

88. *See id.* at 489. The district court's conclusion on this issue is mentioned in the opinion of the court of appeals. *See id.* at 488.

89. 42 U.S.C. § 2000e (1988); *see Reed*, 939 F.2d at 488.

sexual harassment was clearly a revised story. The court of appeals quoted the trial judge:

> "Plaintiff contends that she was handcuffed to the drunk tank and sally port doors, that she was subjected to suggestive remarks . . . , that conversations often centered around oral sex, that she was physically hit and punched in the kidneys, that her head was grabbed and forcefully placed in members' laps, and that she was the subject of lewd jokes and remarks. She testified that she had chairs pulled out from under her, a cattle prod with an electrical shock was placed between her legs, and that they frequently tickled her. She was placed in a laundry basket, handcuffed inside an elevator, handcuffed to the toilet and her face pushed into the water, and maced. Perhaps others."[90]

"The record confirms these and a number of other bizarre activities in the jail office," the appeals court added.[91] "By any objective standard, the behavior of the male deputies and jailers toward Reed revealed at trial was, to say the least, repulsive."[92]

Why, then, did the court go on to conclude that however offensive the conduct of her male coworkers was, it was *not* sexual harassment? Because, the court found, the conduct was apparently not repulsive to Reed *at the time*:[93]

---

90. *Reed*, 939 F.2d at 486 (footnote omitted) (quoting *Reed*, No. EV85-21-C).

91. *Id.*

92. *Id.*

93. *See id.* I should explain something important about this case to put the discussion of this opinion in context. Reed had been charged with trafficking marijuana to some of the inmates in the prison and with encouraging two female inmates to assault another inmate with whom they shared a cell. Apparently, substantial evidence existed to sustain these charges, including a confession, though the evidence does not appear in the appeals court report and the confession was later retracted. *See id.* at 487. The judges apparently believed that Reed was not a terribly sympathetic character in general, and this undoubtedly affected their treatment of her sexual-harassment claims. But the principles of law on which the three-judge panel unanimously relied and the evidence they used to illustrate such principles have implications for the consideration of sexual-harassment claims more generally. I focus on the court's treatment of the sexual-harassment claim in isolation because the reasoning presumably would also apply to more sympathetic victims.

> Reed not only experienced this depravity with amazing resilience, but she also relished reciprocating in kind. At one point during her job tenure Reed was actually put on probation for her use of offensive language at the jail. At the same time, she was instructed to suspend the exhibitionistic habit she had of not wearing a bra on days she wore only a T-shirt to work. She also participated in suggestive giftgiving by presenting a softball warmer to a male co-worker designed to resemble a scrotum and by giving another a G-string. Reed enjoyed exhibiting to the male officers the abdominal scars she received from her hysterectomy which necessarily involved showing her private area. Many witnesses testified that Reed revelled in the sexual horseplay, instigated a lot of it, and had "one of the foulest mouths" in the department. In other words, the trial revealed that there was plenty of degrading humor and behavior to go around.[94]

The court emphasized that this reprehensible conduct did not happen to other women working in the jail, but only to Reed.[95] Three women working there testified that other women had not been further harassed after they asked the men to stop doing these sorts of things to them.[96] But apparently, Reed never told the men to stop. Why? Reed testified at trial:

> Because it was real important to me to be accepted. It was important for me to be a police officer and if that was the only way that I could be accepted, I would just put up with it and kept [sic] my mouth shut. I had supervisors that would participate in this and you had a chain of command to go through in order to file a complaint. One thing you don't do as a police officer, you don't snitch out [sic] another police officer. You could get hurt.[97]

---

94. *Id.* at 486-87.

95. *See id.* at 487.

96. *See id.* The fact that other women had experienced this conduct and had to tell the men to stop was not used by the court as evidence of a hostile working environment. The men, after all, did stop when asked, erasing their prior conduct as far as the court was concerned. *See id.*

97. *Id.* at 492 ([sic]s in original).

court was a revised account, apparently inconsistent with what she and others said about her reactions at the time. And the Seventh Circuit Court of Appeals did not believe her.

Quoting from the Supreme Court's decision in *Meritor Savings Bank v. Vinson*,[98] the Seventh Circuit panel indicated that harassment must be so severe or pervasive as "'to alter the conditions of [the victim's] employment and create an abusive working environment,'"[99] if a claim is to succeed. But to show that this conduct was "in fact" harassing, the victim of such treatment had to indicate *at the time* that she did not welcome the behavior in question.[100] In this case, Reed's claim could not succeed because she had not indicated while these events were occurring that this treatment was unwelcome. In other words, contemporaneous evidence is required to establish any claim of sexual harassment, and this requirement is hard-wired into the doctrine.[101] Judge Manion quoted the trial judge approvingly when he said that the plaintiff had been treated this way "'because of her personality rather than her sex'" (as if the defendants were capable of separating these things) and that the "'defendants cannot be held liable for conditions created by [Reed's] own action and conduct.'"[102] Her failure to object at the time to this behavior and her attempt to deal with it by trying to act like "one of the boys" not only defeated her ability to make a claim, but also justified the conclusion that she had brought this treatment on herself and was therefore the person who was primarily responsible.

But the record sustains another story, one not narrated by her coworkers who were witnesses at the trial. The record documents that Reed was physically beaten, that she was punched in the kidneys, that she had an electric cattle prod shoved between her legs, that she was forcibly restrained by being handcuffed on numerous occasions, that her head was shoved into a toilet, that she was repeatedly tickled, and that she was maced.[103] That was in addition to the extensive and personalized verbal abuse to which she was subjected. Moreover, these individual facts were

---

98. 477 U.S. 57 (1986).

99. *Reed*, 939 F.2d at 491 (quoting *Meritor*, 477 U.S. at 67).

100. *See id.* at 491-92.

101. *See id.* at 492-93

102. *Id.* at 492 (quoting Reed v. Shepard, No. EV85-21-C (S.D. Ind. May 25, 1990)).

103. *Id.* at 486.

all found to be true by the court.[104] The court could have concluded that this evidence supported another story, one that did not erase the violence against Reed by constructing her as a consenting woman, but rather one that presented her as a victim of physical abuse.[105] Although Reed did not explicitly object at the time, the violence to which her coworkers subjected her could be considered felonies anywhere other than in a "friendly" setting.

The court failed to see her claim, I believe, because her sexual-harassment complaint was delayed. Her complaint did not emerge for the first time until after she had been fired. The judges obviously believed a revenge narrative, one in which a bitter employee recast "horseplay" as "abuse" to get back at her coworkers.

But another narrative possibility exists here. Women who have experienced sexual harassment say, as Anita Hill said, that they want to keep their jobs.[106] They want the abuse to stop, but they also do not want to make waves.[107] They want to fit into the workplace environment as if they really belonged there. And to fit in, they endure the abuse.[108] It is as if women are making deals that they will tolerate the abuse if the employer just tolerates their presence.

---

104. *See id.* at 491.

105. *See Meritor*, 477 U.S. at 68. In *Meritor*, the Supreme Court found that the appearance of voluntary participation by the victim did not defeat a successful harassment claim. The behavior that Mechelle Vinson complained of in *Meritor* was so obviously harassment in the view of the unanimous Supreme Court that her failure to object directly to her boss, who had forced her into a sexual relationship with him, did not bar her subsequent claim. *See id.* Why should the Seventh Circuit not consider what happened to JoAnn Reed as harassment also under this standard?

106. As Martha R. Mahoney noted, women generally *need* their jobs and face a hard time finding others in an economy that does not in general pay women very well. *See* Martha R. Mahoney, *Exit: Power and the Idea of Leaving in Love, Work, and the Confirmation Hearings*, 65 S. CAL. L. REV. 1283, 1291-99 (1992).

107. Women fear that they will be retaliated against if they complain, regardless of whether they win a lawsuit. They fear that their careers and their reputations will suffer if they do not put up with the abuse. Tamar Lewin, *A Case Study of Sexual Harassment*, N.Y. TIMES, Oct. 11, 1991, at A18.

108. In one survey, only nine percent of the women quit their jobs immediately after the harassment began, although more women quit once the harassment escalated. *See* LIN FARLEY, SEXUAL SHAKEDOWN: THE SEXUAL HARASSMENT OF WOMEN ON THE JOB 21-22 (1978). Another report found that fewer than five percent of sexually harassed men and women ever report the harassment or take other action. *See* Sandra S. Tangri et al., *Sexual Harassment at Work: Three Explanatory Models*, 38 J. SOC. ISSUES 33, 47 (1982) (noting that most, but not all, sexual-harassment victims failed to report the behavior).

But once a woman has been fired, that deal is off. No longer able to justify to herself that she is at least getting something out of having put up with the abuse, she files suit claiming sexual harassment. If women's greatest fears in complaining about sexual harassment are that they will be fired, then the greatest barrier against bringing a complaint is eliminated when they lose their jobs. Rather than seeing a suit following dismissal as evidence of revenge, judges might see such a suit as the evidence about what the implicit terms of continued employment were. The understandings women have about the conditions under which they work are disturbed by their dismissals. If courts looked at the conduct, like the persistent and abusive conduct to which JoAnn Reed was subjected, and they see only consent, they should ask themselves just why a woman would consent to be treated like that. Perhaps then they would see that the apparent consent reflects a lack of bargaining power and a lack of options rather than the active approval that signifies free choice.

By locking her into a revenge narrative on the sexual-harassment claim, Reed's coworkers and the judges in the Seventh Circuit were effectively penalizing her twice: once for appearing to consent to the abusive treatment in the first place, and again for changing her mind about what it all meant. Reed, in this revenge narrative, then became the problem as the court shifted attention away from the conduct of her male coworkers to Reed's own actions and accounts. It was her conduct in the first place that allowed the harassment to occur, and it was her desire for revenge after the fact that brought the case into court. Her male coworkers were presented as accessories to a story in which the active agent was Reed. It was Reed's motives, actions, and stories that the court took to be the problem. She may have come into court claiming victimization, but she left the process having become the aggressor.

How did this inversion occur? The story JoAnn Reed told in court was inconsistent with her coworkers' interpretations of her actions at the time. Her coworkers' readings of her actions on the job were presented as if those interpretations were her contemporaneous accounts of the events in question.[109] Reed's own story, when she finally got to tell it in court,

---

109. *See Reed*, 939 F.2d at 490. The court also found that she had not been subjected to sexual discrimination in employment and that all the ways in which she was treated differently from her coworkers were due to her rank as a civilian jailer rather than her sex. *See id.* at 490-91. No evidence was given on the relative numbers of men and women who held the ranks of the less prestigious civilian jailer and the more lucrative and privileged position of deputy sheriff in this case, though there were clearly some men and women in each rank. *See id.* Everyone knew, however, how Reed was

was therefore presented as revised, changing over time from a story in which she appeared to enjoy the abuse, to a story in which she abhorred it.

When stories are revised, judges and juries use that very fact as evidence that the later story is false, even when the victim did not grasp the chance to tell the first story herself. In addition, victims whose accounts are revised can be blamed for bringing everything on themselves because their narrative instability makes the later story unbelievable. Such narrative instability casts doubts on the motives of the woman who comes late to her story of blame, and she becomes the aggressive initiator of trouble for others.

While this pattern is the general rule, certain special cases exist in which revised stories can be presented as credible. Such exceptions include cases in which: (1) multiple women establish a pattern of conduct on the part of a particular man; (2) corroborating physical evidence exists to back up the woman's later account; and (3) an expert reconstructs the woman's initial story as a delusion for psychological reasons. It is to these exceptions, the exceptions that demonstrate the solidity of the implicit rule against revised stories, that we now turn.

B. *Safety in Numbers*

If women are to be believed when they revise their stories, they have a better chance if they find other women to do the same. Reconstructing as nonconsensual a sexualized relationship that appeared consensual at the time is very hard to do credibly. Women typically find that they have to establish that their experience was part of a pattern that other women experienced as well. Just as Anita Hill would have been more credible if a parade of former employees of Clarence Thomas had come forward with similar complaints, other women claiming abuse, harassment, even rape, find that there is greater narrative safety in numbers. One example can be found in *Daly v. Derrick*.[110]

---

and women who held the ranks of the less prestigious civilian jailer and the more lucrative and privileged position of deputy sheriff in this case, though there were clearly some men and women in each rank. *See id.* Everyone knew, however, how Reed was treated, and women who testified indicated that they had to explicitly opt out of such treatment themselves. *See id.* at 487. What sort of workplace is this in which a person is held to consent to such violent, dangerous, and abusive treatment?

110. 281 Cal. Rptr. 709 (Ct. App. 1991).

In September 1977, Maura Daly was fifteen-years old:

> Before the start of classes [at a high school in California], [Maura Daly] attended a retreat designed to encourage Alternative School students and teachers to get to know each other. [Tommy] Derrick, who taught psychology, human sexuality, and social studies, also attended the retreat.
>
> One evening, Derrick and several students were giving each other massages. As Derrick massaged Maura, he began to touch her in a sexual manner. His sexual overtures to her continued during the retreat, and she eventually acceded to his request that she orally copulate him. He impressed on her the need to keep their relationship secret.
>
> Following the retreat, Derrick had sexual contact with Maura after school once every few weeks, either at his home or inside his van. Although she was happy to be receiving special attention from a teacher whom she liked and admired, she felt uncomfortable with their sexual activities and consequently experienced confusion. In the spring of her sophomore year, she told Derrick she did not wish to see him any more. After that he sought no further sexual contact with her.[111]

During the time that their sexual relationship continued, Maura described Tommy as her boyfriend:

> The relationship was her first experience of romance and love . . . . He repeatedly told her that she could make her own decision whether to be sexually involved with him, thereby inducing her to believe that she was equally responsible for their relationship. In fact, however, Maura was overwhelmed by his attentions due to her desire for a replacement for the father she had earlier lost through divorce. She did not perceive his conduct as wrong in any legally actionable sense; the only injuries of which she was aware were pain at the distance from her that Derrick maintained at school, jealousy at Derrick's sexual attentions to other students, and from time to time a sense that,

111. *Id.* at 711-12.

rather than being a true friend, he was using her to satisfy his own sexual needs.[112]

In November 1986, Daly sought therapy because she was having "sexual difficulties" with her current boyfriend.[113] In the course of therapy, she mentioned that she had been "molested" by a high-school teacher.[114] "Sometime around March 1987, she began to realize how painful and damaging her relationship with Derrick had been for her."[115] She filed a tort suit against him for damages for the harm he had caused her.

This case is one of a growing number now being brought as a result of the "delayed discovery" of childhood molestation.[116] While most of the cases are not brought against teachers, but are instead brought against male relatives, the gist of the complaint is the same: A minor, usually but not always female, is pressured for sexual favors by a man who has some power over her. She endures the molestation in silence, because the man tells her to be quiet. She may even feel so compromised that she actively engages in preserving the secrecy because the revelation of the activity implicates her as well. Because she does not talk with anyone else about it, she can be influenced strongly by the man's narrative about what is happening. Although she may feel the sexual advances are inappropriate, she does not know how to articulate this as a conscious matter. Sometimes the girl actively claims to enjoy the sexual encounters at the time, valuing the attention they bring. Years later, almost always through therapy, the now-grown woman "learns" for the first time how to name what happened and what these events have done to her.[117]

---

112. *Id.* at 718.

113. *Id.* at 712.

114. *Id.*

115. *Id.*

116. For an explanation of this issue, see Jocelyn B. Lamm, *Easing Access to the Courts for Incest Victims: Toward an Equitable Application of the Delayed Discovery Rule*, 100 YALE L.J. 2189 (1991).

117. California has had a particularly dramatic history with these cases. In DeRose v. Carswell, 242 Cal. Rptr. 368 (Ct. App. 1987), the court rejected the claim of a woman who alleged that her grandfather had molested her repeatedly when she was between the ages of 4 and 11, finding that the statute of limitations had tolled on the case. *See id.* at 377. Because she knew everything she needed to know to file the claim within the statute of limitations, the court reasoned, she should not be allowed to proceed with the case after that time. In 1990, the California legislature enacted a statute designed

In *Daly*, the court was called upon to decide whether the lower court had been correct in throwing out the case on grounds that the statute of limitations had tolled.[118] Ruling that there was a triable issue in the possibility of a delayed discovery of a material fact, the court let the case proceed.[119] But given the judges' emphasis that a new California statute made them do it out of consistency, it is doubtful that the court would have allowed this complaint to proceed without the push from the legislature.[120]

The *Daly* case presents a stark case of a revised story. Daly clearly thought at the time that her relationship with Derrick was romantic, consensual, and wonderful—usually. Only later did she come to believe that this relationship was abusive and that he had taken advantage of her innocence and immaturity. *Daly* starkly presents a case of a complete reframing, in which consent at the time is later cast as consent that was not "real." Though the court allowed her case to proceed, Daly would probably have had a hard time establishing her initial nonconsent. But she had help.

As it turned out, two other women had experienced the same treatment from Derrick while he was their high-school teacher. In fact, all three of these women were friends in high school and had not realized that Derrick had a sexual relationship with each of them at the same time.

---

to supercede *DeRose* by extending the statute of limitations on childhood molestations to eight years from the date the plaintiff attains the age of majority or three years after all of the relevant facts could have been discovered, whichever is later. *See* CAL. CIV. PROC. CODE § 340.1(a) (West 1993).

118. *See Daly*, 281 Cal. Rptr. at 716, 720.

119. *See id.* at 718.

120. In fact, in Marsha V. v. Gardner, 281 Cal. Rptr. 473 (Ct. App. 1991), the court dismissed an action brought by a woman against her grandfather 15 years after the last molestation occurred. The molestations had continued for nine years, during which time her grandfather had allegedly sexually abused, threatened, and used physical violence against her. Nonetheless, the court held that 15 years after the last event was too late to bring the suit because the plaintiff had always *known* that her grandfather had sexually molested her and that his acts were committed against her will and without her consent. *See id.* at 477. The fact that the woman claimed she suffered from "dissociation and psychological accommodation" only created uncertainty as to the amount of damages and did not keep her from knowing enough to file the case within the statutorily defined limits. *Id.* She said that she was not fully aware of the events, however, until she received therapy. *See id.* at 474. The dissent emphasized that Marsha V. could have possibly won in court under the new statute, because she filed within three years of discovering the injury. *See id.* at 478-85 (Johnson, J., dissenting).

Only after Maura Daly had gone into therapy and came to see Derrick's treatment of her as abusive did Daly's mother then call around and find that two other high-school classmates of Maura's had similar stories to tell. They later joined the lawsuit.

Does this change the credibility of the revised narratives of each of the women? For most people, it probably does. But why should three women revising their stories in the same way be more believable than one woman doing this alone? In the case of a lone woman accusing her former lover of abuse, it is easier to tell a stock counter-story about a particular relationship gone sour. But when three such relationships exist that were all being maintained at the same time in an apparently monogamous culture, then each woman appears entitled to adjust her story to take into account that Derrick was misrepresenting to each of them just what the specific relationship was at the time. Derrick's violation of another norm, the norm of monogamy, makes the violation of other norms about abuse seem more plausible. He can be constructed as a deviant all around, not the innocent man whose former lover now takes advantage of a convenient feminism to turn him into a monster after the fact. With three women providing evidence of collective misrepresentation, Derrick looks less like a poor guy with bad judgment in relationships and more like a predator.

Several women, each changing their stories in the same way independently, seem more believable than one woman who does this alone. The sheer volume of the revised stories changes the credibility of each one. Derrick's conduct becomes part of a *pattern* that each individual woman could not have seen alone. This new story is a different story, told for the first time when the narratives of the three women intersect. Taking the three relationships *together*, against backdrop assumptions about monogamous sexual affiliations, Derrick looks less "normal" and the basis of a deviance narrative is laid. There is a way to distinguish him from ordinary men, at least ordinary men in their public presentations. Nothing about the norms of ordinary male conduct is threatened by allowing these women's accounts to be believed as revised. By finding safety in numbers, women may be able to have their revised stories appear credible.

C. *Corroborating Evidence*

Revised stories may also be believed when other evidence, preferably physical evidence, corroborates the changed story. Corroboration requirements may be formally gone in rape law, but their residue remains in the habits of belief. If a revised story is to be credible, it needs something more than itself as proof.

For example, in *Simmons v. State*,[121] the Indiana Supreme Court upheld a rape conviction even though the victim told inconsistent stories.[122] Significantly, however, in both accounts she claimed she was raped.[123] First, she said that she had been taken from the Payless Supermarket to the Grandview Golf Course where she was raped.[124] Later, she said that she had been taken from the Anderson High School parking lot to some nearby railroad tracks where she was raped.[125] She testified at trial that her statements were inconsistent because the defendant forced her to "tell a different version of the incident that he furnished to her."[126] With the introduction of expert testimony from a psychologist and from a social worker to the effect that rape victims often feel under the sway of a rapist even after he is no longer physically present,[127] the defendant was convicted of rape.[128] But the experts did not accomplish this extraordinary feat alone. It helped that the woman had never seen the defendant before the attack, that she had been abducted with the understanding that he had a gun, that he had threatened her with a knife and a heavy pipe during the rape, and that the defendant also stole her car.[129] But crucially, the police found the pipe with which the defendant had allegedly threatened her in the grass by the train tracks. This was, in short, a "real rape"[130] backed up with physical evidence of the pipe and the stolen car.[131] Her revised story did not stand alone.

When a revised account changes some of the elements of the initial story that one would expect to remain invariant across descriptions, the account generally becomes much less credible. In this case, the woman originally said she left voluntarily from the Payless Supermarket parking

121. 504 N.E.2d 575 (Ind. 1987).

122. *See id.* at 577-79, 582.

123. *See id.* at 578.

124. *Id.*

125. *Id.*

126. *Id.* at 579.

127. *See id.* at 578-79.

128. *Id.* at 577, 582.

129. *See id.* at 577-78, 581.

130. ESTRICH, *supra* note 1, at 3.

131. *See Simmons*, 504 N.E.2d at 577, 581.

lot,[132] and then later said she was abducted from the Anderson High School.[133] The "voluntarily left" and "abducted" descriptions can be seen as two plausible interpretations of the same physical events, perhaps relying on different interpretations of her mental state that may not have been easily visible to others. But the Payless Supermarket parking lot was nowhere near the Anderson High School,[134] and so those descriptions seem flat-out irreconcilable, not just a matter of variable interpretation. Had there been no further corroborating evidence, this inconsistency would probably have been fatal to the credibility of the story.

Why is this? Often revisions of the latter type ("flat out") are used as evidence for inconsistencies of the first type ("matter of interpretation"). When a witness reveals inconsistencies in parts of descriptions that are usually matters of general agreement among observers (like where we are physically located when something occurs), this is taken as evidence that she must also be suspect in matters about which there would not necessarily be general agreement among observers (like the mental state of the speaker). Stories look suspiciously reconstructed when some facts that generally produce similar descriptions across observers appear to have been altered since the first account.

But much can be forgiven when physical evidence exists to back up the later story. With corroborating evidence, narrative instability can be "resolved" one way or another. Credibility of the lone woman may be bolstered with some help from physical evidence but otherwise, women's narratives are suspect when they change over time.

D. *Expert Reconstructions*

Sometimes a lone victim's changed story of sexualized abuse can survive scrutiny, even without corroborating physical evidence. But not without some assistance. In recent years, credibility of revised stories has been established through the testimony of expert witnesses. These expert witnesses generally testify that the victims of sexualized violence suffer from a form of post-traumatic stress disorder and therefore have *first* reactions that are not to be trusted, allowing later accounts to be believed. In *State v. Frost*,[135] the expert testimony that was introduced made the

---

132. *Id.* at 578.

133. *Id.*

134. *See id.*

135. 577 A.2d 1282 (N.J. Super. Ct. App. Div. 1990).

victim's revised story credible to the jury, and later to the judges on appeal.[136]

Early one April morning in 1986, L.S. was still sleeping when her former boyfriend, Gregory Frost, tapped on her shoulder.[137] He had broken into her house.[138] As she started to wake up, he started to yell at her. He hit her.[139] Their baby began to cry, so L.S. picked up the child and ran to the front door to escape.[140] Before she was able to open the door, Frost caught up with her and cut her arm deeply with a razor-edged box cutter.[141]

The relationship between Frost and L.S. had been plagued by Frost's frequent outbursts of violence against L.S., and she estimated that he had hit her at least once per month during the time they had been romantically involved, starting on the second day that they knew each other.[142] Police testified that she had called them to the house at least nine times to stop his violence.[143] After suffering through three and a half years of battering, L.S. had left Frost to go to live with her mother. She obtained a restraining order to keep Frost away from her and the baby.[144] Eventually, Frost was sent to prison for theft from another person. L.S. had been responsible for his arrest in that case and, on the day he broke into her house and cut her with the razor, he had just been let out of prison. His first act as a free man was revenge.

Knowing how out-of-control he could be, L.S. tried to talk with him, eventually suggesting that they have sex because "that would calm him down."[145] After they had sex, they went to the place where L.S.'s mother worked to get her car keys to go to the hospital to have the wound treated. L.S. asked her mother not to call the police. At the hospital, L.S. said she had cut her arm on the refrigerator. Her arm needed four sutures underneath the skin and eleven stitches to close the wound.

---

136. *See id.* at 1286-88.

137. *Id.* at 1284.

138. *See id.*

139. *Id.*

140. *See id.*

141. *Id.*

142. *See id.* at 1285.

143. *Id.*

144. *Id.* at 1285.

145. *Id.* at 1284.

After L.S. was treated, she, Frost, and the baby went to Frost's mother's home to get money, and then went to a park where they drank beer and talked together. Eventually, they went back to L.S.'s home again. L.S. was supposed to pick her mother up at work, but never did. When L.S.'s mother arrived, angry at having to find another ride home, she and L.S. got into such a huge fight that neighbors called the police. When the police arrived, they saw Frost running from the apartment wearing no shoes, socks, or shirt. They recognized him as the person against whom a restraining order had been issued, and they arrested him.[146] They charged him with contempt of court for violating the restraining order, as well as burglary for breaking into the house, assault for stabbing L.S., and various weapons charges for possessing the razor.[147] Notably, he was not charged with rape. He was convicted on all counts.[148]

At the trial, Frost had claimed that L.S. had consented to spend the day with him, which he thought should cast doubt on any claim that he had broken in and attacked her that morning.[149] After all, Frost argued, why would this woman spend the whole day with him unless she wanted to? To respond to this, prosecutors introduced expert testimony to the effect that L.S. was suffering from Battered Woman's Syndrome, an identifiable medical condition that was characterized by the court as follows:

> The battered woman places herself in the role of a victim. She blames herself, thereby becoming even more vulnerable to the point where she almost expects it. She is reluctant to tell anybody about what occurs, usually for a variety of reasons. She may be embarrassed, the man might keep her isolated from others, she may hope the situation will change, or she may fear it will get worse if she reports anything. Most significantly, the battered woman cannot just walk away from the situation. She is emotionally dependent on her "man" and is often involved in a love–hate relationship.[150]

---

146. *See id.* at 1285.
147. *See id.* at 1284-85.
148. *See id.* at 1284.
149. *See id.* at 1285.
150. *Id.* at 1287.

The effect of the expert testimony was to provide a context within which a jury could believe that all the things L.S. said on the day of the attack were motivated by fear. Such a fear-induced account could be overridden by a revised story later. Without this expert testimony, however, a jury might reasonably conclude, as Frost tried to argue, that she was now trying to get Frost in trouble because they had had a falling out after a pleasant day. After all, L.S. presented repeated and consistent explanations on the day in question about how she was okay, how she had simply cut herself on the refrigerator, and how no one should call the police because she was fine.[151] But the specific violent history of the relationship between Frost and L.S., as well as the use of expert testimony, convinced the jury that Frost had committed these acts and that L.S. had not consented.[152] On appeal, the admissibility of the expert testimony so crucial to the prosecution's case was upheld.[153]

Expert testimony can be very helpful to women in these situations. But it comes at a price. Such testimony is effective with jurors because it gives them an explanation for a victim's conduct at the time in question by saying she is suffering from a form of mental illness. The victim may have *thought* things were going to get better; she may have *thought* he loved her; she may have *thought* that she wanted to be with him. But she was wrong, deluded, and not a good judge of these things at the time. As a result, whatever she may have *thought* happened on the day in question can be dismissed as the result of temporary mental incapacity. But this sort of transformation from a credible first story to an even more credible revised story is very hard to do without an expert. The expert allows a woman's revised story to be believed, but at the cost of making her out to be a woman who could not know her own mind.

In this case, L.S. apparently wanted Frost convicted for these crimes. But she also visited him eleven times while he was awaiting trial back in prison.[154]

V. The Problem of Truth in Law

So, how do judges and juries know when they have found the truth? It is an astonishing accomplishment that courts as well as ordinary

151. *See id.* at 1284-85.

152. *See id.* at 1285-88.

153. *See id.* at 1288.

154. *See id.* at 1285.

individuals manage to operate on a daily basis as if the bases of factual judgments were clear and solid. While the idea of truth has been a contested subject among philosophers for as long as philosophy has existed, the idea of truth in daily life seems to generate much less debate. When asked to find "the facts" of a case, judges and juries do not puzzle over the meaning of that instruction. Why? The simple answer is that judges and juries, spectators and litigants, ordinary folks in their daily lives and specialists in creating knowledge, "know truth when they see it." Within our own system of truth-finding, some cases may be easier and others harder, but the idea of truth itself is rarely in doubt. If the truth is unclear in a particular instance, default rules, like rules about burdens of proof or about how certain one has to be to convict, are employed to settle matters provisionally so that cases can be resolved with certainty.

American courts rely on the widespread facility of ordinary citizens in reasonably workable practices of truth-finding. The jury system is premised on the idea that citizens, selected to serve on juries, can listen to the presentation of evidence and work out "what happened" independent of any specialized knowledge of the law.[155] Lawyers and trial judges generally receive no special training in determining the credibility of evidence or in discerning truth, and so they too often draw on socially situated, unremarkable methods for determining "what happened." It is generally assumed that anyone who is not connected with the parties to the dispute and who does not have a special interest in the outcome of the case can figure out what to believe from evidence presented in a trial without specialized instruction. This is done because in the business of the evaluation of evidence, almost everyone is thought to be enough of an expert to be entrusted with finding facts.

But as we have seen with the examples explained above, truth-finding is a socially situated practice. We all have a set of interpretive conventions, practices of truth-finding, that tell us when a particular story seems more credible than another and when one witness appears to be telling the truth and another seems to be lying. Most of us engage in the evaluation and construction of truth on a routine basis, finding the activity generally nonproblematic and straightforward. Never mind that we are often dead wrong in assessing credibility, regardless of our experience and professional training.[156] Most of the time, we are successful enough or

155. *See* Scheppele, *Facing Facts*, *supra* note 9, at 42.

156. *See* BENNETT & FELDMAN, *supra* note 9; Paul Ekman & Maureen O'Sullivan, *Who Can Catch a Liar?*, 46 AM. PSYCHOL. 913 (1991).

blind enough to the consequences of our inaccuracies not to reevaluate our practices. Whenever our failures call attention to our inadequacies in this regard, we engage in a patch-up effort to work out what went wrong in the particular case, but we rarely rethink our entire scheme for evaluating the evidence that daily life presents us. Furthermore, when we have to deal with the law, whether as professionals who do this all the time, as jurors or litigants who are called upon to do this on rare occasions, or even as observers or scholars of the judicial process, we bring our interpretive conventions with us.

So, what do people operating in the legal process see when they are presented with evidence? What interpretive conventions do judges and jurors invoke when called upon to figure out "the facts" of cases?

The attribution of truth by judges and juries depends on properties of the stories witnesses tell.[157] Of course, this attribution goes on against a backdrop of cultural expectations about what sorts of stories are credible in the first place, and those expectations are dependent on visions of normality and aberration, drawn from experience and from widely available stock representations. But judges and juries decide whether a witness is telling the truth by evaluating *how the story is constructed* rather than by working out whether the story has a "real" referent. Some of the properties that matter in deciding whether stories are believable include internal consistency, narrative coherence, reliance on "hard" or physical evidence, and perhaps most importantly, the stability of the storytelling over time.

Given that most people have a naive sense that language is supposed to pick out things in the world, this view that the credibility of stories is generally determined by reference to the internal properties of the stories themselves may be disturbing. But it is not new. Clifford Geertz is one teller of a tale that reports a cosmology in which the world rests on the back of an elephant, which stands on the back of a turtle. When asked what the turtle stands on, an informant answered, "[a]h, Sahib, after that it is turtles all the way down."[158] This is not exactly a comforting answer if one wants to believe that some bedrock exists somewhere. But in stories, as with the elephant and its turtles, it is narrative all the way down.[159] Narratives often become their own best evidence.

157. *See* BENNETT & FELDMAN, *supra* note 9, at ix.

158. CLIFFORD GEERTZ, *Thick Description: Toward an Interpretive Theory of Culture*, *in* THE INTERPRETATION OF CULTURES 3, 29 (1973).

159. *See* JEROME BRUNER, ACTS OF MEANING 43 (1990) [hereinafter ACTS]; DAVID

Much historical reconstruction, like the reconstruction in courts, proceeds from narrative evidence. Historians most frequently work with texts and they find themselves composing their own narratives to make sense of the narratives they have encountered. Even those historians who work with physical evidence, like archeological discoveries or other tangible bits of a distant past, make sense of them by placing them in the context of narratives. But saying that historical reconstructions are often narratives "all the way down" is not to say that such reconstructions are fictional. One can have a sense of faithfulness to the records and still be constructing narratives of narratives of narratives as a record of "what happened." Though it is notoriously difficult to draw any distinct boundary between fictional and nonfictional narratives, one can credibly claim to be constructing a narrative of evidence one has not invented out of one's imagination. This is what passes for fact, both in historical research and in courts of law.[160]

Why is this? In courts of law, judges and juries cannot do what a correspondence theory of language would have them do; they cannot hold up testimony against events in the world to see which versions "match" better. The most obvious reason for this is that the events are long over before the cases come to trial and the "reality" in question is not around to hold any descriptions up against, if such a thing could be done. Some procedures would have to be devised for working out when a description corresponds to reality and then those procedures, not the "matching," would be doing all the work. Most of the time, the traces left over from historical events are *accounts* by people who were present at or otherwise involved in the event, and such accounts—narratives—are often the best evidence available.

Even if the descriptions were being constructed simultaneously with events or if the events in question were preserved in some other form—as happened in *California v. Powell*,[161] in which a citizen's videotape

---

CARR, TIME, NARRATIVE, AND HISTORY 4-5 (1986); Theodore R. Sarbin, *The Narrative as a Root Metaphor for Psychology*, *in* NARRATIVE PSYCHOLOGY: THE STORIED NATURE OF HUMAN CONDUCT 3, 9 (Theodore R. Sarbin ed., 1986); Jerome Bruner, *The Narrative Construction of Reality*, 18 CRITICAL INQUIRY 1, 5-6 (1991).

160. For an example of essays providing a range of views on the process of writing history, with a particular focus on what cannot be asserted as true, see PROBING THE LIMITS OF REPRESENTATION: NAZISM AND THE "FINAL SOLUTION" (Saul Friedlander ed., 1992) [hereinafter PROBING THE LIMITS].

161. No. BA035498 (L.A., Cal. County Ct., Apr. 30, 1992) (unpublished opinion of Judge Weisberg).

recorded several Los Angeles police officers beating motorist Rodney King—judges and jurors could not work out which single description best "matched" the world. The whole idea of matching descriptions against the world is misleading because, apart from being metaphorical, it assumes that there is only one perspective, only one point of view, only one ideology, no room for multiple readings, and no potential for disagreement. In short, it assumes no problem with understanding how accounts as socially situated cultural products relate to evidence of the world. But particular "true" stories and particular descriptive statements are often selected from among a set of arguably accurate versions of reality[162]—it is just that other descriptions in the set give very different impressions about what is going on. The vexing question is not just whether the descriptions are accurate in some way, though it is crucially important to screen out lies, but rather, how it is that some particular description instead of some other description comes to be forwarded as the authoritative version of events.[163] This raises questions of power and ideology, of the "situatedness" of the descriptions that pass for truth, and of the social agendas they support.[164]

In law, these questions are not explicitly raised as problems, though practitioners know that they are crucially important. Questions about multiple versions of reality are largely ignored in the subject of evidence, in which the greatest concerns are limits to the sorts of statements that might be taken as accurate. Rules of evidence screen out *types* of information that are thought to be misleading,[165] prejudicial,[166] non-

162. The exceptions to this generalization pose special problems for historians. *See* Carlo Ginzburg, *Just One Witness*, *in* PROBING THE LIMITS, *supra* note 160, at 82.

163. *See* NELSON GOODMAN, WAYS OF WORLDMAKING 20, 97 (1978). In a more distinctly legal context, see Richard K. Sherwin, *Dialects and Dominance: A Study of Rhetorical Fields in the Law of Confessions*, 136 U. PA. L. REV. 729 (1988).

164. *See* Donna J. Haraway, *Situated Knowledges: The Science Question in Feminism and the Privilege of Partial Perspective*, *in* SIMIANS, CYBORGS, AND WOMEN: THE REINVENTION OF NATURE 188-89 (1991). For an account of the truth/ideology distinction in the history of Marxist thought, see MICHELE BARRETT, THE POLITICS OF TRUTH: FROM MARX TO FOUCAULT (1991).

165. *See* FED. R. EVID. 801; *see also* Laurence H. Tribe, *Triangulating Hearsay*, 87 HARV. L. REV. 957, 958 (1974) (explaining that hearsay is excluded because of inaccuracies attributed to ambiguity, insincerity, faulty perception, and erroneous memory).

166. *See* FED. R. EVID. 403 (excluding evidence in circumstances in which its probative value is substantially outweighed by the danger of unfair prejudice).

probative,[167] or just plain unreliable.[168] But the rules of evidence themselves are at best probabilistic judgments about categories of information and their likelihood of being false or irrelevant.[169] Following the rules of evidence is certainly no guarantee of finding truth, especially because most of us frequently use legally excludable evidence in making judgments outside of courtroom settings without apparently being wrong much of the time and because legally admissible evidence may well be unreliable. Rules of evidence proceed on the assumption that individual bits of information can be screened out as unreliable, misleading, or untruthful and that any "reasonable" assemblage of what is left counts as truth. But this is at best a hopeful fiction.

For one thing, rules of evidence provide no guidance about what to do once particular bits of information are admitted as evidence. In practice, judges and juries do the best they can to evaluate evidence the only way they can—through assessing the way the stories hang together with what else they know about the world and through spotting key characteristics in the stories that they hear, characteristics they believe are signs of truth. Judges and juries cannot do anything else. They have to use ordinary conventions of truth-finding.

Given the dependence of law on these ordinary conventions of truth-finding, it is worth asking just what these ordinary conventions are, for several reasons. First, the outcomes of individual cases are highly dependent on what is found to be "the truth" in that instance, so the integrity and reliability of the judicial process depends on these factual determinations. How they are made and what conventions they invoke should be made explicit if law is to be justifiable to those who are subject to it.[170] Second, interpretations of fact and law are not easily separable activities in the process of legal reasoning,[171] and so any theory of

---

167. *See* FED. R. EVID. 402 (excluding evidence that is not relevant).

168. *See* FED. R. EVID. 801 (defining hearsay as, inter alia, "a statement, other than one made by the declarant while testifying [in court], offered in evidence to prove the truth of the matter asserted"; hearsay is not admissible except as provided by the Rules or the Supreme Court); *see also* Tribe, *supra* note 165, at 958 (explaining that hearsay is excluded because of inaccuracies attributed to ambiguity, insincerity, faulty perception, and erroneous memory).

169. *See generally* 1 JOHN H. WIGMORE, EVIDENCE IN TRIALS AT COMMON LAW § 6.5 (Peter Tillers rev. vol. 1983) (arguing that the drafters of the Federal Rules of Evidence did not consider whether the procedural techniques used to regulate the presentation of evidence would be successful in achieving accuracy).

170. STEPHEN MACEDO, LIBERAL VIRTUES 50, 69-70 (1990).

171. *See* SCHEPPELE, *supra* note 8, at 86-102 (detailing the interrelationship between

judging needs to include some account of the interpretive conventions used in the construction of facts to adequately represent the process.[172] Third, law often pretends to be above politics, prejudice, and partiality by virtue of the principled nature of its practices in judging. Insofar as a large part of that practice depends on unexamined and possibly prejudicial conventions for assessing the facts on which judicial judgment depends, the practice of judging can hardly be said to be above these "contaminating" influences. So, we should explore these influences before relying on the assumption that law manages to sanitize bias through its appeal to principle.

In addition to these worries about abstract legal legitimacies, a more immediate practical issue is involved in working out *whose* conventions of truth-finding are to be invoked when more than one set of conventions applies in the social settings that a given legal system embraces. If we have learned anything in recent years about the operation of social practices, it is that they are usually specific to time, place, social location, and embodiment in the lives of particular people. Saying that "we" have a set of conventions for truth-finding begs the questions of who the "we" are and whether "we" share these practices at all.[173] So, working out how information is constituted as fact or, at the risk of creating an unwieldy neologism, how information is "enfacted" requires both looking at the way conventions of practice are historically, socially, and culturally situated in the lives of particular people and asking whose truth is being found when jurors and judges find it. But when we look more closely, we see that the whole metaphor of "finding" rather than "constructing" the truth relies on the assumption that truth is "out there" to be located rather than constituted through the operation of social practices. This way of talking about truth shows how the "facticity" of a truth-claim must be presented as if it is compelled by the "external-ness" of its referent rather than compelled or allowed by the agreement on conventions of description.

---

interpreting facts and laws).

172. *See id.* at 103-04; *see also* Scheppele, *Telling Stories*, *supra* note 9, at 2080-83 (stating that the way people interpret what they see depends to a very large extent on prior experiences, on the ways in which they organize their observations, and on patterns of their daily life; this poses a particular problem in the law because judges and jurors are not first-hand witnesses and can only weigh other people's perceptions).

173. *See* Scheppele, *Telling Stories*, *supra* note 9, at 2079 n.21.

VI. EVALUATING REVISED STORIES

With these theoretical considerations in mind, we can now return to the specific problem of revised stories. If judges and juries generally believe that the first versions of stories are true and that later versions must be suspect unless some special reason exists to distrust the earlier version, what must their picture of truth look like? And how adequate is this picture to the complicated world that judges and juries are trying to represent through the construction of the facts of a case?

To believe initial versions over revised versions, people must have an image of a precarious and fragile truth that decays over time or is subject to the continual risk of subsequent distortion. As a result, information gathered before these inevitable processes of decay and distortion set in is considered to be especially important in figuring out "what happened." If accounts seem to change over time, it must be because something other than the initial, accurate perception of reality is being incorporated into the story.

Some basis for this belief exists, as the work of Elizabeth Loftus on eyewitness testimony makes clear.[174] People do revise their accounts based on new information that insinuates itself into the original memory as if this later information were part of the initial perception. But the possibility of such reconstructions should not eliminate the possibility that victims, particularly those who have been traumatized by the events for which they now want to seek legal redress, may be reinterpreting their experience in a new frame—one that in many ways is more adequate than their initial self-blame and denial.

The distinction people make between initial stories and revised stories obscures an important feature they both share. They are both narratives, and as such, they both represent strategies for organizing and making sense of evidence.[175] Neither story represents "perception without conception." The first version of any story is *not* merely raw material, processed by the mind without interpretation, that revised stories take and then shape through interpretive processes absent in the first version itself. As Wittgenstein showed in the duck-rabbit demonstration, "seeing" initially is often "seeing as."[176] We do not first see things "as they are"

174. *See* ELIZABETH F. LOFTUS, EYEWITNESS TESTIMONY 70 (1979); ELIZABETH F. LOFTUS, EYEWITNESS TESTIMONY: CIVIL AND CRIMINAL (2d ed. 1992).

175. *See* ACTS, *supra* note 159, at 55-59.

176. LUDWIG WITTGENSTEIN, PHILOSOPHICAL INVESTIGATIONS 194-95 (G.E.M.

and then interpret them. We see with the interpretive frameworks we bring to events as much as we see with our eyes. When we change interpretive frameworks, especially when the new frameworks create new accounts of blame, others may see us as making things up.

For example, the woman who sees her abusive husband as revealing his love for her through his violence is not processing raw material that is *then* later interpreted through consciousness-raising. She is interpreting her husband's actions as they are happening—and those initial interpretations feel like untainted perception. But her initial perceptions are already interpretations, though they would be different in their organization from the perceptions of her husband's defense lawyer or a feminist observer seeing those same events unfolding before their eyes. The difference in accounts that the battered woman and the feminist lawyer would give of this event is not the difference between truth and falsehood. Instead, it is the difference in the interpretive framework through which the events are seen in the first place.

Different *versions* of events may be related by different people witnessing the same thing at the same time. For identical reasons, different versions of events may be related by the *same* person who sees what once happened in a new light that only switches on when some time has elapsed since the event. But why should we favor the first framework that the victim happens to have over another framework that might be brought to bear on the event with more reflection?

The puzzle is deepened when we note that most people believe that reflection aids accuracy in everything but reports of perception. Generally, people believe that *considered* preferences are more reliable than preferences listed off the top of one's mind.[177] And ethical judgments that have been weighed for a period of time are better than "snap judgments." Even academic papers that have been through revisions are considered better, more polished, than those that have not been through the process of revision. Why is it, then, that reports of "facts" are not similarly thought to be improved with reflection and thought?

We learn to describe first impressions as *true* because they appear to involve no conscious alteration, even though there may be a physical basis for other reports of those perceptions. Nelson Goodman reports that when most of us report seeing a round table from the side, we still describe it

Anscombe trans., 3d ed. 1984).

177. In an earlier version of this paper, I called revised stories "considered stories" to emphasize their connection with considered preferences.

as round, even though our eyes are perceiving the shape as oval because of the angle of vision.[178] Clearly, there is a large element of construction, however rapid and implicit, even in the most apparently uncontroversial descriptions.

What this all amounts to is that first accounts appear to be *simply true* as if perception were somehow free of organizing concepts and categories that are themselves social products. First versions are the "obvious" way to describe what has happened, while revised versions seem to involve conscious hard work to "make sense" of what has happened and are therefore more obviously contestable. The accounts we take to be "simply true" feel as though they are "straight" read-outs of unbiased perception. The accounts we arrive at by revising our stories to "make sense" of things seem to pull away from those initial perceptions and are consequently distrusted.

But this contrast between a picture of pure and untainted perception and an alternative picture of a contaminated, altered, or revised account should now appear naive. If all narratives are constructions and all descriptions are socially situated, making use of concepts and categories that are made available through the cultural location one occupies, then why should we favor the *first* framework that this particular narrator happens to bring to the description of events? In the context of sexualized violence, in which a victimized population of women has come to see such abuse as a persistent feature of daily life, saying that initial stories are the only believable accounts amounts to saying that a potential defendant's guilt or liability rests on the defendant's choice of victim. Women who have accepted continuing victimization with the resignation of self-blame and denial can be abused without anyone being able to gainsay such women's initial narratives of complicity. When women learn that they do not have to put up with such treatment, however, they see their own pasts differently. But such reconstructions are then discredited as lies.

This is a general problem in the believability of narratives. The preference for first versions of stories looks like a neutral rule. But it falls particularly hard on women. As this article has shown, experience, social-science research, and observation of the legal process tell us that women who are the victims of sexualized violence often need to take time to understand what has happened to them. This is because women have learned both to put up with sexualized violence as a feature of daily life and to blame themselves for it as a first-pass explanation. Courts'

178. GOODMAN, *supra* note 163, at 92.

exclusion of revised stories works disproportionately against women because women are disproportionately the victims of a socialization that masks the immediate recognition of sexualized abuse *as* abuse. Overcoming the first reactions takes time—but it is precisely these delays that courts generally suspect as evidence of lying. The first stories we tell are not constructed in the absence of frameworks that help us to make sense of what has happened; they are simply constructed with our most uncritical frameworks—frameworks that may or may not be the ones we would think best to invoke upon further reflection.

Women's initial reactions in sexually abusive situations may lead others, particularly the men with whom they interact and those who judge women's reactions in court, to conclude that women enjoy the abuse and are encouraging the conduct. In a study of rape victims in Chicago, for example, I was surprised to find out how many women reported that they attempted to fight off their attackers by crying, by telling the rapists their life stories, and by apparently agreeing to sex to lower the violence level in the assault.[179] Each of several of the women in our sample of nearly 100 women said she began to tell the rapist, often a stranger, intimate details of her life in the attempt to get him to see her as a human being. If he saw her as a person, she thought, then he could not do this to her. Many women reported crying and bargaining rather than punching and screaming. Talking, crying, and bargaining very rarely worked, but women viewed these strategies as aggressive attempts to defend themselves while the rapists no doubt interpreted these reactions as a lack of meaningful resistance. In the absense of bruises and scratches that come with a physical struggle, these women often had great difficulty proving their nonconsent in court. Their first reactions were constructed as initial narratives of consent. As a surprising number of first reactions revealed in this study of sexual-assault victims, women are afraid to stop being polite, even when they are being attacked. This may be because women learn to be concerned with maintaining relationships and keeping them from breaking apart.[180] But regardless of the source of these reactions, they make women's later narratives of rape unbelievable.

In cases of sexual harassment, what victims seem to want most is for the conduct to stop. They do not want to leave their jobs, to file formal grievances, or to rip up their lives to avoid what was not their fault to

179. Unpublished study (on file with author).

180. *See* CAROL GILLIGAN, IN A DIFFERENT VOICE 62-63 (1982).

begin with.[181] Women often do not report sexual harassment, hoping it will go away.[182] By the time they decide to fight it, it is too late. The initial story that they were consenting, or at least not objecting, has already stuck.

If we have a legal system that uses rules of evidence and principles that are hostile to revised stories in judging truth, then women will continue to be victims in court when they press cases of sexualized violence. But the few revised stories that *are* currently accepted by courts are not an unqualified good thing in empowering women.[183] In the absence of multiple complaining witnesses and physical corroborating evidence, the revised stories that courts currently accept are generally the versions urged by expert testimony, not just by the woman herself. But the presence of experts may remove a woman's individuality and unique voice by substituting a statistically derived average experience that women typically share for the detailed, potentially idiosyncratic experiences each of us has. What a woman gains in solidarity with other women as a result of being lumped into the averages, she may lose in distinctiveness if her own experience veers from the statistical norm. As the women's movement succeeds in breaking women free from a single conception of femininity, such statistical averages will become less and less accurate as descriptions of particular women's experiences. The reliance on expert witnesses is immensely useful as a transition device between the world today and a world in which women's stories have more power as a source of fact. In the future, however, reliance on such witnesses may be seen as urging another single oppressive image of how women should react to sexualized violence on women who have diverse experiences and diverse reactions.

The use of expert testimony currently allows a woman to win a case against a man by having a "qualified person" testify that she was suffering from trauma or delusion and thus was not in her right mind when she blamed herself, acted from numbness like nothing had happened, tried to

181. *See* Wendy Pollack, *Sexual Harassment: Women's Experience vs. Legal Definitions*, 13 HARV. WOMEN'S L.J. 35, 51 (1990) (stating that women often quit jobs, request transfers, and even request demotions as a result of sexual harassment in their work environment).

182. *See* Mango, *supra* note 13, at 359-60.

183. *See generally* Elizabeth M. Schneider, *Describing and Changing: Women's Self-Defense Work and the Problem of Expert Testimony on Battering*, 9 WOMEN'S RTS. L. REP. 195 (1986) (arguing, in part, that the "battered woman syndrome" defense, as told through expert testimony, often perpetuates gender stereotypes of female incapacity).

show her deluded love for her attacker, or changed her story. What she *really* meant (only the expert can say) was something else. Certifying the later stories, experts succeed in establishing their own credibility while establishing that women are individually unstable at the time of abuse. Such psychologizing of the problem avoids recognition of the scale and scope of sexualized violence against women. Understanding the narrative strategies of women as the result of social and cultural forces larger than the individual case, as this article has tried to do, reempowers women to talk in their own voices and not just through the voices of experts.

Not all revised stories should be believed. Nor should all first drafts of accounts be immediately accepted either. Strategies of belief need to be more complicated than that to do justice to the variety of knowledges present in any given society. Understanding how the stories are socially constituted as believable in the first place is one important step in the process of making the legal system a force for the liberation of women from sexualized violence. At a minimum, fact-finders need to understand that early narratives about sexualized violence may reveal not some deeper truth, but rather the effects of oppression on women. Not allowing women to reinterpret their own experiences as they learn to oppose the abuse is a way of furthering that oppression.

[7]

Theaters of Proof: Visual Evidence and the Law in *Call Northside 777*

Jennifer L. Mnookin* and Nancy West**

The year was 1932. Crime in Chicago had increased sharply during Prohibition, and the city denizens were anxious. On a cold and blustery Friday afternoon in December, two men entered a speakeasy and held its owner up at gunpoint.[1] Shots were fired, and a policeman who happened to be present ended up dead—the eighth Chicago policeman to suffer a violent end that year.[2] Another policeman murdered in broad daylight and

---

* Associate Professor, University of Virginia School of Law. Thanks to Jonathan Cannon, Joshua Dienstag, Daryl Levinson, Jim Ryan, Stephen Robertson, and Bill Stuntz, as well as to participants in a Virginia summer workshop and attendees at a panel at the Modern Language Association annual meeting for helpful comments. Thanks also to Fred Blumberg and Laura Kelly for useful research assistance.

** Associate Professor, Victorian and Cultural Studies, University of Missouri-Columbia. Thanks to Penelope Pelizzon and Sandy Camargo for reading drafts of this Article.

1. People v. Majczek, 195 N.E. 653, 654 (Ill. 1935).

2. Jack McPhaul & James McGuire, *Is He Guilty? Would You Convict Joe Majczek? Here's the Story Behind Slaying of Policeman*, CHI. DAILY TIMES, Nov. 27, 1944, at 3.

in cold blood? It was important that the public believe that the forces of law and order were still in control of the city.[3] The police force and the residents of the city were hungry for justice, or at least vengeance.[4] A Polish immigrant named Joseph Majczek was soon arrested for the murder, and a month later a co-conspirator was also charged.[5] After an uneventful trial, they were both convicted of first-degree murder and sentenced to ninety-nine years in the Illinois State Prison.[6] On appeal, their convictions were upheld.[7] Case solved and case closed, or so it seemed. A short-lived blip on the front pages of the newspapers, this particular cop-killing was relegated to yesterday's headlines, the murder and the trial completely forgotten, at least in the popular imagination.

Eleven years later, however, the case became news once again. The convicted murderer's mother placed a classified ad in the *Chicago Daily Times*, offering a reward of $5000 to anyone with information that could help set her son free.[8] The ad caught the eye of a *Times* reporter, who, thinking there might be a "human interest" story in it, passed it to an editor who then assigned it to two members of his staff.[9] These reporters published a series of investigative articles that generated widespread sympathy for Majczek and eventually led to his release and pardon.[10] In 1948, the case was revisited again, this time by Twentieth-Century Fox in a film named *Call Northside 777*,[11] directed by Henry Hathaway and featuring James Stewart as an investigative reporter named P.J. McNeal, and Richard Conte as Frank Wiecek, the character based on Joseph Majczek.[12]

3. *See National Affairs: Illinois*, TIME, Aug. 17, 1945, at 23 ("Mayor Anton Cermak, who was trying to get Chicago's mildewed reputation scrubbed up for the World's Fair, clamored for a crime cleanup.").

4. As McPhaul and McGuire wrote, "The period was one in which civic groups and newsgroups were agitated over a 'crime wave,' and the local papers were even publishing a 'daily score' on the state's attorney's accomplishments." McPhaul & McGuire, *supra* note 2, at 3; *see also* JOHN J. MCPHAUL, DEADLINES AND MONKEYSHINES: THE FABLED WORLD OF CHICAGO JOURNALISM 195 (1962) (describing how the mayor had ordered a no-holds barred "war on crime" in an effort to clean up the city for the upcoming Century of Progress Exposition).

5. *Majczek*, 195 N.E. at 655.

6. *Id.* at 654.

7. *Id.*

8. CHI. DAILY TIMES, Oct. 10, 1944, at 30. The ad read in full: "$5000 Reward for killers of Officer Lundy on Dec. 9, 1932. Call Gro, 1758 12-7 p.m." *Id.*

9. Jack McPhaul & James McGuire, *Trial Witness Insists Identification False*, CHI. DAILY TIMES, Nov. 28, 1944, at 3; *see also* MCPHAUL, *supra* note 4, at 191.

10. The series of articles began on November 27, 1944, and ran daily until December 5, 1944. The *Times* continued to cover the case extensively through Majczek's eventual pardon on August 15, 1945.

11. CALL NORTHSIDE 777 (Twentieth-Century Fox 1948) [hereinafter *Northside*].

12. During the 1940s and 1950s, Twentieth-Century Fox produced roughly thirty percent of all films now classified as "film noir" and nearly eighty percent of all films now classified as "noir documentaries," *Northside* among them. *See* ALAIN SILVER & ELIZABETH WARD, FILM NOIR: AN ENCYCLOPEDIC REFERENCE TO THE AMERICAN STYLE 5 (1979). Other film noir titles produced by

From a murder trial to a three-line advertisement to a Hollywood feature film: the trajectory of the Majczek case involves an explosion of narratives, each acquiring a greater mass audience than the one preceding it. This Article will focus on the film version, but we analyze the film in relation to the narratives that preceded, inspired, and shaped it—both the trial itself and the newspaper accounts that led to Majczek's freedom. For as we shall show, the film offers a sharp critique of legal rules of evidence, a critique that can best be understood in relation to the evidence presented in the actual Majczek trial. Moreover, through the vehicle of one particular wrongful conviction, the film attempts to tell a grander story of the power of mass media as a protector of freedoms and the righter of legal wrongs—just as the *Chicago Daily Times*'s articles ended up not only freeing Majczek but winning awards for revealing the life-changing power of journalism at its best.[13]

Though it was both popular and critically acclaimed at the time of its release, *Call Northside 777* is no longer much remembered.[14] Today, it is typically a film consigned to a footnote in film history, not a minor film, but not a major one either.[15] It enjoyed substantial popularity on its release, and it features one of Hollywood's most beloved actors; however, while *Northside* is available for rental at many video stores, it remains at

---

Fox include John Brahm's THE BRASHER DOUBLOON (Twentieth-Century Fox 1947), Henry Hathaway's THE DARK CORNER (Twentieth-Century Fox 1946), Otto Preminger's FALLEN ANGEL (Twentieth-Century Fox 1946), and LAURA (Twentieth-Century Fox 1944). For titles of noir documentaries produced by Twentieth-Century Fox, see *infra* note 16.

With directors like Preminger, Hathaway, and Robert Siodmak under contract, Twentieth-Century Fox could claim film noir and the noir documentary as being among its specializations. (Indeed, in a review of *Northside*, *Time* magazine called the studio "the leader" in making what it called "semi-documentary" films. *New Picture:* Call Northside 777, TIME, Feb. 16, 1948, at 99.) A relatively small studio compared to MGM or Paramount, Twentieth-Century Fox specialized in less popular and more "artsy" genres (as did RKO and Warner Bros.) rather than the big-budget musicals, dramas, and comedies that made the other studios so powerful. For discussion of the Hollywood studios and the types of films they made, see generally THOMAS SCHATZ, THE GENIUS OF THE SYSTEM: HOLLYWOOD FILMMAKING IN THE STUDIO ERA (1988).

13. McPhaul and McGuire won the annual Heywood Broun Award of the American Newspaper Guild for their reporting. MCPHAUL, *supra* note 4, between 180-81 (reprinting a photograph of the Heywood Broun Award at a Chicago Newspaper Guild ball in 1945). They also won several other awards, including one from the national journalism fraternity, Sigma Delta Chi, and one from the National Headliners Club. *See* Gary Houston, *A Real Life Chicago Murder Mystery: Few Stories Compare with "Northside 777,"* CHI. TRIB., Jan. 9, 1995, at C1.

14. The *L.A. Times*, for example, called it "engrossing cinema[,] . . . a film triumph." *Time* magazine called it "a good answer to those who generalize too glibly about the superiority of European movies." *New Picture:* Call Northside 777, *supra* note 12, at 100.

15. In comparison to other films starring James Stewart, particularly those directed by Frank Capra and Alfred Hitchcock, *Call Northside 777* has received scant popular or critical attention. More generally, Henry Hathaway has never enjoyed the kind of critical attention devoted to many other American directors. Despite a prolific career (he made sixty-one films between 1932 and 1971) and the critical and commercial success of many of his films, *e.g.*, KISS OF DEATH (Twentieth-Century Fox 1947); HOW THE WEST WAS WON (MGM 1963); TRUE GRIT (Paramount 1969), no scholarly book-length study exists on Hathaway, and the Academy nominated him only once for Best Director—for LIVES OF A BENGAL LANCER (Paramount 1935). *See* EMANUEL LEVY, AND THE WINNER IS . . . : THE HISTORY AND POLITICS OF THE OSCAR AWARDS 170 (1987).

best only vaguely familiar to most moviegoers. Scholars have paid *Northside* some limited attention, focusing primarily on its relation to film noir.[16] But no full-length articles exist on *Northside*, and the rare discussions of it in film criticism are usually limited to a mere paragraph or two.[17] What, then, justifies this Article? Is *Northside* worth so many

16. The three authors who engage with *Call Northside 777* in most detail are film theorists J.P. Telotte and Frank Krutnik, and legal historian Norman Rosenberg. Rosenberg offers a rich analysis of *Northside*'s themes, and he is the only author to date who emphasizes the ways that *Northside* represents "the law" as an institution. Norman Rosenberg, *Law Noir*, *in* LEGAL REELISM: MOVIES AS LEGAL TEXT 281-89 (John Denvir ed., 1996) [hereinafter LEGAL REELISM]. Ironically, given his focus on law, Rosenberg affords no time to *Northside*'s exploration of legal evidence, which is our primary focus.

Telotte and Krutinik both concern themselves with locating *Call Northside 777* within traditional film genres, making the case for the film as a "documentary noir," a hybrid of the film noir and the documentary traditions. *See* J.P. TELOTTE, VOICES IN THE DARK: NARRATIVE PATTERNS IN FILM NOIR 134-35 (1989); FRANK KRUTNIK, IN A LONELY STREET: FILM NOIR, GENRE AND MASCULINITY 202-08 (1991). They identify the film as part of an impressive cycle of movies produced roughly between 1945 and 1950 that purported to offer realistic and objective accounts of urban crime. Also described as "semi-documentary crime thrillers," this cycle of films includes other Twentieth-Century Fox productions like Hathaway's THE HOUSE ON 92ND STREET (Twentieth-Century Fox 1945) and 13 RUE MADELEINE (Twentieth-Century Fox 1946), and Elia Kazan's BOOMERANG (Twentieth-Century Fox 1947). Other titles in this cycle include Jules Dassin's THE NAKED CITY (Universal Pictures 1948), Anthony Mann's T-MEN (Eagle Lion Films 1948) and BORDER INCIDENT (Metro-Goldwyn-Mayer 1949), Alfred Walker's HE WALKED BY NIGHT (Bryan Foy Productions 1949), Maxwell Shane's CITY ACROSS THE RIVER (Universal-International 1949), George Sherman's THE SLEEPING CITY (Universal-International 1950), and John H. Auer's THE CITY THAT NEVER SLEEPS (Republic 1953).

As an attempt to situate the film historically, grouping *Northside* this way makes sense. Like the other films, *Northside* proposed to offer American audiences something different from the Hollywood fare they had been fed on before the war, something as socially charged and informative as the popular newsreel *The March of Time*, which the American public watched in theaters nationwide during the war. Like these films, *March* employed a stentorian voice-over, actual footage, and, as Bosley Crowther once remarked, "the reenactment of an event so effective that it simulates reality itself." Bosley Crowther, *Imitations Unwanted*, N.Y. TIMES, Feb. 22, 1948, at B1, *quoted in* TELOTTE, *supra*, at 135. Aesthetically and methodologically, *Northside* also has much in common with these films. What they share, as Telotte puts it, is their "consistent and calculated slippage from a documentary 'look,'" their deliberate flirtation with the supposed boundaries between Hollywood fiction and documentary. TELOTTE, *supra* at 136.

However, the term "documentary noir" presupposes a hard-edged, even cynical, treatment of its subject, which *Northside* does not offer. The film is too optimistic, too univocal, and too confident about the possibilities for justice to fit comfortably in the category "noir." And although *Northside* possesses important documentary characteristics, some of which we will discuss later, it participates less in the documentary tradition than these other films, which generally cast unknown performers and paid much less attention than *Northside* to such elements as dramatic conflict and narrative closure. *Northside* is at once much more Hollywoodish and, in a sense, more historically accurate than most of these other films. Elia Kazan's *Boomerang* is perhaps the film with which *Northside* shares the greatest affinity: Like *Northside*, *Boomerang* is closely based on an actual murder case; it mixes elements of classical narrative with documentary techniques; and it concerns itself with questions about witnessing, testimony, and the sufficiency of legal evidence. Although *Boomerang* was released on video, it was released in a limited press and is not widely available to viewers at present.

17. Beyond the three authors discussed above, *see supra* note 16, the area of film scholarship that has produced the most commentary on *Northside* is noir studies, which generally upholds the film as marking an important contribution to the genre. It is featured, for example, in Silver and Ward's encyclopedia on film noir, where it is described as a "fine example of what might be called 'newspaper noir.'" SILVER & WARD, *supra* note 12, at 49-50. Stuart Kaminsky includes it as one of 121 "key" film noirs in a list he compiled. STUART KAMINSKY, AMERICAN FILM GENRES 274 (1985). Still, most critics afford it only very brief discussion, no doubt because it lacks so many of noir's typical characteristics. *See, e.g.*, NICHOLAS CHRISTOPHER, SOMEWHERE IN THE NIGHT 15, 44, 52, 91,

words?

We will argue that *Northside* can be read as a study in evidence. It is a film that speaks powerfully to the question of what counts as proof and what persuades, both in the courtroom and in our cultural imagination. *Northside* strongly suggests that legal conceptions of what constitutes good evidence may deviate from more broadly-held ideas of legitimate proof, and that these divergences threaten to lead to injustice. Legal standards of evidence are portrayed as rigid and conservative, too willing to rely on the unreliable and too resistant to novel forms of knowledge.

In this Article, we show in detail how *Northside* sets up a hierarchy of evidentiary forms. Expert evidence is deemed more trustworthy than eyewitness testimony, but the photograph is portrayed as the best evidence of all, offering proof superior to the expert and lay witness alike. Through this hierarchy, the film not only critiques legal conceptions of evidence, but also suggests that visible, technologically produced proof is the most authoritative and reliable. That is, *Northside* suggests that the "cure" for the problems of legal proof can be found in science, in the conclusions of experts, and even better, in the objectivity of new technologies. *Northside* imagines an ideal form of evidence that can provide for narrative closure and moral certainty: The film is in search of proof of innocence, not merely evidence that casts doubt on guilt. In the film, as we shall see, it is a newly discovered photograph that provides this kind of evidence, evidence that rises above the competing narratives of the trial—the witnesses and counter-witnesses and contradictions—evidence that allows no inference but innocence.[18] Or at least, as we shall argue, the photograph

168, 210 (1997); ED GORMAN, LEE SERVER & MARTIN H. GREENBERG, THE BIG BOOK OF NOIR 5, 70 (1998). Other key authors on noir make no mention of *Northside* at all. Indeed, the seminal text on film noir, RAYMONDE BORDE & ETIENNE CHAUMETON, PANORAMA DU FILM NOIR AMERICAIN, 1941-1953 (1955), characterizes noir in such a way that *Northside* is excluded by definition: They argue that film noir can be distinguished from other crime films in that it offers an "inside," psychological perspective on criminality. *Id.* at 1. *Northside* (as well as other crime "semi-documentaries"), by contrast, focuses on the viewpoint of institutional forces like the police, the FBI, and the newspaper industry. Following this line of thinking about noir, some critics do not even mention *Northside* in their study of the genre. *See, e.g.*, JAMES NAREMORE, FILM NOIR AND ITS CONTEXTS (1998). *Northside*'s uneasy fit within the typical categories of genre may help to account for its limited critical attention, as the genre is one of Hollywood's most obvious ways of ensuring, as film historian John Ellis phrases it, "that its films are promotable to the whole of the potential audience." JOHN ELLIS, VISIBLE FICTIONS 200 (1982).

18. Note that in its claim that the techniques of science can provide an antidote to the imperfections of the trial process, *Northside* prefigures current efforts to use DNA evidence to acquit convicted criminals. Like the photographic evidence depicted in *Northside*, DNA evidence appears to offer the possibility of rising above "mere" narrative and accessing truth directly. In this Article, we shall argue that this is precisely the promise of visual evidence in *Northside* (and, we shall suggest, of filmic evidence in actual courts as well), but that it is a promise based, in the end, on illusion. We do not, in this Article, take up DNA evidence directly, but *Northside*, as a story of wrongful conviction, a study in evidence and a critique of law, should be analyzed with DNA—especially its dazzling ability to unravel the stories generated at trials and to turn what seemed to be compelling narratives of guilt into "mere" fictions—in the background. For the dramatic story of the efforts of Barry Scheck and others to use DNA to exonerate the wrongly convicted, see JIM DWYER, PETER NEUFELD & BARRY SCHECK, ACTUAL INNOCENCE (2000).

in *Northside seems* to do so until examined closely.

In fact, in presenting the photograph as the highest form of proof, *Northside* simplifies and ignores the complications posed by photographic evidence. The film thus invites examination of whether confidence in visual and photographic evidence is, in fact, too easily generated, the picture too easily believed. This question of whether cinematic evidence is dangerously seductive is important, too, for the analysis of films as courtroom evidence. In fact, during the two decades preceding the release of *Northside*, films had made their way into actual trials, forcing judges to determine whether they were enough like the "real thing"—or even too much like the "real thing"—to be allowed into evidence. As we shall see, for the most part judges shared the vision set forth in *Northside* of film as a nearly transparent medium of truth.

However, our unpacking of *Northside* suggests that both within legal processes and within cinematic depictions, the power of visual evidence necessarily relies on a kind of illusion, a willingness to ignore the mechanisms by which visual evidence is made, shaped, and constructed. In this sense, the courtroom and the cinema may have more in common than might be expected: Both domains operate as theaters of proof in which the power of sight may be both the most effective rhetorical mode of persuasion and an especially fragile basis for conviction.[19]

---

19. Looking to a popular film for insights about law is not entirely novel. Indeed, in recent years, there has been a groundswell of interest in the relation of law and film. *See, e.g.*, RICHARD K. SHERWIN, WHEN LAW GOES POP: THE VANISHING LINE BETWEEN LAW AND POPULAR CULTURE (2000) [hereinafter SHERWIN, WHEN LAW GOES POP]; LEGAL REELISM, *supra* note 16; Carol Clover, *Movies Juries*, 48 DE PAUL L. REV. 389 (1998); Lawrence Douglas, *Film as Witness: Screening Nazi Concentration Camps Before the Nuremberg Tribunal*, 105 YALE L.J. 449 (1995); Donald H.J. Hermann, *The Law in Cinema: An Emerging Field of Study*, 42 N.Y.L. SCH. L. REV. 305, 306 (1998); Orit Kamir, *Judgment by Film: Socio-Legal Functions of* Rashomon, 12 YALE J.L. & HUMAN. 39 (2000); Carrie Menkel-Meadow, *The Sense and Sensibilities of Lawyers: Lawyering in Literature, Narratives, Film, and Television, and Ethical Choices Regarding Career and Craft*, 31 MCGEORGE L. REV. 891 (1996); Norman Rosenberg, *Hollywood on Trial: Courts and Films, 1930-1960*, 12 LEGAL HIST. REV. 341 (1994); Richard K. Sherwin, *Law Frames: Historical Truth and Narrative Necessity in a Criminal Case*, 47 STAN. L. REV. 39 (1994) [hereinafter Sherwin, *Law Frames*]; Rennard Strickland, *The Cinematic Lawyer: The Magic Mirror and the Silver Screen*, 22 OKLA. CITY U. L. REV. 13 (1997); Symposium, *Legal Reelism: The Hollywood Film as Legal Text*, 25 LEGAL STUD. F. 199 (1993).

This emergence of "law and film" as a topic of scholarly study emerges, broadly, from the more established "law and literature" movement, which has, in recent years, begun to turn to the analysis of less traditional literary forms. Within the law and literature movement, there have been numerous efforts to typologize; one distinction often made (and often criticized) is between the study of "law in literature" and the study of "law as literature." *See, e.g.*, IAN WARD, LAW AND LITERATURE: POSSIBILITIES AND PERSPECTIVES 3 (1995) (detailing the "familiar distinction between law in literature and law as literature").

While the study of law in literature is, to be sure, extensive, surprisingly little of it has focused on the questions of evidence and proof. There are a few notable exceptions. *See, e.g.*, ALEXANDER WELSH, STRONG REPRESENTATIONS: NARRATIVE AND CIRCUMSTANTIAL EVIDENCE IN ENGLAND (1991); Judy M. Cornett, *The Treachery of Perception: Evidence and Experience in* Clarissa, 63 U. CIN. L. REV. 165 (1994); Special Issue, *The Status of Evidence*, 108 PROC. MOD. LANG. ASSOC. (1993). This Article explores how *Northside* represents and critiques legal evidence; in this sense, it emerges from the "law in literature" (or in this instance "law in film") paradigm.

We thus also use *Northside* as a jumping-off point for a broader exploration of the reception of filmic evidence, first by examining *Northside* as a "reenactment," a hybrid form that lies somewhere between drama and documentary, and then, at the end of the Article, by taking a sideways glance at the use of reenactments and other films in actual trials. Reenactments as a form of popular entertainment have grown exponentially in recent years, and they have also begun to receive scholarly attention.[20] No one, however, has yet explored *Northside* as reenactment, or linked the film back to the actual Chicago murder case on which it is based. Moreover, none of the recent work on reenactments links reenactments to law and legal processes. It turns out, however, that reenactments and trials (and their outcomes) have a special relation: They are both, at heart, attempts to recapture the past in an authentic and credible fashion. Neither can claim to capture the past directly, nor even to be true in some grand metaphysical sense, but both verdicts and reenactments want to be seen as being true to the past in all of the ways that count.

We thus have two central purposes in this Article. The first is to examine *Northside*'s exploration of various modes of legal evidence, particularly its privileging of photography as the most valuable form of such evidence. The second goal is to offer a meditation on the hybrid status of the reenactment, both by reflecting on *Northside*'s status as a reenactment and by describing the actual use of reenactments and other films in the courtroom during the 1940s. Looking at judges' decisions regarding reenactments during this time period reveals an unmistakable tendency to simplify the complications posed by the use of film as evidence. This tendency resonates not only with *Northside*'s own simplifying strategies but also with those of the documentary and its related subgenres, demonstrating how both cinema and the courtroom depend on visual naïveté in order to make evidence work.

This Article is divided into four Parts. The first Part looks back to the actual Chicago wrongful conviction case on which the film was based. In addition to bringing back to light the intriguing history of a case that formed the basis of a popular Hollywood film, this discussion provides necessary context for our continued attention to *Northside* as reenactment in Part II. Only by reading the film with attention to the actual case can we show how precisely the film mirrors the case on which it was based—and, importantly, the critical junctures where it does not. The second Part of the Article turns to the film itself. We suggest that the film is best understood as an early exemplar of a reenactment: a retelling of a true story in sufficient detail and with enough fidelity for the audience to understand the film as "fact" instead of, or alongside, "fiction." We then turn to the

20. *See infra* notes 67-71 and accompanying text.

heart of the Article, in which we explore the film's claims and reflections about legal evidence, but with particular attention to those places where the film departs from its source. We argue that the film sets up a hierarchy of evidence, with the eyewitness at the bottom and the photograph on top. We maintain that *Northside*'s depiction of evidence serves both to critique legal conceptions of proof and to buttress the film's own authority as a truthful representation of the actual case. In Part III, we turn to the use of actual films in the courtroom around the time of *Northside* itself, in order to show some of the interesting parallels between *Northside*'s claims about visual proof and the reception of films in actual courtrooms. Finally, in the Conclusion, we suggest that this double examination of *Northside* as a study in evidence and the reception of filmic evidence in court suggests an important affinity between the trial and the filmed reenactment: Both attempt to create believable stories of the past, stories not literally true that nonetheless come to be seen as true, stories that even become substitute depictions for what actually occurred.

I. THE ACTUAL CASE

December 9, 1932 was a cold day, even by the standards of Chicago in the wintertime.[21] It was nearly eleven degrees below zero when, at about 3:00 in the afternoon, two armed men entered Mrs. Vera Walush's speakeasy in Chicago and announced, "This is a stick-up."[22] What began as an attempted robbery ended in a murder: The two men shot seven bullet holes into Officer William Lundy and then escaped unharmed in an automobile.[23] One of the bullets penetrated Lundy's heart and he died immediately; his gun was never fired.[24] Right before Christmas, a twenty-four-year-old Polish immigrant named Joseph Majczek was arrested and charged with the crime, and a few weeks later, a friend of his was arrested as well. At the trial, the two defendants claimed to have alibis for the time of the murder. Though Majczek chose not to testify because he had a police record, witnesses provided him with an alibi, testifying that he had been home at the time of the robbery, helping to carry coal into the house.[25] Several of the witnesses to the crime admitted that they had not seen the two men clearly enough to make a positive identification. In fact, initially, Vera Walush also claimed she had not gotten a good enough look: "I was so scared that I ran away before I could look at them," she

21. Jack McPhaul & James McGuire, *Here's the Story Behind Slaying of Policeman*, CHI. DAILY TIMES, Nov. 27, 1944, at 3.

22. *Id.*

23. *Policeman Slain As He Grapples with Bandits*, CHI. TRIB., Dec. 10, 1932, at 5.

24. *Id.*

25. Jack McPhaul & James McGuire, *Charge Majczek Victim of Bungling*, CHI. DAILY TIMES, Apr. 2, 1945, at 5.

said in her initial statement to the police.[26] The jurors, however, never learned about this earlier statement.[27] And in the courtroom, Vera Walush dramatically fingered the two men as the culprits, and claimed to be certain about it.[28]

Sure enough, after two hours and forty minutes of deliberation, the jury found the two men guilty. [29] The jury declined to impose the death penalty and instead sentenced them to ninety-nine years in prison.[30] The judge indicated subsequently that he believed that the two men were actually innocent and that a second trial would clear them.[31] He began to interview the various witnesses himself, conducting what almost amounted to a second trial in his judicial chambers.[32] He told several people, including one of the witnesses at the trial, that he did not think the trial had been fair, and that he would do whatever it took to get the defendants another trial, even if he had to pay for it himself.[33] However, for reasons that never became clear, but most likely involved the judge's desire to be re-slated in the upcoming election, he eventually stopped pursuing the case, and died without ever helping Majczek and his co-defendant overturn their convictions.[34]

The defendants appealed, but the Supreme Court of Illinois upheld their convictions, finding, "The testimony of one witness may be sufficient upon the question of identity. Even though denied by the accused, the testimony of one witness may be sufficient to sustain a conviction."[35] Moreover, because Majczek's incompetent attorney (who was subsequently disbarred)[36] had failed to make the proper motion for a new trial, necessary to preserve the issue for consideration on appeal, the Supreme Court declined to review the question of whether the sum of the evidence offered was sufficient to support a conviction.[37]

While Joseph Majczek pined away in Joliet—a prison built as a Benthamite Panopticon—Majczek's mother toiled assiduously, scrubbing floors in a Chicago office building, utterly convinced of her son's

26. Jack McPhaul & James McGuire, *Postman's Story at Odds with That of "Finger Woman,"* CHI. DAILY TIMES, Nov. 29, 1944, at 3.

27. *Id.*

28. *Woman Points Out Killers at Slaying Trial*, CHI. TRIB., Nov. 9, 1933, at 7.

29. *Two Get 99 Years for Police Slaying*, CHI. TRIB., Nov. 11, 1933, at 1.

30. *Id.*

31. McPhaul & McGuire, *supra* note 26, at 3.

32. Jack McPhaul & James McGuire, *Trial Witness Insists Identification False*, CHI. DAILY TIMES, Nov. 28, 1944, at 4.

33. *Id.*

34. *See* Jack McPhaul & James McGuire, *Judge's Son Joins Fight To Free Joe*, CHI. DAILY TIMES, Apr. 5, 1945, at 3.

35. People v. Majczek, 195 N.E. 653, 656 (Ill. 1935).

36. Jack McPhaul & James McGuire, *Joe Majczek's Fate up to Board*, CHI. SUNDAY TIMES, Apr. 8, 1945, at 10.

37. *Majczek*, 195 N.E. at 656.

innocence. She saved as much as she could, and on October 11, 1944, she placed a classified ad in the *Chicago Daily Times*, saying "Five thousand dollars reward for killers of Officer Lundy on December 9, 1932. Call Gro-1758, 12-7 p.m."[38] A young reporter noticed it, and, thinking it might contain the seeds of a human-interest story, passed it along to her editor.

Two reporters took an interest in the case and investigated thoroughly. One of the early articles describes how, after reading the prisoner's account of the case,

> The TIMES man found the case history an eye-opener—if. If it could be accepted as gospel, Joe Majczek was one of the world's hard luck guys . . . . But the reporter couldn't forget that a man in prison, brooding long nights over the loss of his freedom, often drifts into the realm of fantasy and delusion, and in time comes to believe the figments of his imagination. And Joe had been in prison for 11 years.[39]

Over time, however, the reporters became convinced of Majczek's innocence. Not only did the prisoner pass a polygraph test,[40] but the reporters found that the police had pressured Vera Walush by threatening her with prosecution for bootlegging, and that she had later told friends that her identification had been false.[41] They also discovered that Vera Walush had failed to identify Majczek the first two times she saw him in a line-up, and that she had been hiding in a closet for the entire duration of the robbery, affording her little chance even to glimpse the two men she later identified as guilty.[42] The reporters even tracked down some of the original jurors at the trial, all of whom said that if they had known about the evidence adduced by the newspaper staff, they never would have voted to convict.[43]

In August 1945, Joseph Majczek was pardoned by the governor of Illinois and released from prison.[44] The Illinois legislature voted to give him $24,000 in partial compensation for his ordeal.[45] His wife had divorced him at his urging and remarried to spare their son the trauma of a

38. CHI. DAILY TIMES, Oct. 10, 1944, at 30.

39. Jack McPhaul & James McGuire, *Trial Witness Insists Identification False*, CHI. DAILY TIMES, Nov. 28, 1944, at 3.

40. Jack McPhaul & James McGuire, *Lie Detector Clears Joe*, CHI. DAILY TIMES, Dec. 4, 1944, at 3.

41. Jack McPhaul & James McGuire, *Swears Joe's Conviction Based on Lie*, CHI. DAILY TIMES, Dec. 3, 1944, at 4.

42. Jack McPhaul & James McGuire, *Frame-Up Seen in Witness' Acts*, CHI. DAILY TIMES, Nov. 30, 1944, at 3.

43. Jack McPhaul & James McGuire, *4 Jurors Would Acquit Joe Today*, CHI. DAILY TIMES, Dec. 5, 1944, at 3.

44. James McGuire & Jack McPhaul, *Joe Majczek Wins Fight for Freedom*, CHI. TIMES, Aug. 15, 1945, at 3.

45. *Green O.K.'s $24,000 for Joe Majczek*, CHI. SUN, June 29, 1947, §1, at 5.

father who was a cop-killer.[46] After his release, Majczek and his wife remarried, and Majczek became a modestly successful insurance salesman.[47] Two years later, Twentieth-Century Fox bought the rights to the story, paying $1000 to Majczek and $2500 to journalist James McGuire, one of the authors of the *Chicago Daily Times* articles that led to Majczek's freedom.[48] (Jack McPhaul, the other author of the series of articles, received no payment.)[49]

II. *CALL NORTHSIDE 777*

A. Northside *as Reenactment*

As it opens onto its first scene, *Northside* promises to offer an explicit recounting of the Majczek story, a promise on which it largely delivers. The film in fact follows the original case to a remarkable degree and in tremendous detail. In order to assure viewers of its fidelity to history, the film begins by appropriating documentary codes and rhetoric. It alerts us (through the opening image of a "shooting script" stamped "urgent") that this is a "true story" whose scenes have all been shot on location in Chicago.[50] Unusually for its time, *Northside* was shot almost entirely on location, and partly in the very settings where the actual case had taken place. A stentorian voice-over guides us through the film's first ten minutes, recounting both the history of Chicago after the great fire of 1871 and the facts of the murder case on which the film is based.[51] With documentary-like style camerawork, including high-grain film, long shots of the city's seedy neighborhoods and buildings, and footage from actual police arrests in Chicago during the 1930s, the clear intention of the film is to appear to reconstruct the crime and the investigation faithfully—both to expose the injustice of Frank Wiecek's conviction and to reveal and

46. Jack McPhaul & James McGuire, *Stork Plays Role in Joe's Defense*, CHI. DAILY TIMES, Dec. 2, 1944, at 3.

47. *Joseph Majczek Dies; Wrongfully Convicted in Killing*, CHI. SUN TIMES, May 31, 1983.

48. Houston, *supra* note 13.

49. *Id.*

50. The film was indeed shot substantially on location, with locations that included a variety of Chicago streets, the 19th precinct, the questioning room in the Chicago Criminal Courts building, and the state penitentiary at Joliet. *See* Exhibitor's Campaign Sheet, CALL NORTHSIDE 777 (n.d.) (on file with authors); *see also* Houston, *supra* note 13. Similarly, Hathaway's *The House on 92nd Street* begins with an introductory title that tells us that the film was "photographed in the actual places the original incidents occurred."

51. The use of this kind of voice-over provides another way in which *Northside* departs from film noir. Noir frequently employs voice-overs by characters whom we discover through the film's diegesis to be unreliable, delusional, or simply uninformed. Classic examples of this pattern include Edward Dmytryk's MURDER, MY SWEET (RKO 1944), Billy Wilder's DOUBLE INDEMNITY (Paramount 1944), and Orson Welles's THE LADY FROM SHANGAI (Columbia 1948). An equally powerful, but less well-known, film noir is Anthony Mann's RAW DEAL (Edward Small Productions 1948), which provides one of the only instances of a female voice-over in the noir canon.

revel in the possibilities of film as a medium for truth.[52] As advertisements for the movie proclaimed, "Every word is true."[53]

Yet, in what will turn out to be the first of several disruptive shifts in the film, the first ten minutes of documentary soon give way to classical Hollywood narrative.[54] *Northside* switches from exterior shots of Chicago that perform as social history to interior shots of the *Chicago Times*, signaling to the viewer that a more personalized, even if institutionalized, perspective will now take over. And, sure enough, the series of interior shots concludes with James Stewart's face in close-up, a shot meant to accentuate his star status and all the associations of honesty it carried with it. The film thus turns to the identifiable and less-threatening terrain of classical narrative, offering a reprieve for audiences from its own documentary strategies and impulses, "making truth both dramatically effective and comfortably acceptable," according to J.P. Telotte, one of the few film critics who has given *Northside* scholarly attention.[55]

But *Northside* does not shift from gritty documentary to classic film narrative simply to appease its audience. By borrowing tropes and visual conventions from two typically distinct genres, the film forces us to recognize the ways in which two supposedly distinct modes of filmmaking, documentary and drama, converge.[56] Moreover, the blending

52. *The House on 92nd Street* also employs footage of the actual investigation on which it was based.

53. Exhibitor's Campaign Sheet, *supra* note 51.

54. Indeed, the documentary "look" does not fully appear again until the last few minutes of the film—an important point, given that what is sandwiched in between is mainly classical narrative, Hollywood style. At the film's ending, the stentorian voice-over returns, as do the long shots, which provide the sense that the film is pulling away from the personal story of Wiecek and McNeal in order to position itself once again as being interested in larger, social problems—in problems, that is, that make up the content of the documentary.

55. TELOTTE, *supra* note 16, at 136. Rosenberg reads this transition as the film's move away from a "distanced," critical look at the police to a sympathetic focus on the private individual, who must fight against the injustices caused by institutional forces such as the police. Rosenberg, *supra* note 16, at 285.

56. Of course, even supposedly "pure" documentaries raise similar questions about the ways in which they are constructed and fictional. Telotte writes of the "uncertainty" and "contradiction" that characterize *Northside* and hybrid films like it in general, but theoretically, these adjectives can describe even the most "truthful" of documentaries, because the genre must always work against and through the fictionalizing tendencies of cinema. *See* TELOTTE, *supra* note 16, at 135-37. Media historian Paula Rabinowitz, describes how documentary films "speak about themselves as contradictory texts. Full of self-doubts about their status as organs of truth and reality, the films and their criticism unravel like so much celluloid on the cutting-room floor." PAULA RABINOWITZ, THEY MUST BE REPRESENTED: THE POLITICS OF DOCUMENTARY 23 (1994). Although not exclusively devoted to documentary film, her study offers an especially fascinating look at the genre because of the way it interweaves multiple modes of representation in Depression-Era America (such as the photographs taken by the Farm Security Administration and populist writing) with documentary film per se. *See also* MICHAEL RENOV, THEORIZING DOCUMENTARY 1-14 (1993). In the introduction to the book, Renov provides a useful list of some of the key "fictive elements" that appear in many nonfiction films: the construction of character, the use of poetic language, narration, or musical accompaniment to heighten emotional impact, the creation of suspense, the use of high or low camera angles, close-ups "which trade emotional resonance for spatial integrity," and the use of editing. *Id.* at 3. Thus, we fully recognize that some of the arguments we make about how reenactments force

of genres invites questions about narrative form: Exactly how should stories be produced? What kind of stories best capture a viewer's attention, documentaries or dramas? Which are most likely to persuade, those that reproduce the actual as literally as possible, or those that smooth out the rough edges of reality, playing to sentiment and even sensation? The inevitably complex relation among representation, reality, and persuasion plays out within the film first in the relation between McNeal's newspaper stories and Wiecek's "real" circumstances. The same questions recur in the second half of the film, when *Northside* dramatically shifts its focus from the newspaper industry and how it produces stories to the legal system and how it weighs evidence. Finally, the film as a whole and its relation to the actual Majczek case invite a similar inquiry into the thorny problem of what it means to represent an event faithfully. We will continue to take up these questions throughout this Article.

The first half of *Northside* looks at how the newspaper industry responds to the Wiecek case, illustrating the newspaper's propensity for sensationalism. Like the actual reporters on whom he was based, the character played by James Stewart, J.P. McNeal, specializes in human-interest stories. And, as Hollywood drama, *Northside* aligns itself with the kinds of stories McNeal produces: stories that reduce the plurality of wills, purposes, and loose ends to a unified narrative of a mother's faith, a son's devotion, and innocence revealed. As McNeal types away at his typewriter, we recognize that the stories' implied readership closely resembles the viewers envisioned by the film: an audience desirous of a seemingly objective point of view, adherence to a cause-effect logic, characters who elicit our sympathies, and a progression toward narrative closure—all the elements, in short, that constitute the stuff of classical film narrative.[57]

Indeed, by spotlighting the stereotyped, sensational stories McNeal writes about the Wiecek case, *Northside* initially takes the production of classical narrative as its underlying subject. Rather than representing the facts of the case, McNeal garners tremendous public interest in Wiecek's case by writing stories with "mass appeal"—what he himself calls "hammering out a sob story." He "plays up" the "mother angle" and the "police corruption angle," for example, even when there is not yet any clear indication that the police acted unprofessionally.[58]

---

epistemological questions could also be applied to documentaries: Still, what interests us in particular about the reenactment is precisely that it is *explicitly* fiction though it claims the authority we associate with the representation of the actual.

57. Much critical discussion has been devoted to the subject of classical narrative cinema. The most insightful work on the subject includes the following: DUDLEY ANDREW, CONCEPTS IN FILM THEORY (1984); ELLIS, *supra* note 17; JAKOB LOTHE, NARRATIVE IN FICTION AND FILM: AN INTRODUCTION (2000); and Laura Mulvey, *Visual Pleasure and Narrative Cinema*, SCREEN 19 (1979).

58. This rather cynical look at how the newspaper industry functions is surprisingly common in film noir. Other films that offer negative representations of the newspaper or magazine industry

Importantly, the very "angles" he takes in his stories are those exploited by the film—the faith and devotion of Wiecek's mother, the loyalty of her son, and ultimately the possibility of police corruption—as if McNeal's hunches for what makes good story material predict the filmic content. To reinforce the connection between McNeal's stories and the cinematic narrative, the camera repeatedly zooms in on McNeal's printed words as they appear in his typewriter. As we see in close-up titles such as "Wiecek places faith in mother" and "Mother slaves to save son," we recognize that these titles perform as textual summaries of what we have just witnessed on film.

At the same time, we also know that these titles, and the stories that follow them, do not accurately represent all that we have seen. We are thus encouraged to believe that we have a privileged viewpoint, privileged not only as compared to that of the film's imaginary readers of the newspaper but also as compared to the viewpoint of the actual readers of the case in 1932.[59] This double viewpoint—the sense that we are being manipulated by the film as if we were newspaper readers, and a simultaneous belief that we are receiving a more "truthful" version of the case—harks back to the film's opening image of a typed page from a manuscript stating that *Northside* is a "true story" and *also* a "shooting script." Documentary and fiction at once, the pages from *Northside's* script are indeed like those of the newspaper's: Both tell truth *and* fiction, even if the film encourages us to see it as somehow coming closer to the real than its textual counterpart.

While McNeal's early stories may attract readers, they cannot directly win Wiecek his freedom because they traffic mainly in narrative devices, not in evidence. "In the world *Northside* sketches, fictionalizing itself becomes the true antagonist, the impulse to veil or disguise reality, the culprit against which the film's documentary strategy is mobilized," Telotte argues.[60] In order to exonerate Wiecek, McNeal must abandon his sensational narratives for facts, or more accurately, for an alternative means of shaping his narratives. Consequently, the film reaches an important turning point when McNeal finally loses his skepticism about Wiecek's innocence and declares that "I'm willing to dig, get the facts." At this halfway point in the film, McNeal becomes an investigator as well as a storyteller, getting affidavits, digging through police files, unearthing

---

include John Farrow's THE BIG CLOCK (Paramount 1948) and Fritz Lang's THE BLUE GARDENIA (Alex Gottlieb Productions 1953), BEYOND A REASONABLE DOUBT (Bert Friedlob Productions 1956), and WHILE THE CITY SLEEPS (Bert Friedlob Productions 1956).

59. A miniature version of this position occurs frequently in film noir, in scenes where the camera provides a close-up shot of the front page of a newspaper. As we read the newspaper's factual account of the storyline that we are following in the film, we realize that we know much more than the newspaper account provides, both in terms of the facts of the case and the psychological motivations of the characters involved. For interesting examples of this technique, see Vincent Sherman's NORA PRENTISS (Warner Brothers 1947), and Arthur Lubin's IMPACT (United Artists 1949).

60. TELOTTE, *supra* note 16, at 149.

photographs. Soon he begins to learn about what constitutes evidence—evidence, that is, according to the law. And in so doing, he transforms into a very different kind of reporter.

Indeed, the law serves as a kind of corrective institution to the newspaper industry here.[61] Though represented as inflexible and severe, its expectations for proof demand a deeper level of investigation and commitment from McNeal.[62] More importantly, they demand the same things from the film itself. By setting up the law's criteria for conclusive evidence as the catalyst for its own climax, *Northside* redefines its own methods and objectives midway through the film. The film moves slightly away from classical narrative—away from emotional scenarios focused mainly on Wiecek's mother and her belief in her son—toward a more scientific, "objective" examination of the Wiecek case. Indeed, *Northside* becomes an exhibition of and meditation on three different kinds of evidence, each of which we will discuss in detail: eyewitness testimony, expert testimony in the form of a lie detector test, and a photograph. The result of this journey through evidence, as we will see in Part III, is a clear hierarchy that privileges image over narrative, or more accurately, upholds the photographic image as offering an ideal type of narrative because it offers a seemingly ideal type of evidence.

While the first half of *Northside* focuses on McNeal and the investigative articles he produces, the second half thus presents an extensive meditation on how the legal system decides what counts as admissible evidence. Like other hybrid crime films of the period, particularly *The House on 92nd Street* and *T-Men*, *Northside* spotlights modern techniques of detection, and in so doing, as Frank Krutnik explains in his book on masculinity and film noir, presents detection "not as a matter of intuitive action but as one of organizational machinery."[63] As we show in the next Part, this concentration on "organizational machinery" bolsters *Northside*'s own documentary claims by suggesting that photography is the most effective of all such machineries.[64]

---

61. This positioning of the law as a corrective force against fiction is, of course, conveniently naïve. Following in a long tradition of scholarship on the subject, Richard K. Sherwin has recently made clear the extent to which law depends on storytelling. *See* SHERWIN, WHEN LAW GOES POP, *supra* note 19, at 41-71. For classic accounts of the importance of narrative and storytelling to the trial process, see W. LANCE BENNETT & MARTHA S. FELDMAN, RECONSTRUCTING REALITY IN THE COURTROOM 62 (1981); and Nancy Pennington & Reid Hastie, *A Cognitive Theory of Juror Decision Making: The Story Model*, 13 CARDOZO L. REV. 519 (1991) (arguing that juries turn evidence into narrative).

62. In this sense, our interpretation of *Northside* differs radically from Rosenberg's. While he sees the film as consistently critical of law, we read *Northside* as offering a more ambivalent representation. On the one hand, the film does portray the legal institution as both narrowminded and inflexible. On the other hand, the law tempers and corrects McNeal's initial penchant for sensationalizing and drawing assumptions without conclusive evidence. Rosenberg, *supra* note 16, at 283.

63. KRUTNIK, *supra* note 16, at 203.

64. Other films that spotlight visual machineries include Anthony Mann's *T-Men*, which presents

This celebration of photography as a machinery of truth, creates a tension in *Northside* between the claims of narrative and those of the image. The film's climax rests on the authority of the photograph: Narrative seems to give way in *Northside* to the silence of a single, indisputable image. As silent witness, the photograph apparently stands opposed to narrative, its evidentiary power seemingly not in need of literary or even verbal accompaniment. Indeed, after the photograph offers the proof Wiecek needs to be set free, we never see the reporter McNeal write a story again. By following this trajectory, the film ultimately resists confronting its own fictional pressures and motivations. For all its exploration of how narrative and evidence work, *Northside* resists exploring the ways in which its documentary impulses are contradicted by its fictional impulses, by its effort to tell a story that, like McNeal's, will possess mass appeal. Just as importantly, it ignores the fact that all photographs, once they are enlisted for evidence, also get enlisted—to however small or great degree—for fiction.

Northside is part tearjerker, part documentary. It is often characterized as a film noir, but in many important ways *Northside* is far from noir, whose narratives generally defy logic, closure, and optimism, embracing ambiguity and cynicism as their modus operandi.[65] We suggest that the best single classification of *Northside* is as a "reenactment."[66] The

---

a dazzling and elaborate scene in which the police construct a life-size image of a criminal suspect on a projection screen as various witnesses provide their physical description of him. Henry Hathaway's *The House on 92nd Street* spotlights the various surveillance techniques, including hidden cameras and two-way mirrors, employed by the FBI.

65. Noirs, of course, range in both degrees of cynicism and narrative experimentation. Interestingly, those films that provide the most complex narrative structures (using such techniques as convoluted time frames, voice-over narrators who withhold or misrepresent information, and flashbacks) often figure as the most cynical in subject matter and tone, since the corruption and decay they spotlight is exacerbated for the viewer by the confusion she feels in following the storyline. Examples of such films include Anatole Litvak's SORRY, WRONG NUMBER (Hall Wallis 1948), Jacques Tourneur's OUT OF THE PAST (RKO 1947), and Orson Welles's *The Lady from Shangai*.

66. Based on an actual murder case, Elia Kazan's *Boomerang* also falls within our classification of "reenactment." Indeed, the parallels between Kazan's film and *Northside* are striking: Both begin with voice-overs that recount the details of the murder; both include documentary-style footage that details police work following the murder, such as the rounding up of suspects, examination of eyewitnesses, and search for clues; both indict eyewitness testimony as unreliable and inaccurate. *Boomerang* also combines the visual style and strategies of documentary and film noir. Like *Northside*, it continually forces its viewers to shift their vantage point as it moves back and forth between the conventions of classical narrative, noir lighting, and unusual camera angles to a realistic documentary style. As in *Northside*, this combination is designed to complicate the film's own claims to truth. *Boomerang* repeatedly admits that its understanding and knowledge of the crime are limited—indeed, like *Northside*, it chooses as its historical basis a case that was never solved.

Boomerang was based on the aftermath of a murder in Bridgeport, Connecticut in 1924, in which a much-loved local priest was shot to death. There was no apparent motive for his murder. A poor vagabond who matched the murderer's description was soon arrested. Numerous witnesses identified him, ballistics experts matched his gun to the bullet used in the killing, and the suspect even confessed to the crime. It appeared to be, as the prosecutor later told the court, "a well-nigh perfect case, affording but very little difficulty in the matter of successful prosecution." Homer S. Cummings, *The State vs. Harold Israel*, 15 J. AM. INST. CRIM. L. 7 CRIMINOLOGY 406, 414 (1925). But when district attorney Homer S. Cummings (who would later become Franklin Delano Roosevelt's Attorney

reenactment as a generic form has, until recently, received little scholarly attention, perhaps partly because it is sometimes seen as low-brow, and partly because it is hard to categorize, belonging comfortably neither to the realm of documentary nor to the domain of fiction. However, academics and cultural commentators have begun to turn their attention to the form. This may be the result of the recent explosion of film and television reenactments of scandals—from Jon-Benet Ramsey to Amy Fisher—and of more serious quasi-historical films like *JFK* or *Mississippi Burning*.[67]

General), arrived to prosecute the case, he announced that he would instead ask for a *nolle prosequi*. Despite the seemingly overwhelming evidence against the suspect, the prosecutor had found after meticulous investigation that the evidence simply did not hold up. The well-nigh perfect case turned out to be as leaky as a sieve. Charges were dropped, and the case was never solved. For the prosecutor's full statement to the court describing the evidence and its flaws, see *id.* On the case more generally, see Anthony Abbott, *A Perfect Case*, 6 THE ROTARIAN 14 (1945). Like *Northside*, *Boomerang* follows the real incident on which it is based in tremendous detail, though like *Northside*, it also departs from the true story in one important particular, designed to provide the viewer with a kind of certainty and closure that the real world story lacked. Instead of leaving the case wholly unsolved, as it was in real life, the film version provides the viewer with an alternative murderer and a theory of the crime, though the details are left murky.

Most importantly for our purposes here, *Boomerang* shares *Northside*'s interest in the epistemological complexities of reenactments; indeed, *Boomerang*'s interest is arguably even more self-conscious and self-reflexive than *Northside*'s. The final third of *Boomerang* focuses on the trial of the suspect, a trial in which the state's attorney proves the man's innocence through various reenactments of the events leading up to the murder. Designed only to prove the innocence of the suspect rather than to identify the actual murderer, these reenactments show that it would have been physically impossible for the suspect to have committed the murder and that the testimony of the witnesses was false. The film presents these reenactments in two ways: in the film's present, with the prosecutor acting out events before the jury in the courtroom, and in the film's past, through flashbacks that show the attorney and his group of assistants reenacting the details of the crime in the actual places where they happened. These reenactments perform two functions: (1) They link film viewers with jury members as they complicate for both groups the details of the crime and, more importantly, (2) They draw attention to the film's own status as a reenactment, alerting us to the fact that, like these individual reenactments, the film can only say what *did not* happen; it cannot offer complete truth. As Telotte remarks in his useful discussion of the film, "It's as if the film itself were on trial, its method for revealing truth called into question." TELOTTE, *supra* note 16, at 142.

In some ways, the challenge presented by *Northside* and *Boomerang* resembles, though not nearly with the same degree of self-consciousness, recent films represented by the "New Documentary" movement. Characterized by self-reflexivity and interactive techniques, the New Documentary marks an attempt to overcome any simple dichotomy between truth and fiction. As film theorist Linda Williams observes in her essay on the movement, these films suggest that there is no "a priori, self-evident truth to be "captured" by the camera, but that there are multifaceted, receding horizons of "truth" that can be constructed within a multivocal (multigazing) form." Linda Williams, *The Ethics of Intervention: Dennis O'Rourke's* The Good Woman of Bangkok, *in* COLLECTING VISIBLE EVIDENCE 176, 183 (Jane M. Gaines & Michael Renov eds., 1999). The foremost figure in this movement is Errol Morris, whose widely acclaimed film THE THIN BLUE LINE (American Playhouse 1988) garnered so much critical attention precisely because it questioned its own participation in the representation of truth. Other directors whose work is representative of this movement are Dennis O'Rourke and feminist filmmaker Trinh T. Minh-ha. For more information on the movement, see generally COLLECTING VISIBLE EVIDENCE, *supra*. *See also* Linda Williams, *Mirrors Without Memories: Truth, History, and the New Documentary*, FILM QUARTERLY 9 (Spring 1993); and Sherwin, *Law Frames*, *supra* note 19.

67. *See, e.g.*, JOHN CORNER, THE ART OF RECORD (1994); DEREK PAGET, NO OTHER WAY TO TELL IT: DRAMADOC/DOCUDRAMA ON TELEVISION (1998); ALAN ROSENTHAL, WRITING DOCUDRAMA: DRAMATIZING REALITY FOR FILM AND TV (1995); WHY DOCUDRAMA: FACT-FICTION ON FILM AND TV (Alan Rosenthal ed., 1999) [hereinafter WHY DOCUDRAMA]. Much of the recent

In a thoughtful discussion of the genre, Steve Lipkin describes how the reenactment (or, as he calls it, the docudrama) functions:

> Even as docudrama departs from documentary proper, the two modes retain a certain semiotic similarity. . . . The documentary image functions as an index; comparable imagery in docudrama remains primarily iconic; however, docudrama asks if, under its terms, the two signs might not be all that different. The films' often high degree of resemblance to [the] actual . . . creat[es] what amount to indexical icons, signs with direct, strongly motivated resemblances to their actual referents. We are offered argument by analogy, the analogies (images) often appearing to be the most literal kind.[68]

In his book on television docudrama in America and Britain, media scholar Derek Paget also emphasizes that the reenactment is "an inherently indexical form," necessarily pointing "beyond the realm of fiction to a realm of non-fiction that is always already-lived."[69] He writes,

> The drama-documentary seeks to overlay the Stanislavskian emotional equivalence of "As If" with a documentary-indexical "See This!". The relation to reality claimed in the solely dramatic "as if" through equivalence and parallel is asserted in dramatic documentary mode through the repetitions of reconstruction/reenactment (these words/actions, in this place—with a gesture back to "that time"). Where one set of actions is in parallel to the real, the other is an attempt to superimpose, to fit with a template, an acted "reality" on film on to a previous, unfilmed one.[70]

Understanding *Northside* as a reenactment emphasizes its dual allegiances: both to representing the true story on which it is based and to telling a powerful and dramatic tale. These theorists of the reenactment offer two useful concepts for examining *Northside*. First, Lipkin's concept of the indexical icon lets us see how the film aims simultaneously to offer both index and icon: a literal telling of a particular truth and something broader, more eternal and allegorical. Divided in purpose, *Northside* necessarily demands a divided response from viewers, who must not forget either that it is a Hollywood drama *or* that it is true. Moreover,

---

scholarship uses the term "docudrama" or "drama-documentary" for that which we term "reenactment." We prefer the term "reenactment," both because it resonates with the filmed reenactments used in trials that we shall discuss in the final part of the Article, and because "docudrama" can suggest a much broader (and for our purposes too broad) range of material. The term "docudrama" can refer not only to dramatic renderings of actual occurrences (or, what we term "reenactments"), but also to dramas inspired only loosely by actual events or drawn from a collection of actual instances, or even to the presentation of wholly fictional material in a documentary-like fashion. For a much broader cultural analysis of the prevalence and significance of copies, doubles, twins, and reenactments, see HILLEL SCHWARTZ, THE CULTURE OF THE COPY (1996).

68. Steve Lipkin, *Defining Docudrama*, *in* WHY DOCUDRAMA, *supra* note 67, at 371-72.

69. PAGET, *supra* note 67, at 136-37

70. *Id.*

Paget's idea that the reenactment operates like a template, fitting over the real while still allowing departure from the actual so long as the basic "shape" is maintained, invites us to explore the correspondence between the film and the material on which it is based, to see when the template fits and when it fails.

Thinking about *Northside* as a reenactment thus focuses attention both on its fidelity to the actual case on which it is based and on its status as a fictional representation. It highlights how the film sets itself up as a Hollywood drama that can nonetheless be trusted as an account of what "really" happened.[71] Reenactments straddle the actual and the fictional, and they necessarily raise questions about belief, persuasion and proof. What makes an audience believe that the story they watch is essentially true? How much dramatic license can a reenactment take before losing the authority that comes from an alliance with the actual? In what follows we will look in detail at how *Northside* treats questions of evidence and proof.

B. *The Question of Evidence in* Northside

The single most remarkable feature of *Northside* is the fact that it takes evidence itself as its subject. Indeed, the film continuously circles around questions of proof, evidence, and facts. In the newspaper reporter's first encounter with the convict, he tells Wiecek that he has read the record and it does not "whitewash you, the way I see it." Wiecek responds, "But you only read what convicted me. All the true facts didn't come out." As McNeal reveals his skepticism, Wiecek asks him, "You don't believe me, do you?" The reporter is unabashed. "Listen, I talked to your mother. She's a very fine old woman. She believes you, I need proof."

Later in the film, McNeal is forced to tell Wiecek's mother that they are going to have to call off the hearing before the Pardon Board because they lack sufficient evidence. She is both outraged and dismissive: "Evidence? They got no evidence when they sent my Frank to prison for ninety-nine years. I got no evidence when I scrub floors every night, go without supper, walk to work, so I save a nickel for Frank. Evidence. What is this evidence?"

By the end of the film, McNeal has had a conversion, and it is his turn to criticize the Pardon Board for its narrow conception of proof:

> Strictly from a reporter's point, you understand, I've assembled what I feel is a very solid case. It consists of such debatable items as a lie detector test. Now I realize that you're unable to accept that. You want evidence. But sometimes the weight of evidence, just because it's in the record, is heavy enough to crush the truth.

71. Lipkin emphasizes that docudramas "warrant": "The viewer is invited to accept the argument that re-creation warrants, that what we see might have 'really' happened in 'much this way.'" Lipkin, *supra* note 68, at 372.

"We'll discuss the shortcomings of the judicial system some other time, Mr. McNeal," a member of the board of pardons replies curtly.

We can see in these three brief moments a complex relation between faith, evidence, and proof. The mother requires no evidence at all. She believes in her son's innocence because she believes in her son. The most incriminating evidence would not dislodge her belief, for it is based on faith rather than inference from evidence. However, when she places the ad offering reward money in exchange for evidence of the real killer, she recognizes that the rest of the world cannot share her faith, and that her only hope of overturning her son's conviction is to locate new evidence, either of her son's innocence or of someone else's guilt. Thus she works for years, saving the money that she hopes may buy the proof she needs: the money that may spur someone to take an interest, to come forward with the evidence that will persuade others of what she already knows.

By contrast, McNeal, the reporter, starts out doubtful about Wiecek's innocence. He is on assignment, and he is initially dubious that there is anything even worth investigating in this now stale murder case. He has to be badgered by his editor into pursuing the matter at all. At first, McNeal figures that because he has been tried and convicted, Wiecek is almost certainly guilty; the legal judgment of conviction is itself adequate proof of guilt to satisfy the reporter. After their exchange in prison, McNeal is intrigued but still skeptical, just like the actual reporters on whom he was based. Over the course of the film, however, McNeal comes to be entirely persuaded that Wiecek has been the victim of a miscarriage of justice. He comes to share Wiecek's mother's faith in her son—but his is a faith that emerges from his reading of the evidence, not from an unshakeable belief in the good character of a particular man.[72] Moreover, he has become a critic of the legal system's too-narrow conception of evidence. There is, he believes, proof that can persuade and reveal the truth, yet that will nonetheless be rejected as legal evidence. As he gains faith in Wiecek's innocence, he loses faith in law and legal processes. He fears that evidence, in the legal sense, can crush the truth. And, as the film progresses, it almost does.

The Eyewitness

In the film (as in Joe Majczek's actual criminal trial), the primary legal

72. The film's depiction of the necessary quantum of proof to persuade is explicitly gendered. It is the female characters—not only Wiecek's mother, but also McNeal's wife—who are prepared to believe without explicit proof, while for McNeal, merely wanting to believe is not enough to persuade him. In a living-room exchange, McNeal's wife asks him, "Why don't you let go? You want him to be innocent, you want him to be free." "Well, maybe you're right. Maybe I do want him to be free, but that doesn't make me believe he's innocent," counters McNeal. "You want to believe. That's enough," his wife insists. This, of course, reflects a classically gendered opposition between faith and proof, or, more typically, emotion and reason. Thanks are due to Fred Blumberg for pointing out to us the significance of gender in *Northside*.

evidence against the defendant was the identification provided by an eyewitness to the shooting, the owner of the speakeasy in which the policeman was killed. And it turns out that this eyewitness was lying. The film never explains *why* the owner was lying. McNeal seeks out the witness and eventually finds her. She is nervous and uncooperative, but she neither recants nor offers any explanation for her original incriminating testimony—nor does she even acknowledge that she failed to tell the truth. Implicitly, the film suggests that she may have been coerced by the police. After all, she was engaged in bootlegging and thus may have been pressured under threat of prosecution to identify Wiecek. In fact, in the actual case, there was strong evidence suggesting that the speakeasy owner was indeed pressured; she subsequently even admitted to a friend that her identification was "improper and false."[73] When her friend prodded her conscience, asking her how she could help convict an innocent man, Vera Walush's response was, "Well, what the hell did you expect me to do? I had to go along with the police, didn't I?"[74] In the film, however, the speakeasy owner's motive for identifying Majczek/Wiecek remains murky, as does her fear and unwillingness to explain herself eleven years later.

By failing to provide a specific explanation for this particular eyewitness's perjury, the film implies that eyewitness testimony in general ought to be viewed with suspicion. The report of one's own eyes may be unreliable and false—and the legal approach to evidence, the film suggests, does not adequately take into account the limits of eyewitnesses' vision. Eyewitnesses may be corruptible or just plain mistaken. Human testimony can be marred by police pressure, the fallibility of memory, fear, the lapse of time, or worst of all, deliberate falsehood.[75] As posed by *Northside,* the unreliability of eyewitnesses is less a problem of inevitable subjectivity than it is a problem of no mechanism for measurement, no way of knowing who—or what—is worthy of credit. Eyewitness testimony is presented as too mediated and too subjective to be trustworthy, especially when that which has been seen is not shared by others, is not part of a larger vision, a corroborated story. The film thus suggests that while eyewitness testimony is sufficient to support a conviction in the legal sense, it ought not to be deemed sufficient to support conviction in the sense of belief.

Concerns about the accuracy and fidelity of eyewitnesses are nothing

73. McPhaul & McGuire, *supra* note 41, at 4.

74. *Id.*

75. A significant literature has emerged on the limits of eyewitness testimony, focusing in particular on the frequency with which eyewitness identification can be mistaken. *See, e.g.*, BRIAN L. CUTLER & STEVEN PENROD, MISTAKEN IDENTIFICATION: THE EYEWITNESS, PSYCHOLOGY AND THE LAW (1995); ELIZABETH LOFTUS, EYEWITNESS TESTIMONY (1996); Samuel Gross, *Loss of Innocence: Eyewitness Identification and Proof of Guilt*, J. LEG. ST. 395 (1987); Gary L. Wells & Eric P. Seelau, *Eyewitness Identification*, 1 PSYCH. PUB. POL'Y & L. 765 (1995).

new. Literary critic Alexander Welsh, for example, has argued that as early as the eighteenth century, novelists, scientists, and judges all came to prefer the evidence of "things not seen"[76] to that of human testimony, viewing inferences from uncontested circumstances as stronger evidence than an eyewitness account.[77] Even though this concern with the fallibility of the eyewitness is longstanding, both crime semi-documentaries and classic film noir evince a particular concern, even obsession, with the limits of the eyewitness, all of the ways in which such evidence can be corrupted or merely mistaken.[78] These film genres thus reflect a growing recognition that human memory is frail and suggestible, that line-ups and photospreads might be tainted by conscious or unconscious signaling on the part of the authorities, and that the passage of time has a negative effect on memory. *Northside* is thus one of a spate of films dealing with crime during the 1940s and 1950s that share a marked concern with the unreliability of human testimony. One of the most notable examples of film noir's treatment of this theme, for example, is Alfred Hitchcock's *The Wrong Man*,[79] in which an innocent man (Henry Fonda) is almost convicted of armed robbery because four separate witnesses make a "positive identification" of him as the culprit. As in *Northside,* all of those who could testify to his innocence are either missing or dead.[80]

Boomerang, a 1947 film directed by Elia Kazan, also emphasizes the unreliability of eyewitnesses. In this film, a beloved priest is murdered one evening on a street corner, and multiple eyewitnesses subsequently identify a suspect, John Waldron, as the killer. Waldron is arrested and brought to trial in what appears to be an open-and-shut case. But after carefully attempting to verify the eyewitnesses' claims and staging reenactments of the crime itself, the prosecutor becomes convinced that the suspect did not, in fact, commit the murder, and asks the judge to drop the charges. Like *Northside*, *Boomerang* was based on a true story, and like *Northside*, the film emphasizes the precariousness of justice. Just as

---

76. WELSH, *supra* note 19, at 7 (citing Hebrews 11:1 ("Now faith is the substance of things hoped for, the evidence of things not seen.").

77. *See generally id.* at 2-42.

78. In addition to the films discussed in our Article, other titles include Robert Siodmak's PHANTOM LADY (Universal 1944), in which a cabdriver, bartender, and singer are all paid off by a wealthy murderer *not* to corroborate the alibi of an innocent man, who is then tried, convicted, and sentenced to die in eighteen days; Robert Siodmak's THE FILE ON THELMA JORDAN (Hall Wallis 1950), in which the prosecuting attorney perjures himself on the stand by lying about evidence so as to defend the woman he is supposedly prosecuting; Jack Arnold's THE TATTERED DRESS (Universal-International 1957), which depicts a notoriously amoral lawyer who is charged by a juror with bribery—only for the film to later reveal that the juror had been lying all along; and Otto Preminger's ANATOMY OF A MURDER (Columbia 1959), in which several eyewitnesses lie on the stand to protect themselves from a man they fear.

79. THE WRONG MAN (Warner Brothers 1956).

80. This is also a recurring motif in Alfred Hitchcock's films, including THE THIRTY-NINE STEPS (Michael Balcon, Gaumont 1935), VERTIGO (Paramount 1958), and NORTH BY NORTHWEST (Metro-Goldwyn-Mayer 1959).

Wiecek would never have been freed but for the enterprising efforts of McNeal, Waldron would surely have been convicted and locked away if it hadn't been for a persevering district attorney who investigated the case with a diligence hardly typical and who refused to cave in to political pressure to prosecute.

In Sidney Lumet's *Twelve Angry Men*,[81] a juror (also played by Henry Fonda) persuades eleven other jurors to change their votes because he consistently demonstrates how easily an eyewitness can be deceived. He points to the case of one woman who swears she saw through a window a son murder his father, even though she was too nearsighted to view anything clearly at such a distance; and the case of an elderly man who stated that he opened his apartment door when he heard a crash and saw the son fleeing the scene of the crime, even though, as Fonda proves, his handicapped leg would have prevented him from walking fast enough to open the door in time.[82] In both cases, the eyewitnesses do not seem to be acting out of malice; they are simply convinced that what they remember is true. Perhaps the most notorious filmic exposé of eyewitness unreliability, Billy Wilder's *Witness for the Prosecution*,[83] focuses on the wife of an alleged murderer (Marlene Dietrich) who appears in court as a hostile witness against her husband, precisely so that she can then create a false identity and appearance, meet with the defending attorney, and produce letters that will discredit her own damaging testimony against her husband.

Whereas crime semi-documentaries of this time period tend to represent eyewitnesses as unreliable so as to promote the need for more scientific means of establishing evidence, classic film noir tends to use the figure of the unreliable eyewitness as a means of illustrating the unreliability of *all* discourse in modern culture. "Through a thematic focus on our discourse," J.P. Telotte writes, "these films [film noir] show how fundamentally our communications, even the movies themselves, carry a certain estranging force, one that renders all discourse precarious and every effort at human communication a risky wager against misunderstanding and alienation."[84] Telotte includes semi-documentaries like *Northside* with such unmistakable noirs as Edward Dmytryk's *Murder, My Sweet* and Anatole Litvak's *Sorry, Wrong Number* as support for this observation. But Telotte fails to recognize that semi-documentaries and classic film noir possess widely different reasons for their focus on narrative unreliability. Semi-documentaries are much more invested in the unreliability of eyewitnesses

81. TWELVE ANGRY MEN (United Artists 1957).

82. Given the fact that only one year earlier, Hitchcock had cast Henry Fonda as a man whose life is nearly ruined by false eyewitness testimony in *The Wrong Man*, it seems highly probable that Lumet was capitalizing on this association by casting Fonda as the juror most skeptical of such testimony.

83. WITNESS FOR THE PROSECUTION (United Artists 1957).

84. TELOTTE, *supra* note 16, at 30.

as a *social* problem that needs to be corrected through more efficient means of detection, while classic film noir is, as a genre, much more interested in the lying or mistaken witness as an *existential* problem that, by its very nature, cannot be corrected.

While *Northside* clearly takes a much more "documentary" approach to crime than a classic film noir allows, its spotlight on the unreliability of eyewitness testimony is the element that brings the film closest to the style, mood, and overall effect of classic film noir. After locating its viewers in generally well-lit, "safe" settings such as McNeal's newspaper office or the domesticated apartment he shares with his wife, *Northside* dramatically plunges us into the noir landscape when McNeal goes in search of Wanda Skutnik in order to persuade her to recant her identification. During these fifteen minutes, the camerawork in *Northside* changes dramatically. Most of the scenes are done in night-for-night shooting; characters' faces, including Stewart's, are shown only half-lit; and physical space becomes much more restricted and, consequently, the individual frames of the film become much tighter.

Although this noir-dominated series of scenes only lasts for fifteen minutes in a film that spans nearly two hours, it resonates throughout the remainder of the film, functioning like *Northside*'s black hole.[85] And, indeed, it *is* the film's black hole, inhabited by a woman who refuses to change her testimony for no given reason, and who will not provide McNeal with any information whatsoever. Despite the film's confidence in its own role in the establishment of truth and justice, for these fifteen minutes *Northside* is pulled into a vortex that it must fight its way out of. Providing that vortex is film noir's work; restoring viewers and the film itself to the possibility of truth and effective social action is the work of both classical film narrative and documentary. At this point, *Northside* leaves noir safely behind and suggests to its viewers the practical need for more certain, more scientific evidence.[86] Like other films focused on crime, *Northside* points to the aspirational possibility for alternatives to the eyewitness, alternatives that seemed, in the 1940s, close on the horizon. One of those alternatives, as we shall see next, was the lie detector test.

But before we turn to this alternative form of evidence, it is important to note that *Northside*'s "noirish" treatment of Wanda Skutnik—its focus on

85. This kind of mini-incorporation of noir elements also occurs in Frank Capra's IT'S A WONDERFUL LIFE (RKO 1946), during the scenes in which George Bailey must revisit his hometown as if he were dead, and in Alfred Hitchcock's SHADOW OF A DOUBT (Universal 1942), where a scene shot in a seedy, darkened bar seems almost like a violation of the rest of the film, which is brightly lit and occurs mostly in domestic spaces.

86. Ironically, these "noirish" scenes, which are much more stylized than those of the rest of the film, could also be read as the most realistic in that they call attention to the extreme poverty and physical degradation that pervaded parts of Chicago. As Rosenberg points out, they "highlight the sociocultural gulf between McNeal's and Wanda's worlds." Rosenberg, *supra* note 19, at 288.

her silence, obstinacy, and perverse sense of complacency in letting a man remain in jail long after, it seems, she could be threatened by the police—means that we never find out in the film if or why Skutnik was forced to lie on the stand. Nor does the film resolve an even bigger mystery: Who actually killed the policeman that day in the speakeasy? The film leaves that mystery (which was also never resolved in the actual case) alone, and in doing so, admits that there are parts of the Wiecek case that *cannot* be reenacted. The focus on Skutnik thus not only exposes the limitations of eyewitness testimony but also makes clear that we may never entirely know what "really" happened. In its quest to recover the past in an authentic and credible fashion, *Northside* has to abandon its interest in Skutnik at this point, leaving behind the thematic strain that most interests film noir—the *impossibility* of ever recapturing the past—for the dubious promises of the reenactment.[87]

The Lie Detector Test

After *Northside* demonstrates so much skepticism about the reliability of human testimony, the film turns to a machine as the next—and better—means of providing evidence.[88] As we will demonstrate, however, the film's representation of the lie detector is marked by a certain degree of ambiguity. If *Northside* seems confident in its stance on the unreliability of eyewitness testimony, its position on the evidential value of the lie detector is much more complicated—a fact that in some ways reflects the larger history of the lie detector in courtroom procedures.

When McNeal asks Frank Wiecek if he would be willing to take a lie detector test, the prisoner quickly agrees: "Mr. McNeal, for eleven years I've been waiting for a chance to get at that box." McNeal emphasizes that it's a dangerous bargain for Wiecek: "You know what you're up against? If it turns out bad, you're cooked. If it turns out good, it's only Leonarde Keeler's professional opinion. It doesn't count legally." But Wiecek is

87. Indeed, the elusiveness and mystery of one's past, or the past of others, haunts the majority of film noir protagonists, including Jeff Bailey in Jacques Tourneur's *Out of the Past*, Rip Murdock in John Cromwell's DEAD RECKONING (Columbia 1947), George Steele in Irving Reis's CRACK-UP (1946), and Vincent Parry in Delmar Dave's DARK PASSAGE (Warner Brothers 1948).

88. Another film noir of this time period that makes interesting use of the lie detector is Joseph Lewis's THE BIG COMBO (Security-Thedora 1955), also starring Richard Conte. In this film, Conte plays Mr. Brown, a powerful mobster who continually outsmarts the detective, Leonard Diamond, on his trail. No method employed by Diamond—harassment, surveillance, and an 18,000 dollar police-force budget—successfully stops Brown's criminal activity until Diamond deploys a lie detector test. During this test, Diamond utters a series of words/names to which Brown must automatically respond with another word/name. While Brown remains calm, even cavalier, throughout most of this test, he falters when he hears the name of a man whom he has managed to silence with money, a man who could provide evidence of a murder Brown committed several years ago. Diamond triumphantly says, "You can't lie with your blood pressure!" Thus, we know that the detective has finally found the one method that, in however minor a way, has located Brown's vulnerability. Though this scene is extremely brief, its revelation of Brown's vulnerability establishes a chain of discoveries that ultimately ends with Diamond killing Brown as the latter resists arrest.

determined, even eager, hoping that the test will persuade others of his innocence. Back in his prison cell, he is warned of the dangers of the test by another convict: "Listen kid, take it from me. Keep away from Keeler and that lie detector. . . . Why, I had the cops, the state's attorney, even my own lawyer believing me. Then they talked me into going against that box." "What happened?" queried Wiecek. "What do you mean what happened. I'm doing life, ain't I?" the prisoner replied. This brief exchange, implying that the convict's attempt to fool authorities was exposed by the lie detector, suggests that the machine can triumph over even the most calculated performances. Given our supposition by this point that Wiecek is telling the truth when he says that he is innocent, it would seem that the scene is constructed so as to reassure viewers that the test will work in Wiecek's favor.

Still, the scene is peculiarly unsettling, for while it appears to be validating the lie detector as a conveyor of truth and justice, it also draws our attention to the machine's potentially devastating and detached power. The fact that the prisoner describes his experience as "going against that box," for example, emphasizes both the seeming absence of a human operator behind the machine as well as the prisoner's ignorance about how the machine works. Cinematographically, this scene is also infused with tension and a vague sense of foreboding, framed as it is in noir's low-key lighting and with the camera lingering in close-up on Frank's anxious face as he meditates on the prisoner's comments. We imagine what Frank must be feeling: that this test could somehow work against him as it did for the other prisoner; that once the machine renders its verdict, his words could be forever discounted; that in one brief session, his fate could be irrevocably decided.

The basic premise behind the polygraph test is that human beings have physical responses to the stress of lying that are beyond their will and control. The body can reveal the mind, and inner mental states can be rendered visible, exposed by the machine.[89] The lie detector continuously measures the prisoner's blood pressure as he or she answers numerous questions, both mundane and significant. The completed test results in a graphic representation of the changes in blood pressure—rendering visible someone's invisible internal states through the intervention of technology. But this seemingly simple procedure belies a whole range of complex questions. How ought one to read the transcript of the body? What do the fluctuations in blood pressure mean? How does one translate the reflection of physical processes to the underlying mental state?[90] Eliciting meaning

89. See the discussion of the lie detector test in RONALD R. THOMAS, DETECTIVE FICTION AND THE RISE OF FORENSIC SCIENCE 21-39 (2000). Thomas traces the rudimentary beginnings of the polygraph in the late nineteenth century, arguing that its development answered the cultural need for, and anxiety over, making the human body readable.

90. Modern polygraphers have developed an elaborate set of approaches—including asking

from a polygraph thus requires interpreters with specialized knowledge. Yet, neither in the 1940s nor at present is there any regulated set of credentials required for one to claim to be a polygraph expert, no specifically mandated course of study nor any testing procedures to assure competence.

Other issues have also made the use of lie detectors controversial. While the test itself is straightforward enough, it rests on highly problematic assumptions. The basic premise behind it is quite simple: Telling lies creates stress or anxiety, and this stress or anxiety is echoed physiologically and recorded on the polygraph. Untruths leave traces.[91] The problem with this reasoning is that physiological responses that suggest stress or anxiety may be generated by a number of factors, only one of which is lying. Perhaps someone is made nervous merely by taking the test. Perhaps the anxiety generated by the accusation is itself sufficient to generate a physiological response that mimics that typically generated by a liar. Perhaps some liars feel no anxiety and register no change in physiological response even when they fail to tell the truth. The physiological response measured by the polygraph can only record that some response is taking place; it cannot determine the cause of that response or its meaning without interpretation.

On several occasions, the film reminds its viewers that the lie detector is not legitimate legal evidence—and indeed, even up to the present courts have been quite reluctant to authorize lie detector tests as legal proof.[92] In

---

suspects unusual and embarrassing "control" questions to gauge their physical responses or instructing them to lie when asked a particular question or questions—to attempt to create test methods that can provide secure knowledge. For a thorough discussion of the strengths and weaknesses of the polygraph today, compare David C. Raskins, Charles R. Honts & John C. Kirchner, *The Scientific Status of Research on Polygraph Techniques: The Case for Polygraph Tests*, *in* MODERN SCIENTIFIC EVIDENCE 565 (David Faigman et al. eds., 1997), with William G. Iacono & David T. Lykken, *The Scientific Status of Research on Polygraph Techniques: The Case Against Polygraph Tests*, *in* MODERN SCIENTIFIC EVIDENCE, *supra*, at 582.

91. The premises behind the polygraph test, in this sense, are strikingly similar to the premises behind police uses of photography in the nineteenth and early twentieth centuries. Both in Britain and America, the police took photographs of criminals and criminal suspects not only for identification purposes but because it was still widely assumed in both these countries, thanks to the extraordinary popularity of physiognomy as a mode of social science, that the physical features of a person revealed his or her internal traits. Thus, if one studied the details of a photograph closely, one could "read" a person's guilt or innocence in his or her face. In both photography and the lie detector, then, the body betrays its owner. For contemporaneous examples of this belief in photography's revelatory powers, see THOMAS BYRNES, PROFESSIONAL CRIMINALS OF AMERICA (1886); and CESARE LOMBROSO, CRIMINAL MAN (1911). For the seminal discussion of this phenomenon, see Alan Sekula, *The Body and the Archive*, *in* THE CONTEST OF MEANING: CRITICAL HISTORIES OF PHOTOGRAPHY 343, 348-52 (Richard Bolton ed., 1990).

92. *See, e.g.*, United States v. Scheffer, 523 U.S. 303 (1998). In the last few years, however, there has been a slight softening toward the polygraph in some jurisdictions, with some courts holding that polygraphs ought to be analyzed on a case-by-case basis rather than presumed inadmissible. *See, e.g.*, United States v. Cordoba, 104 F.3d 1997 (9th Cir. 1997); United States v. Posado, 47 F.3d 428 (5th Cir. 1995); United States v. Pulido, 69 F.3d 192 (7th Cir. 1995); United States v. Glabreth, 908 F. Supp. 877 (D.N.M. 1995); United States v. Crumby, 895 F. Supp. 1355 (D. Ariz. 1995).

fact, *Frye v. United States*,[93] a 1923 case that remains influential as a standard for approaching expert evidence even today,[94] examined the admissibility of an early lie detector test. The judge determined that the lie detector test was not yet sufficiently reliable to be used as legal evidence:

> Just when a scientific principle or discovery crosses the line between the experimental and demonstrable stages is difficult to define. Somewhere in this twilight zone the evidential force of the principle must be recognized, and while courts will go a long way in admitting expert testimony deduced from a well-recognized scientific principle or discovery, the thing from which the deduction is made must be sufficiently established to have gained general acceptance in the particular field in which it belongs. We think that the systolic blood pressure deception test has not yet gained such standing.[95]

In 1948, when *Northside* was released, courts typically based their exclusion of lie detectors on a variety of arguments: The experiments were still uncertain, the details of interpretation too murky, and the general reliability of the test insufficiently established. On extremely rare occasions, individual judges did permit such evidence. In one 1938 case, for example, a judge allowed a polygraph into evidence, reasoning thus:

> For hundreds of years our courts have deemed the examination and cross-examination of witnesses in open court to be the best method so far devised for the ascertainment of the truth . . . . It seems to me that this pathometer and the technique by which it is used indicate a new and more scientific approach to the ascertainment of truth in legal investigations.[96]

But this case was atypical, an outlier criticized and dismissed by other judges.[97] More generally, courts and legal commentators acknowledged that if the lie detector were perfected, it would be a useful tool, but they steadfastly asserted that its time had not yet arrived.[98] However, throughout the last half-century, courts have been noticeably more stringent in applying this general acceptance standard to the polygraph

93. 293 F. 1013 (D.C. Cir. 1923).

94. In *Daubert v. Merrell Dow Pharms.*, 509 U.S. 579 (1993), the Supreme Court ruled that *Frye* was not incorporated into the Federal Rules of Evidence. Nonetheless, *Frye*'s test of "general acceptance" remains one of the factors to which judges can look in determining the admissibility of expert evidence, and a number of state courts have chosen to continue to use *Frye* as their standard for admissibility even post-*Daubert*. *See generally* Heather G. Hamilton, *The Movement from* Frye *to* Daubert*: Where Do the States Stand*, 38 JURIMETRICS J. 201 (1998).

95. *Frye*, 293 F. at 1014.

96. People v. Kenny, 3 N.Y.S.2d 348, 351 (1938).

97. *See, e.g.*, People v. Forte, 4 N.Y.S.2d 913, 916 (1938) (rejecting *Kenny*'s claim that there is sufficient scientific basis for admitting the polygraph into evidence).

98. *See, e.g.*, 2 JOHN HENRY WIGMORE, A TREATISE ON THE SYSTEM OF EVIDENCE § 875 (2d ed. 1923) (declaring that "[i]f there is ever devised a psychological test for the valuation of witnesses, the law will run to meet it," but also admonishing that "[t]here must first be proof of general scientific recognition that [the test is] valid and feasible").

than to numerous other forms of evidence.[99]

Hence, the history of the lie detector's evidentiary status is fraught with complications. The film never goes into these complications, other than to refer to the detector's general exclusion from the courtroom. Since these difficulties with the polygraph are largely absent from the film, the legal system's refusal to accept the polygraph as legitimate evidence seems somewhat odd in *Northside*, even perverse. Just as the film offers no compelling explanation for the speakeasy owner's refusal to tell the truth (and thereby seems to be an indictment of eyewitness testimony in general), the film provides no explanation for the legal system's reluctance to embrace the lie detector test. As represented in the film, the lie detector is entirely reliable, so its unreliability cannot serve as an explanation for its exclusion from trials. In fact, it is the polygraph that persuades McNeal: It is precisely at this point in the film that the reporter's skepticism is transformed into full-fledged conviction, his wavering belief in Wiecek's innocence now a matter of faith. The film invites its viewers to ask how the courtroom's exclusion of such technologies of truth can be justified.

Implicitly, the suggestion is that the lie detector is too threatening—it provides a technology for truth-detection more effective and more efficient than the legal system's reliance on the jury can ever be. It must be kept out precisely because it threatens to replace the trial process altogether, substituting trial by jury for trial by machine. It is the lie detector's potential as *pure* technology, therefore, that makes it a problematic form of evidence—for the judges, attorneys, and arguably for the film viewers themselves. For while the film represents the lie detector as reliable and accurate, and the legal system as antiquated and myopic in rejecting it as evidence, *Northside*'s representation of the lie detector is nevertheless constructed in such a way as to mystify its functions and epistemological assumptions. This mystification effectively distances viewers from the very machine they are apparently being encouraged to admire, instilling in them a mistrust of its scientific complexity, and therefore, its inaccessibility.

Nowhere is this more evident than in the elaborate, eight-minute scene in which Wiecek takes the test, a scene that demonstrates a peculiar remoteness from the instrument it spotlights. Interestingly, the scene begins *in medias res*. As a close-up shows us the machine's intricate wiring and gauges, we can hear the voice of someone who sounds like a highly knowledgeable person explaining to McNeal how the machine works. The voice is actually that of Leonarde Keeler, an inventor and advocate of the lie detector, who plays himself on-screen. In fact, it was Keeler himself who had administered Majczek's actual lie detector test,

99. For the continued contemporary debate over the reliability of the polygraph, see the competing perspectives offered in MODERN SCIENTIFIC EVIDENCE, *supra* note 90.

concluding both in the actual case and on the screen that the test strongly suggested that the man who had spent more than a decade in prison was telling the truth when he denied any involvement in the crime for which he was convicted. Keeler's appearance in the film thus helps to invest the machine with particular authority, while simultaneously lending the film an even greater documentary aura through this bit of verisimilitude.[100] Keeler's undoubted expertise also allows the film to skirt around the obvious issue of interpretation and the human mistakes that can potentially come with it. By having Keeler administer the test, the viewers are apparently assured that the reading will be fair and accurate, that the polygraphist brings both integrity and knowledge to the examination. If Wiecek is the author of the text, in that it is produced by his body, its interpretation is authorized by Keeler, whose expert judgment cannot be questioned.

At the same time, however, Keeler's presence in the film ultimately reinforces the film's tendency to mystify the functions of the lie detector. This is evident in several ways, including the fact that, as noted earlier, we only hear *part* of his explanation to McNeal about how the lie detector operates because the scene begins *in media res*. Moreover, the *mise-en-scene* repeatedly draws our visual attention to the machine rather than to Keeler, with individual shots framed to place a fragmented figure of Keeler in the background (with only his lower torso visible) while the machine itself looms large in the foreground. The relationship between sound and image is also striking in this sequence of shots, since Keeler's voice is both monotone and jargon-filled; his explanation to McNeal refers to such scientific concepts as "the electrical conductivity of the skin" and "the systolic measurements of the heart." His voice does not attract our interest: What *does* attract our interest is the *spectacle* of the machine itself.

In making the workings of the lie detector so visible to viewers, then, the film manages both to enlighten and to mystify us about the machine. We hear Keeler's explanation to McNeal, we hear him ask questions of Wiecek and we hear Wiecek answer them, we watch the machine produce its graph as the two men talk, but we cannot understand how the machine is interpreting the exchange. We observe carefully, aided by the camera's frequent close-ups, but this privileged entry into the production site of the lie detector tells us very little about the machine itself. Nor do Keeler's explanatory comments provide much guidance.

As Keeler administers the test, McNeal, his boss, and the prison warden

---

100. Some critics of dramadocs and reenactments have singled out for particular criticism the use of small, seemingly genuine details (such as an actor's replication of a real person's mannerisms or the participation of an actual participant) to give the film the semblance of authenticity: "Falseness of gesture and falseness of appearance drive authenticity from docudramas. This is why those who admire these forms of dramatic life find the most trivial touches of verisimilitude so entrancing." Jerry Kuehl, *Lies About Real People*, *in* WHY DOCUDRAMA, *supra* note 67, at 119, 122.

all watch from behind a window that allows them to see but prevents them from hearing the questions or answers, and the viewers assume this vantage point for a brief period of time as well. This spectatorial foregrounding dramatizes the cinematic dimensions to the scene, which, by placing such stress on instruments and instrumentality, invites a comparison between the lie detector and those of the camera.[101] Like the lie detector, the camera provides its own recording of Wiecek's physical responses as he answers the questions, focusing on the heaving of his chest, the inadvertent moving of his fingers, the sighs he emits as he answers, and the sweat on his face and hands. Yet, while only Keeler can understand the graphics produced on the white sheet of paper, viewers can read Wiecek's emotional response simply by watching carefully. While the lie detector needs an intermediary to interpret its signs, film does not.

To some degree, the film thus spotlights the lie detector so as to undermine its technology as inferior to its own—inferior, that is, because it is too sophisticated, too scientific, too inaccessible, and, finally, too *visible*. One could argue, in other words, that the decision to show viewers the scene of the lie detector's production serves the ulterior purpose of masking the film's own site of production. As a wide range of critics have discussed, classical narrative film depends on the invisibility of its mechanisms; its success, in other words, hinges on its own transparency—on the illusion of effortlessness with which it seems to give us its recreated world.[102] By visualizing the mechanisms of the lie detector test, in all their complex and mystifying glory, *Northside* simultaneously maintains its own status as a transparent medium onto a "real" world—one that needs no intermediary, no agent.

These observations become especially interesting in light of cultural historian of science Bruno Latour's arguments about how science gets made and disseminated. According to Latour, scientific findings are generated through the use of instruments that create visual displays of various sorts, graphs, charts, gauges, and so on, or what Latour terms "inscription devices."[103] Latour argues that scientific truths are made persuasive precisely through a reliance on these inscription devices: They make it appear as if the viewer, whether fellow scientist or layperson, sees

101. Another fascinating example of a film that spotlights the workings of the lie detector so as to draw attention to its own epistemological status is the much more recent movie, THE POLYGRAPH (Cinea 1996). The opening scene of the film begins with a lie detector test in operation. At the end of the test, the polygraphist informs the suspect that the "results were inconclusive"—a phrase that is repeated several times. As the film progresses, we learn that while the suspect is not guilty of the murder, his intense hatred of the victim and his past behavior toward her complicate his innocence. This revelation is not straightforwardly given in the film's narrative; rather, it comes through a series of intricate visual clues. Hence, the inherent properties and functions of the film's camera perform the same role as the lie detector, rendering the "results" of a close investigation of the protagonist "inconclusive."

102. *See, e.g.*, DAVID A. COOK, A HISTORY OF NARRATIVE FILM, (2d ed. 1990).

103. BRUNO LATOUR, SCIENCE IN ACTION 68 (1987)

the results for herself, while the scientific author "behaves as if he or she were [just] the mouthpiece of what is inscribed on the window of the instrument."[104] The viewer's confrontation with the instruments that produce these inscriptions—gauges, meters, physiographs, and all the other instruments of the modern laboratory—is, according to Latour, an "audio-visual spectacle" that generates "conviction." That is to say, visual inscriptions and verbal commentary are far more persuasive in tandem than either would be alone.[105] But this seeming attempt to make science accessible turns out to mystify its processes even further, since very few people can actually make sense of the inscriptions they are viewing, or even the verbal explanations that accompany them.

Although the lie detector test does not figure into Latour's discussion, its representation in *Northside* certainly provides an excellent example of the type of inscriptions he analyzes. Viewers see in close-up the graph the lie detector produces, but we have no comprehension of what it means, nor do we fully understand the explanatory words offered by Keeler. Our technological and scientific ignorance is precisely why, the film implies, we need an alternative form of evidence—one that everybody can make sense of and understand, or at least believe that they can. And, hence, the film makes a climactic shift to the final form of evidence it explores: the photograph.

When the film elevates photography as the most accessible and therefore most valuable form of legal evidence, its own self-promotion is thus cemented, as we shall see next. Photography becomes *Northside*'s means of selling its own supposedly simple and simplifying technology. Like classical narrative film, photography also depends on the invisibility of its site of production; it presents itself as natural transcript, ready and waiting to be read and interpreted without need of expert assistance or explanation. And, unlike the lie detector test, which can record only present history as it charts the body's immediate responses to questions in the here-and-now, photography's supposed capturing of the past also means that *Northside* has finally arrived at the form of evidence that, like itself, aspires to reenactment.

The Photograph

In the last quarter of the film, *Northside* explores a third kind of

---

104. *Id.* at 71.

105. *Id.* Much of Latour's study focuses on the role of the "black box," which, according to him, is a device whose accurate functioning can be taken for granted, a device believed to "work" so that the user need only be concerned with what is put into the box and what is taken out, rather than what goes on inside it. *See id.* at 2-3, 131-32. According to Latour, to challenge seemingly established science, one inevitably begins to open these black boxes and peer inside. *See id.* at 29. Although he does not discuss it specifically, the lie detector, as it is presented in the film, functions as a perfect example of the "black box," while legal decisions questioning the machine's authority present an example of how the "black box" can be re-opened and contested.

evidence that lacks the defects of the first two, a kind that is portrayed as both reliable and legally legitimate. The photograph is the film's "solution" to the evidentiary conundrum. Unlike the lie detector, the photograph is permitted within legal processes. Unlike an eyewitness, the photograph is trustworthy. The existence of the photograph thus provides the critical evidence that guarantees that Frank Wiecek will go free, the evidence that can force the pardon board to recognize and rectify the grave injustice of Wiecek's conviction for murder.[106]

As photographic historian John Tagg has argued, assumptions about photographic veracity have little to do with the "natural" qualities of the photograph.[107] Rather, they have been produced and sustained by discursive systems aimed at advancing the authority of certain institutions or forces—such as the media, the penal system, the law, and more specifically, the documentary movement that began in the 1920s. "That a photograph can come to stand as evidence, for example, rests not on a natural or existential fact, but on a social, semiotic process," claims Tagg.

But in *Northside*, the photograph's evidentiary status is also hard-won.[108] The first mention of a photograph occurs late in the film, when McNeal explains to his employers and the *Chicago Times* attorney that he has unearthed a photo from the files of the *Times*'s former rival, and now defunct, newspaper, *The Herald Examiner*. The photograph depicts a handcuffed Wiecek walking into the police station; in the background is the owner of the speakeasy, Wanda Skutnik, who testified that she saw Wiecek for the first time since the murder when she identified him in a police line-up on December 23. The photograph offers proof that Skutnik was lying, McNeal believes, because he assumes that the picture was taken before the time of the lineup. McNeal is thrilled with his discovery, certain that he has found the critical piece of evidence that will cement Wiecek's claim of innocence.

The attorney dismisses some of McNeal's evidence as inadequate, telling him, "Look here McNeal, I'm an attorney. I know what it is to go up in front of the pardon board. They go on facts." McNeal answers,

106. In this way, *Northside* provides a similar view of photography to that found in other noir documentaries. Henry Hathaway's *The House on 92nd Street* and Anthony Mann's *He Walked by Night*, for example, represent photographically based technologies such as surveillance cameras as invincible, modern forms of detection. In this sense, noir documentaries differ radically from other films noir, which tend to treat photography with much more skepticism. In films ranging from Steve Sekely's THE SCAR (Bryan Foy Productions 1948) to Edward Dmytryk's *Murder, My Sweet*, the photograph is presented as a highly unreliable piece of evidence. In direct contrast to the strategy of *Northside*, these types of film noir focus on the misleading nature of photographic images as a means of drawing attention to their own visual unreliability. For other examples of this pattern, see Fritz Lang's *Beyond a Reasonable Doubt* and Edwin L. Marin's NOCTURNE (RKO 1946).

107. JOHN TAGG, THE BURDEN OF REPRESENTATION: ESSAYS ON PHOTOGRAPHIES AND HISTORIES 7 (1988).

108. Rosenberg makes the important point that McNeal demonstrates unequivocal faith in technology while the attorneys in the film are at first quite dubious about the photograph's evidentiary status. *See* Rosenberg, *supra* note 16, at 286.

"Facts, okay, I'll give you something better than facts. I'll give you a picture."[109] He presents the photograph to the attorney, who takes a quick glance at it, looks to see if anything is written on the back, and hands it back to McNeal, explaining that the photo is useless without a date—without some kind of self-positioning device that could verify its exact moment in history and thus legitimize its documentary status.[110] Deflated, McNeal folds the picture and puts it away in his vest pocket.

In this particular scene, Hathaway's pedestrian camerawork, consisting entirely of medium shots, underscores the photo's status as object rather than symbolic image.[111] Seen through the eyes of an attorney whose tough, dismissive attitude is intended to influence our response, the photograph does not compel. As viewers of a film with documentary impulses, we may wish to side with McNeal, but we necessarily wind up on the side of the attorney, realizing that without a date, the photo cannot fulfill its documentary role. Until it is linked to a particular moment in time, this photograph means nothing.

The photograph then disappears from the film's plot until the day that the pardon board is due to convene to consider Wiecek's fate. Even though McNeal is absolutely certain of Wiecek's innocence, he is resigned to defeat before the pardon board, for he lacks the sort of proof that counts legally. But then, riding in a taxi, he happens upon a headline on the front page of a newspaper describing a "police enlargement process."[112] The

---

109. This is precisely the stand that the film ends up taking: Pictures are better than facts, or, more precisely, pictures are the best possible way to prove contested facts.

110. This is also in direct contrast with many noir films' treatment of photography, which tend to use elaborate close-up shots and montages to draw our attention to the physical and symbolic properties. Emphasis on the importance of the date and context recalls Barthes's observations about the function of the photographic caption, which, according to him, guides our vision, even to the extent that "sometimes . . . the text produces (invents) an entirely new signified which is retroactively projected into the image." ROLAND BARTHES, IMAGE-MUSIC-TEXT 27 (Stephen Heath trans., 1977).

111. This dismissive treatment of the photograph contrasts sharply with most representations of photography in classic film noirs. In Robert Siodmak's *The File on Thelma Jordan*, for example, a district attorney jeopardizes his professional career by falling in love with and helping a murder suspect, Thelma Jordan, whom he believes to be innocent. In a dramatic moment that utilizes a zoom lens and a series of increasing close-ups, the lawyer discovers a photo of Jordan as a former prostitute in the police files and realizes for the first time that the woman he thought he knew is not what she seems. The photograph fills the entire screen, its evidentiary status in effect displacing for both the betrayed attorney and the film viewers a former impression of Jordan—one carefully constructed by the film's cinematography—as a respectable, naïve, and sincere young woman. Paradoxically, then, the police photograph, magnified by Siodmak's camera, offers us a new image of Jordan that possesses far more potency than any previously offered by the film. Watching a film noir, viewers may be seduced by the seeming potency of the photographic image, forgetting about dates, context, and general reliability, but within the perimeter of a quasi-documentary, we are forced to adopt a much more critical stance.

112. To our knowledge, no new enlarging processes had been invented around the time of the film that would have made news headlines. Although photographs can, in fact, be enlarged by 1000% as the film suggests, the resulting image would almost certainly have been much too grainy for any details to appear clearly. Thus, the film's representation of this technique is quite exaggerated. A relevant discussion may be found in MORRIS GURRIE, THE COMPLETE BOOK OF ENLARGING 19-21 (1949), which was published only one year after *Northside* was released.

previously useless photograph now has the potential to assume vital importance, as McNeal hurries down to a police photo lab and begs the technician to enlarge it as quickly as possible. He hopes that the process will reveal the date of a newspaper held by a newspaper boy in the far left corner of the photo, which would determine the date of the photo's origin and thus possibly offer conclusive evidence that Wanda Skutnik was lying. Wiecek's fate thus comes to rest not on the photo itself, but upon the use of a technology that may allow the photograph to "speak." Note, too, the charmingly self-referential twist here: Not only does McNeal find the key to proving Wiecek's innocence by reading a newspaper headline, but within the photograph itself it is a newspaper that may provide the reporter with the evidence he needs to persuade the parole board.

After making the request of the technician, McNeal travels to Springfield, the state capitol, to plead with the pardon board to wait for the enlarged photograph over the AP wire as it is sent from Chicago's police headquarters. In the film's most dramatic scene, six members of the pardon board—along with the film's actual viewers—wait in a state of suspense for the enlarged image to appear. Hathaway sets the scene in a photo lab, the scientific look of the police laboratory lending an authoritative aura to the process. The board members, not up-to-date on the latest procedures for enlarging photographs, listen intently to McNeal's explanation of what the enlargement process can do—that it can magnify an area of a photograph to many times the original size and that the quality of the resultant image will depend on such variables as the "condition of the dup. negative" and the "density of the print." McNeal also tells the board that he's been "praying, too."

As we gaze into the solution bath, the image slowly starts to appear. The film's camera zooms in on the image as it develops, mirroring the enlargement process itself. The cinematic close-up and the enlargement process thus combine to make visible what had previously been left invisible, enacting Walter Benjamin's observation that "[t]he enlargement of a snapshot does not simply render more precise what in any case was visible, though unclear: it reveals entirely new structural formations of the subject."[113] Through this dazzling and extended scene of development, the photograph is transformed from worthless to indispensable: Locating it temporally transforms it into the most reliable of witnesses. As Benjamin explains, the enlargement process has not simply made the image "more precise." The photograph's original subject—Wanda Skutnik and Frank Wiecek entering the police station—is now recast, and the photograph now has a new subject: time itself, verifiable and irrefutable history. The film's enlargement of the photograph, in other words, functions as a kind of *reenactment*, allowing for a revisiting and reinterpretation of the site of

113. WALTER BENJAMIN, *The Work of Art in the Age of Mechanical Reproduction*, *in* ILLUMINATIONS 217, 236 (Hannah Arendt ed., 1968).

the original image. No longer is the photo just an image of an inscrutable instant. Now it can be placed within a narrative context. Like a single frame pulled from a film, it is one moment captured, but it is now a moment with a clear before and after.[114]

Once the critical date is revealed, everyone—McNeal, the parole board, and the film viewer—knows that Frank Wiecek will go free. No one doubts the authority of the photograph. Even the attorney opposing the prisoner's pardon is silenced by the evidence of the photograph. Moreover, the photograph is portrayed as the exclusive form of evidence that can cross between the various arenas of proof. It is valid both within legal processes and outside of them. In the film, then, the eyewitness is authoritative in the legal setting, but unreliable; the lie detector is authoritative outside the courtroom but irrelevant within it. Only the photograph is capable of commanding authority across domains, equally trustworthy in the theater of the courtroom and in the theaters of the 1940s presenting *Northside*. It is effective, it would seem, precisely because it lacks the totalizing power of the polygraph—it does not threaten to displace legal process altogether, but only to check it by tempering human judgment with mechanical objectivity. The photograph links together legal proof with lay conceptions of evidence; in both realms, it can be deemed persuasive, legitimate, even dispositive. The photograph not only saves Frank Wiecek, but it redeems legal proof as well, by showing that in the end, legal evidence can suffice to bring the truth to light.[115]

Moreover, this climactic scene, in which the enlarged photograph becomes visible before our eyes (note, here, that the film's audience and the film's characters all view the newly legible photograph together), serves a critical purpose within the film. By presenting the photograph as utterly authoritative, this scene warrants that *we can believe what we see*. In this sense, the photograph is a stand-in for the film itself. The authority of the mechanically produced visual image is maintained in a double sense: The truth of the photograph affirms the truth of the film as a whole.

---

114. Looking at a film still, for Roland Barthes, takes place at a divide—at a point where the image, or our perception of the image, undergoes a transformation. Liberated from the narrative impulse of the film, the still nevertheless retains the illusion of movement. Barthes calls this "the possibility of configuration," the "armature of a permutational unfolding." BARTHES, *supra* note 110, at 77.

115. But note that while the photograph assures that Frank Wiecek will receive justice, it certainly does not completely exculpate the legal system. The existence of the photograph, that McNeal was able to locate it, that he serendipitously discovered in the cab that it might be possible to have it sufficiently enlarged, and that he was able to find someone who could enlarge it quickly enough in order to reveal the crucial date on the newspaper, are all portrayed as contingent facts, lucky breaks. The photograph might never have been found; or McNeal might never have realized its significance. Without it, Frank Wiecek might well have remained in prison. So Wiecek's release from prison does not turn *Northside* into a "justice will win out" morality tale; rather, we continue to see how fragile and accidental the rendering of justice can be. Still, the fact that the parole board does respond to the photograph softens the film's critique of law: Legal processes are not viewed as inherently corrupt, but merely rigid.

Just as the members of the parole board can believe in the authority of the enlarged photograph, the members of the audience can believe in the authority of *Northside*'s retelling of a true crime tale. According to the film, both the photograph and the film itself can be trusted.

Whatever *Northside* wishes us to believe, however, neither documentary films nor photographs are inherently trustworthy. In fact, *Northside*'s conflation of documentary film and authoritative photograph is an interesting one, in part because the very device that affirms the film's realism turns out to be pure fiction: *In the actual Majczek case, there was no photographic evidence, no visual image that helped to secure the actual defendant's release.* Rather, in the actual case, though the evidence was compelling, it was murkier and more circumstantial—hardly the stuff out of which film climaxes are made. The film's representation of the photograph as an authoritative means for truthtelling thus turns in on itself ironically, revealing the fabrication of both film and photograph alike. The Majczek case received a great deal of media attention—in addition to the *Chicago Daily Times*'s nearly daily reports, the case got attention from the national press and magazines like *Time* and *Newsweek*.[116] Many of *Northside*'s viewers thus certainly had some previous knowledge of the facts of the case itself, and may even have recognized the irony of the fictionalized climax.

This use of a "fictional" photograph necessarily challenges the film's own claim to be something other than "fiction," suggesting that in the end, drama or narrative impact outweighs any concern for verisimilitude. (And why not?—it is a Hollywood film, after all.) For those viewers who had closely followed the actual Majczek case, those who eagerly read the actual articles in the *Chicago Daily Times*, this use of a photograph is a kind of a nod and a wink, a gesture to say "Okay, we admit it. Reality isn't quite dramatic enough for film even when reality is at its most dramatic." Genre makes demands that reality cannot live up to.

This takes us back, once again to the question of certainty.[117] The film seeks to offer a form of proof—both to the parole board and to the viewers—that would eliminate all doubt about Wiecek's innocence. In so doing, the film carries its viewers from doubt to assurance as the narrative progresses: from the mother's faith, to the reporter's polygraph-inspired conviction, to the eventual knowledge that Wiecek is in fact innocent beyond a shadow of a doubt. The photograph turns the mother's faith and McNeal's justified belief into certain knowledge. And yet, ironically, this certainty is built atop a fiction.

It is interesting, however, to recognize how narrowly *Northside* circumscribes its turn to fiction. We can imagine, for a moment, some of

116. *See, e.g.*, *National Affairs: Illinois*, TIME, Aug. 27, 1945, at 23.

117. For discussion of the relation between faith and certainty in the film, see *supra* Section II.B.

the other ways that the film could have provided dispositive proof of Wiecek's innocence. Most obviously, McNeal's digging might have uncovered the actual perpetrator, necessarily exculpating Wiecek. Alternatively, McNeal might have located another eyewitness to the murder—someone who saw it all, and who could therefore confirm that Wiecek was the wrong guy. Or Wanda Skutnik might have recanted her original testimony, admitting that she had indeed perjured herself out of fear that the police would have arrested her for bootlegging had she failed to identify Wiecek as the guilty man. This list could, of course, go on. Had the film offered any of these forms of proof of Wiecek's innocence, it would have been manufacturing evidence that did not exist in the actual case, just as it did with the photograph. (In point of fact, in the actual case, Majczek's release marked the first time in the state of Illinois that a convicted man was pardoned even without an alternate suspect for the crime.)

But although there was no photograph in the actual Majczek case, the photograph manufactured by the film did not itself manufacture evidence absent from the actual case. The photograph showed Skutnik and Wiecek together outside the courthouse the day before Skutnik's identification of Wiecek. The photograph proved, therefore, that when Skutnik said under oath that she had not seen Wiecek at any time between the day of the murder and the day she identified him in the police station, she was lying. The substance of what was suggested by the photograph was, in fact, suggested by the evidence in the actual case as well. In the actual case, the reporters found Majczek's original arrest slip, and it was dated one day prior to Walush's identification.[118] Why didn't Walush see Majczek for purposes of identification the very day of the arrest? The one-day delay suggested the plausibility of—though obviously did not prove–Majczek's claim that Walush saw him several times and had to be pressured by the police into making identifying him.

So the photograph did not offer proof that differed in substance from evidence in the actual case, but only evidence that differed in representational form. Instead of merely having Majczek's say-so, corroborated by slight circumstantial evidence, to suggest that Skutnik was lying, the photograph established the same thing in starker, less contestable form. The fiction of the photograph, then, is merely a fiction of form: The contents of the photograph are consistent with what happened in the actual case, but no photograph ever emerged to operate as a "silent witness" to corroborate and confirm Majczek's story.

But the closer we look at the photograph, the less certain it appears. All that the picture actually depicts is people walking in and out of the courthouse. The blown-up newspaper, transmitted almost magically across

118. McPhaul & McGuire, *supra* note 42.

space to take us back in time, situates the photograph as having been taken in a particular and critical moment. It does show that Wanda Skutnik was lying when she said she had never seen Wiecek before identifying him, but Skutnik's lie is not necessarily inconsistent with Wiecek's guilt. It could be that Skutnik lied *and* Wiecek was guilty: The one in no way precludes the other. Indeed, the mere fact that Skutnik had in fact seen Wiecek prior to her December 23 identification of him does not even prove that her identification of Wiecek as the murderer was incorrect.

The photograph thus impeaches Skutnik's credibility by contradiction, showing by extrinsic evidence that her testimony was inaccurate, at least in one particular. Note that the film has in fact already suggested the importance of contradiction to the evaluation of credibility by both the police and the jury: It was partly Wiecek's own contradictions about minor matters that led to his arrest and subsequent conviction. Now, however, the viewer is supposed to believe that Wiecek's contradictions meant nothing; they were innocent mistakes or trivial mistruths deriving from the pressure of interrogation: As Wiecek explained to McNeal, "When they question you hour after hour, you're bound to get mixed up on a lot of little things, the way I did." Skutnik's contradiction, by contrast, is seen to be positive proof of her perjury. While the film entirely elides the difficult question of when and to what extent inconsistency should impeach credibility, it is true that if Skutnik is discredited, the evidence linking Wiecek to the murder, already gossamer, dissolves entirely. Skutnik's identification was the only substantial proof against Wiecek: Without it, there is no longer sufficient evidence to justify a belief in Wiecek's guilt. In the actual Majczek case, the reporters interviewed some of the jurors who had decided Majczek's fate. All of those interviewed claimed that had they been informed about some of what the *Chicago Daily Times* had managed to dig up, they never would have convicted Majczek in the first place.[119] Certainly had such a photograph been displayed to the original jury, the probability of Majczek's conviction would have decreased substantially.

And yet, powerful though the photograph's attack on Wanda Skutnik's credibility may be, the proof offered by the photograph is much more circumstantial and attenuated than the film makes it out to be. It does not in fact speak for itself, but rather requires a context in order to be understood.[120] Only by understanding why the date matters can we

119. McPhaul & McGuire, *supra* note 43.

120. Because of the frequent testimonial use to which photographs are put, photography is often described as possessing narrative qualities. But the crucial element in any narrative is agency, which, in the case of the photograph, may be located in the viewer. The viewer of any discovered photo may endow the image with storytelling abilities. According to Barthes, the most compelling photographs are those that resist the viewer's imposition of a narrative through their "stupidity"—their refusal to "speak." ROLAND BARTHES, CAMERA LUCIDA 9 (1980). For other discussions of the relation between photography and narrative, see W.J.T. MITCHELL, PICTURE THEORY: ESSAYS ON VERBAL AND

appreciate the significance of the date revealed on the front page of the newspaper. The movement from the photograph to a belief in Wiecek's innocence requires the viewer to make a chain of inferences. Placed into a broader narrative, the photograph shows that Wanda Skutnik's testimony was inaccurate; however, the viewer must therefore infer that her inaccuracy was intentional, a lie rather than a misunderstanding or an honest mistake, and then further infer that a witness who lied about this detail cannot be believed when she identifies Wiecek as the guilty man. Alternatively, the viewer might infer that Skutnik's inaccuracy may have been inadvertent, but that a witness who misremembers whether she had previously seen the suspect cannot be trusted when she claims to remember his identity from the crime scene itself. The point is that although the miraculously enlarged photograph does impeach Skutnik's credibility, it does not, when analyzed carefully, speak dispositively about Wiecek's innocence. The film, however, treats it as if it does, as if the photograph makes Frank Wiecek's innocence *self-evident.*[121]

The film's resolution of the evidentiary conundrum is problematic from another angle as well. In fact, in actual courtrooms, the photograph lacked the clear-cut authority granted to it in the film. The photographic image had never been granted the legal status of irrefutable proof that the film suggests. Rather, from the time of their earliest use in the 1850s and 1860s, photographs had often provoked an ambivalent response on the part of judges, who saw them as offering potentially compelling evidence and simultaneously feared the very vividness of their displays.[122] This

VISUAL REPRESENTATION (1994); and ROLAND BARTHES, *The Photographic Message*, *in* IMAGE-MUSIC-TEXT, *supra* note 110, at 15.

121. Barry Scheck and his co-authors make similar claims for properly administered DNA tests, claims that are, on their face, much more plausible than *Northside*'s claims about the photograph. *See, e.g.*, DWYER, NEUFELD & SCHECK, *supra* note 18, at 92 (calling DNA tests "indisputable proof"). But note that even DNA profiling does not necessarily prove innocence or stand outside the narratives produced at trial: For example, the lack of a DNA match may just show that another party was present as well, in addition to the defendant. And proof, even DNA evidence, is almost never "indisputable"; the acquittal of O.J. Simpson (in which Scheck himself was one of the defendant's attorneys), for example, shows how significant quantities of DNA evidence found at the crime scene may be explained in ways consistent with innocence. It is worth remembering that a critical piece of evidence in the civil suit against Simpson was, in fact, a series of photographs: images of Simpson wearing Bruno Magli shoes, the Lorenzo model, at a football game. (Bloody treadmarks from Bruno Magli shoes, the Lorenzo model, in Simpson's size, were found at the scene of the crime, and only 299 pairs of such shoes in the proper size were sold in the United States, and Simpson had denied owning any such shoes.) For the testimony on this photograph and its authenticity, see, for example, the transcripts from the civil trial of O.J. Simpson for Dec. 18 and Dec. 20, 1996, *available at* http://www.courttv.com/casefiles/simpson/transcripts/dec/dec18.html; http://www.courttv.com/casefiles/simpson/transcripts/dec/dec20.html. Like the photograph in *Northside*, this image (if believed to be authentic) showed that a witness's statements were incorrect (in this case Simpson's testimony that he had never owned Bruno Magli shoes). The photograph did not, of course, prove that Simpson murdered Nicole Brown Simpson; it simply showed that one of Simpson's testimonial claims was mistaken. Nonetheless, while we cannot know for certain, it seems likely that this photograph, by challenging Simpson's credibility, played a significant role in the jury's finding of liability.

122. Jennifer L. Mnookin, *The Image of Truth: Photographic Evidence and the Power of Analogy*, 10 YALE J.L. & HUMAN. 1, 53-59 (1998).

ambivalent response to the photograph was part of a much broader judicial ambivalence toward technologically-produced ways of knowing that both promised and threatened to provide authoritative knowledge—and thus both promised and threatened to eliminate human judgment from the process of legal fact-finding. (The judicial reluctance to allow the polygraph, as we have seen, also reflects this ambivalence.)

In the case of the photograph as evidence, the judicial response to this ambivalence was to construct a doctrine that deemed the photograph to be mere illustration, rather then independent proof.[123] Photographs were understood to be the depiction of an eyewitness in visual form, rather than substantive evidence in and of itself.[124] This doctrine meant that in order to use a photograph, it first had to be "authenticated" by someone who had first-hand personal knowledge of that which was represented in the image. A witness had, in essence, to claim the photograph as his or her own testimony in visual form. Photographs were not generally permitted to serve as "silent witnesses"—they could be used as evidence only when they had a testimonial sponsor, some witness who claimed to have seen whatever was depicted.[125]

A photograph found in a newspaper archive, taken long ago by an unidentified and hence unavailable photographer, enlarged to reveal details unknown to any human being, would, therefore, not have been permitted into evidence by most judges.[126] While *Northside* suggests that the photograph can be the evidentiary form that retains its authority both for the everyday man on the street[127] and within the legal sphere, in fact, the photograph that provided the definitive evidence in the film would have been excluded, like the polygraph, from many courtrooms.[128]

What is most striking about the use of the photograph in *Northside* is just how comfortable, how sanguine, the film seems to be about its

123. *Id.* at 43-45.

124. *See, e.g*, 1 JOHN HENRY WIGMORE, A TREATISE ON THE SYSTEM OF EVIDENCE, § 790 (1st ed. 1904).

125. Mnookin, *supra* note 122, at 43-45.

126. The on-the-ground realities were more complicated. Although doctrinally, photographs were understood as merely illustration, in fact, as courts sometimes recognized, they were, once admitted, also treated as if they had independent probative value. *See id.* at 47-50. However, it was only with the advent of the x-ray that judges had to construct grounds for admissibility that emphasized that the authority of visual evidence might come from the process by which it was made rather than because of authentication by a witness. On the important shift that occurred with the rise of x-ray evidence, see Jennifer Mnookin, Images of Truth: Evidence, Expertise and Technologies of Knowledge in the American Courtroom 367-404 (1999) (unpublished Ph.D. dissertation, M.I.T.) (on file with M.I.T. Library and with the author).

127. Given *Northside*'s gendered conception of proof, we use "man" advisedly. *See supra* note 72.

128. This of course does not mean that it would have been excluded from a Board of Pardons hearing, where the formal rules of evidence that govern trials would not in fact have applied. But *Northside* makes no distinction between the evidence that might be received in different legal settings, and generally constructs "legal evidence" and "evidence admissible in court" as equivalent.

authority. In stark contrast to most noir films that examine the meaning or truth-value of the photograph, *Northside* urges no cautions regarding the photograph in particular, nor technologically produced knowledge more generally.[129] Rather, the film celebrates and even glorifies technological processes as offering privileged access to truth, access even (as with the polygraph) to the seemingly impenetrable interiors of the human mind. The film archly criticizes the legal system for resisting these technologies, for failing to recognize that they are superior to the imperfect and corruptible lay eyewitness who reports what she allegedly saw.[130]

As a reenactment, *Northside*'s claims to epistemological authority are necessarily precarious, and it is the photograph that acts as a warrant, warranting that we can indeed believe what we see. The photograph becomes a stand-in for the film itself: The authority of the photograph buttresses the authority of the film. And at the plot level, the photograph quashes all dissent, carrying every reasonable viewer inexorably toward the conclusion that Frank Wiecek is innocent. It is the photograph alone, among all the forms of evidence displayed in the film, that can compel conviction by operating as legitimate evidence both within the legal arena and outside of it.

In the end, however, it is precisely the film's strong realist claims that undermine its defense of machine-made knowledge. For as we have seen, the crowning moment of technological triumph, the development of the photograph that confirms a man's innocence and persuades doubters, is a fiction. By turning to a blatant fiction at the most critical moment of the film, *Northside* undermines its own authority, revealing that in fact its own representation of the case cannot necessarily be trusted. This climactic scene manifests the disjunction between seeming real and being real, the tension between verisimilitude and evidence. These tensions in turn rehabilitate the legal system's hesitation and ambivalence regarding technologically-produced forms of evidence, a hesitation borne, in part, precisely out of the fear that machine-produced vision risks looking more real than the real itself, that visual evidence may be too persuasive, too compelling.

And yet, as we shall see next, many judges during the 1930s and 1940s were more easily seduced by the moving image than their predecessors were by the photograph. Perhaps this suggests that the courtroom and the cinema may share more in common than we might think.

---

129. *See* Nancy West & Penelope Pelizzon, Smile, My Lovely: Photography, Film Noir, and Identity (2001) (unpublished manuscript, on file with authors).

130. In this sense, *Northside* follows classical film narrative's tendency to make the individual into a heroic figure. Like the Western hero or the private detective, McNeal is portrayed as emerging triumphant over rigid social forces by following his own instincts and codes of conduct. For further discussion of this point, see Rosenberg, *supra* note 19, at 284-85.

III. FILM AS LEGAL EVIDENCE

So far, this Article has striven to show how *Northside* is a film that centers upon questions of evidence. On the one hand, the film itself is a study in evidence. It interrogates three distinct modes of proof, critiques legal conceptions of evidence, and concludes by offering up the photograph as the evidentiary ideal, a seemingly "pure" form of knowledge that retains its power even when it is enlarged, sent over a wire, and reconstituted somewhere else. On the other hand, as a reenactment, *Northside* sets itself up *as* evidence, or, at a minimum, as a true retelling of an actual case. That is, recognizing *Northside*'s status as a reenactment invites precisely the same questions *Northside* asks about proof, but this time at a meta-level. What makes a filmic depiction credible? What makes the viewers of *Northside* know that even if *Northside* isn't "real," it indeed portrays "real" events in a manner that can be trusted? Do not be misled—while the film is simultaneously fact and fiction (just as the photograph in the film is both the critical fact and itself a fiction), *Northside* is not, in fact, particularly reflexive. Rather than interrogating its own authority or generating skepticism about the possibilities for knowledge, the film simply wants viewers to believe in its authority.[131] In short, the film is about two spheres of evidence, the lay and the legal. The film portrays the limits of legal evidence—the willingness to be satisfied by unreliable eyewitness testimony, the unwillingness to see the evidence of machines of judgment. It shows both the unrivalled persuasive power of visual proof and reveals that finding the proof that will satisfy the law can be a serendipitous enterprise. At the same time, while the film is neither documentary nor fiction, it is itself a form of proof. It is designed to be a persuasive rendition of a true story of justice nearly denied, revealing indisputably both Frank Wiecek's innocence and the precariousness of justice. Reenactments, we might say, offer a kind of lay evidence. As one of the advertisements for the film on *Northside*'s press sheet put it hyperbolically, "Every word is true."[132]

And so, in this final section of the Article, we will turn to look at the third side of this triangle of evidence: films as legal evidence. We shall see that there are, in fact, interesting parallels between *Northside*'s claims about visual proof and the reception of films in actual courtrooms. Just as *Northside*'s credibility, both at the plot level and as the reenactment of a true story, depends on retaining a certain naïveté about the meaning of the visual image, judges who confronted filmic evidence elided the complexities of the form. Moreover, the conflation between the

131. Our reading of the film, in this sense, departs substantially from that of Telotte, who sees *Northside*, as well as other noir documentaries, as possessing a great deal of self-reflexivity. *See* TELOTTE, *supra* note 16, at 141.

132. Exhibitor's Campaign Sheet, *supra* note 50.

photograph and the film, implicit in *Northside*, becomes explicit when films become a form of legal proof. Finally, on those few occasions when filmed reenactments were used in trials, they were often seen to be as powerful as the real thing. Actually, these filmed reenactments were even more successful at operating simultaneously as fiction and as fact than *Northside*, not only standing in for the actual event but offering a form of proof that was seen to be, in fact, superior to it.

Films were offered into evidence in court as early as 1913—merely seventeen years after the first motion pictures were displayed to audiences. For the next twenty years, juries in a number of states viewed the occasional film in evidence, but few appellate courts ruled on their admissibility. Though films appear to have been used without objection on occasion in trials, the only two reported appellate cases before the end of the 1920s that analyzed their use both supported their exclusion.

The earliest appellate case to examine the admissibility of a film was *Gibson v. Gunn*, decided in 1923.[133] The plaintiff was suing to recover for damages resulting from having been struck by the defendant's automobile. The plaintiff was a vaudeville dancer who, at some point prior to the current accident, had lost his leg and had been forced to use a prosthesis but was nonetheless able to continue in vaudeville with his artificial leg. He displayed to the jury a motion picture that he used as the opening entertainment in his vaudeville show; the film portrayed the plaintiff on crutches, walking into a shop that sold artificial limbs, and leaving the store walking under his own power. In the following scene, he encountered two friends, dancers who performed certain tricks—the plaintiff performed these same tricks as well as other stunts that his able-bodied buddies viewed as too difficult for them.[134] Though the opinion does not detail the plaintiff's motivation for displaying the picture, presumably he wanted the jury to see how competent and sure in movement he was despite his artificial leg, in order to rebut either an explicit or implicit claim that his new injuries did not cause him much additional damage or loss in income considering his prior one-legged condition.

Whatever his justification for showing the film, the appellate court was not impressed. The opinion deems the admission of the film "a radical departure from the rules of evidence," notes that "moving pictures present a fertile field for exaggeration of any emotion or action," and complains that no evidence was presented "as to how this particular motion film was prepared."[135] Worse, the film "brought before the jury irrelevant matter, hearsay and incompetent evidence, and tended to make a farce of the

133. Gibson v. Gunn, 202 N.Y.S. 19 (1923).

134. *Id.*

135. *Id.*

trial." It is as if the performer had performed on the wrong stage: "The plaintiff's ability as a vaudeville performer was not the issue, and his eccentric dancing, comic songs and the dialogue and remarks of his fellow-performers had no place in the trial in the Supreme Court of the state."[136] While some of their specific criticisms of the film are not without merit (one might, for example, be legitimately concerned about the lack of proof of how the film was made and about the fact that the statements made by the vaudevillian's buddies within the film may have been hearsay), the judges' discomfort does not seem to stem from these particular concerns, but rather from something deeper and less inchoate. Showing a film at a trial? A vulgar entertainment in the arena of judgment, vaudeville theater invading the theater of proof? It is more than the judges can bear. They say so themselves: The film threatened to make the trial itself into a farce.

The next appellate discussion of an attempted use of film also came down in favor of exclusion. This case, decided in 1926, involved alleged stock fraud.[137] One of the issues in the case was whether glass caskets could feasibly be manufactured; the defendant sought to introduce a film that purported to show the actual manufacture of these caskets at the defendant's Oklahoma plant. The trial court refused to allow the defendants to show the film, declaring, "A motion picture does not of itself prove an actual occurrence. The thing reproduced must be established by the testimony of witnesses."[138] The court said that determining whether the film was sufficiently verified to warrant its admission was up to the trial court. But the opinion then offered a circular argument, one that, if taken at face value, would mean that the exclusion of a motion picture as evidence could never constitute error: "[I]f, as contended by counsel for appellant, the testimony relative to the process of manufacture completely verifies the picture, then he cannot successfully claim injury from the refusal of the court to repeat this testimony by a moving picture display of the facts already in evidence."[139] Essentially, the court suggests, quite reasonably, that a film has to be verified by testimony to be admissible. But if testimony verifies the film in every particular, then the exclusion of the film cannot harm the party, for it is by definition cumulative—what the film shows is already in evidence, through the testimony necessary to verify the film in the first place. A film is thus either insufficiently verified or inherently cumulative.

Unfortunately, the opinion in the case provides little detail on the facts underlying the criminal charges. One imagines, however, that the trial judge may have been concerned that the perpetrators of an elaborate stock

136. *Id.*

137. De Camp v. United States, 10 F.2d 984 (D.C. Cir. 1926).

138. *Id.* at 984-85.

139. *Id.*

fraud might well have also "manufactured" a film showing the company's manufacturing plant. The film might have been authenticated, in the sense that a witness vouched for its accuracy, and yet nonetheless be nothing more than fiction. The circular approach taken by the appellate court thus provides a tool for upholding the exclusion of a film of dubious reliability by giving the trial judge unlimited discretion. The appellate court does not merely think the trial court had the discretion to exclude the film; it views the trial court as having been right to exclude the film: "[T]he admission of the motion picture would have amounted to nothing more than a spectacular display of a situation based upon facts in evidence."[140] The tone of this opinion is far less outraged than that of *Gibson v. Gunn*, but we still see hints of the same concern: A film may be a "spectacular display" that debases legal process and turns the courtroom itself into a spectacle.

Films as spectacles: This observation demands pause for reflection. Spectacle is part of a long tradition of popular forms, such as the circus or magical acts of traveling fairs dating back centuries.[141] Spectacles are sensational; they are designed to provoke sensation, to appeal to the viewer's emotions. It is this sensational response that the judges are leery of, and while their reaction may be unduly alarmist, it reflects a serious concern: that films may be so powerful, so persuasive, that they will carry along the viewers toward a conclusion that would not be warranted by reason. In fact, we can tease out three separate anxieties: first, that films as evidence may cheapen the trial, demeaning its seriousness by importing a form of popular entertainment, delegitimating verdicts by association with vaudeville. Second, that evidentiary films may encourage juries to make determinations based on emotion rather than reason. (Jurors may be lured by sensation and fail properly to sift the evidence.) Third, that films carried the risk of seeming too real, eliminating the distance between a representation and the actual event. Leading evidence scholar John Henry Wigmore cautioned judges about this risk in the 1923 edition of his treatise on evidence: "Theoretically, of course, the motion picture can never be assumed to represent the actual occurrence. . . . And yet, any motion picture is apt to cause forgetfulness of this and to impress the jury with the convincing impartiality of Nature herself."[142]

The opinions of these early judges, however, do not represent the approach that came to typify judicial response to motion picture evidence. For the most part, those judges who were faced with this new

140. *Id.*

141. Much has been written on the cultural history and operation of "spectacles." *See, e.g.*, JONATHAN CRARY, TECHNIQUES OF THE OBSERVER (1993); Jean-Luc Comolli, *Machines of the Visible*, *in* THE CINEMATIC APPARATUS 121 (Stephen Heath & Teresa de Lauretis eds., 1980); and Elizabeth Cowie, *The Spectacle of Actuality*, *in* COLLECTING VISIBLE EVIDENCE, *supra* note 66, at 19.

142. 2 WIGMORE, *supra* note 98, § 798.

technological form of proof resisted the notion that films as evidence raised any complicated evidentiary or interpretive questions. The typical response was simply to analogize the film to a collection of photographs, and to argue that, since photographs were admissible so long as a proper foundation was established, then films should be as well. There was, to be sure, still occasional continued discomfort with the "spectacular" nature of film, as well as soft murmurs of concern over whether film might be too lifelike a medium, too vivid and too convincing. But these moments of anxiety were the exception. Most of the time, judges saw movies as nothing more than a series of still photographs, a sequence of individual frames made into one seamless whole, and they saw the whole as no more and no less than its constituent parts.

The basic logic is well illustrated, for example, by a 1937 California case, *Heiman v. Market*: "[I]t is established beyond question that photographs may be admitted in evidence, that moving pictures are but a series of single pictures, and that as single pictures may be received in evidence, there is no reason why moving pictures may not be admitted."[143] The description of film as a "series of photographs" is obviously intended to make filmic evidence unproblematic, for by the 1920s, photographs had been regularly used as legal evidence for more than forty years. More importantly, this rough equation of film with photography serves to minimize film's "spectacular" quality—taming film, as it were, into possessing one of the most desirable characteristics for the courtroom: immobility. It suggests that the viewers of cinematic evidence possess more control over what they watch than they actually do, since photographs, because they depict one frozen moment in time, allow for careful and repetitive inspection far more easily than films do. And, by linking film with photography, the description also capitalizes on the latter's historical associations with accuracy and objectivity, a point to which we will return shortly.

Unlike the two early judges who were repelled by films as evidence, then, most of the judges who considered them were quite taken with the extraordinary probative value of the proof they offered. And though Wigmore's warning that the representation might be mistaken for the real was frequently cited, it was generally not viewed as a reason to exclude the film from evidence. What accounts for the surprising lack of anxiety about filmic evidence? Why did the early concerns—that films were frivolous, spectacular, and too persuasive—come to seem less pressing?

We shall return to this question at the conclusion of this Section, but we can begin to offer one answer here: Judges may have been influenced by the particular nature of the films that were used in the courtroom. Most of the motion pictures that made their way into evidence in the 1930s and

143. Heiman v. Market, 69 P.2d 178 (Cal. App. 1937).

1940s fell into two broad categories. The vast majority were films taken surreptitiously by insurance companies (or other defendants), exposing the plaintiff as a malingerer who was overstating or downright faking injuries.[144] Or, on occasion, they were reenactments or recreations of matters at issue in the trial, including, in a few instances, filmed reenactments of the crime itself. For reasons that we shall explore, both of these sorts of films seemed especially "safe" to use as legal evidence, seemingly exempt from the concerns that led a few early judges to voice serious concern about the use of filmic evidence.

Judges generally allowed defendants to present motion picture evidence that revealed that a plaintiff's injuries were less severe than the plaintiff claimed.[145] Indeed, some appellate courts found that if such a film had been properly authenticated, its exclusion constituted reversible error. In *Boyarsky v. Zimmerman*, a plumber working on a building was hit on the head by a bolt that crashed down from fifty-five feet above, where steelworkers, employed by a different subcontractor, were also at work. Eight months after the accident, the defendant secretly filmed the plaintiff walking along the street carrying a parcel, in order to show that the "plaintiff's claim that he was physically incapable of working was untrue."[146] The court writes,

> In view of the claim of the plaintiff that he was totally disabled and unable to work or earn a living at any useful employment this case is a striking illustration of an instance where moving pictures are not only admissible but very important. . . . In the present case the defendant, appellant, properly points out that the pictures taken of the plaintiff, who contends that he received very severe injuries, will show that he went to live in another city and there evidently conducted himself as a perfectly well man instead of the invalid

144. This courtroom use of surveillance film constitutes the logical outcome of nearly fifty years of using photography and film to make private and furtive acts public. As the work of film scholar Tom Gunning has shown, a series of interlocking inventions—beginning with the invention of the "detective camera" in the early 1880s—came to popularize the use of surreptitious picture-taking as entertainment. Indeed, as Gunning points out, cinema was "born out" of this form of entertainment, since actuality-films, rather than fictional films, constituted the main product of the cinema for over ten years. Within this climate, Gunning writes,

> The apparatus of the cinema allows the passage from private to public space, and its role as simultaneously witness and record endows it with a juridical effect, providing both evidence of wrongdoing and the occasion for judgment and punishment. The viewer of the film negotiates this propulsion of private deeds into public exposure, positioned as both voyeur-witness and moral judge through the surrogate apparatus.

Tom Gunning, *Embarrassing Evidence: The Detective Camera and the Documentary Impulse*, *in* COLLECTING VISIBLE EVIDENCE, *supra* note 66, at 46, 46 (1999).

145. *See also* Kortz v. Guardian Life Ins. of Amer., 144 F.2d 676 (10th Cir. 1944); Bethlehem Steel v. Foy, 108 P.2d 698 (Cal. App. 1940); Heiman v. Market, 21 Cal. App. 2d 311 (1937); Wallendorf v. N.Y. Life Ins., 12 S.2d 585 (Fl. 1943); Equitable Life Assur. Soc. v. McDonald, 134 S.W.2d 953 (Ky. 1939); Denison v. Omaha 7 C.B. St. R. Co., 280 N.W. 905 (Neb. 1938); Mason v. Evans, 69 A.2d 33 (N.J. Sup. 1949).

146. Boyarsky v. Zimmerman, 270 N.Y.S. 134 (1934).

which he claimed to be.[147]

On occasion, judges allowed these secret movies even when the defendant "entrapped" the plaintiff into conducting the activities that were filmed. First, it is worth quoting at length the detailed description of the film in one of these cases, to see just how damning these motion pictures could be:

> The first picture shows the plaintiff at a golf course, what is commonly called a driving range. He and his lady friend are using a bucket of balls and the plaintiff especially, is driving the balls out into the field. The plaintiff stoops over to take a ball out of the bucket or basket, places it on a tee and strikes the ball with splendid form and carry through. The plaintiff is next seen tossing a basketball. Next he is seen throwing baseballs at a doll rack, or some similar device. Next he is rowing a boat. He is next seen at the lake front preparatory to going swimming. He had his swimming trunks on under his clothes, and the camera discloses that he undressed at the beach, but was not wearing his leather jacket. He and his blonde lady friend go in swimming, and he is shown teaching her how to swim, and lifting her almost out of the water, and as the picture ends it is as though he were rescuing her from drowning, with his left arm under her chin and supporting her and swimming around with his right arm.[148]

So much for the plaintiff's claims of incapacity.

The plaintiff, however, claimed that he had only engaged in these activities because the woman who also appeared in the film had urged him to, and that (unbeknownst to him at the time of their frolicking) she was actually an agent of the defendant. The court was not impressed: "We do not think it is material what part this girl took in persuading the plaintiff to do what the pictures disclose he did do. The pictures speak for themselves and show that the defendant could do things that he claimed at the trial he could not do."[149] The pictures speak for themselves: They impeach the plaintiff, showing his testimony to be composed of lies, just as the photograph in *Northside* seems to show that Wanda Skutnik lied upon the stand.

These movies, taken secretly and then made public before the jury, are particularly interesting because they reveal the theatrical aspects of all legal proof. They show up plaintiffs as actors: When they appear in court, looking ragged or stooped, injured and miserable, they may simply be putting on a show for the jury. Is the seemingly injured plaintiff a genuine

147. *Id.*

148. McGoorty v. Benhart, 27 N.E.2d 289 (Ill. App. Ct. 1940).

149. *Id.* Courts did occasionally evince some concern that defendants could "entrap" plaintiffs into appearing on film, but the courts usually admitted the film evidence nonetheless. *See, e.g.*, Maryland Cas. v. Coker, 118 F.2d 43 (5th Cir. 1941).

victim, or merely a malingerer? Can the jury be trusted to tell exactly which plaintiffs are acting, to separate fact from fiction? The films taken by detective agencies and other commercial filmmakers let the jury spy on plaintiffs when they are unsuspecting, going about the daily business of life. There is a certain irony in using film—the medium of actors—to reveal what these plaintiffs are like when they are not posing for a jury.[150]

These films did not seem to be spectacles themselves: In fact, the subjects of the film did not even know that their actions were being caught on film, and clearly there was no risk that they were playing to the camera or unconsciously influenced by the presence of the recording instrument. Rather than appearing as spectacles themselves, these films revealed the spectacular aspect of the plaintiff's in-court behavior. They showed that the plaintiff was playing to the jury's sympathies, preying on emotion and sensation. These films seemed to bring reality into the courtroom; to exclude them would have meant allowing the plaintiff to stage a dramatic performance unchecked and unconstrained by the contradictory evidence of his or her actual out-of-court behavior. Given this choice between allowing the film into evidence and allowing the plaintiff to dramatize with impunity, it is not surprising that judges almost always saw these films as legitimate evidence.

Reenactments were not nearly so common as these spy films; in fact, there are only a handful of appellate decisions discussing their use in the 1940s. But occasionally, defendants would, astounding though it may seem, agree to reenact their own crimes for the police and before the camera. In one such case, there had been a fatal shooting at DiCioda's liquor store in Los Angeles in 1947. The defendants allegedly committed another robbery a few hours later, and then, when the police stopped them to ask some questions a few weeks later, they shot and wounded one of the officers. Six weeks afterward, they were arrested, and implicated themselves in the liquor store homicide. They also agreed to reenact their crime and have this reenactment recorded on film. At trial, the defendants repudiated their confessions, and claimed that they had made them under coercion.[151] The three motion pictures—each one showing a reenactment of one of the alleged crimes, the homicide, the robbery, and the shooting of the police—were shown at trial. Testimony was introduced to show how the films were set up and made:

---

150. These courtroom films are a version of cinema vérité; like vérité they endeavor "to render the film-making itself invisible and to give viewers the sense of unmediated access to the contingencies of an actuality uncompromised by the camera." CORNER, *supra* note 67, at 44. One of the key qualities of vérité, it has been argued, is "a firm commitment to the 'evidentiality' of film." *Id.* Corner further argues that the reenactment (or, in his terms, the drama-documentary) and vérité together "put pressure on documentary 'look' and 'truth' by developing specific generic characteristics and aspirations to an extreme degree," though obviously in quite different ways. *Id.* at 55. It is interesting to recognize that the two forms of films used as legal evidence are precisely those kinds of films that both partake in and problematize documentary's naïve claims to truthful depiction.

151. People v. Dabb, 197 P.2d 1 (Cal. 1948).

> There was first a rehearsal of each incident, at which the defendants were asked to show what they had done. From this it was determined where the camera should be set up in order to embrace all of the action, and the entire scene was then photographed, with the sound and pictures being simultaneously recorded on the same strip of film.[152]

The court noted that motion pictures are susceptible to fabrication, but thought that the way to handle this risk was by requiring adequate foundation evidence to establish that the film was properly taken, developed, and not tampered with, as a prerequisite to admissibility. The court further recognized that films might be misleading, or unduly vivid, but emphasized that a voluntary reenactment was unlikely to suffer from these dangers:

> A motion picture of the artificial recreation of an event may unduly accentuate certain phases of the happening, and because of the forceful impression made upon the minds of the jurors by this kind of evidence, it should be received with caution. . . . However, when the events which are being photographed consist of a voluntary reenactment by the accused of what occurred, there is little, if any, danger of misleading emphasis which is unfavorable to him. Moreover, as a method of presenting confessions, sound motion pictures appear to have a unique advantage in that, while presenting the admission of guilt, they simultaneously testify to facts relevant to the issue of volition.[153]

It is worth dwelling for a moment on the strangeness of these reenactment films. Why, one wonders, would a criminal suspect agree to let the police make a movie of his crime? Is he or she lured by the desire to play a starring role in a two-bit drama? Is it the same dynamic that drives criminal suspects to confess: an urge to tell their stories, an urge for someone to know what has happened?[154] In some of these films, the criminal suspects and the police return together to the actual scene of the crime, and sometimes a cop plays the victim, the police and the perpetrators performing together in a spectacle of proof.[155]

What exactly are these reenactments? They are, in fact, spectacles of proof. They are extremely persuasive evidence that the defendant committed the crime because they simultaneously show and tell: They literally show the defendant committing the crime, and they also show, by the fact of their existence, that the defendant was willing to tell everyone that she or he committed the crime. They are not just proof, but also

152. *Id.* at 7-8.

153. *Id.* at 9.

154. For an analysis of the role of the confession in law and literature, see PETER BROOKS, TROUBLING CONFESSIONS: SPEAKING GUILT IN LAW AND LITERATURE (2000).

155. *See, e.g.*, People v. Rowe, 99 Cal. App. 3d 1023 (1975).

spectacle: a compelling display before the jury of the police and the criminals together engaged in a form of cinema vérité. As reenactments, these films show the jury what it was like when the defendant committed the crime. His actions are replayed before the jury's eyes, turning the jurors into virtual witnesses[156] to the events underlying the trial. Of course, these reenactments do not "actually" reveal what the crime looked like; they are post-hoc representations, not filmed depictions of the event itself. In fact, though, they may offer even more persuasive evidence than a film that actually caught the criminal in the act. Films that capture the actual moment on camera might indeed be powerful evidence—but they are subject to reinterpretation, or to reinscription within a larger narrative, or to analysis that makes what looks clear on film seem more complicated or muddy once it is explained or contextualized.[157] By contrast, when a suspect agrees to participate in a reenactment of his own crime, it is a form of confession, but a confession by demonstration rather than simply by words. Of course, such a film could itself be placed within a larger context (as those defendants who claimed coercion were attempting to do), but it is hard to make such a context stick, for the films themselves *demonstrate* the defendants' guilt.[158]

Courts continued, on occasion, to register discomfort about the "spectacular" nature of filmic evidence. In a case where the appellate court insisted that a film be excluded because it was misleading, the judge writes dryly, "Doubtless the show was highly entertaining to the jury, but entertainment of the jury is no function of a trial. And why all this fuss to prove a fact susceptible of easy, exact, and indisputable demonstration by actual measurement?"[159] But for the most part, courts seemed complacent about cinematic evidence, confident that films, becoming ever more popular as a medium of news and entertainment, could offer reliable evidence in court as well. They were appreciative of the evidence that

---

156. The term "virtual witness" is borrowed from STEVEN SHAPIN & SIMON SCHAFFER, LEVIATHAN AND THE AIR PUMP (1985).

157. The acquittal of the officers in the state criminal case resulting from the beating of Rodney King is an obvious example of how a videotape that seems upon first viewing to show something clearly—in this instance the use of excessive force by the police—can be read differently when it is explained frame-by-frame. *See, e.g.*, Kimberlé Crenshaw & Gary Peller, *Reel Time/Real Justice, in* READING RODNEY KING/READING URBAN UPRISING 56 (Robert Gooding-Williams ed., 1993); Chuck Hagen, *Photography View: The Power of a Video Image Depends on the Caption*, N.Y. TIMES, May 10, 1992, §2, at 32; *How the Defense Dissected the Tape*, NEWSWEEK, May 11, 1992, at 36.

158. Reenacted depictions of the crime, like any other form of confession, might of course be false. On the phenomenon of the false confession, see Saul M. Kassin, *The Psychology of Confession Evidence*, 52 AM. PSYCHOLOGIST 221 (1997); Saul M. Kassin & Katherine Keichel, *The Social Psychology of False Confessions: Compliance, Internalization and Confabulation,* 7 PSYCHOL. SCI. 125 (1996); Richard J. Ofshe & Richard A. Leo, *The Decision To Confess Falsely: Rational Choice and Irrational Action,* 74 DENV. U. L. REV. 979 (1997); and Richard J. Ofshe & Richard A. Leo, *The Social Psychology of Police Interrogation: The Theory and Classification of True and False Confessions*, 16 STUD. L. & SOC'Y, 189 (1997).

159. Hadrian v. Milwaukee, 1 N.W.2d 755 (Wisc. 1942).

films could offer—seemingly direct access to critical matters ranging from the way the crime was actually committed to the plaintiff's actual physical condition—and were strikingly unconcerned about distortion, either the distortions that might be present within the filmic representation, or distortions of the trial process that might result from the growing use of such "spectacular" evidence. Of course, trials can be spectacles themselves, and the presentation of evidence is a show that one side puts on before the factfinder; in this sense, filmic evidence within a trial is like a play-within-a-play. But filmic evidence walks a very fine line between fact and fiction, between reconstruction and representation. Like the filmed reenactment of *Northside*, a film made in order to be legal evidence is simultaneously real and unreal, documentary and drama.

We will return now, at more length, to the central puzzle raised by this brief look at the use of actual films as legal evidence: Why did judges overcome their early concerns about this spectacular form of proof and decide that films were a legitimate form of proof? It is tempting, fifty years later, to position these judges as naïve—too easily awed by visual technology to see through it. If such a reading is fair, a certain irony emerges, given that photography, in its early days, received a substantially more critical evaluation from judges. Why, in other words, would late-nineteenth-century judges express such informed skepticism about photographic authority, while their counterparts some decades later were relatively sanguine about filmic evidence?

We will offer four arguments, all of them admittedly speculative, for why judges latched onto filmic evidence relatively uncritically. First, judges may have been influenced by the contemporaneous emergence of a form of film that claimed to offer truthful representation: the documentary. In fact, shortly before judges were starting to embrace film as possessing the authority of a "series of photographs," the documentary movement had begun its development in Britain and the United States.[160] From its very beginnings, the rhetoric surrounding the documentary film focused on such key concepts and nouns as "knowledge," "information," "sobriety," "objectivity." The intention, of course, was to associate documentary film with the serious, to position it—along with law, science, and other information-oriented fields—as what Bill Nichols calls a "discourse of sobriety."[161] In so doing, documentary filmmakers even referred to their individual films as "possessing all the authority and close attention of the photograph. . . . [O]ur aim is not to offer light entertainment but to show the raw truth, exposed and frozen forever as image, just as Jacob Riis and

160. The date of "origin" for the documentary movement is generally accepted as 1926, the year in which the leading figure of the movement in Britain and America, John Grierson, coined the term. *See* BILL NICHOLS, REPRESENTING REALITY: ISSUES AND CONCEPTS IN DOCUMENTARY 4 (1991).

161. *Id.* at 2.

others have done with their photographs."[162] This echo of the very description deployed by judges to legitimate films as evidence (film as a "series of photographs")—an echo that we can hear in other descriptions of documentary film as well—alerts us to the possibility that the documentary movement may, in fact, have helped shape legal notions about the evidential usefulness of cinema. Between the late 1920s and early 1940s, the documentary film enjoyed a powerful reputation in American culture as objective, earnest, and trustworthy—characteristics which proponents of the movement reinforced by setting the sobriety of the documentary against the "spectacle" of mainstream Hollywood cinema.[163]

Yet, as film scholar Elizabeth Cowie describes, even documentary films, simply because they *are* films, possess elements of the spectacle. "For all its seriousness, the documentary film nevertheless also involves more disreputable features of cinema usually associated with the entertainment film, namely, the pleasures and fascination of film as spectacle."[164] These pleasures arise not through make-believe or fictional enactment but by the representation of actuality. Thus, inherent in the viewing of any film, no matter what its purpose, audience, method, or genre, are two desires: a desire for reality captured, securely contained for dissection and analysis, and a desire for the real not as knowledge but as image, as spectacle. In the early days of the documentary movement, however, such a recognition was rarely articulated; what was articulated, over and over again, and often by analogy to photography, was the documentary's seriousness of purpose. And, while the judges of the two early appellate cases anticipated Cowie's observations by warning the legal community of film's "spectacular" nature, later judges—those writing some time after the development of documentary film in America—seemed willing enough to see film as a "discourse of sobriety." Whether or not judges were in fact influenced by the rise of documentary filmmaking, surely documentary filmmakers could not have asked for a more powerful alliance.

The second argument for why judges came to accept filmic evidence with relative ease is quite straightforward: By analogizing films to photographs, judges made the film into a comprehensible—and

162. *Id.* at 7; *see also* ERIK BARNOUW, DOCUMENTARY: A HISTORY OF THE NON-FICTION FILM 254-55 (1974) (discussing these analogies to photography).

163. As Bill Nichols observes, "A deep-rooted response in documentary filmmaking has been vigorous disassociation from the distracting shadow-play of fiction. Early documentarists were particularly vehement in their judgments of the fiction film." NICHOLS, *supra* note 160, at 4. Among these filmmakers were Dziga Vertov and John Grierson, who "drew harsh and unflattering comparisons between the fiction film industry and both the formal potential of cinema and the social purpose of the documentary. They lambasted Hollywood as a symbol for escapist, meretricious spectacles." *Id.*

164. Cowie, *supra* note 141, at 19.

admissible—form of evidence. If photographs were admissible (and they long had been so) and films were nothing more than a series of photographs, then films did not pose tricky problems of categorization or analysis. This process of analogizing the new to the known is, of course, a mainstay of legal reasoning as well as a commonplace judicial reaction to new technological forms.[165] In fact, when confronted with the photograph decades earlier, judges made a similar conceptual move: They analogized the photograph to maps, models, and diagrams, thus making the new into the familiar.[166]

Analogical reasoning, however, involves emphasizing similarity and eliding difference. If x can be analogized to y, it means that the two items are the same in all the ways that count; the battleground, of course, becomes determining which, exactly, are the ways that count. When judges analogized photographs to drawings, the analogy foregrounded the ways in which the photograph was a constructed representation, a human creation rather than a mirror of nature. It was, in significant part, this analogy that led judges to resist any simplistic notion of the photograph as an unmediated depiction of the real.[167] Over time, as photographic admissibility became taken for granted, the power of the analogy faded, and judges began to see the photograph both as an illustration and, at times, as a silent witness.[168] Still, the key point is that the analogy circumscribed the way that the photograph was understood. The analogy between films and photographs may have had a similar circumscribing effect. It provided judges with a way to ignore some of the differences between photography and film: that films captured movement and the passage of time instead of a single instant; that films were typically edited into their final form; that the process of "reading" a film was less familiar to a lay juror than "reading" a photograph. But even this list is misleading,

165. For the classic account of case-by-case reasoning in the law, see EDWARD H. LEVI, AN INTRODUCTION TO LEGAL REASONING (1949). For how analogy operates in legal discourse, see, for example, Scott Brewer, *Exemplary Reasoning: Semantics, Pragmatics, and the Rational Force of Legal Argument by Analogy*, 109 HARV. L. REV. 925 (1996); Cass Sunstein, *On Analogical Reasoning*, 106 HARV. L. REV. 741 (1993).

166. Mnookin, *supra* note 122, at 24-27, 45-50, 54-55.

167. In this sense, legal discourse was vastly different from other nineteenth-century discourses, which tended to exaggerate the novelty of photography as a medium. As photo historian John Tagg notes, "What is striking in the earliest articulated responses to the invention and dissemination of photography is how often the images it began to pour forth are hailed (or alternatively denounced) as a totally new currency, not only quantitatively but qualitatively different from any previous kind of image production." JOHN TAGG, GROUNDS OF DISPUTE: ART HISTORY, CULTURAL POLITICS, AND THE DISCURSIVE FIELD 122 (1992).

168. *See, e.g.*, People v. Bowley, 382 P.2d 591, 594 (Cal. 1963) (declaring that photographs can be "silent witnesses" that provide substantive evidence and not merely illustrate someone's testimony); Sisk v. State, 204 A.2d 684, 685 (Ct. App. Md. 1964); John H. Anderson, Jr., *Admissibility of Photographs as Evidence*, 7 N.C. L. REV. 443 (1929) (suggesting that a case excluding a photograph as substantive evidence was incorrectly decided); Dillard S. Gardner, *The Camera Goes to Court*, 24 N.C. L. REV. 233, 245 (1946) (arguing that photographs properly verified can be silent witnesses).

for the power of the analogy was to make analysis of the similarities and differences between films and photographs *optional*. Judges could, and often did, simply make the analogy and then admit the film, as if it were syllogistic logic in action: Photographs, when verified by an attesting witness, are admissible; films are a series of photographs; therefore, films, when verified by an attesting witness, are admissible.

The third argument for why judges became comfortable with filmic evidence focuses on the particularly persuasive power of the types of films—surveillance films and reenactments—that were used in the courtroom. We have already discussed this point, so we shall simply recap briefly here. Surveillance films carried the weight of *exposure*; reenactments, when performed by the actual criminals, carried the weight of *confession*. To have excluded surveillance films would have been to allow the plaintiff to lie with impunity. These films, instead of seeming fictional or spectacular themselves, seemed to reign in otherwise dangerous, in-court performances of injury.

Further support for the argument that judges admitted filmic evidence because of the particularly persuasive nature of the films involved can be gleaned by recalling those films that were excluded from evidence, such as a manufacturing process that might never have existed, and a vaudevillian's opening act. When the films themselves seemed to be either fictional creations or performances, judges barred them.[169] When the use of fiction in court became too obvious, judges resisted because one of the fictions of law is that trials are places for the determination of facts, not (or at least not merely) the construction of stories.[170] So long as films promised to counteract other fictions—the fiction of the injured plaintiff, the fiction of the innocent defendant—they were a legitimate and desirable form of evidence, for they could provide tales of truth rather than encouraging flights of fancy.

Finally, there is a fourth, related reason why judges may have found filmic evidence difficult to resist. This has to do with the conception of what kind of evidence courts prefer, and the implicit epistemology of legal evidence. Our system of rules governing the admissibility of evidence rests upon a set of basic assumptions, and fundamental among them is that we prefer that proof which comes closest to direct sensory perception. We have built a regime of legal evidence that is deeply Lockean, that assumes

169. This is not to say that the law and fiction operate in different realms; in fact, as Sherwin claims in the opening of his recent book on popular culture and law, "The law is shot through with fiction." SHERWIN, WHEN LAW GOES POP, *supra* note 19, at 3.

170. There is in fact a large recent literature analyzing the trial as a process of narrative construction. *See, e.g.*, BENNETT & FELDMAN, *supra* note 61; Pennington & Hastie, *supra* note 61. Even the Supreme Court has given a nod to the critical role that the making of narratives plays in the trial process. *See* Old Chief v. United States, 519 U.S. 172 (1997) (arguing that "a syllogism is not a story," that the jury expects stories, and that parties have the right to present their evidence in a compelling way).

that knowledge must derive from the experiences of the senses.[171] Hence, as a general rule, witnesses can testify only to things about which they have personal knowledge. And even if they have personal knowledge they must testify only to their perceptions—they are to report what they saw or heard directly, without gloss or interpretation.[172] As Robert Burns describes it in his recent book on the trial as a cultural form, our legal system requires, as "more a first principle than a rule of evidence," that the jury hear "an artificially stripped-down, value-free account of the witness's perceptions."[173] Why this emphasis on direct perception? According to Burns, the typical explanation ("the received view") is that it contributes to the functioning of the rule of law, by giving the jury the basic building blocks for their decision in a form that makes it less likely that the jury will simply adopt the value judgments or conclusions of the witnesses.[174]

This explanation is clearly part of the story. But equally important is that what we are striving for, our ideal form of evidence, is that which will somehow give the jury direct access to the past: genuine knowledge, whatever that is, of what actually occurred. In this sense, the trial and the reenactment share an important similarity. Both aim to produce knowledge of a past event, knowledge that counts as true despite the inability of both trials and reenactments to capture the past directly. (We shall return to this similarity shortly.) And implicit in the rules of evidence is the belief that this knowledge is most likely to emerge from that evidence which is closest to the event itself—a direct eyewitness rather than a second-hand account, or an immediate description of what happened rather than a later one made after the witness had time for reflection. Legal scholar Kim Scheppele has invoked a wonderful metaphor for precisely this point: We strive to reach ground-zero, the physical and temporal location of the events that gave rise to the litigation. In her words,

> The point of American evidence law is to enable the reproduction of the ground-zero moment and its aftermath to assess what truly happened. . . . [G]round zero is the moment when "the trouble" occurred and the law of evidence strives to admit facts that were generated as close in time and space as possible to the moment when this trouble happened.[175]

Since the jury can't see the ground-zero moment for itself, we want the

171. JOHN LOCKE, AN ESSAY CONCERNING HUMAN UNDERSTANDING (Peter H. Nidditch ed., Oxford Univ. Press 1979) (1690).

172. These conceptions are embodied in the Federal Rules of Evidence, but they come from common-law conceptions of admissibility. *See* FED. R. EVID. 602, 701.

173. ROBERT P. BURNS, A THEORY OF THE TRIAL 20-21 (2000).

174. *Id.* at 21.

175. Kim Scheppele, *The Ground Zero Theory of Evidence*, 50 HASTINGS L.J. 321, 322 (1998).

jury to see and hear the next best thing: the direct sensory report of percipient witnesses, those who were in fact at ground-zero.

We have detailed so far two basic epistemological assumptions built into our rules of evidence: first, a preference for direct perception, and second, a preference for direct perception of the underlying events themselves, the ground-zero moment. But there is a third assumption as well, not quite so explicit in the evidence rules but equally real. And that is, quite simply, that among various forms of sense perception, seeing is best: that visual perception is both most authoritative and most persuasive.[176] This preference is implicit, not explicit. No rule avows the primacy of the visual. Nevertheless, we can recognize it in a variety of ways: in the far greater attention paid to issues of eyewitnessing than earwitnessing; in the assumption that juries can judge credibility in part because they see the witness's demeanor; in the dominance of visual metaphors; and, perhaps especially, in the widespread use of visual evidence.[177] One advocacy manual describes our fixation with evidence that can be seen as

> "the wax museum" effect. People are fascinated by the real thing. The bullets that were found lodged in the victim's heart, the actual handwritten memorandum that was used to seal the agreement, the remains of the automobile gas tank that ruptured on impact burning the occupants of the car. . . . Until we see something tangible, [the event] is something that did not happen, or at least did not happen to real people.[178]

It isn't real until we see it. This, at last, brings us back to films as evidence. Films offer an especially powerful medium for making experience seem real: to watch a film of an event or occurrence provides the almost-illusion of having been there ourselves. In contemporary courtrooms, there are, on occasion, films that actually do capture ground zero: videos taken at the scene itself, capturing the moment in question for posterity and for courtroom scrutiny.[179] Although there were not such films in the 1940s courtroom, the surveillance films do offer a kind of access to ground zero. They do not show the scene of the plaintiff's injury,

---

176. Whether this is a legal preference or simply the byproduct of a more general cultural belief in the primacy of the visual is not important for our purposes. On the traditionally central role of visuality in law and culture, see Bernard Hibbits, *Making Sense of Metaphors: Visuality, Aurality, and the Reconfiguration of American Legal Discourse*, 16 CARD. L. REV. 229 (1994) (arguing that vision has been central to law, but that aurality is now growing more important). On the hegemony of vision in modernity (and the existence of an anti-visual discourse), the classic work is MARTIN JAY, DOWNCAST EYES: THE DENIGRATION OF VISION IN TWENTIETH CENTURY FRENCH THOUGHT (1993).

177. *See generally* Hibbits, *supra* note 176, at 241.

178. *Id.* (quoting ASHELY S. LIPSON, ART OF ADVOCACY: DEMONSTRATIVE EVIDENCE § 2.02 (1994)).

179. Of course, whether these films actually make the legal determinations clear or easy is another question altogether, as the Rodney King incident and its aftermath powerfully shows.

but they do show the plaintiff him or herself, captured on camera during an ordinary day, showing the "real" plaintiff going about his or her business. But more generally, filmic evidence lets the jury see matters for itself; it turns the spectators into virtual witnesses.

Of course, these points elide a central question: Should the jury believe what is before its eyes? Film as a medium simultaneously reflects a belief in the primacy of the visual and challenges it. The experience of film watching is affectively powerful, and this power comes, in part, out of how genuine-seeming, how real, a film can seem. And yet a film is directed, staged, edited, acted—it is an elaborate production, an artifice that nonetheless feels real. As Siegfried Kracauer once famously claimed, "what the camera captures seems more real than reality itself."[180] The point, however, is that film as a medium plays to some of the significant assumptions embedded within our rules of evidence, and it has the added advantage of letting the jury see for itself.

Of course, it is precisely the way in which film seems real that makes it simultaneously powerful and dangerous. Through the medium of film, the real and the image can become so inextricably intertwined that jury members watching a film may forget the present of the courtroom to enter the past of the crime, or put aside their own identities to identify with an imagined witness. At the same time, they may see the reenactment of a crime or event as somehow *more real* than the original, and their viewing of it as somehow *more legitimate* than a mere witness's account—more real and more legitimate, that is, because of the heightened attention to the subject a film can provide, because of the heightened opportunity to *see* more carefully, more effectively, more conclusively. But despite these dangers—reflected precisely in Wigmore's warning as well as judicial concerns about the spectacular—judges may have felt that films simply could not be kept out. As a medium that gave the jury direct sense perception of relevant matters, that let them see events for themselves, it may have seemed too powerful, too persuasive, too appealing, to exclude.

CONCLUSION

This final argument, that films were an appealing form of evidence precisely because they give the viewer such a powerful perception of really being there, of witnessing, of approaching ground zero, takes us to our concluding point: that there is in fact a significant affinity between the filmed reenactment, as a cultural form, and what takes place in the courtroom.

If, as Richard Sherwin has recently argued, the "symbolic drama" played out by trials casts jurors into "a mythic space and time," where

180. SIEGFRIED KRACAUER, THEORY OF FILM: THE REDEMPTION OF PHYSICAL REALITY 23 (1960).

"ordinary conventions drop away together with the ingrained habits of thought, feeling, and belief that maintain them," then surely the use of filmic evidence plays a part in this casting.[181] Sherwin's description of a trial resembles, in fact, the ideal cinematic experience as constructed by Hollywood. In both, the viewer is asked to leave the circumstances of her own world behind in order to enter as fully as she can into the "virtual" world before her. In both, she is invited to *see* much more attentively than she does outside the perimeters of their spaces. In film, as in a trial, reality becomes compelling, not because it is ordinary, but because it is suddenly strange—because it invites the viewer to watch with an extra-ordinary kind of attention.

While films and trials may have certain parallels, our claim is more particular: that trials are in fact a kind of reenactment. In a filmed reenactment like *Northside*, typically a singular, largely consistent version of events unfolds on screen, ensuring that the audience, whether they sit in a court of law or a theater, reads the evidence in a certain way.[182] By contrast, within a trial, multiple reenactments of the past compete. Each side offers its story, and the verdict is a judgment about which reenactment is more persuasive. The verdict affirms one side's story as the more plausible one, the one that bears a better correspondence to reality. Moreover, as evidence scholar Charles Nesson has persuasively argued, the verdict is not seen, in the end, as a comment on the strength or weakness of the evidence; rather, it is taken to be a judgment about what "really" happened.[183]

The key point is that both reenactments like *Northside* and the stories told at trials are, aspirationally, substitute depictions of what actually occurred. The reenactment and the representations presented at a trial both endeavor to stand in for the real. They do not do this through misrepresentation: They do not claim to be a literal depiction of what happened, but rather, acknowledge explicitly that they are retellings. They do not give us direct access to ground zero, but they nonetheless give us the essence of ground zero. The claim of a reenactment like *Northside*—that which makes it a reenactment rather than just a fictional story inspired by real events—is that it is true to the actual past in all the ways that count. (Note that in this sense a reenactment's relation to the actual is, in fact analogical: Like an analogy, the reenactment claims to correspond to the real in the ways that matter, without professing an identity between the reenactment and the event itself.) Similarly, an attorney making a closing

---

181. SHERWIN, WHEN LAW GOES POP, *supra* note 19, at 50-51.

182. Of course, some films are in fact about the problem of perception and interpretation, and generate multiple versions of events precisely to illustrate the incomplete nature of perception and the fragility of memory: any list of such films would start with RASHOMON (Daiei 1950). For a thorough analysis of *Rashomon* as a socio-legal text, see Kamir, *supra* note 19.

183. Charles Nesson, *The Evidence or the Event? On Judicial Proof and the Acceptability of Verdicts*, 98 HARV. L. REV. 1357, 1357 (1985).

argument endeavors to make the factfinders feel that they know what must have occurred even though they were not there. Reenactments and representations at trials *become,* at least in part, our account of what happened, *even though* we know that they do not give us transparent access to the events themselves.[184] In fact, if they fail to become substitute depictions of the actual, they are failures in their own terms. The filmed reenactment that strays too far from reality loses credibility; it becomes at best, fiction, at worst misleading or propagandist.[185] The trial verdict that cannot stand as a judgment about what actually happened can become a social problem, leading to cynicism about legal process (think O.J. Simpson) or in the extreme, unrest or riots (think Rodney King).

This excursion into films as evidence and the deep affinity between the reenactment and the trial itself has taken us some distance away from *Northside* itself. But it is worth nothing that *Northside* is itself a successful reenactment of just such a failed trial. That is, *Northside* tells the story of a verdict that in the end could not be believed as an account of what really happened. By the end of the film, Wiecek's conviction cannot stand, for it is no longer a plausible judgment about what actually occurred in that speakeasy so many years before. Note, however, that Wiecek's conviction does not simply collapse under its own weight: It takes an investigative reporter's diligent effort to bring forth the evidence that shows the mismatch between the verdict and reality. In this sense, *Northside* is an unusual reenactment: It is not merely, or even primarily, the story of a crime or the story of a trial. Rather, it is the story of the making of a story out of the crime and the trial. It is a reenactment of the making of a narrative, a narrative that revealed the original judgment of guilt to be nothing more than fiction.

If *Northside*'s starting point is a trial in which the verdict and reality failed to correspond, as a reenactment the film largely succeeds. We do not mean by this to make an aesthetic judgment, but rather a practical one: Though *Northside* is not terribly well known, it seems nonetheless fair to say that it is all that remains of the original story of Joseph Majczek's wrongful conviction. The film has come to stand in for what really happened, and, with the passage of time, even the fictional photograph that the film uses to generate both a climax and evidentiary certainty has, on occasion, been seen as real. For example, in an annual report in 1994, a journalism foundation used *Northside* to illustrate the power of photographic evidence in a pre-digital era—and in a delicious irony, given

184. The film *Boomerang* makes this point explicitly. The reenactments within the film show the film's viewers all that they can ever know about what really happened—which is mostly that they cannot really know what happened. The film shies away from its epistemological skepticism, however, by implicitly (and unfortunately) giving the viewers an alternative (and never fully proven) theory of the crime.

185. This is precisely the debate, for example, over some of Oliver Stone's films, such as NIXON (Hollywood Pictures 1995), or JFK (Warner Brothers 1991).

that it was, after all, a report on the future of *journalism*, simply assumed that the photograph had really existed:

> In the 1948 film *Call Northside 777*, Jimmy Stewart obtained an innocent man's freedom from prison by means of the latest technological advance—the Associated Press Wirephoto. . . . In real life, Chicago Times reporter James McGuire received a Pulitzer Prize for the reporting on which the movie was based. His hard work—his clever use of the latest technology—succeeded in freeing the unjustly convicted Joe Majczek from prison, where he had served 11 years for a crime he didn't commit.
>
> In the 1940s, modern technology performed the miracle of transmitting irrefutable photographic evidence almost instantaneously from one location to another. In the 1990s, technology has made it possible for all existing means by which information is imparted from one human being to another—sounds, images, printed words—to be converted into digital form—the 0s and 1s used by computers. . . . Would the photo McGuire used to prove Majczek's innocence prove anything at all anymore?[186]

We ought not to overinterpret an annual report. But still, this example shows how, especially with the passage of time, the reenactment can indeed become the real thing, or at least, all that remains of it.

Creating a believable story of the past is the raison-d'être of reenactments and trials alike. Both the stories told at trials and those told in reenactments like *Northside* admittedly provide only a partial, subjective, mediated, and even fictional account of what occurred. They cannot and do not claim truth in any grand sense, but their purpose is truth nonetheless: Both verdicts and reenactments attempt to capture the past in the ways that matter most. Recognizing this affinity between the trial and the reenacted film provides one final reason for why judges were reluctant to engage in a sustained critique of film as evidence: Perhaps such a critique would lead to a reflective examination of the trial process itself, exposing the theater of proof as, well, theater.

186. The ROBERT R. MCCORMICK TRIBUNE FOUND., 1994 (JOURNALISM PROGRAM), *available at* http://rrmtf.org/journalism/j94ar.htm. Note also that McGuire did not in fact receive a Pulitzer for his reporting on Majczek, though he did receive several other awards. *See supra* note 13.

[8]

Film as Witness: Screening *Nazi Concentration Camps* Before the Nuremberg Tribunal

Lawrence Douglas[†]

> And then they showed that awful film, and it just spoiled everything.
>
> Hermann Goering[1]

INTRODUCTION: FILM AS WITNESS AND THE PROBLEM OF REPRESENTATION

November 20, 1995 marks the fiftieth anniversary of the beginning of the most unusual judicial proceedings of the century, the Nuremberg war crimes trials. After a day devoted to entering the indictment and the pleas, Robert H. Jackson, a sitting Justice of the U.S. Supreme Court and the chief counsel for the Allied prosecution, opened his address to the Tribunal with the words, "The wrongs which we seek to condemn and punish have been so calculated, so malignant, and so devastating, that civilization cannot tolerate their being ignored, because it cannot survive their being repeated."[2] A week later, on the afternoon of November 29, 1945, Sydney Alderman, associate trial counsel, prepared the Tribunal for the presentation of the prosecution's most dramatic evidence of the Nazis' malignancy: "At this point it is planned by our staff to show a motion picture, and it will take some few minutes to make the physical

---

† Assistant Professor of Law, Jurisprudence & Social Thought, Amherst College. I would like to thank Robert Bezucha, Robert Burt, Frank Couvares, Owen Fiss, Stephen Gardbaum, Leah Hewitt, Nancy Pick, Austin Sarat, Martha Umphrey, Sue Vice, and James Young for their helpful comments and suggestions. William Connelly, Research Librarian at the U.S. Holocaust Memorial Museum; William Murphy, former director of the Motion Picture and Sound Department at the National Archives; and Stephen Porder provided valuable research assistance. The writing of this Essay was generously supported by a Karl Loewenstein Fellowship in Jurisprudence.

1. *See* G.M. GILBERT, NUREMBERG DIARY 49 (1947).

2. 2 TRIAL OF THE MAJOR WAR CRIMINALS BEFORE THE INTERNATIONAL MILITARY TRIBUNAL 98–99 (1947) [hereinafter IMT].

arrangements in the courtroom, so that if the Court should feel like recessing, those arrangements could be made."[3]

After the short recess, Thomas Dodd, executive counsel to the American prosecutorial team, described the purpose of the screening: "[T]his film which we offer represents in a brief and unforgettable form an explanation of what the words 'concentration camp' imply."[4] Jackson himself had mentioned the film during his opening statement, as he offered the first description of the evidence that would introduce Nazi genocide to the law's ken:

> We will show you these concentration camps in motion pictures, just as the Allied armies found them when they arrived . . . . Our proof will be disgusting and you will say I have robbed you of your sleep. . . . I am one who received during this war most atrocity tales with suspicion and scepticism. But the proof here will be so overwhelming that I venture to predict not one word I have spoken will be denied.[5]

News of the camps, of course, had been broken months before the trial: British and American newspaper reports from Buchenwald and Belsen in late April and early May of 1945 had created a sensation.[6] "'It is my duty,'" one British journalist had begun his dispatch, "'to describe something beyond the imagination of mankind.'"[7] Generals Patton and Eisenhower, as was well publicized, had ordered every soldier not committed to the front line to visit the camps.[8] Eisenhower himself had issued a terse statement, now etched into slabs of gray granite at the entrance to the U.S. Holocaust Memorial Museum in Washington, D.C.: "The things I saw beggar description . . . . I made the visit deliberately, in order to be in a position to give *first-hand* evidence of these things if ever, in the future, there develops a tendency to charge these allegations merely to 'propaganda.'"[9]

But rather than call Eisenhower to the stand, or any of the other thousands of soldiers who had been commanded to bear witness to Nazi atrocities, the prosecution turned instead to a novel witness—a documentary film.[10] This

---

3. 2 *id.* at 431.

4. 2 *id.*

5. 2 *id.* at 130.

6. Historians, however, have demonstrated that news of the Nazi camps had found its way into the American press long before the liberation of the camps. Both the *New York Times* and the *New York Herald Tribune* had published accounts of the camps as early as 1942. *See* WALTER LAQUEUR, THE TERRIBLE SECRET: SUPPRESSION OF THE TRUTH ABOUT HITLER'S "FINAL SOLUTION" 74, 93 (1980).

7. *Id.* at 2.

8. ROBERT H. ABZUG, INSIDE THE VICIOUS HEART: AMERICANS AND THE LIBERATION OF NAZI CONCENTRATION CAMPS 128 (1985).

9. Letter from General Dwight D. Eisenhower to General George C. Marshall (Apr. 15, 1945), *reprinted in* THE PAPERS OF DWIGHT DAVID EISENHOWER: THE WAR YEARS 2616 (Alfred D. Chandler ed., 1970).

10. Jackson in particular favored the use of captured documentary evidence, material he considered "harder" and less vulnerable to being discredited by defense attorneys practiced at the art of tendentious

use of film in a juridical setting was unprecedented.[11] Crime scene photography was well established in Anglo-American courts; and while the turn to filmic proof was perhaps a logical extension of available technology, it nevertheless marked a wholly new method of documenting criminality. Though motion pictures had been submitted as trial evidence as early as 1915,[12] prior to Nuremberg, one can find no records of any court using graphic film of atrocities as proof of criminal wrongdoing. The use of film was necessitated, so the prosecution argued, by the nature of the crimes the Allies had assumed the burden of proving.

The Nazis themselves had recognized that the incredible nature of their atrocities would cast long shadows of doubt upon any allegedly eyewitness reports. Primo Levi describes how inmates at concentration camps heard the frequent taunt from their captors that should they survive, their stories would not be believed: "And even if some proof should remain and some of you survive, people will say that the events you describe are too monstrous to be believed: they will say that they are the exaggerations of Allied propaganda and will believe us, who will deny everything, and not you."[13]

The concern that allegations of atrocities would be dismissed as propaganda troubled the prosecution as well. Serious evidentiary questions, after all, had plagued the war crimes trials convened after World War I. While French, British, and American newspapers covering the Great War had routinely reported rumors of German acts of civilian slaughter, rape, and infanticide, most such stories were later exposed to be the prevarications of propagandists.[14] The failure of the complaining parties (the French and British agitated to prosecute German war criminals over American objections) to support their allegations with credible evidence eroded the legitimacy of judicial proceedings anchored upon uncertain legal and jurisdictional

---

cross-examination. Prosecution counsel William Donovan's vehement argument that a greater reliance upon eyewitness testimony would have provided the trial with "an affirmative human aspect" led to his unceremonious removal from the prosecution team after the first week of the trial. *See* TELFORD TAYLOR, THE ANATOMY OF THE NUREMBERG TRIALS: A PERSONAL MEMOIR 146–49 (1992).

11. *See* ERIK BARNOUW, DOCUMENTARY: A HISTORY OF THE NON-FICTION FILM 173–75 (2d rev. ed. 1993). *See generally* ILAN AVISAR, SCREENING THE HOLOCAUST: CINEMA'S IMAGES OF THE UNIMAGINABLE (1988) (discussing representation of Holocaust in different film genres).

12. Pierre R. Paradis, *The Celluloid Witness*, 37 U. COLO. L. REV. 235, 235 (1965). In a famous early case, a "moving picture of plaintiff's performance in a vaudeville entertainment" had been introduced as evidence of the plaintiff's condition before a debilitating accident. Gibson v. Gunn, 202 N.Y.S. 19, 20 (App. Div. 1923) (per curiam), *aff'd on reh'g*, 202 N.Y.S. 927 (App. Div. 1924). The appellate court held that the film showing plaintiff's "eccentric dancing" and "comic songs" "tended to make a farce of the trial," as evidenced by the "excessive verdict returned by the jury." *Id.*

13. PRIMO LEVI, THE DROWNED AND THE SAVED 11–12 (Raymond Rosenthal trans., Vintage Int'l 1989) (1986) (paraphrasing SIMON WIESENTHAL, THE MURDERERS AMONG US (Joseph Wechsberg ed., 1967)).

14. *See* TAYLOR, *supra* note 10, at 13 (discussing reports of conduct of German troops in Belgium); *see also* JAMES F. WILLIS, PROLOGUE TO NUREMBERG: THE POLITICS AND DIPLOMACY OF PUNISHING WAR CRIMINALS OF THE FIRST WORLD WAR 12–13 (1982).

principles.[15] Concerned about this precedent, Jackson, in a report sent to the President in June 1945, wrote, "We must establish incredible events by credible evidence."[16]

In response to this dilemma, the prosecution turned to documentary film. As the prosecution readied the Army's documentary for the Nuremberg Tribunal, James Donovan, an assistant trial counsel, expressed the idea succinctly. "[T]hese motion pictures," he announced, "speak for themselves in evidencing life and death in Nazi concentration camps . . . ."[17] The filmic witness could offer pictures where speech failed; it could produce visual knowledge of atrocities that resisted summary in the words of eyewitness testimonials. Such a view echoed an understanding that both saw documentary film as capable of offering a more complete and transparent window upon the "real,"[18] and anticipated the crisis of representation that has come to characterize efforts to find an idiom capable of capturing the Holocaust's central horror.

The representational problems raised by Nazi genocide are familiar to Holocaust scholars. As Anton Kaes has observed, "The insistence on the impossibility of adequately comprehending and describing the Final Solution has by now become a *topos* of Holocaust research."[19] Lawrence Langer, to take one important example, has argued that the conventions of nineteenth-century literature rendered it "inadequate for the representation or evocation of the physical, moral, or psychological chaos" of the Holocaust.[20] Langer's examination of literature's engagement with the Holocaust finds its analog in the works of scholars such as Lucy Dawidowicz[21] and Zygmunt Bauman,[22] who have studied the struggles of historical and sociological discourses to find

15. Article 228 of the Versailles Treaty required the German government to hand over its own citizens for war crimes trials to be conducted before tribunals of the victors. An initial Allied list of individuals to be surrendered named 854 persons, including many leading military and political figures. The storm of indignation unleashed in Germany led to a compromise between the Allies and the Germans: The Germans would try those accused of war crimes before the German Supreme Court in Leipzig. The Leipzig trials concluded in acquittals or short sentences, before being formally abandoned. *See* TAYLOR, *supra* note 10, at 16–18; *see also* WILLIS, *supra* note 14, at 126–47.

16. ROBERT H. JACKSON, THE NÜRNBERG CASE 10 (Cooper Square Publishers 1971) (1947). This concern also troubled Eisenhower. His famous statement, "The things I saw beggar description," poignantly expressed the dilemma of the observer who felt the ethical obligation to bear witness, yet whose language failed to provide the means to articulate what he had seen. As such, it powerfully anticipated George Steiner's aphorism, "The world of Auschwitz lies outside speech and it lies outside reason." GEORGE STEINER, *K*, *in* LANGUAGE AND SILENCE 118, 123 (1966).

17. 2 IMT, *supra* note 2, at 433.

18. In the words of the early film critic W. Stephen Bush writing about the First World War, "The only real and incorruptible neutral in this war is not the type but the film. . . . It is utterly without bias and records and reports but does not color and distort." W. Stephen Bush, *War Films*, 21 MOVING PICTURE WORLD 1617 (1914); *see* Anton Kaes, *Holocaust and the End of History: Postmodern Historiography in Cinema*, *in* PROBING THE LIMITS OF REPRESENTATION 206, 208 (Saul Friedlander ed., 1992) (suggesting that what is not available to cognition through conventional idioms may be made available through film).

19. Kaes, *supra* note 18, at 207.

20. LAWRENCE L. LANGER, THE HOLOCAUST AND THE LITERARY IMAGINATION 15 (1975).

21. *See* LUCY S. DAWIDOWICZ, THE HOLOCAUST AND THE HISTORIANS (1981).

22. *See* ZYGMUNT BAUMAN, MODERNITY AND THE HOLOCAUST 1–30 (1989).

a form and grammar appropriate to the task of expressing the Holocaust experience.

The Nuremberg prosecution's turn to the filmic witness can thus be understood as an attempt to secure an adequate representation of "an order of reality which the human mind had never confronted before."[23] This straightforward ambition, however, yielded less than straightforward results. The film *Nazi Concentration Camps*, as we shall see, was anything but an unambiguous document, and its use by the prosecution exemplifies how imperfectly evidence of Nazi genocide was presented and digested at Nuremberg. To appreciate this, it is important to consider the unique challenge that Nazi genocide presented to the law. Distinct from history, literature, and those disciplines burdened with finding an appropriate manner of representing the Holocaust, the law had to locate an adequate idiom of both representation *and* judgment. The Nuremberg prosecution could not simply gesture toward evidence of unspeakable atrocities by darkening a courtroom and showing a film; it had to present proof that would support the pronouncement of a legal judgment.

Yet as an examination of the documentary *Nazi Concentration Camps* and the legal case in which it was enlisted as proof reveals, the task of shaping an adequate idiom of both representation *and* judgment often pulled the prosecution in opposite directions. While the film offered visual proof of astonishing atrocities, the very unprecedented nature of the crimes to which it bore witness complicated attempts at assigning blame and seemed to undermine the jurisprudential theories upon which the Allied prosecution was based. For the horror of the Nazis' crimes lay not only in their concrete detail, but also in their symbolic content. By challenging the capacity of the Nuremberg Tribunal to comprehend the practice of genocide in terms of conventional violations of ordered legality, Nazi practices threatened to expose law's limits.

A study of the prosecution's response to this challenge—its attempt to reconcile the task of representation with the burden of judgment—will highlight the power of legal discourse to frame our understanding of visual images. It will also, however, reveal how the extraordinary effort to accommodate Nazi genocide to prior conceptions of legality and criminality resulted in a failure to grasp the nature and meaning of the effort to exterminate Europe's Jewish population. Ultimately, this failure can be seen as the predictable, if not inevitable, consequence of an attempt to comprehend an unprecedented evil through an idiom whose authority is anchored in the concept of precedent—and in the belief that all crimes can and must be judged according to familiar principles filtered through past practice.

---

23. LANGER, *supra* note 20, at 3.

Yet the very failure of the Nuremberg prosecution to represent adequately the nature and meaning of Nazi genocide also constituted a juridical success. By translating evidence of unprecedented atrocity into crimes of war, the Nuremberg prosecution was able to create a coherent and judicially manageable narrative about crimes so radically alien that they seemed to defy rational and juridical explanation.

I. SCREENING *NAZI CONCENTRATION CAMPS*

If filmic testimony could supply credible, indeed irrefutable, evidence of unprecedented crimes, what exactly did the Tribunal see when the prosecution screened *Nazi Concentration Camps*? This seemingly straightforward question is critical if we are to understand how the prosecution attempted to translate images of atrocity into a coherent legal idiom. While the official transcript of the proceedings before the International Military Tribunal is helpful in reestablishing the circumstances surrounding the showing of the documentary, it also frustrates the effort. James Donovan (the assistant prosecutor who claimed the film would speak for itself) informed the court that the footage had been "compiled from motion pictures taken by Allied military photographers as the Allied armies in the West liberated the areas in which these camps were located."[24] Some 80,000 feet of tape had been edited into about 6,000 feet of film with a running time of a little over an hour.[25] The accompanying narration, Donovan noted, had been "taken directly from the reports of the military photographers who filmed the camps."[26]

According to the official transcript, "photographs were then projected on the screen showing the following affidavits while at the same time the voices of the respective affiants were reproduced reading them."[27] The first affidavit belonged to Lieutenant Colonel George C. Stevens, who was already a well-known Hollywood director before he joined the Army Signal Corps, and who in the 1950s would reach greater fame through films such as *Shane*, *A Place in the Sun*, and *The Diary of Anne Frank*. Responsible for the "photographing of the Nazi concentration camps and prison camps as liberated by Allied Forces," Stevens certified that "these motion pictures constitute a true representation of the individuals and scenes photographed."[28] The second affidavit, that of E.R. Kellog, a "director of film effects" who had examined the film, certified "that the images of these excerpts from the original negative have not been retouched, distorted or otherwise altered in any respect."[29]

24. 2 IMT, *supra* note 2, at 432–33.
25. 2 *id.* at 434.
26. 2 *id.* at 433.
27. 2 *id.*
28. 2 *id.*
29. 2 *id.* at 434.

Yet after the dramatic buildup preparing the court for the documentary, the trial transcript suddenly turns laconic:

> *[The film was then shown.]*
> COL. STOREY: That concludes the presentation.
> *[The Tribunal adjourned until 30 November 1945 at 1000 hours.]*[30]

The morning session on Friday, November 30, began without any mention of the film, as the prosecution turned from an earlier discussion of the Austrian *Anschluss* to the seizure of the Sudetenland. Yet the failure to refer to the film does not indicate that the documentary left the court unmoved. As one news account filed from the trial makes clear, the spectators were so disturbed that "[t]he presiding judges retired without a word and without announcing as usual the time set for the next session."[31] Even contemporaneous journalistic accounts, however, as well as memoirs written years later, fail to make clear what the Tribunal saw. Under the title "War-Crimes Court Sees Horror Films," the *New York Times* ran an article on November 30 that observed:

> The coolest and most collected spectators were the prisoners, whose rapt expressions were illuminated by the dimmed lights along the front of the dock. All but Schacht followed every scene of the film, leaning forward to get a better view. . . . The only other prisoner affected . . . was von Ribbentrop, who watched the first third of the film and then turned away and closed his eyes for most of the remainder, taking only an occasional glance at the screen as if urged to it by some horrible fascination.[32]

G.M. Gilbert, who served as the prison psychologist at Nuremberg, offers, however, a dramatically different account of the screening in the diary that he kept at the time:

> Funk covers his eyes . . . Sauckel mops brow . . . Frank swallows hard, blinks eyes, trying to stifle tears . . . Frank mutters "Horrible!" . . . Rosenberg fidgets, peeks at screen, bows head, looks to see how others are reacting . . . Seyss-Inquart stoic throughout . . . Speer looks very sad, swallows hard . . . Defense attorneys are now muttering, "for God's sake—terrible." . . . Fritzsche, pale, biting lips, really seems in agony . . . Doenitz has head buried in his hands . . . Keitel now hanging head.[33]

30. 2 *id.* Though this short sequence was the only description of the film's presentation in the actual trial transcript, a transcript of the film's narration was included in the volume titled "Documents and Other Material in Evidence," which was appended to the trial transcript. *See* 30 *id.* at 462–72.

31. *Atrocity Films in Court Upset Nazis' Aplomb*, N.Y. HERALD TRIB., Nov. 30, 1945, at 11; *see also Nazis on Trial See Horror Camp Film*, WASH. POST, Nov. 30, 1945, at 2.

32. Raymond Daniell, *War-Crimes Court Sees Horror Film*, N.Y. TIMES, Nov. 30, 1945, at 6.

33. GILBERT, *supra* note 1, at 45–46.

In his 1978 memoir, Airey Neave, who as a twenty-nine-year-old Oxford lawyer assisted the British prosecutorial staff at Nuremberg, described the impact of the screening upon the courtroom in somewhat different terms:

> Several in the darkened courtroom were faint or sobbed quietly at the scenes described by a burly British lieutenant-colonel as he stood among the dead and dying of Belsen. . . .
>
> . . . During the showing of the film, the dock, as a measure of security, was picked out by small spotlights. Few of the defendants could bear to watch the whole film. . . .
>
> I cannot forget the sudden vision of those twisted guilty faces . . . with tears on their cheeks. I sometimes dream of it.[34]

More recently, Telford Taylor, who served as associate trial counsel, remembered the screening in his 1992 memoir *The Anatomy of the Nuremberg Trials*:

> Dr. von der Lippe recorded that the film would rob its viewers of sleep and that he had heard one of the defense counsel say it had become intolerable to sit in the same room with men like Kaltenbrunner and Frank. Schacht turned his back on the screen to show that he had had no connection with such bestiality; Goering tried to brazen it out; the weaker ones like Ribbentrop, Frank, and Funk appeared shattered.[35]

Despite their differences, all four accounts share an interesting rhetorical feature. We are supplied with the barest description of the actual images projected in the film. Instead, we are asked to see the film voyeuristically through the eyes of not just any viewers, but of those allegedly responsible for the very atrocities captured on film. Such a technique thus supports the idea that the atrocities projected on the screen defeat and silence efforts of verbal summary. Indeed, the technique itself partakes of a cinematic logic, as the spectator, caught between voyeurism and revulsion, finally breaks his gaze away from the images of atrocity and turns toward the perpetrators. Their agitation seems baffling: We are left wondering whether the defendants had never before seen or imagined the atrocities they had orchestrated, or whether the realism of the filmic representations, their construction from an outsider's perspective, produced an awareness among the defendants greater than that gained through their engagement as Nazi functionaries.[36] The melodrama of the scene is underscored by Neave's description of the defendants' dock discreetly illuminated by small spotlights. And while Taylor recalls that the

34. AIREY NEAVE, ON TRIAL AT NUREMBERG 247 (1978).

35. TAYLOR, *supra* note 10, at 187.

36. Martha Umphrey suggested this insight in conversation.

defense counsel von der Lippe feared the film would deprive its viewers of sleep, it is not the images from the documentary that recur in Neave's dreams, but the expressions on the defendants' faces.

By focusing on the Nazi defendants, both the transcript and the memoirs unfortunately leave us in the dark about what the Tribunal saw in *Nazi Concentration Camps*. This, of course, is not accidental, as the authors of the memoirs do not resolve the defendants' legal culpability as much as presuppose it. They ask us to see the defendants through the reflection of atrocities in their eyes. By neglecting to make clear what the court actually saw in *Nazi Concentration Camps*, the journalists and memoirists only reinforce an understanding that the images "speak for themselves" as to the defendants' guilt.

Yet guilty of what? If the question seems misplaced or even grotesque given our knowledge of Nazi atrocities, it is worth recalling that the Nuremberg trial was dedicated to proving, not assuming, that the accused had engaged in criminal acts as defined by relevant law. As Taylor himself has observed, "The public showing of the film certainly hardened sentiment against the defendants generally, but it contributed little to the determination of their individual guilt."[37] Indeed, the very unnamed repulsiveness of the film's images can be seen to have complicated rather than simplified the legal issues before the Tribunal. If evidence of Nazi atrocities exhausted linguistic reserves, then how can such images be assimilated into a meaningful juridical decree? How can images of unprecedented horrors be used to support a legal judgment whose legitimacy is anchored in the concept of precedent? To answer these questions, it is necessary to turn attention away from the problem of representation to the problem of judgment, and to examine the legal idiom used by the prosecution to translate images of atrocity into a discourse of illegality.

II. Arendt on Nazi Atrocities: Exploding Law's Idiom

Even in the waning moments of the war, it was far from clear that the Allies would use the arm of the law to punish the Nazi leadership. The British, for example, resisted the idea of trying the various heads of state, favoring instead the summary execution of a dozen or so leading members of the Nazi apparatus—a symbolic yet tangible punishment of a criminal state's most visible functionaries.[38] The proposal enjoyed the virtue of simplicity. It would

37. Taylor, *supra* note 10, at 187.

38. The British proposal also enjoyed Soviet support; indeed, Stalin, in a "half-serious recommendation," suggested that 50,000 German general staff officers be shot. Such proposals arose from American circles as well: Joseph Pulitzer, the newspaper tycoon, urged in May 1945 the shooting of 1,500,000 Nazis. Morgenthau also prominently recommended that major war criminals be summarily executed. *See* István Deák, *Misjudgment at Nuremberg*, N.Y. Rev. Books, Oct. 7, 1993, at 48 & n.8 (reviewing Taylor, *supra* note 10). For histories of the competing proposals, see Taylor, *supra* note 10,

spare the Allies the tedious process of quickly organizing a vast amount of material into a legal case, and would deprive the guilty of an opportunity to vex prosecutors through dilatory tactics and legalistic casuistry. As the jurisdictional bases of any formal action against former heads of state would be vulnerable to legitimate dispute, summary execution also had the added attraction of candor: The victors would not attempt to rationalize or disguise a punishment exacted by one sovereign upon another by appeal to the neutral instrument of the law.

The British position implicitly found support among various thinkers who expressed deeper doubts about the efficacy of relying upon a legal response to atrocities perpetrated on such a vast scale. Commenting on the Nuremberg proceedings years before she would serve as the *New Yorker*'s correspondent on the Eichmann trial, Hannah Arendt observed:

> The Nazi crimes, it seems to me, explode the limits of the law; and that is precisely what constitutes their monstrousness. For these crimes, no punishment is severe enough. It may well be essential to hang Göring, but it is totally inadequate. That is, this guilt, in contrast to all criminal guilt, oversteps and shatters any and all legal systems. That is the reason why the Nazis in Nuremberg are so smug. . . . We are simply not equipped to deal, on a human, political level, with a guilt that is beyond crime . . . .[39]

While Arendt's statement remains question-begging—she never offers an understanding of "normal" criminal guilt and as a consequence fails to specify the manner in which the Nazis' crimes "explode the limits of the law"—she also gives voice to the important insight that the Nazis' crimes threaten to unsettle the most fundamental conceptions of personal responsibility, moral choice, and legal normativity upon which Western jurisprudential understandings are predicated. As such, her statement resonates with, and helps elaborate, the reasoning behind the British proposal.

Arendt does not, for example, argue that the enormity of the Nazis' crimes supplies an argument against punishment. Quite to the contrary, the need for the most extreme punishment can never be seriously questioned. Indeed, the insufficiency of even the most violent sanctions to fit the crimes only underscores the inadequacy of a legal response. If the controlling trope of Anglo-American law is the scales of justice,[40] this device is meant not only to measure the formal proof in a given case, but also to strike a balance between the wrong committed and the sanction imposed. The common

at 25–40, and Steven Fogelson, Note, *The Nuremberg Legacy: An Unfulfilled Promise*, 63 S. CAL. L. REV. 833, 836–45 (1990).

39. HANNAH ARENDT, KARL JASPERS CORRESPONDENCE 1926–1969, at 54 (Lotte Kohler & Hans Saner eds., Robert Kimber & Rita Kimber trans., 1992) (footnote omitted).

40. *See* Dennis E. Curtis & Judith Resnik, *Images of Justice*, 96 YALE L.J. 1727, 1731 (1987).

challenge to legal justice comes from the failure to strike this balance in a fair manner: The requirements of a just resolution are not satisfied when the scales are tipped in the direction of violence imposed in the law's name. The Nazis' crimes, by contrast, offer a more extraordinary challenge to this concept of legal justice, as no amount of juridically authorized violence will ever even the scales against the impossible burden of genocide. Thus the problem, as Arendt conceives it, is not that the law will fail to do justice to the defendants; rather, it is that the crimes of the defendants have so distorted the meaning of legal justice that the law will not do justice to *itself*. The Nazis' crimes, as captured in material such as *Nazi Concentration Camps*, make futile the effort to unite a jurisprudential vision with the imposition of a violent sanction.

In this regard, Arendt's critique remains metadoctrinal. The Nazis' crimes, she suggests, make embarrassingly visible the shortcomings of any jurisprudential theory that seeks to locate and anchor law's normativity in the commands of a sovereign.[41] Moreover, Nazi atrocities undermine and erode confidence in many of the foundational concepts upon which the rule of law is predicated. The belief that the state can be relied upon as the locus of legal authority, that wrongdoing proliferates only in the absence of societal rules, and that criminality is no more than an anomalous and discrete state of affairs, are all notions that can barely survive contact with the images of the concentration camps. Arendt's argument thus implicitly supports the British proposal in questioning the law's capacity to provide an adequate response to Nazi atrocities.

III. Jackson and the Prosecution's Idiom of Judgment

The Americans, however, insisted upon a juridical response to the Nazis' crimes. Murray Bernays, who largely shaped the case's jurisdictional and substantive framework, understood, in important respects, the insight that the Nazis' crimes threatened to expose law's limits.[42] For Bernays, however, it was the very seriousness of the challenge that intensified the need for a legal response. Bernays pioneered the use of the concept of criminal conspiracy as the organizing principle of the prosecution. Such a charge, he argued, could effectively link a diverse group of defendants to a broad array of crimes.[43]

Jackson formalized the broad principles of Bernays's approach into the four-count indictment: first, the conspiracy charge; second, "Crimes Against

41. For a classic statement of the positivist position, see John Austin, Lectures on Jurisprudence or the Philosophy of Positive Law (London, John Murray 1885); H.L.A. Hart, The Concept of Law 181–207 (1961).

42. The gradual rallying of support—in both American circles and abroad—for Bernays's juridical solution is well documented. *See* Taylor, *supra* note 10, at 35–42; Fogelson, *supra* note 38, at 861–67; *see also* Whitney R. Harris, Tyranny on Trial (1954).

43. Taylor, *supra* note 10, at 35–36.

the Peace," that is, the crime of waging aggressive war; third, "War Crimes"; and fourth, "Crimes Against Humanity."[44] Jackson understood that the Allies invited the charge of conducting a victor's trial by bringing criminal proceedings against former heads of state.[45] Sensitive to this critique, he insisted that it was incumbent upon the proceeding to rebut, in its form and substance, the charge that it was no more than a partisan exercise in the relativity of justice. Only in so doing, he argued, could the Tribunal claim that power and the "hand of vengeance" had been disciplined and checked by reason.[46]

For the purpose of understanding the prosecution's provocative use of *Nazi Concentration Camps*, however, it is necessary to consider how Jackson sought to rebut the objection that the Nuremberg proceeding represented no more than the imposition of the standards of one sovereign upon the leaders of another. This critique, as articulated by scholars such as Hans Kelsen,[47] specifically questioned the legal adequacy of Article I of the indictment, "Crimes Against the Peace"—the charge that emerged as the gravamen of the prosecution's case.

Whether waging a war of aggression constituted a punishable crime in positive law was a question that aroused intense debate within the prosecution itself. The French, in particular, resisted the inclusion of "Crimes Against the Peace," and argued instead that "War Crimes" and "Crimes Against Humanity" should be the focus of the Allies' case.[48] Although sound doctrinal grounds seemed to support the French position—international law and custom seemed less ambiguous in their condemnation of extermination than in their rejection of aggressive militarism—the Americans, and in particular Jackson, vehemently argued that belligerent militarism remained the greatest threat to world peace and could be understood as the proximate cause of the Nazis' other crimes.[49]

One consequence of this approach can be seen in the Tribunal's restrictive reading of the fourth count of the indictment, "Crimes Against Humanity." While such a count would seem to provide the Court with sweeping power to

44. The definitions of "Aggressive War," "War Crimes," and "Crimes Against Humanity" are provisionally offered in the "Indictment." *See* 1 IMT, *supra* note 2, at 27–68. The Americans were responsible for presenting the case for the first count, the British presented the second, and the French and Russians jointly presented the third and fourth counts.

45. Some legal scholars have attempted to answer the victor's trial charge by pointing out that all criminal trials are, in a sense, victor's trials—as the presence of any defendant in a courtroom already speaks of the victory of the state's powers of detection and discipline over the accused. More specifically, Herbert Wechsler, who served as a legal adviser to Judge Biddle, pointed out that crimes such as treason rely upon a logic not dissimilar from that employed by the Tribunal. *See* HERBERT WECHSLER, *The Issues of the Nuremberg Trial*, *in* PRINCIPLES, POLITICS, AND FUNDAMENTAL LAW 138, 144–45 (1961). A rejoinder and fresh elaboration of the victor's trial critique is offered by Deák, *supra* note 38, at 51–52.

46. 3 IMT, *supra* note 2, at 99.

47. Hans Kelsen, *Will the Judgment in the Nuremberg Trial Constitute a Precedent in International Law?*, 1 INT'L L.Q. 153, 154–59 (1947).

48. *See* TAYLOR, *supra* note 10, at 64–67.

49. *See id.* at 76–77.

act in defense of "universal" human rights, the Tribunal interpreted the London Charter (the international agreement that called into being the Nuremberg proceedings and defined the Tribunal's jurisdiction) as restricting its authority and allowing punishment of such offenses *only* if committed in furtherance of "planning, preparation, initiation or waging of a war of aggression."[50] As Jackson expressed the idea: "Th[e] attack on the peace of the world is the crime against international society which brings into international cognizance crimes in its aid and preparation which otherwise might be only internal concerns."[51] Thus, under this interpretation, whatever crimes against humanity the Nazis committed against German citizens before the Wehrmacht crossed the Polish border did not fall under the jurisdiction of the Nuremberg court. At the heart of this position were the Allies' (principally the Russians', though the Americans' as well) worries that too robust a concept of crimes against humanity would supply a potentially unattractive precedent for challenging a sovereign's control over its own domestic population. As a jurisprudential matter, then, the prosecuting authorities' decision to focus on aggressive warfare led to a restrictive reading of the charge that covered the Nazis' worst atrocities.[52] Against the rights of humanity, Nuremberg deferred to the superior claims of sovereignty.

The result of refusing to consider crimes against humanity as a punishable offense independent of any connection to the crime of waging aggressive war was that the soundness of this count of the indictment rested upon the legitimacy of the "Crimes Against the Peace" count.[53] On one level, this

50. 1 IMT, *supra* note 2, at 11. The reasons for the Tribunal's restrictive reading of the fourth count are largely a result of the Charter's restrictive definition of the conspiracy charge which, in its final form, only applied to the aggressive war charge. Thus Article 6 of the Charter, as finally agreed on, did not include a charge of conspiracy to commit war crimes or other atrocities. As Taylor has argued, this was a "disastrous blow" to Bernays's original proposal, as the very logic of the conspiracy charge was to criminalize prewar atrocities. Why Jackson acceded to this modification of the Charter is not completely clear. Taylor argues that Jackson "either overlooked the effect of the change or did not care; for him the conspiracy charge had always been important primarily in aid of proving individual guilt for waging aggressive war, and its role as a device for criminalizing prewar atrocities may not have been in the forefront of his mind." TAYLOR, *supra* note 10, at 76. Though the prosecution during the trial tried to include prewar atrocities as actionable under the conspiracy charge, the Tribunal interpreted Article 6 to apply exclusively to the charge of waging aggressive war.

51. 2 IMT, *supra* note 2, at 103.

52. Of course, the Allies also had sound doctrinal reasons for restricting the crimes against humanity charge to acts committed in furtherance of the war of aggression, as international law and custom did not offer firm support for the authority of one sovereignty to pass judgment on the leaders of another sovereignty for their treatment of their own domestic population. *See* ROBERT K. WOETZEL, THE NUREMBERG TRIALS IN INTERNATIONAL LAW 184 (1960). As Woetzel put this point:

> Thus, even if the acts of nationals of one state against citizens of the same state amounted to the most flagrant violations of fundamental principles of civilised behaviour as recognised by most nations, it is not certain that this fact alone would constitute sufficient legal basis for holding individuals criminally responsible for them.

Id.

53. Unfortunately, however, this count has not escaped vociferous challenge. This attack, a variation of the positivist critique, insists on the basic similarity between the actions of the vanquished and the victor. Nations throughout history, the argument goes, have used warfare as a means of advancing diplomatic and strategic ends; to treat such behavior as criminal is simply to increase the penalties for the defeated's

appeared a questionable move, as notwithstanding Jackson's attempts to appeal to a body of international law, treaty, and custom,[54] many commentators have remained unconvinced by the attempt to criminalize aggressive war.[55] On another level, however, Jackson's jurisprudential argument can be understood as mindful of Arendt's concern that the Nazis' crimes glaringly revealed law's limits. By treating crimes against humanity as ancillary to the principal crime of military aggression, Jackson's approach shifted attention away from those atrocities that presented, in Arendt's mind, the greatest challenge to the concept of ordered legality. While criminalizing military belligerence can be dismissed as an exercise in futility, the *acts* that Jackson sought to punish can be seen as less disruptive of jurisprudential assumptions than genocide. Genocide, as Arendt suggests, undermines confidence in all jurisprudential understandings, be they inspired by natural or positive law traditions. The criminalization of aggressive warfare, unusual as this may be, represents no more than the extension of legal principles that control domestic conduct into relations between nations. As Sir Hartley Shawcross declared in his opening statement for the British prosecution: "If murder, rapine, and robbery are indictable under the ordinary municipal laws of our countries, shall those who differ from the common criminal only by the extent and systematic nature of their offenses escape accusation?"[56]

This attempt to cast extraordinary legal arguments in terms of conventional legal understandings is best captured in the analogy Jackson drew between international and common law:

> [International law] grows, as did the common law, through decisions reached from time to time in adapting settled principles to new situations. The fact is that when the law evolves by the case method, as did the common law and as international law must do if it is to

ultimate crime: losing. A victor's trial represents no more than the attempt to exact punishment for the defeated's failure to win. Indeed, this argument found widespread sympathy within the allied prosecution, particularly among the French. As one member of the French prosecution declared, "'We do not consider as a criminal violation the launching of a war of aggression.'" TAYLOR, *supra* note 10, at 65–66. Though the French ultimately agreed to the American plan, they continued to believe that the "war crimes" and "crimes against humanity" charges should have remained the gravamen of the complaint. For a positivist critique of the aggressive war charge, see Kelsen, *supra* note 47, at 156–59, and for a more general polemic against the trial, see WERNER MASER, NÜRNBERG: TRIBUNAL DER SIEGER 517–608 (1977).

54. Though the Americans were formally charged with presenting the first count of the indictment (the conspiracy count), this charge essentially presented Jackson with the opportunity to examine extensively the second count (waging aggressive war). *See* Fogelson, *supra* note 38, at 850.

55. Jackson was correct that the Briand-Kellogg Pact, adopted by the League of Nations in 1928 with Germany as a signatory, banned the waging of aggressive war, and thus seemed to tender the positive law basis for criminalizing the waging of aggressive war. But the Pact also famously failed to define the meaning of "aggressive war," neglected to specify who may supply the missing definition, and left unanswered what sanctions could be levied against a violator and by whom. *See* Kelsen, *supra* note 47, at 156–59; *see also* Otto Kranzbuhler, *Nuremberg Eighteen Years Afterwards*, 14 DEPAUL L. REV. 333, 343–45 (1965) (noting difficulty in defining and assigning blame for crime of aggressive war).

56. 3 IMT, *supra* note 2, at 92.

> advance at all, it advances at the expense of those who wrongly guessed the law and learned too late their error.[57]

By appealing to the example and positive presence of the common law, Jackson brilliantly attempted to preserve the available idiom of the law while enlisting it to give order to a realm that had never been adequately and intelligibly subjected to legal administration and judgment. In so doing, Jackson extended the common law method to a metadoctrinal level: The specific case no longer supplies the precedent to the subsequent holding; now it is the very method of lawmaking through judicial accretion that supplies the precedent for, and thus legitimizes, the Tribunal's power to reach a legal decision. Thus, by asking his audience to imagine international law as a subspecies of domestic common law (instead of vice versa), Jackson was able to stretch the law's power of legitimate sanction without altering its basic and familiar idiom.

Nuremberg, for Jackson, was ultimately an exercise in law's self-reconstitution. The Tribunal, he argued, had not only to demonstrate that it was a neutral forum of judgment; it had to demonstrate law's power to reintroduce its ordering effects—both administratively and normatively understood—into a space of spectacular excess and egregious lawlessness.[58] By conceptualizing the pathologies of modern warfare as legally cognizable and punishable crimes, and by legitimatizing the Tribunal's power to exercise jurisdiction over these wrongs through appeal to the common law, Jackson showed how law's conventional idiom could be modified to discipline the most extreme excesses. In contrast to Arendt's focus on genocide, Jackson shifted the Tribunal's attention to the widespread, but judicially manageable, crimes of belligerent militarism.

IV. The Tension Between Representation and Judgment: The Plight of the Camera

If Jackson attempted to justify criminalizing aggressive militarism by speaking the familiar (at least in Anglo-American circles) language of the common law, how does this explain the prosecution's use of *Nazi Concentration Camps*? We have already observed that the statements of the prosecution that the images "speak for themselves," while perhaps useful in justifying the introduction of the film as a witness, also threatened to unsettle

57. 2 *id.* at 147.

58. Arendt, by contrast, seems to understand the application of positive laws in much the same way as the modern physicist understands the application of physical laws. They are capable of controlling the behavior of conventional objects, yet become stretched beyond meaning when they are applied to extraordinarily large and refractory phenomena. Jackson, however, believed the law's power to control conventional situations demonstrated its power to control extremes.

any effort to reconcile the outrages captured on film with Jackson's theory of the prosecution's case. Indeed, for his theory to be consistent, Jackson had to maintain exactly what the prosecution tacitly called into question by introducing the filmic testimony. He had to claim that the images did not exhaust law's capacity to unite proof of criminal wrongdoing with a just and measured punishment. With this tension in mind, how can one harmonize the evidence presented to one's eyes with Jackson's unusual, yet in many respects, deeply conventional, idiom of criminality?

To view *Nazi Concentration Camps* today unfortunately provides an imperfect idea of what the Tribunal saw fifty years ago. The horror captured in *Nazi Concentration Camps* is by now so familiar that it is difficult to imagine an original screening—that is, a screening that shocks not simply because of the barbarity of the images, but also because of their novelty. By familiar, however, I do not mean to suggest that the actual images shown in the film trigger the same visual recognition of, for example, the Zapruder film of the Kennedy assassination—though the scenes of British soldiers bulldozing heaps of rotting corpses into mass graves at Bergen-Belsen certainly remain among the most harrowing and recognizable documentary footage associated with the end of the war. Rather, I mean to suggest that the filmic landscape that we inhabit is very much the visual legacy of films such as this, a cultural universe defined by the production and circulation of graphic images of extreme violence.

Film had, of course, discovered the allure of warfare on the battlefields of the First World War, when battle sequences were shown in weekly British and American news reels.[59] Yet these films rarely showed graphic shots of the war dead.[60] Indeed, as George Roeder has observed, because of "the technical limitations of early twentieth century photography, the most striking images to come out of World War I were written ones."[61] Earlier still, Mathew Brady's photography of the Civil War had demonstrated the special relationship between photography and death: how the stillness of the image demonstrates formal affinities with death's repose (in an age of slow shutter speeds, the dead struck the most cooperative poses).[62] Perhaps not coincidentally, George C.

59. MICHAEL T. ISENBERG, WAR ON FILM: THE AMERICAN CINEMA AND WORLD WAR I, 1914–1941 *passim* (1981).

60. *See id.* at 74.

61. GEORGE H. ROEDER, JR., THE CENSORED WAR: AMERICAN VISUAL EXPERIENCE DURING WORLD WAR TWO 17 (1993).

62. A pictorial album of Brady's photography is provided in JAMES D. HORAN, MATHEW BRADY: HISTORIAN WITH A CAMERA (1955). Barthes, for example, drew attention to "that rather terrible thing which is there in every photograph: the return of the dead." Michael Renov, *Toward a Poetics of Documentary*, *in* THEORIZING DOCUMENTARY 12, 25 (Michael Renov ed., 1993) (citing ROLAND BARTHES, CAMERA LUCIDA: REFLECTIONS ON PHOTOGRAPHY 9 (Richard Howard trans., 1981)). But the relationship between photography and death that Barthes named is very different from what I have in mind. If Barthes intended to identify the eerie temporality of photography, the image's resistance to the decay of that which it represents, war photography discovers a disturbing harmony between the dead subject and the still image. (For a remarkable study of the aesthetics of the photographed murder victim, see LUC SANTE, EVIDENCE

Stevens was a great admirer of Mathew Brady's work—he owned, at the end of his life, a large collection of the Unionist's photographs.[63] But by ushering film into a new, and at the time, unknown terrain of violence and horror, Stevens's *Nazi Concentration Camps* did less to extend Brady's legacy than to exhaust it.[64]

In this regard, the magnitude of the atrocities committed as well as the clarity and immediacy of the film's representations seemed unprecedented.[65] Commenting on the photographic stills from the camps, Susan Sontag writes:

> Nothing I have seen—in photographs or in real life—ever cut me as sharply, deeply, instantaneously. Indeed, it seems plausible to me to divide my life into two parts, before I saw those photographs (I was twelve) and after . . . . When I looked at those photographs, something broke. Some limit had been reached, and not only that of horror . . . .[66]

By providing a visual register of atrocity, *Nazi Concentration Camps* crossed a threshold of representation from which there was no turning back. But if our presence in a culture saturated with images of extreme violence makes it difficult to view the documentary with the innocence of the contemporaneous spectator, it also makes it easier, less sacrilegious, to consider critically what we have seen. Because we have seen these images before, we are free, as the first observers were not, to examine their structure, meaning, and uses as representations.

Nazi Concentration Camps begins by testifying to its own authenticity. The trial transcript, as we have seen, notes that pictures of various affidavits

---

(1992)). Film, by contrast, provides the documentation not of death's stillness, but of the instant of its violent intrusion.

63. *See* MAX HASTINGS, VICTORY IN EUROPE 10 (1985).

64. One could argue that it is only fitting that George C. Stevens should be credited with the film, as the very innocence of the cinematic art is registered upon the prewar work of this popular Hollywood director. Esteemed for his romantic comedies, Stevens's work typified a cinematic vision that united an at-times edgy critical eye with a fundamentally benign outlook on the nation. If he searched for fresh and entertaining twists on the romantic struggle between individual and society, the range of reality known to Stevens's films largely exhausted the world as known to American film: Images of frustrated courtship and working class hardship were digested in a larger mosaic of honest individuals searching for meaning among local attachments. Although *Nazi Concentration Camps* displays many of the virtues that distinguished Stevens's filmmaking—classically framed panoramas that dissolve into fastidiously composed close-ups, arresting stills, unsettling juxtapositions—these technical gifts find themselves now enlisted to create a work that explodes the very filmic universe his Hollywood career had served to build. *See generally* DONALD RICHIE, GEORGE STEVENS: AN AMERICAN ROMANTIC (photo. reprint 1985) (1970).

65. Yet as George Roeder has demonstrated, the censoring and suppression within the United States of horrific battlefield images from the American theater in World War II intensified and complicated the response to film of German atrocities. Pictures of horrors from culturally remote areas—such as those committed by the Japanese upon the Chinese—were, by contrast, more widely circulated. ROEDER, *supra* note 61, at 125–27.

66. SUSAN SONTAG, ON PHOTOGRAPHY 20 (1977). Yet, once this limit has been reached, Sontag notes how quickly the individual becomes immune to any effect the photographs might originally have had: "Once one has seen such images, one has started down the road of seeing more—and more. . . . The shock of photographed atrocities wears off with repeated viewings . . . ." *Id.*

supporting the film's accuracy were projected before the Nuremberg court. What the transcript fails to make clear, however, is that these affidavits are part of the film itself, and the voice that reads them aloud is part of the sound track. This gesture of self-authentication thus supports the novel understanding of the documentary as a privileged witness independently competent to swear to the truth of its own images.

On a procedural level, however, this unorthodox submission of affidavits remains significant, as it draws our attention to the relaxed rules of proof that governed the Tribunal's proceedings and permitted the prosecution to introduce the film as evidence.[67] The standard of admissibility of filmic proof, at least in Anglo-American jurisprudence, centered on the doctrine of the authenticating witness.[68] This doctrine, which continued to control in certain jurisdictions until well after Nuremberg, maintained that "[t]he motion picture does not of itself prove an actual occurrence but the thing reproduced must be established by the testimony of witness."[69] As a piece of "demonstrative evidence" (evidence used to represent a state of affairs, as distinct from "real" evidence such as hair samples, etc.[70]), film was admissible "when it [was] shown that it [was] a correct likeness of the persons or objects which it purport[ed] to represent . . . ."[71] Not surprisingly, what constituted a "correct likeness" was a question that excited considerable judicial debate.[72] Yet because film was conceptualized as dependent upon the corroboration of eyewitness testimony,[73] it was often barred not because of its inaccuracy, but

67. The Nuremberg prosecution, of course, did not wholly eschew the use of eyewitnesses. As already noted, Jackson, in a notable struggle with other members of the prosecution, sought to restrict the use of eyewitnesses. The prosecution's heavy reliance upon affidavits and documentary evidence had, however, the consequence of quickly turning the spectacular proceeding into a terrifically tedious affair. For an evocation of this tedium, see, e.g., REBECCA WEST, A TRAIN OF POWDER 1–22 (1955). For a discussion of the prosecution's use of documentary evidence, see JOHN MENDELSOHN, TRIAL BY DOCUMENT: THE USE OF SEIZED RECORDS IN THE UNITED STATES PROCEEDINGS AT NÜRNBERG 15–18, 95–109 (1988); John Mendelsohn, *Trial by Document: The Problem of Due Process for War Criminals at Nuernberg*, 7 PROLOGUE 227, 227–34 (1975). Finally, *Nazi Concentration Camps* was not the only film screened at Nuremberg. The prosecution showed sections of films made by the Nazis themselves (including footage from Leni Riefenstahl's *Triumph of the Will*, *see* 3 IMT, *supra* note 2, at 400–02; TAYLOR, *supra* note 10, at 200), as well as films documenting atrocities in the east, *see* 7 IMT, *supra* note 2, at 601, and a pogrom in a Jewish ghetto, *see* 3 *id.* at 536. These films, however, were not placed at the rhetorical center of the prosecution's case as was *Nazi Concentration Camps*.

68. *See* Paradis, *supra* note 12, at 235–47.

69. *Id.* at 250 (citing UAW v. Russell, 88 So. 2d 175 (Ala. 1956), *aff'd*, 356 U.S. 634 (1958)); *see also* Beattie v. Traynor, 49 A.2d 200, 204 (Vt. 1946) ("A photograph . . . is merely a witness' pictured expression of the data observed by him . . . and its admission when properly verified, rests on the relevancy of the fact pictured.").

70. *See* Paradis, *supra* note 12, at 250.

71. *Id.* at 237 (quoting Kortz v. Guardian Life Ins. Co. of America, 144 F.2d 676 (10th Cir. 1944)).

72. Although the Nuremberg prosecution conceptualized film as the ideal neutral and veracious witness, early courts evinced a wariness toward filmic testimony. *See, e.g.*, Massachusetts Bonding v. Worthy, 9 S.W.2d 388, 393 (Tex. Civ. App. 1928) ("It is a matter of common knowledge that pictures showing a person in action may be made very deceptive . . . .").

73. "[T]he mere picture . . . cannot be received except as a non-verbal expression to the *testimony of some witness* competent to speak to the facts represented." 3 JOHN H. WIGMORE, WIGMORE ON EVIDENCE § 790, at 218–19 (James H. Chadbourn ed., rev. ed. 1970).

because of its redundancy: It offered no more than a needless repetition of information already supplied by the superior eyewitness.[74] Furthermore, the failure to support filmic evidence with eyewitness testimony was also fatal, as the film would then be barred as hearsay. Without in-court corroboration, such evidence would provide no more than a declaration of material fact made by an out-of-court witness unavailable for adversarial cross-examination—the very definition of hearsay. Finally, of importance to the Nuremberg Tribunal, certain American jurisdictions had barred photographic proof not because it was cumulative or hearsay, but because it was "gruesome": Graphic pictures of injuries had been declared inadmissible in certain suits because their relevance as evidence was outweighed by their potential for prejudicing a jury.[75]

The enabling charter of the Nuremberg Tribunal solved these evidentiary problems by the simplest means possible: It declared that the trial would "not be bound by technical rules of evidence." The Tribunal, the charter declared, "shall adopt and apply to the greatest possible extent expeditious and non-technical procedure, and shall admit any evidence which it deems to have probative value."[76] The application of these relaxed evidentiary conventions was tested early in the trial when the defense vigorously objected to the prosecution's use of sworn affidavits of persons who could have been called to testify in court (a practice which, as we shall see, played a significant role in the screening of *Nazi Concentration Camps*). In response to the defense's objection, Jackson argued: "This Tribunal sits under a Charter which recognized the impossibility of covering a decade of time, a continent of space, a million acts, by ordinary rules of proof, and at the same time finishing this case within the lives of living men."[77] Exigency alone, however, did not justify these relaxed conventions of proof. The absence of a jury, Jackson argued, supported the idea that the war crimes trial was "no occasion for applying jury rules";[78] judges, as distinct from lay persons, could weigh the relevance of hearsay testimony and would be less susceptible to being swayed by tendentious or prejudicial arguments. The very idea of convening a military tribunal "instead of an ordinary court of law," he argued, "was in order to avoid the precedent-creating effect of what is done here on our own law and the precedent control which would exist if this were an ordinary judicial body."[79] Thus, while the trial itself was meant to supply a critical precedent for the articulation and defense of principles of international law, the

74. *See* Paradis, *supra* note 12, at 257–60.

75. *See, e.g.*, United States v. 88 Cases, More or Less, Containing Bireley's Orange Beverage, 187 F.2d 967, 975 (3d Cir.), *cert. denied*, 342 U.S. 861 (1951) (holding that trial court erred in admitting into evidence pictures of guinea pigs dying in agony from Vitamin C deficiency after being put on diet of orange drink).

76. London Agreement, Aug. 8, 1945, sec. V, art. 19, *reprinted in* 1 IMT, *supra* note 2, at 15.

77. 3 IMT, *supra* note 2, at 543.

78. 3 *id.*

79. 3 *id.*

procedures that governed the conduct of the trial were deemed to except themselves from ordinary rules of evidence. Remarkable in this argument is the implication that ordinary evidentiary conventions both slow a trial and render it a blunter instrument for securing historical truth. By permitting evidence such as that supplied by the documentary *Nazi Concentration Camps*, the Tribunal acted not only in the interest of efficiency, but also in the interest of securing the most reliable and complete representations of unspeakable atrocities.

This observation is reinforced by the film's interesting soundtrack. The stentorian voices that read aloud the two affidavits lead us to assume that we are hearing George Stevens and E.R. Kellog in person, until the documentary's narration begins, speaking in the same professional voice we took to be Kellog's. It is only then that we realize that the transcript is wrong in reporting that "the voices of the respective affiants were reproduced reading them."[80] In fact, we are listening to an unnamed narrator, who, by standing in for Stevens and Kellog, claims a central omniscience as the speaker of what the camera sees. The narrator thus supplies the voice not of a military historian or soldier witnessing the liberation of the camps, but of the camera itself. As such, it seems to speak with the same objectivity that the images claim for themselves.

The film fades to a map of Europe, marked by its prewar borders, upon which appear, in rapid proliferation, the names not of nations and capitals, but of obscure locales, until the center of the continent is crowded with the names of the *Lagers* (concentration camps). During the course of its presentation, the documentary visits a dozen of these camps, each of which is treated discretely and introduced with a graphic of a chipped brick wall upon which is superimposed, in block letters, PENIG (sic) CONCENTRATION CAMP, OHRDRUF CONCENTRATION CAMP, NORDHAUSEN CONCENTRATION CAMP, BUCHENWALD CONCENTRATION CAMP, DACHAU CONCENTRATION CAMP. Upon this brick wall appears what looks like a splattering of blood, though it is difficult to say, as the film is shot entirely in that finely shaded black and white that has powerfully overdetermined our images of the period. *Nazi Concentration Camps*, however, could have been a color film. Technicolor, though an expensive process, was available at the time of the liberation of the camps; and Stevens filmed much of the footage from Dachau with the same hand-held color camera with which he had kept a personal filmic diary of the making of his popular *Gunga Din*.[81] The Army, however, fearing that the three-track projectors necessary for showing Technicolor films would be unavailable in courtrooms and movie

80. 2 *id.* at 433.

81. *See* GEORGE STEVENS: A FILMMAKER'S JOURNEY (Castle Hill Productions 1984). Stevens's color footage can be seen at the U.S. Holocaust Memorial Museum.

houses, decided to rely exclusively on monochrome for its documentaries, a decision that was instrumental in shaping persistent cultural images of the Holocaust as an event that unfolded in black and white.[82]

The film begins with the camp in Leipzig, where shortly before the liberation hundreds of prisoners were locked in a barrack and torched alive by the retreating Nazis. The camera shows the scar of the building upon the blackened earth surrounded by dirty snow, and then draws close, examining the brittle remains of burnt corpses. It is an image that defines the visual legend of the film, which does not capture the active commission of atrocities, but focuses instead on the wounds they leave behind—upon the earth, the dead, and the survivors. Such images powerfully suggest belatedness: The liberators have arrived, but they have come too late. No specific regimen of punishments could have reduced the victims to this horrific state, the film seems to say. Only a vast and systematic pattern of perverse cruelty could account for the magnitude of the wounds seen by the camera.

At times the camera rebels against its own belatedness, as when it relies upon reenactments to make vivid the horror. Yet these moments are the film's least effective: Russian POWs, recreating how they would scavenge for food in camp garbage, turn what was a cruel competition for survival into a comradely jostling for the camera, their faces creased with smiles. Equally awkward are those moments when the camera overly aestheticizes its subject. The film offers a close-up through the camp's fence of a bearded camp survivor, his head framed by a rectangle of barbed wire. The frame within the frame, a perfectly adequate and appropriate technique for a Hollywood shot, seems in this context mannered and indecent.[83] Indeed, the man's grim vanquished stare haunts not simply because it abandons any pretense of posturing for the camera, but because it suggests contempt toward this self-conscious effort to aestheticize his experience. The image succeeds despite itself, for it draws attention to the horror of the survivor through the plight of the camera.

The camera struggles to find the proper perspective, the appropriate angle from which the camps should be seen. While it is commonplace today to speak of the camera's exclusions and aggressions,[84] in *Nazi Concentration Camps* we catch glimpses of a more unusual phenomenon: the camera's confusion and

82. Steven Spielberg, for example, describing his choice to film *Schindler's List* in black and white, stated, "I knew *Schindler's List* had to be black and white, the moment I decided to make the movie." Zoë Heller, *The Real Thing*, THE INDEPENDENT (London), May 23, 1993, at 24. By contrast, Alain Resnais relied upon the juxtaposition between documentary footage in black and white and contemporary footage in color for much of the unsettling force of his 1955 film, *Night and Fog*.

83. For an instructive discussion of the difficulty and indecency of aestheticizing horror in photographs, see JANET MALCOLM, *The View from Plato's Cave*, *reprinted in* DIANA AND NIKON: ESSAYS ON THE AESTHETIC OF PHOTOGRAPHY 75 (1980).

84. *See, e.g.*, BILL NICHOLS, REPRESENTING REALITY: ISSUES AND CONCEPTS IN DOCUMENTARY 7 (1991); *see also* SONTAG, *supra* note 66, at 7 ("There is an aggression implicit in every use of the camera.").

embarrassment. Its efforts to occupy a position of detached neutral observation—the putatively privileged position of the realist documentary[85]—merely call attention to a central confusion that leaves its traces throughout the film. Even those moments when the survivors treat the camera as invisible are unnerving, as we are so accustomed to posing for a photograph that the subjects' capacity to stare past the camera's gaze becomes revealing. Close-ups of former inmates show the twisted facial geometries and afflicted eyes of the demented. Their very obliviousness to the filming eye, the absence of any defense against the camera's intrusions, makes their isolation and despair manifest. The camera functions, then, less as the invisible witness imagined by theorists of realist documentary and members of the Nuremberg prosecution. Instead, it serves to provoke—we learn of the survivors' world through their reaction (or lack of one) to the lens's awkward probings.

At other times, it is the survivors' awareness of the camera that provides moments of inadvertent revelation. In a peculiar shot, three former inmates are caught posing not for the filmmaker, but for a still photographer also captured within the documentary's frame. In the shot within the shot, we see the three survivors—two emaciated men, stripped to their waists, seated on either side of a third, standing, clothed in layers of rags—directing gaunt and macabre smiles toward the photographer, like three members of a grotesque reunion. Here, however, it is the absurdity of their efforts to satisfy the roseate expectations of the camera that creates a haunting image.

In another shot, an attractive woman lifts her skirt to reveal puncture wounds upon her buttocks inflicted by Nazi torturers. She is filmed, for unknown reasons, standing on the rooftop of an apartment building, and as she stares over her shoulder back at the camera, her skirt gathered at her waist, we can see, stretching behind her, the ruins of a bombed and ravaged township. The film thus connects the woman's body to the townscape: All forms of property have been violated by the Nazis. Yet the very effort to document the Nazis' sexual cruelty inadvertently creates a pornographic moment, as the film offers her body as an object to be voyeuristically surveyed.[86]

But the most remarkable, if not grotesque, instance of filmic posturing occurs in a sequence in which the camera interrogates a former American POW at the Mauthausen camp. Up until this point, the film has been guided exclusively by the voiceover of the invisible narrator. Now, as the camera focuses upon this handsome young American who towers above the other liberated POWs crowding about him, we hear, for the first time, the voice of a person *in* the film. Compared to the walking corpses and bedridden patients that largely people the film, the American soldier makes a healthy, even robust

85. *See* WILLIAM GUYNN, A CINEMA OF NONFICTION (1990).

86. For an examination of how efforts to critique the pornographic recapitulate its representational logic, see SUSAN STEWART, CRIMES OF WRITING: PROBLEMS IN THE CONTAINMENT OF REPRESENTATION 235–72 (1991).

impression. As he stands before the camera, he begins his grim narrative with a rather buoyant introduction—"'I am Lt. (senior grade) Jack H. Taylor, U.S. Navy, from Hollywood, California'"—and then adds, "'Believe it or not, this is the first time I have ever been in the movies.'"[87] The burden of credibility falls, then, not upon his enumeration of the various forms of execution used at the Mauthausen camp—"by gas, by shooting, by beating, that is beating with clubs, by exposure, that is standing out in the snow naked for 48 hours and having cold water thrown on them in the middle of winter—starvation—dogs—and pushing over a hundred-foot cliff"[88]—but rather upon the fortuity of his appearance on the big screen. And as the camera moves from his healthy complexion to mass graves, we glimpse the perverse logic behind his ironic celebration of his filmic debut.

The horrors mount and intensify as the film journeys to the camps at Buchenwald, Dachau, and Bergen-Belsen. The camera lingers upon naked, emaciated bodies strewn upon a barrack floor. Suddenly, one twitches and we realize that unlike the other mounds of corpses, these people are, in fact, alive. It is a jarring moment, as what appears a "still" turns into a moving image. "These are the survivors,"[89] comments the narrator laconically. The documentary concludes with the now-famous footage of British bulldozers pushing a veritable mountain of bodies into a mass grave. As the dead and dirt cascade down the deep pit, the narrator ends with the flat declaration, "This was Bergen-Belsen."[90] The horrific images render any additional verbal summary or commentary superfluous.

Yet just as the documentary calls attention, however inadvertently, to the camera's intrusions, it relies upon a final, notable rhetorical technique to authenticate what it has seen: Lest anyone doubt the veracity of its images, the documentary provides shot after shot of eyewitnesses viewing the very legacy of atrocities that the film records. We watch Generals Eisenhower, Bradley, and Patton examine, ashen-faced, the camps; we track the journey of a delegation of congressmen; we follow the footsteps of GIs filing past rows of bodies. The technique harks back to the affidavits that swear to the film's authenticity. Again, the documentary supplies within its own frame witnesses to corroborate the truth of its representations.

The spectacle of witnessing the act of witnessing serves a further end distinct from evidentiary interests. Many of the film's most powerful images are shots of Germans forced to bear witness to Nazi barbarity. From a field of rotting exhumed corpses, the film cuts suddenly to a promenade of smiling Weimar women, dressed in their Sunday best, strolling along a tree-lined road, on their way to view the camps by "invitation" of the Americans. Compelled

87. 30 IMT, *supra* note 2, at 462, 467.
88. 30 *id.* at 468.
89. 30 *id.* at 470.
90. 30 *id.* at 472.

to witness the legacy of Nazi atrocities, the "good" German citizens are later captured in various attitudes of disgust and distress, stifling sobs or nausea by burying their faces in handkerchiefs.[91] These scenes reappear throughout the film. The memoirists' device of depicting the screening of the film at the trial through a description of the reaction of the defendants[92] thus powerfully echoes the visual structure of the film itself. And if the scenes of Germans pressing tightly balled kerchiefs to their faces anticipate the memoirists' portraits of the defendants, they also present the same problems implicitly raised by the works of Gilbert, Neaves, and Taylor. For the trial eschewed precisely the argument to which the film and the memoirists seem committed: that the German people shared in the deeper culpability for the atrocities perpetrated by their leaders and state. In his opening statement, Jackson specifically declared that the prosecution did not seek to condemn a nation in its entirety: "[W]e have no purpose to incriminate the whole German people."[93] The film, by contrast, offers no such guarantees, as it disperses responsibility for what happened to those who became complicitous in crimes through the tacit and cowardly tolerance of places they chose to know nothing about.[94]

Yet the sanction imposed upon the citizens living in the environs of Dachau and Buchenwald ultimately is no more than the punishment of *witnessing*. It is, in certain respects, an odd punishment, for although we might take grim satisfaction in watching the Germans forced to confront the legacy of their shame and quiescence, the film places the "innocent" viewer in much the same position as the German civilians. While there is presumably a significant difference between being forced to witness such horrors first-hand and viewing them through the camera's mediation, we have also noted that the prosecution's very reliance upon film was meant to belie this distinction. If we think of the act of viewing as a sanction, then the film seems to impose virtually the same punishment upon us.

The act of coerced witnessing suggests itself as an appropriate response to the civilians' quiescence, less because the punishment fits the crime than because it violently abrogates it. Whatever evasions and duplicities permitted a person to sweep the camps from his or her frame of vision during the war

91. The documentary erroneously attributes this footage, which includes shots of Germans filing past a table displaying flayed human skin and shrunken heads prepared by the Nazis, to the liberation of Arnstadt Concentration Camp. In fact, the footage is from Buchenwald, a fact corrected in the published transcript of the documentary. *See* 30 *id.* at 469.

92. *See supra* notes 32–37 and accompanying text.

93. 2 IMT, *supra* note 2, at 102.

94. In a remarkable column in *The Nation*, James Agee condemned the showing of clips of atrocity films in the United States precisely because such films "pin the guilt for these atrocities on the whole German people." James Agee, *Films*, THE NATION, May 19, 1945, at 579. Dismissing the films as mere "propaganda," Agee pointed out "I have not felt it necessary to see the films themselves." *Id.* He further claimed that the showing of such pictures makes Americans worse "in some respects, than the Nazis," for such screenings have the effect of spreading blame over the entire German citizenry. *Id.*

cannot survive contact with the world captured on film. The film does not simply instruct or produce visual knowledge of atrocity; rather, it overwhelms one's senses, creating an irrefutable imprint upon the mind, a trauma of sight. The ultimate coercion issues not from the conquering army that commands the act of witnessing, but from the tangible evidence of atrocity itself. The corpses force their memory upon the coward's mind.

The film, however, provides few clues as to who is responsible for the atrocities in a more tangible, i.e., juridical, sense. The camera focuses briefly on the face of Josef Kramer, the former commandant of Belsen, whose unusually brutal appearance—small eyes cast to the side; thick neck; beefy cheeks ribboned with *Schmiesse*, the dueling scars that were points of pride for members of the fraternal *Burschenschaften*—makes him a helpful exemplar of the kind of person responsible for such crimes. But besides its brief focus upon this specimen of evil, the film fails to clarify more specific questions of legal responsibility. Indeed, the camera's struggles to find an adequate visual idiom suggest the difficulties of enlisting the evidence of such atrocities to support a criminal case organized around the charge of aggressive militarism. These difficulties are only underscored by the circumstances of the film's awkward insertion at the trial, bearing no ostensible connection to the testimony about either the Austrian *Anschluss* that preceded it, or the seizure of the Sudetenland that followed it. But if the film unsettles both the very conventions of documentary representation through which its images are discomfittingly framed, and the legal argument it was meant to support, how was Jackson able to see his way to enlisting this evidence into his legal case?

V. Harmonizing the Evidence with the Argument

An answer can be hazarded by considering more closely the relationship between the film's principal constitutive elements—its images and narration. Commenting on the role that captions play in news photography, the French director Jean Luc Godard once observed, "'This photograph, like any photograph, . . . is physically mute. It talks through the mouth of the text written beneath it.'"[95] By contrast, in the theory of documentary realism, sound is meant to be "'merely a supplementary support of representation; it must integrate itself docilely with the mimed object.'"[96] Yet the closer we study *Nazi Concentration Camps*, the more it becomes clear that the narration does not simply strengthen the verisimilitude of the image;[97] on the contrary, the voice of the commentary comes ultimately to assert control over the film's

95. SONTAG, *supra* note 66, at 108 (quoting film A LETTER TO JANE (1972)).
96. GUYNN, *supra* note 85, at 155 (quoting Roland Barthes, *Upon Leaving the Movie Theater*, *in* APPARATUS: CINEMATOGRAPHIC APPARATUS: SELECTED WRITINGS 2 (Theresa Hak Kyung Cha ed., Bertrand Augst & Susan White trans., 1981).
97. *Id.*

images. While the pictures captured by the camera's eye produce a "'visual impact . . . such as will nullify explanation,'"[98] the narration attempts to restrict and secure the meaning of the evidence that has been presented to our eyes.

In *Nazi Concentration Camps*, the narrator, as we have observed, remains nameless, and often seems to do no more than clarify what the camera sees: "Some have gangrenous wounds."[99] "They see the woodshed where lime-covered bodies are stacked . . . ."[100] "Victims bear the marks of violent deaths."[101] "There are two heads which have been shrunk to one-fifth their normal size."[102] "Large pieces of skin have been used for painting pictures, many of an obscene nature."[103] At other times, however, the narrator's omniscience is clearly greater than the film's, as he is able to provide information unavailable to the camera: "The victims are mainly Poles and Russians with considerable numbers of French and other nationalities also included in the camp roster."[104] "The Nazis maintained a building at the camp for medical experiments and vivisections with prisoners as guinea pigs."[105] The narration is relatively flat and laconic, free of the histrionics and rhetorical flourishes one often finds in wartime documentaries made for weekly newsreels. In fact, the entire text of the seventy-minute film takes up no more than eleven pages of the Tribunal's massive published catalogue of "Documents and Other Material in Evidence."[106] Indeed, it is the very flatness and terseness of the commentary that most powerfully creates the impression that it is the images, and not the words, that are speaking.

Yet this terseness, upon closer inspection, calls attention to certain interesting omissions. The word "Jew," for example, is mentioned only once in the entire film, and in such a manner as to obscure any suggestion that Nazi terror was directed against Jews as a group: "The 4,000 Ohrdruf victims are said to include Poles, Czechs, Russians, Belgians, Frenchmen, German Jews and German political prisoners."[107] Any further mention of terror directed specifically against Jews is suggested in a highly elliptical manner: "Under the guise of an insane asylum this had been the headquarters for the systematic murder of 35,000 Poles, Russians, and Germans sent here mainly for political and religious considerations."[108] This is not to suggest that the film deliberately failed to specify the special atrocities reserved for Jews; the camps

98. SONTAG, *supra* note 66, at 111 (quoting Robert Frank).
99. 30 IMT, *supra* note 2, at 462.
100. 30 *id.* at 463.
101. 30 *id.* at 466.
102. 30 *id.* at 469.
103. 30 *id.*
104. 30 *id.* at 467.
105. 30 *id.* at 469.
106. 30 *id.* at 462–72.
107. 30 *id.* at 464.
108. 30 *id.*

liberated by the British and Americans were not, technically speaking, centers of extermination. Nor, however, were the liberators lacking evidence of the Nazis' vast genocidal project directed against European Jewry. The Germans' retreat before Soviet advances had led to the liquidation of the death camps in the East, and by the time the Allies reached Bergen-Belsen, for example, the camp was already hideously overcrowded with Jews forcibly marched westwards.[109] If we now know that *Lagers* such as Bergen-Belsen and Dachau were not death camps *per se* (Belsen ironically was a "model" camp until late 1944, when it began receiving internees from the East[110]), the photos and film of the liberation of these camps "more than any other aspect of the Holocaust imprinted on the Western consciousness the images which have come to characterize the Final Solution."[111] Indeed, as Neal Ascherson has observed, "[I]t was to be many years before the word 'Auschwitz' (implying the gassing of millions), replaced 'Belsen' . . . as the ultimate metaphor of evil."[112]

The film's understanding of its own images is revealed, then, in a small but telling description. As the camera moves across the corpses littered about Buchenwald, the narrator declares, "Pictorial evidence of the *almost* unprecedented crimes perpetrated by the Nazis at Buchenwald Concentration Camp."[113] Noteworthy in this characterization is the insertion of the word "almost." Whether the Nazis' genocidal campaign was "unique" or "unprecedented," has, of course, emerged as one of the most contentious issues in Holocaust studies. While some scholars continue to emphasize the monstrous singularity of the Nazi genocide and question the motives of those who would challenge such an understanding,[114] others have attempted to assimilate the extermination of the Jews into a more "conventional" history of atrocity, one that finds ample precedents in Stalin's gulags and echoes in Pol Pot's killing fields.[115] Yet regardless of one's position in this debate, it

109. At the time of its liberation, roughly 40,000 Jews were interned at Belsen—roughly two-thirds of its final population. *See* JON BRIDGMAN, THE END OF THE HOLOCAUST: THE LIBERATION OF THE CAMPS 34 (1990); *see also* MARTIN GILBERT, ATLAS OF THE HOLOCAUST 206–26 (1993) (documenting death marches towards end of war leading up to Allied liberation of Belsen and other camps).

110. *See* BRIDGMAN, *supra* note 109.

111. *Id.* at 14.

112. Neal Ascherson, *The Film Britain Hid from Germany*, THE OBSERVOR (London), Sept. 8, 1985, at 7. Recent publications commemorating the fiftieth anniversary of the end of the war continue to associate Buchenwald and Belsen with centers of genocide. *See, e.g.*, Tom Infield, *Witness*, PHILA. INQUIRER MAG., Apr. 9, 1995, at 12, 15 ("This is how America learned of the Holocaust. It was only when U.S. troops began stumbling onto concentration camps as they overran the heart of Germany in April 1945 that America came to realize the absolute evil of the Nazi regime.").

113. 30 IMT, *supra* note 2, at 468 (emphasis added).

114. *See, e.g.*, DAVIDOWICZ, *supra* note 21, at 15–19; STEVEN T. KATZ, *The "Unique" Intentionality of the Holocaust*, *in* POST HOLOCAUST DIALOGUES 287, 290, 310 (1983).

115. For a revisionist account of the Holocaust arguing against the thesis of uniqueness, see ERNST NOLTE, DER EUROPÄISCHE BÜRGERKRIEG, 1917–1945, at 503 (1987) (noting parallels between German National Socialism and Russian Communism, especially with regard to deportation of ethnic minorities). For a discussion of the controversy within German academic circles about the causes and nature of the Holocaust (the so-called *Historikersstreit*), see CHARLES S. MAIER, THE UNMASTERABLE PAST: HISTORY,

should be clear that the narration's use of "almost" to modify "unprecedented" does not indicate a historically nuanced acknowledgment of other instances of extreme organized cruelty.

The crimes perpetrated by the Nazis at Buchenwald are "almost" unprecedented not because genocide has its historical antecedents, but because the film does not understand itself to be a document about genocide. The insertion of "almost" serves purposes that are at once strategic—the modest qualification appeals to the naturally incredulous mind that associates the rhetoric of the "unprecedented" with the ends of propaganda—and revelatory. It reveals that the film does not perceive its images as bearing witness to the astonishing crimes perpetrated against Europe's Jewish population.[116] The visual organization of the film insists on the veracity of its images, yet the narration suggests that the film itself remains deeply confused by what it has seen.

But if *Nazi Concentration Camps* is not about genocide, then what is it about? The narration offers no unequivocal answers or rigid explanatory framework to make intelligible its accompanying images. Yet in the terse words that narrate the camera's entry into each camp, a larger understanding begins to emerge:

> More than 200 political prisoners were burned to death in this concentration camp near Leipsig [sic].
>
> . . . .
>
> At this concentration camp in the Gotha area, the Germans starved, clubbed and burned to death more than 4,000 political prisoners over a period of 8 months. . . .
>
> . . . .
>
> This is Breendonck prison in Belgium. It offers evidence of Nazi brutality imposed on Belgian patriots during the period of German occupation.
>
> . . . .
>
> The slave labor camp at Nordhausen liberated by the 3rd Armored Division, 1st Army.
>
> At least 3,000 political prisoners died here at the brutal hands of SS troops . . . .
>
> . . . .
>
> The report lists the surviving inmates [of Buchenwald] as representing every European nationality. . . .
>
> . . . .
>
> In the official report, the Buchenwald camp is termed an "extermination factory." . . . By these means, the report continues,

HOLOCAUST, AND GERMAN NATIONAL IDENTITY (1988).

116. *See* Jacob Robinson, *The International Military Tribunal and the Holocaust: Some Legal Reflections*, 7 ISR. L. REV. 1, 8–12 (1972).

> many tens of thousands of the best leadership personnel of Europe have been exterminated.[117]

By its own terms, then, *Nazi Concentration Camps* is a film about political terror and the excesses of war. It documents a barbaric campaign to exterminate political enemies of a brutal regime. It exposes the horrific mistreatment of prisoners of war, and the enslavement of civilians to service a ruthless war machine. It bears witness to spectacular excesses of cruelty and reveals the administrative and technological apparatus that made possible campaigns of mass murder. It does so, however, in a manner that understands extermination in terms of the perverted logic of political control and military conquest. The film understands the crimes to be the consequence of aggressive militarism rather than genocide. Yet the question remains: Did the film misinterpret its own images?

The question raises interesting issues about the meaning of documentary evidence. Writing about a British film team's documentary covering the liberation of the camps, Neal Ascherson has observed, "The filmmakers had not, in fact, had time to grasp the horror within the horror. The scale of the 'Final Solution of the Jewish Problem' had scarcely dawned on them . . . ."[118] Whether this also explains the narrative posture of *Nazi Concentration Camps* ultimately, however, is of marginal concern. More interesting remains the fact that some fifteen years after its screening at Nuremberg, *Nazi Concentration Camps* was shown at the Eichmann trial as evidence of the Nazis' campaign of extermination directed specifically against the Jews.[119] At roughly the same time, *Nazi Concentration Camps* made its own Hollywood debut, appearing as the film within the film of Stanley Kramer's *Judgment at Nuremberg*.[120] Starring Spencer Tracy and Burt Lancaster, *Judgment at Nuremberg* offered a dramatization of the trial not of the major war criminals before the International Military Tribunal, but of a follow-up trial involving defendants in the Reich Ministry of Justice and other legal functionaries.[121] Devoted to examining how members of a legal apparatus, in particular judges, could pervert institutions of justice, *Judgment at Nuremberg* reaches its dramatic peak when the prosecution screens documentary footage of the liberation of the concentration camps. The film within the film is, of course, none other than *Nazi Concentration Camps*, and director Stanley Kramer drives home its power by using precisely the

117. 30 IMT, *supra* note 2, at 462–68.

118. Ascherson, *supra* note 112, at 7.

119. *See* 3 THE TRIAL OF ADOLF EICHMANN: RECORD OF PROCEEDINGS IN THE DISTRICT COURT OF JERUSALEM 1283–85 (1993).

120. JUDGMENT AT NUREMBERG (Metro-Goldwyn-Mayer 1961).

121. United States v. Josef Altstoetter et al. (also known as the Justice case), *in* 3 TRIALS OF WAR CRIMINALS BEFORE THE NUERNBERG MILITARY TRIBUNALS UNDER CONTROL COUNCIL LAW NO. 10 (1949–53).

techniques used by the memoirists: He cuts from the film within the film back to the Hollywood drama, as we now see shock and revulsion etched on the faces of Richard Widmark and Burt Lancaster. In *Judgment at Nuremberg*, however, *Nazi Concentration Camps* is again comprehended as it was at the Eichmann trial—as irrefutable evidence of the Holocaust.

We find this understanding of Nazi Concentration Camps also at work in the film's most recent use in a trial setting. In 1985, some forty years after the film's Nuremberg "premiere," a Canadian prosecutor again called *Nazi Concentration Camps* to the stand—this time in the criminal trial of Ernst Zundel, a notorious Holocaust denier.[122] Zundel, who had arranged for the publication of *Did Six Million Really Die?*, a tract that claimed the Holocaust was a Zionist swindle, was charged with violating a little-used portion of the Canadian criminal code prohibiting the publication of false statements "likely to cause injury or mischief to a public interest."[123] Because the indictment charged Zundel with knowingly publishing false statements, the court reasoned that it was incumbent upon the prosecution to prove the falsity of Zundel's Holocaust denials. Toward this end, *Nazi Concentration Camps* was shown to the jury, now as evidence of precisely those crimes against the Jews that the film fails to mention. Indeed, at the film's conclusion, the prosecutor announced to the court, "'That is the case for the Crown, Your Honour.'"[124]

Ironically, then, *Nazi Concentration Camps* has been used as irrefutable proof of an event the film did not originally see itself as documenting.[125] Though ironic, this is not entirely surprising, as we are reminded of the plasticity of visual evidence, the way identical images can sponsor multiple interpretations and support different legal arguments. Yet regardless of how *Nazi Concentration Camps* has been comprehended in other contexts, of interest for our purposes is how the documentary's narration—the understanding that it supplies of its own images—made the film available for juridical use at Nuremberg. By framing its horrific scenes in a narrative about perverted militarism and war's excess, the film harmonized its imagery with Jackson's legal argument.

---

122. Regina v. Zundel, 58 O.R.2d 129 (Ont. Ct. App. 1987).

123. R.S.C., ch. C-34 §177 (Supp. 1970) (Can.).

124. Leonidas E. Hill, *The Trial of Ernst Zundel: Revisionism and the Law in Canada*, 6 SIMON WIESENTHAL CENTER ANN. 165, 184 (1989). Zundel was convicted and sentenced to two years in prison. On appeal, however, the conviction was overturned. The appellate court reasoned, inter alia, that *Nazi Concentration Camps* had been improperly shown to the jury at trial. Because the nameless screenplay writer and narrator were unavailable for cross-examination, the documentary failed under the rules of hearsay. *See* Regina v. Zundel, 58 O.R.2d 129, 195–200 (Ont. Ct. App. 1987). For additional discussion of the Zundel case, see Lawrence Douglas, *Wartime Lies: Securing the Holocaust in Law and Literature*, 7 YALE J.L. & HUMAN. 367, 387–89 (1995). As noted above, the relaxed rules of evidence that controlled the Nuremberg trial permitted the film's showing.

125. As a related matter, it seems ironical that Eisenhower's famous words should be inscribed upon the entrance to the U.S. Holocaust Memorial Museum, as it is far from clear that by speaking of things that "beggar description" Eisenhower meant the mass extermination of Europe's Jews.

Jackson, as we have seen, understood the Nazis' central crime as the waging of aggressive war. This offense, though supported by an unsteady scaffolding of positive and customary law, nevertheless left intact deeper concepts of ordered legality and provided, so the prosecution argued, the proximate cause for other Nazi crimes. Granted, the Nuremberg prosecution extensively detailed the Nazis' savagery toward the Jews in later stages of the trial,[126] and Jackson, to his credit, devoted a lengthy section of his opening statement to detailing "Crimes against the Jews,"[127] during which he powerfully declared, "It is my purpose to show a plan and design, to which all Nazis were fanatically committed, to annihilate all Jewish people."[128] Yet his understanding of this design of annihilation is noteworthy:

> Nor was [the policy of starvation and extermination] directed against individual Jews for personal bad citizenship or unpopularity. The avowed purpose was the destruction of the Jewish people as a whole, as an end in itself, as a measure of preparation for war, and as a discipline of conquered peoples.[129]

At this critical moment, Jackson invoked, if not the term, then the logic of genocide—the extermination of an entire people as an end in itself. He was close at this point to following the lead of the indictment, which specifically used the word "genocide" to describe the Nazis' annihilation of European Jewry.[130] But the neologism, first coined by Raphael Lemkin in 1944 to describe the extermination of the Jews,[131] was never again used at Nuremberg. Indeed, Jackson himself listed "the destruction of the Jewish people" not simply as an end unto itself, but also as a means. The Jews, he argued, were used as exemplars of Nazi discipline to other citizenries under Nazi subjugation,[132] and their persecution eliminated an obstacle to aggressive war.[133] His reasoning, of course, is question-begging—how can such annihilation be understood as a "measure of preparation for war"?—and historically suspect. Scholars of the Holocaust, for example, have amply demonstrated how the Final Solution not only did not serve any military end,

126. The prosecution's presentation, however, suffered from remarkable omissions: The French prosecution, responsible for presenting evidence under the fourth count of the indictment ("Crimes Against Humanity"), mentioned the Jews as a target of Nazi violence on but one occasion. *See* TAYLOR, *supra* note 10, at 296.

127. 2 IMT, *supra* note 2, at 118–27.

128. 2 *id.* at 118.

129. 2 *id.* at 119.

130. The indictment's description of genocide includes the extermination of "Jews, Poles, and Gypsies and others." 1 *id.* at 44. Yet consistent with Jackson's approach, the crime of genocide is named under the third count, "War Crimes," and not under the fourth count, "Crimes Against Humanity." 1 *id.* at 43–44.

131. *See* Robinson, *supra* note 116, at 6 (citing RAPHAEL LEMKIN, AXIS RULE IN OCCUPIED EUROPE 79–95 (1944)).

132. 2 IMT, *supra* note 2, at 118 ("The ghetto was the laboratory for testing repressive measures.").

133. 2 *id.* at 127 ("The purpose . . . of getting rid of the influence of free labor, the churches, and the Jews was to clear their obstruction to the precipitation of aggressive war.").

but channeled away critical resources from the war effort.[134] Yet the very vulnerabilities of Jackson's argument highlight his attempt to translate shocking images of genocide into an idiom consonant with, and supportive of, the prosecution of functionaries responsible for a campaign of renegade militarism.

CONCLUSION

In *The Reawakening*, Primo Levi describes his first encounter after his liberation from Auschwitz with a man from "the civilized world." Standing before a well-dressed lawyer—an "extremely courteous and benevolent" person—Levi recalls feeling a powerful need to unburden himself of all that he had witnessed:

> I had a torrent of urgent things to tell the civilized world: . . . things which (it seemed to me) ought to shake every conscience to its very foundations. . . . I spoke at dizzy speed of those so recent experiences of mine, of Auschwitz nearby, yet, it seemed, unknown to all, of the hecatomb from which I alone had escaped, of everything. The lawyer translated into Polish for the public. Now I do not know Polish, but I know how one says 'Jew' and how one says 'political'; and I soon realized that the translation of my account, although sympathetic, was not faithful to it. The lawyer described me to the public not as an Italian Jew, but as an Italian political prisoner.[135]

Astonishing in its own detail, Levi's story brilliantly captures the small strategic distortions that both made possible, and resulted from, the effort of the Nuremberg prosecution to comprehend the extermination of European Jewry. In translating schemes of annihilation into excesses of war, Jackson and the narration of *Nazi Concentration Camps* protected not only the jurisdictional reach of the Tribunal, but also preserved the underlying jurisprudential vision that sought to extend international law into the conflicts between nations but not into the darkest bowels of a reprobate sovereign. By treating genocide as ancillary to the crime of militarism, Jackson and the documentary's narration supplied the formal links between the legal case and the visual evidence enlisted to support it. Like the actions of the lawyer whom Levi encounters, Jackson's efforts remained sympathetic, though less than faithful, to the history his arguments had to defend.

One can, of course, claim it is unfair to condemn prosecutorial teams, burdened with shaping a vast amount of evidence into a complex legal case in a short period of time, for failing to be fully attentive to the crimes against Europe's Jews. Yet the failure to address Nazi genocide adequately was not

134. *See* RAUL HILBERG, THE DESTRUCTION OF THE EUROPEAN JEWS 644–46 (Harper Colophon 1978) (1961).

135. PRIMO LEVI, THE REAWAKENING 54 (Stuart Woolf trans., Little, Brown & Co. 1965) (1963).

simply an example of overtaxed prosecutors revealing the same indifference to the fate of the Jews that the Allies had shown during the war. Indeed, on a juridical level, the prosecution's efforts can be seen as a success. By "reading" *Nazi Concentration Camps* in a manner that recuperates the power of law to assimilate the atrocities on film into a novel, though comprehensible, idiom of criminal transgression, Jackson performed something of a legal tour-de-force. Just as the narration of *Nazi Concentration Camps* comes to exercise control over the images it is meant simply to clarify, so the voice of the law, as uttered by Jackson, came to exercise authority over evidence that threatened to expose the law's limits. If this success came at the cost of misreading the film's images, this merely underscores the extraordinary difficulty of accommodating a crime that "lies outside speech and . . . outside reason"[136] to available conceptions of justice and legality. And it reveals that in a trial, even evidence that claims to speak for itself of atrocity ultimately must be spoken for. The legal meaning of such evidence must be secured even as what it shows cannot be denied.

136. STEINER, *supra* note 16, at 123.

[9]

A REPORTER AT LARGE

DOUBT

Even in an apparently simple assault-and-robbery case, it was impossible for the jury not to speculate about the defendant and the young women who provided his alibi. But what happens when a juror returns to his role as a journalist and investigates the details that never came out in court?

BY WILLIAM FINNEGAN

MARTIN KAPLAN, subway mugger. It sounded like a setup line from an early Woody Allen routine about a bully in the third grade. Nobody laughed, though, while Marc Agnifilo, a young prosecutor, led the victims through their tale of violent assault and robbery at the Astor Place station. The crime had occurred on the night after Christmas, 1991. John Leamy and John Solder, friends since college—they both attended the Pratt Institute, in Brooklyn, in the early nineteen-eighties—had spent the evening in the West Village, and were on their way back to the apartment of Solder and his wife, on the Upper East Side. Leamy was living in San Francisco; he had just stopped in New York for the weekend, on his way home from Europe, to see Solder. Then he planned to take a bus west across the country. At the entrance to the Astor Place station, Leamy and Solder found their way blocked by three young men, belligerently arrayed. Leamy tried a technique he had learned as a bartender: he shook hands and made eye contact with each of the men. Then he and Solder went around them and into the station, ignoring the obscene threats that followed them down the stairs.

Toward the bottom of the stairway, they were attacked from behind. Both men were knocked to the ground and repeatedly punched and kicked. Both fought back, to little effect. Leamy remembered yelling, "Enough! Enough!" and seeing something shiny—a knife, he thought—in the hand of Solder's main assailant. Eventually, one of the attackers headed back up the stairs and—according to an eyewitness, who also testified—waved a wallet and shouted, "I got it! Let's get the fuck out of here!" Leamy was by then flat on his face, unaware of his surroundings, and was bleeding heavily from the mouth. "My bottom lip was . . . hanging off, hanging down," he recalled. The two remaining attackers finished their work and fled. The mugging was over. Leamy's face was cut and battered, one eye blackened, his skull a mass of knots, his ribs badly bruised. Solder's face was also battered and swollen, one of his eyes also blackened, his ribs also bruised. He had not been stabbed, but he had lost his wallet.

The eyewitness, Carroll Wilder, had already called 911. His testimony corroborated Leamy's and Solder's on all the main points. A tape recording of his 911 call was played in court. Shouts and blows could be heard in the background, and Wilder, who was clearly standing very near the assault, was asked to describe the assailants. "White! All white!" he said. "Five guys! Quick, get somebody here!"

The police arrived before Wilder got off the phone. He and Solder and Leamy, who had recovered his senses, were driven to St. Mark's Place and Second Avenue, two blocks away, where the police already had a suspect in custody. It was Martin Kaplan, a twenty-three-year-old white male. The victims and the eyewitness all identified Kaplan as one of the assailants at Astor Place. Kaplan had not been the one with the knife—Wilder, too, had seen a knife, more clearly than Leamy had—but Kaplan had been, according to Wilder, "particularly violent." Kaplan didn't have Solder's wallet on him, but his hands were bloody, and his boots were spattered with something that looked like blood. He was arrested and charged with assault and robbery.

Now, almost sixteen months later, Kaplan was on trial in New York State Supreme Court, in a windowless, blondwood courtroom on the sixth floor at 111 Centre Street, in downtown Manhattan. I, for my sins, was on the jury. Kaplan's alleged fellow-muggers had never been caught, and he was facing two counts of second-degree robbery and two of third-degree assault. If Leamy and Solder had agreed, on the night of the attack, to go to a hospital—they were examined by paramedics but were treated at home by Solder's wife, a physician—the assault charges might have been more serious. As it was, though their injuries troubled them for many weeks, and left scars inside Leamy's mouth that still bothered him as he testified, the assault charges were only misdemeanors. The robbery charges, however, were felonies, though the amount of money stolen had been insignificant.

In his remarks during jury selection, Agnifilo, the prosecutor, emphasized a legal idea that he called "acting in concert," meaning that even if Kaplan had not himself taken the wallet, he was responsible for its being taken, because he and his confederates had acted together with the same intent. But the prosecution witnesses—the victims, the eyewitness, and two police officers involved in the arrest—were now forced to reidentify the suspect from photographs, for Kaplan attended only the jury-selection phase of his trial. He then, according to Judge Frederic S. Berman, who was hearing the case, exercised his "right to choose not to be present."

Jerald Rosenthal, Kaplan's lawyer, tried to shake Leamy's and Solder's identification of his client by suggesting that they had been drunk at the time of the attack or had been too groggy afterward to think clearly. He dwelt on discrepancies in their and Wilder's descriptions of the boots that had been applied to Leamy's face and ribs. In Wilder's 911 call, in the testimony of the three men before a grand jury, and in their trial testimony, the boots appeared, variously, as Army boots, combat boots, commando boots, and motocross boots. Kaplan's boots had been confiscated and were admitted as evidence. Rosenthal told the jury in his opening remarks, "Those of us who were in the service know what combat boots look like, and they are nothing like the boots that will be shown to you today." The boots were of black leather, nearly knee high, with many buckles and a big metal shin guard. Rosenthal, who was short, stout, natty, and white-maned, had a habit of addressing the jury over a pair of half-glasses perched on his nose. He was aggressive with Leamy and Solder, but he also had to be careful. They were attractive characters: Solder, fair-haired and easygoing, programmed computers for an investment bank; Leamy, black-haired and intense, let it be known, earnestly, that his latest painting was an eight-by-eight-foot allegorical work about Vincent van Gogh. The two men were effective witnesses, low-key and articulate, and they had been, after all, victims. As such, they were not well cast—both men were good-sized and athletically built—but photographs of them taken immediately after the attack and admitted as evidence left no doubt about how badly they had been beaten. Their handsome faces were gruesome, abraded masks. When Leamy spoke of the "mortal terror" he had felt during the attack, no one had to wonder what he meant.

Photographs of Martin Kaplan taken shortly after his arrest were also admitted as evidence and circulated among the jury. Two at a time, we studied the pictures. They showed a slim, sour face, high-cheekboned and pale-eyed; punk hair; and a leather jacket—the street version of the rangy, silent defendant in the cheap black suit who had dozed his way through jury selection.

Rosenthal also had to be careful with Wilder, for he, too, was an attractive character—a big, young, well-spoken African-American computer programmer and bridge player, who after an evening of bridge had been on his way uptown. Wilder was plainly a hero. Other bystanders had run off down the platform when the mugging started; Wilder had stayed and called 911. He had gone with the police to Second Avenue—travelling, incongruously, in a city bus driven by one Officer William Ungro, who had been using the bus on plainclothes patrol, and who testified in the Kaplan trial but failed to explain how a bus functioned in undercover work—and then to the police station, where he was kept until 5 A.M. By the time he was allowed to leave, he testified, "I was tired, I was angry, because I thought I had done the right thing to help these two guys, and I was kept in the Police Department all morning." Wilder nonetheless turned up to testify before the grand jury, and then, of course, at the trial itself, where Rosenthal, while careful to keep his questioning amiable, proceeded to read out a portion of Wilder's sixteen-month-old grand-jury testimony in order to show deficiencies in his original description of the assault. Wilder doggedly testified for most of an afternoon, his exchanges with the lawyers filling nearly seventy pages of trial transcript, before he finally wailed, in answer to a stream of questions from Rosenthal about the disposition of the effects of Solder and Leamy and their attackers on the floor of the subway station after the attack, "My life has been going on since then!" He was excused, and as he hurried away from the courtroom he was heard to observe, to a startled group of bystanders, that it was certainly true that no good deed goes unpunished.

SUE COE

Marc Agnifilo had led his witnesses carefully through their testimony. Compactly built, wearing what seemed to be the same baggy dark suit each day, he had a boyish, equable, slightly abashed manner—like a New York–Italian version of Wally Cleaver. He was well prepared and seemed to believe he had a strong case. I had no notion what my fellow-jurors were thinking—we were always instructed not to discuss the case during our frequent breaks from hearing testimony—but Agnifilo's confidence was certainly justified insofar as I was concerned. I had been ready to convict since Leamy stared at the photographs of Kaplan, swallowed hard, and said, "Absolutely."

KAPLAN offered an alibi defense. Or, as Jerald Rosenthal memorably put it in his opening remarks, "obviously, the person who committed the horrible act, which seems senseless to us when we think about it, looked exactly like my client or enough like him that they would be able and continued to say that he is the person who did it, for there is an episode from 'Star Trek' where people can beam all over the place, but it's physically impossible for us to be virtually two places at once." The word "alibi," Rosenthal explained, means simply "elsewhere," and Kaplan had indeed been elsewhere—specifically, in a taco bar on Second Avenue called San Loco—at the time of the attack on Solder and Leamy.

Two young women got up and testified to that effect. The first, Leah Tagliaferri, had been Kaplan's live-in girlfriend at the time. She was in her early twenties, brown-haired, pretty, clear-eyed, and strong-voiced, more Irish-looking than Italian. She described a rather aimless evening of wandering around the East Village—Kaplan, she said, "has been pretty much in that area for a while." Kaplan had left her and two other friends at a table in San Loco "maybe a couple of minutes before he got arrested" on the street outside—not nearly enough time for him to go to Astor Place, two cross-town blocks away, commit a robbery, and return. Questioned about his bloody hands, she said that they were often that way. "He is not a very clean person," she said. "He is always picking things on his hands." She shed little light on why she, a well-scrubbed, good-looking child of the suburbs—she wore a black cotton skirt and a neat black blouse sewn with red flowers, and her mother, whose presence the prosecutor noted, came in from Long Beach, Long Island, every day to watch the trial—would have been living with the unkempt likes of Kaplan. They had met in early 1991, she said, when she was living in Tudor City, across from the United Nations, and Kaplan, who was a friend of a roommate, had come to stay with them. Within "like a week," she said, they were lovers. The couple later moved out to Long Beach, where they were living when Kaplan was arrested. Tagliaferri's parents had originally put up seventy-five hundred dollars to bail Kaplan out of jail. The money had since been returned to them, but Leah herself, though she and Kaplan were no longer romantically attached, and though she had very little in the way of savings (she was working as a horse-carriage driver in Central Park), had helped put up further bail. When she was asked why she had done so, and why she was testifying—she had not been subpoenaed, and a transit-police detective had visited her at home and warned her of the consequences of perjury—she replied stoutly, "Because I don't think it's right that he should go to jail for something he didn't do."

Luciente Castellano was the second alibi witness. She was about the same age as Tagliaferri and Kaplan, and had long, dark hair, which she wore straight down; a pale, heart-shaped face; and big dark eyes. She wore a black suit over a white blouse, and she seemed nervous. She and Kaplan had been friends, she said, since they were about thirteen years old, and she, too, had been in the taco bar with him at the time of the mugging. Castellano's account of the evening included a stroll that she and Kaplan took along St. Mark's Place, which Tagliaferri had not mentioned, but otherwise she corroborated Tagliaferri's testimony. Castellano, too, had been visited by the transit-police detective, Jerry Lyons: he had come to see her three times, in two offices where she worked. Much of the questioning of Castellano focussed on her exchanges with Detective Lyons, including a telephone conversation immediately after his first visit, in which she apparently claimed that she had not even been with Kaplan on the night in question. If she had said that, Castellano now explained, it was only because she was afraid of getting involved with the case, afraid that her family and her boyfriend would be angry with her for being "involved with Martin at all." She had subsequently decided that it was her duty to testify. Why? "Because I know that Mr. Kaplan is innocent."

When the defense had rested its case, the prosecution called a rebuttal witness: Detective Lyons. He described his visits with Castellano in less dramatic terms than she had, leaving out elements of threat and intimidation, which she had emphasized, but adding the claim that during his first visit with her she confided that Tagliaferri had asked her to lie to help Kaplan construct an alibi. Detective Lyons had brought to court his notes from that conversation, however, and they turned out to contain nothing about Tagliaferri's alleged request. Lyons had also, it emerged, tape-recorded, without Castellano's knowledge, the conversation they had on his third visit to her. When that tape was played in court, the jury heard the veteran detective telling the frightened secretary that her story about Tagliaferri asking her to lie was already part of a written report that "the lawyers are entitled to see." On the tape Castellano could be heard denying, just as she had denied on the witness stand, that anyone had ever asked her to lie, or that she had ever told such a story to Lyons; and her description of the events on the night of the crime was, again, exactly the same one she had given in court. Rosenthal, in his cross-examination of Lyons, was at pains to point out that the detective's statement to Castellano that he had a written record of her alleged remarks about an invitation to perjury had been false.

"When I first saw your mother, she was bathed in moonlight."

The two lawyers then gave

"Excuse me, I'm lost. Can you direct me to the information superhighway?"

their summations, Rosenthal proclaiming that "there is no more horrifying thing in human events than being charged with a crime that you didn't commit," and Agnifilo attacking the credibility of the alibi witnesses, recapping the crime (he again played the tape of Wilder's 911 call), and recalling the three eyewitness identifications of Kaplan that we had heard. Then the judge gave his charge to the jury. For more than an hour, he explained the charges against Kaplan and spelled out our responsibilities. Finally, nine days after the beginning of jury selection, we were allowed to retire to our deliberations.

THE jury was a grab bag of Manhattanites. There were two bankers, an engineer, an architect, an insurance agent, a retired teacher, a legal secretary. The twelve of us had already spent a formidable amount of time together—reading and chatting and twirling our thumbs, since we were forbidden to discuss the one thing we had in common: the case that had taken over our days. Now, free at last to talk about it, we first agreed to take a voice poll to see if we had anything to talk about. The polling showed ten people ready to convict. I was one of the dissenters: something had happened to my certainty since the prosecution presented its case. The other dissenter was the retired teacher: she said she had found Kaplan's alibi credible.

We started discussing the alibi, and were soon busily contravening Judge Berman's instruction that we "must not, under any circumstance, indulge in speculation or guesswork, nor are you to consider anything outside of the evidence." We guessed and speculated about the lives and motives of the alibi witnesses, trying to put "the evidence" into some narrative context that made sense. Those with more experience of the East Village tried to evoke the neighborhood's street life for those with less. Odd details got pawed over. Detective Lyons had testified, for instance, that Luciente Castellano told him during one of his visits that Kaplan, just before his arrest, had left San Loco with a flashlight he hoped to sell on the street. To at least one juror—a young white businesswoman, a native of Alabama, who had come to court every day impeccably dressed—this seemed somehow implausible. "I mean, come on—a *flashlight*?" To others, the flashlight simply conjured a world. It was clear already that each juror was seeing a cast of characters formed out of his or her own life and preconceptions. The Alabamian saw Kaplan and his friends as creatures of an urban underworld, not to be trusted. The schoolteacher saw them as just a bunch of kids, aimlessly hanging out.

Meanwhile, the impossibility of considering only "the evidence" was so obvious it was hardly mentioned. As jurors, we had been kept firmly in the dark throughout the trial, allowed to hear only what the judge deemed fit for our ears. We had no idea who Martin Kaplan really was. We didn't even know whether he had a criminal record, whether he was a career mugger, or what. It was right and just, of course, that we didn't know such things—Kaplan was charged with this crime, and not others—but it was also frustrating, and the disputed facts before us would make sense only if we could imagine the worlds around them. And so we told each other stories.

My reluctance to convict, which had been stirred by the alibi testimony, had been only strengthened, I realized, by the prosecution's rebuttal case. I tried to take my fellow-jurors through the surprise calls by Detective Lyons on Luciente Castellano, to show how they served to bolster her story. If she had in fact told him that Tagliaferri asked her to lie, would he really have forgotten to include that in his notes? And why did the story she told him during his last visit, when she did not know she was being taped, comport so exactly with the story she told on the witness stand? Finally, why did he mislead her about having a written record of her alleged claim that Tagliaferri had asked her to lie? Not all the jurors recalled that the tape had caught Lyons intimidating and misleading Castellano, so we asked to hear it again. Even after hearing it, some of them, including our foreman, an engineer and Vietnam veteran who seemed otherwise skeptical-minded, declined to agree with my interpretation of the detective's motives. I said that the prosecution was plainly trying to discourage Kaplan's friends from testifying. The prosecution wouldn't do that, the foreman muttered. But a young architect named Timothy Hyde, who was emerging as the spokesperson for the conviction camp, said quietly, "I think Lyons' testimony has been discredited," and the detective was not mentioned again.

A second voice poll revealed that, my efforts notwithstanding, the jury was still ten to two to convict.

We turned to the positive case: the

evidence placing Kaplan at the scene, committing the crime. We had requested earlier that various exhibits, including the boots he had been wearing that night, be delivered to us in the jury room. Now we passed the boots around the table, peering dubiously at the brown stains on the metal shin guard. Were they in fact blood? It was generally regretted that they had not been sent to a serology lab for testing. If the stains had turned out to be blood, of John Leamy's type, there would have been, it was generally agreed, nothing more to discuss. As it was, the positive case against Kaplan was still extremely strong.

Nearly everyone on the jury was contributing regularly to the discussion. The only exception was a middle-aged white woman who sat in a corner, knitting. During one of the few lulls in our deliberations, someone suddenly asked her what she thought. She looked up, startled. She worked her mouth, searching for words. She was shy, and she was not, she had already made clear, an educated woman. Finally, she said, "Well, it seems to me like these two girls are lying so their friend won't go to jail."

There was a deflated silence, then a couple of appreciative titters. "So," I said, after a minute, feeling foolish. "That's the prosecution's case. But have they really disproved the alibi?"

We went back to work on the alibi, detail by detail. Attention was concentrated, naturally, on the schoolteacher and me. Did we really not see the little hole here, the implausibility there? The women, in particular, chided me. "You don't understand what these girls will do," the fashionable Alabamian said. "They'll say *anything*." She found an ally in Lily, a young black legal secretary, who had sat on my left throughout the trial and now, in the jury room, continued to do so. "When their man is in trouble, they don't care," Lily said. She studied me. "You *don't* know what they're like," she said. At the trial's emotional high points, and at some of its low points as well, she had gently but eloquently elbowed me in the ribs. Now, when my arguments got too fanciful, she snorted and backhanded me across the upper arm.

The discussion veered occasionally into the seriously fanciful, as when it began to concentrate on Leah Tagliaferri's mother, who had silently watched the entire trial from the public benches: an enigmatic figure well cast for our favored pastime—speculation and guesswork.

But Timothy Hyde helped keep us on track. Precise and self-effacing, he took us through the alibi testimony again and again, carefully drawing out the discrepancies between the two women's accounts. We asked to hear a section of Tagliaferri's testimony about the night of the crime read again. The schoolteacher seemed inclined to view any small discrepancies as the inevitable confusion of separate recollections of mundane events by imprecise youths, and I was inclined to agree with her. But I was also reaching the conclusion that, while the burden of proof lay always with the prosecution, an alibi defense presented special difficulties. The judge, in his charge, had told us that "the people must disprove the alibi to your satisfaction beyond a reasonable doubt." But wasn't the standard of reasonable doubt that we were supposed to apply to the positive case different from the standard we should apply to the alibi? That is, the two stories were inextricably related, so didn't they need to be weighed against each another? Considered on its own, the alibi, it seemed to me, was virtually impossible to disprove conclusively.

As I was trying to sort out these questions, a court officer knocked on the jury-room door. The judge wanted to see us. We filed back into the courtroom, and there the court clerk asked if we had reached a verdict. Our foreman said we hadn't, and the judge informed us that we had been deliberating for five hours. I was amazed; I would have said half that much time had passed. It was getting late, the judge said. He was going to sequester us for the night. Our families would be informed.

SEQUESTRATION seemed absurd. It wasn't as though we needed to be shielded from the press, or from bribery attempts, or from mob hit men. And if the notion was that with the threat of sequestration hanging over our deliberations we might reach a verdict sooner rather than later, then why had no threat been made, no deadline set? Instead, we were suddenly taken into custody. And I, along with the schoolteacher, was responsible. I felt awful, and braced myself for a wave of coldness from the group as we gathered our things and were herded into an elevator behind the courtroom. But the

SHAME

Shame left me when I was very sick
unprotesting I uncovered to strangers' hands gave up to strangers' eyes

the poor secrets of my body

They strutted into me sharply increasing the abasement

My professor of forensic medicine old man Mancewicz
when fishing the suicide's corpse from out the pool of formalin
bowed over it as if to apologize
and then with an expert movement spread open the splendid thorax
the silenced basilica of breath

delicately almost tenderly

Thus—faithful to the dead respecting ashes—I understand
the ire of the Grecian princess her stubborn no
she was right—brothers deserve dignified burials

earth's winding sheet drawn carefully over
the eyes

—ZBIGNIEW HERBERT

(Translated, from the Polish, by Charles Kraszewski.)

mood was giddy, mock-woeful, off-to-summer-camp. Jokes flew back and forth about Officer Ungro and his undercover bus waiting for us outside. My mumbled apologies were jovially rebuffed.

We ate dinner in a gaudy old downtown haunt called Peggy Doyle's. Conversation at my end of the table was about recent books and films; a banker named Chris, who had just seen "Indecent Proposal," contributed a thoughtful review of Demi Moore's postpartum body. I tried to make a quick call on a public phone at the back of the restaurant, hoping to apprise my girlfriend, Caroline, of my plight, but one of the court officers accompanying us appeared, wagging his finger. No calls.

On the van ride out to a Holiday Inn in Queens, I found myself wondering if our sequestration was not, indirectly, Caroline's fault. That is to say, she is a lawyer, specializing in criminal defense, and she and I had had some bruising arguments about her work. I would be appalled by the foul deeds attributed, sometimes with good reason, to her clients, and flabbergasted by her energetic representation of them. Confused and angry, with a picture of the victims stuck in my mind's eye, I could lose sight entirely of her clients' right to a fair trial and competent counsel. So now that I was a juror I wondered if I wasn't perhaps trying to make amends, giving the defendant the benefit of a little extra doubt, imagining that Caroline would approve.

Or was I just being gullible? I remembered that Caroline had once said, laughing, "You believe anything a good-looking female says. If it's a girly girl, you just can't imagine that she would really do anything wicked." Leah Tagliaferri and Luciente Castellano were both good-looking females—they probably even qualified as girly girls, whatever those were—and it was true: I found it difficult to accept that they might simply be lying.

My roommate for the night was a man in his mid-fifties. He was a Mason, a photographer, and an insurance agent on the Upper West Side. While a court officer sat outside our room insuring we didn't escape, and the LaGuardia air traffic roared ceaselessly overhead, my roommate, who was a sweet talker, told me stories about growing up black in rural Georgia in the nineteen-forties. Later, he slept soundly. I counted the hours.

In the morning, at breakfast, Lily sat as usual on my left. She was now monitoring me, it seemed, for the rest of the jury. In the van the night before, I had said something to her about how abruptly the judge had sequestered us, and how I thought we might have reached a verdict if he had given us a little more time—and Lily had turned and given a thumbs-up sign to those in the seats nearby. Now, over breakfast, I made an aside to her about having a reasonable doubt about what was actually in the eggs. Lily didn't like the sound of that. She turned and stared at me. She shook her head. "Bill, Bill, Bill," she said, and lightly knuckle-punched me in the arm.

On our second day of deliberations, the schoolteacher and I quickly caved in. I don't know what her rationale was, but I cobbled together a little theory about reasonable doubt and an alibi defense. My notion—which was only common sense—was that the strength of the positive case, placing the defendant at the scene committing the crime, set a standard of proof that the alibi then had to clear. In this case, the standard had been set quite high: an identification by three eyewitnesses. Was the alibi sturdy enough to clear that standard? On close examination, I decided, it was not. It wasn't necessary to decide that the alibi witnesses were lying—only that there was enough room within the frames of their separate accounts for Kaplan to have slipped away for ten or fifteen minutes and participated in the attack. (Another way to put this might be that I had at first thought the burden of disproving the alibi fell entirely on the prosecution's rebuttal case, which had not, in my view, succeeded. More realistically, it fell on the prosecution's entire case, which had been far more persuasive.) And so, after ninety more minutes of discussion, I changed my vote. The schoolteacher did the same. And thus we found Martin Kaplan guilty on all counts.

Judge Berman, after hearing our verdict, thanked us and discharged us. Then he visited us in the jury room as we were collecting our things. Until then, we had seen him only across the courtroom. Tall and gaunt in his robes, with a fine head of white hair and a slow, formal, civics-lesson manner, he had been an exceed-

ingly judgelike judge. Now, at close quarters, we could see that his eyes, deep-set under thick white brows, were red and inflamed-looking. This revelation changed his whole presence, somehow. He distributed a set of school-award-type Certificates of Jury Service, signed by him, and asked if we had any questions.

Yes, our foreman said. Where was Martin Kaplan?

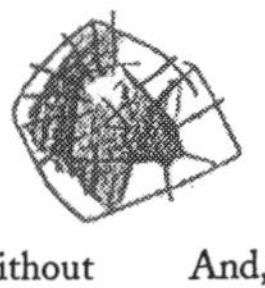

The judge chuckled. "I thought you might be wondering that," he said. Kaplan had skipped bail after jury selection, he said, and it had been decided to proceed without him. "I issued a warrant for his arrest, of course, as soon as he disappeared."

But what about his right not to be present?

The judge shrugged. He didn't have a right to skip bail. The judge had put the best face on Kaplan's absence when he explained it to us in the courtroom not only because he wanted to avoid prejudicing us against him but because, he said, "I thought the defense case was weak enough as it was."

I was stunned. While the judge's admonition that we infer nothing from Kaplan's absence had been, perhaps, the only part of his instructions concerning speculation and guesswork that the jury actually followed, and while I had been careful about not discussing the case, I had once mentioned to Caroline that it was an empty-chair trial. She had seemed surprised. "Yes," I said. "The defendant is exercising his constitutional right not to be present." She had made a strange face and abruptly left the room. Now I realized that she had been struggling not to laugh. I had pictured Kaplan down the street somewhere, strategizing over the phone with Rosenthal during breaks. She had known immediately that he had skipped.

As it happened, the judge went on, Kaplan was now in custody. He had been picked up on another charge, and was on his way from Riker's Island to the courthouse to hear our verdict.

Though we had been discharged, few of the jury members seemed inclined to leave. We milled in the corridor outside the courtroom, lingering over our good-byes. A group of us buttonholed Marc Agnifilo, who was quietly enjoying his triumph. I asked what Martin Kaplan had been rearrested for.

"Breaking into a car, apparently," Agnifilo said. "That's what he does. The guy's got like thirty convictions."

Were they for violent crimes?

"He's not usually violent," Agnifilo conceded. "Only if you catch him breaking into your car. Then he might beat the hell out of you."

Any narcotics convictions? (Our speculation during deliberations had featured a lot of drug abuse, with addiction a possible robbery motive.)

"Many. He's a heroin addict, and apparently a heroin dealer."

And, I thought, my mind now reeling, the alibi witnesses were no doubt drug customers. And Tagliaferri's mother, it suddenly occurred to me, seemed to have a wasted look. Was Kaplan, perhaps, her connection? That would clear up *that* mystery. I found my face getting hot with chagrin at the thought that I had wanted to acquit this thug, sending him back out to beat someone else to a pulp.

I asked what had happened to Kaplan's first lawyer. (We had heard testimony about a lawyer who had preceded Rosenthal. My assumption was that this was a public defender and that Kaplan's friends, believing that his chances would be better with a private lawyer, had decided to hire Rosenthal.) Agnifilo said his impression was that the first lawyer, who was indeed a public defender, had been confronted with an ethical dilemma after Kaplan insisted on mounting an alibi defense. "You're not allowed to put somebody on the stand who you think is going to lie," Agnifilo said. So the public defender had withdrawn. Rosenthal, a private attorney, was also paid by the state in this case, he added.

I had heard enough.

Four or five of us, including Timothy Hyde, the schoolteacher, and the Alabamian, went across the street for a deli lunch. We had decided to stay to see Kaplan. After lunch, we returned to the courtroom, sitting now on the public benches. Kaplan was brought in. He was handcuffed, and dressed in jail dungarees. He looked angry and distant. The judge informed him of our verdict, and scolded him for having risked the bail money put up by his friends, Tagliaferri and Castellano. Kaplan curled his lip and said nothing. The judge set a date for sentencing, and warned Kaplan that he would be sentenced as a "predicate felony offender," citing a prior conviction for attempted grand larceny. As the trial officially ended, I noticed that my ally, the schoolteacher, was weeping. I was surprised, for I was by now feeling relieved and righteous about our verdict.

THREE weeks later, at Kaplan's sentencing, my feelings were much the same. I wasn't sure why I was there; I was the only jury member who had turned up. Luciente Castellano was also there, dressed in a black leather jacket, jeans, and sandals. Kaplan was brought in, looking strikingly healthier after three weeks in jail. He winked at Castellano, and she blew him a kiss. Two armed guards stood at his sides while his handcuffs were removed. Jerald Rosenthal and Marc Agnifilo were back at their accustomed posts.

First, Rosenthal asked, in his fulsome, perfunctory way, for the verdict to be set aside and Kaplan granted a new trial. The reason? Kaplan had not been brought immediately, after he was rearrested and discovered to be "in the system," to the courtroom where his case was being heard. Judge Berman denied the request, and ordered that the sentencing proceed.

Kaplan stood.

Agnifilo, asked for his views, recommended a sentence of six to twelve years, citing the violence of the assault and Kaplan's lengthy criminal record, which included no fewer than four convictions *since* the Christmas mugging. Castellano, who was sitting near me, muttered angrily during the prosecutor's remarks, disputing sotto voce each detail of his version of Kaplan's record.

Rosenthal then asked that Kaplan be allowed to make his plea for leniency in camera. This request denied, he announced, rather dramatically, that any sentence longer than the three-to-six-year minimum that Kaplan faced would be "a life sentence," for "it seems Mr. Kaplan has been found H.I.V.-positive and has a very low blood count."

The judge asked Kaplan if he cared to speak.

"I don't have anything to say," Kaplan mumbled.

Judge Berman drew himself up and pronounced Kaplan's crime "unprovoked" and "vicious." ("Too bad he didn't do it," Castellano whispered.) As the latest and most serious of a long string of crimes, the judge continued, this offense deserved to be "appropriately" punished. He was therefore sentencing Kaplan to five to ten years in prison.

The handcuffs went back on. Kaplan

"Do you, Edward and King, take Susan and Fluffy, to have and to hold . . ."

• •

turned and looked into Castellano's face, his expression more rueful than tragic, as he was led away.

Leaving the courtroom, I found myself in an elevator car with Castellano, who was wiping her eyes, and taking deep breaths. I introduced myself.

She stared at me. "I thought I recognized you," she said. She turned away. "Martin really got railroaded."

I asked what she meant.

"It wasn't a fair trial," she said. "I can't believe he got convicted. I was thinking about going to law school, but not after seeing this. Both my parents are lawyers. My sister's a lawyer."

We left the courthouse together, walking west. As we went on talking, I found that many of my (and the rest of the jury's) assumptions about Castellano were being rudely overturned. Both her parents were lawyers? I offered to explain how we had reached our verdict, and Castellano said she was interested. She listened closely, nodding, sighing, shaking her head, as we slowly walked through Tribeca and then caught the uptown I.R.T. at Franklin Street. "I understand," she said. "I understand. And Martin *is* a criminal. He really is. But he didn't do this. We *know* he didn't do it."

When Castellano rose to leave the train, at Thirty-fourth Street, I asked if we might talk again.

"Sure," she said, wearily, and she gave me her number.

NOW I knew why I had come back for Kaplan's sentencing. Serving on the jury had been gratifying in its way, but it had also been profoundly irritating. I wanted to learn more about the real story, the fuller, truer tale that we jurors, with a man's freedom hanging on our judgment, had been forced to guess at lamely.

I met Castellano for lunch in a noisy midtown bistro. (At her insistence, I have changed her name.) She seemed calm and cheerful, watchful, eager to please. She wore a black leather jacket and jeans, with a chain slung from one hip. Kaplan, she said, had been sent to a prison up on the Canadian border, and he was fiercely miserable there, as she learned again each time he called her, collect. She was back living with her parents, in Queens, still working at two jobs, and going full time to college, where she was majoring in Romance languages. I asked how many languages she spoke—I had noticed her ordering lunch from the French menu. "Five," she said. "But only three fluently. My Russian and my German have got pretty mediocre."

For what it was worth, my assumption during the trial, seemingly shared by the rest of the jury, had been that Castellano was from a working-class background, probably Dominican or Puerto Rican. Now it turned out that she was Chilean. (And I found myself wondering how many languages our jury's Alabama delegate, who had been so certain about the insular out-of-court identities of the alibi witnesses, spoke.) Her family had left Chile, Castellano said, shortly before Allende was overthrown, in 1973. Her parents both worked for international organizations, and the family had lived all over. Luciente had especially loved Kenya, where they had lived for two years. Her oldest sister, now a lawyer, had gone off to live with Masai cattle herders. "When she came back, she smelled like *smoke*." Castellano laughed. "And this Masai man who wanted to marry her came to see my father. He wanted to give us two cows for her." Castellano planned to start travelling again. She needed to finish school first, though. Also, she needed to support herself. That was why she was working at two jobs—one as a doctor's secretary, the other as a freelance translator for various government agencies. "I probably shouldn't talk about the translating, but it's really fun. They give me all these tapes of people who don't know they're being taped."

"Detective Lyons rides again."

Castellano grimaced. "What a shock, hearing I'd been taped."

I asked where she'd met Martin Kaplan.

"Washington Square Park," she said. She had been a young teen-ager, living on the Upper East Side, going to the United Nations International School, and had been drawn downtown by the punk scene of the early nineteen-eighties. Her crowd had followed bands like Agnostic Front and Murphy's Law, had hung out at clubs like the Rock Hotel, on Jane Street. "Most of the kids had, like, really permissive parents, who let them stay out all night. The others were runaways, living in abandoned buildings on the Lower East Side. My parents were pretty permissive, I guess. But we fought a *lot*." Castellano gave a pained little laugh at the memory. She had, I noticed, a tattoo running around her left wrist—what looked like a bracelet of thorns. "Martin was the tough kid," she went on. "The wild one. It's so corny when you think about it now, but we were just teen-agers, and everybody thought he was so cool. The girls really liked him, and we all followed him around. He was always the most daring kid: climbing buildings, climbing trees. He was a big showoff, really. He'd play tricks on people—sneak up and stick wet fingers in your ear. He was only about fourteen, but he was already living in abandoned buildings.

"But you know how people tell you the horror stories of their childhood, and you always have to take them with a grain of salt? Well, Martin was given up for adoption when he was born, and adopted by this Jewish couple out in the projects in Canarsie. Then, when he was seven, his mother flipped out on Valium, so they put Martin in the Infants Home of Brooklyn, which was run by the Jewish Board of Guardians, for, like, four years. He started getting into trouble. In fact, his father used to send him out to steal things. There's a picture of him and Martin with a car that Martin stole when he was twelve. Finally, Martin's mother left, and his father had to move across the hall to live with this old man, and they didn't want Martin around. So he's been on his own, basically, since he was really young. I've actually *heard* his father say, 'I never wanted you. Your mother wanted you, and now she's gone, so why don't you get lost.' I couldn't believe he would say that in front of me. We were seventeen at the time. Have you ever been to Canarsie? It's like out on these docks, in a swamp, way out past the end of the L line. Martin's father is in a nursing home now, in Brooklyn. He had both his legs amputated. Anyway, Martin never even got to high school. He was always broke, always hungry, never had a place to live. He used to help other kids, though. Runaways. Especially girls." Castellano laughed lightly. "He used to live off girls—N.Y.U. students, F.I.T. students."

What about drugs?

"These old hippies used to give us acid," Castellano said. "It was a really bad thing to do, I realize now, but they did it. And everybody smoked pot, of course." Cocaine and heroin came along later, she said.

Did Martin become a drug dealer?

"Martin?" Castellano looked amused. "No. He's too irresponsible. Drug dealing takes responsibility."

Agnifilo, I thought, had apparently given Kaplan too much credit.

Martin did become an addict, however, Castellano said, and after he and she became romantically involved, when they were seventeen, she became an addict, too. Eventually, she began living with him in abandoned buildings. "Horrible squats. One on Ninth Street. Another one on Eighth Street. People used to steal electricity from an outlet in the street. They used to tap into the telephone lines, and the runaways would make long-distance calls to their parents. I used to see my parents sometimes, and they were desperate about what I was doing, but they couldn't do much. They used to really hate Martin." Kaplan had by then found his vocation—breaking into cars—and was constantly being arrested. He twice spent a year in jail. Finally, after five years together, Castellano left him. She was twenty-two. She entered drug rehab, got a job and an apartment, and started college.

"But somehow Martin and I stayed friends, even though we broke up, ah, nonamicably," she said. "I left because of drugs, and because he was using needles, and wouldn't stop—I never used needles—but I felt like I still had to take care of him. Martin can't take care of himself. He gets girls to take care of him."

Like Leah Tagliaferri?

"Exactly. Leah was a college girl, going to Hunter, living in an apartment paid for by her parents. I felt sorry for her. People warned her about Martin. But she was like a typical case in a self-help book: 'Leah, a woman who loved too much, and believed that he would change.' Martin *couldn't* change. He didn't know anything else. Also, he's too self-destructive. So he just lived off her, always getting high, disappearing for days—the same old thing. And she just used to stand on the corner, literally, waiting for him. People used to imitate her: 'This is Leah.'" Castellano let her arms fall to her sides and made a hangdog face, looking forlornly from side to side. "That's why I felt sorry for her. But she and I were never friends. She felt threatened by me, even though Martin and I had broken up at least a year before they met."

I recalled that during the trial the prosecutor had seemed extravagantly surprised and skeptical when Tagliaferri said that she and Castellano were not really friends. Were they, perhaps, trying to hide the fact, he seemed to wonder, that they had cooked up their

"I did a 'Kojak,' two 'McCloud's, and some voice-overs. Right now, I'm doing my laundry."

little alibi story together? Some members of the jury had thought that it was a ridiculous ruse, too—their pretending not to be friends—and that it had damaged their credibility.

I asked about Tagliaferri's mother. Was she, by any chance, into drugs?

"No! She's just a regular mom!" Again, Castellano seemed to find my question amusing. She grinned and then guffawed. "I do think she's got some psychological problems, though, that she needs to work on. I mean, she's so co-dependent it's unbelievable. She just attaches herself to people. Like Martin. He lived with them for a while. *My* mother would have had him arrested if he'd done to me what he did to Leah. He never even told Leah he was H.I.V.-positive—and he denied it after somebody else told her. But Leah's mom still bailed him out of jail, and she went to his trial every day. She still talks to him on the phone from jail. I mean, it's nice of her, but . . ."

What did her own parents think about Kaplan now?

Castellano shrugged. "They accept that he's part of my life. I mean, they hope I'll get over him. But there's nothing to get over. He's my friend. They don't know I testified at his trial. And, to tell you the truth, I would *really* have preferred not to. I just couldn't avoid it. It was my obligation. I *had* to do it."

I asked about her bracelet-of-thorns tattoo—probably not, I guessed, her parents' favorite sight—and said that at Kaplan's sentencing I had noticed something similar around his wrist.

"Actually, the one on Martin's wrist is skulls. But he got a tattoo like mine on his upper arm the same day I got this."

Castellano's current boyfriend, who was also probably not delighted about the tattoo she shared with Kaplan, was a musician and writer (and former friend of Kaplan's). She told me that he filled notebooks with poems and stories that she and her sister thought were fantastic but he refused to try to publish. "He should have lived in the eighteenth century," she said, laughing and blushing bright red.

Castellano was curious about the eyewitness descriptions of Kaplan that had convinced the jury of his guilt. I said that they had been only slightly more detailed than the descriptions of his companions.

"Companions?"

It seemed that she had never heard—or had forgotten—that there were three attackers. She pushed her plate away. "Now I'm absolutely positive," she said finally. "There *weren't* two other guys around that night. And who would hang out with Martin, anyway? It's not like he has a *crew*, or anything." She shook her head and sighed. "On the other hand, it never made sense that Martin would do a mugging alone, either. I mean, he's a wimp. Most junkies are. Mugging takes courage. Martin breaks into cars. It's easy, it's safe. He can *look* intimidating, especially after he's been in jail, but he's not violent. He runs away from fights. Once, this Puerto Rican couple tried to mug us. They had baseball bats, and everything. And Martin just *ran*. And the people were so surprised, to see him leave me standing there, that I had time to get away, too. You know, I thought about saying in court what I really thought—that Martin's a wimp. But Martin would have been really mad. So I didn't. Anyway, they never asked my opinion. They just wanted facts. And then they didn't believe us."

I tried to explain that it had been possible to convict Kaplan without first concluding that she and Tagliaferri had deliberately lied. But the truth was that most of my fellow-jurors had thought they were lying.

As we left the restaurant, I asked Castellano to ask Kaplan, the next time they spoke, to call me. She looked uncomfortable. "I'll ask him," she said. "But I told him I was coming to see you, and you don't want to know what he said."

"What did he say?"

"Well . . . he said, 'Fuck that reporter.' He's just angry, you know. Angry at the world."

THINGS weren't getting any clearer, but the picture was at least filling in. I got a transcript of Kaplan's trial—at six hundred and eighty pages, it was three inches thick—and, unexpectedly, the picture congealed some more. Much of the expurgation of the story that the jury heard had occurred, I discovered, in open court, during the various "colloquies" that took place while we were banished to the jury room. The fact that Kaplan had been arrested on a new charge while he was awaiting trial, for example, had been discussed during a break in Leah Tagliaferri's testimony. The judge had at that point come up with a description, acceptable to both lawyers, of Kaplan's bail situation which would not reveal the rearrest; and, upon our return, he had smoothly laid it on us.

Later, with Detective Lyons on the stand, we had been abruptly sent out after Lyons mentioned that a relative of his was a former cocaine addict. In the colloquy that followed, with Jerald Rosenthal repeatedly asking for (and being denied) a mistrial, the judge declared himself determined to find some way, in his words, "to clear up any possible thought in the jury's mind that Mr. Kaplan is a drug addict." Since Lyons had actually been making an oblique reference to Luciente Castellano's drug problem, not Kaplan's, the judge decided to tell us when we returned that the discussion between Lyons and Castellano had been about drug problems in their respective families, thus removing the inference farther from Kaplan. Rosenthal, while noting that "we are doing a deception on the jury"—Judge Berman disputed this description, but it was clearly accurate—had no objection. And again we were glibly gulled.

The colloquies contained some odd gems, including vintage weird riffs by Rosenthal. On, for instance, the secret taping of Castellano by Lyons: "It's a gratuitous act on his part which to me is a violation of everything that we hold sacred on our privacy and everything else." Judge Berman seemed to feel less compunction about rebuking Rosenthal during colloquies than he did in front of the jury, at one point exclaiming, "You get so carried away with your own voice and speech that you are not aware I am about to grant you what you request."

But the gist of the colloquies revolved around a powerful irony, which, I now realized, had suffused the entire trial. The great care taken to exclude certain matters from evidence had but one purpose: to protect the rights of the accused. Everyone, starting with the judge, had been intent on providing Martin Kaplan a fair trial. And yet the net effect had been to weaken his case. At least, I found that his alibi, once the judicial veils were removed, and Kaplan and his world were shown in far more detail (however sordid), was only getting stronger. Castellano had been credible as a witness, I thought, and she was even more so off the stand.

LEAH TAGLIAFERRI, it turned out, had also thought about saying in court something different, something more candid, than what she had said. "Maybe I should have just got up there and said,

'Martin's a junkie,' " she told me. "Said, 'His hands were bloody when they stopped him because he'd been shooting up in his wrists. He couldn't have beat up anybody if he wanted to—he was too high. Anyway, Martin does cars. He doesn't rob *people*. He knows that's a felony. He's not stupid. He makes a living from cars, and he's a creature of habit. He does the same cars on the same streets, every night. Plus, nobody from the neighborhood would try that shit at Astor Place, because the station is crawling with plainclothes cops. You jump a turnstile there, they'll get you. So there's no way Martin could have done it.' Maybe that would have worked better."

"Mama and I fixed a lovely dinner. I used the right side of my brain, and she used the left side of her brain."

Tagliaferri seemed to believe, however, that in the end no defense could have succeeded. Why? "Because that jury had no brain," she told me. "All they had to do was look at the evidence. It was *impossible* that Martin could have done it. But they were just too stupid. They wanted to convict him from the first time they saw him. 'Street punk? He must have done it.' "

We were sitting in Tagliaferri's horse-drawn carriage, a graceful maroon-colored landau, on Central Park South. It was a raw December night, and she had spread a heavy blanket over our knees. She wore a head scarf against the cold, and a nose ring that I hadn't noticed in court (had she removed it for the occasion?) now glinted in the street light. The well-mannered suburbanite from the courtroom seemed, indeed, quite transformed by a pugnacious, vaguely Cockney charm. At the same time, Luciente Castellano's depiction of Tagliaferri as a lovelorn doormat seemed suddenly way off the mark—the wishful putdown, perhaps, of a romantic rival. I had surprised Tagliaferri earlier, picking her out of a group of drivers talking near their carriages. She hadn't recognized me from the trial, and her wariness had only increased after I introduced myself. But she had slowly warmed to her subject, and now she seemed entirely unconcerned that I might take personally her low opinion of my intelligence as a juror.

I asked about her relationship with Kaplan.

"The first time I saw him was years ago, at the Lismar Lounge, on First Avenue," she said. "He was dressed like the Road Warrior. Black leather, boots, with, like, a Mohawk. I said to my friend, 'Who is that? He's *hot*.' He was with this girl, though—Lucy." Tagliaferri pronounced "Lucy" with exaggerated disdain. She and Kaplan finally met, she said, in 1991, when she came home one day and found him, courtesy of her then roommate, asleep in her bed. They took up with each other, but, as she soon discovered, "Martin was a *terrible* boyfriend." She explained, "He was always disappearing, always strung out, getting arrested. He wasn't a womanizer—I just could never count on him. So I used to be *mean* to him. But, the whole year we lived together, Martin never said a mean thing back to me. I'd be yelling at him, and he'd just say, 'Come on, don't be like that.' Because Martin is a truly sweet person. I've never seen him be violent. Which is another reason he couldn't have done this robbery."

Did she, too, get into drugs?

"No. Martin wouldn't even let me see him buy drugs. He didn't want me to smoke pot. He didn't even want me to *drink*."

What about his H.I.V. status?

"I don't know he's H.I.V.-positive," Tagliaferri said tightly. "I know I'm not. And my new boyfriend's not."

Kaplan's attempts to kick his heroin addiction had all been doomed by his circumstances, Tagliaferri recalled, her voice bitter. "Somebody like Lucy, she had her family to fall back on when she wanted to clean up," she said. "But Martin has nobody. He got into a methadone program once, and when they found out he was homeless they just kicked him out. Before he was even detoxed. Have you ever been around somebody that's trying to kick? The smell is *horrible*. It comes out through their skin. We used to spend whole days sitting in the welfare office, trying to get Martin on welfare. You'd sit there the whole fucking day, then they'd tell you, 'Come back tomorrow.' "

Once, Tagliaferri said, she took Kaplan upstate. "My cousins live up near Kingston, and every summer they have this thing they call the Swampathon. They live next to a swamp, and they have like a big party, and everybody has to run through the swamp. It's really gross, really fun. Martin didn't want to go, but I told him there was no *way* I wasn't going upstate. So he came, too, and he had *so much fun*. He did the Swampathon. He rode a pony. He raced go-carts. He climbed a tree to get a snake that was up there. And he was like 'Leah, let's just stay here. Not go back to the city.' I've never seen Martin so happy."

Had Kaplan ever been gainfully employed?

"He was a bicycle messenger, before I met him. And he was a roofer down in Florida once, when he was a teen-ager. And a dishwasher. That's about it. I tried to get him on here at the carriages. He got dressed up, in a nice shirt, and everything. But the guy I was working for then wouldn't hire him. He said he looked too intimidating. He was a real prick, that guy.

"But the worst part of this job right now," she went on, "is this little fat fuck from the A.S.P.C.A. running around out here writing tickets. Five people in your carriage? Boom, five-hundred-dollar fine. A couple of times, the animal-rights people were out here, spraying drivers with Mace. Can you believe that? What assholes!"

The subject of animal-rights activists got Tagliaferri started on "political correctness," which had plagued Hunter College, she said, and had ultimately caused her to drop out.

Her current boyfriend, she said, was also a carriage driver. "He's, like, the complete opposite of Martin," she said. "He's really clean. Doesn't drink or smoke or do drugs. Can't go to bars, because he has asthma. Drinks fruit juice, and this protein stuff. He works out." Tagliaferri rolled her eyes as she said "works out." I gathered that physical fitness didn't rate much higher with her than political correctness did. "He's in Ireland right now," she said. "I just got back from there."

The conversation turned back to Kaplan, sitting in prison far upstate. "There's *nothing* up there," Tagliaferri said. "Nobody to talk to. Nothing to do. I want to go visit him, but my boyfriend wouldn't like it. Also, it's, like, ten hours on the bus, overnight, and it's a really cold ride, I heard. Plus, the visits are for six hours. And, I mean, what's there to talk about for six hours? Martin's always saying, 'My life's not worth living.' And I never tell him it's true, of course." Tagliaferri stamped her boots against the cold, which had long since robbed my feet of all feeling. "It was different when he was in Riker's, or the Tombs," she said. "It was easy to visit him, take him things. Books. He loves to read." I remembered Castellano telling me that Kaplan liked Edgar Allan Poe. "Martin's artistic," Tagliaferri said. "He made me these carvings out of soap when he was in Riker's. They were really good. One was a picture frame, with a skull and crossbones. Another one he made from two bars of soap. It was a coffin, with a skeleton inside."

The many short sentences Kaplan had served in local jails had all been the upshots of plea-bargain agreements. His being sent upstate for a long stretch now was, Tagliaferri knew, a direct result of his refusal to follow the usual procedure. "They tried to get him to cop out, to take a sentence of two to four years," she said. "But I told him, 'That's getting pretty low, when they can make you cop out to something you didn't even do.' That's why Martin wouldn't go along. His first lawyer, Armstrong, didn't want it to go to trial. The prosecutor didn't want it to go to trial. Armstrong thought we would lose and Martin would get more time. And he was right. But we never thought they could railroad him the way they did."

A car backfired, and Tagliaferri sprang from the carriage bellowing, in a surprisingly deep voice, "Hercules! Hercules!" She ran toward a muscular horse behind us, which had spooked and was pulling a driverless carriage up onto the sidewalk. Tagliaferri caught his reins, led him back to the street, and tied him firmly to a grate. She checked the line ahead of us before she climbed back in her carriage. "Unbelievable," she muttered. "I'm going to end up making a total of one trip tonight." She lapsed into a disgruntled silence.

When she spoke again, her voice was querulous, almost angry. "You know, my mother, who watched the whole trial, said something funny was definitely going on in there. Like, she said that all three of the witnesses against Martin were just lying sacks of shit. I mean, what is this bullshit about one of the so-called victims trying to shake hands with these three guys who want to kick his ass? When was the last time you saw that happen? And who were these two other guys Martin supposedly had with him, these phantoms? Why did the cops never try to find them?

My mother said she thought the whole thing might have been a drug deal gone bad. Or else these guys just got in a fight and lost and wanted to cover it up."

I bit back an impulse to ridicule this interpretation of the trial—I was a reporter now, I reminded myself—and instead asked Tagliaferri about her mother's background. "She used to be a ticket agent for Pan Am," she said. "So we used to fly all over for free. She lost her job when Pan Am got bought by Delta. So she's got an age-discrimination lawsuit against Delta. And a class-action suit against them, too. My stepfather was a fireman. He just retired. They're talking about moving to France for a year with my half sister."

We sank into silence again. Eventually, Tagliaferri piped up, "You know, Martin is going to be mad at me for blabbing to you. Whenever he used to disappear, and I'd go around asking people if they'd seen him, he'd show up eventually and hear about it, and get all mad. 'Everybody on the whole Lower East Side knows my business now! I don't want you telling people my business!' "

Tagliaferri used a huffy Brooklyn whine to imitate Kaplan, and I realized that I had heard him say only a very few words.

"But it's *scary*," she said suddenly. "Don't you think?"

"What?"

"How a couple of rich yuppies from the Upper East Side can just say you did something, and, even if you didn't, that's it—you go to jail. For five to ten years!"

I remembered something Castellano had told me. "Leah and I had this joke going at the trial," she said. "We were like 'They don't have twelve junkies sitting on that jury, so they don't know what's going on.' That's why I don't believe in the jury system. Somebody's fate shouldn't be decided by a bunch of people who aren't trained in the law. They should be professionals." While the idea of twelve professional junkies sitting in judgment on their peers had been more surreal than compelling, Tagliaferri's contention that class prejudice had been crucial to Kaplan's conviction—a bourgeois jury identifying with bourgeois victims, and being relatively deaf to the arguments of street scufflers—was less easily dismissed.

I didn't know what to say. So I tried to reassure Tagliaferri that she wasn't the only friend of Kaplan's who had talked to me.

"Oh, but Lucy's weird, don't you think?" she said. I didn't reply, and she widened her eyes and tilted her head in an imitation of Castellano. "I mean, it was good of her to come and testify," Tagliaferri said. "But I don't trust her. I think she's catty. All women are. They talk about you whenever your back's turned. That's why I don't like women. I have hardly any women friends."

I didn't tell Tagliaferri that her theory of female character had been shared by some of my fellow-jurors, and that the theory had helped send Kaplan up the river. Instead, I said that I had to go home—it was past midnight—and climbed down from the carriage. Talking to Tagliaferri had left me feeling like a character in a nineteenth-century novel—Inspector Bucket, perhaps, from "Bleak House," but more classbound. She, meanwhile, was the fiery, intelligent, undereducated working lass, her general sense of grievance sharpened by the injustice she saw being done to her beloved Kaplan. As we stretched our legs and said good night, I gave Tagliaferri my number and asked her to have Kaplan call me collect. She said she doubted he would, but she would try. Then, as I turned to leave, she cocked her head, put an index finger to her cheek, and said, mock-coyly, "So, was it better than talking with Lucy?"

I wondered how many times she must have asked Kaplan a version of the same question.

I CALLED Mrs. Tagliaferri, and asked why she had been so interested in Kaplan's trial.

"I wanted to give Martin moral support," she said. "Who was there for him? How would you like to be on trial, and nobody showing up in court for you? I felt terrible for him, seeing that courtroom. I hadn't seen Martin for almost a year, and I didn't know what was going on with him, but I brought a bag of clothing for him every day, just in case he showed up. And then I got interested in the trial. I got nosy. There was something phony about that trial. My feeling was: this was not a robbery. It was either a fight or they were there buying drugs. The one guy was Wall Street, which is very heavy cocaine use. The other guy was a bartender. Out here in Long Beach, a lot of the bartenders are involved."

In fact, among her greatest fears, Mrs. Tagliaferri said, was that one of her children would become a drug addict. "I was very worried that Leah would get into drugs, or some kind of trouble," she said. "And when Leah first brought Martin home I did not know he was a drug addict. If I had known, I might not have let him stay here. It wasn't obvious. But, you see, she had brought another guy home with her once. His mother had thrown him out. And we let him stay here, and he got his G.E.D., and we really straightened him out. He's in college now, doing fine. So we trusted Leah's judgment—that she wouldn't bring home anybody who wasn't a decent person. So I put Martin in for a G.E.D., too. But his concentration was about five minutes. We were trying to teach him fractions. He's very smart. He just couldn't concentrate.

"Then we found out he was a drug addict, and I was horrified. I was afraid for my daughter. One thing I know about drug addicts is that they try to get other people to use drugs. Luckily, Martin wasn't like that. He's really a very nice person. The drugs just got in the way. If he wasn't using drugs, he'd be perfectly fine. I was never, ever afraid of him. He never stole from me—that's another thing addicts usually do. All he did was eat. He was eating me out of house and home!" Mrs. Tagliaferri laughed. "He'd eat anything. One night, he ate a box of dried stuffing."

I could hear Leah guffawing in the background.

"He stayed with us for about a year," her mother went on. "My seven-year-old daughter liked him. He was good with her. But I asked him to leave in May, because by then I knew he was on drugs, and that I wasn't helping him by letting him stay here. I was just making it easy for him. He wasn't doing anything for himself. He wasn't looking for a job. He was causing friction in the house. My husband wasn't happy. So Martin left, and went back to the city. Back to squatting. Then Leah went, and was staying with him, and I was very worried, so I went looking for her. We convinced Martin to go into drug treatment, at St. Barnabas Hospital, in the Bronx. We arranged it through some group in Grand Central. We took a taxi up to the Bronx, and then it took all day to get Martin admitted. They didn't want to take him, because he fell asleep and when they woke him up he was disoriented, and they thought he was psycho. But we finally got him in, for five days of detox. After that, we took him to Odyssey, in the East Village. But it

SIXTH SENSE

Something told him she was near. In the same room,
Even. Wearing the blue polka-dot dress he'd given her,
With the pearl choker and the sapphire earrings,
Holding a Kir Royale. He looked at her left hand.
No ring. And knew he had to get out of there
Fast, before one of them did something irrevocable,
Like the time she slapped his face in the bus
And he wasn't sure why, or the day they stood
In front of the dress-shop window, and when
She said she liked the yellow kimono he went
And bought it on the spot. What an amazing day
That was. Everyone he met that day was someone
He had known before, a decade ago or more,
And the statue of Alice the gigantic girl
In Central Park turned out to be his sister
When they were small. Mama was in the kitchen
Waiting for the phone to ring, and Daddy was still
On the road, checking the rearview mirror
In the old green Chevrolet, when the hurricane hit.
One of the other men drowned that night, but Daddy
Came back safely, with gifts for all the kids
If they agreed to go to sleep and dream of him.

—DAVID LEHMAN

turned out that he really hadn't detoxed long enough, so it didn't work. And that was the last time I saw Martin. That was, oh, eighteen months ago, at least."

Mrs. Tagliaferri paused, and Leah, who had been tossing in comments throughout this account, was also silent. "It's a ruined life," Mrs. Tagliaferri said softly. "And you look at this guy and say, 'He really could've *been* something.' And I think, if he changes his mind, he still could be. He still calls here. I talk to him. I yell at him. I tell him to straighten out."

A FEW days after my conversation with Leah, Martin Kaplan surprised me with a collect call. His voice sounded just like her imitation of him.

"I got two things to say," he said. "First, I wasn't guilty of doing this. Second, I was stuck in the system from Monday onward. I only missed two days on my own."

I couldn't recall offhand where Monday had fallen in the trial, so I asked why he had been absent to begin with.

"I was strung out," he said.

There was a rising clatter in the background, then shouting. "Hold on," Kaplan said. "There's gonna be a count."

A soundtrack from Pandemonium filled the phone for several minutes while I jotted down questions.

When Kaplan returned, I had him confirm the details of his background as I had heard them from his ex-girlfriends. (He agreed that his father had sent him out to steal when he was a child; however, his father, when I reached him by telephone, denied that he had ever approved Martin's stealing.) Then he resumed his *mea exculpa*, echoing both the alibi that had been offered in court and the more nuanced version I had heard since. "I walked out of San Loco, I'm standing there, and the cops pull up in an unmarked car and throw me against the car," he said. "My entire record is for stealing cars. I don't mug people."

So why did the victims and the eyewitness identify him?

"They didn't," he said. "Not at first. It was only after we'd been at the station for two and a half hours. The cops were talking to them in the back room the whole time, and then they came out and looked at me in the cage and said I was the one. I only saw them for a couple of seconds. But if you ever talk to them I wish you'd ask them if they *really* think it was me, and if the cops didn't coerce them. I mean, they looked like young, decent guys, could be in college. They were pretty lumped up, but they didn't seem like bad guys. Not enough to deserve the beating they caught. It's something you see a lot in the East Village, though. Hang around, you see a couple of those a night. Just another bashing."

Kaplan had the voice, I thought, of someone who had been on the receiving end of more than his share of bashings. But he also had a casual, palooka authority.

"I've heard of people being picked up for things they didn't do before," he went on. "But nothing as serious as this. Of course, I'm the only fool who ever took it to trial. I shoulda taken the two-to-four, because I coulda done that standing on my head, and I'd be home now. But I'm just not gonna cop out to stuff that I haven't done."

On a hunch, I asked about the flashlight.

"You heard about that?" Kaplan seemed amused. "Yeah, I was trying to sell it. It— I guess I can't get in trouble for it now. It came out of a car. I wanted to do a nickel of coke, and I was trying to sell it for two dollars. But that's the biggest joke of all. The cops said I just robbed this guy of sixty bucks, and here I am with no money, trying to scrape up five bucks."

Perhaps his accomplices had taken off with the sixty, I thought, without much conviction. I asked Kaplan what the police had offered him in exchange for his help in finding the other attackers.

"They never mentioned 'em," he said. "You don't understand. It was obvious to the cops that I wasn't there."

What about his bleeding hands?

"There was blood running down my left arm when I was arrested," he said. "There was an abscess on my arm where I had been sticking a needle in it. The paramedics took a look at it. It was obvious where the blood was coming from. I had some little cuts and abrasions on my hands, but on my fingertips, not on my knuckles. Those were from messing with car locks and stuff, undoing bolts on radios with my fingers. I always had those cuts, because I didn't have tools. The cops took pic-

"You know what I think, babe? Seven on the Richter scale."

tures of my hands. Didn't you see them?"

No, I said, we hadn't seen them. I asked about his health.

"It's O.K.," he said. "You mean the H.I.V. thing? I don't think I'm positive. I wasn't actually tested at any point in time. My lawyer said I had it at my sentencing, but that was just, like, a last-ditch bid to get my time down. They tested me in here. I'm waiting for a result now."

I wished him luck with the test results.

"I'll be O.K.," he said evenly. "I never used too many dirty needles. I've always come up negative before."

I didn't point out that he had just told me, less than a minute earlier, that he had never been tested previously for H.I.V.

The time permitted for an inmate's call was running out. Kaplan urged me to relay to Solder and Leamy his questions about their identification of him. "You have a good Christmas," he said in parting.

I mumbled something similar as the line went dead.

EVEN after allowing for the excellent possibility that I was being conned, I was now quite rattled. I called Detective Lyons, who had conducted the police investigation, and asked whether Kaplan had ever been asked about his accomplices. Not that he knew of, he said. "See, what the D.A. tries to do is clear the calendar, not add to it," he said. "Of course, I never dealt directly with Kaplan. Once he has a lawyer, it's pointless." Lyons had shown John Solder mug shots of "guys from that area with that m.o.," he said. "But I woulda had a better chance if I coulda talked to the guy in California. He was better at I.D."

The only reason he even got involved with the case, Lyons added, was that the defense was planning to present an alibi. "And they had two decent-looking girls. If I was in the jury, I would've acquitted him, because of the reasonable doubt. So that's why I went out to talk to them—to try to tie them to a story that they can't change later. That way, it's my word against hers. And if you believe her and not me, you're going to acquit. That's why integrity is so important. It's all I really got at that point."

Another thing Lyons had, and mentioned to me, was his "success rate," or "clearance rate." "Detectives are graded on their success rate, and the powers that be consider a ten-per-cent clearance rate good," he said. "I don't."

I wondered if I was supposed to congratulate Lyons on his success in the Kaplan case. I didn't.

I called Solder and Leamy. Solder on the phone was much as he had been in court, expressing a rather detached satisfaction that "some part of the system in New York actually worked," and saying that "determining guilt or innocence was secondary" (I assumed he meant that his primary goal was to see justice done, not Kaplan convicted), while declining to elaborate much on his testimony.

Leamy, on the other hand, was vastly more vehement and dramatic than the witness we had heard. "I'm a tough son of a bitch," he said. "But did you see those boots? Weren't they murderous? I caught some serious blows. I can't believe to this day that I didn't lose an eye, or something. I'm not on a vendetta—if you knew me, you'd know that I don't want to be responsible for putting anybody in jail—but this guy is an evil son of a bitch. I mean, the scumbag from Hell. I didn't want to go back and testify. I didn't want to face him again. I've had to deal with that pride aspect, see. I feel shame that I was wounded by some dooky character like himself. I mean, one on one, come *on*, baby. But I was whamboozled. Bushwhacked. Ambushed."

Rock music and loud voices rose and fell behind Leamy in the San Francisco bar where he worked. I asked him about the identification process.

"When we found him on the street, I was dead set," he said. "Some things register in your soul. Like when someone tries to murder your ass. I *knew* that motherfucker. And I went up to him in the cage there, next to the desk, in the station, and he was in there, behind those solid, steely-eyed bars, and I said, 'I will remember you.' I'm an artist. I notice things."

Had the police said anything to him and Solder about Kaplan?

"The cops said absolutely nothing to me about Kaplan," he said. "Except that he was a junkie and had a rap sheet and they weren't surprised he was there."

In saying "absolutely nothing," I thought, the police had said a mouthful, including everything they should not have said. And Leamy, for all his attention to detail, clearly had a passion to avenge the beating he had received. Like the news of Lyons' devotion to his "success rate," these were not reassuring revelations.

Solder had also mentioned that the police had told him, in the station that night, "We've seen this guy before." But when I phoned him back he changed his story, denying that the police had said anything to him about Kaplan. And any doubts that he might have had about Kaplan being one of the attackers, he said—doubts perhaps raised in the course of preparing for the trial, "because the D.A. just keeps asking you, and you have to ask yourself, 'Am I absolutely sure?' "—had been resolved before he testified, he said, his voice now grim and defensive.

I asked Leamy who had told him that Kaplan was a junkie. He said that it had been Officer Ungro, who, he added, had done a wonderful job that night. " 'Dedicated' is the word I would use."

I called William Ungro. He said he had never seen Kaplan before that night, and had had no idea who he was. I asked if he had taken any photographs of Kaplan's hands after his arrest. "Yeah, I did," he said. "But they didn't come out too good."

What was wrong with them?

"You couldn't really see the blood," he said.

A FEW nights later, I had a dream. A dark, sticky substance coated my hands and arms. I had been making liquor—or some sort of drug, or dessert—with the stuff, and now I was trying to wash it off under a tap. But it just got thicker and stickier. I was in a little house in the country, and I began to hear, above the sound of the water, Caroline screaming somewhere outside. I had been planning to go look for her after washing up. She had stumbled off earlier, looking for something in the woods. I rushed outside, unable to tell which direction the screaming was coming from. Panic filled my throat, and I woke up.

Lying in the dark, trying to calm down, I saw, in my mind's eye, Martin Kaplan's ravaged arms and bloody hands. The image was drenched with horror, and it was not the simple horror of a gory sight. It was moral horror—the now distinct possibility that we had put Kaplan in prison for something he did not do. The comfortable gulf between juror and accused, journalist and subject, cheerful audience and characters in torment had suddenly filled with ordinary sympathy,

THE DETECTIVE'S SUCCESS RATE

and even this referred distress was shockingly intense.

I WENT to the District Attorney's office. Marc Agnifilo, I was told, was not permitted to talk to me now that I was press. The public-information officer who could talk to me was polite but could answer virtually none of my questions. She did get copies of the two tape recordings that had been played during Kaplan's trial but had not appeared in the trial transcript—Carroll Wilder's 911 call and Lyons' interview with Luciente Castellano—and she let me listen to them in a corner of her office.

The 911 call was as I remembered it: chaotic, upsetting, not very informative.

Lyons' tape was another matter. I played it loud and slow, and was able to make out many bits that had been inaudible in the courtroom. I also played it right through passages that had been excised from the evidence version. The public-information officer had instructions to prevent me from hearing those passages, but it was easy to slip them past her. I was no longer a juror, and I felt justified in trying to learn whatever I could. And what I learned was that Lyons had gone considerably farther in his efforts to confuse and intimidate Castellano than the jury had been allowed to hear. The tension between them, and his relentlessness, were far more palpable with the volume turned up and with sections replayed. What had sounded like background noise and sociable chuckling by Castellano now emerged as a series of nervous, ingratiating, desperate moans, more like sobbing than like laughter. Several times, she had tried, very timidly and politely, to end the interview, and had been ignored.

The passages that had been excised were those in which Lyons talked about his relative being a former cocaine addict. The reason for bringing up Castellano's drug problem, Lyons had explained to the judge during one of the colloquies we didn't hear, had been merely to establish some common ground with her. On the tape, however, it was painfully clear that he had also brought up the subject of her struggle with addiction to scare her. "You've come a long way, Lucy," Lyons said avuncularly. "I don't know. Sometimes people fall back. I don't know if you have or not."

"No, I haven't," Castellano said, laughing miserably.

In a breathtaking gambit, Lyons turned Castellano's decision to testify into a failure in her recovery from heroin. "I don't know what you do as far as the steps," he said, referring to the standard twelve-step recovery program. "But with my [relative] . . . there are certain steps. And I don't think [testifying] is part of the steps. You know what I'm saying? And you know it's not, either."

When Castellano, in the face of repeated threats that she would be charged with perjury, refused to change her mind about either Kaplan's innocence or her own determination to testify, Lyons finally took his leave, saying, "You've come a long, long way, and I hate to see something like this happen to you, that's all. For what? For what?"

I gave the tapes back to the public-information officer, feeling thoroughly sick. Listening to them hadn't really told me anything new about Kaplan's guilt or innocence. But the experience had redoubled my feeling that if I could somehow vote again on the case, I would now vote to acquit.

IT wasn't that I had come to believe unshakably that Kaplan had not been one of Solder and Leamy's assailants. Nor was it that I believed that, as Kaplan put it, "the police and the D.A. built a phony case" against him. The District Attorney and the police almost certainly believed that they had caught and convicted a guilty man. And their failure to pursue the other muggers was not, in fact, unusual, I discovered. Even Kaplan's first lawyer on the case, Richard Armstrong, who was an experienced public defender, said that it didn't strike him as strange that they weren't interested. "It's the regular course of business," he said.

Neither was it that I swallowed whole the picture of Kaplan as a nonviolent criminal, as his ex-girlfriends painted him. He continued to phone me, and while I couldn't tell how much of it was prison bluster, his answers to some of my questions were decidedly rough. When, for instance, I tried to check with him Castellano's contention that she had never used needles, he growled, "I told her if I ever caught her with a fuckin' spike in her arm I'd break her arm." It was true that he had no previous convictions for violent felonies, but ten months before the Astor Place mugging he had been arrested for felony assault. Kaplan described that incident as a self-defense

"Do you think this would have happened even if we weren't the last two smokers in the office?"

Another old street buddy of Kaplan's, whom I met the same day, said the same thing. And when I told him what Armstrong had said he laughed. "His lawyer said that? 'The third guy to stomp someone.' That's perfect." He also recalled Kaplan's arrest for stabbing somebody. The word on the street, he said, was that the charges had been reduced only because the car owner and victim didn't pursue it.

I noticed, though, that the customers standing at the counter in San Loco when I walked in were young men in black jackets, jeans, and heavy black boots—the same East Village uniform that had helped tie Kaplan to the Astor Place mugging. San Loco was an odd little place, with walls painted blood red and canary yellow, Latino laborers and white students streaming in and out, music blazing from a cheap sound system, and one wall covered with a manifesto about all the fresh and natural ingredients used in the kitchen. I tried to picture Kaplan in there, hanging out at a table with his friends, wired on cocaine or nodding on smack, blood running down his arms—the dashing, battered, nominally Jewish casualty from Canarsie. He might have cut a fairly formidable figure, I thought, among the more impressionable college kids. (And no taint of political correctness clung to *him*, to put off the tough nuts like Tagliaferri.)

But back to the facts: Agnifilo had been both right and wrong, it seemed, about why Armstrong left the case. He had indeed been in a quandary about whether to put Luciente Castellano on the stand, but not because he believed that her story was a lie. It was, rather, because he had been told that Castellano had "cracked"—that the D.A.'s office had caught her telling two different stories. Armstrong had spoken to her only over the phone, and he thought she sounded like a solid witness,

• •

stabbing—he had, he said, been fighting off two thugs who jumped him—and told me the charges had been dismissed. But his rap sheet showed that he had in fact pleaded guilty to a lesser charge of weapons possession. (Kaplan's rap sheet, even before his assault-and-robbery conviction, was at least twenty-five pages long and showed thirty convictions, and it covered only the eight years since he had turned sixteen. Numerous convictions for drug offenses contradicted his contention that his "entire record is for stealing cars.") More likely, I later thought, this incident had been what Agnifilo was referring to when he said, immediately after the trial, that Kaplan got violent if you caught him breaking into your car.

My problem was simply that I was now racked with doubt, reasonable and otherwise.

Armstrong seemed to have had similar problems. "I went through different periods of what I thought and didn't think about whether Kaplan did it or not," he said. "A lot of my clients do stay in one field, so to speak. A burglar doesn't become a robber, and a robber doesn't become a burglar. They're different mind-sets. So Martin's theory that he's a car booster and not a robber may have been right. You could even say he was building his alibi by getting arrested repeatedly for breaking into cars while we were preparing this case!" But Armstrong, too, had begun to wonder about Kaplan's capacity for violence. "He had a streak, like a bad temper. And while I never could see him being the instigator of a robbery, I could see him, after I got to know him, as an accomplice, maybe following his friends into something, being the third guy to stomp someone."

None of the witnesses of the assault in Astor Place had depicted Kaplan as a follower, though. Quite the contrary.

Unable to leave all this unknowing alone, I went looking for more alibi witnesses. Both Castellano and Tagliaferri had said that there were others who could place Kaplan with them at the time of the crime but that they had all been, for various reasons, reluctant to come forward. I found one of them in San Loco. He agreed to talk to me on the condition that I not publish his name. He said he had told Castellano, who had approached him about two weeks after Kaplan's arrest, that he simply could not remember the night in question, let alone Kaplan's precise movements. A few months later, he said, Castellano had relayed a message to him from Kaplan, who was by then in jail. "Martin said he was gonna kick my ass when he got out," he said, shrugging.

I asked if he believed that Kaplan was capable of a violent robbery.

He thought about it for a long time. "Yeah," he said finally. "It doesn't take much to jump somebody when you've got two other guys with you."

but his confidence in her was also being undermined by Kaplan and Tagliaferri, who had described her as "unstable." However, when Armstrong told Kaplan that he was now reluctant to put Castellano on the stand, because she just might wreck their case, Kaplan was adamant that she should testify. It became a breaking issue, and Armstrong left the case. Hearing from me that Castellano had in fact been a strong witness, Armstrong sighed. "I guess I should have been more skeptical," he said. "About what I was hearing from the D.A. *and* Kaplan."

And from Tagliaferri, I thought, when it came to her rival, Castellano.

But I was also becoming familiar with Kaplan's penchant for disparaging Castellano, despite all she had done for him. He had maligned her several times during our conversations, for no apparent reason. I finally said something about it, and he said, sheepishly, "I'm just mad at her because she said she'd stay with me while I was in jail, and she didn't."

"But you two haven't been together for years."

"We haven't?" he said sharply. He let that hang in the air. Finally, he said, "Yeah, I guess we haven't, for a while."

I mentioned the bracelet of thorns on Castellano's wrist.

"Yeah, that's the other side of the tribal on my arm."

The tribal?

"It's a black tattoo. It originally started in tribes."

Both of Kaplan's lawyers had been impressed by the lasting hold he seemed to have over Castellano and Tagliaferri. "He's some kind of Svengali," Jerald Rosenthal said, when I called him.

I asked Rosenthal if he thought the women had told the truth in court. He said he did. But he also thought that Kaplan had probably committed the crime. "The girls didn't believe he had enough time to get up to this mischief, but he did." It was the same theory I had used to vote to convict, but I was amazed to hear that Rosenthal subscribed to it. Kaplan had complained to me that Rosenthal had never really cared about the case, but I thought he had fought hard. And Armstrong had said, when I told him about the trial, "Rosenthal must have done a good job, to keep the jury out overnight on that one."

I was happy to share the credit for keeping the jury out overnight. But that was all I was happy about, for I would probably never, I realized, attain anything like Rosenthal's seemingly settled mind about what had happened, or about my own role in it.

KAPLAN keeps calling. I come home from a weekend in the country and there are fifteen messages on my answering machine: all of them a recorded female voice intoning that I have a collect call from an inmate at a New York state prison. Sometimes, when he reaches me, he mutters that he shouldn't have phoned: he was just calling all the numbers on a list of those he is permitted to call, hoping to talk to anyone. We talk about his life in prison, his trial, his childhood, the story I'm writing. He frets that he will "look like a piece of shit" in this article, that people will now think he's H.I.V.-infected, that Castellano "is saying stuff about me, trying to break up me and Leah." He dreams ardently that I will somehow exonerate him. Once, he says, "Leah says you think I'm innocent."

I say that's not strictly true.

The truth is that I now have no idea whether Kaplan committed the crime for which I and my fellow-jurors sent him to prison.

We talk about his routine. "I'm studying for my G.E.D.," he says. His voice is flat. "I was working in the mess hall. That's real specialized training. I'll know how to wipe tables when I get out of here." The prison is thick with racial tension, he says, and there are too few white inmates to give him any protection. "If you ever wanted to write any stories on jail, I got some fuckin' funny stories," he says.

But none of the stories he tells me are funny.

I ask Kaplan what he's been reading.

"This place ain't got no kind of library," he says.

I offer to send him a box of books. What kind would he like?

"Horror," he says.

On another occasion, he asks me point-blank if I believe he received a fair trial.

I think for a long time. Then I say, "Yes." ♦

"Hobart, this is Merlin, my science adviser."

Part III
Dialogics of Law and Culture

[10]

Story and Transcription in the Trial of John Brown*

Robert A. Ferguson

Legal critics have long noted that trials are narratives that arbitrate between conflicting stories about a controversial event and that, consequently, the legal process often takes on a larger cultural meaning through the idea of story. But acknowledgment, as such, does not imply an effective analytical understanding of the connection, and it has not led to a perception of the way in which legal stories become cultural narratives. We can only tell the stories we know how to tell, and the degree of our understanding—our appreciation—depends on issues of narrative and genre often present but usually missed in studies of the legal process.

Famous trials, trials that capture the imagination of a community, are particularly useful for observing the nature of legal-literary-cultural connections and dependencies. This essay uses one such trial, that of John Brown in 1859, to suggest that a better understanding of the way trial narratives and larger communal perceptions intersect is important to legal studies. At issue is a much closer analysis of cultural context than many legal critics are willing to undertake. For example, Ralph Waldo Emerson said of John Brown, on the second day of Brown's trial, "he is a hero of romance & seems to have made this fatal blunder only to bring out his virtues."[1] Emerson's words are still familiar, but we no longer quite comprehend what they meant at the time. Americans of later generations have accepted Emerson's appraisal, but without an informed sense of the cultural assumptions at work in his language.

Recovering the cultural context of a major trial, particularly one generating as many narratives as the trial of John Brown, is no easy matter. There is, however, a reward for perseverance. Since trials involve the transcription of everything that is said in a courtroom they

---

1. Ralph Waldo Emerson to Sarah Swain Forbes, 26 October 1859, in *The Letters of Ralph Waldo Emerson*, ed. Ralph L. Rusk, 6 vols., (New York: Columbia University Press, 1939), 5:179-80.

make excellent cultural barometers.[2] Indeed, the payoff of this trial is particularly attractive because of what the trial reveals about a still mysterious figure in American history, especially because John Brown's extraordinary reputation comes almost entirely from the events of his trial. We will see that underlying homologies between courtroom performance and the genre of the American Romance helped to turn Brown into Emerson's "hero of romance." The result was a story of mythopoeic proportions, one which transcription and reiteration imprinted on the American mind in a remarkably short period of time. Brown's trial became the first event in American history to receive intense and daily multimedia coverage and validation—from newspaper journalists, from leading essayists, from poets, and from that most magical of antebellum inventions, what contemporaries called "the voice of God," the telegraph.

The homologies between courtroom performance and Romance reveal how the trial itself generated a more permanent cultural narrative. Brown's courtroom became the setting in which previously condoned or ignored ideological inconsistencies about slavery suddenly became unavoidable. On trial for his life, John Brown achieved a special imaginative power by mixing legal artifice with religious understanding. He was able to mix them with particular effect because of the special license of the Romance as a narrative frame of reference.[3] The largely self-educated Brown first came to grips with the possibilities of Romance in an autobiographical fragment that he wrote in 1857. This fragment is useful because it illustrates Brown's power as a storyteller as well as the specific nature of his contemporary audience in antebellum American culture.

We move next, in the middle sections of the essay, to the ways in which Brown used his powers of self-dramatization to manipulate trial procedures and decorum. These manipulations established the con-

2. The law, as barometer, operates as both a positive and a negative gauge. In the words of legal historian Lawrence Friedman, "law reflects the agenda of controversy—the things that are in actual dispute. It also gives strong negative evidence about which issues are not in dispute, the things that nobody questions." See "Notes toward a History of American Justice," in *American Law and the Constitutional Order: Historical Perspectives*, ed. Lawrence Friedman and Harry N. Scheiber (Cambridge: Harvard University Press, 1978), 24-25.

3. *The Oxford Companion to American Literature*, 4th ed. (New York: Oxford University Press, 1965), 724, defines the nineteenth-century "romance" as the "generic name applied to prose fiction that is conceived in terms of the fanciful and idealistic, rather than in terms of observation and faithful description of fact." Central to this definition of romance is the notion of a narrative that allows the combination of different levels of reality on a single plane of observation for a heightened affect. Henry James defines romance as "experience liberated, so to speak" in the name of "the greatest intensity," where experience is like a balloon tied to earth by a cable. "The art of the romancer," writes James, "is 'for the fun of it,' insidiously to cut the cable, to cut it without our detecting him." The overall goal is "the disconnected or uncontrolled experience . . . which romance alone more or less successfully palms off on us" as a higher reality. Henry James, *The Art of the Novel: Critical Prefaces* (1907; reprint, New York: Charles Scribner's Sons, 1937), 33-34.

text for Brown's final statement before the court at sentencing. Acknowledged to be one of the great set speeches in nineteenth-century oratory, this statement is seldom analyzed for the underlying nature of its power. Throughout the trial, John Brown uncannily surpassed himself. Reactions to his performance in the courtroom were overwhelming by any measure, and this fact tells us something about the imaginative power and expansiveness of trial scenes in American culture. This power leads to a final insight into what might be called "the migratory patterns" of trial narratives in a republic of laws.

I

The failure of the raid on Harper's Ferry had everything to do with John Brown's ultimate success as a historical figure. The fatal blunder, to paraphrase Emerson, brought out his virtues; it also suppressed his vices. The raid was, in typical narratives of the event, an "ultimate triumphant failure."[4] Brown himself quickly came to see it in these terms. "The great bulk of mankind estimate each other's actions and motives by the measure of success or otherwise that attend them through life," he wrote from prison a month after the raid. "By that rule, I have been one of the worst and one of the best of men." Two days before his execution, he added, "I have now no doubt but that our seeming disaster will ultimately result in the most glorious success."[5]

The raid as planned could not have succeeded, but the significance of immediate failure to later cultural formations has not been appreciated. Certainly, it failed as soon as it began on October 16, 1859. John Brown and his twenty-one followers held their objective, the U.S. Arsenal at Harper's Ferry, for less than thirty-six hours before federal troops under Brevet Colonel Robert E. Lee easily overwhelmed them. Not a single local slave chose to join Brown's attempt "to free the slaves."[6] Of the seventeen who died at Harper's Ferry,

4. David Potter summarizes this rhetorical line in *The Impending Crisis 1848-1861*, The New American Nation Series (New York: Harper & Row, 1976), 358. For a more historical account, see Frederick Douglass's claim that "the hour of [Brown's] physical weakness was the hour of his moral strength." Douglass, "John Brown," in *A John Brown Reader*, ed. Louis Ruchames (New York: Abelard-Schuman, 1959), 322. Douglass, who knew Brown and also knew of his plans before the raid, delivered this comment at Harper's Ferry, Virginia, 30 May 1881.

5. John Brown to Judge Daniel R. Tilden, 28 November 1859, and John Brown to his family, 30 November 1859, quoted in *John Brown*, ed. Richard Warch and Jonathan Fanton (Englewood Cliffs, N.J.: Prentice-Hall, 1973), 98, 100.

6. This description of the purpose of the raid is John Brown's on the day that he was captured. "A Conversation with Brown: Harper's Ferry, October 19, 1859," in *The Life, Trial and Execution of Captain John Brown, known as "Old Brown of Ossawatomie," with a full account of the attempted Insurrection at Harper's Ferry*, ed. Robert M. De Witt (1859; reprint, New York: Da Capo Press, 1969), 45. In describing the public record of Brown's comments, I generally cite from this source because it is the first relatively complete record of all of the events in the Brown saga, and because this collection of materials contains the trial transcript.

ten belonged to Brown's party; two were his sons. The whole project was ill-conceived and poorly executed. Harper's Ferry, in the Blue Ridge Mountains of northern Virginia, had no large slave plantations nearby, and free whites outnumbered slaves in the surrounding six counties by a ratio of almost seven to one. None of the circumstances were propitious for a slave rebellion. The raiders neglected to bring so much as a day's rations to sustain their enterprise, and their first shots killed a black railroad worker who was already free.[7]

But every failure contributed to another kind of success. The act of imagination behind the raid stimulated reactions that still need to be explained and that reveal much about the cultural sensitivities of antebellum Americans. In a curious reversal, the attack on Harper's Ferry held the nineteenth-century mind in part because it could *not* hold physical terrain. There was, in consequence, little need for anyone except the court to dwell on the messy and often absurd details of Brown's plot. Instead, imagined possibilities dominated all accounts, providing an intrinsic fascination unconfined by reality.

John Brown, the protagonist of every account, loomed large because of his capacity to dare. He roused visions in the American psyche of both cultural fulfillment and purification. These visions in turn competed with nightmares of armed invasion and racial warfare in simultaneous and compelled narratives that made Brown both hero and villain. None of these narratives had much to do with the facts of Harper's Ferry. The narratives conflated political, religious, legal, and racial perceptions in formulaic patterns that, in turn, exaggerated every possibility—and especially exaggerated the character of Brown. This strategy of exaggeration transfigured Brown from lifelong bungler, bankrupt, narrow extremist, murderer, and border fugitive into a cultural icon. This essay attempts to illuminate Brown's strategy in a new way by demonstrating how it paralleled, thematically and historically, the development and the highest expressions of the American Romance.

The homologies between John Brown's appeal and the American Romance can be seen most vividly in the comments of Nathaniel Hawthorne.[8] Hawthorne expressed a prevalent communal reaction

---

De Witt's collection also appears to have had a great immediate impact on American thought at the time of its publication.

7. The information as well as the inferences about the raid in this paragraph are taken from Warch and Fanton, *John Brown*, 59, and Stephen B. Oates, *To Purge This Land with Blood: A Biography of John Brown*, 2d ed. (Amherst: The University of Massachusetts Press, 1984), 294-302. For a minority view in the scholarship, defending the feasibility of the raid, see Karen Whitman, "Re-evaluating John Brown's Raid at Harper's Ferry," *West Virginia History* 34 (1974): 46.

8. In stressing Hawthorne's understanding of the Romance, I inevitably enter current controversies about the very definition of the Romance and about the possibly exaggerated role assigned to Hawthorne in supplying those definitions. Regardless of those controversies, my

when he said that Brown "preposterously miscalculated the possibilities."[9] Hawthorne knew that the preposterous described an essential form of American literary comprehension and expression in his time. As he told his publisher in 1850, "the fact is, in writing a romance, a man is always—or always ought to be—careering on the verge of a precipitous absurdity, and the skill lies in coming as close as possible, without actually tumbling over."[10]

John Brown appeared on just such a verge, and his tumble, when it came, turned into an extraordinary ascension. Moreover, that transformation involved techniques that corresponded to the license, disengagement, symbolism, and performative dialectic, which Hawthorne brought to the craft of fiction. Nineteenth-century Americans exalted or vilified John Brown for some of the same reasons they read romancers like Hawthorne.

John Brown contributed to his own figuration. Historians routinely refer to Brown's "remarkable sense of words" or his ability "to create an image of himself as a man," and the best of them recognize that "this strange disguised romanticist," in "holding the mirror up to art," "had romanticized himself quite as much as others romanticized him." Missing from these accounts, however, is a precise understanding of how Brown's words worked—how they electrified his countrymen by using popular forms of expression.[11] Missing, as well, is a realization of how strategic these uses were for the times. Brown may be the first figure in American culture to have controlled the perception of a

---

own emphasis can be justified in terms of Hawthorne's direct influence on the other intellectual figures that I examine in regard to John Brown. Hawthorne alludes directly to these figures—Theodore Parker, Richard Henry Dana, Jr., William Ellery Channing, Ralph Waldo Emerson, Henry Thoreau, and Henry Wadsworth Longfellow—in the very prefaces in which he gives his version of the Romance, and all of these figures were clearly familiar and apparently comfortable with his definition. At the same time, I try to restrict my own definition of the Romance to those characteristics accepted today by all parties as generally prominent in the 1850s. For the best recent syntheses in the ongoing debate about the Romance, see George Dekker, "Once More: Hawthorne and the Genealogy of American Romance," *ESQ: A Journal of the American Renaissance* 35 (1989): 69-83, and John McWilliams, "The Rationale for 'The American Romance,'" *Boundary 2* 17 (Spring 1990): 71-82. For the best argument questioning the overall clarity of the term in the 1850s and the nature of Hawthorne's general influence on it, see Nina Baym, "Concepts of the Romance in Hawthorne's America," *Nineteenth-Century Fiction* 38 (March 1984): 426-43. For a partial counter, see J. Lasley Dameron, "Hawthorne and the Popular Concept of the Prose Romance," *English Studies* 68 (April 1987): 154-59.

9. Quoted in James R. Mellow, *Nathaniel Hawthorne in His Times* (Boston: Houghton Mifflin, 1980), 551-52. See also Nathaniel Hawthorne to H. Woodman, 26 June 1862, *The Letters, 1857-1864*, vol. 18, *The Centenary Edition of the Works of Nathaniel Hawthorne*, ed. Thomas Woolson et al. (Columbus: Ohio State University Press, 1987), 463-64.

10. Nathaniel Hawthorne to James T. Fields, 3 November 1850, in *The Letters, 1843-1853*, vol. 16, *Centenary Edition of the Works of Nathaniel Hawthorne* (Columbus: Ohio State University Press, 1985), 371.

11. Louis Filler, *The Crusade Against Slavery 1830-1860*, The New American Nation Series (New York: Harper & Row, 1960), 241, and Potter, *The Impending Crisis*, 357-62. Of the positive reactions of Boston literati to Brown, Potter notes: "They saw him, as by nature and instinct, a man of action, utterly devoid of artistry and rhetoric, and they never sensed at all that he was, in some ways, more of an artist and a man of words than any of them."

major event entirely through self-dramatization and media control. As he put the matter while pondering his own execution, "I have been *whiped* as the saying *is*; but am sure I can recover all the lost capital occasioned by that disaster; by only hanging a few moments by the neck; & I feel quite determined to make the utmost possible out of a defeat."[12]

Success from failure is the very stuff of the Romance, and the quantum shift in the opinions of contemporary Americans shows how completely Brown used his trial for this effect. Students of the raid and its aftermath generally agree that the apotheosis of Brown would have been mitigated, perhaps obviated altogether, if Brown had died in the raid or if he had received a prison sentence instead of the death penalty at trial. They also agree that most antebellum Americans were not in sympathy with Brown's immediate goals. North as well as South feared a slave insurrection of the kind Brown tried to instigate at Harper's Ferry. That the slaves did *not* rebel was a relief everywhere in white America, one of the many levels on which failure functioned as a license for the imagination.

It was Brown's performance at trial that led so many to identify so closely with him. In the first hundred years of the Republic only the deaths of leading presidents—of George Washington in 1799, of John Adams and Thomas Jefferson prophetically together on July 4, 1826, and of Abraham Lincoln on Good Friday in 1865—matched the paroxysms of emotion unleashed by the death of John Brown. In 1859, between October 18th (the day of Brown's capture) and December 2nd (the day of his execution), the public image of the man moved from that of an outlaw on the radical fringes of abolitionist politics to what can only be called a moral touchstone in American life. But how did these shifts in sentiment achieve such range when the vast majority of Americans, Northern and Southern, remained suspicious of Brown's goals, and how did the sentiments reach such intensity over a relatively obscure figure in the course of a mere six weeks?

The answers to these questions lie in Brown's words and behavior during his six-day trial, and his ultimate conviction on counts of conspiracy, treason, and murder at Charlestown in the Circuit Court of Jefferson County, Virginia. While a long string of witnesses under the direction of special prosecutor Andrew Hunter supported all three charges with vivid accounts of the raid during the first three days of

12. John Brown to Mary Ann Day Brown, 10 November 1859, quoted in Oswald Garrison Villard, *John Brown 1800-1859: A Biography Fifty Years After* (Boston: Houghton Mifflin, 1910), 540.

the trial, Brown stubbornly resisted the advice of his own lawyers in ways that kept him at the center of attention in his own defense.[13]

Answers lie, as well, in the extensive reportage given to colorful eyewitness accounts and to the peculiar nature of Brown's performance during them. In 1859, the press was just reaching the technological capacity to narrate the immediacy of daily events to a national audience. Brown's movement from utter marginality to, in Henry Thoreau's phrases, "the greatest and best" and "the most American of us all" came through the orchestrated theatricality of the trial as it appeared in newspaper lead after newspaper lead.[14] Reporters necessarily repeated the essential facts of the raid every day but always through the filter of the trial experience. Their reiteration literalized the story in what has been since termed "the story line," and turned the trial itself into a synecdoche of Brown's overall achievement.

II

What happened in Brown's trial grew out of nineteenth-century understandings of the purpose of a republic of laws. John Brown used his constitutional right to be heard at public trial to dramatize a central contradiction in the culture around him, that of slavery in a society where all men were declared to be equal. The contradiction was hardly new in 1859. Americans had recognized the problem in 1776, and they had accepted a presumed inconsistency between republicanism and slavery when they included the "peculiar" institution in their acts of national formation.[15] John Brown and other radical abolition-

13. During the six-day trial, Brown was represented by six lawyers in all, none of whom were formal defense counsel for more than half of the proceedings. Charles J. Faulkner and Lawson Botts, of the Virginia Bar, were originally assigned by the Court to represent Brown, but Brown rejected each in turn at strategic moments. When Faulkner resigned at the end of the first day, the court responded by adding Thomas C. Green, another member of the Virginia Bar. Northern lawyers, George H. Hoyt of Massachusetts, Henry Griswold of Ohio, and Samuel Chilton of Washington, arrived on the third and fourth days of the trial to take up the defense. Green and Botts resigned at the end of the third day of the trial with the arrival of this "foreign counsel." Each new lawyer asked for a delay in trial to prepare a proper defense, a request that the court consistently refused. Brown clearly followed the advice of his lawyers only when it was convenient for his own purposes. See De Witt, *The Life, Trial and Execution*, 55-78.

14. Thoreau reached his high opinion of Brown immediately after the raid on Harper's Ferry. The quotations are from "The Last Days of John Brown," delivered on 2 December 1859, the day of Brown's execution, and "A Plea for Captain John Brown," delivered on 30 October 1859, the fifth day of Brown's six-day trial. Both speeches relied heavily on newspaper coverage to make their points. See Wendell Glick, ed., *Henry D. Thoreau: Reform Papers* (Princeton: Princeton University Press, 1973), 145, 125.

15. For crucial aspects of the uncomfortable inclusion of slavery in the U.S. Constitution in 1787, see the debates of 8 August and 25 August in the Federal Convention, in *The Records of the Federal Convention of 1787*, ed. Max Farrand, rev. ed. (New Haven: Yale University Press, 1966), 2:220-23, 415-19. See also Gary B. Nash, "The Failure of Abolitionism," in *Race and Revolution* (Madison: Madison House Publishers, 1990), 25-55. For one of the first national defenses of slavery as a "peculiar" institution or exception to republican principles, see "The Federalist No. 54," *New York Packet*, 12 February 1788 in *The Federalist* (1787-1788; reprint, New York: Random House, 1937), 356-57.

ists had long repudiated that compromise, but they were a minority in antebellum politics and had difficulty finding a forum at once congenial and official for articulating views that their contemporaries regarded as extreme.

Brown's trial represented something of a dividing line in the debate over slavery. Before the trial, Congress and state legislatures had managed to evade radical abolitionist polemics through informal or formal "gag rules" that kept antislavery petitions unheard, and many citizens ignored or repressed their own sense of the ideological inconsistency in slavery by restricting their frustrations to the political sphere.[16] Suddenly, in Brown's trial, the context of exchange was neither occasional and consensual nor loosely political, but officially adversarial. Formal scrutiny was imposed here by the rigor of legal rules, and the issues of universal rights and protection of property were starkly presented. Duty to conscience challenged obedience to law in a prolonged debate.

Although Brown suffered discrimination as an abolitionist in a Virginia courtroom, he achieved certain advantages for his cause when he entered the formal protection of trial rituals. The exclusive focus in the courtroom on charges resulting from the events at Harper's Ferry enabled Brown to erase unseemly events in his unheroic past. On trial for his life, he became what he appeared to be in the moment, the courageous leader of a doomed but exciting mission. Gone from view were earlier incidents of personal cruelty, his many vocational failures, the previous legal difficulties in which he was clearly and inexcusably culpable, his limited standing in the political circles of abolitionism, his inept role as a military commander, and even his unprovoked murder of five proslavery men just three years before in "bleeding Kansas."[17] In their place was the man who was willing to die for his cause.

When they did appear in the publicity surrounding the trial, Brown's weaknesses ended up as strengths. Insensitivity appeared as fixed principle, financial failure became superiority to material concern, atrocities blurred and then reinforced the image of the veteran warrior defending freedom in Kansas. Everything combined to prepare the defendant for the final role he chose to play. Humiliated for years by constant litigation and bankruptcy proceedings over fifteen

16. The historian David Donald estimates that only one of every twenty Northern voters was an abolitionist in the 1840s and early 1850s. For this estimate and for commentary on the official "gag rules" that tabled discussion of slavery in legislative assemblies, see David Herbert Donald, *Liberty and Union* (Boston: Little, Brown & Company, 1978), 16-20 and Glyndon G. Van Deusen, *The Jacksonian Era 1828-1848*, The New American Nation Series (New York: Harper & Brothers, 1959), 108, 133-35.

17. For good summaries of these negative aspects of Brown's life, see Filler, *The Crusade Against Slavery*, 239-43; Warch and Fanton, *John Brown*, 1-12. Villard's assessment of Brown's clear responsibility for what is called "the Pottawatomie Massacre" on the night of May 23-24, 1856, is now generally accepted. See ibid., 170-88.

business failures in four states, Brown knew his way around an American courtroom.[18] In 1859, he turned those bitter lessons to account, manipulating trial rituals (the procedural sense of formal collective participation) into a confrontation between moral positions and competing discourses. Helpless in previous trials, he was master of this one. Even the normally intimidating question of guilt or innocence suited his rigid moralistic temperament better than the flexibility of political compromise ever could.[19]

At trial, Brown translated innocence and guilt into terms of good and evil, thereby evoking powerful rhetorical themes—themes familiar and persuasive in themselves but much more powerful when woven together. By resisting the charge of guilt through an appeal to higher truth and by trying to destroy the evil of slavery in the name of good, Brown followed his own penchant for religious explanation and moral certitude. Simultaneously, he activated an affinity to the literary modes of the Romance, where good and evil battle toward inevitable conclusions in a narrative freighted with symbolism and exaggeration. The mixture of legal and religious frames of reference with the elements of the Romance proved explosive in awakening sympathy for Brown and in magnifying his cause. Thereafter, whether as diabolical invader of the peace or as first martyr of republican freedom, he was always larger than the life he led, always above the legal decision to take that life, always somewhere beyond the facts.

III

Not known as a master rhetorician before his trial, John Brown nonetheless belonged to a generation that made a singular contribution to American literature. Tracing the connection is essential to understanding a man who spoke and wrote so much better than he knew. Brown, after all, made himself a cultural symbol overnight, and language was his primary tool. Granting, for the moment, that the man on trial surpassed himself, what were the skills and cultural congruences that supported his effort? Brown's own writings and comments outside of the courtroom are especially useful because they reveal affinities with the writers of the American Renaissance and because they allow us to avoid the tautology of explaining Brown's impact through his impact.[20] The same writings demonstrate Brown's

18. For the details on Brown's business failures and lawsuits, wherein he was the frequent loser between 1837 and 1854, see Oates, *To Purge This Land with Blood*, 37, 45-49, 76-77.

19. Brown's contempt for politicians and the flexibility of political response was clear from very early in his career. A measure of his disenchantment was his apparent failure to vote in any national presidential election after 1832. For a brief discussion of these issues, see Oates, *To Purge This Land with Blood*, 20-21.

20. When investigators explain Brown's appeal by concentrating on his seeming prescience about the evolution of sectional strife and about the eventual destruction of slavery, as most of

capacity for expression and his relationship to contemporary literary forms, and prefigure his eloquence at trial.

A deliberate, even meticulous, care with language is apparent in Brown's short autobiography, written on July 15, 1857, in the form of a letter to the thirteen-year-old son of an abolitionist financial supporter, the wealthy Massachusetts merchant George Luther Stearns.[21] Simply but shrewdly crafted, the letter must be read with the historian David Potter's general warning in mind: "[H]ardly anything can be said with certainty about John Brown."[22] Brown couched the autobiography as an outright fiction. "[I] have concluded to send you a short story of a certain boy of my acquaintance," Brown tells young Harry Stearns, "& for convenience & shortness of name, I will call him John." The writing, in other words, is a fabrication meant for several levels of understanding. Written so simply as to be boy-to-boy, it is also a man's cautionary tale in admonition of youth, a sophisticated narrative pitched to the influential father behind the son, and, over all, Brown's communication to the world of what he wants it to know about him.

Significantly, the idea of fabrication, inscribed in the notion of story, was not necessarily a pejorative one for Brown's several audiences. Antebellum Americans were taught to look for a higher truth in what they read, and they learned to accept and engage in distortions of mundane reality to achieve that goal. As Ralph Waldo Emerson described his own reading procedures, "[I read] for diversion & a mechanical help to the fancy & the Imagination. I read for the lustres as if one should use a fine picture in a chromatic experiment merely for its rich colours. It is not Proclus but a piece of Nature & Fate that I explore."[23] The cultural thirst for drama in these words, for imaginative projection and the crystallization of effect, and particularly, for the possibility of self-dramatization were part and parcel of the American Renaissance. John Brown and his publicizers could craft a mythic persona out of the ruins of repeated failure in part because their countrymen recognized and accepted similar performative strategies in other aspects of the culture.

---

them do, they tend to conflate his ideas in support of his actions and his subsequent ideological achievement. The result, while not always inaccurate, is a circularity of explanation that leaves out of the equation Brown's immediate influence in 1859. Lost in these emphases is the separate importance of his trial.

21. John Brown to Harry Stearns, 15 July 1857, in *The Life and Letters of John Brown*, ed. Franklin B. Sanborn (Boston: Roberts Brothers, 1891), 12-17. All quotations and references to the Brown "autobiography" in the next paragraphs are from this source. Brown's supporters—and especially Ralph Waldo Emerson—gave the autobiography wide circulation during his trial.

22. Potter, *The Impending Crisis*, 356.

23. Ralph Waldo Emerson, "July 12-14, 1842," in *Emerson In His Journals*, ed. Joel Porte (Cambridge: Harvard University Press, 1982), 287. Emerson's choice of an example is relevant to his meaning here. Proclus (410-485 A.D.), one of the last major ancient Greek philosophers, was a Neoplatonic idealist who emphasized that thoughts, not things, comprise reality.

Brown's autobiography takes the problem of fabrication as a central thematic concern. The boy John's greatest fault, one to which he is "somewhat addicted," consists in "*telling lies*." Inasmuch as the penchant continues in the man, John finds himself "(in afterlife) obliged to struggle *so long* with so *mean* a habit." The implication is that John, "so often guilty of this fault," has managed to overcome it, and yet the storyteller frequently hides the truth for larger ends. The man of many failures brags repeatedly of "the degree of success *in accomplishing his objects*," of "his close attention to *business*; & success in its management," and of how "he rarely failed in some good degree to effect the things he undertook."[24] If the need to appear successful is an understandable one in an autobiographer, the strain shows in Brown's own definition of success.

To Benjamin Franklin's formula of frugality, unceasing industry, and emulation of the virtuous, which he admires, Brown adds consistency of conduct and character in the name of "*some definite plan*," "plan of life," or "greatest or principal object." Elsewhere, the formulation took a more melodramatic and decidedly un-Franklinian turn: "Death for a good cause was glorious," he told one family friend, in words that revealed Brown's "capacity to become greatly excited when his mind fixed on one idea."[25] Success as a consistency of high purpose lay within Brown's ken in a way that evidence of material advance did not. It fit abolitionist purposes as well as Brown's monomaniacal personality, and it set a different standard—in the words of his autobiography, "the consciousness that our plans are right in themselves." In addition, the *idée fixe* allowed for a dramatically represented self that did not need to conform to the realities of daily life, much less to its own unexciting past.[26]

In keeping with the flexibility allowed in a represented or constructed self, Brown's short autobiography juxtaposes a series of competing images. He is not only the serious, young businessman on the road to success, but also an isolated, swashbuckling Western adventurer dressed in buckskins who consorts with Indians and who takes on the persona of "a rambler in the wild new country," a direct

24. Brown's biographer documents both his tendency to lie and his general ineptitude as a businessman. See Oates, *To Purge This Land with Blood*, 10, 45, 56-57, 76-77, 187, 203-04.

25. Stephen B. Oates notes Brown's great familiarity with Franklin, and Brown's autobiography owes much to Franklin's. The comment by Brown to a family friend, George Delamater, and Brown's fascination with single controlling ideas, noted by a number of contemporaries, are also from Oates's definitive biography. See Oates, *To Purge This Land with Blood*, 20, 53.

26. For a recent discussion of the general movement in American expression from an immanent self (one beneath mere appearance and beyond manipulation) to a represented self (one that is necessarily constructed and so made identical with appearance), see Larzer Ziff, *Writing in the New Nation: Prose, Print, and Politics in the Early United States* (New Haven: Yale University Press, 1991), xi, 77, 114.

descendent of Revolutionary warriors, a pacifist whose "disgust . . . with military affairs" leads him to get "along like a Quaker," a humble shepherd ("*it being* a calling, for which *in early life* he had a kind of *enthusiastic longing*"), an imperious leader of men ("A King against whom there is no rising up" who is "much disposed to speak in an imperious or dictating way"), and, inevitably, the abolitionist and the religious zealot ("the firm believer in the divine authenticity of the Bible"). Each of these images entered the larger myth of John Brown. The more immediate point, however, is that Brown feels rhetorically free to present any one of them, or any combination, when it suits the integrity of his "principal object."

A more revealing theme balances the conventional topic of success. Over and over, Brown stresses the fact of loss in his life. The losses of a toy, of a pet, of another favorite animal leave the subject of this narrative in a "protracted *mourning season*"—all transmogrified in the unresolved trauma of his mother's death; John at eight is "left a Motherless boy which loss was complete & permanent." Of even the least in this series, a marble lost by the boy of six, Brown tells us "*it took years to heal the wound*." Not surprisingly, this mournful figure is a loner separated by inclination and circumstance. "To be sent off through the wilderness alone to very considerable distances," Brown writes in the autobiography, "was particularly his delight."

Unremitting loss generates the obsessive personality of this writer, with grief and anger interacting and feeding upon each other. When the unresolved grief of the child finds a home in the undifferentiated and permanent anger of the adult (what the narrator calls "his haughty obstinate temper"), both emotions fix on abolitionism. Only one figure, in a telling parallel, appears less fortunate than young John. Forced to watch the beating of a "*negro boy* (who was fully if not more than his equal)," John is led "to reflect on the wretched, hopeless condition, of *Fatherless & Motherless* slave *children*." The psychological repercussions are fierce identification and a very tenuous social equilibrium. Brown's rhetoric is helped by the fact that loss operates as a fairly pervasive and dominant cultural theme in early America.[27] Even though Brown's compulsive rendition of "*sore trials*" borders on the grotesque, he achieves a social balance of sorts by channeling his sorrow and anger into protest against the evil of slavery.

These passages reveal Brown for what he was in another sense, an unsophisticated writer who depended on standard literary conventions for the appeal of his prose. Virtually every strategy in the autobiogra-

27. For a detailed analysis of the theme of loss in early American culture, see generally Fred Somkin, *Unquiet Eagle: Memory and Desire in the Idea of American Freedom, 1815-1860* (Ithaca: Cornell University Press, 1967).

phy appeared prominently in the popular literature of the times. Brown's calculated appeal to separate audiences (one reading a surface narrative and the other probing beneath), his stress upon intensity or excess of feeling, his claim of spirituality in the consciousness of righteousness, his intrusive and openly manipulative narrator, his selectivity and willingness to exaggerate event through symbolism, his readiness to inflate a represented self through a bewildering range of character traits and alternative experiences, and above all, his assumption of a rhetorical license to mix and match—these were the characteristics of the American Romance.

While Brown brought no special craft to these devices, he understood them well enough to enhance his capacity for self-dramatization. Here again, his autobiography resembles the nineteenth-century Romance and its folkloric corollaries, the tall tale and ballad. The narrator triumphs in "the school of *adversity*," he celebrates the isolated but dedicated individual, he resists the commonplace, he summons the sorrows and the terrors of death, he tells stories about cruelty to children and the healing domesticity of the virtuous woman, he yokes the romantic adventurer to the responsible citizen, he conjures up the Revolutionary past as well as the Wild West, and he purveys the timeless battle of good against evil (in his "*Eternal war* with slavery"). These themes were also the preoccupations of the nineteenth-century historical and domestic Romance.[28]

To be sure, Brown was no accomplished romancer: he gave no single theme a unique rendering, and offered no imaginative equivalents of the tortured Dimmesdale and demonic Chillingworth in *The Scarlet Letter*, nor of the multivalent Holgrave in *The House of the Seven Gables*, nor of the monomaniacal Hollingsworth and inquisitive Coverdale in *The Blithedale Romance*. Still, Brown inserted these character types in embryonic form.

Both Hawthorne and Brown realized that the pressing issues of their time demanded the language and the psychology of spiritual engagement. As Hawthorne was on the edge of what remained a Bible culture, so Brown was steeped within it, and each saw—Hawthorne with irony, Brown with conviction—that the intrusion of secularization required a rhetoric of excess where materiality and spirituality could mingle.[29] Symbolism, in particular, took on a double

28. See generally George Dekker, *The American Historical Romance* (Cambridge: Cambridge University Press, 1987), and Gillian Brown, *Domestic Individualism: Imagining Self in Nineteenth-Century America* (Berkeley and Los Angeles: University of California Press, 1990).

29. The essential point of how the deterioration of a sense of the sacred leads to a "literary aesthetic of excess" or melodrama is made by Peter Brooks, *The Melodramatic Imagination: Balzac, Henry James, Melodrama, and the Mode of Excess* (New Haven: Yale University Press, 1976), 1-23, 198-206. Brooks identifies, in melodrama, many of the elements that make up the American Romance, including pressure on a surface reality through levels of understanding, an

significance in the material and spiritual worlds. Brown, with Hawthorne, assumed that he was "allowed a license with regard to every-day Probability," that the rhetorician looked for "an available foothold between fiction and reality," that fact and invention necessarily intersected in achieving a higher truth, and that the ultimate integrity of a narrative lay not in the details but in "the authenticity of the outline."[30]

In keeping with these predilections, Brown reached for the "moral" of the far more cynical Hawthorne in *The House of the Seven Gables* when the failure at Harper's Ferry required an instantaneous reconfiguration of his own understanding. That moral was predictably half-political and half-spiritual in nature. In Hawthorne's words, "the wrong-doing of one generation lives into the successive ones, and, divesting itself of every temporary advantage, becomes a pure and uncontrollable mischief."[31] The threat of curse, and the implied necessity of sacrifice and expurgation are the underlying concepts that reach across levels of reality in this statement. Lying wounded on the engine-room floor of the armory at Harper's Ferry, Brown was able to raise himself through just such "an available foothold," addressing his captors with perfect equanimity and, hence, considerable eloquence. "You may dispose of me very easily;" he told them, "I am nearly disposed of now; but this question is still to be settled—this negro question I mean—the end of that is not yet."[32]

This speaker could easily have been a character in *The House of the Seven Gables*. "God will give him blood to drink," cries Matthew Maule from the gallows, and John Brown, on the way to his own execution, sounded a similar note. "I John Brown am now quite *certain* that the crimes of this *guilty land*: *will* never be purged *away*; but with Blood."[33] Crime, guilt, and purgation conflated legal and religious explanations with Brown fused in the roles of judge, prophet, and sac-

---

intrusive narrative voice that needs to tell all, a dramatic rendering of the battle of good and evil, as well as menace and suspense in representation. That the American Romance has been hospitable to melodrama has been clear since Richard Chase, *The American Novel and Its Tradition* (1957: reprint, Baltimore: Johns Hopkins University Press, 1980), 1. See also Michael Taylor, "Reluctant Romancers: Self-Consciousness and Derogation in Prose Romance," *English Studies in Canada* 17 (March 1991): 89-105.

30. These quotations and paraphrases are taken from Hawthorne's prefaces to his Romances and describe his understanding of the genre. See respectively *The Blithedale Romance*, vol. 3, *The Centenary Edition of the Works of Nathaniel Hawthorne* (Columbus: Ohio State University Press, 1964), 2; and *The Scarlet Letter*, vol. 1, *The Centenary Edition of the Works of Nathaniel Hawthorne*, (Columbus: Ohio State University Press, 1962), 33-36. Subsequent references to these works refer to these editions.

31. Hawthorne, *The House of the Seven Gables*, vol. 2, *The Centenary Edition of the Works of Nathaniel Hawthorne* (Columbus: Ohio State University Press, 1965), 2. Subsequent references to this work refer to this edition.

32. "A Conversation With Brown," in De Witt, *The Life, Trial and Execution*, 49.

33. Hawthorne, *The House of the Seven Gables*, 8. Quoted in Oates, *To Purge This Land with Blood*, 351. The biblical reference for Brown's comment is *Hebrews* 9:12-25.

rificial object. The Civil War soon removed the ironies from these identifications and instructed others in their use. Five years later, the trope of sacrifice reached its ultimate expression in Abraham Lincoln's Second Inaugural Address, where again the language, neither specifically religious nor entirely political, would be a deliberate and crafted concurrence of possibilities.[34]

Where Brown fell short of Hawthorne was in the romancer's adroit orchestration of the variables. Hawthorne was a master in combining ingenuous and ironic ways of reading, in crossing while sustaining the boundary between the domain of the senses and the world of imagination, in exercising the dark inner drives of the Romance, in subversively exploring the inconsistency between the ideal and the real in American life, and in coming to grips with the spectral and yet human quality of all experience.[35] Discrepancy was the common element in these procedures, and Hawthorne used it to stress disjuncture and the realm of the grotesque.[36] The grotesque was often his calling card, his method of alerting and holding his reader.[37]

34. Roy P. Basler, ed., "Second Inaugural Address: March 4, 1865," in *The Collected Works of Abraham Lincoln*, 9 vols. (New Brunswick: Rutgers University Press, 1953-1955), 8: 333. "[I]f God wills that [this mighty scourge of war] continue until all the wealth piled by the bondsman's two hundred and fifty years of unrequited toil shall be sunk, and until every drop of blood drawn with the lash shall be paid by another drawn with the sword, as was said three thousand years ago, so still it must be said, 'The judgments of the Lord are true and righteous together.'"

35. In this sentence, I include the major assumptions of current leading interpreters of the Romance. For the interplay between ingenuous and ironic ways of reading, see Dekker, "Hawthorne and the Genealogy of American Romance," 78-79. For an interpretation of the crossing or transgressive mode in a performative dialectic between boundary lines, see Evan Carton, *The Rhetoric of American Romance: Dialectic and Identity in Emerson, Dickinson, Poe, and Hawthorne* (Baltimore: Johns Hopkins University Press, 1985). For a summary of the extensive scholarship on "all those dark, inner, asocial drives of the self which the very notion of the 'American Romance' has encouraged us to ponder," see John McWilliams, "The Rationale for 'The American Romance,'" *Boundary 2* 17 (Spring 1990): 72-73. For the subversive tendencies of the Romance and its tendencies in sacrificing the relation between levels of reality, see Michael Davitt Bell, *The Development of American Romance: The Sacrifice of Relation* (Chicago: University of Chicago Press, 1980), and Frederick Newberry, "A New Perspective on the American Romance: A Review Essay," *Poe Studies* 14 (December 1981): 33-39. For the pivotal connection of the spectral and the human in the Romance, see E. Miller Budick, "The World as Specter: Hawthorne's Historical Art," *PMLA* 101 (March 1986): 225ff.

36. For a recent emphasis on the grotesque in the American Romance, see generally Robert S. Levine, *Conspiracy and Romance: Studies in Brockden Brown, Cooper, Hawthorne, and Melville* (Cambridge: Cambridge University Press, 1989). For a specific explanation of how the grotesque works in literary representation, see generally Robert A. Ferguson, "The Grotesque in the Novels of F. Scott Fitzgerald," *The South Atlantic Quarterly* 78 (Autumn 1979): 460-77.

37. Thus, for example, Hawthorne turns literally to "the corpse of dead activity" in "The Custom-House" preface to *The Scarlet Letter*. The deceased surveyor Jonathan Pue, or rather his "imperfect skeleton" under "a wig of majestic frizzle," rises from the grave to enjoin Hawthorne to tell his tale. It is "as if the ancient Surveyor, in his garb of a hundred years gone by, and wearing his immortal wig,—which was buried with him, but did not perish in the grave,—had met me in the deserted chamber of the Custom-House." This "ghostly hand" and "ghostly voice" are more than matched by other corpses, which are still caught in "the convulsive throes of cholera" or which "stared me in the face with a fixed and ghastly grin of contemptuous defiance." See Hawthorne, *The Scarlet Letter*, 29-33, 39, 34. Ghosts, of course, appear everywhere in Hawthorne's stories, but for particularly powerful renditions of the grotesque in his Romances, see "Governor Pyncheon," where the narrator dances for an entire

Brown could lack all of Hawthorne's talents and still achieve the effect. Character and circumstance supplied the grotesque at Harper's Ferry, and they needed no orchestration. The discrepancy that arrested antebellum Americans depended on the vexed aura of slavery—Northern horror of it and Southern fear of insurrection within it—but the grotesque also depends on the concrete, and the events at Harper's Ferry supplied that ingredient in abundance. Take, for example, John Brown under siege pacing the armory with two of his sons dying around him and responding to one's cries of agony with the rebuke "if you must die, die like a man." Or, alternatively, see the enraged local populace slicing off the ears and beating one dead raider, Dangerfield Newby, with sticks before allowing hogs to root at the body. Consider the mob seizing and slaughtering Will Thompson, another raider held captive, and then using his corpse for target practice. In eyewitness accounts, "the cries and screams [of the dying] made one's flesh creep." Watson Brown, for one, was shot through under a flag of truce. Later, his body was taken to the Winchester Medical College, where it was "skinned, and the skin varnished, after which a dispute arose whether it should be kept whole or stuffed, or cut up for game pouches."[38] There was no shortage of the grotesque at Harper's Ferry, and over it all impended the bizarre personality of John Brown himself.

The figure of Brown occupied the boundary line between worlds: "an angel of light" to his supporters, and among "the foes of the human race" to his executioners.[39] His skill at trial and during punishment came in his recognition and use of this liminality. A transgressor by definition, he turned the courtroom into an exploration of discrepancies where the ideal and the real changed places, and where the spiritual supplanted the merely legal. The fact of transgression forced either a re-articulation of values or an enunciation of new ones in the moment of reversal, and the relation to formal literary expression in this game of levels did not go unnoticed. Henry Thoreau's appraisal in "The Last Days of John Brown" insisted on Brown's literary character. Brown's commentary from prison and while on trial formed

---

chapter on the corpse of Jaffrey Pyncheon, or the description of Zenobia's suicide in *The Blithedale Romance*.

38. The best overall source for these details is Oates, *To Purge This Land with Blood*, 294-99, 356; see also "The Last Hours of the John Brown Raid: The Narrative of David H. Strother," ed. Cecil D. Eby, *Virginia Magazine of History and Biography* 73 (April 1965): 169-77. The quotation about the treatment of Watson Brown's body is from Truman Nelson, "John Brown Revisited," *The Nation* 135 (August 31, 1957): 86-88.

39. The first quotation in this sentence is from Henry Thoreau, "A Plea for Captain John Brown," 190. Thoreau delivered these words on 30 October 1859, in Concord in one of the first public defenses of Brown. The second comment, from Colonel J. T. L. Preston of the Virginia Military Institute, came at the moment of Brown's execution. In full, the comment reads: "So perish all such enemies of Virginia! All such enemies of the Union! All such foes of the human race!" Quoted in Oates, *To Purge This Land with Blood*, 352.

"an American book" like no other. "I do not know of such words, uttered under such circumstances, and so copiously withal," concluded Thoreau, "in Roman or English or any history."[40]

Literature operated as more than an analogy in Thoreau's explanation of Brown's importance. "[S]ee what a work this comparatively unread and unlettered man wrote within six weeks," observed Thoreau. "Where is our professor of belles-lettres, or of logic and rhetoric, who can write so well?" Brown succeeded because he understood that "the *art* of composition is as simple as the discharge of a bullet from a rifle" and because his own transition from lawless raider into courtroom defendant transformed "a material weapon, a Sharp's rifle" into "the sword of the spirit."[41] The power and immediacy of Thoreau's images should not disguise their standard place within the literary parlance of the times. The goal of interpretation is, once again, self-dramatization (words as bullets) and the hope for transformations between the material and spiritual realms. The ascendancy of the spiritual within the material, thought Thoreau, was precisely the quality that allowed Brown to "answer more wisely than all his countrymen beside."

Brown, like Hawthorne, resolved the competition of different realities into an expression of higher truth, but where Hawthorne relied on aesthetics and artistic control, Brown emphasized the exercise of principle in action. What was it that separated Brown from others who attempted to rescue slaves and who were executed for it? Thoreau answered the question by emphasizing the "devotion to principle" in Brown's words at trial. Brown "forgot human laws, and did homage to an idea." In this expression of principle, "the North, I mean the *living* North was suddenly all transcendental" in a context where "transcendental" signified the courage to see past the failure of human law in a recognition of "eternal justice and glory."

For Thoreau, anyone's inability to accept Brown's words indicated a larger failure of comprehension in a reader. Again the terms of reference were ones of literary interpretation. Those who thought of John Brown "as an ordinary felon" had lost their spiritual way and their aesthetic bearings. It was no accident that Thoreau's condemnation of the merely material opponent in "The Last Days of John Brown" was a virtual paraphrase of Hawthorne's similar mockery of insensitivity in "The Custom-House" of *The Scarlet Letter*. "They have either much

40. The quotations here and in the next four paragraphs regarding Thoreau's critique of Brown are all from Thoreau's short address read at John Brown's official burial service in North Elba, New York on 4 July 1860, "The Last Days of John Brown," 192-98.

41. Thoreau uses the same metaphor in a slightly different way but with the same sense of Brown's higher consciousness of expression in his earlier essay on Brown, "A Plea For Captain John Brown," 182-83: "He could afford to lose his Sharp's rifles, while he retained his faculty of speech—a Sharp's rifle of infinitely surer and longer range."

flesh," wrote Thoreau of those who did not understand Brown, "or much office, or much coarseness of some kind. They are not ethereal natures in any sense." The true reader of Brown, like Hawthorne's romancer, who tried "to live throughout the whole range of his faculties and sensibilities," matched contrasting worlds in the name of the spirit. "How can a man behold the light who has no answering inward light?" Thoreau asked.[42]

In transcendentalist circles, deciding for or against Brown reflected directly on a general literary capacity. "Show me a man who feels bitterly toward John Brown, and let me hear what noble verse he can repeat," sneered Thoreau. "He'll be as dumb as if his lips were stone." For the same reason, mutual recognition of Brown's achievement supplied a form of literary solidarity. Thoreau, Ralph Waldo Emerson, Bronson Alcott, Louisa May Alcott, Lydia Maria Child, Theodore Parker and others lionized Brown in part because they identified in him an intellectually and emotionally kindred enterprise. They wanted to see him in their own terms, and Brown's unfolding trial gave them the means.[43]

When Thoreau wrote that he knew "of nothing so miraculous in our history" as the "meteor-like" last six weeks of Brown's life, he meant that communal responses had acclaimed Brown's importance in an unprecedented fashion during his trial and punishment. "No theatrical manager," he concluded, "could have arranged things so wisely to give effect to [Brown's] behavior and words." The trial, in effect, became a providential stage for testing affinities, something best appreciated in the actual juncture of theatricality and legal procedure practiced in the courtroom at Charlestown, Virginia.[44]

42. Compare Thoreau's unworthy readers with Hawthorne's uncomprehending companions in the Custom-House: "the Collector, our gallant old General" with his "weight, solidity, firmness," the narrow "man of business," "men of traffic," and the other inspectors, none of whom "share in the united effort of mankind." Compare, as well, each writer's search for the true reader, the "heart and mind of perfect sympathy," in Hawthorne's phrase. Behind both writers' comments was Hawthorne's recognition that "thoughts are frozen and utterance benumbed unless the speaker stand in some true relation with his audience." Hawthorne, *The Scarlet Letter*, 3-4, 20-25, 38-40, 44.

43. For one reading of Thoreau's "selective vision" of Brown, one in which Thoreau is found to identify more powerfully with Brown than with any other figure in history, see Michael Meyer, "Thoreau's Rescue of John Brown from History," *Studies in the American Renaissance, 1980*: 301-16. For a more general treatment of how the writers of the American Renaissance reached for communal solidarity, see Donald Pease, *Visionary Compacts: American Renaissance Writings in Cultural Context* (Madison: University of Wisconsin Press, 1986).

44. Although many commentators have noted the power of Brown's words while on trial, most ignore the formal context of those words and, curiously, give the trial itself cursory treatment. The compilation of materials on John Brown by Richard Warch and Jonathan Fanton devotes less than five of 178 pages to the trial. Stephen Oates' definitive biography of Brown describes the trial itself in four pages. See Warch and Fanton, *John Brown*, 79, 81-84 and Oates, *To Purge This Land with Blood*, 324-27.

IV

The Circuit Court of Jefferson County, Virginia labored under an enormous strain during the trial of John Brown. A community is always on trial in the courtroom of a republic of laws, but when a community is seriously divided, as this one was, the pressure on courtroom procedures increases dramatically. The raid on Harper's Ferry by abolitionists had unleashed fears of rampant illegality in Virginia—so much that more than a thousand armed troops were guarding Brown in Charlestown from the daily rumored terrors of the lynch mob and the rescue party, with the possibility of a slave insurrection thrown in. Criticized from all sides, local leaders feared that Jefferson County was about to become "the seat of war."[45] They were, in consequence, particularly anxious that legal decorum, the minimal public test of a functioning community, be preserved in Brown's trial.

At the outset, Judge Richard Parker, speaking for the Circuit Court on October 21st, articulated the crucial connection between legal decorum and communal identity in charging the Grand Jury of Jefferson County to help provide "a fair and impartial trial" for Brown and his men. "We owe it to the cause of justice as well as to our own characters," he observed, "that such a trial should be afforded them."[46] In the North, the *New York Times* spelled out the implications of Parker's words:

> We know of no better test of the civilization and soundness of a State than the tone of her judges and Bar, in dealing with a case of this kind in a time of great popular excitement. . . . The world will always take it for granted that a community which produces judges, who preserve their composure, their honor, in the midst of tumultuous passions, is sound at the core.[47]

Composure was a struggle for any Virginian on October 21, 1859, two days after Brown's raid. Judge Parker told the Grand Jury:

> I will not allow myself to give expression to any of those feelings which at once spring up in every breast when reflection upon the enormity of the guilt in which those are involved who invade by force a peaceful unsuspecting portion of our common country,

45. See, in particular, Kenneth L. Smith, "Edmund Ruffin and the Raid on Harper's Ferry," *Virginia Cavalcade* 22 (1972): 28-37; Craig Simpson, "John Brown and Governor Wise: A New Perspective on Harper's Ferry," *Biography* 1 (Fall 1978): 15-38; Isaiah A. Woodward, "Document: John Brown's Raid at Harper's Ferry and Governor Henry Alexander Wise's Letter to President James Buchanan Concerning the Invasion," *West Virginia History* 42 (1981): 307-13; and Donald Brooks Kelley, "Harper's Ferry: Prelude to Crisis in Mississippi," *Journal of Mississippi History* 27 (November 1965): 351-72. By the time of Brown's execution on December 2nd, there were 4,000 additional men under arms in Virginia and thousands more in the other Southern states.

46. De Witt, *The Life, Trial and Execution*, 50. All further references to this account of the trial are noted parenthetically in the text.

47. "The Virginia Judiciary," *New York Times*, 24 October 1859.

> raise the standard of insurrection amongst them, and shoot down without mercy Virginia Citizens, defending Virginia soil against their invasion (p. 50).

These words shed light on the complex relation between decorum, fairness, and communal identity in Judge Parker's courtroom, and they help explain how decorum there became the pivotal term *between* fairness and identity. Parker wanted to exclude from deliberation the potent emotions that Virginians possessed on the issue under investigation ("those feelings which at once spring up in every breast"). By the same token, Parker's personal denial ("I will not permit myself") readily attested to negative emotions supposedly banished from the courtroom. When the Judge talked of "the enormity of the guilt" of those "who invade by force," who "raise the standard of insurrection," and who "shoot down without mercy," his own feelings could not have been clearer. A controlling narrative was already in place before the Grand Jury heard a shred of evidence.

Decorum, in this construct of denial and assertion, signified not the absence of emotion but a hermetically sealed zone of restraint and order. Legally, it meant confining public behavior within procedurally sanctioned norms and formal conventions. Anything else, local authorities feared, might induce communal breakdown. The ritual acceptance by all participants of the constraint of an assigned role in the courtroom closed out the extraordinary circumstances in question, demonstrating fairness and re-articulating communal values.

In typical expressions of this theme, Judge Parker appeared "desirous of trying this case precisely as he would try another, without any reference at all to outside feeling" (p. 83), and the prosecution promised "to avoid anything by way of argument or explanation not immediately connected with the particular issue to be tried" (p. 67). Only in this way could the procedure of Brown's trial and conviction "vindicate the majesty of the law" (p. 93). Communal patience was essential, in the words of the prosecution, "in preservation of the character of Virginia, that plumes itself on its moral character, as well as physical, and on its loyalty, and its devotion to truth and right" (p. 93).

Virginians realized through such statements that Virginia joined Brown on trial in Charlestown, and their realization led them to act out the strictest rule of legal decorum in defense of their communal reputation. A minor incident recorded in the trial transcript underscores the point. As Brown, easily the most hated man in Virginia on November 2, 1859, formally received the sentence of death, the "perfect quiet" of the courtroom was broken by "the clapping of the hands of one man in the crowd." But if proprieties had been shattered, the celebrant, in the trial stenographer's gloss, "is not a resident of Jefferson County," and he "was promptly suppressed, and much regret is expressed by the citizens at its occurrence" (p. 95). Elsewhere, the transcript pauses to congratulate the trial audience for hiding emotions out of respect for "the forms of the Court."[48]

Every courtroom formally depends upon the careful observance of protocol and ritual, but the standard established in Charlestown left the Circuit Court of Jefferson vulnerable from two directions. First, the idea of excluding from the legal process the imaginative thrust of events that totally absorb a community was inherently defective. Courtrooms, as arbiters of social conduct, are extensions of the community in which they function. Virginians needed to express the very feelings they suppressed, as Judge Parker's statements already have illustrated. Second, decorum requires the participation of everyone, and Brown, who openly sought martyrdom through the court's ultimate capacity to punish, had few incentives to cooperate on anything but his own terms—terms that were quite distinct from those imposed upon him. Just as the Virginia court wished to protect the events in the courtroom from outside, so Brown's personal needs led him to open those events to the largest possible communal discussion and debate.

Several consequences followed from the vulnerabilities of the court, and they all favored Brown's capacity to make the most of his situation. When intrusions from the outside came, they reinforced extant questions about the fairness of Brown's trial; the very concept of a sealed-off fairness invited these criticisms. Furthermore, the accents on decorum converted Brown's occasional disruptions in the courtroom into especially effective, even sensational episodes at trial. Only Brown could *be* dramatic in the courtroom. The court had already assigned itself as mundane a role as possible ("without any reference at all to outside feeling"), and Brown quickly established that the price of any display by the prosecution would be either disengagement or further disruption on his part.

The result was a curious imbalance. Brown lost his formal case at each stage of the decision-making, both procedurally and substantively, but his threats of disruption led to concession after concession from the prosecution and the court, both of whom were anxious to obtain and keep his minimal cooperation as matters proceeded. Brown gradually became an independent agent in his own trial, left to pursue his own ulterior purposes. By the fourth day of the adversarial proceeding, he was freely instigating and carrying on "a general collo-

48. Thus, at the announcement of the jury's verdict, we find the following: "Not the slightest expression of elation or triumph was uttered from the hundreds present, who, a moment before, outside the court, joined in heaping threats and imprecations on his head; nor was this strange silence interrupted during the whole of the time occupied by the forms of the Court." De Witt, *The Life, Trial and Execution*, 93.

quy" with witnesses and the prosecution. "No objection was made," runs the transcript of these moments, "to Brown's asking these questions in his own way, and interposing verbal explanations relative to his conduct" (p. 80).

Here is one key to Brown's sudden cultural transformation. Crossing boundary lines and assuming control amidst the necessarily unimaginative rigidities and official constraints of the courtroom, Brown became the figure of romance that Ralph Waldo Emerson described. He entered that "medium the most suitable for a romance-writer" of Hawthorne's description, "a neutral territory, somewhere between the real world and fairy-land, where the Actual and the Imaginary may meet, and each imbues itself with the nature of the other."[49] Neutrality, in this sense, implies converging but still fundamentally divergent possibilities that inform each other; or, in another similarity between the courtroom event and the Romance narrative, it reflects the intrinsic and necessary ambiguity of opposing interpretations.

The decorum of the courtroom was a starting point, a baseline for the imagination to rest upon while it searched other realities for answers to the fantastic and the bizarre in Brown and his raid. Disruptions of that decorum encouraged speculation beyond it. Those in favor of Brown quickly grasped the exaggerations of his effect. Those against him found plenty of scope for casting him back into the darkness from which they thought he had come.

Since the decorum of a trial embraces the extremity of competing interpretations as part of the essence of the advocacy system, it often contains other worlds of interpretation in embryonic form. When, for example, the South demonized Brown, it needed to look no farther than the trial transcript for confirmation.[50] The conventions of Brown's indictment for treason specified that he and his followers acted "not having the fear of God before their eyes, but being moved and seduced by the false and malignant counsel of other evil and traitorous persons and the instigations of the devil" (pp. 59-60). The prosecution easily advanced this discourse of evil incarnate. It wanted to punish "those who have raised the black flag on the soil of this Commonwealth" (p. 66), a crime after which "there could not be a female in this country who, whether with good cause or not, was not trembling with anxiety and apprehension" (p. 83). In the prosecu-

49. Hawthorne, *The Scarlet Letter*, 35-36.

50. The Southern need to demonize Brown is virtually automatic in its workings. In the typifying words of one eyewitness recollecting his first reactions to the raid, "I must confess that through my mind floated vague visions of horns and hoofs and forked tails, for be it remembered I was very young, had never been north of Mason and Dixon's line, and from my tenderest years had been led to regard *abolitionists* as being nearly allied to his Satanic Majesty." Edward White, "Eyewitness at Harper's Ferry," *American Heritage* 26 (1975): 57.

tion's proof of malice, Brown "glories in coming here to violate [Virginia's] laws" (p. 93) and everything those laws protect. Even a prospective attorney for Brown from the North occupied a zone of magnified possibilities. "We know not," warned the prosecutor, "whether he is to come here as counsel for the prisoner, or whether he wants to head a band of desperadoes" (p. 65).

These statements and others like them bespoke a melodrama of fire and brimstone against a backdrop of desperadoes and frightened maidens. Two artifacts, in particular, controlled the demonizing narrative. Brown's provisional constitution, written out for an abolitionist state, proved his premeditated and overarching malignancy; there was simply "too much method in Brown's madness" (p. 92). Doubly horrifying as symbols were the pikes that Brown had brought to Harper's Ferry to arm the slaves. They, in fact, substituted for narrative.[51] "When you put pikes in the hands of the slaves, and have their masters captive," intoned the prosecutor in his final summation, "that is advice to slaves to rebel, and punishable with death" (p. 92). The duty of the court was clear, though even death proved a temporary measure in the prosecutor's scheme. As he told the jury, "let retributive justice, if he is guilty, send him before that Maker who will settle the question forever and ever" (p. 93).

From the other side of the case, Brown figured as God's agent. He set the tone himself on the first day of the trial by claiming that "God has always been at his side" (p. 58). Procedurally, "full confidence in the goodness of God" removed any need for a legal confession of criminal action; Brown "knows God is with him and fears nothing" (p. 58). The statement immediately established the defendant's spiritual explanation of his own courage during his trial and later execution. That courage was considerable, and not even Brown's enemies denied its significance.[52] When Virginia Governor Henry A. Wise, who orchestrated Brown's trial, employed the colloquial terminology of the cockfight to admit that Brown is "the gamest man I ever saw," the

51. These pikes held attention in the South like no other aspect of the Brown raid, and regional firebrands, understanding as much, sent them for prominent display to each of the governors of the fifteen slaveholding states. Edmund Ruffin, the Southern extremist who travelled to Harper's Ferry and went to great lengths to witness Brown's execution in Charlestown, led the way. He inscribed his gifts of these weapons with slogans like "Sample of the favors designed for us by our Northern Brethren" and "The most precious benefit derived from the Northern states by the Southern, if, rightly using it, 'out of this nettle danger we plant the flower *safety*.'" The pikes were to remind all Southerners of the need for "defence against all assaults from the unscrupulous and measureless enmity of Northern Abolitionists." Smith, "Edmund Ruffin and the Raid," 37.

52. Even Edmund Ruffin, who attended Brown's execution in the hope of seeing the doomed man falter, grudgingly admitted that "the villain whose life has thus been forfeited, possessed but one virtue (if it should be so called) or one quality that is more highly esteemed by the world than the most rare and perfect virtues. This is physical or animal courage, or the most complete fearlessness of and insensibility to danger and death. In this quality he seems to me to have had few equals." Quoted in Smith, "Edmund Ruffin and the Raid," 36.

earthy validation had a higher integrity. "He is a bundle of the best nerves I ever saw. . . . He is a man of clear head, of courage, fortitude and simple ingeniousness," noted Wise. "He is cool, collected and indomitable . . . and he inspired me with great trust in his integrity as a man of truth."[53]

With the connection between physical courage and truthful integrity acknowledged by all, the next step, from physical courage toward the superiority of the spirit in moral courage, was an automatic one for Brown's defenders and later followers.[54] In the trial transcript, Brown's behavior in crucial moments confirmed at least the appearance of that superiority. A dramatic description of the verdict, "terrible to look upon," gave Brown "the only calm and unruffled countenance" in the courtroom: "There he stood, a man of indomitable will and iron nerve, all collected and unmoved even while the verdict that consigned him to an ignominious doom was pronounced upon him" (p. 93). As ritual, the penultimate moment of conviction on October 30th was a ceremonial and accurate precursor for the execution on December 2nd. Completely "calm and cheerful" on the way to the gallows, Brown would bid "an affectionate adieu" just before taking the final plunge.[55] "I am waiting the hour of my public murder with great composure of mind and cheerfulness," he had explained in a last letter to his family, "feeling the strong assurance that in no other possible way could I be used to so much advantage to the cause of God and of humanity. . . . [O]ur seeming disaster will ultimately result in the most glorious success."[56]

Martyrdom marks the ultimate boundary between flesh and spirit—between the grotesque reality of total bodily humiliation and the sublime imagination of eternal life. Brown's courage allowed supporters to predict his martyrdom from the moment of his capture, and their foreknowledge contributed to his own performance on the boundary line. "Let Virginia make him a martyr!" cried Henry Ward Beecher in

53. Quoted in Simpson, "John Brown and Governor Wise," 17.

54. Emerson and Thoreau both used Wise's acknowledgement of Brown's courage to paint a portrait of the latter's inherent superiority. "High courage, or a perfect will superior to all events, makes a bond of union between two enemies," wrote Emerson. "Inasmuch as Governor Wise is a superior man, he distinguished John Brown." Quoted in John J. McDonald, "Emerson and John Brown," *The New England Quarterly* 44 (1971): 385. See also Thoreau, "A Plea for Captain John Brown," 175-76. During the trial, Brown's attorneys made much of their client's integrity through his courage. Brown, in their words, was "actuated by the highest and noblest feelings that ever coursed through a human breast. . . . He is a man of indomitable will, of sleepless energy, and of purpose, possessed of a spirit of perseverance that turns back from no difficulty, and endowed with a constitution that will endure and overcome everything." The defense explicitly asked the jury to make its decision by following the same upward trajectory from physical to moral courage. De Witt, *The Life, Trial and Execution*, 67, 89.

55. De Witt, *The Life, Trial and Execution*, 100-101. This account of the execution received extensive circulation at the time.

56. John Brown to his Family, 30 November 1859, quoted in Warch and Fanton, *John Brown*, 100.

a sermon on October 30, 1859. "Good," wrote Brown on his own copy of a newspaper report of the suggestion.[57] Writing letters in the weeks before his execution, Brown carefully located himself within the hagiographical tradition. He was Peter armed with the sword, Paul in prison, Samson overturning the house of slavery around him, even Christ on the cross. Lest a precise religious allusion be missed, Brown supplied parenthetical references.[58] The letters reached for a sense of station as God's chosen servant—and something more. With a humble demeanor that would help Emerson to compare the gallows to the cross, Brown concluded: "Let them hang me; I forgive them, and may God forgive them, for they know not what they do."[59]

The dramatic potential of such language was vast in the religious culture of antebellum America, and Brown wielded it to achieve a purification in martyrdom. At work in the borrowed words of Jesus—"for they know not what they do"—was yet another indication in levels of meaning. For if an earlier age might have found presumption in Brown's appropriation, the Americans of the 1850s had been schooled to accept a rhetoric of excess. Brown as Christ was a theatrical effect rather than a blasphemous gesture. At the same time, Brown's courage represented a natural fact in a world that still believed natural facts prefigured spiritual truths.[60] The language of

57. Quoted in Oates, *To Purge This Land with Blood*, 319. From Italy, writing a week before Brown's death, Theodore Parker summarized the ingredients in the claim:

> Brown will die, I think, like a martyr, and also like a saint. His noble demeanor, his unflinching bravery, his gentleness, his calm, religious trust in God, and his words of truth and soberness, cannot fail to make a profound impression on the hearts of Northern men; yes, and on Southern men.

Theodore Parker to Francis Jackson, 24 November 1859, in Ruchames, *A John Brown Reader*, 265-66. Thoreau, writing "A Plea for Captain John Brown" while Brown was still alive, observed, "I am aware that I anticipate a little . . . I have all along found myself thinking and speaking of [Brown] as physically dead." Thoreau, "A Plea for Captain John Brown," 181.

58. These biblical references are frequent and varied in Brown's prison letters. See Brown to "E.B.," 1 November 1859, in Warch and Fanton, *John Brown*, 90. ("You know that Christ once armed Peter. So also in my case I think he put a sword into my hand"); Brown to his family, 30 October 1859 ("I am in charge of a jailer like the one who took charge of Paul and Silas"), ibid.; Brown to Reverend James W. McFarland, 23 November 1859 ("I think I feel as happy as Paul did when he lay in prison"), ibid., 96; Brown to Reverend Dr. Heman Humphrey, 25 November 1859 ("If the cause in which I engaged in any possible degree approximated to be 'infinitely better' than the one which Saul of Tarsus undertook, I have no reason to be ashamed"), ibid., 98; Brown to his family, 8 November 1859 ("Remember, my dear wife and children all, that Jesus of Nazareth suffered a most excruciating death on the cross as a felon, under the most aggravated circumstances"), ibid., 92; Brown to Reverend H.L. Vaill, 15 November 1859 ("I, at least, am on the 'brink of Jordan.' (See Bunyan's 'Pilgrim')"), ibid., 94.

59. Brown to Reverend James W. McFarland, 23 November 1859, in Warch and Fanton, *John Brown*, 96. Emerson's comment that John Brown "will make the gallows glorious, like a cross" appeared in a Boston lecture entitled "Courage" on 7 November 1859, quoted in McDonald, "Emerson and John Brown," 386-87. Emerson removed the comment from the published version of the essay.

60. Peter Brooks's study of melodrama includes an analysis of the way that the idea of the sacred gives way to melodrama or "a literary aesthetic of excess." In America, still basically a revivalist culture in the 1850s, the sacred and the melodramatic interact with a peculiar intensity. Also, the forms of belief (specifically, a framework of typological reference) remain as much a part of Ralph Waldo Emerson's prose as of Jonathan Edwards's writing a century before. In

prophecy and of religious parallels fell within familiar parameters of belief that appealed to friend and foe alike. One way or the other, the display of Brown's courage at trial was going to have another meaning, and his followers used this assumption to transfigure his image fundamentally.[61]

V

With the complex variables of secular and religious explanation more firmly in mind, we are now in a position to understand how Brown's intrusions and disruptions during the trial process provided him with "a neutral territory" for accessing multiple frames of reference. The prospect of martyrdom freed him from the puny civic threats in the criminal action against him. Brown was *in* but not *of* the world, *in* but not *under* the constraints of legal procedure. "I am ready for my fate," Brown announced at the beginning of his first day in court, a *pro forma* preliminary hearing before a magistrate's court. Five times in this first short appearance he would ask "to be excused from the mockery of a trial" (p. 55). The opportunity to speak came because the court had to inquire if the prisoner had counsel, and Brown seized the occasion. "If you seek my blood," he answered, "you can have it at any moment, without this mockery of a trial" (p. 55). Brown's only other formal request was also rhetorically aimed: "I have now little further to ask, other than that I may not be foolishly insulted, only as cowardly barbarians insult those who fall into their power" (p. 55).

No opening strategy could have been better calculated to put the Virginia authorities on the defensive. The perception of fairness through decorum was important to Charlestown leaders as a symbol of their own civilization. Brown began by challenging their claim and the very notion of fairness in forms: "But if we are to be forced with a mere form—a trial for execution—you might spare yourselves that trouble" (p. 55). Brown, as would-be martyr, needed the ritual of the trial as much as the authorities did, but he first had to secure the event for his own purposes.

Indifferent to the actual procedures that were leading toward his execution, Brown challenged them closely in the courtroom (and with

Emerson's words from "Nature," "every natural fact is a symbol of some spiritual fact." Brooks, *The Melodramatic Imagination*, 200-202. See also Perry Miller, "From Edwards to Emerson," in *The Errand into the Wilderness* (1956; reprint, New York: Harper & Row, 1964), 184-203; Ralph Waldo Emerson, "Nature" in *The Complete Essays and Other Writings of Ralph Waldo Emerson*, ed. Brooks Atkinson (New York: Random House, 1940), 15.

61. The purification of Brown's image is an interesting separate topic. For just two quick examples from an enormous literature, see Louisa May Alcott's "With a Rose that Bloomed on the Day of John Brown's Martyrdom" ("And the gallows only proved to him/ A stepping-stone to heaven"), and John Greenleaf Whittier's "Brown of Osawatomie" ("And round the grisly fighter's hair/ The Martyr's aureole bent!"), both in Ruchames, *A John Brown Reader*, 271, 295.

an impunity born of indifference) in order to put himself above them. The prosecution wanted to prove the criminality of Brown's behavior at Harper's Ferry. He responded with a legal *non sequitur*, proclaiming the selflessness of his own actions. Of no use to the defendant, the strategy was crucial to the parallel agenda of the martyr, but Brown could implement this plan only after he had extracted an extralegal right of procedural flexibility from the court. Accordingly, his earliest challenges established a position from which he could successfully resist the prosecution's later charges of irrelevancy.[62]

A single sentence from the transcript best captures the essence of Brown's overall position as well as his awareness of his adversaries' vulnerability in Charlestown: "I wish for counsel if I am to have a trial," he observed in the first stage of a continuous battle over the assignment of counsel, "but if I am to have nothing but the mockery of a trial, as I have said, I do not care anything about counsel" (p. 56).[63] His real concern, as he eventually admitted, was that "if he has counsel he will not be allowed to speak himself," and he cooperated only after court and assigned counsel, in the first of many concessions, promised to "give him the advantage of every privilege that the law will allow" (p. 58). Throughout, Brown also used these extended debates over the right to counsel to serve notice that any "insult" would trigger a challenge to the fairness of the proceedings and the authority of the court.

Brown disrupted proceedings once each day that he was in court—just often enough to maintain the threat. Quiet most of the time, he chose his moments carefully, and this restraint is suggestive since violations of due process and other opportunities for protest proliferated in the course of the trial. Afraid of the incendiary atmosphere in Charlestown, Governor Wise ordered the prosecution of Brown and his followers within a week of their capture, and this was done even though Brown, wounded during the raid, could not stand unassisted at his own arraignment and declared himself seriously incapacitated (pp. 58, 62).[64] Possibilities for challenge were everywhere. Brown had no

62. Most of Brown's defense, on the fourth day of his trial, deals with his fair treatment of his hostages, his "purely defensive" use of weapons, his bravery, and the absence in him "of any malicious feeling." The prosecution, in exasperation, conceded all of these points while dismissing the whole strategy "as merely calculated to waste time." It was a waste of time for the defendant, but not for the martyr. In return for the court allowing these defenses, Brown tacitly withdrew from a position of procedural non-cooperation. De Witt, *The Life, Trial and Execution*, 79-81.

63. For Brown's manipulation of his own legal counsel, see note 13 above.

64. The court's explicit admissions of the need for haste, in the trial transcript, are questionable procedurally in themselves and should have supplied grounds for delay, change of venue, and later, for prejudicial error. "The reason given for hurrying the trial, is, that the people of the whole country are kept in a state of excitement, and a large armed force is required to prevent attempts at rescue." De Witt, *The Life, Trial and Execution*, 58. See also ibid., 62-63, 78-79.

real chance to consult with his attorneys before trial (p. 55), defense counsel changed completely three times during the course of the six-day event without benefit of recess (pp. 55, 72, 78), and the Governor's special prosecutor, Andrew Hunter, should have disqualified himself on the grounds of a conflict of interest.[65] Brown and his attorneys raised each of these issues except the last, but they did not stress them (pp. 55, 62, 63, 65, 66, 76). Brown, for his part, deliberately ignored other apparent chances to object. He failed, for instance, to challenge a single person during jury selection.[66]

Obviously, Brown's motivation for disruption had nothing to do with due process. Brown wanted instead for trial rituals to dignify spiritual objectives and for them to broadcast his mission beyond the courtroom; somehow these rituals had to be extended to reach the separate narratives accessible to him. The courtroom had to serve as a catalyst, and it had to do so over the prosecution's complaints of "outdoor effect and influence" (p. 75) and over its specific objections to Brown's tactics "outside of what the laws recognize" (p. 65). It is significant, then, that the most blatant manipulation also fed the claim of martyrdom. Brown exploited the wounds he had received from the fighting at Harper's Ferry. Forced to stand trial while still suffering from painful sword cuts, he reacted by refusing to walk. The ensuing compromise allowed the defendant to be carried into the courtroom on a cot—an arrangement the prosecution quickly came to regret (pp. 63-64, 66).

Whether languishing or rising in rejoinder, Brown used his bed of pain to repropose the extraordinary circumstances that the court wanted to exclude from the legal process. The cot was an emblem of current affliction and a symbol of final suffering to come, and it turned Brown's presence at trial—"laid down on his cot at full length within the bar" (p. 64)—into a visible act and constant reminder of his courage. Inherently theatrical, this cot in the courtroom was the prop of a knowing performer. In those trial moments Brown appeared to be prostrate, exhausted, and seemingly indifferent. Such moments included his indictment (p. 66), the march of prosecution witnesses on the second day of trial (pp. 68-71), the closing arguments of counsel (pp. 84, 93), and the jury's verdict (p. 93). Brown could disregard what he pleased. Sometimes he dismissed the trial altogether—cover-

65. Andrew Hunter, the special prosecutor of Governor Henry A. Wise, was a relative of a militiaman from Charlestown, Henry Hunter, who openly admitted on the witness stand that he murdered a defenseless captured raider, Will Thompson, at Harper's Ferry. Prosecutor Hunter was also related to one of the victims at Harper's Ferry, the mayor of the town, Fontaine Beckham. De Witt, *The Life, Trial and Execution*, 74-76; Oates, *To Purge This Land with Blood*, 296-97, 309, 325. Oates gives his own summary of violations of procedural due process.

66. Oates, *To Purge This Land with Blood*, 309.

ing himself completely, closing his eyes, and, after one dramatic outburst, feigning sleep (pp. 63, 93, 77).

The same cot was also a pulpit for guarding Brown's sense of mission from more explicit challenges in the courtroom. On the second day of trial, as assigned defense counsel introduced evidence of insanity, Brown apprehended a threat to his plan of ultimate sacrifice and moved quickly to refute it.[67] "Brown then raised himself up in bed," runs the court transcript, and declared, "I reject, so far as I am capable, any attempt; to interfere in my behalf on that score." He "disdain[ed]" the plea and those who made it: "I look upon it as a miserable artifice and pretext of those who ought to take a different course in regard to me . . . and I view it with contempt more than otherwise" (pp. 64-65). References to his own helplessness were peculiarly available to the man on the cot, and they tempered an anger that was now poignant rather than offensive. Thus, when hostile witnesses boasted of shooting "those villainous Abolitionists," Brown, weeping for his dead followers, staggered again from his mattress to do battle. Although a doomed man "ready for anything that may come up," he was a more formidable adversary because of it, and he rose without fear or hope to confront everything by relating his physical plight to the procedural imbalances around him (pp. 75-76).

Brown also understood that his own counsel was the best target for demonstrating "that nothing like a fair trial is to be given me." Provoked, he now exercised that option in stronger terms. "I have no counsel, as I before stated, in whom I feel that I can rely," he exclaimed, this time in rage and exasperation. Standing feebly by his cot, he was the iconographic verification of the complaint that followed: "I am myself unable to attend to [my defense]. I have given all the attention I possibly could to it, but am unable to see or know about them [the witnesses], and can't even find out their names; and I have nobody to do any errand, for my money was all taken when I was sacked and stabbed, and I have not a dime" (p. 76). This outburst overwhelmed the court. As Brown collapsed once again on his bed, his lawyers resigned, and Judge Parker necessarily declared a postponement until the following morning (pp. 77-78).[68]

67. The charge of insanity clearly negates all thought of altruistic service and self-sacrifice. Procedurally, if successful as a plea, insanity also thwarts the execution that brings martyrdom as long as Brown behaves properly on the gallows; hospitalization or even imprisonment were clearly ignominious alternatives for this defendant. Brown worries enough about the larger imputation to mount a public relations campaign against it in his letters from prison. See Brown to Reverend Dr. Heman Humphrey, 25 November 1859, and Brown to Judge Daniel R. Tilden, 28 November 1859, in Warch and Fanton, *John Brown*, 97, 99.

68. In the words of the transcript, "Brown then lay down again, drew his blanket over him, and closed his eyes and appeared to sink in tranquil slumber." Thomas C. Green, assigned as Brown's lawyer with Lawson Botts, announces that "Mr. Botts and myself will now withdraw from the case, as we can no longer act in behalf of the prisoner, he having got up now and

This incident underlines the fragility of courtroom procedure in general. Adversarial in form, trials nonetheless depend on a high level of cooperation in practice, and any substantial disregard of that cooperation brings the interactive mechanism to a halt. The Circuit Court of Jefferson County asked for the trouble it received by rushing Brown to trial in prejudicial circumstances, but now, in the face of his rejection of its forms, it coped with Brown's disruption by doing everything possible to induce him back to the level of cooperation needed for the trial to proceed.

The prosecution responded immediately. It withdrew all of its objections to the submission of irrelevant evidence by the defense, granting the latitude that Brown needed to present himself in his own spiritual terms: "we are perfectly willing to admit these facts in any form [the defense] desire[s]" (p. 77). The facts in question had to do with "the conduct of Captain Brown in the treating of his prisoners with leniency, respect, and courtesy" (p. 77), and their formal submission went a long way toward creating the impression of Brown as an efficacious moral force at Harper's Ferry in place of the confused raider who crouched indecisively in the armory on October 17th.[69]

The concessions continued: On the morning after Brown's outburst, the prosecution withdrew every document that Brown's new team of lawyers disputed (p. 79). The state subsequently agreed not to cross-examine a single witness called by the defense (p. 81), and even offered to forego a final summation before the jury if the defense would do likewise (p. 83). Nothing in these courtroom acquiescences influenced the formal judgment of Brown, but the change in narrative outcome for the listening nation was immense.

Imbalance in the adversarial process helped yield an image of Brown that was larger than life. While the defense emphasized Brown's restraint, his bravery, his kindly attentions to his hostages, his high moral character, and his indomitable will (pp. 79-81, 89), the prosecution magnified the scope and importance of the raid itself and Brown's characterological singleness of purpose (p. 92). Lost from both were the petty and ridiculous sides of Brown and in their place a consensus that Brown's actions carried momentous consequences for all Americans. A blend of these embellished trial perspectives entered the popular imagination. It would be what history bestowed on John Brown—but not before Brown himself gave it a final turn.

declared here that he has no confidence in the counsel who have been assigned him." De Witt, *The Life, Trial and Execution*, 77.

69. "The speed with which the countryside had mobilized had taken Brown completely by surprise; flustered, he did not know what to do. . . . To Osborn P. Anderson [one of the raiders] the old man seemed 'puzzled' as he watched the bustle of armed men in the streets and the gray sky beyond." Oates, *To Purge This Land with Blood*, 293-94.

VI

The undramatic stresses of legal procedures—their arcane forms, their avoidance of surprise, their insistence on repetition, their claim upon regularity, and their complexity—are stubborn trial ingredients, but they eventually give way to moments of high tension and vital suspense, and the highest, excepting the verdict, is the moment of sentencing. Only here does the public trial allow the person or persons under scrutiny something like free reign. Here defendants receive the right to speak on their own, within but beyond the forms of the law. It is a liminal moment for all concerned. The defendant, found guilty, is passing from the community that made the negative determination to a separate state of isolation in punishment. This moment distills emotion in a way that is otherwise foreign to the rationality of the legal process. It encourages contrition, shame, sorrow, despair, realization, sometimes defiance, and, of course, revelation. In every other aspect of the trial, defendants are encouraged to protect themselves from the world, to hide even from themselves if necessary, protected by the right against self-incrimination. Asked why sentence should not be imposed upon them, they enter a different realm of presumed candor and conscience, without intermediaries, unimpeded by the intrusion of counsel.

John Brown was the perfect master of this moment. Throughout the trial, he had been striving to speak without benefit of counsel, to separate himself from others, to dwell on the meaning of his punishment, and to engage in revelation. The spiritual resonances he had struggled to create elsewhere in the legal process were now his for the asking. As much as the gallows, Brown's speech at sentencing was a necessary platform, and he made the most of both. Emerson would later place Brown's words alongside Lincoln's Gettysburg Address as "the two best specimens of eloquence we have had in this country."[70] It was much earlier, however, that he conveyed most succinctly what eloquence might mean. "The high prize of eloquence may be mine, the joy of uttering what no other can utter & what all must receive," wrote Emerson in 1834.[71] Brown seized that prize before the bench in Charlestown on November 2, 1859. He uttered what no other person could and what all then must receive, and his oration is best examined as living speech.

Brown's words are all the more remarkable in that they begin and end in falsehood. Brown presented twenty-six short, simple sentences; they fill less than a printed page, and ten contain fifteen

70. Ralph Waldo Emerson, "Eloquence," in *The Complete Works of Ralph Waldo Emerson* (Boston: Houghton Mifflin, 1903-04), 8:125. See generally, McDonald, "Emerson and John Brown," 393-96.

71. Journal entry for 6 October 1834, Porte, *Emerson in His Journals*, 128.

words or less.[72] Yet no less than eight of Brown's most declarative sentences, including five of the first six, asserted that he never planned an insurrection of the slaves—a claim that contradicts the facts. His sincerity in court notwithstanding, Brown talked at length about his plans to instigate a slave uprising, and his intentions at Harper's Ferry made no sense without the hope of an insurrection.[73] Why should a small but heavily armed band of raiders take an armory unless they were looking for weapons for other people? Brown, at trial, had admitted that he already possessed sufficient weaponry to arm 1,500 men, a figure that included the 950 sharpened pikes designed expressly for freed slaves to handle (p. 71).

A second puzzle in the speech may help to explain the first. With his trial nearly over, Brown abruptly disowned his former statements about it: "I feel entirely satisfied with the treatment that I have received on my trial." This admission was part of a subtle recalibration of his strategy of confrontation. With his objective in sight and the whole nation in mind, he was the guardian of freedom everywhere rather than the raider and nightmare of the South. "I never had any design against the liberty of any person," Brown informed a riveted audience. Mission and sacrifice, not insurrection and anger, were his closing messages for the scaffold.

The speaker's realization took the normal sting from his tones, replacing acrimony with elegiac power and stately acceptance. Brown took his life in his hands and told why he must die. God's law in the injustice of a slave land required it of him, and this explanation, cast in the simplest language that biblical cadence will allow, lifted the speaker and his subject well above court and country. It was from the spheres that Brown delivered his firmest rebuke:

> Had I interfered in the manner which I admit, and which I admit has been fairly proved—for I admire the truthfulness and candor of the greater portion of the witnesses who have testified in this cases—had I so interfered in behalf of the rich, the powerful, the intelligent, the so-called great, or in behalf of any of their friends, either father, mother, brother, sister, wife, or children, or any of that class, and suffered and sacrificed what I have in this interference, it would have been all right, and every man in this Court would have deemed it an act worthy of reward rather than punishment. This Court acknowledges, too, as I suppose, the validity of the law of God. I see a book kissed, which I suppose to be the

72. The analysis and quotations in the next four paragraphs use the version of Brown's last formal speech before the court as it appears in De Witt, *The Life, Trial and Execution*, 94-95.

73. For a summary of the evidence that Brown meant to start an insurrection at Harper's Ferry, see Potter, *The Impending Crisis*, 365-68. As Brown told Frederick Douglass, in trying to recruit Douglass for the raid, "I want you for a special purpose. When I strike, the bees will swarm, and I shall want you to help hive them." Oates, *To Purge This Land with Blood*, 283.

> Bible, or at least the New Testament, which teaches me that all things whatsoever I would that men should do to me, I should do even so to them. It teaches me further to remember them that are in bonds as bound with them. I endeavored to act up to that instruction. I say I am yet too young to understand that God is any respecter of persons. I believe that to have interfered as I have done, as I have always freely admitted I have done in behalf of His despised poor, is no wrong, but right. Now, if it is deemed necessary that I should forfeit my life for the furtherance of the ends of justice, and mingle my blood further with the blood of my children and with the blood of millions in this slave country whose rights are disregarded by wicked, cruel, and unjust enactments, I say let it be done.[74]

Americans, Brown wanted his audience to realize, had been listening to the wrong stories. Their popular tales of injustice had concentrated on the rich and the powerful, the so-called great or the domestic circle, to the exclusion of both the greatest story, Christ's willing sacrifice for humanity, and the greatest injustice, slavery in America. The terms of Brown's reprimand, like his autobiography, catalogued the themes of the American Romance, but missing from the injustices that his fellow citizens have been willing to entertain in stories was a true spiritual empathy for the human soul in naked distress. This much of Brown's rebuke was aimed at all regions of the country, and his own story was meant as a counterweight. For Brown, the "interference" that produced either high reward or low punishment was the very stuff of dramatic narrative, but the moral conventions of this narrative had been debased all through the land. The ignored slave undermined every other story worth telling.

The speaker understood that even his supporters failed to respect the personhood of African Americans. Few Americans in 1859 would have disagreed with Emerson's brutal summary of his own priorities in 1851: "The absence of moral feeling in the whiteman is the very calamity I deplore. The captivity of a thousand negroes is nothing to me."[75] The real calamity was deeper than Emerson could see, and Brown, knowing that, reached for all of its implications by insisting on metaphors of attachment that link him directly to black men and women. He was "bound with" those in bonds and agreed "to mingle my blood further with the blood of my children and the blood of millions in this slave country whose rights are disregarded." Both conceptions, the victim bound and mingling blood, evoked Brown's claim to the sacrificial altar. He was to become what he has suffered for. "I

74. This passage is the heart or middle of Brown's speech, sentences eight through fifteen of the twenty-six that he offered to the court.

75. Entry from May-July 1851, Porte, *Emerson in His Journals*, 426.

say let it be done," he concluded quietly, turning his own death into a logical step toward legal and spiritual emancipation.

Brown never forgot that the clash of peoples around him was also a clash of different worlds. An expression of the 1850s, his five-minute speech before the court placed those separate levels of meaning in a careful spiritual continuum where ambiguities explain each other. Once again, imagination and dramatic effect lie in different levels of reading. The Bible glorifies God's "despised poor" when properly perceived, and Brown, by referring directly to the Sermon on the Mount, draws attention to the message in its most eloquent form.[76] But unfortunately, a correct reading of that message was not possible in the Virginia courtroom or, by extension, in an America that tolerated slavery. If the court acknowledged the law of God, it did not follow it. The witnesses at trial who sealed their oath of testimony with the Bible could not possibly know its contents, which was why Brown could only guess at the nature of the "book kissed" in front of him. ("I see a book kissed, which I suppose to be the Bible.") The qualifications illustrated Brown's rejection of Christian authority in a slave state. "There are no ministers of Christ here," the condemned man wrote of Charlestown, after rejecting the services of several.[77]

Facing judgment, Brown made each of these points with a delicacy foreign to his character and writings. There may be no better indication of how completely he had risen to the occasion. Not irony but a gentle awareness pervaded his understanding of the forces around him, an awareness in which spiritual mission and courtroom decorum finally merged. The quality of his recognition was mirrored in the acceptance that came after him. In one of those rare conjunctions of legal ritual and consummate literary expression, Brown's final courtroom speech touched the highest aspirations in the culture.

VII

It would be a mistake, however, to leave the last word to John Brown on the matter of his significance, a common enough shortcoming in interpretations of his mythological status in American culture. Our subject all along has been the peculiar power of the conjunction

76. *Matthew* 7:12 reads "Therefore all things whatsoever ye would that men should do to you, do ye even so to them." Brown's paraphrase, "all things whatsoever I would that men should do to me, I should do even so to them" is quite close. Four of the nine formal beatitudes announced in the Sermon on the Mount (*Matthew* 5:3-11) refer specifically to those in low distress and the blessings that they will receive.

77. Brown to Reverend James W. McFarland, 23 November 1859, in Warch and Fanton, *John Brown*, 96. "These ministers who profess to be Christian, and hold slaves or advocate slavery," wrote Brown, "I cannot abide them. My knees will not bend in prayer with them, while their hands are stained with the blood of souls." Consistent with this understanding, Brown refused the presence of a state-sanctioned minister at his execution. See Brown to Mrs. George L. Stearns, 29 November 1859, ibid., 99.

of law and literature—the power, and also the license, in the cultural formations that the conjunction inspires. Brown's presentencing speech may live on its own, but the circumstances of its transcription and subsequent transmission increase its power and eloquence. Recognizing the importance of the original context requires a brief return to the actual aesthetics of reading a trial transcript.

Anyone who has scanned such a record understands how the repetition, the circularity, the technicality, the occasional opacity, and the sheer minutiae in transcription inflict a special burden on the reader. Of course, some kind of burden always exists in comprehension. Contemporary critics talk frequently of "horizons of expectation" in a reader's interaction with a text and of the "tenacious" search for "textual unity or wholeness," but these problems of expectation and unity are compounded in the looseness and bulk of trial records.[78] In the case before us, the transcript of Brown's trial in general and the capstone of his final speech in particular welcome a generic appropriation that helps to give them larger meaning.[79] Left for demonstration is the process by which these appropriations take on a life of their own.

We have seen that John Brown's behavior and words in the Circuit Court of Jefferson County invited generic reconstruction about his place in American culture. Ralph Waldo Emerson, returning somewhat compulsively to the idea of the Romance a month after Brown's execution, saw the likelihood of further imaginative production quite clearly. "Thus was formed a romantic character absolutely without vulgar trait," Emerson observed of Brown's trial, "living to ideal ends, without any mixture of self-indulgence or compromise. . . . And, as happens usually to men of romantic character, his fortunes were romantic. Walter Scott would have delighted to draw his picture and trace his adventurous career."[80]

Emerson understood that the character "formed" in the courtroom would be formed again and again in accordance with the imaginative requirement of "living to ideal ends." He could intuit this much because he had already measured in himself the irresistible impulse. In the act of speaking about Brown, he and others already "delighted

78. For discussions of these concepts within the enormous subject of reader reception in contemporary criticism, see Hans-Robert Jauss, "Literary History as a Challenge to Literary Theory," *New Literary History* 2 (1970): 7-19, and Susan R. Suleiman, "Introduction: Varieties of Audience-Oriented Criticism," in *The Reader in the Text: Essays on Audience and Interpretation*, ed. Suleiman and Inge Crosman (Princeton: Princeton University Press, 1980), 35-40.

79. One might also explain this phenomenon as a relation between historical narrative and story in the way that historian Hayden White does. In White's words, "historical narratives are not only models of past events and processes, but also metaphorical statements which suggest a relation of similitude between such events and processes, and the story types that we conventionally use to endow the events of our lives with culturally sanctioned meanings." Hayden White, "The Historical Text as Literary Artifact," *Tropics of Discourse: Essays in Cultural Criticism* (1978; reprint, Baltimore: The Johns Hopkins University Press, 1990), 88.

80. "John Brown," in *The Complete Works of Ralph Waldo Emerson*, 11:279.

to draw his picture." We need not rehearse again how Brown's own language in Charlestown summons an answering language beyond the trial of "living to ideal ends." It *is* important to see that the combination consolidates the trial itself in the popular mind—that it subsumes and collects all other narratives about the event like a magnet sweeping across a field of iron filings.

For while the trial and execution always remain the necessary backdrop of the picture of John Brown, the finality of legal constructions has been refashioned in the reconstruction of Brown "living to ideal ends." Brown in his final speech emphasizes that "the law of God" will take account of what he has "suffered and sacrificed" and turn punishment into reward, death back into life. Here, if anywhere, is Emerson's "romantic character absolutely without vulgar trait." So powerful is this construction as a mode of cultural understanding that even vulgar forms are transformed to serve it. And nowhere is that shift more apparent than in the mode of memory most frequently summoned, that of the popular song "John Brown's Body."

The paradox of the most frequently voiced lyric in American history lies in its lost origins. The song we sing reinvokes the decisive rhetorical device of John Brown's major speeches at trial. Just as the defendant in the Charlestown courtroom framed physical defeat within a claim of spiritual victory, so, in balladic terms, the phrase "John Brown's body lies a'mouldering in the grave," receives an exultant qualification with "his truth is marching on." But this parallel must also be understood against a startling discrepancy. The original figure in "John Brown's Body" is *not* the legendary raider of Harper's Ferry in 1859 but Sergeant John Brown of the Second Battalion, Boston Light Infantry, Massachusetts Volunteer Militia in 1861. The song begins as a jibe from the ranks at the expense of a feckless noncommissioned officer of the same name. Compelled by the swelling narratives about the abolitionist hero, it soon migrates to its more dramatic and now familiar placement, and, notably, this migration requires a complete shift in meaning. Lost entirely is the low humor and comic incongruity, hero against anti-hero, that gave birth to the jingle. Sergeant Brown of Boston would, in fact, die pathetically rather than in pathos, drowning by accident while crossing the Rappahannock River with his regiment on June 6, 1862.[81]

The transformation from earthy jingle into triumphant marching song can serve as a final illustration of the urgencies that turned John Brown into something he had not previously been. To understand what he became requires a double act of interpretation: of the legal

81. For the story of "John Brown's Body" and its migration from Sergeant Brown into the legend of the abolitionist hero, see Boyd B. Stutler, "John Brown's Body," *Civil War History* 4 (September 1958): 251-60.

counts of treason, conspiracy, and murder on the one hand, and of narrative on the other. "Narrative," Roland Barthes tells us, "is first and foremost a prodigious variety of genres, themselves distributed amongst various substances."[82] Legal studies needs to grapple a little more carefully with this assertion of "first and foremost."

Genre is the hidden presence in the transcription and interpretation of trial event. True, trial records are literal transcriptions, but people can only speak through the stories they understand, and the customarily massive record of what *has actually been said* always demands an answer to what Wolfgang Iser, in another context, calls "the vacancy within the referential field."[83]

Once again, the issue is double in nature and exists on both conscious and unconscious levels: speakers will use generic forms to explain themselves in a courtroom, while trial observers will impose available generic understandings on what they hear or read in order to make sense of what is happening. Not surprisingly, the ensuing relation between cultural and legal understanding is often haphazard.

The trial of John Brown, in this sense, exemplifies a vital component in cultural and legal history. Seemingly extraneous generic considerations enter the trial process as inevitable engines of comprehension, and they remain to control perception, then and later. The John Brown who emerges from Charlestown exists almost entirely within a context of cultural Romance. At the same time, "the substance" or transcript that holds that narrative needs to be better understood by cultural critics. At stake is a balanced understanding of the ongoing courtroom events that regularly absorb the American culture. We need to retain the accuracy in trial forms without losing sight of cultural projections and their impelled variations on legal themes.

82. Roland Barthes, *Image, Music, Text*, trans. Stephen Heath (New York: Farrar, Straus, and Giroux, 1977), 79.

83. Wolfgang Iser, "Interaction between Text and Reader," in Suleiman and Crosman, *The Reader in the Text*, 113-18.

[11]

RATS, PIGS, AND STATUES ON TRIAL: THE CREATION OF CULTURAL NARRATIVES IN THE PROSECUTION OF ANIMALS AND INANIMATE OBJECTS

PAUL SCHIFF BERMAN*

INTRODUCTION

In 1522, in the district of Autun, France, a village was incensed to find that rats had eaten its barley crops.[1] The townspeople took the matter to the ecclesiastical court,[2] which duly investigated the "crime" and then delivered a summons to the rats ordering them to stand trial.[3] A court official went to an area of the countryside where the rats were believed to live, and served notice in a loud and solemn declaration.[4]

This seemingly bizarre case then proceeded to an actual trial. The court appointed a young lawyer named Bartolomée Chassenée to

---

* A condensed version of this Note was presented at a conference sponsored by the Group for Early Modern Cultural Studies at the University of Rochester on November 4, 1994. The author wishes to thank Professors William Nelson and Burt Neuborne for their many helpful comments on previous drafts of this Note, and Deborah Lewittes for her valuable research assistance.

1 See Walter W. Hyde, The Prosecution and Punishment of Animals and Lifeless Things in the Middle Ages and Modern Times, 64 U. Pa. L. Rev. 696, 706 (1916) (describing trial of rats by ecclesiastical court of Autun). For additional accounts of the proceedings, see Esther Cohen, Crossroads of Justice 120-21 (1993) [hereinafter E. Cohen, Crossroads]; E.P. Evans, The Criminal Prosecution and Capital Punishment of Animals 18-19 (Faber and Faber 1988) (1906); see also Esther Cohen, Law, Folklore and Animal Lore, 110 Past & Present 6, 14 & n.26 (1986) [hereinafter Cohen, Folklore] (describing proceedings against animals in the context of debate concerning the universality of human justice).

2 Throughout the medieval period, ecclesiastical courts exercised independent jurisdiction from the secular courts. "[T]he two parallel legal systems existed side by side, formally independent of each other, but in reality constantly interpenetrating and influencing each other. The very vagueness of the dividing line provided a dynamic, developmental element." E. Cohen, Crossroads, supra note 1, at 18; see also Wendy Davies & Paul Fouracre, The Settlement of Disputes in Early Medieval Europe 215 (1986) (summarizing importance of the Church to the development of dispute settlement procedures); 2 Frederick Pollock & Frederic W. Maitland, The History of English Law 478-80 (2d ed. 1968) (describing procedures for excommunications in ecclesiastical courts).

3 Hyde, supra note 1, at 704.

4 Id.

defend the rats.[5] When the defendants failed to appear in court in response to the summons, Chassenée intervened to save his clients from a default judgment. He argued that there had not been proper service of process because in fact "the salvation or ruin of all rats was at stake" in the case, and so *all* rats (and not just those in the village with the crops) deserved to be informed.[6] Following his demand, the priests of each and every parish within the diocese of Autun announced a new summons.[7] When the rats once more failed to appear, Chassenée urged that because the rats were dispersed across the countryside, more time was needed for them to make the migration to the courthouse.[8] Having been granted another delay, Chassenée pressed his case for the still-absent rats. He argued that a summons implied the full protection of the law on the way to the courthouse; however, his clients, though anxious to appear, feared they would be attacked by hostile cats and could not be expected to risk death in order to obey the summons.[9]

Although this story may sound like an absurdist satire created by Ionesco,[10] the trial described above actually occurred. And it was not an isolated case. Records indicate that trials of animals took place throughout Europe and elsewhere from the ninth through the nineteenth centuries.[11] Individual animals were tried—usually for killing human beings—in secular courts according to common law precedents dating back to the Book of Exodus.[12] And, as with the rats of Autun, many animals were tried in groups as public nuisances before ecclesiastical tribunals.[13]

---

[5] E. Cohen, Crossroads, supra note 1, at 121; E.P. Evans, supra note 1, at 18.

[6] Quoted in E. Cohen, Crossroads, supra note 1, at 121 (citing Auguste de Thou, 1 Histoire Universelle Depuis 1593 Jusqu'en 1607, at 414-16 (1734)); see also E.P. Evans, supra note 1, at 19; Hyde, supra note 1, at 706.

[7] E. Cohen, Crossroads, supra note 1, at 121; E.P. Evans, supra note 1, at 19; Hyde, supra note 1, at 706.

[8] E. Cohen, Crossroads, supra note 1, at 121; E.P. Evans, supra note 1, at 19; Hyde, supra note 1, at 706.

[9] E. Cohen, Crossroads, supra note 1, at 121; E.P. Evans, supra note 1, at 19; Hyde, supra note 1, at 706-07.

[10] In Ionesco's play, Rhinoceros, people are slowly transformed into animals while keeping up the stuffy formality of cocktail party chatter. See generally Eugene Ionesco, Rhinoceros (Derek Prouse trans., 1960).

[11] See E.P. Evans, supra note 1, at 265-86 (listing animal prosecutions). For a discussion of the extant evidence, see text accompanying notes 51-65 infra.

[12] See J.J. Finkelstein, The Ox That Gored, 71 Am. Phil. Soc. (pt. 2) 5, 48-73 (1981) (linking the animal trials to the Biblical story of the ox that is slaughtered for having killed a man). See generally Exodus 21:28-32.

[13] See E. Cohen, Crossroads, supra note 1, at 110. But see Finkelstein, supra note 12, at 64-66 (arguing that the ecclesiastical trials can be discounted because they "were *not* proper trials but were ritual procedures"). His distinction, however, is not grounded in the medieval experience, which seems to have viewed both secular and ecclesiastical proceed-

The historical evidence indicates that communities viewed these trials seriously. Many jurists and philosophers debated the propriety of holding animals responsible for crimes, with Thomas Aquinas being the most celebrated critic of the practice.[14] But despite scholarly arguments that animals could not summon the requisite intent to be found guilty, the practice continued.

It would be impossible to discover with any certainty the reasons for this seemingly irrational custom. No doubt the motivations—psychological, economic, religious—varied from community to community, and from one social class to another. Nevertheless, it would be unwise to dismiss the animal trials as the unenlightened custom of a bygone era.[15] As one commentator has noted, the trial of an animal "was not a game. It was undertaken for the good of society, and if properly conducted it was intended to bring *social benefits* to the community—benefits, that is, to human beings."[16] Certainly the trials cost the community a great deal of money. Defense lawyers were engaged on behalf of the animal, which was detained and fed in a jail at the community's expense,[17] and, of course, the hangman was paid just as he was for all other executions.[18] It would have been easier and cheaper simply to kill an animal that had become a menace.

Nevertheless, communities all over Europe turned to the mechanism of the trial to bring these animals to justice. If we can understand what social benefits the trials brought to the people of these towns, we may begin to see that trials even in our own time fulfill cultural needs that extend far beyond dispute resolution and adjudication.

This Note's discussion of animal trials begins not in the medieval era, but in ancient Greece. On the north side of the Athenian Acropolis stood a law court known as the Prytaneion, which tried not only animals but inanimate objects such as statues and pillars.[19] Part I

ings as serious judicial events. Moreover, this Note argues that trials *are* in fact ritual forms, so Finkelstein's distinction is particularly unhelpful in the context of this analysis.

14 See text accompanying notes 106-13 infra.

15 See Nicholas Humphrey, Foreword to E.P. Evans, supra note 1, at xix:

> [W]e must be wary of . . . assuming that people of mediaeval Europe were so different from ourselves that it is not worth trying to apply any of the standards of rationality we have today . . . . [T]o suggest, for example, that the grown-up people involved really could not tell the difference between animals and human beings, cannot be right. Other people may be other, but they are not necessarily stupid.

16 Id. at xx.

17 See text accompanying notes 67-69 infra.

18 See E.P. Evans, supra note 1, at 141-42 (citing bills listing amount of money received by a hangman for executing pigs).

19 See John W. Jones, The Law and Legal Theory of the Greeks 256-57 (1977); Hyde, supra note 1, at 696. (Both authors use the Latin spelling, "Prytaneum."). See also

of this Note first sketches the sparse historical data that exists from antiquity and shows how fatal accidents were reconceptualized as crimes through these proceedings, thereby creating both a guilty party and a societal ritual for expiating the death. This Part then describes the history of the animal trials in Europe, focusing on how the proceedings precisely mirrored the trials of human beings. By integrating animals within a human scheme of justice, these trials allowed the community to affirm a rational order and assign a role for animals within the hierarchy of creation.

Part II reveals that the animal trials took place against the backdrop of a widespread societal debate concerning how best to explain and understand chaotic and destructive events caused by nonhuman actors. This Part then describes in more depth a typical proceeding in order to explore how the various competing narratives found expression in the arguments made by lawyers at the trials.

Having surveyed this elliptical history, the Note then uses the trials of animals and inanimate objects as case studies in a more speculative and theoretical analysis of the role and function[20] of trials within a society. In addition to adjudicating the actual dispute involved, popular trials may also adjudicate among various discourses for describing the world by creating narratives[21] that help to shape the social con-

---

Finkelstein, supra note 12, at 58-59 (providing examples of classical sources mentioning trials at the Prytaneion).

20 Critics have often attacked functionalist arguments for implying an unproved causal link. See, e.g., Jon Elster, Ulysses and the Sirens: Studies in Rationality and Irrationality 32 (1979) ("A large body of sociological literature seems to rest upon an implicit regulative idea that if you can demonstrate that a given pattern has unintended, unrecognized and beneficial effects, then you have also explained why it exists and persists."). However, the social functions of trials are not discussed in this Note for the purpose of showing why trials exist, nor does this Note assert that the possible beneficial function of animal trials explain why they took place. Rather, a discussion of social function is useful in order to recognize the various cultural roles trials may fulfill.

21 Over the past several decades, anthropologists, literary critics, and legal scholars have increasingly studied the role of narratives in structuring our experience of the world. See, e.g., Vincent Crapanzano, Tuhami: Portrait of a Moroccan (1980) (exploring conflicting storytelling styles between anthropologist and subject); Jacques Derrida, Of Grammatology (Gayatri C. Spivak trans., 1974) (drawing on the work of linguist Ferdinand de Saussure to argue that language provides no direct access to reality and therefore what we call "reality" is really only a set of narrative conventions); Renato Rosaldo, Culture and Truth: The Remaking of Social Analysis (1989) (advocating that social science acknowledge the role of conflicting narratives and subjectivity in descriptions of reality); The Anthropology of Experience (Victor W. Turner & Edward M. Bruner eds., 1986) (collecting essays exploring the relationship between experience and narratives used to describe experience); Roland Barthes, Introduction to the Structural Analysis of Narratives, in Image—Music—Text 79 (Stephen Heath trans., 1977) (using linguistics to construct, describe, and classify a theory of narratives); Claude Lévi-Strauss, The Effectiveness of Symbols, in Structural Anthropology 186 (Claire Jacobsen & Brooke G. Schoepf trans., 1963) (describing the use of narratives to encapsulate pain); Hayden White, The Value of Narra-

struction of reality. In this view, trials serve as a genre of public discourse and storytelling; their social function stretches well beyond either the concern for discovering the truth of an event, the need to resolve disputes, or the imposition of retributive or deterrent justice. Trials not only adjudicate the conflict that arises from the breach of a social norm, but also provide a ritual[22] mechanism that can help to heal the community.

Part III identifies two ways in which trials can facilitate a community's healing process beyond the primary adjudication. First, trials allow the community to domesticate chaos by providing a consensus explanation of social reality to replace what would otherwise seem to be frightening and uncontrollable activity. Chaotic and painful events are thus brought within human jurisdiction and control through the construction of a narrative that reflects the moral values of the community. Second, trials allow this consensus narrative to emerge through a process that is inherently multivocal, as different points of view are articulated on a moral stage prior to decision. Just as religious institutions create cultural stories to provide meaning in times of crisis, so too trials, with their elaborate procedures and formal rules,

---

tivity in the Representation of Reality, in On Narrative 1, 2 (W.J.T. Mitchell ed., 1981) (finding that "[n]arrative is a metacode, a human universal on the basis of which transcultural messages about the nature of a shared reality can be transmitted"); Robert M. Cover, *Nomos* and Narrative, 97 Harv. L. Rev. 4, 4 (1983) (arguing that "[n]o set of legal institutions or prescriptions exists apart from the narratives that locate it and give it meaning"). Narratives are now seen as encompassing almost any form of social discourse and not just traditional narrative forms such as folk tales. See, e.g., Barthes, supra, at 79:

> The narratives of the world are numberless. Narrative is first and foremost a prodigious variety of genres . . . . [U]nder this almost infinite diversity of forms, narrative is present in every age, in every place, in every society; it begins with the very history of mankind and there nowhere is nor has been a people without narrative.

The focus on narratives allows critics to study how the vessel by which we impart social knowledge—conversational forms, gestures, news items—itself constitutes our understanding of reality.

22 The term "ritual" will be used throughout this Note to mean a formal, socially standardized, and repetitive action wrapped in a web of symbolism that serves to channel emotion, define experience, and guide understanding. This relatively broad definition follows the conceptual understanding employed by most contemporary anthropologists. Until a generation ago, the term ritual was more often used only to describe supernatural or religious rites. This earlier definition stemmed from Emile Durkheim's influential statement that rituals are "rules of conduct which prescribe how a man should comport himself in the presence of . . . sacred objects." Emile Durkheim, The Elementary Forms of Religious Life 56 (Joseph W. Swain trans., 1915). Durkheim believed that rituals were coercive moral forces dictating right behavior and, as such, identified rituals with organized religion. Because most contemporary cultural scholars focus on how all members in a culture use the narratives produced by various social institutions to construct meaning, Durkheim's more limited view has had less influence. Instead, ritual has become "an analytical category that helps us deal with the chaos of human experience and put it into a coherent framework." David I. Kertzer, Ritual, Politics and Power 8 (1988); see also id. at 1-14 (examining interplay of politics, symbolism, and ritual).

create a mythic arena for expressing the great tensions and moral battles of the community.

In conclusion, this Note explores how an understanding of the social function of trials may allow us to rethink their value in contemporary society. Although many of the postmodern political and critical strategies of the past thirty years have quite effectively exposed old historical "truths" as mere products of hierarchy,[23] the resulting cacophony of competing voices threatens to dissolve any unified cultural value system. By creating a coherent community vision from the competition of diverse cultural narratives, trials may help to reinstill new consensus values that do not simply return to the old oppressive ones. If so, then trials, particularly those that receive widespread publicity, may be seen as essential to maintaining the sense of a unified culture. Far from being a quaint historical curiosity, the animal trials may provide important insights for our own legal system.[24]

I
Trials of Inanimate Objects and Animals in Ancient Greece and Medieval Europe

The way in which we describe or conceptualize an experience ultimately creates the meaning we discover in that experience.[25] As anthropologist Edward Bruner notes, "[i]f we write or tell about the French Revolution, for example, we must decide where to begin and where to end, which is not easy, so that by our arbitrary construction of beginnings and endings we establish limits, frame the experience, and thereby construct it."[26] In extreme cases, we may even change our actions based on the way we plan to describe them later.[27] The

---

23 "The skeptical and disrespectful rhetorical, antifoundational, and antiessentialist moves of postmodernist writers are partly strategic devices. They are meant to disrupt and erode the power of the grand normalizing discourses . . . ." Jane Flax, The Play of Justice, in Disputed Subjects: Essays on Psychoanalysis, Politics and Philosophy 111, 114 (1993); see also Joyce Appleby et al., Telling the Truth About History 1 (1994):

> Once there was a single narrative of national history that most Americans accepted as part of their heritage. Now there is an increasing emphasis on the diversity of ethnic, racial, and gender experience and a deep skepticism about whether the narrative of America's achievements comprises anything more than a self-congratulatory story masking the power of elites.

24 Professor John Langbein likewise has used medieval European judicial practices to illuminate contemporary American criminal procedure in the context of plea bargaining. See John H. Langbein, Torture and Plea Bargaining, 46 U. Chi. L. Rev. 3, 3-22 (1978).

25 See Edward M. Bruner, Experience and its Expressions, in The Anthropology of Experience, supra note 21, at 3, 7-12.

26 Id. at 7.

27 See Renato Rosaldo, Ilongot Hunting as Story and Experience, in The Anthropology of Experience, supra note 21, at 97 (describing the Ilongot of the Philippines, who some-

narrative a culture creates to understand an event is an important part of the meaning assigned to that event.

When faced with an act that transgresses society's norms, but no culpable human actor, the community has various conceptual options for explaining the occurrence. For example, it may view the event as an act of God and construct a narrative about human sin and punishment; it may create order and rationality by trying to construct physical laws of cause and effect; or it may believe that the world is simply random and chaotic. The following discussion demonstrates, however, that various cultures, including our own, have at times created a narrative that redefines the accident as a crime and punishes an object or animal as the guilty party.[28]

Cultures have ascribed guilt even when there was no real belief that the object could manifest intent or malice. Grafting a notion of moral blame onto random misfortunes is a symbolic way of understanding and conceptualizing pain.[29] The process not only expiates the sadness and irrationality of the event itself, but also draws the community together by asserting a moral order.[30]

This Part begins with a brief survey of historical evidence about the trials of inanimate objects in ancient Greece, and then describes the trials of animals in Europe from the ninth to nineteenth centuries. These trials scrupulously adhered to all the legal norms established for human criminals. From the stay in prison to the appointment of counsel, from the weighing of evidence to the ultimate judgment, the trials demonstrate the extreme ways in which communities incorporated animals into their sense of procedural justice.

A. *Trials of Inanimate Objects*

> If some soulless thing should take away the soul from a human being, except in cases where it's a lightning bolt or some such missile coming from a god, but in the case of any of the other things that may kill someone through his falling upon it or its falling upon him—the next of kin should appoint the closest neighbor to be

times change their behavior in the forest during a hunt so as to return to the home camp with a good story to tell).

28 Psychologist Nicholas Humphrey in fact proposes this function as his explanation of the trials of inanimate objects and animals. See Humphrey, supra note 15, at xxvi.

29 See Lévi-Strauss, supra note 21, at 197-98 (arguing that cultural narratives give shape to pain and allow for effective response to crisis).

30 See text accompanying notes 198-206 infra. Later sections of this Note argue that trials can aid in the creation of a unifying cultural narrative because they create a ritual forum for adjudicating competing discourses and then assert a consensus description of social reality. Even when a trial serves no practical purpose, this social function may still be present.

> judge, and thus remove the impious impurity from himself and the whole family. The convicted party they should cast beyond the borders, just as was stated in the case of the class of living things.[31]

In ancient Athens, one of the buildings on the acropolis, the Prytaneion, was used as a ceremonial center of the city and as a site for special social functions. In addition, a law court located in the building was dedicated to hearing only three kinds of cases: those in which 1) the murderer was unknown or could not be found; 2) the death was caused by an inanimate object; or 3) an animal had killed a human being.[32]

Classics scholar Walter Woodburn Hyde has gathered together the few references to the Prytaneion that exist in the extant Greek literature. He concludes that though ceremonial in character, the trials observed ordinary procedural requirements.[33] The proceedings at the Prytaneion, like all other murder trials, took place in the open air so that the judges would not be contaminated by moral pollution emanating from the accused.[34] In addition, if the accused were found guilty, the court issued an order banishing the offending object or animal beyond the borders of the city.[35] As in other judicial proceedings, jurisdiction was sometimes an issue at the Prytaneion. In one instance, a boy was killed by a javelin while watching a man practice in the gymnasium.[36] The court was forced to determine whether the boy, the man, or the javelin was to blame. Only if it were deemed to be a trial of the javelin could the case be heard at the Prytaneion.[37]

---

31 The Laws of Plato 269 (Thomas L. Pangle trans., 1980). Other Greek writers that mention the practice are quoted in Finkelstein, supra note 12, at 58-59; see also Leo Strauss, The Argument and the Action of Plato's Laws 136 (1975) (arguing that the punishment for such murders "does not serve the purpose of improvement or deterrence but that of expiation of the family of the killed man"). Oddly, Strauss does not mention that the act might be seen as a crime against the community's order despite the fact that he focuses on punishment in general as a means of safeguarding the health of the regime elsewhere in his discussion of murder. See id. at 134.

32 Finkelstein, supra note 12, at 58; Hyde, supra note 1, at 696.

33 Hyde, supra note 1, at 696.

34 Id. at 696-97. See generally Jones, supra note 19, at 254-57 (discussing the conception of pollution in Ancient Greece and methods used to diminish its danger).

35 Jones, supra note 19, at 256-57. As recently as February 1994, the Governor of New Jersey banished from the state a dog that bit a person, ending the dog's three-year incarceration on death row. Robert Hanley, Taro Leaves Death Row, Jail, and New Jersey Soil, for Good, N.Y. Times, Feb. 11, 1994, at B4; see also Jeff Stryker, The Dog Walks, N.Y. Times, Feb. 3, 1994, at A21 (comparing the case to the medieval animal trials). Although the dog was never formally charged with a crime or put on trial, the banishment mirrors the Greek custom of exiling guilty objects beyond the boundaries of Athens.

36 Hyde, supra note 1, at 697-98.

37 Id. These jurisdictional questions were taken very seriously. According to Plutarch, the great statesman Pericles once spent a whole day arguing with the sophist Protagoras about just such an issue. See 1 Plutarch's Lives 260 (Arthur H. Clough ed., 1961).

Although there are no records of any Greek trials of animals,[38] Aristotle refers to the fact that such trials were held at the Prytaneion: "When [one] does not know who committed the offense, he institutes proceedings against 'the [unknown] who did the deed.' The [officials at the Prytaneion] conduct prosecution[s] of inanimate things and animals also."[39]

Evidence exists that many societies throughout the world have held formal proceedings and rituals against inanimate objects. Hyde presents examples of actions against trees, rocks, arrows, swords, axes, houses, boats, wooden idols, and even glaciers, for the damage done to mountain valleys.[40] Hyde argues that these trials were necessary to restore the "moral equilibrium" of the community after a killing.[41] For the Greeks, guilt and punishment had to be ascribed to some person or thing lest the Furies, avenging spirits of the dead person, create misfortunes throughout the land.[42] Indeed, whether the killing was intentional or premeditated seems to have been irrelevant, for the primary purpose was to remove the moral pollution in the air created by the murder.[43]

This search for a narrative of guilt in accidents caused by inanimate objects has survived in the British common law rule of the deo-

---

38 Hyde, supra note 1, at 700.

39 Aristotle, Constitution of Athens and Related Texts 135 (ch. 57) (Kurt Von Fritz & Ernst Kapp trans., 1950).

40 See Hyde, supra note 1, at 724-26. Hyde states: "The . . . notion, that lifeless things are . . . responsible agents like animals and men, can be evidenced from every stratum of human society from the lowest to the highest." Id. at 724. With only his anecdotal evidence to support his statement, however, we must regard it as an overly broad generalization.

Psychologist Nicholas Humphrey has found that the practice even extended to instances when the bodies of criminals already dead were placed on trial. See Jack Smith, Putting Animals, Bugs and Corpses on Trial Sounds Weird, But What's a Body to Do?, L.A. Times, July 21, 1987, § 5, at 1 (discussing Humphrey's discoveries). For example, on his accession in 896, Pope Stephen VI accused his predecessor, Formosus, of sacrilege. The dead Pope's body was exhumed, dressed in papal robes, and placed on a throne in St. Peter's. A deacon was assigned to defend him. On his conviction his body was stripped and thrown into the Tiber River. Id.

41 Hyde, supra note 1, at 698. This sense of equilibrium is expressed frequently in Greek dramas, where plagues, famine, storms, and other misfortunes in the natural world are usually attributable to an unexpiated wrong within the society. See, e.g., Sophocles, King Oedipus, in The Theban Plays 26-27 (E.F. Watling trans., 1947).

42 E.P. Evans, supra note 1, at 9. In the last play in Aeschylus's Oresteia trilogy, it is to placate the Furies of the slain Clytemnestra that Athena "remands" the case of Orestes to a human court at Athens, beginning the age of human rather than divine law. See Aeschylus, The Eumenities, in Oresteia 133, 151-52, ll. 470-89 (Richmond Lattimore trans., 1953); see also Burt Neuborne, Ghosts in the Attic: Idealized Pluralism, Community and Hate Speech, 27 Harv. C.R.-C.L. L. Rev. 371, 372 (1992) ("The Oresteia ushers in the luminous idea of law, not force, as the mediator between self and community.").

43 See Hyde, supra note 1, at 698.

dand[44] and its philosophical progeny,[45] which survive even in contemporary American jurisprudence. Under the law of the deodand (literally meaning "given to God") an inanimate object that caused the death of a human being was considered guilty, handed over to the King, and ultimately forfeited to God.[46]

What is most striking about the cases involving deodands is that the narrative ascribing guilt to inanimate objects persisted.[47] The judgments forcefully declare that actions involving deodands were not mere forfeitures meant to punish owners of objects for their carelessness: "The thing is here primarily considered as the offender, or rather the offense is attached primarily to the thing."[48]

In the United States, the imputed guilt of the deodand remains a part of the common law of forfeitures. Thus, the Supreme Court upheld the forfeiture of a vessel involved in piracy even though the innocence of the owner was clearly established.[49] The Court even referred to the vessel as "the offender."[50]

---

44 F. Pollock & F. Maitland, supra note 2, at 473.

45 See Jacob J. Finkelstein, The Goring Ox: Some Historical Perspectives on Deodands, Forfeitures, Wrongful Death and the Western Notion of Sovereignty, 46 Temp. L.Q. 169, 195 (1973) (arguing that some contemporary American legal doctrines are influenced by the concept of the deodand).

46 See Hyde, supra note 1, at 726 n.104 (the thing "'was forfeited to God, that is, to the King, God's Lieutenant on earth, to be distributed in works of charity for the appeasing of God's wrath'" (quoting Edward Coke, Third Part of the Institutes of the Laws of England 57 (1817))); see also F. Pollock & F. Maitland, supra note 2, at 473 (also quoting Coke to explain deodands).

The law of deodands was not abolished in Great Britain until the nineteenth century. See Finkelstein, supra note 45, at 170-80 (discussing the passage of legislation abolishing deodands). Because the law was a major boon to the King's coffers, the longevity of the practice may be explained, in part, on economic grounds. See Finkelstein, supra note 12, at 75-76. This Note, however, is not intended to address the causes for the practice; rather, it attempts to identify the cultural significance of the narrative of guilt that often accompanied the procedure.

47 Finkelstein rejects the notion that assigning guilt was the primary motivation, preferring to explain the phenomenon as a kind of tax collected by the King. See Finkelstein, supra note 45, at 182. Nevertheless, even he acknowledges that "a notion of [guilt] might have played *some* role in the development of the institution." Finkelstein, supra note 12, at 74. Hyde rejects economics as the primary motivation for the practice, arguing that the real object of the deodand was to atone for manslaughter in accordance with medieval concepts of justice. See Hyde, supra note 1, at 728.

48 The Palmyra, 25 U.S. (12 Wheat.) 1, 14 (1827).

49 See Harmony v. United States, 43 U.S. (2 How.) 210, 233 (1844) (a vessel involved in piracy could be "treated as the offender," without regard to the owner's conduct). Such treatment was seen "as the only adequate means of suppressing the offense or wrong." Id. at 238.

50 Id. at 233. For a more recent example, see Calero-Toledo v. Pearson Yacht Leasing, 416 U.S. 663, 680-84 (1973) (justifying a forfeiture in part by reference to the deodands); see also Christopher D. Stone, Should Trees Have Standing? — Toward Legal Rights for Natural Objects, 45 S. Cal. L. Rev. 450, 456 (1972) (invoking law of deodands to support

B. Trials of Animals: Historical Background

E.P. Evans, in *The Criminal Prosecution and Capital Punishment of Animals*,[51] has gathered the most complete listing of animal trials to date.[52] He cites over two-hundred cases, occurring between 824, when moles were tried in the valley of Aosta,[53] and 1906, the year of his writing, when a dog was sentenced to death in Switzerland.[54] The trials occurred in nearly every country in continental Europe (as well as isolated cases in Great Britain, Brazil, Canada, and the United States).[55] A majority of the cases involved pigs that ran freely through the streets of medieval towns and so were frequently involved in altercations, particularly with small children.[56] Pigs were not the only defendants, however, for there are records of proceedings against asses, beetles, bulls, caterpillars, cocks, cows, dogs, dolphins, eels, fieldmice, flies, goats, grasshoppers, horses, insects, leeches, locusts, moles, rats, serpents, sheep, snails, termites, turtledoves, weevils, wolves, worms, and unspecified vermin.[57]

The bulk of the recorded cases arose in France during the sixteenth and seventeenth centuries, but it cannot be assumed that the list of recorded trials is exhaustive or that the patterns indicate anything more than that there were better court records kept in some eras and locations than others.[58] Moreover, the routine nature of the extant trial records seems to indicate that there were many more trials held than the two hundred Evans was able to discover. For example, the earliest French record of an animal trial is from 1266, but historian Esther Cohen believes that the matter-of-fact manner in which the proceedings are described makes it likely that the custom had long been in existence by that time.[59]

---

notion of legal rights of trees in environmental litigation). References to the animal trials have also been used to bolster animal rights claims. See, e.g., Rosalind Hill, Both Small and Great Beasts (1955); Jeff Stryker, supra note 35, at A21 (linking medieval animal trials to contemporary movement aimed at recognizing animal rights).

[51] E.P. Evans, supra note 1.

[52] Because we must rely on fragments of court reports and written documentation preserved in archival records of small towns around Europe, it is impossible to determine just how many trials were held. Finkelstein, supra note 12, at 67-68. The evidence does indicate, however, that the practice was widespread and long-lived.

[53] Evans consistently identifies place names by province or town, presumably based on the name listed in the actual court records. Because some of these towns may no longer exist or may have changed names, it is often difficult even to identify the present-day country that corresponds to Evans's appellations.

[54] E.P. Evans, supra note 1, at 265-86.

[55] Id.

[56] Cohen, Folklore, supra note 1, at 11.

[57] E.P. Evans, supra note 1, at 265-86.

[58] See id. at 137; Finkelstein, supra note 12, at 67-68.

[59] See Cohen, Folklore, supra note 1, at 20.

In addition, we can find references to animal trials in the literature of the period. In his nineteenth-century novel *Notre-Dame de Paris*, Victor Hugo describes the trial of a goat belonging to the gypsy Esmeralda.[60] Likewise, Gratiano refers to animal trials in Shakespeare's *The Merchant of Venice*:

> Thy currish spirit
> Governed a wolf who, hanged for human slaughter,
> Even from the gallows did his fell soul fleet . . . .[61]

In 1688 French playwright Jean Racine devoted an entire play to a parody of animal trials. In *Les Plaideurs*,[62] a dog is tried for stealing and eating a capon. The prosecution and defense lawyers address the court in flowery and bombastic rhetoric complete with quotations from the Bible and Aristotle. The accused is condemned to the galleys. As his last plea for mercy, the defense counsel brings into court a litter of puppies, and appeals for clemency:

> Come, you desolate family,
> Come wretched children whom he would render orphans,
> Come to speak your innocent souls.[63]

As a father, the judge is moved by the plea and cannot let the young puppies grow up as orphans.[64] Not only does Racine's parody indicate that he knew the custom of trying animals would be familiar to his audience, but it is also one example of the criticism that seems to have accompanied the animal trials from the inception of the practice.[65]

C. *Trial Procedures: Human Justice Applied to Animals*

When a domesticated animal caused the death of a human being, the beast was treated in all ways possible as a human criminal.[66] Animals were confined in human prisons and subjected to the same treat-

---

60 Victor Hugo, Notre-Dame de Paris 330 (Alban Krailsheimer trans., Oxford University Press (1993) (1832) ("At that time nothing could be simpler than putting an animal on trial for sorcery.").

61 William Shakespeare, The Merchant of Venice act 4, sc. 1, ll. 133-35, at 114 (Kenneth Myrick ed., Signet Classic 1965). As editor Kenneth Myrick noted, "wolves, dogs, and other animals were sometimes hanged for killing or attacking people; hence the phrase 'hangdog look.'" Id. at 114 n.134.

62 Jean Racine, Les Plaideurs, in Théâtre Complet de Racine 195 (Jacques Morel & Alain Viala eds., 1980).

63 Id. at 241 ("*Venez, famille désolée, Venez, pauvres enfants qu'on veut rendre orphelins, Venez faire parler vos esprit enfantins.*") (translation by author).

64 Id. at 241-42.

65 See text accompanying notes 102-31 infra.

66 For a description of European criminal procedure with regard to human beings, see generally Adhemar Esmein, A History of Continental Criminal Procedure 55-174 (John Simpson trans., 1913) (discussing criminal procedure in feudal era through sixteenth cen-

ment as human prisoners. In the town of Pont de Larche, for example, records from the fifteenth century indicate that the sheriff at one time paid a particular prison keeper the sum of nineteen *sous* six *deniers tournois* "for having found the king's bread for the prisoners detained, by reason of crime, in the said prison."[67] The jailer listed the names of the persons in custody, and concluded with: "Item, one pig, conducted into the said prison and kept there from the 24th of June, 1408, inclusive, till the 17th of the following July," when it was hanged "for the crime of having murdered and killed a little child."[68] The jailer even charged the same daily rate for the pig's board as for boarding human prisoners.[69]

Once the trial began, it too was conducted just as if the defendant were a human being. The prosecution was represented by professional advocates, and defense lawyers were also hired.[70] Witnesses and evidence were heard prior to judgment. And though the animals were usually found guilty, such a verdict was certainly not assured. For example, in 1457, the sucklings of a sow that had murdered a five-year-old child were included in the indictment. They had been found at the scene of the crime stained with blood, but "in lack of any positive proof that they had assisted in mangling the deceased, they were restored to their owner, on condition that he should give bail for their appearance, should further evidence be forthcoming to prove their complicity in their mother's crime."[71] Likewise, in 1750 at Vanvres, France, a man and a donkey, discovered in an act of copulation, were both charged with bestiality, but while the man was sentenced to death, the donkey was subsequently acquitted on the ground that she was the victim of violence and had not participated in her master's crime of her own free will.[72] At the trial, the defense had presented a statement signed by many inhabitants of the community stating that they had known the donkey for four years, and that "she had always shown herself to be virtuous and well-behaved both at home and abroad and had never given occasion of scandal to anyone, and that therefore, 'they were willing to bear witness that she is in word and

tury); O.F. Robinson et al., An Introduction to European Legal History 44-70, 335-76 (1985) (discussing legal developments in western Europe during feudal period).

67 Quoted in E.P. Evans, supra note 1, at 292 ("[P]*our avoir trouvé (livré) le pain du roi aux prisonniers debtenus, en cas de crime, es dites prisons.*") (translation by author).

68 Id.

69 Id.

70 See, e.g., id. at 38 (noting name of defense lawyer for group of insects in a trial in 1545).

71 Id. at 153-54.

72 Id. at 150.

deed and in all her habits of life a most honest creature.' "[73] This document seems to have had a decisive influence upon the judgment of the court.[74]

As with human beings, animals also could receive a pardon prior to punishment. On September 5, 1379, as two herds of pigs were feeding together near the town of Saint-Marcel-le-Jeussey, three pigs mortally wounded the son of the gamekeeper.[75] The three sows were tried and condemned to death.[76] Both the herds were believed by their cries and aggressive action to have encouraged the crime and "approved" of the attack.[77] Therefore, all the pigs were arrested as accomplices and sentenced by the court to death as well.[78] But the prior,[79] Friar Humbert de Poutiers, not wanting to lose his entire herd, sent a petition to Philip the Bold, Duke of Burgundy, asking for clemency for all but the three instigating pigs.[80] The Duke pardoned the animals and released them.[81] Significantly, the language of the remission does not question the legitimacy of the practice of trying animals at all. The Duke proclaimed that the Mayor had arrested the pigs "in order to execute reason and justice in the proper manner."[82] Nevertheless, because only the three pigs were truly guilty, the Duke's order concluded that "while justice was done to the three or four said pigs, the rest should be released."[83]

If there were no such pardon, the offending animals were executed. Even the customs for punishment were the same for animals and human beings. The usual method was hanging, although there are also recorded instances of animals having been burnt at the stake or buried alive.[84] Sometimes the animal was actually dragged through the streets as was the practice with a human criminal.[85] If it managed to escape, an effigy was burned, again mirroring the treatment of human defendants.[86] Animals were even put in the rack prior to the

---

73 Id.

74 See id. at 150-51.

75 For an account of this trial, see id. at 144-45.

76 Id. at 144.

77 Id.

78 Id.

79 A "prior" is an officer in a monastic order, next in rank below an abbot. Webster's Third New International Dictionary 1804 (1986).

80 E.P. Evans, supra note 1, at 144-45. For the original French text of the petition, see id. at 294-95.

81 Id. at 145.

82 E. Cohen, Crossroads, supra note 1, at 112.

83 Id.

84 E.P. Evans, supra note 1, at 147.

85 E. Cohen, Crossroads, supra note 1, at 113.

86 Id.

execution in order to extort confessions.[87] "It is not to be supposed that, in such cases, the judge had the slightest expectation that any confession would be made; he wished merely to observe all forms prescribed by the law, and to set in motion the whole machinery of justice before pronouncing judgment."[88]

In contrast to the murder and bestiality cases, many other trials of animals involved large groups of pests that caused hardship throughout the community or created a public nuisance. In these instances, there was neither a single victim nor one animal to hold responsible, and so the entire rural commune prosecuted the case, and the proceedings—even more than the murder trials—demonstrated the direct community participation in judicial rituals.[89]

Unlike the murder prosecutions, the pests before the court in these cases had not committed any specific crime, and defense counsel often argued that the animals were merely obeying God's command to be fruitful and multiply throughout the land. The trials thus served as the scenes for "extremely thorough debates concerning the roles and interchanging relationships of God, man, animals and the vegetable world that fed all of God's creatures."[90] Because no individual animal could be punished, these trials often ended with anathemas[91] and excommunications placed on the guilty party by an ecclesiastical tribunal. Another common resolution was to order that the offending animals limit themselves to a certain portion of the crops while leaving alone the food intended for human consumption.[92]

All of these trials evince a scrupulous concern for ensuring procedural justice to the animals. For example, in a fourteenth-century Swiss case brought against a swarm of Spanish flies, the judge ordered the appointment of counsel to represent the flies "in consideration of

---

87 E.P. Evans, supra note 1, at 139.

88 Id.

89 It should be noted that these animal trials were conducted as public spectacles with the active participation of the community.

> [T]he public watching legal rituals was, despite its ostensible passivity, perhaps the most important element in the entire picture. Unless the spectacle spoke the language of the audience, used its symbols and cultural perceptions, the entire purpose of the exercise was lost. The judge in his gallery viewing a stage set at his orders and the spectator in the crowd looking, jostling and being jostled, shouting assent or dissent, were both participants in the legal drama.

E. Cohen, Crossroads, supra note 1, at 74.

90 Id. at 119.

91 "Anathemas" were formal ecclesiastical curses, usually accompanied by excommunication. Webster's Third New International Dictionary 78 (1986).

92 See E. Cohen, Crossroads, supra note 1, at 123 ("'I exorcize you . . . that you should immediately retreat from these fields . . . nor should you further reside there, but should move to such places where you cannot harm any of God's servants.'" (quoting from a typical judgment in such cases)).

their small size and the fact that they had not yet reached their majority."[93] Similarly, at the conclusion of a 1519 trial against some fieldmice in western Tyrol, an agreement was reached whereby the mice would be moved to a new tract of land.[94] The defense lawyer demanded that they should be provided with safe conduct, securing them against harm or annoyance from dog, cat, or other foe.[95] The judge agreed to the safe conduct, but only for the weakest and most vulnerable fieldmice. He mitigated the sentence of perpetual banishment by ordering that "a free safe-conduct and an additional respite of fourteen days be granted to all those which are with young and to such as are yet in their infancy; but on the expiration of this reprieve each and every [mouse] must be gone, irrespective of age or previous condition of pregnancy."[96]

II
Animal Trials as a Forum for Articulating Competing Narratives

From a twentieth-century perspective, it seems hard to imagine that people really believed a judicial proceeding would encourage rats to stop ravaging the crops or that by hanging a pig, other animals would be deterred from committing crimes.[97] Although we might be tempted to dismiss the proceedings as a product of superstitious or religious thinking,[98] the significance of these trials cannot truly be un-

[93] E.P. Evans, supra note 1, at 110-11.

[94] See id. at 111-13.

[95] Id. at 112.

[96] For the original German record of these proceedings, see id. at 259-60.

[97] Not surprisingly, the seemingly fanciful nature of the trials has inspired several fictionalized accounts, including a feature film, a novel, and a video work. See The Advocate (Miramax Films 1994); Julian Barnes, A History of the World in 10 1/2 Chapters 61-80 (1989); Rhyme 'em to Death (The Wooster Group 1994) (video work created by the New York theater company The Wooster Group).

[98] Of the very few scholarly accounts of the animal trials in the twentieth century, most have dismissed the phenomenon as part of a primitive and barbarous past. See, e.g., E.P. Evans, supra note 1, at 186 (explaining these trials as indicative of "[t]he childish disposition to punish irrational creatures and inanimate objects . . . common to the infancy of individuals and races"). Other writers viewed the trials in connection to the "animism of primitive man." According to this theory, human beings erroneously endowed inanimate objects with both a soul and human (or superhuman) mental facilities. See Finkelstein, supra note 12, at 48 (quoting Hans Kelsen, General Theory of Law and State 3-4 (Anders Wedberg trans., 1945)). Still another view is that the trials were an outgrowth of the superstitious belief that the Devil could inhabit offensive beasts. See Cohen, Folklore, supra note 1, at 16 n.31. For additional commentary dismissing the trials in similar ways see 3 James G. Frazer, Folk-lore in the Old Testament 415-45 (1918); Frank A. Beach, Beasts Before the Bar, 59 Natural History 356 (1950); Joseph P. McNamara, Animals at the Bar, 3 Notre Dame Law. 30 (1927-28); E.V. Walter, Nature on Trial: The Case of the Rooster That Laid an Egg, in Civilizations East and West 51 (E.V. Walter et al. eds., 1985).

derstood without analyzing how communities used the forms of legal procedure to resolve their problems.[99] Even if we agree that there was widespread belief in the Church's power to excommunicate those animals found guilty at trial, we must still try to understand why people insisted that the court proceeding itself was necessary.[100] After all, it would have been much simpler to have a holy person curse the offending animals without any prior judicial ritual.[101]

By looking at the philosophical opinions of the period, this Part will argue that the animal trials were actually the forum for a much broader debate among conflicting visions of the natural world and various conceptualizations of the interrelationship of God, human beings, and animals. These competing narratives all were present at the trials, either through the explicit appeals of the advocates for both sides or implicitly through the very application of human justice to the animal world. By examining lengthy excerpts from actual trial records, this Part will describe how the arguments put forth during the court proceedings allowed the trial to adjudicate among the available scholarly and popular narratives.

---

99 Surprisingly, even Walter Woodburn Hyde, in his 1916 article on the animal trials, ignored these jurisprudential questions even though he was writing in a legal journal. Instead, Hyde merely recycled the ideas of philosopher Edward Westermarck, stating that "[t]he savage, in his rage, obliterates all distinctions between man and beast, and treats the latter in all respects as the equal of the former." Hyde, supra note 1, at 722 (discussing Edward Westermarck, The Origin and Development of Moral Ideas (2d ed. 1924)).

In contrast, Jacob Finkelstein, a professor of ancient literature, proposed in 1981 that the trials did not indicate that people thought of the animals as rational beings. Instead, he argued that people were extremely conscious of the fact that animals existed on a lower level in the hierarchy of creation. By killing a human being, the animal infringed on that order and was subject to punishment. See Finkelstein, supra note 12, at 73 ("The visible evidence of the breach of this order had to be removed—and removed in solemn public procedure—in order that the cosmologic equilibrium would be widely recognized as having been restored."); see also text accompanying notes 202-06 infra.

Esther Cohen's recent book, Crossroads of Justice, supra note 1, is distinctive because it explores the relationship between the community and the judicial ritual of the animal trials. Her analysis interweaves law and culture to create the most complex, nuanced picture of the proceedings to date. Because Cohen focuses only on the medieval period, however, she does not raise broader questions about the social function of trials. This Note poses some of these more general questions.

100 It is important to note that the animal trials, like all criminal procedures of the medieval era, were public. In the feudal period, for example, "[t]he hearing was usually held in the open air, at the gate of the castle or at the public meeting-place of the town." A. Esmein, supra note 66, at 56. Likewise, Hugo sets the trial of Esmeralda's goat in *Notre-Dame de Paris* before a large crowd at the Great Chamber of the Palais de Justice. V. Hugo, supra note 60, at 323-32; see also note 89 supra.

101 In fact, most of the so-called precedents cited in favor of the trials were instances of holy people cursing animal nuisances without any judicial procedures. See text accompanying notes 127-28 infra.

A. The Debate About Animal Trials

From the outset, substantial scholarly criticism accompanied the practice of trying animals. The earliest commentary on animal trials in Europe is found in the "customals" of the region of Beauvaisis by Philippe de Beaumanoir.[102] The "customals" were manuals designed to instruct judges and litigants on courtroom activities and strategies.[103] In 1283 Beaumanoir described the custom of animal trials in a section on "Misadventure":

> Some people with jurisdiction on their lands punish animals who have killed someone: for example if a sow or other animal kills a child, they hang it and draw it. But this should not be done, for dumb animals have no discrimination of good and evil, and for this reason the punishment is lost on them, for punishment should be executed to avenge the offense, and so that the offender will know and understand that he has a certain penalty for a certain crime; but dumb animals do not have this understanding, and for this reason a person who puts to death a dumb beast as a kind of punishment for an offense is doing something to no effect; but the lord should take charge of the animal as of his own, for it is his by right; and in any case if it is a bull or a pig or a sheep or an animal of whatever kind that has gone wild, it is better for him to kill it and take his profit from it, so that it will not do the same thing again . . . .[104]

Beaumanoir thus condemned the trials as meaningless and invalid, and he intimated that the only purpose served was the greed of the elites who profited from the custom. Social historian Esther Cohen has shown, however, that though his theoretical argument might have validity, Beaumanoir's cynical view of profit by the feudal lords was false. Because the incarceration, trial, and execution cost as much for an animal as for a human being, and because the profit of the animal's

---

[102] See generally Philippe de Beaumanoir, Coutumes de Beauvaisis (A.M. Salmon ed., 1970).

[103] Cf. A. Esmein, supra note 66, at 611 (finding Beaumanoir's work valuable for acquainting readers with the legal institutions of the period); O.F. Robinson, supra note 66, at 335 (describing Beaumanoir's *Coutumes* as one of the important unofficial compilations of territorial customs in areas of France).

[104] See P. de Beaumanoir, supra note 102, at § 1944 (translation by author):

> *Li aucun qui ont justices en leur terres si font justices de bestes quant eles metent aucun a mort: si comme se une truie tue un enfant, il la pendent et trainent, ou une autre beste. Mes c'est nient a fere, car bestes mues n'ont pas entendement qu'est biens ne qu'est maus, et pour ce est ce justice perdue, car justice doit estre fete pour la venjance du mesfet, et que cil qui a fet le mesfet sache et entende que pour tel mesfet il en porte tele peine; mes cis entendemens n'est pas entre les bestes mues, et pour ce se melle il de nient qui en maniere de justice met beste mue a mort pour mesfet; mes face ent li sires son pourfit comme de sa chose, car ele li est aquise de son droit; et toutes voies est il bon, se c'est tors ou pourceaus ou moutons ou beste enragie, quele qu'ele soit, qu'il face qu'ele muire en son pourfit fesant, pour ce qu'ele ne face une autre fois autel* . . . .

labor was lost to the lord as well as to the beast's owner, the trials and executions of animals were clearly a financial loss for all concerned.[105]

Beaumanoir's more jurisprudential argument, that animals could not summon the requisite intent to be charged with crimes, was a recapitulation of arguments made by other critics. Earlier in the thirteenth century, Thomas Aquinas, in his *Summa Theologiae*,[106] questioned whether it was even permissible to curse irrational creatures.[107] He argued that curses and blessings should only be pronounced on beings that could receive evil or good impressions from them, and so such spells could only be aimed at rational and sentient beings.[108] Because animals were devoid of understanding, they could not, in Aquinas's view, commit a wrong.[109] Although he acknowledged the existence of Biblical spells visited upon nonrational beings, Aquinas explained that these curses were actually aimed at the human beings who would be affected.[110] Thus, when God cursed the earth, the true targets were human beings who would be punished by its sterility.[111] Aquinas concluded that if animals are regarded as creatures coming from the hand of God and employed by Him as agents for the execution of His judgments, then cursing them constitutes blasphemy.[112] On the other hand, if animals are treated as lesser, nonrational creatures, then cursing them is "idle and futile and therefore wrong."[113]

Most ecclesiastical opinion agreed with Aquinas. If animals were ravaging the communities, it must be the Devil's work, and so the proper course of action was for the people to repent their sins rather than put the animals on trial.[114] Indeed, defense counsel at many of these trials argued that because the pests clearly were sent to punish sinful human beings, they should be regarded as agents of God, making it useless and indeed blasphemous to prosecute them. Instead, repentance would be the only effective means of combating the beasts, for only then might God remove the scourge.[115]

The evidence indicates, however, that this argument was rarely successful. Instead, the validity of animal prosecutions was upheld,

105 See E. Cohen, Crossroads, supra note 1, at 115.
106 St. Thomas Aquinas, Summa Theologiae (Blackfriars 1975).
107 Id. at 201 (2a-2æ, q. 76).
108 Id. at 207.
109 Id. at 205.
110 Id. at 207.
111 Id.
112 Id.
113 Id.
114 See E. Cohen, Crossroads, supra note 1, at 126.
115 See E.P. Evans, supra note 1, at 52-53.

and the trials were combined with various rites of religious purification. Thus, prior to any trial that would involve an exorcism, the entire commune formed processions of prayer and repentance. It was only if these religious means failed that the trial could begin. If the beasts were then found guilty, the community would again take part in the disposition of the case. In 1487, after a trial at Autun that ended in the conviction of a group of snails, the bishop instructed the rectors of all parishes in the diocese:

> We hereby order that you convoke your parishioners, one and all, of both sexes, and march in procession with holy water and the standard of the cross throughout and around the boundaries of your parishes, while sprinkling holy water within the said boundaries, chanting the litany, and exhorting your people to come with you devotedly, [carrying] burning candles, and humbly to exhort and beg of God, the glorious Virgin Mary and all of God's saints that they should deign to free them of this tribulation; and you should warn and adjure the said snails damaging the land and its fruits by virtue of our Lord Jesus Christ and his most glorious passion, and the blessed apostles Peter and Paul, that they should desist within three days' time from the destruction and devastation of the said fruits and transfer themselves to deserted places, where they shall not be able to damage creatures and the fruits of the earth, under threat of the divine majesty's anger and eternal curse. And you shall conduct such processions for three continuous days without interruption, exhorting your people to devotion insofar as possible, and thus cursing the snails, so that by God's mercy we may be freed of this scourge.[116]

These activities might seem to indicate that animals were punished because they were seen as the embodiment of Satan. However, the sentences against the animal pests usually stated only that the animals were harming human beings, not that they were agents of the Devil.[117] Even the precedents cited invariably were curses of earthly animal nuisances, with no mention of any supernatural element at work.[118]

In contrast to ecclesiastical scholars, secular jurists such as Bartolomée Chassenée and Gaspard Bailly did not treat the animals as agents of the Devil. They recommended excommunication not to cast out supernatural forces, but to protect human beings against harm.[119] For example, Chassenée acknowledged that it might seem

116 E. Cohen, Crossroads, supra note 1, at 131 (quoting Bartolomée Chassenée, Concilium (1531)).

117 See E. Cohen, Crossroads, supra note 1, at 130.

118 See id.

119 See Cohen, Folklore, supra note 1, at 30-31.

unlawful to curse animals, but added that one could curse them insofar as they harmed the human population.[120] He reasoned that because the failure to exorcise the beasts would cause famine and lead to the death of human beings, *not* to curse the pests would be tantamount to homicide and surely a far greater evil than the one that Aquinas articulated.[121]

Other leading jurists of the time, who took part in these trials on a regular basis, likewise saw nothing wrong with applying overarching rules of justice to animals. For example, one judge asked rhetorically "'whether a brute beast, if it commit[ted] a crime as pigs sometimes do in devouring children, ought to suffer death,' and answered the question unhesitatingly in the affirmative."[122] Similarly, another jurist wrote in 1573 that

> if beasts not only wound, but kill and eat any person, as experience has shown to happen frequently in cases of little children being eaten by pigs, they should pay the forfeit of their lives and be condemned to be hanged and strangled, in order to efface the memory of the enormity of the deed.[123]

Not all legal commentators were so certain, however. One Belgian jurist, for example, took a more equivocal view. He wrote in 1562 that "a beast is punishable, if it commits the crime through natural malice, and not through the instigation of others, but that the owner can redeem it by paying for the damage done."[124]

Chassenée, the leading jurisprudential proponent of the trials, wrote a treatise, first published in 1531, defending the practice.[125] He began his work with a discussion of the legality of an excommunication of locusts at Autun. He wrote:

> The principle question is whether one can by injunction cause such insects to withdraw from a place in which they are doing damage, or to abstain from doing damage there, under penalty of anathema and perpetual malediction. And although in times past there has never been any doubt on this point . . . I thought that the subject should be thoroughly examined anew . . . .[126]

---

120 See E. Cohen, Crossroads, supra note 1, at 126.

121 See id.

122 E.P. Evans, supra note 1, at 108 (quoting Guy Pape, Decisions of the Parliament of Grenoble, 254-55 (qu. 238) (2d ed. 1667)).

123 E.P. Evans, supra note 1, at 108-09 (quoting Jean Duret, Treatise on Pains and Penalties 250 (1573)).

124 E.P. Evans, supra note 1, at 109 (summarizing views of Jacodus Damhouder).

125 See id. at 21.

126 Id. at 22.

As a lawyer, Chassenée argued from precedent. Evans reports that Chassenée cited Biblical events as examples of anathemas against the nonhuman world:

> the cursing of the serpent in the Garden of Eden . . . ; David's malediction of the mountains of Gilboa, so that they had neither rain nor dew; God's curse upon the city of Jericho, making its strong walls fall before the blasts of trumpets; and . . . the withered fig-tree of Bethany [in the New Testament].[127]

Chassenée interpreted the words of Jesus, "Every tree that bringeth not forth good fruit is hewn down and cast into the fire," as a condemnation and punishment of the tree for its delinquencies, and added: "[i]f, therefore, it is permitted to destroy an irrational thing, because it does not produce fruit, much more is it permitted to curse it, since the greater penalty includes the less."[128]

Recognizing that his precedents were instances of curses, not of trials, Chassenée argued that animals could also be considered guilty of a legal crime. First, he defined a crime as the commission of deeds hurtful to other sentient beings knowing such actions to be wrong.[129] Then he observed that birds, beasts, and insects have certain clearly established laws of their communities, and that those members who do not conform are punished.[130] In addition, he noted that domestic animals often showed a knowledge of guilt when caught by their master while committing some offense.[131] Thus, to Chassenée, because the animal could tell right from wrong, justice required that any wrong be prosecuted.

These debates about animal trials indicate that there was no uniformity of opinion, no blind belief in the powers of religion and magic. The arguments demonstrate that skepticism about the efficacy of animal trials existed alongside the proceedings. During the trials themselves, the lawyers echoed these philosophical positions, and the proceedings therefore became a primary forum for debating the various descriptive narratives. Ultimately, the trials allowed the community to apply its notions of justice to the animal kingdom by constructing a narrative that could harmonize the needs of the society with the natural forces it could not control.

---

127 Id. at 25.

128 Id. (quoting B. Chassenée, supra note 116).

129 See E.P. Evans, supra note 1, at 34.

130 See id. at 34-35.

131 See id. at 35.

B. *Adjudicating Conflicting Narratives in the Trial of the Weevils*[132] *at Saint Julien*

The philosophical debates and competing explanations of animal behavior described in the previous Section surfaced again and again in the trials themselves. The proceedings became a forum for judging the validity of the conflicting narratives present in those debates. In order to examine how the trials echoed the larger public discussion, this Section will examine an action against weevils that had been destroying vineyards in the town of Saint Julien.[133] This trial, which seems typical of the conduct of most animal trials, provides a particularly clear example of how the proceedings adjudicated among differing social constructions of reality even as they addressed the stated issue of guilt or innocence.

The prosecution of the weevils was actually divided into two trials, spaced some thirty years apart. The original complaint was made by the wine growers of Saint Julien in 1545.[134] Attorneys were hired to defend the animals. After an initial presentation by both sides, the ecclesiastical court dismissed the case in a proclamation dated May 8, 1546, recommending public prayers as the requisite first step in the proceedings.[135] After first declaring the court's desire not to act rashly against God's creatures, the order then gave instructions prescribing a series of prayers. The required rituals included three consecutive days of high mass followed by a religious procession around the vineyards, to be joined by at least two persons of every household. A signed document in the court records attests that the prayers were given and that the weevils disappeared soon after.[136]

Even in this first stage of the trial we can see how the court shaped a narrative for understanding the destruction brought on by the weevils. Like Aquinas, the court viewed the animals as God's creatures; therefore the devastation was seen as a sign passed from God to human beings through the animals.

---

132 The term "weevil" refers to any of a variety of species of snout beetle. Webster's Third New International Dictionary 2592 (1986).

133 See E.P. Evans, supra note 1, at 37-49 (providing a detailed description of the proceedings); see also Hyde, supra note 1, at 705-06 (summarizing the trial).

134 E.P. Evans, supra note 1, at 38.

135 See id. at 38-39:

> Inasmuch as God, the supreme author of all that exists, hath ordained that the earth should bring forth fruits and herbs . . . not solely for the sustenance of rational human beings, but likewise for the preservation and support of insects, which fly about on the surface of the soil, therefore it would be unbecoming to proceed with rashness and precipitance against the animals now actually accused and indicted; on the contrary, it would be more fitting for us to have recourse to the mercy of heaven and to implore pardon for our sins.

136 Id. at 39.

The second stage of the trial began thirty years later when the weevils returned to the same vineyard. In the complaint, the petitioners stated that the animals had "resumed their depredations and are doing incalculable injury."[137] Because the original defense lawyers had died, the petition asked that new advocates be appointed to defend the weevils in excommunication proceedings.[138]

After a brief adjournment, the weevils' newly appointed counsel, Pierre Rembaud, answered the complaint with a plea to dismiss the case. Rembaud stated that the animals had done nothing to deserve excommunication.[139] Referring to the Book of Genesis, he argued that the lower animals were created before Man and that God blessed all the living creatures of the earth. The Creator would not have given this blessing unless He intended that the creatures would be able to sustain themselves. In fact, the Bible states that God ordered that "to every thing that creepeth upon the earth every green herb has been given for meat."[140] Therefore, Rembaud argued, the weevils had a prior right to the vineyards, conferred upon them at the time of creation. In addition, the defense counsel contended that because animals could only be subject to natural law and instinct, bringing them within human jurisdiction would be absurd and unreasonable.[141]

Rembaud thus introduced two alternative narratives on behalf of the animals. The first conceptualized the acts of the weevils as part of God's ultimate scheme for all creatures of the earth. The second declared that animals could not be understood or judged at all in human terms.

When the prosecuting attorney presented a document detailing the misery suffered by the villagers on account of the weevils, the defense requested, and was granted, a second adjournment to review the submission.[142] In the meantime, François Fay, the commune's advocate, offered his reply. Fay argued that although the animals were created before human beings, they nevertheless were made subservient to the needs of human beings who maintain dominion over the earth.[143] According to Fay, this view had been held "from time immemorial by our ancestors."[144] Fay's narrative asserted a hierarchy and

137 Id. at 41-42.
138 Id. at 42.
139 Id.
140 Genesis 1:30.
141 E.P. Evans, supra note 1, at 42-43.
142 Id. at 44.
143 Id.
144 Id. Many advocates in other trials cited the historical and Biblical precedents at far greater length. The seventeenth-century jurist Gaspard Bailly constructed a series of model speeches in order to demonstrate the proper procedure for trying animals. In his

order to the universe that insisted on human jurisdiction over animal behavior.

The defense answered only by stating that it had not yet received a copy of the document that had been presented, and so the case was adjourned again.[145] When the parties returned to court, Antoine Filliol, an attorney for the insects, responded to Fay by arguing that the subordination of the lower animals to Man did not confer a right to excommunicate them.[146] In addition, he returned to the argument that animals could only be subject to natural law, "a law originating in the eternal reason and resting upon a basis as immutable as that of the divine law of revelation, since they are derived from the same source, namely, the will and power of God."[147] Filliol's narrative, like Fay's, acknowledged a hierarchy and order to the universe, but positioned God as the only dominant adjudicator.

While this legal wrangling continued, the inhabitants of Saint Julien organized a public meeting in the town square.[148] At the meeting, the villagers decided to set aside land outside the vineyards for the weevils, so that the insects might live freely away from the town.[149] After selecting a piece of property, the townspeople drew up an elaborate contract with the weevils, giving the insects the right to an area known as La Grand Feisse (which, according to Evans, is specified in the document by its location, dimensions, and the character of its foliage and herbage).[150] The contract reserved for the villagers the right to pass through the tract of land "without prejudice to the pasture of the said animals," and to make use of the springs of water contained therein, which were also to be at the service of the weevils.[151] In addition, the town would retain the right to take refuge in the area during time of war and the right to extract minerals from the area as long as the insects were not harmed.[152]

By creating this contract, the townspeople implicitly asserted that the weevils possessed free will. According to this narrative, rational negotiation could lead to the peaceful coexistence of human beings

versions, the prosecutor quotes Moses, Paul, Pliny, Ovid, Silius Italicus, and Pico di Mirandola on the glory and excellence of mankind and then declares that it would be absurd to deprive such a being, made in God's image, of the fruits of the earth for the sake of "'vile and paltry vermin.'" See id. at 103 (quoting Gaspard Bailly, De l'excellence des monitoires (1668)).

145 E.P. Evans, supra note 1, at 45.

146 Id.

147 Id.

148 Id. at 46.

149 Id.

150 Id. at 46-47.

151 Id. at 46.

152 Id.

and animals in the natural world. If the animals could be convinced to leave through the use of incentives that would appeal to human beings, the human order would be restored, and the necessary crops would be preserved.

When the commune's counsel appeared in court and demanded the enforcement of the contract, the defense requested another delay to review the agreement, and the proceedings were adjourned for an additional six weeks.[153] After the court reconvened, Filliol, the weevils' attorney, objected that the land offered to his clients was sterile and not able to fulfill the weevils' subsistence needs. When the commune insisted that the land was suitable for insects, the court adjourned again after hiring experts to examine the area and to submit a written report of its fitness as a home for the weevils.[154] The court's actions evince a concern that the contract be fair, thereby implicitly adopting a narrative that abstract principles of justice could be applied to animals, and that the weevils would likewise acknowledge the supremacy of such principles.

Ironically, the final decision of the case cannot be ascertained because apparently some insects destroyed the last page of the trial records. Evans fancifully suggests that the weevils might have been dissatisfied with the decision and eaten the paper in retaliation.[155]

Regardless of the outcome, the trial of the weevils at Saint Julien articulated many of the different popular and scholarly narratives for explaining and understanding the depletion of crops in a rural community. By raising these narratives in a court of law, the parties were implicitly submitting their philosophical proposals to the judges for a decision on their merits. The next Part will argue that the ability to adjudicate among such conflicting conceptions of reality is a key element of the social function of trials.

III
The Role of Trials in Adjudicating Popular Narratives and Enacting Social Knowledge

Most modern writers who have discussed the social function of trials have emphasized the courts' chief role as dispute resolvers.[156]

153 Id. at 47-48.

154 Id. at 48-49.

155 See id. at 49.

156 See, e.g., Theodore Becker, Comparative Judicial Politics: The Political Functionings of Courts 26 (1970) (viewing disputes as the justification and focus of court work and therefore stressing impartiality as "the heart of the judicial process"); Disputes and the Law (M. Cain & K. Kulcsar eds., 1983) (arguing that the more complex the society, the greater the need for disputes to have institutionalized resolutions according to legal pat-

Indeed, Roger Cotterell, in his review of the literature, finds that the focus on dispute resolution is almost universal.[157] As a result, though courts have sometimes acknowledged the importance of the jury trial to the community,[158] there has been little serious discussion of the ability of trials to adjudicate among different narratives for describing the broader social or political reality.

Once we focus our attention on the role of trials as cultural storytellers, we can view the judicial process as a constitutive element in a broader social drama. Anthropologist Victor Turner has defined social dramas as performative rituals that allow a community to respond to the breach of a social norm.[159] He has outlined a four-part sequence to explain the process:

> 1) *breach* of regular norm-governed social relations; 2) *crisis*, during which there is a tendency for the breach to widen . . . . ; 3) *redressive action* ranging from personal advice and informal mediation or arbitration to formal juridical and legal machinery . . . to the performance of public ritual . . . . ; [and] 4) . . . either . . . the *reintegration* of the disturbed social group or the social recognition and legitimation of *irreparable schism* between the contesting parties.[160]

While the judicial process clearly fulfills the third, redressive stage of the social drama by resolving the actual conflict, the ritualized

---

terns); J.A.G. Griffith, The Politics of the Judiciary 220 (1981) (discussing British courts as fora for resolving political controversies); Richard L. Abel, A Comparative Theory of Dispute Institutions in Society, 8 L. & Soc'y Rev. 217 (1973) (describing courts as primarily dispute-resolving institutions); M. Cain & K. Kulcsar, Thinking Disputes: An Essay on the Origins of the Dispute Industry, 16 L. & Soc'y Rev. 375 (1982) (arguing that any general theory about disputes should begin with the presumption that courts should settle disputes); Simon Roberts, The Study of Dispute: Anthropological Perspectives, in Disputes and Settlements 1 (John Bossy ed., 1983) (discussing different ways dispute institutions intervene in a quarrel to reach a resolution).

157 See Roger Cotterell, The Sociology of Law 220 (1984).

158 See, e.g., Richmond Newspapers, Inc. v. Nevada, 448 U.S. 555, 571 (1980) (noting that public trials are necessary for "community catharsis"). The Court, however, describes the social value only in terms of the community's need to watch the process of justice in order to strengthen confidence in the judicial system, id. at 572, or to provide a check on governmental power, id. at 592 (Brennan, J., concurring). This Note focuses instead on the process by which trials construct social knowledge by telling a particular descriptive narrative. While that narrative might well be a general story about justice and the balance of power, it might be far more complicated and specific, as in a decision between scientific or religious narratives in the Scopes monkey trial. See text accompanying notes 194-96 infra. See generally Popular Trials: Rhetoric, Mass Media, and the Law (Robert Hariman ed., 1990) [hereinafter Popular Trials] (arguing that popular trials should be recognized as a genre of public discourse).

159 See Victor Turner, Dramas, Fields, and Metaphors 37-42 (1974) (describing the four phases of social dramas); see also Victor Turner, The Anthropology of Performance, in Process, Performance, and Pilgrimage 60, 63 (L.P. Vidyarthi ed., 1979) (defining social dramas as "units of aharmonic or disharmonic social process, arising in conflict situations").

160 Turner, The Anthropology of Performance, supra note 159, at 63-64.

theatrical nature of the trial may fulfill the fourth stage as well. Ideally, the trial creates a way for the community to adjudicate among conflicting narratives before constructing a new, unifying story that allows for the reintegration and healing of the society. Both of these functions are equally important.

In order to fulfill its reintegration function, the trial must not only resolve the dispute but also "perform the laws" so that the community may have a framework for extracting meaning from the crisis event.[161] Trials, therefore, may function not only as adjudicatory procedures but also as cultural performances[162] that allow a group to scrutinize, portray, understand, and then heal itself. The adjudication, stage three of the social drama, cannot be the end of the cycle. In order for society to reconstitute itself after the breach of a norm, there must be some ritual that allows the community to create its own understanding of the crisis experience.

Once trials are seen as playing a vital role in the reintegration stage of the social drama, then we must examine how trials discharge that role. Drawing on the proceedings against animals and inanimate objects, this Part argues that trials can fulfill at least two important ritual functions that help a community heal itself after a breach of society's norms. First, trials may provide a narrative presenting a consensus[163] explanation of social reality to replace what would otherwise

161 See Robert Hariman, Performing the Laws: Popular Trials and Social Knowledge, in Popular Trials, supra note 158, at 17.

162 See Charles Fried, An Anatomy of Values: Problems of Personal and Social Choice 131-32 (1970) (arguing that trials, like artistic performances, have inherent value apart from material consequences of litigation); Thurman Arnold, The Criminal Trial as a Symbol of Public Morality, in Yale Kamisar et al., Criminal Justice in Our Time 137, 143 (A.E. Dick Howard ed., 1965) ("Trials are like the miracle or morality plays of ancient times. They dramatically present the conflicting moral values of a community in a way that could not be done by logical formalization."). Certainly, the practice of having judges sit higher than the other participants while wearing wigs or robes, as well as the maintenance of painstaking decorum within the courtroom demonstrate that courts depend at least in part upon the power of theater to fulfill their social role. See Milner S. Ball, The Play's the Thing: An Unscientific Reflection on Courts Under the Rubric of Theater, 28 Stan. L. Rev. 81, 83 (1975) (suggesting that "the design and appointment of the courtroom, enhanced by costuming and ceremony, do create a dramatic aura which has even been described in hyperbolic religious terms").

Sociologist Harold Garfinkel has also recognized the theatrical nature of trials, arguing that trials function as "status degradation rituals" that draw on the moral indignation of the community. See Harold Garfinkel, Conditions of Successful Degradation Ceremonies, 61 Am. J. Soc. 420, 421 (1956) ("Moral indignation serves to effect the ritual destruction of the person denounced. Unlike shame, which does not bind persons together, moral indignation may reinforce group solidarity. . . . [A] degradation ceremony must be counted as a secular form of communion.").

163 Of course, it is difficult to determine whether any explanation embodied in a legal decision truly creates a consensus in the public at large. Nevertheless, the resolution of a trial does endorse a particular understanding of reality that may, in time, become the gen-

seem to be irrational and uncontrollable activity. Second, trials produce this consensus narrative only after adjudicating among many different discourses that are constantly competing for recognition as the best descriptive understanding of the event.

This Part begins with a discussion of how cultural narratives structure our understanding of reality by creating explanatory stories to encapsulate pain and chaos. Then this Part argues that because there are always many possible narratives available to describe any given event, trials inevitably present not only a battle among the parties, but also a clash of descriptive stories. Ideally, the court's final judgment both resolves the dispute and produces a consensus narrative that helps to reunify the community. Finally, this Part returns to the animal trials to show that these proceedings ultimately constructed a narrative asserting the universality of human justice and thus incorporated inexplicable acts of irrational actors within the moral scheme of the society.

A. *Understanding Reality Through Narratives*

Philosopher Wilhelm Dilthey wrote that "reality only exists for us in the facts of consciousness given by inner experience."[164] But for every experience there is a wide range of possible meanings that can be assigned. And for every possible meaning there are a range of stories one can tell. Anthropologists have long realized that the kind of narrative form with which we describe an event shapes the meaning we draw from it.[165]

---

erally accepted community standard. In contrast, the first trial of the police officers accused of beating Rodney King is an example of a legal proceeding that was rejected by the community. See Seth Mydans, Los Angeles Policemen Acquitted in Taped Beating, N.Y. Times, Apr. 30, 1992, at A1 (reporting riots in aftermath of verdict); see also Tony Mauro, L.A. Residents Strongly Condemn Verdict, Reuters News Serv., May 6, 1992 (reporting telephone poll indicating that almost 70% of Los Angeles residents believed that predominantly white jury was biased in favor of police officer defendants); Darci McConnell, King Verdict: Around the Country, Shock, Dismay, and Bewilderment, Gannett News Serv., Apr. 29, 1992.

The shaping of a consensus narrative can be closely linked to Ronald Dworkin's notion of interpretation. In Dworkin's view, the best legal decision will identify the principles that both best "fit" or cohere with the settled law and practices of a legal system and also provide the best moral justification for them, thus showing the law "in its best light." See Ronald Dworkin, Law's Empire 90 (1986). If Dworkin is right, then good legal decisions will tend to be in harmony with the community's deepest understanding of reality even if it might not meet with immediate acclaim. And, the decision will, in turn, shape that understanding and slowly alter the consensus reality. See id. at 228-38 (likening the legal decisionmaking process to a chain novel in which the person creating the legal rule must construct the best understanding of past writing while creating a new reality for future decisionmakers to interpret).

164 Wilhelm Dilthey: Selected Writings 161 (H.P. Rickman ed. & trans., 1976).

165 See generally, e.g., The Anthropology of Experience, supra note 21.

These cultural narratives provide a "shield against terror."[166] By providing a framework to interpret what we experience and a language for describing reality, they are the vehicle by which we construct the meaning we take from the world around us. "Every telling is an arbitrary imposition of meaning on the flow of memory . . . every telling is interpretive."[167] It is only in the performance of an expression that we reexperience, relive, recreate, retell, reconstruct, and refashion our culture.[168]

At times of stress, social institutions provide narratives for encapsulating pain and chaos and constructing meaning.[169] Claude Lévi-Strauss, in a pioneering study of childbirth in several Central and South American cultures, found that a mythological narrative told by a shaman invoking supernatural monsters and magical beings was used in some communities as a cure for the pain accompanying particularly difficult deliveries.[170] According to Lévi-Strauss, the fact that the shaman's story did not correspond to any objective reality was irrelevant.[171] Because the tale drew on popular conceptions of reality, the narrative provided a mechanism for the woman to integrate the seemingly incoherent, arbitrary, and alien pains within a meaningful understanding of the universe.[172]

> The shaman provides the sick woman with a *language*, by means of which unexpressed, and otherwise inexpressible, psychic states can be immediately expressed. And it is the transition to this verbal expression—at the same time making it possible to undergo in an ordered and intelligible form a real experience that would otherwise be chaotic and inexpressible—which induces the release of the physiological process, that is, the reorganization, in a favorable direction, of the process to which the sick woman is subjected.[173]

According to this theory, narratives do not merely describe reality but actually constitute reality itself. Lévi-Strauss stresses that the shamanic tale not only allowed women to endure the pain of childbirth but actually cured them.[174] Anthropologist Mary Douglas adds that the language used to describe experience frames and limits the

---

166 D. Kertzer, supra note 22, at 4.

167 Bruner, supra note 25, at 9.

168 Cf. Roland Barthes, S/Z 4-6 (Richard Miller trans., 1974) (arguing that no given text contains a fixed meaning and that through the act of interpretation the reader actually "writes" the text, constructing its meaning in a perpetual present).

169 See, e.g., Lévi-Strauss, supra note 21, at 180-201.

170 Id.

171 Id. at 197.

172 Id.

173 Id. at 198.

174 Id. at 197.

experience itself merely by the choice of words. "The speech has created something, a [new] thought which might not have been the same [as the experience]."[175]

Narratives are relied upon particularly in times of change, disorientation, and trauma. Thus, a disaster will stimulate "pronouncements, prayers, eulogies, addresses, white papers, and other formal offerings that later dissolve back into the welter of conversation characterizing the ordinary business of living together."[176] The society's primary social institutions must function as storytellers during such moments of crisis. Religious narratives and their accompanying rituals are the clearest example of an institution constructing meaning out of death and other irrational and frightening events.[177] The rites link us to our past and future by enacting enduring and underlying patterns.[178] And the narratives provide explanations, or affirmations of faith, or parables, all of which create a framework for understanding the crisis event and healing psychological wounds. For example, Michel Foucault has noted that in the medieval world,

> the ravages of disease and hunger, the periodic massacres of the epidemics, the formidable child mortality rate, the precariousness of the bio-economic balances—all this made death familiar and gave rise to rituals intended to integrate it, to make it acceptable and to give meaning to its permanent aggression.[179]

Courts, too, are social institutions that tell cultural stories about chaotic events. By definition, crimes are breaches of societal norms. In order to heal the social rift, trials provide a formal, rational discourse that allows the community to reassert order and control.

The judicial proceedings against animals and inanimate objects help us see how trials can act to create rationalizing narratives. When statues fall from the sky or pigs kill a small child or rats destroy the crops, there is a sense of disorder and irrationality which the society's primary institutions must address. Random acts of violence caused by insensate agents bring a deep feeling of lawlessness: not so much the fear of laws being broken, but the far worse fear that the world might not be a lawful place at all. The courts allow the community to establish cognitive control, to impose order on a world of random violence, and to create a narrative that makes sense of inexplicable events by

175 Mary Douglas, Purity and Danger: An Analysis of the Concepts of Pollution and Taboo 64 (1966).

176 Hariman, supra note 161, at 19.

177 See Lévi-Strauss, supra note 21, at 186-204.

178 See D. Kertzer, supra note 22, at 9-10.

179 Michel Foucault, Discipline and Punish 55 (Alan Sheridan trans., 1979).

redefining them as crimes and placing them within the rational discourse of the trial.[180]

Sociologist Pat Carlen, after studying English magistrate courts, concluded that the defendant in a criminal trial is a secondary consideration. The trial involves the defendant only as far as his presence and participation are necessary to the court's "plausible performance of justice."[181] Carlen suggested that the construction of social reality by the trial is often a performance for public consumption as much as one designed to persuade the defendant.[182] Therefore, insofar as the trial is concerned with developing shared understandings of events and actions, it may be the community that is most affected by the judicial ritual.

B. *The Trial as a Clash of Narratives*

If narratives actually constitute how a society comes to understand reality, then such social knowledge is inevitably dynamic, as new narratives are "always being created, tested, changed, and abandoned or amplified."[183] Anthropologist Renato Rosaldo points out that the study of narratives resists any frameworks that claim a monopoly on truth.[184] Rather, because there are always a variety of cultural narratives for describing any one phenomenon, the focus must be on the interaction of various conflicting conceptualizations.[185] This view stresses the constantly shifting nature of social knowledge.

For a trial to create any kind of reunification, the proceedings must, therefore, first account for the "diffuse and unprivileged character of narrative" itself.[186] With so many possible versions of reality available, any single story is bound to seem incomplete. The trial,

---

180 Psychologist Nicholas Humphrey has noted a parallel between the animal trials and the recent proceedings against Nazi war criminal Klaus Barbie:

> Aren't we seeing again nothing other than people's need to make sense of nonsensical events—to close the book on a chapter of otherwise inexplicable calamity. Barbie's living presence in the courtroom has almost no significance. If he were dead, his corpse would serve the role of the defendant just as well. At the end of it, Barbie's body will metaphorically be thrown into the Rhone. We shall all feel curiously relieved . . . .

Quoted in Smith, supra note 40, at 1. For more on the cultural narratives produced in war crimes proceedings, see generally Hannah Arendt, Eichmann in Jerusalem: A Report on the Banality of Evil (1963).

181 Pat Carlen, Magistrates' Justice 64 (1976).

182 See id. at 64-65; cf. Neil P. Cohen, Trial in Absentia Re-Examined, 40 Tenn. L. Rev. 155 (1973) (arguing that trials in absentia should be permitted in many instances).

183 Hariman, supra note 161, at 28.

184 R. Rosaldo, supra note 21, at 93.

185 See V. Crapanzano, supra note 21, at 21-22 (contrasting Western and Moroccan narratives for conceptualizing reality).

186 Cover, supra note 21, at 4 n.3.

however, has the distinct advantage of being a social practice particularly well-suited to comparing and adjudicating among competing discourses.[187]

When trials ultimately construct a narrative by rendering a decision, they do so after first enacting a performance in which the society "creates, tests, changes, and judges" the various competing discourses that could make up our social knowledge.[188] James Boyd White argues that law's strength is in providing a forum for testing the persuasive power of competing narratives.[189]

> The multiplicity of readings that the law permits is not its weakness, but its strength, for it is this that makes room for different voices, and gives a purchase by which culture may be modified in response to the demands of circumstance. It is a method at once for the recognition of others, for the acknowledgment of ignorance, and for cultural change.[190]

In White's vision, law must provide a set of institutions that emphasize the fact that "we are a discoursing community, committed to talking with each other about our differences of perception, feeling, and value, our differences of language and experience."[191]

Trials, because they are inherently multivocal,[192] can fulfill this vision. We have seen that participants in the animal trials provided many different popular and scholarly interpretations. The proceedings allowed the community to weigh the competing discourses before attempting to develop any consensus narrative. As one commentator has pointed out, "justice . . . involves reconciling diversities into a restored and new multiple unity. Justice requires a unity of differences; mutuality and incorporation rather than annihilation of opposites and distinctions."[193]

Perhaps the most prominent twentieth-century example of how trials adjudicate competing discourses is the 1925 prosecution of John Scopes for teaching the theory of evolution in a public school.[194] Although the strict legal issue in the case was not in dispute, the trial

---

187 See Popular Trials, supra note 158, at 29.

188 See id.

189 See James B. White, Law as Language: Reading Law and Reading Literature, 60 Tex. L. Rev. 415, 444 (1982).

190 Id.

191 James B. White, Justice as Translation 80 (1990).

192 James B. White, Is Cultural Criticism Possible?, 84 Michigan L. Rev. 1370, 1373 (1986). For further discussion of this perspective, see generally James B. White, Heracles' Bow (1985).

193 Flax, supra note 23, at 123-24.

194 For an extended discussion of this case, see Lawrence M. Bernabo & Celeste M. Condit, Two Stories of the Scopes Trial, in Popular Trials, supra note 158, at 55.

became an "argument about the orders of knowledge,"[195] in which the language of religious fundamentalism battled with the new narrative of science. Though the State won the case, Clarence Darrow won the battle of the discourses, and the consensus narrative that emerged from the Scopes trial was that science would be America's preeminent language for describing the world in the twentieth century.[196]

If law not only issues edicts but also constructs narratives, then law is suggestive, and not merely coercive. Just because a trial reaches a verdict or a judge renders a decision does not mean that a new consensus is magically created. Rather, the law *attempts*, through a unifying narrative, to reintegrate the community or mend rifts in the social fabric. If a decision strays too far from most people's intuitive understanding of reality, the resulting narrative will fail, just as the rigid formalism of nineteenth-century contract doctrine failed ultimately to reflect the society's sense of fairness and so gave way to more tort-like remedies.[197] Nevertheless, as White makes clear, trials do at least possess the *potential* to construct unifying narratives for conceptualizing reality.

C. The Underlying Narrative of the Animal Trials

The criminal prosecution of animals can thus be viewed as an attempt by a community to apply its own moral scheme to the natural world and create an integrated universal sense of justice. From this perspective Bartolomée Chassenée's many procedural excuses in defense of the rats of Autun are not merely clever delaying tactics, but pleas for "the order and forms of justice."[198] Chassenée's arguments reflected the conviction that justice was universal, applicable to animals as well as human beings.[199]

But the trials of animals and inanimate objects reflected more than just a global *notion* of justice. By trying an animal or an object using the exact formula applied to a human murderer, the court was incorporating the human and nonhuman within one *community* of justice. The trials applied formal court rules to what otherwise would

[195] Richard M. Weaver, Dialectic and Rhetoric at Dayton, Tennessee, in The Ethics of Rhetoric 30, 30 (1953) (noting that the defense, "pleading the cause of science, was forced into the role of rhetorician; whereas the prosecution, pleading the cause of the state, clung stubbornly to a dialectical position").

[196] See Popular Trials, supra note 158, at 25.

[197] See generally, e.g., Grant Gilmore, The Death of Contract (1974).

[198] See E. Cohen, Crossroads, supra note 1, at 121 (citing A. de Thou, supra note 6, at 414-16).

[199] In fact, Cohen points out that dead bodies were also incorporated into the medieval scheme of justice. See E. Cohen, Crossroads, supra note 1, at 134-45; see also note 40 supra.

seem to be random and inexplicable acts of irrational actors. In this way the community integrated the offender within its moral scheme,[200] thereby healing the breach of the social order.

Turner's discussion of social dramas thus seems readily applicable to these trials. According to his analysis, stage four of the social drama must lead to a "reintegration" of the disturbed social group.[201] Only a ritualized trial that maintained strict fidelity to procedural norms could fulfill this role. Simply slaughtering the offending animal might have been simpler and less costly, but such an act by itself would not have healed the psychic trauma of the community.

It is not surprising, therefore, that even in the Bible, crimes committed by animals required their own particular rituals of punishment. In the Book of Exodus, for example, the Bible commands that an ox who gores a human being should be stoned to death.[202] The punishment of stoning is a distinctive sentence in the Bible, reserved for only a few types of crimes.

> In those cases, there was no designated "executioner," for the community assembled would act as the common executioner of the sentence. Offenses which entail this mode of execution must therefore be of a character that, either in theory or in fact, "offend" the corporate community or are believed to compromise its most cherished values to the degree that the commission of the offense places the community itself in jeopardy.[203]

The Biblical treatment of the ox indicates that at least as far back as the Book of Exodus, crimes of animals against human beings were viewed as a threat to the moral and religious fibers of the community. Punishment was an insufficient remedy for such a transgression; some ritual was needed to reassert a sense of order.

Thus in 1576, when a hangman, without legal authority, killed a pig at the gallows after it had bitten the ear off a child, the community viewed the act as being to "the disgrace and detriment of the city."[204] The hangman was forced to flee the town. An execution without a formal judicial ritual was intolerable. Chassenée, too, railed against human beings who chastised their domestic animals and put particularly dangerous animals to death. To him, such an act was arbitrary and autocratic, and if systematically applied to human beings would be denounced as intolerable tyranny. Chassenée insisted that under no circumstances was a penalty to be imposed except by judicial deci-

200 See id. at 83-84.
201 See text accompanying notes 159-61 supra.
202 Exodus 21:12-14.
203 Finkelstein, supra note 12, at 26-27.
204 E.P. Evans, supra note 1, at 146-47.

sion and, in support of the principle, referred to the Apostle Paul, who had declared in the Bible that sin is not imputed where there is no law.[205]

The safeguarding of justice itself, therefore, was part of the trial's function.[206] These trials of animals and inanimate objects weighed the various possible explanations of reality and then constructed a narrative to assert cognitive control over chaos.

Conclusion

Law functions as one of the most pervasive discourses in our society.[207] As Alexis de Tocqueville wrote, "[t]here is hardly a political question in the United States that does not sooner or later turn into a judicial one."[208] If so, then we must recognize the role of the popular trial in creating the narratives through which we understand reality. Once we take seriously the idea that trials exist as much for the community as for the disputants, then there are many ramifications and avenues for further study. Both academicians and legal practitioners need to chart the range of narrative strategies available for inducing belief within a popular trial.[209] There might also be increased study of the social knowledge enacted in various historical trials, beyond the four corners of the legal issues. Finally, there might be further discussion about the efficacy and justice of trials conducted for primarily symbolic reasons.

Likewise, there are important jurisprudential policy questions: Do the rules of procedure and rules of evidence ensure the most effective expression of the various narratives at play in the trial?[210] Does the heightened role of lawyers inhibit the expression of nonprofessional or subversive narratives?[211] Will the increased dissemination of

---

205 Id. at 34-35; see also Romans 6:14.

206 See E. Cohen, Crossroads, supra note 1, at 110 (arguing that the animal trials, like all rituals involving animals, were meant to affirm the "perception of justice in the universe").

207 See Popular Trials, supra note 158, at 7.

208 Alexis de Tocqueville, Democracy in America 270 (J.P. Mayer ed., George Lawrence trans., 1969).

209 For some examples of such scholarship, see generally Popular Trials, supra note 158; see also Anthony G. Amsterdam & Randy Hertz, An Analysis of Closing Arguments to a Jury, 37 N.Y.L. Sch. L. Rev. 55 (1992) (examining attorneys' use of storytelling techniques).

210 See, e.g., Edgar Lustgarten, The Murder and the Trial 3-4 (1958) (arguing that failure of the discourse of trials to understand and account for human psychology led to an unjust conviction); William Finnegan, Doubt, The New Yorker, Jan. 31, 1994, at 48 (expressing frustration that jurors may make incorrect judgments because rules of evidence preclude them from hearing the full story).

211 See, e.g., John M. Langbein, The Criminal Trial Before the Lawyers, 45 U. Chi. L. Rev. 263, 282-83 (1978) (discussing forms of discourse prevalent in the "old Bailey" from

trials on television and the simultaneous increase in public awareness and debate enhance the ability of court proceedings to adjudicate national social issues?[212] Do we need trials in product liability and mass tort cases so that victims of sudden sadness can construct narratives to encapsulate pain?[213] How much do we lose by the fact that the vast majority of cases, civil and criminal, never go to trial at all?[214] Will trials be better able to construct consensus narratives if the juries that author those narratives represent diverse cultural backgrounds?[215]

Perhaps most important is the social question: in a multicultural, post-deconstructionist society, where there are more available narra-

---

the 1670s to the mid-1730s that were later silenced as a result of the increased role of lawyers at trial).

212 If Carlen is right that trials are primarily cultural performances for public consumption, see text accompanying notes 181-82 supra, then it would seem that the more members of the community with access to the event, the better. Throughout American history, popular trials such as the prosecutions of Scopes, Sacco and Vanzetti, the Rosenbergs, the Chicago Seven, and the police officers accused of beating Rodney King have been catalysts for major public debates and provided an effective way of defining and crystallizing important social issues that might not have been achieved elsewhere in the political arena. See Popular Trials, supra note 158, at 1.

213 See Lévi-Strauss, supra note 21, at 197-98; see also text accompanying notes 169-74 supra.

214 Martin Shapiro writes that as of 1981, 90% of American criminal cases were settled by a guilty plea or its equivalent. See Martin Shapiro, Courts: A Comparative and Political Analysis 53 (1981). Thus, "[t]he basic business of American criminal courts is not the triadic resolution of disputes." Id. Likewise, on the civil side, most lawsuits end in some form of settlement. See Ellen J. Pollock & Edward Felsenthal, Federal Civil Cases Rarely Reach a Trial, Wall St. J., June 27, 1990, at B2 ("Almost 95% of all private civil cases filed in Federal courts never reach trial, ending instead in settlements or other pretrial dispositions, according to a study by Rand Corp. Moreover, the percentage of cases tried appears to be declining rapidly.").

215 If so, then the recognition that trials construct narratives provides an additional justification for the Supreme Court's recent limitations on the use of peremptory challenges based on race and gender. See, e.g., Batson v. Kentucky, 476 U.S. 79 (1986) (forbidding prosecutors from challenging jurors solely on the basis of race); J.E.B. v. Alabama, 114 S. Ct. 1419 (1994) (extending *Batson* to peremptory challenges based on gender). The discussion of this issue has generally been framed in terms of the rights either of defendants or of the excluded jurors themselves. See, e.g., *J.E.B.*, 114 S. Ct. at 1421 ("potential jurors, as well as litigants, have an equal protection right to jury selection procedures that are free from state-sponsored group stereotypes"); *Batson*, 476 U.S. at 85 ("defendant does have the right to be tried by a jury whose members are selected pursuant to non-discriminatory patterns"). The role of trials in constructing cultural narratives suggests, however, that a more diverse jury panel is also necessary so that the broader community can accept the resulting narrative as the product of true consensus. For example, if the jury in the first trial of the police officers accused of beating Rodney King had been more racially-integrated, it is likely that an identical verdict would have met with much less community resistance. See Mauro, supra note 163; see also note 163 supra.

tives[216] than ever before and no fixed notion of truth[217] or morality,[218] can popular trials play a role in adjudicating discourses and creating consensus visions of reality that will help unify an increasingly diffuse culture?[219]

Asking such questions allows us to reexamine the value of trials as instruments of social understanding, rather than merely as a means of discovering the truth of an event or resolving disputes efficiently. Often, trials may not be the best mechanisms for reaching the objective truth,[220] and they are almost never the quickest way to resolve a dispute. The logic of trials may well rest elsewhere, and this Note has attempted to indicate how further reflection on that social logic can lead to a more inclusive understanding of the cultural narratives law constructs.

An appreciation of the community's participation in trials will also allow us to make more nuanced normative judgments about whether the narrative function of trials should be encouraged or resisted. The need to assert community values to understand irrational events may seem relatively benign in the context of animal trials, but the same social functions were also fulfilled by the witch trials,[221]

---

216 See R. Rosaldo, supra note 21, at xviii ("[C]lassic modes of analysis, which in their pure type rely exclusively on a detached observer using a neutral language to study a unified world of brute facts, no longer hold a monopoly on truth. Instead, they now share disciplinary authority with other analytical perspectives.").

217 The recognition of multiple voices has eroded the authority of many of the historical verities underlying western culture. See, e.g., James D. Hunter, Culture Wars 215 (1991) ("[The multiculturalist argument is that] [k]nowledge, in a word, is inherently biased. The solution today, therefore, is to be more inclusive of different experiences, perspectives, and truths, particularly those that have been ignored or silenced in the past . . . ."); see also note 23 supra. For a particularly blistering critique of postmodernist scholarship, see generally Gertrude Himmelfarb, On Looking Into the Abyss: Untimely Thoughts on Culture and Society (1994).

218 See Amitai Etzioni, The Spirit of Community 24 (1993) ("The problem is that the waning of traditional values was not followed by a solid affirmation of new values; often nothing filled the empty spaces that were left when we razed existing institutions.").

219 See J. Appleby et al., supra note 23, at 8 ("We . . . see skepticism and relativism as two-edged swords. They can be wielded against the powers that be to promote greater inclusiveness, but they can also wound those committed to pursuing any kind of knowledge whatsoever.).")

220 See Louis S. Raveson, Advocacy and Contempt: Constitutional Limitations on the Judicial Contempt Power, 65 Wash. L. Rev. 477, 531 (1990) (arguing that "our entire system of trial procedure and ethics compels any thinking person to wonder whether there isn't something else going on in judicial proceedings besides a serious search for the truth").

221 For a discussion of the parallels between the trials of animals and witches, see Cohen, Folklore, supra note 1, at 31-32; see also E. Cohen, Crossroads, supra note 1, at 85-99 (characterizing trials of women and Jews as rituals of exclusion). For an overview of European witch trials, see Brian P. Levack, The Witch-Hunt in Early Modern Europe (1987); see also M. Douglas, supra note 175, at 102-03 (describing the tendency to view witches as

which most of us would be quick to condemn. We may not always want a judicial system that places the immediate needs of the community ahead of other fundamental values. A consensus narrative may not always be a just one. Yet, we cannot accurately conceptualize this normative question until we understand the symbolic and narrative impact of trials.

The proceedings discussed in this Note allow us to see that trials can fulfill social roles distinct from what we usually view as the traditional function of courts. By examining the trials of animals and inanimate objects—behavior that seems so foreign to us—we may well gain insight into our own psychological and social need for rituals of justice.

marginalized figures possessing powers and characteristics different from and dangerous to mainstream society).

[12]

Constructing a Common Language: The Function of Nuremberg in the Problematization of Postapartheid Justice

Stéphane Leman-Langlois

This paper analyzes the function acquired by the historical Nuremberg trial in the constitution of a specific discourse about transitional South Africa and about what should be done about the brutality of the past. This function is best described as mythical: *emptied of content,* Nuremberg *was a blank slate on which all parties to the debate could write their conflicting representations of the situation and their respective proposed solutions. The organization of fundamentally incompatible representations of reality around unifying myths such as Nuremberg was key to the production of visible consensus on the proper evaluation of the sociopolitical situation and the basic characteristics of the right course of action, and thus the appearance of effective state administration in a reconciled nation.*

The Nuremberg trials are probably the most important legal precedent in the continuing international effort to address the reality of state-sponsored crime. While equally solid legal arguments can and have been made both in support of and against the principles, goals, or procedures the trials represented, by all accounts they certainly marked the beginning of a new conceptualization of the rule of law and its area of application. What is considerably less clear, however, is the actual, practical manner in which

---

Stéphane Leman-Langlois is a criminologist with interests in state-sponsored crime, terrorism, and international law and currently teaches at the University of Montreal's School of Criminology. The research for this paper was conducted with the help of a grant from the *Fonds pour la formation de chercheurs et l'aide à la recherche* (FCAR) of the Government of Québec.

the experience of Nuremberg becomes useful in dealing with specific contemporary sociopolitical problems involving state-sponsored crime.

These problems arise most often in the context of political transitions where repressive regimes have been replaced by more democratic forms of dispensation. This is a context in many ways different from that of the end of the Second World War, mainly because it usually involves a negotiated transfer of power and a much less obvious "legitimacy gap" between the parties' past actions (Hayner 1994; Huyse 1995; Jung and Shapiro 1995; Nel 1995). However the very need for a transition is commonly understood to imply that the previous organization of the state was corrupt and that those responsible should account for their actions (Cohen 1994; Ensalaco 1994). I think it is safe to assume that the idea of former state officials having to face the nation immediately *sounds* like Nuremberg and that because of this conceptual proximity in such contexts the memory of Nuremberg is bound to be invoked. How it will be invoked, and for what purpose, is central to my investigation: Will it be a positive example of one possible remedy, or a warning of a pitfall to be avoided? It is the use of this comparative potential I wish to explore here. Postapartheid South Africa is a prime example of the function of popular knowledge about Nuremberg in the creation of an institution intended to deal with injustices linked to political conflict and a past antidemocratic government. And as it turns out, during the elaboration of that institution, Nuremberg contributed much more than its baggage of legal knowledge or its nature as a quasi precedent in international law.

The South African National Assembly voted in 1995 to create a special institution, the Truth and Reconciliation Commission (TRC), to deal with the remnants of apartheid-era violence. From the title and with some knowledge about other "truth commissions" around the world, the reader can already guess that this institution was in no way to follow the Nuremberg precedent. In fact it was designed and sold to the public as a better solution than conventional retributive criminal justice and precisely as avoiding "a" Nuremberg. In this case, *Nuremberg* acquired the function of reflective myth; it was adopted by opposing groups as an image (i.e., rather than an *example*) of various possible perils embodied by conventional justice. It was one of the basic materials needed in the construction of a unified discourse in favor of a "truth commission." Its power laid not in the legal knowledge it provided but in the way it afforded speakers the ability to rhetorically unify diverse and in fact contradictory positions about the past, postapartheid society, and the nature of justice, and thus overcome potential administrative paralysis.

For my present purposes it suffices to mention that the resulting TRC was meant to investigate the past, to collect the testimony of victims, and to take the confessions of wrongdoers in exchange for granting them individual immunity from prosecution and indemnity from civil action (together referred to as "amnesty"; see South African TRC 1998). It was also to make recommendations to the government as to how to best compensate victims of brutality. This followed a clause in the historic 1993 interim constitution enjoining that amnesty be granted in relation to "conflicts of the past," which is widely thought to have been a *sine qua non* condition to the transfer of power from the old government.

While the subsequent TRC-supporting discourse generally contained multiple and forceful references to this constitutional guideline as legally forcing a departure from conventional retributive justice, the constitution is in fact rather vague as to who should be eligible for what kind of "amnesty" and under which conditions. Further, this was not South Africa's first dabbling in criminal immunity laws: there had already been two separate Indemnity Acts in 1990 and 1992, and the 1957 Defense Act contained provisions for secret immunity for state agents (art. 103*ter*). On the whole it is far from clear what exactly the constitution added to this context or made mandatory for the new government, and therefore this argument was severely crippled from the start. However, there existed an alternative way to organize a public legitimating discourse for the TRC, and without the complexity of constitutional analysis: this is where Nuremberg was of great help.

I. MYTH AS BUILDING BLOCK OF REALITY

"Legitimating discourse" refers to the institution's internal logic or rationale, where its goals, methods, and principles are articulated in harmony with prevalent norms and may be presented as "right" (or lesser evils) or "good" (or the best possible) to the concerned social groups. Following Foucault (1972, 1984), this does not entail the eradication of any competing discourse and in fact if it did our vocabulary would not contain a word like *controversy*. Rather, it is sufficient that a context arise where a critical mass of individuals (1) perceive a discrepancy between current practice and the dominant conceptualization of the social context and (2) adopt a sufficiently unified way to define the "problem" and the new solution it appears to demand. The original moment of "problematization" may be instigated by social, economic, or political processes (Foucault 1984, 388) that make the conventional at odds with new empirical realities—and the abandonment of apartheid is certainly an extreme example of such change. What is then needed is an adjustment of the intellectual tools we use to understand reality, in order to repair the broken consistency between the world and our actions.

In Foucault's writing, as well as in subsequent literature using the concept, problematization generally appears to start slowly, with a few or even one individual thinker articulating a new model of representation, which is eventually taken up by mainstream society (for example, the modern idea of "government," see Foucault 1991). But what we see in a context of political transition is a much shorter "acclimation" time, where a major revision of practice must defuse resistance and reduce controversy long enough to constitute a solution to what is usually an enormous and pressing problem; this with the added administrative necessity to make government appear effective and to show that the nation's politics are moving forward and making the transition successfully. This sense of urgency is probably why cogent popular images are recycled in public speech and transformed into mythical examples of resounding, history-defining successes—or in this case impending doom. The function of such myths is not to remind us of historical truths but rather to illustrate concerns, fears, desires and various normative positions that are of immediate importance to parties and individuals concerned (see Carbonell and Rives 1990; Edelman 1964; Flood 1996; Thompson 1985). One further benefit is that, as an intricate part of what Edelman (1964) calls "hortatory language" (a form of speech meant to reassure, to convince, and to co-opt), the widespread use of a few central myths is a powerful way to show that basic, functional agreement exists and that all differences between the groups in power are limited to the details of the projects, the methodology, and so forth and never undermine the fundamentals (1964, 138). This is very important in the wider discourse of the "new South Africa" where the "conflicts of the past" are over and where democracy is relatively functional.

Nuremberg, then, was a very important element in the building of a narrative of a just and well-governed postapartheid South Africa. However, it was obviously not the only such element, and I am not arguing that it was the sole, or even the primary determinant in the construction of a new social reality around the TRC. Through it, we can glimpse at the mechanism by which the building takes place: a new problematization, a new language, a new reality are being built, and this building is in no way limited to the institution itself as a "solution." Rather, it includes the context, the people, the problems, and the solutions. But let us be careful when speaking of the creation of new realities. First, "new" should be taken as a rearrangement of previously existing elements, with rarely anything created *ex nihilo*; and as we will see below, the novelty of the TRC project, by far, lies in the way it makes use of old ideas and not in the way it reinvents justice. Second, the way powerful individuals or groups shape reality is, as Foucault might say (see Dreyfus and Rabinow 1983, 187), at the same time voluntary and unexpected: all intellectual activity involved, while clearly willfully directed at fulfilling personal or organizational goals, leads to a created reality mostly through the unforeseen consequences of the infinitely re-interpretable discourses being reproduced and the inevitably flawed practices being designed. Discourse has no masters and it has a way of escaping the narrow confines of immediate necessity and creating new ways of understanding reality independent of its originators' intentions.

II. THE NUREMBERG VARIATIONS: CREATING CONSENSUAL SPACE

Without getting into the details, I have already noted that the rationale represented by the TRC is fundamentally at odds with conventional thinking about the "crimes" it is meant to address. But that is part of the question: What if those were not really crimes, or not primarily crimes after all? The "one-best-way," Taylorist language used by government officials to describe projects such as the TRC (see Crozier and Friedberg 1977) holds reality as objectively given and good administration as the proper arrangement of things for maximum benefits (including morality) to the nation. But far from a simple descriptive and prescriptive tool, this language has intense creative power, and its use results in significant readjustments of the working definitions of *all* elements of reality, after much discussion and negotiation.[1] And it so happens that the best way to deal with apartheid brutality implied creating and observing restrictions on the use of the word *crime*.

This section explores three broad themes in the building of postapartheid justice, as illustrated, organized, and conveyed by *Nuremberg*. These themes were focal points around which a few basic facets of the new institution could be constructed in relation to the objects they were to address. They helped neutralize dissent and harmonize contradictory political strategies. Naturally there is much politicking in the events I describe. But what is particularly interesting is how this continuous effort to match a solution with a problem, beyond serving more obvious utilitarian goals (the ordinary power grabs, enhanced party political marketing, as well as the more straightforward desire to avoid punishment), was also more or less unwittingly creating and consolidating a number of fundamental truths about South Africa and postapartheid justice. I have explored the consequences of some of these truths elsewhere (Leman-Langlois 2000). In many ways this is the story of short-term strategy creating long-term reality. Throughout, Nuremberg was used in public speech as a reflection and amplification of those characteristics of criminal justice that were thought to be detrimental to truth, reconciliation, peace, and the proper administration of the country.

1. Negotiation here does not refer to the simple, immediately obvious meeting of parties around discussion tables, but to the determination of what may or may not be held and spoken as competent discourse about the world. It is important to bear in mind that the negotiated production of social reality and the haggling associated with setting the technicalities of projects are two very different things.

The direct effect was to strip all these signifiers of many possible alternate meanings and to redirect them in very specific ways.

A. Moral Condemnation and Administrative Objectivity

At the time of the debate over the truth commission the government of South Africa was organized as a Government of National Unity (GNU). This meant that while the African National Congress (ANC) had gained a landslide majority in the elections, the rival regional Inkatha Freedom Party (IFP) and the newly freshened up National Party (NP, the one party/government/state of the apartheid past) were constitutionally entitled to participate in government. This power-sharing arrangement was in fact only the logical extension of the dynamic of negotiation and compromise that was at the heart of the transition from the start. One of the most important effects of this dynamic is that any agreement reached either around a negotiation table or between "sides" in Parliament is only as legitimate as the least legitimate of the parties involved (Nel 1995). Therefore all participants have a stake in insuring a minimum respectability for the others, in affirming the other sides' right to be there as an integral part of the appropriateness of dealing with them, and making the GNU a morally sound and effective mode of administration.

Bearing this in mind, our first theme in the perils of retributive justice is one that may be described as "apprehended mutual accusation." It makes wielding the criminal justice system a very delicate exercise, because it spontaneously awakens questions about "fairness," objectivity, political neutrality, and at what stage of the process they are most important, and ultimately who should be allowed to participate in government and the creation of law. For instance, some critics have used actual *numbers* of TRC investigations to reject the process as unfair (Giliomee 1997, and personal communication), the implication being that it would be better to make sure that a roughly equal number of government officials and resistance fighters were investigated in order to avoid an "unbalanced" account of the past. This view of fairness is widely held, and it is the direct consequence of a narrative of the past with two clearly defined "sides" equally involved in, equally affected by, and equally responsible for all past violence. This narrative reinforces the all-important moral equality of the major parties that justifies their participation in a democratic South Africa—"raw" historical fact being secondary.

In general, within the ANC, Nuremberg was used to demonstrate that unrestrained, simplistic, "wild" accusations would be avoided, while still reiterating superior moral standing and actually enhancing it with the appearance of calm, effective government:

> I think the ANC has throughout . . . gone out of its way to make sure that this commission will be a balanced and an even-handed one. Unlike other liberation or resistance movements that overthrew evil systems of government, we have not—and we have said that we will not—instituted war crimes trials. We have not had Nuremberg trials. (W. Hofmeyr [ANC], South Africa 1995a, 1397)

Hofmeyr was involved in the original drafting of the TRC bill, and he later sat on the joint Assembly-Senate Committee on Justice, which reviewed and redrafted the bill before the final vote. His reference to war crimes trials, of which Nuremberg is taken as the epitome, shows how the powerful image can serve to demonstrate that moral superiority existed then—and still does now, in a different context of political "fairness." It also underlines that rationality, calm and pragmatism will prevail in the treatment of wrongdoers. Hofmeyr continues:

> [A] few weeks ago, we ourselves honoured some of those pilots ["who bombed innocent German women and children in cities"] in and outside this House. They were not vilified and they were not named for maiming and killing innocent people, because it is recognised that they did it in furtherance of a struggle that was for the greater good. Nonetheless, in an effort to make sure that this commission will work, and to make sure that it keeps our country together, the ANC has said that everybody should be investigated. (W. Hofmeyr [ANC], South Africa 1995a, 1397–98)

The idea of the "greater good" is another very important part of this discourse, from all sides of the debate. It allows the ANC to investigate itself out of fairness but with no implication or admission of wrongdoing. It also defines truth finding as establishing moral superiority or "the proper moral order," as the euphemism goes, because it will shed light on the nature of the greater good and the struggle for it. Minister Omar put it this way: "in the same way that we honour and salute those who fought against Nazism, we honour and salute our freedom fighters" (A. Omar [ANC], South Africa 1995b, 2210). Since "a Nuremberg" will be avoided, it is demonstrated that despite the moral superiority (there *could* be a string of trials), political-administrative realism has prevailed and a pragmatic and "neutral" half-point situated before the full use of criminal justice has been found. This half-point is at the same time between the terms of the invented dichotomy of arbitrary punishment and ignorance of the past, as well as between the ANC and the NP, confusing agendas with groups, methods with goals, and legal fairness with moral neutrality.

"Saluting the freedom fighters" of course has other uses. By the time the TRC was being debated in the National Assembly, the ANC had released the findings of two internal investigations (ANC 1992, 1993), which had uncovered some abuse in its internment camps abroad and had already led to limited disciplinary action against some of its members. The first commission had not named any of the perpetrators, but the media had soon recognized those responsible and published their names (e.g., *Weekly Mail*, 23 Oct. 1992, 4-5). The second commission (the Motsuenyane Commission; ANC 1993) had simply gone ahead and named the perpetrators. Naturally, there might have been some qualms about the prosecution of ANC members from its military wing, uMkhonto weSiswe (or MK, "Spear of the Nation"), and presumably some of its higher-level members who were involved in its command structure. The commanders had accepted responsibility even before the first commission's report, further underlining the difficulties and dangers of going full steam ahead with the justice system. In short, the ANC was forced to admit, comparatively early on, that even just causes could lead to abuses of power and crimes; but it was also evident that the greater good gives the abuses a different, more acceptable meaning. The Nuremberg-Nazi comparison had the power to rehabilitate their intentions, if not their actions.

As for the NP ex-government, we must note right away that the entire idea of Nuremberg had a very special cultural resonance. It so happens that the NP itself was born out of the ashes of Nazi-supporting political formations after the Second World War. Further, there is an unavoidable connection between apartheid and various policies of the Third Reich, especially with the "Nuremberg Laws" of 1935 (not to be confused with the trials later held there, precisely for the symbolic effect), that immediately springs to mind. The fairness discourse is therefore deeply modified by this glaring metaphorical proximity: even if all violators of human rights, including those from the ANC, had been processed through a Nuremberg-like system, only the nationalists would be likely to bear the "Nazi" stigma.

In order to undermine the comparison, pro-apartheid, pro-government fighters also embraced the idea of the "just war" or "greater good" wholeheartedly, avoiding the Nazi analogy by recasting themselves as anti-Communist fighters (although ironically this was also a favorite Nazi claim during the war, one used to recruit *WaffenSS* in occupied countries and send them to the Eastern front, e.g., the Charlemagne division from France). Not that the idea of a "Communist threat" was entirely an after-the-fact justification; it was and still is at the forefront of South African politics. One can find full-page NP newspaper ads for the 1994 elections showing the Communist Party wolf in ANC sheep clothing. Still, this allowed the complete eradication of race segregation or any past or present racist conceptualization of society from the NP's history. In their first submission to the TRC, the NP and former president F. W. de Klerk as its only spokesperson made no mention of race segregation, presenting a "sanitized" version of apartheid. In his second submission to the TRC, de Klerk had this to say: "those who fought on the government side were motivated by a number of factors . . . all these factors are, in my opinion, legitimate and had nothing to do with racism or apartheid per se" (National Party 1997, 25).

And if the eradication of racism is not complete, at least the contrast is less clear: which was worse, apartheid or *Stalinism*? Who is more condemnable? "Yes, apartheid has been referred to as a crime against humanity, but communism is not a lesser crime against humanity" (B. Geldenhuis [NP], South Africa 1994, 3911).

> He [Minister of Justice A. Omar] spent his time on another emotional and uncontrolled attack on so-called apartheid. In many debates a one-sided perception is being created, namely that the NP were the bad guys and the ANC the good guys in this story. In my contribution, I shall put the record straight on the real issue, namely the fight against communism. (F. van Heerden [NP], South Africa 1995a, 1414)

Extremists in the party never fail to make de Klerk and others sound reasonable; theirs is, though, the same discourse (also to be noted is how the "loss of emotional control" reproach is never far in the administrative discourse about postapartheid justice). Again, this discourse was possible because it was compatible with a wider effort at leveling the moral playing field, which was crucial to the legitimacy of the government as a whole. Consequently, the future commission could appear to avoid political entanglements by disregarding the matter of guilt and retribution. In the words of a member of the already mentioned committee that reviewed the TRC bill:

> [I]f there is any suggestion that a distinction is to be made between persons who fought for or against the previous government, it can only be perceived as being discriminatory. Then it is not reconciliation on equal terms, but a witch-hunt or inquisition. (M. Schutte [NP], South Africa 1995a, 1371)

In the words of a senator, also from the justice committee:

> [I]f these actions [ANC terrorism] are morally right, what sort of questionable basis does such morality in fact have? If we are looking to the Truth Commission as a springboard to Nuremberg trials, we are in for a dreadful era of recrimination and to quote, "a fate too ghastly to contemplate." I wish to say to the Hon Minister that forgiveness is not and cannot be only one-sided. This is not the spirit of this legislation. There are many innocent victims of the ANC as well. (R J Radue [NP], South Africa 1995b, 2251)

In perfect logic, the political problem also applies to *forgiveness*. If calls to forgive should be "one-sided" it would imply that only one side was wrong, which amounts to accusation.

Nuremberg helped articulate a specific relationship between crimes of the past and political affiliation, in which retribution (or even forgiveness) was a dangerous power wielded against political opponents: if there are trials, they will be Nuremberg-like group trials and some will find themselves declared guilty by association. By contrast, the reality offered was that all parties were equally blamable, and all criminals equally justified. And as a result, the future commission would demand to hear adequate "political motivations" in order to pardon human rights violations.

So Nuremberg was not rejected as a solution because it did not fit the context of postconflict South Africa; it was used *to* reject a specific conception of this context as a typical criminal justice one and instead re-emphasize the negotiation-compromise ethos, national unity, the legitimacy of rejecting convention, and granting amnesty for politically motivated acts. All the while it also permitted a strong, unequivocal moral discourse to be held against *apartheid* (even though the NP have been timid in their rejection of it so far), something which has already officially and legally disappeared, and for "exposing the truth" about it, telling the story of the wrongs endured by its victims. This condemnation of apartheid was important because it constituted the administrative rationale necessary for doing anything about it in the first place.

In this context of symbols and metaphors any actual knowledge of legal precedent the speaker may or may not have is not relevant to the discourse he or she is reproducing: what is useful here is the image, the emotional charge linked to the well-known historical event and how it can transform the way one thinks of reality, the way postapartheid justice can appear as a problem beyond the capacity of conventional practical solutions to deal with it. In short, Nuremberg is used to disqualify a particular perception of reality.

B. Legitimacy through the Dispersal of Blame

I subsume under this theme all rationales that conclude that Nuremberg, because of its accusatory and condemnatory nature, would not work because *everyone* must bear some blame for the "conflicts of the past." While speaking of victory over the old government implied that only ex-officials were corrupt, a victory over *apartheid* (and this is the only discourse that allowed "victory" to be claimed by both the "new" NP, the ANC, and other less important formations)[2] implied that anyone who ever supported apartheid or the political parties that defended it was responsible for conflicts of the past, along with anyone who supported violent opposition movements. I suspect that in reality this still leaves out most of the population, and in a way the fundamental nature of amnesty as political self-pardon is most apparent in this aspect of the discourse. Be that as it may, dispersing blame makes any moral or legal judgement less significant and less rational. It reinforces the tragic-inevitable view of apartheid and the brutality that accompanied it and makes any project of redress seem overly ambitious, time-consuming, and costly if it is to reach beyond surface issues or fails to stay focused exclusively on the extreme.

The problem of scale is of course very real: for instance, the TRC itself was concerned with a relatively large slice of South African history, namely, from the Sharpeville massacre in 1960 to the inauguration of President Mandela in May 1994, but, significantly, only as far as "gross human rights violations" were committed, that is, the bloody tip of the apartheid iceberg. Even with this reduced scope, many feared the number of people involved would be too massive to handle, as is almost always the case in transitional situations (see Cohen 1995). But at the time the commission was taking shape, all possibilities were still open and the problem appeared nearly unsurmountable. For example, the TRC had to decide whether to address questions such as, Were apartheid laws and policies "criminal," as the UN proclaimed? And if so, how many people were to be held responsible for creating and enforcing them? How far back in time?

But scale is at once a problem and a *solution*. A (pre)determination of scale serves to support some methods and to evacuate others from the debate. This not done with actual numbers; remember that the truth isn't known yet. But simply discussing it evacuates or displaces the matter of individual responsibility from the center of the question. It further contributes in creating a narrative of group responsibility.

There are two aspects to the matter of scale. There is the obvious administrative one about the handling of such large numbers of cases, how much it is going to cost, how many qualified people will be needed, and so forth. But there is the even more complex problem of attempting to define limits to the application of criminal justice, which is contrary to its internal logic. Under a criminal justice rationale one can neither *predict* nor *control* the number of accusations, the time needed to reach a definitive result or the costs involved: once the train is out of the station, it cannot be stopped

2. Less important at the time, that is. The NP is currently losing its opposition status to the Democratic Party, a trend that seems irreversible.

until the end of the tracks.[3] In the words of Minister Omar, in an early speech in the new National Assembly:

> I want to give assurance to those who have fears and who may have perpetrated human rights violations and want to join in reconciliation, that in respect of politically motivated crimes there will be no Nuremberg-type trials. There will be no vengeance or witch-hunts, there will be no revenge and there will be no humiliation of any person. . . . The advantage of a commission, whatever its name—we must avoid any connotation which suggests revenge or witch-hunts—is that it can facilitate disclosure within a framework that provides amnesty with acknowledgement, justice and dignity. Far from being an instrument of vengeance and humiliation, it has the advantage of forestalling a multiplicity of criminal prosecutions and civil claims (A. Omar [ANC], South Africa 1994, 188–89)

If the problem of limits is made a crucial one, then the offered solution must be (relatively) swift and definitive: "before we can close the book on our past, we must have one last, fairly rapid but penetrating look at it" (K. Asmal [ANC], South Africa 1995a, 1381). By comparison, given free rein, retributive justice has no intrinsic limit: we are told that apartheid only worked because tens of thousands of individuals did their part, including ordinary members of the NP. Maybe all members of the NP should be barred from employment in the civil service and, *a fortiori*, from government. At the time, this principle of "lustration," of "disinfecting" the public service and the state from its bad elements was being discussed in the former East Germany, in Czechoslovakia, Poland, and in some Latin American countries (see Łós 1995)—as well as having been the main rationale behind post-Nuremberg "de-Nazification" trials, which are all integrated under the metaphor.

Of course, Nuremberg could just as well stand for the *opposite* of witch-hunts: the trial of the 24 "major criminals" was more like a swift eradication of group responsibility, a concession to the "handful of Nazis misleading the nation" theory of Hitlerism (see Goldhagen 1996), in other words, the purification of the nation through the personification of the crimes and of the ethos, which is the opposite of the dispersion we are seeing here. Finding a middle ground between the two extremes of personification or blaming everyone/no one would have involved defining and circumscribing blameworthiness and responsibility—difficult conceptual and political work with little chance of success. Personification was out of the question because the potentially accused and sacrificed were those negotiating the deal. This left

3. In Argentina, for example, the eventual scramble to put an end to the prosecution of former security forces personnel and former state officials with "due obedience" and *punto final* ("final stop") laws transformed a democratic process into an authoritarian one (see Feitlowitz 1998, 142).

blaming everyone/no one, and it was easily carried in a wide enough political consensus as "not a Nuremberg." Without the very cogent myth of Nuremberg to help reduce the dilemma to these two options, reaching a consensus on postapartheid justice would probably have been intensely divisive or impossible. Since it was not only readily available but practically unavoidable because of the conceptual proximity I have already mentioned, it was possible to disqualify any nuance or redefinition of the acts or any alternative approach under a criminal justice logic.

Not that the vocabulary of crime, punishment, and justice was abandoned altogether. It was merely circumscribed. It became a *problem* to be solved instead of an indisputable, spontaneously suggested solution. Nuremberg helped transform any conventional justice argument into a nonstarter. In a speech given before the adoption of the TRC law, the minister of justice thus explained his intellectual point of departure:

> I would like to point out that international law requires crimes against humanity to be prosecuted and punished . . . it provides further that international criminal responsibility applies, irrespective of motive, to individuals and representatives of the state. . . . [T]hus there is little doubt that in so far as the acts envisaged under the amnesty provisions were part and parcel of the apartheid strategy, they ought to be prosecuted and punished in accordance with the requirements of international law. (A. Omar [ANC], South Africa 1995b, 2215)

There is obvious strategy here: in other words, all things considered, the TRC bill is a good deal for old regime supporters. Considering the alternative, what in the end really should be done, the ANC has been reasonable and accommodating. However, at the center of the thinly veiled threat is also a genuine legal problem: strictly speaking international law is of no help in evaluating the depth of responsibility. Between the Geneva conventions and protocols, the convention on apartheid, crimes against humanity, there is no telling how many should be accused, and of what, or when it will all end: much work would be needed to articulate a criminal justice approach, work that is already disqualified. In this speech Omar is speaking about a problem that has already been solved: he is actually using the threat of limitless prosecutions to support the solution he has tabled in the Senate, precisely within the dichotomy already established and reinforced by the Nuremberg myth. The question of limits has been solved through circumvention, the "legalism," the "moralism," have been replaced by rational, objective, and effective statesmanship.

C. Avoiding Revenge

One last discursive tool created with the help of Nuremberg was the confusion of uncivilized, undemocratic revenge with retributive justice. For the government, the danger was to appear to have "lost emotional control" and abandoned the proper administrative attitude, thus opening itself to the already mentioned impression of fitting widespread racial stereotypes. On the NP side, the role of protector of the white minority's "rights," also claimed by the rival DP, implied constant surveillance of the probational one-person-one-vote government, and no anti-TRC speech could leave the impression that this basic mission of the NP had been a failure. In short, this was a delicate balancing act for all formations, who had to find a proper equilibrium between ostentatious dissension over what Edelman (1964) calls "transient issues" and functional congruence with regards to the fundamentals of legitimate participation in government. The added difficulty in this case, of course, was that the problem being discussed itself concerned that legitimacy immediately and directly, which is not the case with ordinary criminal justice debates.

In such a chaotic and unpredictable context, achieving consensus on a course of action entirely depends on the ability to articulate the problematic in "hortatory" terms (Edelman 1964): the type of discourse that enables supporters to speak in a single voice and critics to find satisfactory "cover" for following a path not directly or entirely compatible with their traditional political position. "National reconciliation" of course was a major component of this new public knowledge being constructed. It remains undefined to this day—which helps avoid dissention—but whatever it is, surely it must be the opposite of Nuremberg. So the myth had two very helpful functions under this theme: on one hand, it helped define, or rather helped avoid having to define the declared reconciliatory objective of the projected institution; on the other, it helped TRC supporters defuse the accusation of being vengeful while at the same time underlining the extent of wrongdoing (and thus the need for action) by pointing to the *potential* for revenge.

In his very first speech in Parliament, the minister of justice said that "the reason for dealing with the past in an open, orderly and systematic way is that we must avoid any recrimination, vendetta or attempts at finding scapegoats" (A. Omar [ANC], South Africa 1994, 24). J. de Lange, one of the drafters of the original bill, said in August 1994:

> [I]f we do not provide a legislative framework through which our citizens are able to deal with their respective pasts, we will be leaving them to their own devices. This will most certainly lead to persons taking the law into their own hands, or, at the very least, it will lead to continuous prosecutions, counter-prosecutions, civil proceedings and counter-civil proceedings. And at the end of the day the pressure will

> rise in society and I am not sure in my own mind whether we will be able to avoid even going as far as the way in which matters were dealt with in the Nuremberg trials. (J. De Lange [ANC], South Africa 1994, 862)

There is hyperbole here (a series of trials would actually be worse than "persons taking the law into their own hands"), but the point is clear: Nuremberg would be entirely wrong and out of place, obviously exaggerated, unjust, and arbitrary in the South African postapartheid context. By contrast, "this Bill represent[s] a historic act of generosity on the part of the victims of apartheid, such as President Nelson Mandela, towards those who committed gross violations of human rights during the apartheid years" (A. Omar [ANC], South Africa 1995b, 2209-10). Again there is an element of moral superiority to this reconciliation; according to later deputy chairperson of the TRC Alex Boraine:

> [T]here are many, many South Africans who would want the state to go much further, who would opt for a Nuremberg-style approach, who would want prosecutions and revenge, but in our wisdom, I think, we have opted for amnesty and reconciliation. (A. Boraine, oral submission to the Joint Senate/House Committees on Justice, Feb. 1995, trans. p. 55)

From the other side of the house, the discourse is practically the same: "to a great number of people out there the name 'truth commission' is synonymous with persecution, reprisals, and even Nuremberg-style trials and a witch-hunt" (R. H. Groenwald [NP], South Africa 1995a, 1411). Against it, it must be reaffirmed that true morality must be pragmatic:

> The last thing we need in this country is a lust for retribution. I know that there are people who want some form of Nuremberg trials. Fortunately, the majority of citizens would resist such a move. The irony of the situation is that those who clamour for such retribution are those who did the least in the liberation struggle. They are the ones who are suddenly more radical. (C. Redcliffe [NP], South Africa 1995b, 2228)

The senator is trying to articulate an antiscapegoating argument, implying that those who felt most guilty for not opposing apartheid were actively trying to cleanse their mistake at the expense of others—and risking peace and order in the process. Nuremberg, as "lust for retribution," would be worse than the crimes it was meant to address, and the intentions behind such a plan are highly suspicious. The theme is clear: vengeance/retribution is a disproportionate and devious response to apartheid brutality.

Sometimes excessive retribution can come from less likely places. This is how the leader of the extreme-right Freedom Front (FF), Constand Viljoen, put it:

> [Nongovernmental organizations workers] are people with a specific psychological makeup. They are invariably moralists and some even sentimentalists and it is good that they have such people, but their judgement in the field of public life is exactly because of their prejudices, not always to be trustfully with undeniable high ideals they tend to suffer from frustration. On these ideals which ends up with some form of frustration. (Oral submission to the Joint Senate/House Committees on Justice, Feb. 1995, trans. p. 4-5)

Unsurprisingly, there is total agreement among all parties that radical, uncivilized revenge would be a problem. But whether the revenge is an instinctual, violent one, one manifested through excessive use of the courts, or one instituted in an *ad hoc* solution such as a special commission—each option, it seems, likened to "Nuremberg"—it is always made up as a determining part of the problem, and potential solutions must be evaluated by their capacity to contain it. I think it is clear that the problem being defined is not only about the nature of the crimes or the response: it is primarily about the social situation of the country and the nature of the postapartheid government as the context of the future solution. It is related to many elements, but mainly: (a) it played on the fundamental distrust of nonwhites' ability to administer unbiased justice (Gobodo-Madikizela 1996); (b) it was morally condemnatory in that the fight against the old government was invariably put in terms of human rights and international law; and (c) not only did the Mandela-driven "rainbow nation" approach of the ANC need to be inclusive in terms of ethics but also, whites still held the economic levers, and their exodus would have been catastrophic. In all cases, the danger of revenge, whether from frustrated human rights types, from the great unwashed, or from "radicals," found a convenient home in the Nuremberg myth, which gave power to the rhetoric without the need for articulation of the argument (while entirely avoiding attacking or questioning the conventional criminal justice system running in the background).

The problem of recriminations and vendetta is more than a strategic, political question: it conveys significant adjustment or reinforcement of some fundamental concepts. By facilitating the interchangeability of "retribution" and "revenge," Nuremberg effectively negated the legitimacy of conventional criminal justice in this particular context by redrawing its contours. This is a context where any judicial action is uncalled for, where the word *crime* does not appear in the TRC law, replaced by "gross human rights violations." The myth has made it possible to redefine the past as a struggle where all sides were both right and wrong and where subsequent condemnation is impossible or at least illegitimate. What is left to do is to separate the right from the wrong outside of the responsibility of actors, that is, to find the truth. The hope was that truth would provide normative conclusions without raising the matter culpability.

For the most part, *reconciliation* has only been negatively defined, as the opposite of revenge, which only marginally narrows down the range of possible meanings—thus keeping everyone on board. But the putative need for airing the past in public adds to this definition that either revenge happens in ignorance of the past or that official knowledge is revenge enough. In either case, knowledge, or truth, is made the central concern, displacing the matter of retribution: establishing truth is more important than retributive—or in fact any kind of corrective justice—because it serves as correction in itself. So reconciliation, because it is only defined as the absence of revenge, starts to be indistinguishable from truth—we air the truth so there is no revenge. Later, the commission's motto would be, "truth, the road to reconciliation," entirely in keeping with this particular understanding of the past as a festering, tension-producing, generalized misunderstanding.

III. TRANSFORMING CONTRADICTORY POLITICAL OBJECTIVES INTO ADMINISTRATIVE ACTION

Nuremberg left many questions unanswered: there were still very few, and at best embryonic, parameters for the future truth commission. More definitional work was needed, and in reality many other mechanisms came into play to shape the final institution. It was, however, instrumental in settling a few truths: first, the project should avoid direct condemnation of individuals because it is counterproductive or plain wrong to blame apartheid brutality on individuals or politically identifiable groups; in fact, apartheid is not to be addressed as significant wrongdoing at all, and its brutality is to be understood as an unavoidable consequence of a "war" between opposed factions. Second, and as a corollary, the commission should not actively seek or investigate individual wrongdoers, because it would look threatening and vengeful (criminal justice and retribution having been made incompatible with the situation). Rather, it should be left to those responsible to actively seek the commission, so some benefit must be offered (amnesty) and unpleasant or otherwise negative consequences must be kept to a minimum. Third, the commission should in no way interfere with *already existing* national reconciliation, peace, and order.

This emerging TRC discourse did much more than settle some questions about what to do with the remnants of the apartheid era: it transformed and strengthened a specific understanding of the context where the truths became dominant, at least temporarily. Clearly the solution, the course of action to be taken was being defined in conjunction with the problems, with multiple readjustments and new "findings" bringing new nuances and new meanings to the existing context, transforming it. The appearance of these truths does not require or even imply a conspiracy or other directed efforts at rewriting history: it is simply the result of compromises made at other levels to meet other goals and make the administration appear to solve problems and address public concerns. The inclusion of a handful of easily recognizable myths in the rhetoric of all parties to the debate formed a basis for administrative action by *de facto* reducing the problem in a specific way: the question of retribution became no longer separable from irrational revenge, conventional justice was irremediably vengeful in postconflict situations, and the remedy to all would be "truth" (that is, truth within extremely strict boundaries). The myth also served to crystalize a series of contradictory positions and to demonstrate reconciliation at the level of the nation's politics: it married a condemnatory and moralistic discourse to judicial pardon, denunciation to compromise, responsibility and accountability to an amnesty process free of corrective obligations, and so forth.

Later, the actual practices and achievements of the TRC, while in fact not entirely in keeping with the politicians' plans, largely supported and further reinforced this new reality. Edelman (1964, 8) has spoken cogently of this standardizing mechanism: "controversial political acts . . . are bound to become condensation symbols, emotional in impact, calling for conformity to promote social harmony, serving as the focus of psychological tensions." I think this is easily extracted from its psychological assumptions into a more social perspective: "psychological tensions" are simply difficulties of incoherence, or gaps in common sense, representations and mentalities which make further action problematic in an unpredictable situation. Symbols and myths—of which Nuremberg was only a single example—help smooth out the contingent sources of problematization by introducing open-ended abstractions that can be used in a variety of ways to make sense of the situation for different observers: it allows the thinking individual to take pieces of different puzzles and make them fit together to form a new picture, a new structuring of society where contingency has been evacuated.

IV. RHETORICAL POWER AND PROBLEMATIZATION

In essence, Nuremberg contributed to the transformation of a large set of objective but meaningless potentialities and uncertain, overly complex, contradictory or unclear notions into a very small range of valid options and proper attitudes. It was of great help in reducing the appearance of arbitrariness in decision making and it created post-transition South Africa as a series of easily identifiable, specific necessities that had to be met while solving unanswerable, paralyzing questions by eradication. The Nuremberg myth allowed this reconstruction by providing key elements of a new discourse, used to convince a critical mass of the population of the reasonableness of a drastic departure from what is conventionally accepted as justice in criminal matters.

Following the rhetorical "career" of a myth such as that of Nuremberg provides new insights into the process of construction of a logical model of action. It shows how the significant elements of a situation are conceptually and rhetorically bound together in a sufficiently convincing way and may be used in support of a unified institutional blueprint (whether the actual institution will later comply is a separate question). I used the concept of "institution" here as a set of practices that, taken together, form a consistent whole both in terms of objectives and methods: in other words it is a system with two essential parts, a set of practices and a discourse about them. What we have explored here is the creation of the rationality of this institution, that is, how it became a coherent plan of action—replacing an older one that used to be equally convincing but is now judged to be inadequate. If at first glance Nuremberg was used to *illustrate* a number of parameters of the socio-politico-cultural context and the possible solutions, it did much more. In addition to the powerful symbols it carried, it helped exclude a number of traditionally obvious, "go-without-saying," "common sense" truths about criminal justice by supporting an alternative discourse where they were non-starters. Because Nuremberg was understood as an example of perverted legalism and counterproductive judicial excesses, it portrayed the situation as potentially explosive and in need of solutions of appeasement rather than solutions of "justice."

This process of displacement of conventionally accepted practice is particularly interesting under a Foucaultian light. Thinking of this phenomena as the "problematization" of an area of the social, the moment where a discrepancy between context and practice appears, easily explains why the process of redefinition involves both. The way the situation is constructed and understood is inseparable from the concomitant construction of its solution. On one hand, the matter of the consequences—and indirectly but unavoidably the *nature*—of apartheid had to be defined in ways that a large number of actors could agree on. What was really left after the transition? A few hardened criminals? A multitude of misled people? A huge cover-up that needed to be aired? A pent-up desire for revenge? Two reconciled political parties? On the other hand, the basic principles of any compatible and acceptable courses of action had to be articulated in rational, Taylorist language as the best solution for the problem, immediately reinforcing it, but also clearly having influenced its construction from the beginning. Finding a "solution" to a "problem" is not difficult: there are plenty of alternatives and models floating around, all potentially valuable (note that a series of trials was the ANC's preferred response to apartheid until the late 1980s).

What is truly demanding is the articulation of a discourse where both the situation and one of the possible actions are represented coherently, and that will be cogent enough to impose itself.

That is what problematization is all about: deciding that the old mentality is no longer adequate and attempting to replace it. But of course the mentality is what serves to describe both the world and our actions within it. Foucaultian problematization is simply the moment where an object calls for attention and triggers intellectual work on a process of reconstruction. But this is a reconstruction from the inside, with the available tools: there are no outside, objective, Taylorist observers. But it is our desire that such objective observation and analysis be possible that makes symbols such as Nuremberg so powerful. Its representation as a historical precedent erased the contingency of the construction process and reinforced the Taylorist rational model of observation-analysis-action of administrative processes, where solutions always follow problems, glossing over the fact that reality is a socially structured accomplishment and that both aspects were defined together. Nuremberg comes complete with a situation (historical Nazi crimes), followed by a solution to it (the application of retributive justice), clearly laid out in a progressive problem-solution sequence. It implies that it was considered and analyzed as such by the speaker, in a universally objective, rational evaluation of its flaws and benefits. By extension, this mantle of rationality also covers the preferred solution supposedly taken after careful analysis and given in contrast to it.

Further, I think it is clear that in many ways myths can speed up and homogenize the way we detect and build problem situations. First, myths and metaphors make communication easier and therefore will tend to spread through public speech rather quickly; and, once available, they will tend to shape, limit, and direct problematization by providing the same intellectual tools to all observers and thus reduce the creativity (or "discursive incompetence") of individual thinkers. Not that all will miraculously agree on how the problem should be defined and addressed, and that was obviously not the case here. Rather, it subtly caused large numbers of individuals to see the same slices of routine mentality and practices as problematic, at the same time—whatever their initial conclusions were. Evoking widely held popular images in a specific context, with a specific rhetorical purpose, probably helps a greater proportion of people think of the situation in compatible ways and adopt or at least accept a problematization without thinking about it too long: it immediately sounds right, proper, necessary, or inevitable. The use of Nuremberg as a symbol and as a specific form of knowledge—among other factors—provided the power to determine which issues would be raised at what time and imposed a specific understanding of the problems of fairness, revenge, and so forth. More than simple conveyors of representations, using and thinking in or with myths also influences our capacity to think of the new object in new ways, by providing, and thus by *limiting* the conceptual tools available.

V. CONCLUSION

The objective of this paper was to understand the process of displacement of a mentality by another and to describe the creation of the fundamental principles of a new administrative project. In the end the reader may be disappointed to find few normative conclusions or even signposts, but that was precisely part of the intent: to see normativity itself being developed. Ethically speaking, I think the debate is open: one could argue that the image of apartheid given by the political TRC discourse was severely skewed; that politicians requiring "political motivation" as condition for amnesty was a direct throwback to the old "act of state" defence. At the same time, conventional retributive justice is far from a perfect, or indeed an entirely adequate solution, in *any* context: and all things considered this is probably the worst imaginable context.

However I think it is clear by now that asking, debating, and answering such questions is part of the way we continuously make up our reality. And this is not simply a somewhat convoluted restatement of the truism that morality is relative; morality is not relative, it is not even set: it is continuous, never-ending *work*.

REFERENCES

African National Congress [ANC]. 1992. Skweyiya Commission Report: Report of the Commission of Enquiry into Complaints by Former African National Congress Prisoners and Detainees.

On the web: http://www.anc.org.za/ancdocs/misc/skweyiya.html

———. 1993. Report of the Commission of Enquiry into Certain Allegations of Cruelty and Human Rights Abuse against ANC Prisoners and Detainees by ANC Members. Motsuenyane Commission, ANC internal documents.

Carbonell, Charles-Olivier, and Jean Rives, eds. 1990. *Mythes et politique*. Toulouse, France: Presses de l'Institut d'Études Politiques.

Cohen, Stanley. 1994. Social Control and the Politics of Reconciliation. In *The Futures of Criminology*, ed. David Nelken, 63–88. London: Sage.

———. 1995. State Crimes of Previous Regimes: Knowledge, Accountability and the Policing of the Past. *Law and Social Inquiry* 20 (1): 7–50.

Crozier, Michel, and Erhard Friedberg. 1992. *L'acteur et le système*. Paris: Seuil.

Dreyfus, Hubert, and Paul Rabinow. 1983. *Michel Foucault: Beyond Structuralism and Hermeneutics*. Chicago: University of Chicago Press.

Edelman, Murray. 1971. *Politics as Symbolic Action: Mass Arousal and Quiescence*. Chicago: Markham.

Ensalaco, Mark. 1994. Truth Commissions for Chile and El Salvador: A Report and Assessment. *Human Rights Quarterly* 16:656–75.

Feitlowitz, Marguerite. 1998. *A Lexicon of Terror: Argentina and the Legacies of Torture.* New York: Oxford University Press.

Flood, Christopher. 1996. *Political Myth: A Theoretical Introduction.* New York: Garland.

Foucault, Michel. 1982. The Discourse on Language. In *The Archaeology of Knowledge.* New York: Pantheon.

———. 1984. Polemics, Politics and Problematizations: An Interview. In *The Foucault Reader*, ed. Paul Rabinow, 381–90. New York: Pantheon.

———. 1991. Governmentality. In *The Foucault Effect: Studies in Governmentality*, ed. Graham Burchell, Colin Gordon, and Peter Miller, 87–104. Chicago: University of Chicago Press.

Giliomee, Hermann. 1997. TRC Report, Academics and History. *Cape Times*, 23 Oct., 8.

Gobodo-Madikizela, Pumla. 1996. Reenactment of Old Identities and Implications for Reconciliation. Paper presented at the Fortieth Annual Convention of the Institute of Personnel Management, 21 October. TRC internal documents.

Goldhagen, Daniel Jonah. 1996. *Hitler's Willing Executioners: Ordinary Germans and the Holocaust.* New York: Alfred A. Knopf.

Hayner, Priscilla. 1994. Fifteen Truth Commissions: A Comparative Study. *Human Rights Quarterly* 16:597–655.

Huyse, Luc. 1995. Justice after Transition: On the Choices Successor Elites Make in Dealing with the Past. *Law and Social Inquiry* 20 (1): 51–70.

Jung, Courteney, and Ian Shapiro. 1995. South Africa's Negotiated Transition: Democracy, Opposition and the New Constitutional Order. *Politics and Society* 23 (3): 269–308.

Leman-Langlois, Stéphane. 2000. Mobilizing Victimization: The Construction of a Victim-centred Approach in the South African Truth and Reconciliation Commission. *Criminologie* 33 (1): 145–65.

Łós, Maria. 1995. Lustration and Truth Claims: Unfinished Revolutions in Central Europe. *Law and Social Inquiry* 20 (1): 117–62.

National Party. 1997. Second Submission to the Truth And Reconciliation Commission. Original distributed on 23 March 1997.

Nel, Philip. 1995. Transition through Erosion: Comparing South Africa's Democratisation. *Aussenpolitik* 46:82–93.

South Africa. 1994. *Hansard Debates of the National Assembly; Interpellations, Questions and Replies of the National Assembly.*

———. 1995a. *Hansard Debates of the National Assembly; Interpellations, Questions and Replies of the National Assembly.*

———. 1995b. *Hansard Debates of the Senate; Interpellations, Questions and Replies of the Senate (Hansard).*

South African Truth and Reconciliation Commission [TRC]. 1998. *The Report of the Truth and Reconciliation Commission.* Cape Town: Juta Books. Also available on unofficial website: www.struth.org.za.

Thompson, Leonard. 1985. *The Political Mythology of Apartheid.* New Haven, Conn.: Yale University Press.

[13]

'THE TRIAL':[1] A PARODY OF THE LAW AMID THE MOCKERY OF MEN IN POST-COLONIAL PAPUA NEW GUINEA

David Lipset

University of Minnesota

According to students of legal pluralism, the relationship between Western law and local dispute management processes, remedies, and so on is multiple and complex. Legal pluralism studies have not ventured very far outside the arenas of conflict resolution, be they authorized or private. In this article, I argue that legal pluralism has imposed methodological blinders upon significant expressive dimensions of its problem. In a satirical mock-trial that took place in rural Papua New Guinea, legal and indigenous constructions of order met not, as one might expect, instrumentally in the context of negotiating the resolution of a 'trouble case', but creatively combining in play to result in a multi-voiced, comic discourse. The law is shown to have rhetorical value, particularly in colonial and post-colonial settings where it may be deployed or invoked to represent and convey ambivalent attitudes about both justice and local constructions of personhood.

Legal pluralism reflects a view of social order as being made up of multiple regulatory agencies. Legal pluralism studies have particularly, although not exclusively, focused on political situations, such as those in colonial or post-colonial states, where indigenous and judicial institutions remain largely foreign in relationship to the other – for instance, independent – even after prolonged periods of interaction with colonial rulers and Western-style legal systems.[2] Of the many points one can take from three decades of legal pluralism scholarship,[3] among the least controversial, yet certainly the most important, is that the influence of Western law on colonized cultures is neither as all-encompassing as the state might try to claim it to be, nor as contemptible and incompatible as anti-colonial activists might insist.

My aim in this article is to show that, despite their many successes, legal pluralism studies have tended to overlook an expressive dimension of their problem. That is, they have ventured little attention beyond the arenas of conflict resolution, be they authorized, private, or mixed. To do so, I discuss an episode that took place in post-colonial Papua New Guinea (PNG), during which legal and indigenous constructions of order met, not instrumentally, say, to contribute to the settlement of another trouble case (Lipset 1997: 217-76), but in creative play, combining to result in a multi-voiced parody. One of my conclusions is that the law may not only be used politically, but may also have rhetorical value, particularly in colonial and post-colonial settings, where it may be deployed to represent and convey ambivalent attitudes, not only about justice, but no less about local constructions of personhood.[4] In other words, instead of adopting a unilateralist or dialectical view of the relationship of law to local concepts of order, a view which privileges the law, I conclude that this relationship may also give rise to a decentred discourse, a discourse in which multiple voices simultaneously assert and contest plural versions of authority, creating a legal heteroglossia that is 'forever being shaped and yet never congealing' (Bakhtin 1984*a*: 16). In this moment of PNG history, I should add, the state itself has become decentred rather than dominant.

While such leading students of play-related phenomena as Bateson (1953) and Goffman (1974) focused on its microcosmic dimensions, namely, how play may be cognized or situationally communicated, my purpose requires a somewhat broader historical and political contextualization of the relationship between play and culture. The view of this relationship which I favour is one that Bakhtin has called 'dialogism'. In Bakhtin's view, forms of discourse that emerge in diverse and politically complicated circumstances are 'unfinalized', rather than subordinate to a definitive authoritative position. In other words, to a certain extent at least, they remain independent of a ruling monologue, such as those issued by state or church (Bakhtin 1984*a*: 32). Among favoured Bakhtinian imagery we find 'unmerged voices', 'carnival', 'thresholds', 'double-voiced discourse', 'contrapuntal voices', 'combined images', 'ambivalence', and 'two-in-one images'. These reveal a view of discourse as anything but reductionist, static, or structural. Dialogism, moreover, construes discourse as not just composed of actual voices talking back and forth. Discourse is made up of voices that are saturated with the words of others, whether or not dialogue is actually taking place. Dialogism therefore refers to both present and absent interlocutors. It therefore focuses not only on the ways in which language may be used socially, but also on how metaphor, style, intonation and so forth may themselves be understood as rejoinders, typically between opposing regimes, rejoinders, that is, which struggle with and against each other to compose an open-ended discursive field.

In this article, I consider a relationship between forms of indigenous satire, irony and parody and the law as dialogical.[5] My text is an improvised, mock 'trial' that was 'convened' in a village in the Murik Lakes region in rural PNG in 2001. In my use of such terms as 'satire' and 'parody,' I am employing terms and categories which derive from local usage; it should not be thought that I am imposing classical Western tropes on this PNG context.[6] It is important to avoid reducing Murik parody, however, either to emphasize the law, as some legal anthropologists might prefer, or to emphasize the element of comic discourse in it, as students of play might want to do. 'The trial' did not take place at random. Nor was it merely a script (Nelson & Seidmen 1984; Schank & Abelson 1977) 'about' a 'judge' weighing the 'guilt' or 'innocence' of a 'defendant'. It was 'convened', as I show below, by means of and in the parodic scripts of Murik joking relationships, ethos, and images. Rather than being deployed as a threat, or a bargaining chip, 'the trial' became a metaphor that drew upon Murik satire and creativity, mocked local order, and mocked the judicial system of the post-colonial state. In other words, the dialogicality of this performance saturated 'the trial' so thoroughly that neither the metaphor of the law nor the comic rendition of Murik personhood which informed local voices should be privileged either exegetically or by the actors who created it. 'The trial', as a representation, was dialogically absorbed by, just as it simultaneously absorbed, an ongoing genre of indigenous parody. Murik joking partners assimilated 'the law', for their comic purposes, just as 'the law' informed their comic discourse mocking personhood. 'The trial' stood for both an historical moment in PNG and an ongoing cultural dynamic within Murik society.

The precise significance of 'law' depicted below therefore remains refractory, unfinalized, and reflexive. The imaginative caricature of 'a trial' might well be understood as an insubordinate mockery of the state's claim that it, and only it, may define the rights and judge the conduct of the citizen; alternatively, it might be understood as an indirect acknowledgement of its sovereignty. Or it may, perhaps, be both. The caricature of the moral person might also be construed doubly, as both insubordinate and unequivocal. Either way, this creative mixing of the prosaic and the formal did not reflect a moment or a phase that would or should eventually defer to the official, monologic voice of legal authority. It was not a passing moment on the road towards that, or any other inevitable end. The contrapuntal imaginations, the one answering the other, belong to a labyrinthine situation in Papua New Guinea, a situation in which the significance of the law remains subject to interpretation, a situation whose future is indeterminate and unpredictable.

Legal pluralism in a weak state

The history of state-based law and unofficial forms of social control in PNG ought properly to be traced back to *Crime and custom in savage society* in which Malinowski (1926) argued that although moral order in Trobriand society was stateless, it was none the less safeguarded by interdependent, reciprocal relationships and the obligations created by them. 'Law and order', Malinowski concluded, 'arise out of the very processes which they govern' (1926: 122-3).[7] During the colonial era (1884-1975), representatives of which were largely absent in *Crime and custom*, villagers were subject to a regime of petty, paternalistic rules and ordinances which were known in official parlance as Native Regulations. They were intended to keep Papua New Guineans 'obedient and unobtrusive' (Kituai 1998: 7) by restricting movement from villages, imposing night-time curfews, banning gambling and alcohol consumption, and even requiring the wearing of clothes on the upper body. The official policy of the chief administrator of the territory of Papua, Sir Hubert Murray, 'vigorously opposed the setting up of tribunals composed of indigenes and administering customary law' (Epstein 1974: 3). Murray held that indirect rule was impossible due to the barbaric nature of local-level authority.[8]

It is true that both the German and Australian colonial authorities appointed village officials who heard complaints. In both cases, the system of government was generally undifferentiated and decentralized, with most functions being carried out by district officers (*kiap*), who operated as administrators, policemen, magistrates, and jailers, in other words, as multi-powered bosses at local levels (Gordon & Meggitt 1985: 52ff., Kituai 1998: 19-41;

McPherson 2001; Rowley 1965: 76). Multi-powered, but at the same time manipulable: 'in this environment, *kiap* courts provided additional fora that could be incorporated into local political strategies' (Dinnen 2001: 23). In the early 1950s, Paul Hasluck (1976), who served as Australia's Minister for Territories between 1951 and 1963, instituted a system of democratically elected Local Government Councils; this was part of a move to begin the unification of the country[9] by increasing indigenous participation. The Councils appeared in a few areas at first and then, over the years, became more prevalent (Lynch 1969). In 1966, the separate court system for native affairs, which had been presided over by district officers, was abolished and replaced by an integrated, pyramidal court system – national, district, and local – that was based on English common law (Derham 1963; see also Fenbury 1978: 116 ff.). The Supreme Court soon became known as the 'White Court', whose efficacy and import, of course, depended on one's perspective.[10] The new system guaranteed equal legal access and orientated itself to the preference for mediation and consensus settlements in indigenous custom, but contained no reference to specific offences. Schemes were introduced to train local men in procedures and rules of evidence so that they could serve as full-time magistrates in local courts (Barnett 1969: 159). Three indigenous magistrates were appointed in 1967. Ten years later, there were a total of about 140 serving at local and village levels.

At Independence in 1975, the post-colonial state adopted this structure, preserving the form as it existed during the final decade of Australian rule (Chalmers & Paliwala 1977: 67 ff.). At the top remained a supreme court. Each region had a district court, and below it, local courts, which were originally designed to serve the populace. Local courts were located in town centres at considerable distances from villages. Villagers rarely went to them for justice (Scaglion 1976). Village courts were instituted in 1973 as part of the run-up to Independence. By 1985, about 75 per cent of the country had access to them (Keris 1987: 71). They were intended to apply customary rules and procedures to dispute settlement. Magistrates were selected from among local leadership, and were familiar with customs, people, and events. These courts were meant to be less formal and imposing than the urban courts. 'Wide variation in modes of procedure and styles of operation is permitted, in keeping with the variability of Melanesian customary law' (Scaglion 1990: 19-20; see also Hutchins 1990; LiPuma 2000).

Many courts did not conform to this expectation. Some magistrates, styling themselves after the judges in urban courts, tended to impose judgments rather than using mediation techniques (Iamo 1987; A. Strathern 1981: 16). A number of communities rejected the system altogether because of its association with state control; others resisted it, either on the grounds that the village courts would serve only the interests of a rising, local elite or because of their domination by a local male gerontocracy (Fitzpatrick 1980). Another criticism of the village courts, particularly in the highlands, has been that they have reinforced the subordination of women and children (Garap 2000). By the 1980s, however, the village courts were held to be making use of both formal mediation and custom in creative ways (Scaglion 1979; Zorn 1991). They had not displaced indigenous remedies, but had come to occupy 'a regulatory position somewhere in between' (Goddard 2000: 243) local society and the state.[11]

However village court practices may be evaluated, the overall effectiveness of the legal system in PNG has been in persistent decline; this is part of the more general process of deterioration which many commentators see as afflicting PNG's endemically 'weak state' (Dinnen 2001; see also Larmour 1998; Migdal 1988; Morauta 1987; Standish 1994, 2001; cf. Lipset 1989). Criminal violence and lawlessness, the renewal of tribal warfare in the highlands (Gordon & Meggitt 1985), election-related fighting, and rampant petty theft, armed robberies, rapes, and homicides perpetrated by urban youth gangs who are popularly known as *raskols* in Tok Pisin,[12] have given rise to ever increasing fears about personal security throughout the country (see also Dinnen 1998; Dinnen & Ley 2000). Curfews and special policing operations[13] have had little or no effect. Although longitudinal data confirming the breakdown of order in PNG are sadly lacking, there can be little doubt that confidence in the state has been declining steadily since Independence. On the one hand, the perceived failings of PNG state institutions may be measured in terms of institutional ineffectiveness and lack of resources. On the other hand, Dinnen rightly notes that the weakness of the justice system must take 'deeper dislocations' into account, namely the 'context of rapid, often bewildering change ... [and] new forms of social and economic marginalization' (2000: 69).

The year 2000 was the Silver Jubilee of PNG's Independence. While a large-scale celebration was staged in the national capital, Port Moresby, in the provinces little was done to mark the occasion and only a minimum of government support was provided. At Kundiawa in Simbu Province, dance groups performed

> largely ignoring the rather jaded speeches of local dignitaries apologizing for limited government support paid to the dancers. A platoon of women ... also marched and drummed, their ... bodies glistening with black tree oil, satirizing colonial policemen while demanding public order. In effect denying the ability of the state to assist their community, they were asserting that they would themselves keep their own young people under control (Standish 2000: 1).

An enfeebled, fragile, corrupt, deeply underfunded, post-colonial state faced many challenges in 2001. Chief among them was the task of trying to rebuild a system of law and justice, both in terms of recreating its legitimacy and rehabilitating its institutional abilities, so as to combine the legal-bureaucratic functions of the state together with the polyphony of local-level values and processes to which the overwhelming majority of rural Papua New Guineans still adhered.

Law and order in a Sepik village

The village of Darapap is situated on the remote outer margins of this weak state and its overextended, deeply compromised legal system. Darapap is one of five communities located on the Murik Lakes, a system of brackish coastal lagoons in the delta of the Sepik River into which the Pacific Ocean ebbs and flows. The local people, who are known in Papua New Guinea (as well as in the ethnographic literature) as 'Murik', speak a common language and share a common ethnohistory; they also share a common network of kin and

FIGURE 1. Dwelling in Darapap Village, 2001. Photo: D. Lipset.

affinal ties and a distinctive adaptive strategy. The big, dugout outrigger canoes that were once built by the Murik male cults have given way to fibreglass dinghies (see Figure 1) and powerful outboard motors, which have reduced the time it takes to travel the 60 miles between the village and the provincial capital by more than half. Darapap nevertheless remains little more than a backwater of the global village. The community is not in receptivity mode, awaiting the imminent arrival of modernity; it is instead a place where modernity has already come and gone, leaving in its wake a few services and then moving on.

Darapap is populated by just over 600 people who still live in the same kind of buildings that their ancestors constructed. It is a village of pile-houses built out of 'bush' materials, thatch, posts, poles, and floorboard, all bound together by cane lashings. These materials are still gathered from the shallow swamps and the mangrove forests along which the people live. The villagers go to town regularly to buy foodstuffs and other commodities. But they also still practise aquatic foraging, supplemented by hereditary, inter-tribal trade based upon gift exchange and/or barter. While battery-operated 'boomboxes' are plentiful, there is no electricity or running water in the village. There is no hospital or aid post. There is no primary school. There is a Seventh Day Adventist Church, which has had a continual missionary influence in the community since the early 1950s. The church building is also built from bush materials. Linguistic and economic changes are certainly taking place within the community; for one thing, the Murik vernacular slowly seems to be giving way to Tok Pisin (or PNG Pidgin English), but outwardly the village looks much the same as in 1981, when I first visited it.[14]

The sociology of Darapap remains lived out in kin groups. Families – sibling and cognatic descent groups – serve both as units of reproduction and production and still fulfil ritual obligations, largely during mortuary rites. The male and female cults go on modulating the tenor of daily life through relent-

FIGURE 2. Age-grade masker on the beach. Photo: D. Lipset.

less joking relationships (cf. Knauft 2002: 32). The people practise elaborate ceremonial relationships as part of these two secret societies, relationships they call the *mwara yakabor* in Murik and *pilai kandere* in Tok Pisin. Women, as nieces with classificatory fathers' sisters, and men, as nephews with their classificatory mothers' brothers, mercilessly prod and tease one another about alleged sexual indiscretions and supposedly boundless appetites in the same way (see Barlow 1992; cf. Lipset 1997: 135-76).

Meanwhile, *Gaingiin* spirits, representing the masking society, constantly patrol the avenues and walking paths of Darapap with great delight (see Figure 2). This society allocates the privilege of donning a particular masked costume to each of its constituent age-grades. In costume, the masker may chase and spear anyone junior to himself. In pre-colonial times, this masking society served as a training-ground for the male cult. Today, although the latter remains housed in its own building, the power and frequency of its ritual activity have diminished, much like that of the post-colonial state. No longer are the young initiated and sent off to war. No longer does the state reliably regulate daily urban life.

Village governance is conducted by a ceremonial gerontocracy, comprising the men and women who head descent groups, together with democratically elected officials: a councillor, his committee man and a magistrate who is appointed by the councillor. The locality remains in semi-autonomous control of the negotiation of dispute-resolution processes (Moore 1979); these are managed in both Murik and Western terms (Lipset 1997: 135-76). Customary social control involves direct negotiation; this can give rise to avoidance relations which are normally concluded by ritual commensality involving private meetings during which disputants exchange dishes of food, air differences and pay compensation. Although village courts are not convened, moots are held by councillors and magistrates when needed. Disputants and onlookers assemble in the public space which is normally used for village meetings. Every few years, on secondment from the district seat or the provincial capital, police appear in the village, in response to one kind of crime or another, either to drag an individual or a handful of people off to face a regional court, or else to engage in some other dramatic, and often brutal, show of force.[15] All this might seem to suggest a society imbued with deeply conservative cultural traditions. It should be remembered, however, that Darapap has experienced over a century of interactions with the forces of modernity, most notably those enshrined in state judicial systems with their time-honoured principles of professed impartiality.

It is true that Murik youths joined the colonial police services both before and after the First World War with a steady trickle of men taking service as policemen, prison-warders, and so forth not only under the Australians and in the forces of post-Independence PNG, but also under the Japanese occupation forces during the Second World War. And it is no less true that the long shadow cast by Sir Michael Somare, the first prime minister of the post-colonial state of Papua New Guinea (1975-81), and native son of the Murik Lakes, has loomed large over this somewhat attenuated but persistent relationship (Somare 1975). Sir Michael has affected Murik identity in and orientation towards the state in a culturally distinctive way. On the other hand, he is thought to have occasioned very little in the way of concrete development gains in any significant area of PNG life. In 2001, like so much of rural Papua New Guinea, the moral imagination of Darapap village remained deeply embedded in local constructions of personhood even though villagers had no choice but to recognize the legal requirements of citizenship, however poorly equipped the state actually was to penalize those who defied its authority.

A peoples' 'court'

Although the village looked much as it did in 1981, one building on the foreshore stood out for me when I returned there for the fifth time in 2001. Rather than being constructed from bush materials, it had a wooden planking frame and walls made of aluminium sheeting. On the corrugated metal roof of this architectural anomaly were bolted three solar panels (see Figure 3). Referred to in Tok Pisin as the 'Haus Sola', the building had been constructed by local carpenters in 1999 as part of a government-sponsored project to stimulate a commercial fishery in the Lower Sepik. It had been equipped with two freezers in which fish were to be stored before being ferried to market in the provincial capital. Off to one side of its porch were about ten automobile batteries linked by cable to the solar panels, and opposite it was a counter with a built-in metal sink. Inside, a single room with plank floorboards was rimmed with a bench meant to facilitate the process of weighing and cleaning fish. The two freezers were kept in the interior room, which was illuminated by a couple of flourescent lights. The commercial fishing scheme had not yet been implemented. Most of the time, the building therefore remained empty except for the young people who sometimes loitered there during the day.

Late one morning in early January 2001, I found myself on the porch of the Haus Sola among about six young and middle-aged men who were doing

FIGURE 3. The 'Haus Sola' where 'the trial' took place. Photo: D. Lipset.

FIGURE 4. Judge Smith, Frankie, and Beldon at play before 'the trial'. Photo: D. Lipset.

just that. They were all joking partners, related matrilaterally and with ties to the male cult. As is often the case, the horseplay and quick, irrepressible banter of Murik comedy commenced (see Figure 4). All of a sudden, an impromptu 'peoples' court' convened itself inside the building before a self-proclaimed 'judge', a middle-aged man named Smith Jakai Tamau, who was barefoot and clad casually, like everyone else, in shorts and a button-down shirt. 'Judge Smith' was a former village councillor and the heir of an important headman.

FIGURE 5. Markus, Judge Smith and Frankie in 'court'. Photo: D. Lipset.

The 'defendant', Frankie, related as classificatory sister's son and joking partner to 'Judge Smith', was to stand 'trial' (see Figure 5). Others in attendance were Luke, who was another one of Frankie's senior joking partners, Beldon, Jeffrey Marabo, and two or three more young men.[16] Other people came and went. At one point, Gaingiin, the most junior spirit in the men's masquerade, stopped by. And I, also classed as one of Frankie's senior joking partners, was present. Rumors about which these self-same joking partners had been gossiping, to the effect that Frankie had had an affair with his wife's mother while visiting the 'bush Murik' village of Boig, were to be levelled as 'charges' against him. As the group improvisation began to develop (Sawyer 2002), and realizing that something of special interest to me was taking place, I turned on my untrusty little tape recorder.

The ongoing direction of linguistic change being what it is, the 'trial' took place primarily in Tok Pisin laced with the Murik vernacular. The following excerpts have been culled from a much longer transcript. I present it so as to preserve the integrity of the moment as much as possible. Without altering the overall sequence, I have sought to aid intelligibility by presenting the transcribed material in separate short sections, following each with a brief exegesis. Each utterance is numbered and followed by an English translation, where appropriate.

1. Luke:	Harim, eh! Man ia em i trebel i stap! [Hear ye! The accused is here!]
2. Voice:	Mipela stap long kes bilongem, dispela nau. [We have got to his case now.]
3. … Frankie:	Yu gat ol witnes!? Husat witnes nau? [You have witnesses!? Who is a witness?]
4. Voice:	Mi yet mi wanpela i stap. [I am here.]

5. Voice: Kom!
[Come!]
6. Frankie: Yu laik ploim kon!
[You like to plough corn!]
7. Voice: Mipela no toktok long toktok belong kot!
[We are not talking properly for court, or talking in proper court language!]
8. … Frankie: Juj i stap, inap long em kom long harim kot bilong …
[The judge is here. He will come and hear [my] … case.]
(*Someone pounds the wall*)
9. Voices: Kundu … patim em. Bai i pairap strong, bai ol i harim.
[Beat the hand-drum. The drumbeat of the hand-drum should be loud, so everyone will hear it.]

The dialogized play of law and Murik comedy is instantly audible and intelligible in this initial segment. On the one hand, in lines 1-5, a mock-attempt was being made, through the call for special language and the use of percussion, to mimic the script of 'a trial'. That is, the convening of an official gathering of credible 'facts', with witness confirmation, before an impartial adjudicator, was being simulated. On the other hand, in line 6, *kon*, the Tok Pisin word Frankie may have used to mean 'corn', as part of his insulting rejoinder to his accuser, might actually have been *kan*, the word for 'cunt'. The repartee of Murik joking partners is called *gwaga'iin* in their vernacular, which means 'play talk', and is translated as *tokpilai* in Tok Pisin. But 'to play' in Murik always has a lewd and sexually charged connotation. So Frankie's gibe, 'You like to plough corn!', might just as well have been, 'You like to plough cunt!'. The voice in line 7 would seem to confirm this interpretation. Certainly, men's joking discourse consists in large part in creating and reveling in just this kind of bawdy *double-entendre.* It is an antic discourse in which Murik ribaldry mocks Murik virtue. Interpreting dialogical relations between the discourse of 'court' and Murik comedy challenges both me and the reader, who would emphasize either the legal or the comedic metaphor whenever it comes into play, with a tricky methodological problem. The law may radiate influence beyond its official confines (Santos 1987), but, in the local setting, so does Murik comedy. Clearly, the voices of one and the other were immersed within each other so thoroughly on this occasion that neither may be afforded a clear analytical priority. The entertainment was not in any ultimate sense 'about' the law, a 'judge', or 'a trial'. It was a satire, simultaneously 'about' both the law and Murik personhood.

10. 'Judge' Smith: Mama bilong meri bilong yu salim tok tasol em laik maritim yu ken?
[The mother of your wife sent word that she wants to marry you again?]
11. Frankie: Mi, eh?
12. 'Judge' Smith: Yeah.
13. … Voice: Na yu lukim, em krongutim mauntin na em i lukim em.
[Look, he tramped up 'the mountain' and went to her.]
14. … 'Judge' Smith: Em i nogut. Dispela meri ia, em mama ia. Em karim em. Na yu kisim em, yutupela slip, kerap. Yu gat pikinini. Wai bai yu go ontap long mama ken?
[He is immoral! This woman, she is a mother. She gave birth [to your wife]. You took her, you slept with her, got up. You have a child. Why did you mount this mother again?]

In Murik, affinal decorum between mother and daughter's husband should be shame-ridden and deferential. Largely mute, in this avoidance relationship only a minimum of face-to-face, direct communication ought to take place. Moreover, as I argued in *Mangrove man* (1997), concepts of the 'good' and the 'right' are a part of an ongoing dialogue about the reproduction of moral personhood. In Murik culture, an idealized vision of new motherhood, particularly in 'her' qualities of nurture, unconditional generosity, and chastity, contends against, and runs counter to, the assertion of more self-centred aspects of experience. Frankie, having allegedly had an affair with his wife's mother, was accused of having gone 'up the mountain' to her in line 13, which is to say, he had climbed an inclined path to Boig village, located just inland from the Murik Lakes, or had climbed up onto her 'mountain'. Line 6 refers to a major theme of the incessant parody that goes on between the classificatory mother's brother and his sister's son: the scandals and grotesque embodiments of 'immoral men' (*nor mwaro*). Endowed with a huge phallus and boundless appetite for erotic intrigue, his id answers the quietist, maternal ethics enacted in siblingship, conjugal fidelity, and affinal etiquette. The accusation levelled in lines 10 and 14 by 'Judge' Smith against 'defendant' Frankie immersed 'the court' in the moral imagination of Murik comedy and momentarily removed it from judicial mimicry. Was this an actual, 'real' allegation? Or, was the 'judge' creating it in the spirit of cultural whimsy? Whether true or false, Frankie was willing to 'play' with the charge levelled against him in two ways: first, he was willing (below, in lines 15 and 19) to oblige his mother's brother, whom he would otherwise tease in kind, and, secondly, he was willing to reject the charge as if it were genuine.

15. ... Frankie:	Em i no mama tru bilong dispela meri nau mi maritim. [[She] is not the 'true' mother of the woman I just married.]
16. Beldon:	Sapos olesem – [If so –]
17. ... Frankie:	(*laughter*) Mi nogat wanpela rong bilong mi, tasol yupela pointim mi ... [(*laughter*) I have not committed a crime, yet you accuse me ...]
18. Voice:	(*inaudible*) ...
19. Frankie:	Em mama bilong dispela meri ... [She is the mother of this woman ...]
20. DL:	Em konpes! [He confessed!]

As a result of difficulty in making out the words on my tape, it is not clear to me what exactly was going on during this sequence. But I think that two key points can be made here. One is that Frankie was drawing the ordinary Murik distinction between a biological and adoptive relationship which is evident in his use of the word, 'true'.[17] The other is that while using this term to try to dispute the mock-allegation, Frankie code-shifted in line 17 back to mock 'trial' mimicry. Here, the desire to repudiate 'the charge' against him and to defend his honour has motivated a movement away from joking discourse and back to the caricature of official, legal language. A third, less evident point, but one about which I am also reasonably confident, is how much the ethos of this moment was one of merriment and farce. I must 'confess': I too was in its thrall, and my enchantment is demonstrated by the sudden, peremptory report of my verdict upon the 'proceedings' (line 20).

21.	... 'Judge' Smith:	Nau, dispela meri bilong we? [Now, where is the girl from?]
22.	Frankie:	Em bilong Boig. [She is from Boig.]
23.	... 'Judge' Smith:	Yu wet, yu yet. Yu save olsem dispela. Hau bai dispela meri i kom na i stap long Boig? [You wait a second! You know this. How did [your wife] end up in Boig?]
24.	Frankie:	OK, mi stori pastaim na yu bai yu harim, eh? [OK, I will tell you and you will hear it, eh?]
25.	... 'Judge' Smith:	Dispela pikinini taim ol i kisim em, hau ol i kisim em? Em kom olsem wanem? Em kom stap long Boig? – [When they took this child, how did they do it? How did she come ... to Boig? –]
26.	Frankie:	Taim liklik boi bilongem i dai, OK, em kisim dispela pikinini meri i kom, no kom stap wantaim ol. Na taim mi maritim meri ia tu, mi no maritim em long Boig. [When the little boy died, OK, they adopted this little girl and she came and stayed with them. And when I married her, I didn't marry her in Boig.]
27.	'Judge' Smith:	Yu maritim em we? [Where did you marry her?]
28.	Frankie:	Mi maritim em autsait, long Angoram. [I married her in Angoram, outside of the village.]
29.	... 'Judge' Smith:	Long Angoram, em bin stap wantaim husat? [In Angoram, with whom was she staying?]
30.	Frankie:	Em stap wantaim bikpela susa bilongem, marit long Joseph Aigut ia. Stori ia, em i klia nau? [She was staying with her elder sister who is married to Joseph Aigut. Is the story now clear?]
31.	... 'Judge' Smith:	Nogat, em i no go stret long tingting bilong mi yet. [No, I still haven't sorted this out yet in my head.]
32.	Frankie:	Yu tok. [You talk.]
33.	... 'Judge' Smith:	OK, lukim, sapos na meri bilongyu kom na mi askim em? [OK, what if your wife comes here and I myself ask her?]
34.	Frankie:	OK, mi bai mi go long Point na bai mi kisim meri ia i kom na bai mi askim em, 'yu kom long wanem ples tru?' [OK, I will go to the Point and I will get her and ... ask her, 'Where do you truly come from?']

Epistemologically, contexts of legal pluralism engender a labile view of knowledge. Notice that laughter, and the moral imagination of Murik comedy, have subsided and yielded to a relatively earnest, magisterial mode of investigation throughout this segment. 'The judge' critically examines Frankie's claim that his wife was adopted (lines 21 ff.) and in so doing assumes control and asserts his mock-authority. He wants to establish how mother and daughter came to their relationship and implies that Frankie can provide 'objective' answers to his questions (line 23). Notice as well how unevasive Frankie is. He willingly complies with 'Judge' Smith (line 24). His wife, he grants, was adopted by a woman from one of the horticultural villages inland from the Murik Lakes.[18] However, Frankie emphasizes the disconnection in her relationship to Boig village by citing 'the fact' that he married her elsewhere, namely, in Angoram, the district seat (lines 26-30). As the questioning develops, Frankie, 'the defendant', seems to be winning his case. He agrees to bring his wife to 'court' and have her 'testify' about her origins (line 34). Previously,

Frankie switched from Murik parody to judicial parody. In what ensues below, 'the judge' takes the opposite tack for a moment before combining the two voices with a non-verbal flourish. In response, Frankie answers in the voice of official mimicry, but quickly returns to that of Murik parody.

35. 'Judge' Smith:	Yu harim tu? Na olesem adoptim pikinini, tasol, em i adoptim pikinini, em i stret. Em mama pinis bilongen. Na yu rong! Em i rong long komantap longen! ... [Did you hear? Adopted the child. They adopted the girl! ... She is her mother. You are immoral! It was immoral to mount her!]
36. Frankie:	OK.
37. ... 'Judge' Smith:	Rong i kamap olsem; (*sotto voce*) yu kwapim mama bilongyu! [A crime has been committed; (*sotto voce*) you screwed your mother!]
38. Frankie:	Na mi laik save, husat tru i lukim mi kwapim em? [I want to know, who really saw me screw her?]
39. Voices:	Ehhhhhh!
40. Frankie:	Mi laik save. [I want to know.]
41. 'Judge' Smith:	Andrew i lukim yu. [Andrew saw you.]
42. ... Frankie:	Yu holim stik bilongem liklik tu? [Have you held his stick a little too?]
43. 'Judge' Smith:	Mi no holim stik bilongem. Nau [Andrew] i tokim mi olesem, mi lukim – [I haven't held his stick. Now [Andrew] has spoken to me, 'I saw –]
44. Frankie:	Ah. Em i tokim yu. [Ah. He spoke to you.]
45. 'Judge' Smith:	Em tokim mi, yu kwapim mama bilong meri bilongyu. [He told me that you screwed the mother of your wife.]

In line 37, the voice in which 'the judge' makes his accusation – namely, that Frankie had 'screwed his mother' – combined judicial parody with Murik affinal terminology according to which a man's mother-in-law may both be addressed and referred to as 'mother.' When Frankie demands to know the identity of 'the witness' to his alleged indiscretion (line 38), the thought of watching such an act provoked a squeamish chorus of culturally normative revulsion (line 39). This is a particularly notable moment in the dialogue. Frankie's demand for an eyewitness testimony is asserted in both a Murik and legal voice, which overlap momentarily, the Murik also being absorbed, like the court, in maintaining a cultural distinction between representation, appearances and reality, beginning in early childhood. Retreating, Frankie shifts from this double parody back to the conventional script and the pseudo-aggressive ethos of Murik male comedy (line 42). Citing the reported speech of a corroborating witness as authoritative, the 'judge' reiterates the charge, no longer in a stage whisper, but now in an uncompromising double voice, which was at once a mock 'formal allegation' delivered in terms characteristic of Murik parody (line 45). He goes on in the latter.

46. ... 'Judge' Smith:	Yu kon man! Harim, yu kon man, kon man! [You are a *kon* man! Listen, you are a *kon* man, a *kon* man!]
47. DL:	(*laughs*)
48. Frankie:	(*laughs*) Hey!

49. 'Judge' Smith:	Luke, yu kom! OK, [*to Frankie*] toktok bilongyu em i go olsem, yu laik papa long dispela mama bilongyu ken! [Luke, come here. OK, the complaint against you [Frankie] has gone this way: you are accused of having wanted to be a father with your mother again!]
50. Frankie:	No!
51. ... 'Judge' Smith:	Na sapos yu wokim em olsem, yu mas kalabus! [If you did this, you must go to jail!]
52. Frankie:	No, na yu rong olegeta [No, you are completely wrong.]
53. ... 'Judge' Smith:	Olsem, yu man bilong haitim tok! Dispela em i bikpela rong!! [You keep secrets! This is very immoral!]
54. Frankie:	Kot i save olsem mi wanpela hanes man! [The court knows that I am an honest man!]
55. 'Judge' Smith:	Yu kon man! [You are a *kon* man!]
56. Frankie:	(*laughs*)
57. 'Judge' Smith:	Kot i tok olsem, yu kon man. [The court has spoken: you are a *kon* man.]
58. Frankie:	(*laughs*)
59. 'Judge' Smith:	Long kon bilong yu, yu mas kalabus! [On account of your [interest in] *kon*, you must go to jail!]

Frankie stands 'accused' of having been and wanting again to be 'a father' with the woman again (line 49). In other words, he is 'charged' with having asserted and wanting to reassert the sexual privileges of a husband in a wife, except that 'the wife' was, in the event, his wife's mother. 'The judge' concludes that 'the defendant' must be incarcerated should this be so (line 51). The playful *double-entendre*, involving the use of the word for corn, returns us to the conventional repartee of Murik joking, which is now expanded to impugn the character of 'the defendant' as a whole (line 55). This reproach is joined with an insubordinate caricature of the judicial authority of the state. 'The court has spoken,' the 'Judge' declares to Frankie, 'you are a *kon* man!' (line 57). Frankie continues to protest. Again, the two voices have become dialogically fused to the great amusement of the actors (line 59). A double parody of both Murik personhood and law has been momentarily synthesized. In what follows, Frankie and 'Judge' Smith persist in this double-voiced play.

Frankie, amused, brashly likens himself to a 'one-fish' man. In *Tok Pisin*, 'one-fish' refers to a loner (a fish, who doesn't swim with the school); it refers, perhaps, to a shameless rake, or a rogue, that is, to an individualist who is above both custom and law (see also Epstein 1999: 24). 'Judge' Smith takes a dubious view of the tag, and instantly translates it into the terms of Murik comedy.

60. Frankie:	(*laughs*) Mi papa bilong wan pis! [(laughs) I am the greatest 'one-fish' man of all!]
61. ... 'Judge' Smith:	Wan pis man nogut ia. Yu save kisim K2 na passim long kok bilongyu na soim long meri. Long dispela kain pasin olsem, mipela tok olsem 'wan pis'. Long dispela pasin nogut yu wokim bai yu mas kalabus! Yu harim! [You are a deviant 'one-fish' man. You like to take a 2 Kina note and tie it to your cock and show it to women. For this kind of decadence, we call you 'one-fish'! For this immoral behaviour, you must go to jail! You hear!]

62. ... Voice:	Wan pis kalabus wan wik pinis. ['One-fish' has already served one week in jail.]
63. Frankie:	Em lait, eh? [It is late, eh?]
64. ... 'Judge' Smith:	Pasin nogut bilongyu ia long soim samting bilongyu long ples klia. [What perversity! You exposed yourself in public!]
65. Frankie:	Kot i pinis eh? [Court is over, eh?]
66. 'Judge' Smith:	Kot i pinis ia. [Court is over now.]

While imputations of depravity and sexual licence are staple fare in Murik male comedy, one particular detail in 'the judge's' redefinition of a 'one-fish' man deserves further comment (line 61). 'The judge' suggests that 'the defendant' solicited his wife's mother to perform an act of prostitution by tying a currency note to his penis, a '2 kina woman' being slang for a prostitute. Both the language of the investigation, the colonial lingua franca, Tok Pisin, and the monetized phallus, as an image of procurement, remind us of the thorough embeddedness of Murik culture within the post-colonial state.

'Judge' Smith then went on to reiterate his view that 'the defendant' ought to serve time and put an end to 'the deliberations'. The real world returned to awareness: Frankie announces that time has passed and a moment later, word arrived that some trading partners would not show up as expected to sell sago. People dispersed anyway. Nothing more happened, although in subsequent days I heard a number of people making mock threats to resume 'the trial'.

Play and legal reality in a post-colonial moment

In the 1960s and 1970s, studies of legal change explored the ways in which law can sometimes reshape local culture (e.g. Burman & Harrell-Bond 1979). Law was widely thought to be a strong force for modernization. Since the 1980s, it has been viewed more cautiously. Its influence on indigenous order has been construed as incremental, sometimes even negligible. Indigenous cultures have come to be seen as possessing the resilience to 'resist and circumvent penetration or even capture and use the symbolic capital of state law' (Merry 1988: 881). There are, as I have shown, expressive dimensions of this resilient relationship, as well as instrumental ones. However, so far as I know, the law as a discursive medium, particularly as imagined from the standpoints of such vital cultures – whether comically, inquisitively, defiantly, or fearfully – has not been theorized at all.

In anthropology, understanding the relationship between comedy and moral order has posed a long-standing problem for social theory. Durkheim's disciple, Radcliffe-Brown, viewed mock-disrespect in joking relationships as a means by which individuals related through marriage might substitute sham conflicts for real ones (1940). Gluckman developed the orthodox view of the relationship of comedy to political hierarchy in analyses of Swazi and Zulu 'rites of rebellion'. Ritual licence, expressed in mock-contempt for and mock-denunciations of the king, ultimately results in the preservation of a status quo. 'The conflicts can be stated openly when the social order is ... indubitable – when there are rebels and not revolutionaries. In such a system, the licensed statement of conflict can bless ... order' (Gluckman 1956: 134). This, then, is an approach which treats rites of rebellion – including their satirical and comic elements – in a way that presupposes the sovereignty of authority, thus providing a model of social control in which potential fissures within the polity are invariably neutralized.[19]

This rather conservative view of the relationship of adult joking, as well as ritual licence, to socio-political structure echoes or adheres to the two-level Aristotelian model – consisting of play that mimics, responds to, and supports the wider values of society – long favoured in psychological and anthropological studies of pretending among children (see e.g. Garvey & Berndt 1977; Groos 1901; G.H. Mead 1934; Schwartzman 1978; cf. Raum 1940). In these studies, play is generally represented as an activity through which children represent, reproduce and thus begin to experience cultural reality by means of make-believe. As Piaget put it, by first pretending to be themselves and then to be others, children start vicariously to learn to assimilate the ego to the demands of role-play in the wider world (1962: 145). However, 'the trial' not only mimicked the post-colonial court system, but constituted an additional flight of fancy from it. It was a parody, that is to say, of both Murik male joking relationships and of the legal world. 'The trial' engendered a double transformation of reality rather than a single one. It played on everyday relations in village Murik culture and on the legal institutions of the post-colonial state. L. Goldman has made an analogous argument about the play of Huli children, which he has singled out as 'double-play' (1998: 101). When these children enact a theme of play, such as hunting or going to the hospital, they sing about it in melodies drawn from Huli mythology (*bi te*). 'Players are ... enmeshed in symbolic play both within the underlying ... fantasy and at the level of the overlaying genre modality' (Goldman 1998: 101). According to Goldman, the propensity to juxtapose voices indicates a dynamic willingness to 'play with the playframe' (Bretherton 1989: 384), a disposition that provides them with a means or a device to refresh their pretending. 'The cultural repositories of fantasy are raided and reinvented ... not just with respect to themes, but also with respect to aspects of form, motif and performance' (Goldman 1998: 143).

The disposition creatively to bring in and combine voices in play – possibly new voices with old – raises the question of how play may be related to history. As it happens, this is a question that is now in the foreground of contemporary anthropological theory about comic licence. Functionalist views of comedy as supporting the status quo have now been displaced by the view that comedy may express ambivalent attitudes about external forces and foreign authority. '[T]his is the heuristic significance of ... clowning: the clown – a highly opinionated moralist – points baldly ... to ... prickly issues of everyday life and beyond' (Mitchell 1992: 19, 24).The open-ended power of state-based and globalized forces has inspired the weak to use what Fernandez has called 'tropes of indirection' (2001: 87). Satirical or ironic voices today resist and defy officialdom and globalization. Instead of consolidating moral order in the locality, play is now widely seen to provide marginal citizens with a brief illusion of mastery over worlds that are becoming ever more intractable and unresponsive (Herzfeld 2001).[20]

Some years ago, the literary critic Northrop Frye (1957: 33-5) created a view of the relationship of modes of fiction – including comedy – to figures of authority which I find useful, as it is more comprehensive than that developed in socio-cultural anthropology. Building on interpretation of Aristotle's *Poetics* (1953: 18-19), Frye argued that fictional heroes should not be classified on the basis of their moral standing, but instead according to the degree to which their power to act is superior, equal, or inferior to that of the audience or of other men in their social and natural environments. If superior in kind, then the hero becomes a divine being and the story about him Frye classed as mythic. If superior in degree, the hero is merely an human who moves through worlds, the rules of which are only slightly suspended for him. Prodigious acts of courage and endurance which are unnatural to most are taken for granted by him, and the enchanted weapons, talking animals, terrifying ogres, and talismans of power violate no rule in this world. These stories are legends, folk-tales, and so forth. If superior in degree to other men, but not to nature, the hero is just a leader. He has authority, passion, and power which outweigh those of other men, but what he does is nevertheless subject to criticism and to the laws of nature. Such men are heroes of what Frye calls 'the high mimetic mode' of epic and tragedy. 'If superior neither to other men nor to his environment, the hero is one of us' (Frye 1957: 34). Such a hero is found in 'low mimetic' modes of fiction, to which he assigns 'most comedy and realistic fiction'. The hero is subject to the same laws of probability that we find in our own experience. When, lastly, a fictional hero is represented as inferior in power or intelligence to others, so that the audience receives a sense of looking down on a scene of slavery, frustration, or absurdity, 'the hero', says Frye, 'belongs to the ironic mode' of fiction.

In this final section, I wish to use Frye's correlations, not to produce a typology of European fiction as he did, but as an heuristic device to help in clarifying representations of the law in colonial and post-colonial political settings. I tabularize these relationships in the Table.

TABLE. Northrop Frye's adaptation of Aristotle's classification of fiction-correlated, changing political-legal orders

Culture	Historical moment	Relationship of the state/ hero to society		Fictional mode
Modern	First contact	Superior	In kind	Myth
	Colonial	Superior	To a great degree	Legend
Post-modern	Post-colonial	Superior	To a small degree	High mimetic mode: tragedy or epic
	Post-colonial	Equal	–	Low mimetic mode: comedy or realistic fiction
		Inferior	–	Ironic mode of fiction

My central claim, in brief, is this: as power relations between indigene and the state become less differentiated, popular representations of the law may shift, possibly reflecting the increased symmetry. In order to show how this point may relate to my Murik data, I need to turn back to a moment of high colonialism, when Papua and New Guinea were separate Mandated Territories which were both administered by Australia. I mentioned earlier that Sir Hubert Murray served as head administrator for the Australian government (1908-40). In Papua and New Guinea, unlike many African colonies, no deliberate effort was made to bring indigenous forms of conflict resolution into the colonial justice system. As was noted above, Murray viewed Melanesian societies as primitive, vulnerable, and in need of paternalistic protection. He himself had received legal training and held the position of chief judicial officer of the Territory. He held that Western law was a powerful transformative force but stressed the need to limit the use of force in pacification, dismissing punitive expeditions as 'swift injustice' (Murray 1925: 6).

In 1930, while in the Papuan Gulf, Murray – who was devoted to the pioneering task of extending government control through patrolling – spent a day with members of the London Missionary Society at Fyfe Bay. He was entertained by a little performance staged by villagers which he described in a letter to a son.[21] In the skit, an old woman is murdered by four men. The woman's son tries to gain revenge, but the perpetrators escape.

> ... [A] village constable ... appeared ... who reported the crime; and then appeared the Assistant Resident Magistrate – the quaintest figure you can imagine with a white cardboard mask, a shocking bad hat, a worse coat, and trousers and boots that were simply impossible. He sat down on a chair at a table (which suddenly appeared from nowhere in particular) with two half coconuts connected by a piece of string to denote a telephone. He rang up the Resident Magistrate and told him of the murder, and sent the Village Constable away to make the necessary arrest.
>
> A regular policeman now turned up and he and the Village Constable [VC] brought in the culprits on a rope, and the trial began. It was a queer trial. The Assistant Resident Magistrate [ARM] told the VC to 'shut up', called one of the prisoners a monkey, convicted them all, and sent them to Daru. As they were led away he suddenly remembered that he had not passed sentence and shouted 'six months' after them as they disappeared. Then the ARM danced ... among the audience, all the actors ... bowed their acknowledgments of the wild applause ... It was quite fun; some of them were ... natural comedians, especially one boy who took the part of the old woman, and who afterwards appeared during the trial with a beard and moustache, playing the fool ... and being hit on the head by the ARM (West 1970: 123-5).

In this visit by Murray to Fyfe Bay, what kind of Aristotelian hero was he personifying to the villagers and what kind of heroes were the villagers playing for him? As lieutenant-governor, he would have been classed by the villagers, at the very least, as superior in degree to them. From their point of view, he moved through a world in which he made the rules, in other words, one in which the rules were slightly suspended for him. Thus he might well have been seen as the stuff of legend. But for Murray, the villagers were inferior 'primitives', inferior in power and intelligence to himself and his civilization. Their 'queer trial' was absurd to him. They were 'natural comedians' whom Frye might have classed as staging an ironic mode of fiction.

Of course, I must concede that the contexts of Murray writing informally to his son in 1930 and me writing for a disciplinary audience in 2003 are not in the least equivalent. Still, I think interesting and obvious power differentials emerge between Fyfe Bay and Darapap when we look at the contrasting socio-political contexts behind the two performances. The post-colonial state is no longer a foreign sovereignty but a Melanesian one. I return to the village, not as legendary colonial official, but merely as anthropologist and fictive kin, who is classed by the Darapap as a member of the employed, urban middle class. The performance is staged not for me but for the amusement of the villagers themselves. Of course, I tape-recorded it, but, like everyone else present, I engage in 'the prosecution' of Frankie, who is also viewed as one of my classificatory joking partners. Power differentials, in short, have been reduced.

This greater equality also finds representation in the plots of the two performances. The Fyfe Bay villagers caricature colonial law realistically. 'The defendants' are brought in tied to a rope. The satirical figure of the ARM, with his 'shocking bad hat', 'impossible' clothes, and coconut telephone, is also that of a bully. Rough and insulting, he hits 'a man' and orders the actor playing the constable to keep quiet. Unilaterally, he convicts all 'the defendants', sends them off to serve a sentence in an urban jail, but, evincing a moment of human fallibility, he forgets to specify its length. The skit was 'great fun', according to Murray, and was greeted by 'wild applause'. The villagers mocked the colonial administration, reducing the degree of its superiority to create a momentary illusion of equality.

By introducing the metaphor of 'a trial' into their incessant cultural comedy, the Darapap (or at least a few men, on a particular day)[22] suggest that the generic ridicule and fantasy with which they conventionally tease each other could be easily identified as a legal institution. From Frye's point of view, we might say that this act of metaphorization is an implicit nullification of difference: the one court of law is being held up as socially, politically, and conceptually equivalent to the other. At the same time, the alleged indiscretion committed by Frankie, the sister's son, was no less the object of his mothers' brothers' mockery than were courts and judges. Parodic attitudes to both the state and its judicial system, as well as Murik personhood, were simultaneously at play that day. Thus we heard 'the judge' savouring the salaciousness of his double-voiced accusation when he declared to 'defendant' Frankie, not in the full voice of judicial authority, but under his breath: 'You screwed your mother.' And we heard 'the defendant' happily questioning 'the judge' about whether a witness had 'held his stick'. In Bakhtin's view (1984*b*), this kind of carnivalesque revelry transgresses and disrupts ordinary hierarchy and canon. Through what he called 'grotesque realism', norms might be undermined, and all that was marginalized and excluded might take centre stage. By admitting an image of 'the judge' into their ongoing Melanesian carnival, the Murik were simultaneously mocking and acknowledging his elevated status, denying yet affirming the unbridgeable inequities that would otherwise separate and estrange them from the state. The contrast between the ambivalent colonial performance at Fyfe Bay in 1930 and the post-colonial one in Darapap in 2001 could hardly be rendered more plainly. The one exclusively satirized the state and the villagers' powerlessness in relationship to it, while the other mocked the weakened, post-colonial state and Murik personhood.

In this article, I have shown that the relationship between law and culture may be dialogical, dialogical in the sense that both may assimilate each other (cf. Galanter 1981). An ambivalent attitude about both law and culture emerged that day in the villagers' comedy. Their impromptu 'trial' provided a pleasurable – though deeply contradictory – illusion of mastery shared between a group of people at a difficult and daunting post-colonial moment. 'The trial' became dialogized as both a Murik institution and a state institution. Yet it was neither of these, since, of course, the performance was a fantasy.

Appropriately, the 'court-house' stood as the only evidence of state-sponsored economic development in their community, but the Haus Sola was empty at that time. Nevertheless, their world remained problematically dependent upon the state's resources, above all on its economy and system of education. The makeshift 'trial' held on an ordinary day in January 2001 transformed the drift of rural alienation and subordination into a moment of low mimetic comedy (cf. Limon 1989). In their simulated world, the legal system was no longer foreign, but was locally administered and no longer beyond their command or criticism. Ironically, the law in PNG had become so unreliable as to be worthy of only just this kind of now-you-see-it-now-you-don't sort of emulation.

In the late 1960s, Peter Lawrence concluded that 'the ordinary villager [in PNG] cannot be expected to assimilate a legal system which is entirely foreign to his social system' (1969: 35). However, if Gilbert Ryle is correct (1949: 244, 250; see also Bateson 1956), the cognitive shift to mockery and make-believe reflects a higher order of attitude, sensibility, and belief than those of realism and authenticity. The meanings of mockery or parody, however creative and critical, must fail without a prior structure, that is without rules defining a prior reality. I take Ryle to exemplify a major position within the study of play: a view that play rehearses and makes imaginative sense of prototypical roles and value frameworks in as well as of the social world (Fortes 1938; Furth 1996; Goldman & Smith 1998). In the light of this perspective, it would seem that thirty years on, Lawrence's characterization invites reassessment. The foregoing, albeit ephemeral, moment of street-theatre drew upon a post-colonial environment that was informed by dialogized concepts of order, rather than unrelated ones. As many have observed, this state of legal heteroglossia has disrupted order and 'weakened' the law, and, no doubt, they are right. But the circumstances ought to be defined more comprehensively. Semiotically, I should say, PNG has itself become a dialogized form in local discourse, a state whose meaning is both Melanesian and Western, rather than either the one or the other.

I have argued in this article that the focus of legal pluralism, and more generally, that of legal studies in PNG and elsewhere, might well become somewhat less literal. In addition to the ways in which law and local remedies may be deployed to resolve disputes and regulate behaviour so as to maintain the status quo, it might attend to the ways in which the law may become a metaphor in constructions of the relationship of both the sovereignty of the state and local personhood. In the case of Murik parody, the image of 'a trial' disclosed ambivalences about these two institutions. That is, it conveyed not just resistance to or acceptance of the law and Murik morality, but gave voice to contradictory attitudes towards both at once. Although 'the prosecution' of Frankie was incorporated into an ongoing genre of indigenous satire, and was not intended as serious or 'real', I must emphasize that I do not view the law as either a tactical resource or a discursive one. The mock 'trial' staged by Murik comedians should rather be seen as possessing multiple significances, each of which may be analytically distinguishable while yet belonging to a single, dialogized reality. Here, however, for the purpose of advancing what I take to be this new, or at least underappreciated, methodological point, I have chosen to foreground the expressive over the political dimension of the law.

NOTES

Fieldwork for this article was conducted between December 2000 and January 2001 and was funded by the Anthropology Department of the University of Minnesota. It benefited from generous criticism by Jamon Halvaskv, Simon Harrison, Mary Huber, Mischa Penn, Stephen Gudeman, Geoffrey White, and two anonymous *JRAI* readers. It stands in memory of A.L. 'Bill' Epstein, who inadvertently encouraged me in developing the idea for it shortly before he died.

[1] My choice of title is with dubious acknowledgement of, and obvious apologies to, Kafka (1937/1955).

[2] Several solutions to the plural relationship between law and society have been proposed: see Griffiths (1986), Fitzpatrick (1984), Moore (1978), and Santos (1977; 1987).

[3] There were two initial phases in legal pluralism studies (Merry 1988). In the first, the focus was on colonial and post-colonial contexts, where 'whole legal systems' have been imposed 'across cultural boundaries' (Benda-Beckmann [1979]; Hazlehurst [1995]; Hooker [1975: 1]); in the second, the concern has been with legal pluralism in modern, capitalist societies (Moore [1978]; Merry [1986]). In a more recent third phase identified by Santos (1995: e.g. cf. Teubner 1997), the focus has turned from indigenous, local-level, legal orders pre-existing the state to an emphasis on legal orders that coexist in the world system over and above both state and intrastate societies. In contrast, Tie (1999) has identified three different types of legal pluralism: post-realist, post-modern, and post-pragmatist. Benton (1999) has pointed out that in India and elsewhere, judicial practices changed during the colonial period from being permissive and open to closed and hierarchical.

[4] Lips, however, did not see ambivalence in the figure of a judge created by a West African that he found in a collection in Cologne: 'All the terror which [the artist] ... may have felt, on learning the verdict, has found its concentration in the heavily conventional form, which he has placed in rigid symmetry on the judge's bench. The expression of the eyes, which is not altogether human, was obtained by inserting pieces of glass. The mouth shows no trace of kindly impulse. Above the stony face is poised the tupê. The enormous projecting ears hear everything, while the shoulders are exaggerated in breadth, and denote the power and efficiency of the jurist' (1937: 209-10).

[5] I do not mean to essentialize the notion of indigenous discourse as static or immune to transformation. Eberhard refers to relativist legal communication as 'dialogical' (2001), but this usage is very different from mine.

[6] See M. Mead (1935) on Mundugumor joking relationships, Bateson (1953) on Iatmul mockery, and Barlow (1992) on the clowning of Murik women. See also Lipset & Silverman (forthcoming) for a comparison of Iatmul and Murik ritual comedy, and the well-known film, *Trobriand cricket*, for satirical images of Western tourists and sports. And see Counts & Counts (1992) on the performances of ritual clowns during weddings and other rites among the Lusi-Kaliai of New Britain, and Sinavaiana (1992) on the performances of comic sketches that ridicule both local and Western figures of authority in Samoa.

[7] Subsequent studies catalogued remedies practised elsewhere in Melanesia, as if they were uninfluenced by the colonial state (e.g. Burridge [1957]; Epstein [1974]; Fortune [1947]; Sack [1972]; Young [1974]). Recently, Papua New Guineans have been seen as an oppressed

peasantry (Fitzpatrick [1980]) negotiating legally plural contexts (Scaglion [1976]; A. Strathern [1972]; M. Strathern [1972]; Westermark [1986]). See also Watson-Gegeo & White (1990) for a Pacific-wide anthology of conflict-resolution practices.

[8] 'I do not know of any tribe ... [in the country] by whom anything even remotely resembling administration of justice has been attempted, nor do I know of any part of [it] ... where native administration of justice could be introduced, with any prospect but the certainty of absolute failure' (Murray quoted in Mattes 1969: 79).

[9] To the east was the Trust Territory of the United Nations and to the west was the Australian colony of Papua. Both were separately administered by Australia. They were divided by language differences, colonial resentments, and lack of travel by both indigenes and officials.

[10] Thus Hasluck wrote that, '[t]rials, conducted in the district where the alleged crime took place, with ... full ceremony ... and with ... due care ... introduced the idea of justice and the idea of substituting punishment by the State for revenge in the hands of the individual' (1976: 81). A district officer, by contrast, concluded that '[t]o the indigene, the Supreme Court is part of the Government, and its aloofness, incomprehensibility, inconsistency, and weakness are the faults of the Government, and justice is manifestly not done' (Fenbury 1978: 138).

[11] Other courts have been created including local land mediators, Local Land Courts, and District Land Courts which arbitrate conflicts between Incorporate Land Groups, the legal entities empowered via legislation in 1974 to recognize customary land-holding groups. These groups have become increasingly popular since 1992, with large increases in registration taking place. These courts have not been established, however, either in the Murik Lakes or in the Lower Sepik District.

[12] See Goddard (1992; 1995; 1996; 1998), Harris (1988), Kulick (1993), Roscoe (1999), and Sykes (2000).

[13] And private security companies.

[14] While doing doctoral research together with Kathleen Barlow.

[15] In 1999, for example, police appeared in Darapap in connection with marijuana use and beat up several young men.

[16] These were young to middle-aged, village-raised men with four to six years of primary education as well as various work experiences throughout PNG.

[17] The 'true', or *nogo*, relationship is contrasted in the Murik vernacular with either 'taken' (*sangait*), the adoptive relationship, or with nonsense and fantasy (*kakowi*) or humour (*gwaga'iin*). The latter is the discourse of matrilateral joking partners who belong to the male cult.

[18] Historically, a marriage taboo existed between the gardening and the fishing villages. This broke down to a limited extent after the imposition of colonial rule.

[19] See Apte (1985), Douglas (1975), Handelman and Kapferer (1972), and Turner (1982).

[20] See Basso (1979) and Errington and Gewertz (1995: 77-106).

[21] My thanks to Michael Goddard for alerting me to this incident.

[22] How typical is the idiom of 'the trial'? The mockery between classificatory mothers' brothers and sisters' sons is absolutely typical of daily Murik life. The import of the legal metaphor is one of a perpetual flow of metaphors, both local and modern, that are brought into the discourse of this joking relationship, some others being touristic, religious, maternal, political, and overseas trading.

REFERENCES

Apte, M.L. 1985. *Humor and laughter: an anthropological approach*. Ithaca, NY: Cornell University Press.

Aristotle 1953. *Aristotle on the art of fiction: an English translation of* The poetics (trans. L.J. Potts). Cambridge: University Press.

Bakhtin, M. 1984*a*. *Problems of Dostoevsky's poetics* (trans. C. Emerson). Minneapolis: University of Minnesota Press.

——— 1984*b*. *Rabelais and his world* (trans. H. Iswolsky). Bloomington: Indiana University Press.

Barlow, K. 1992. Dance when I die! context and role in the clowning of Murik women. In *Clowning as critical practice* (ed.) W. Mitchell, 58-87. Pittsburgh: University Press.

Barnett, T.E. 1969. The local court magistrate and the settlement of disputes. In *Fashion of law in New Guinea* (eds) B.J. Brown & G. Sawer, 159-80. Sydney: Butterworths.

Basso, K. 1979. *Portraits of 'the whiteman': linguistic play and cultural symbols among the Western Apache*. Cambridge: University Press.

Bateson, G. 1953. The position of humor in human communication. In *Cybernetics: circular, causal and feedback mechanisms in biological and social sciences: transactions of the ninth conference* (ed.) H. von Foerster, 1-47. New York: Josiah Macy Jr. Foundation.

——— 1956. The message: 'this is play'. In *Conference on group processes: transactions of the second conference* (ed.) B. Schaffner, 145-242. New York: Josiah Macy Jr. Foundation.

Benda-Beckmann, F. von. 1979. *Property in social continuity: social continuity and change in the maintenance of property relationships through time in Minangkabau, West Sumatra*. The Hague: Martinus Nijhoff.

Benton, L. 1999. Colonial law and cultural difference: jurisdictional politics and the formation of the colonial state. *Comparative Studies in History and Society* **41**, 561-88.

Bretherton, I. 1989. Pretense: the form and function of make-believe play. *Developmental Review* **9**, 383-401.

Burman, S.B. & B.E. Harrell-Bond (eds) 1979. *The imposition of law*. New York: Academic Press.

Burridge, K. 1957. Disputing in Tangu. *American Anthropologist* **59**, 763-80.

Chalmers, D.R.C. & A.H. Paliwala 1977. *An introduction to the law in Papua New Guinea*. London: Sweet & Maxwell.

Counts, D. & D. Counts 1992. Exaggeration and reversal: clowning among the Lusi Kaliai. In *Clowning as critical practice: performance humor in the South Pacific* (ed.) W. Mitchell, 88-103. Pittsburgh: University Press.

Derham, D. 1963. Law and custom in the Australian Territory of Papua and New Guinea. *The University of Chicago Law Review* **30**, 495-506.

Dinnen, S. 1998. Law, order and state. In *Modern Papua New Guinea* (ed.) L. Zimmer-Tamakoshi, 333-50. Kirksville, Mo.: Thomas Jefferson Press.

——— 2000. Breaking the cycle of violence: crime and state in Papua New Guinea. In *Developing cultural criminology: theory and practice in Papua New Guinea* (ed.) C. Banks, 51-78. Sydney: Sydney Institute of Criminology.

——— 2001. *Law and order in a weak state: crime and politics in Papua New Guinea*. Honolulu: University of Hawaii Press.

——— & A. Ley. 2000 *Reflections on violence in Melanesia*. Annendale: Hawkins Press.

Douglas, M. 1975. *Implicit meanings: essays in anthropology*. London: Routledge & Kegan Paul.

Eberhard, C. 2001. Towards an interlegal legal theory: the dialogical challenge. *Social and Legal Studies* **10**, 171-201.

Epstein, A.L. 1974. Moots on Matupit. In *Contention and dispute: aspects of law and social control in Melanesia* (ed.) A.L. Epstein, 93-112. Canberra: Australian National University Press.

——— 1999. *Gunantuna: aspects of the person, the self and the individual among the Tolai*. Bathurst: Crawford House.

Errington, F. & D.B. Gewertz 1995. *Articulating change in the 'last unknown'*. Boulder, Colo.: Westview Press.

Fenbury, D.M. 1978. *Practice without policy*. Canberra: Australian National University.

Fernandez, J.W. 2001. The irony of complicity and the complicity of irony in development discourse. In *Irony in action: anthropology, practice and the moral imagination* (eds) J.W. Hernandez & M.T. Huber, 84-102. Chicago: University Press.

——— & M.T. Huber (eds) 2001. *Irony in action: anthropology, practice and the moral imagination*. Chicago: University Press.

Fitzpatrick, P. 1980. *Law and state in Papua New Guinea*. London: Academic Press.

——— 1984 Law and societies. *Osgoode Hall Law Journal* **22**, 115-38.

Fortes, M. 1938. Social and psychological aspects of education in Taleland. In *From child to adult* (ed.) J. Middleton, 14-74. New York: Natural History Press.

Fortune, R. 1947. Law and force in Papuan societies. *American Anthropologist* **49**, 244-59.

Frye, N. 1957. *Anatomy of criticism: four essays*. Princeton: University Press.

Furth, H.G. 1996. *Desire for society: children's knowledge as social imagination*. New York: Plenum Press.

Galanter, M. 1981. Justice in many rooms: courts, private ordering and indigenous law. *Journal of Legal Pluralism* **19**, 1-37.

Garap, S. 2000. Struggles of women and girls: Simbu Province, Papua New Guinea. In *Reflections on violence in Melanesia* (eds) S. Dinnen & A. Ley, 159-71. Annendale: Hawkins Press.

Garvey, C. & R. Berndt 1977. The language of social pretend. *Developmental Review* **9**, 364-82.

Gluckman, M. 1956. *Custom and conflict in Africa*. New York: Harper & Row.

Goddard, M. 1992. Big man, thief: the social organization of gangs in Port Moresby. *Canberra Anthropology* **15**, 20-34.

——— 1995. The rascal road: crime, prestige and development in Papua New Guinea. *The Contemporary Pacific* **7**, 55-80.

——— 1996. The snake bone case: law, custom, and justice in a Papua New Guinea village court. *Oceania* **67**, 50-9.

——— 1998. Off the record: village court praxis and the politics of settlement life in Port Moresby, Papua New Guinea. *Canberra Anthropology* **21**, 41-62.

——— 2000. Three urban courts in Papua New Guinea: some comparative observations on dispute settlement. In *Reflections on violence in Melanesia* (eds) S. Dinnen & A. Ley, 241-53. Annendale: Hawkins Press.

Goffman, E. 1974. *Frame analysis*. New York: Harper & Row.

Goldman, L. 1998. *Child's play: myth, mimesis and make-believe*. Oxford: Berg.

——— & C. Smith 1998. Imagining identities: mimetic constructions in Huli child fantasy play. *Journal of the Royal Anthropological Institute* (N.S.) **4**, 207-34.

Gordon, R.J. & M. Meggitt 1985. *Law and order in the New Guinea Highlands*. Hanover, NH: University Press of New England.

Griffiths, J. 1986. What is legal pluralism? *Journal of Legal Pluralism* **24**, 1-55.

Groos, K. 1901. *The play of man*. New York: Appleton.

Handelman, D. & B. Kapferer 1972. Forms of joking activity: a comparative approach. *American Anthropologist* **74**, 484-517.

Harris, B. 1988. The rise of rascalism: action and reaction in the evolution of rascal gangs. Port Moresby: Institute of Applied Social & Economic Research.

Hasluck, P. 1975. *A time for building: Australian administration in Papua and New Guinea, 1951-63*. Melbourne: University Press.

Hazlehurst, K.M. (ed.) 1995. *Legal pluralism and the colonial legacy*. Brookfield, Vt.: Ashgate Publishing Co.

Herzfeld, M. 2001. Irony and power: toward a politics of mockery in Greece. In *Irony in action: anthropology, practice and the moral imagination* (eds) J.W. Fernandez & M.T. Huber, 63-83. Chicago: University Press.

Hooker, M.B. 1975. *Legal pluralism: an introduction to colonial and neo-colonial laws*. Oxford: Clarendon Press.

Hutchins, E. 1990. Getting it straight in Trobriand land litigation. In *Disentangling: conflict discourse in Pacific societies* (eds) K. Watson-Gegeo & G. White, 412-58. Stanford: University Press.

Iamo, W. 1987. Customary law in Keakalo Society: implications for legal development. *Customary law and legal development in Papua New Guinea* (ed.) R. Scaglion (*Journal of Anthropology* **6**), 95-125.

Kafka, F. 1937. *The trial*. New York: A.A. Knopf.

Keris, P. 1987. The role of village courts. In *Law and order in a changing society* (ed.) L. Morauta, 70-5. Canberra: Australian National University.

Kituai, A.I. 1998. *My gun, my brother: the world of the Papua New Guinea colonial police, 1920-1960*. Honolulu: University of Hawaii Press.

Knauft, B. 2002. *Exchanging the past*. Chicago: University Press.

Kulick, D. 1993. Heroes from hell: representations of 'raskols' in a Papua New Guinea Village. *Anthropology Today* **9**, 9-14.

Larmour, P. 1998. State and society in Papua New Guinea. In *Modern Papua New Guinea* (ed.) L. Zimmer-Tamakoshi, 21-30. Kirksville Mo.: Thomas Jefferson Press.

Lawrence, P. 1969. The state versus stateless societies in Papua and New Guinea. In *Fashion of law in New Guinea* (eds) B.J. Brown & G. Sawer, 15-38. Sydney: Butterworths.

Limon, J. 1985. Carne, carnales and the carnivalesque: Bakhtinian bathos, disorder and narrative discourse. *American Ethnologist* **16**, 471-86.

Lips, J. 1937. *The savage hits back*. New Haven, Conn.: Yale University Press.

Lipset, D. 1989. Papua New Guinea: the Melanesian ethic and the spirit of capitalism, 1975-86. In *Democracy in developing countries*, vol. 3 (eds) L. Diamond, J.J. Linz & S.M. Lipset, 383-423. Boulder, Colo.: Lynne Rienner.

——— 1997. *Mangrove man: dialogics of culture in the Sepik estuary*. Cambridge: University Press.

——— & E.K. Silverman forthcoming. The grotesque and the moral: the dialogics of the body in two Sepik societies. *Journal of Ritual Studies.*

LiPuma, E. 2000. *Encompassing others: the magic of modernity in Melanesia.* Ann Arbor: University of Michigan Press.

Lynch, C.J. 1969. Aspects of political and constitutional development and allied topics. In *Fashion of law in New Guinea* (ed.) B.J. Brown, 39-69. Sydney: Butterworths.

Malinowski, B. 1926. *Crime and custom in savage society.* Paterson, NJ: Littlefield, Adams & Co.

Mattes, J.R. 1969. The count system. In *Fashion of law in New Guinea* (ed.) B.J. Brown, 71-82. Sydney: Butterworths.

McPherson, N.M. 2001. *In colonial New Guinea.* Pittsburgh: University Press.

Mead, G.H. 1934. *Mind, self and society.* Chicago: University Press.

Mead, M. 1935. *Sex and temperament in three primitive societies.* New York: Morrow.

Merry, S.E. 1986. Everyday understandings of the law in working class America. *American Ethnologist* **13**, 253-70.

——— 1988. Legal pluralism. *Law and Society Review* **22**, 869-96.

Migdal, J. 1988. *Strong societies and weak states: state-society relations and state capabilities in the third world.* Princeton: University Press.

Mitchell, W. (ed.) 1992. *Clowning as critical practice: performance humor in the South Pacific.* Pittsburgh: University Press.

Moore, S.F. 1978. Law and social change: the semi-autonomous social field as an appropriate subject of study. In *Law as process: an anthropological approach,* S.F. Moore, 54-81. London: Routledge & Kegan Paul.

Morauta, L. 1987. Law and order in Papua New Guinea: a tenth anniversary report. In *Law and order in a changing society* (ed.) L. Morauta, 7-19. Canberra: Department of Political and Social Change, Research School of Pacific Studies.

Murray, H. 1925. *Papua of to-day: or an Australian colony in the making.* London: King.

Nelson, K. & S. Seidman 1984. Playing with scripts. In *Symbolic play: the development of social understanding* (ed.) I. Bretherton, 45-71. Orlando, Fla.: Academic Press.

Piaget, J. 1962. *Play, dreams and imitation in childhood.* New York: Norton.

Radcliffe-Brown, A.R. 1940. On joking relationships. In *Structure and function in primitive society,* 90-104. Glencoe, Ill.: The Free Press.

Raum, O. 1940. *Chaga childhood.* London: Oxford University Press.

Roscoe, P. 1999. Return of the ambush: 'raskolism' in rural Yangoru, East Sepik Province. *Oceania* **69**, 171-83.

Rowley, C.D. 1965. *The New Guinea villager.* Melbourne: F.W. Cheshire.

Ryle, G. 1949. *The concept of mind.* Chicago: University Press.

Sack, P. 1972. *Land between two laws.* Canberra: Australian National University Press.

Santos, B. de Sousa 1977. The law of the oppressed: the construction and reproduction of legality in Pasargada. *Law and Society Review* **12**, 5-125.

——— 1987. Law: a map of misreading: toward a postmodern conception of law. *Journal of Law and Society* **14**, 279-302.

——— 1995. *Toward a new common sense: law, science and politics in the paradigmatic transition.* New York: Routledge.

Sawyer, R.K. 2002. Improvisation and narrative. *Narrative Inquiry* **12**, 319-49.

Scaglion, R. 1976. Seasonal patterns in Western Abelam conflict management practices. Ph.D. diss., University of Pittsburgh.

——— 1979. Formal and informal operations of a village court in Maprik. *Melanesian Law Journal* **7**, 116-29.

——— 1990. Legal adaptation in a Papua New Guinea village court. *Ethnology* **13**, 17-33.

Schank, R. & R. Abelson 1977. *Scripts, plans, goals and understanding.* Hillsdale, NJ: Lawrence Erlbaum.

Schwartzman, H.B. 1978. *Transformations: the anthropology of children's play.* New York: Plenum Press.

Sinavaiana, C. 1992. Where the spirits laugh last: comic theatre in Samoa. In *Clowning as critical practice: performance humor in the South Pacific* (ed.) W. Mitchell, 192-221. Pittsburgh: University Press.

Standish, W.A. 1994. Papua New Guinea: the search for identity in a weak state. In *Papua New Guinea: issues for security planners* (ed.) A. Thompson, 51-97. Canberra: Australian Defence Studies Center, Australian Defence Force Academy.

——— 2000. Papua New Guinea reflects. *Journal of Pacific Society* **23**, 1-10.

——— 2001. Papua New Guinea in 1999-2000. *Journal of Pacific History* **36**, 277-83.

Strathern, A. 1972. The Supreme Court: a matter of prestige and power. *Melanesian Law Journal* **1**, 23-8.

——— 1981. Compensation: should there be a new law? In *Homicide compensation in Papua New Guinea: problems and prospects* (ed.) R. Scaglion, 8-24. Port Moresby: Law Reform Commission.

Strathern, M. 1972. Official and unofficial courts: legal assumptions and expectation in a Highlands community. (Bulletin 47). Port Moresby: New Guinea Research Unit.

Sykes, K. 2000. Raskolling: Papua New Guinean sociality as contested order. In *Developing cultural criminology: theory and practice in Papua New Guinea* (ed.) C. Banks, 174-94. Sydney: Sydney Institute of Criminology.

Somare, M. 1975. *Sana*. Hong Kong: Niugini Press.

Teubner, G. (ed.) 1997. *Global law without the state*. Aldershot: Darmouth.

Tie, W. 1999. *Legal pluralism: toward a multicultural conception of law*. Brookfield, Vt.: Ashgate Publishing Co.

Turner, V. 1982. *From ritual to theatre: the human seriousness of play*. New York: Performing Arts Journal Press.

Watson-Gegeo, K. & G. White. 1990. *Disentangling: conflict discourse in Pacific societies*. Stanford: University Press.

West, F. (ed.) 1970. *Selected letters of Hubert Murray*. Melbourne: Oxford University Press.

Westermark, G. 1986. 'Court is an arrow': legal pluralism in Papua New Guinea. *Ethnology* **25**, 131-49.

Young, M. 1974. Private sanctions and public ideology; some aspects of self-help in Kalauna, Goodenough Island. In *Contention and dispute* (ed.) A.L. Epstein, 40-66. Canberra: Australian National University Press.

Zorn, J. 1991. Customary law in Papua New Guinea village courts. *The Contemporary Pacific* **2**, 279-312.

« Le procès » : une parodie de droit parmi les parodies des hommes dans la Papouasie-Nouvelle-Guinée post-coloniale

Résumé

Les recherches consacrées aux formes de pluralisme juridique montrent la multiplicité et la complexité de la « relation » entre le droit à l'occidentale et les procédures, résolutions et autres démarches de gestion locale des conflits. Ces études ne se sont guère aventurées au-delà du cadre de la résolution des conflits, qu'ils soient d'ordre administratif ou privé. L'auteur avance ici l'idée que d'importantes dimensions expressives de la problématique du pluralisme juridique ont été occultées. Dans une parodie de procès satirique organisée dans une zone rurale de Papouasie-Nouvelle-Guinée, les constructions juridique et indigène du droit ne se sont pas rejointes, comme on aurait pu le penser, au niveau instrumental, dans le contexte d'une négociation visant à résoudre un litige, mais à un niveau créatif, en se combinant pour produire un discours polyphonique d'effet comique. Il apparaît ainsi que la loi a une valeur rhétorique, notamment dans les contextes colonial et post-colonial, dans lesquels elle peut être appliquée ou invoquée pour représenter des attitudes ambivalentes à propos de la justice aussi bien que des constructions locales de l'idée de personne.

Dept of Anthropology, University of Minnesota, 301-19th Av. S. Mpls. MN 55455, USA. Lipse001@umn.edu.

[14]

Forms of Judicial Blindness, or the Evidence of What Cannot Be Seen

Traumatic Narratives and Legal Repetitions in the O. J. Simpson Case and in Tolstoy's *The Kreutzer Sonata*

Shoshana Felman

This paper will reflect on a famous case of law that has impacted on our times—the O. J. Simpson (criminal) trial—together with a famous literary text that bears, surprisingly, many resemblances to this contemporary case: Tolstoy's *The Kreutzer Sonata.* In both the legal drama of the case and in the literary drama of the text, what is at issue is a marriage that ends up in murder. In both, a jealous husband is arrested and is put on trial for the murder of his wife—and is acquitted. And yet the husband in Tolstoy's work acknowledges his guilt, and is precisely telling us the story to explain not only why, but *how* he killed his wife.

A trial and a literary text do not aim at the same kind of conclusion, nor do they strive toward the same kind of effect. A trial is presumed to be a search for truth, but, technically, it is a search for a decision, and thus, in essence, it seeks not simply truth but a finality: a force of resolution. A literary text is, on the other hand, a search for meaning, for expression, for heightened significance and for symbolic understanding. I propose to make use of this difference in literary and legal goals, by reading them *across* each other and against each other. I propose, in other words, to draw the questions of "the trial of the century" (and the general significance of trials) into Tolstoy's text, but even more importantly, to *draw out Tolstoy's insight,* so to speak, *into* the O. J. Simpson case in order to illuminate legal obscurities with literary insights and to reflect on ambiguities the trial has left by using textual issues that will turn out (surprisingly) to be quite relevant to them.

The dialogue between the disciplines of law and literature has so far been primarily thematic (that is, essentially conservative of the integrity and of the stable epistemological boundaries of the two fields): when not borrowing the tools of literature to analyze (rhetorically) legal opinions, scholars in the field of law and literature most often deal with the explicit, thematized reflection (or "representation") of the institutions of the law in works of the imagination, focusing on the analysis of fictional trials in a literary plot and/or on the psychology or the sociology of literary characters whose fate or whose profession ties them to the law (lawyers, judges, or accused). My own inquiry will be quite different. I will attempt here to illuminate reciprocally not just the themes, the thematized meanings of the literary and the legal narratives of crime and trial, but (most important) the structure and the process of these narratives; and not just the structure and the process of the stories but their actual impact, their historical reception. I will thus compare a work of fiction whose impact has in turn generated passionate polemical reactions and a great deal of obsessional discussion with an actual criminal affair that has made legal history and yet whose legal haunting has not stopped; a real case that has been legally decided and yet continues to translate itself obsessively into new legal and nonlegal channels. Right now, the civil trial draws us back into the story's literary and dramatic spell and legally authorizes an official repetition—a reactivation—of the judicial process. But the outcome of the civil trial, I predict, will in turn be incapable (whatever it might be) of truly closing this affair, which keeps reclaiming our interest and our historical attention and thus presents itself, quite strictly (technically, judicially), as an interminable trial.[1]

1. [Footnote added March 1997:]—These lines were written prior to the ending of the civil trial (January 1997). But their prediction holds true. The conclusion, in the meantime, of the civil trial, by a unanimous verdict of liability does not in its turn bring an ending to the case, first, because there will be an appeal or a request for a new trial, and, second, because the civil verdict cannot cancel out its contradiction by the criminal acquittal, whose historical impact cannot be undone and whose outcome is, thus, irreversible (not merely legally but epistemologically), in that society now knows it cannot produce, on Simpson's guilt, an *undivided* justice (a legal truth not subject to a systematic—and systemic—legal crisis). Indeed, the force of the unanimous decision of the civil verdict has immediately

Shoshana Felman is the Thomas E. Donnelley Professor of French and Comparative Literature at Yale University. She is the author of *The Literary Speech Act: Don Juan with Austin, or Seduction in Two Languages* (1984), *Writing and Madness* (1985), *Jacques Lacan and the Adventure of Insight* (1987), and *What Does a Woman Want? Reading and Sexual Difference* (1993). She is also the editor of *Literature and Psychoanalysis: The Question of Reading—Otherwise* (1982) and coauthor, with Dori Laub, of *Testimony: Crises of Witnessing in Literature, Psychoanalysis, and History* (1992). The present essay is part of a book in progress entitled *Dilemmas of Justice.*

This essay will propose a study and a theory of the phenomenon of legal repetition as internal to the structure and the logic of a case, or as the legal outcome of the literary/psychoanalytic principle of the traumatic narrative that constitutes, as I will show, at once the literary story and the actual legal case.[2]

The dramatic mirroring between the hard facts of the law and the imaginary facts of literature will thus result in a far reaching lesson consisting, among other things, in a new model of perception of legal events and in the conceptual articulation of a new analytic tool (focused on the relation between the traumatic nature of a case and its compulsive legal repetition), an analytic tool that will here help us not just to rethink the meaning of the legal case but to displace the very terms and the very questions through which we interpret cases, both in fiction and in the reality of legal life. This lesson, based on the contaminating interpenetration of the story and the case, will in effect become compellingly informative and dramatically, surprisingly instructive only through a destabilization of the boundaries that epistemologically define and separate the territory of the law from that of literature. In actual life, the living entities of law and literature—trial and story—relate to one another not as reality to fiction or as empiricism to aestheticism but as two narratives of trauma, two enigmas of emotional and physical destruction, two human responses to the shock of an unbearable reality of death and pain, and two linguistic acts of cultural and of social intervention.

In reading law through literature, and in deciphering the meaning and the impact of the literary speech act through the meaning and the impact of the trial of the century; in asking how Tolstoy illuminates the O. J. Simpson case and how the real case speaks from inside Tolstoy's novella, my interest, however, is not simply—not primarily—to add as yet another commentary to a much debated and much commented-on case but to articulate—through the example of the case—an innovative theo-

been challenged and interpreted (explained away) as a "white verdict." There will be other, as yet unanticipated, legal sequels. "The case is far from over," Simpson prophetically announced in response to the conclusion of the second trial.

2. [Footnote added March 1997:] This study as a whole was conceived and written in the aftermath of the Simpson criminal trial, and its first draft was completed several months before the beginning of the civil trial (in June 1996; the preceding lines referring to the civil trial were added later, in December 1996). My analysis of the phenomenon of legal repetition as internal to the structure of the case was thus initially based only on the similarity between the Simpson criminal trial and Tolstoy's text. It is, in other words, the relation among trial, repetition, narrative, and trauma in Tolstoy's text that has informed my initial insight into the (historically) repetitive traumatic legal structure of the Simpson case and that has instructed me—before the fact—about the structural interminability of such a trial and the historical inexorability of its legal repetition. The subsequent reincarnation of the repetition in the civil trial has strikingly confirmed the analysis and rendered all the more acute, compelling, and dramatically self-evident the multi-layered vision of its historical perspective.

retical perspective on the highly problematic and yet, in my view, absolutely fundamental relation of the law to the larger phenomenon of cultural or collective trauma. Through a philosophical analysis of the criminal trial of the century, I will demonstrate the ways in which the law remains professionally blind to this phenomenon with which it is nevertheless quite crucially and indissociably tied up. I argue that it is because of what the law cannot and does not see that a judicial case becomes a legal trauma in its own right and is therefore bound to repeat itself through a traumatic legal repetition. This compulsion to a legal repetition (like the one that is now demonstrated through the O. J. Simpson case) is accounted for by narratives of trauma (Tolstoy's story will in turn address this issue and highlight it in its own specific literary way).

Legal memory is constituted, in effect, not just by the "chain of law" and by the conscious repetition of the precedent but by a forgotten chain of cultural wounds and by compulsive or unconscious legal repetitions of traumatic, wounding legal cases. My analysis will show how historically unconscious legal repetitions inadvertently play out in the historical arena the political unconscious of the law (the unconscious of past legal cases). These traumatic repetitions illustrate, therefore, in history, the Freudian notion of "a return of the repressed"; in the ghost of the return of a traumatizing legal case, what compulsively, historically returns from the forgotten legal past is the repressed of the judicial institution.

The relevance and the significance of this comprehensive theoretical perspective extend far beyond the limits of the O. J. Simpson case and its particular parameters. As a singularly eloquent example, the trial of the century becomes itself not just a vehicle, a leverage for this larger understanding, but an allegory of its need and of its urgency.

1

A Trial for Our Times

How does a trial come to claim the status of "the trial of the century"? What was it in the O. J. Simpson case that has been grasped as so revealing, momentous, and uniquely symptomatic of the very nature of our times?

In a cover story that presents the case under the heading, "A Trial for Our Times," *Time* magazine suggests two definitions of the concept of legal event: "1) what really happened, the facts, and 2) what people believe happened, the immense tapestry of folklore and conviction and myth that surrounds an event like the Simpson-Goldman murders. Category number 1 addresses the needs of justice and history. But category number 2 is important . . . in its own way." The purpose of a trial is, presumably, to transmute events from category number 2 to category number 1. But even if the legal process in this case has not achieved the transformation of the striking mythic images and witnessing beliefs into undoubted facts, the event behind the trial nonetheless remains sufficiently significant and sufficiently defined to *define the era* as a master narrative, the key plot of "an unbeatably lurid end-of-the-millennium American" mixture of "race . . ., sex, celebrity, media hype, justice and injustice." "Sometimes," the essay goes on to reflect, "a trial plays out like a culture's collective dream," acting out "society's deepest passions: its fears, prejudices and desires."[3]

The dream, of course, is not just fantasy but is composed—like any dream—of fragments of reality . To render even more acute this reading of the O. J. Simpson trial as a cultural dream, I would add that a *collective* dream is, paradoxically enough, an unconscious and yet *public secret:* a secret that, while remaining unconscious, translates itself into a public spectacle—that of the courtroom ritual—which then becomes the ritual of an obsession or of an obsessional dream. It was, then, as an acting out of society's unconscious and of the culture's open or collective secrets that the brutal murders of Simpson's ex-wife, Nicole Brown, and of her companion Ronald Goldman, have set the stage for "the defining trial of the 1990s."

An editorial in the *Boston Globe* entitled "Sad but True: Titillating Case Defines Our Times" agrees emphatically, if with a different emphasis; it describes the way in which the impact of the O. J. Simpson case has overshadowed the more consequential impact of major political events. "History textbooks of the future will make much of the Republican realignment. . . . They will talk about the lightning victory in the Gulf War. . . . They may even linger on the travails of Bill Clinton. But we will tell our children that, more than any of those things, our world . . . was shaped by the O. J. Simpson trial. Like it or not, it is the defining event of our time." "Many commentators are arguing that America, not simply Simpson, was on trial. . . . That's too big a thought," the article concludes. "We know one thing, though: America, even if not on trial, was at the trial. And we will be there for a long time."[4]

In the *Los Angeles Times,* the trial as the event that marks the century is read not through the fascination of the crowd of its spectators, nor through the crime that the proceedings put on trial (Simpson's or America's), but through the very legal execution or performance of the trial: the way in which the diversity of race and sex defines not just the secret crime scene but the spectacular scene of the trial. Only in the twentieth century, indeed, could a trial take place with a woman at the head of the

3. Lance Morrow, "A Trial for Our Times," *Time,* 9 Oct. 1995, p. 28.

4. David Shribman, "Sad but True: Titillating Case Defines Our Times," *Boston Globe,* 8 Oct. 1995, p. A32.

prosecution and a black attorney at the head of the defense.[5] The trial defines the century not through its statements but through its utterance; what is distinctive in the trial is its *voice:* "*We heard the American voice* in so many registers and using so many different kinds of diction, sounding itself in so many accents. . . . These days, both sexes and an astonishing cross-section of this country's ethnic resources are right in the middle of major events as significant players."[6]

Law and Trauma

I would suggest, for my part, that what gives "the trial of the century" its philosophical dimension (beyond its social meaning) and its historic depth (beyond the moment's fascination), what makes it a landmark trial of historical significance are three profound features: (1) its *complex traumatic structure;* (2) its *cross-legal nature,* or the repetition it enacts of another trial; and (3) its *attempt to define legally something that is not reducible to legal concepts.* I would suggest, moreover, that these three features are perhaps in general characteristic of every major trial with historical significance and certainly of major controversial trials that immediately grow into public or political "affairs" and whose symbolic impact is immediately perceived in the intensity with which they tend at once to *focus* public discourse and to *polarize* public opinion.

1. The Complex Traumatic Structure of the Trial (Race and Gender)

Every trial is related to an injury, a trauma for which it compensates and which it attempts to remedy and overcome. The three features I have mentioned (by which I am attempting to define at once the historic singularity and the archetypal theoretical significance of the trial of the century) are all related to the ostentatious way in which the structure of the trial, in this case, has revealed itself to be supported by the structure of a trauma. The trial has attempted to *articulate* the trauma so as to *control* its damage. But it is the structure of the trauma, I submit, that in the end controlled the trial. The trial has become itself a *vehicle of trauma:* a vehicle of aggravation of traumatic consequences rather than a means of their containment and their legal resolution. I argue, therefore, that the case encapsulates the drama and the mystery, not simply of a link, but of a real *parallel between traumatic structures and legal proceedings:* a parallel which is at once disquieting and thought provoking and which the present essay will attempt to analyze.

5. Not to speak of a presiding judge who is neither black nor white.

6. Stanley Crouch, "The Agonizing Whine Down," *Los Angeles Times,* 8 Oct. 1995, p. M1.

What makes the Simpson trial both unforgettable and unforgettably complex, moreover, is the way in which *two* traumas—that of race and that of gender—have been set *in competition* with each other in the adversarial structure of the lawyers' arguments in such a way as to confuse and radically complicate both the *perception of the trauma* that the trial strived to remedy and the very question of *who was the victim* of the case: the abused and murdered wife or the wrongfully or hastily accused black husband? At the focus of the trial, therefore, *two* forms of victimization and abuse (race abuse and sex abuse) paradoxically enter into competition and mobilize their anger and their pain to dispute each other's claim for justice; *two traumas* paradoxically attempt to overpower one another and to silence each other's outcry.

But in these two competing narratives of trauma—in the conflicting stories of the prosecution (which blames an abusive husband for the murder of his wife) and of the defense (which blames the justice system for its racial bias and an abusive law enforcement body for a rush to an arrest and an unfounded inculpation of the husband)—there is an ironic symmetry: both the husband and the agents of the law are supposed to give protection but end up inflicting harm (confusingly, deceptively) precisely under their protective guise.

Civilization and Domesticated Violence, or History and Repetition at the End of the Millennium

It is perhaps not a coincidence that such a trial takes place at the close of the twentieth century, a century whose history of wars and violence has taught us how to recognize traumatic symptoms and events of trauma (that once seemed extraordinary) as part of *normal,* ordinary life; a century of civil rights but also of unprecedented *civilized abuses.* It is, thus, not by chance perhaps if the trial of the century comes up, in parallel, with two (contradictory) interpretations of *deceptive* violence and with two legal demystifications of the confusing, intimate, domestic, *civilized* kind of abuse that masks itself as closeness or protection.

What stands at the center of the trial, therefore, is not only the trauma but the blindness it induces, the radical confusion with which the trauma is tied up because of the deceptive package of the violence (marriage, love, police protection, justice). The trial strives to cancel out this blindness, to give the hidden trauma legal visibility. Yet, in the adversarial structure of the litigation, the two "domestic" traumas (gender, race) also dispute, deny each other's claim to visibility. Each trauma, in competing for exclusive visibility, at the same time *blinds* us to the other. The result is that the trial can by no means *totalize,* or give to see in its totality, the trauma underlying it. The complexity of the traumatic structure of the trial thus effectively prevented the trauma from becoming fully visible, in creating a specific form of judicial *blindness* that, paradoxically, was part of the legal achievement of the trial.

2. *The Cross-Legal Nature of the Trial*

I forge the concept of "cross-legal" (on the model of "cross-cultural") to designate a trial's reference to another trial, of which it recapitulates the memory, the themes, the legal questions or the arguments, and whose legal structure it repeats or reenacts—unwittingly or by deliberate design.

Indeed, in everyone's perception, black or white (although in different manners and with different readings), the Simpson trial looked like a return of the ghost of the Rodney King trial. For the defense, which underscored the repetition for its own strategic purpose through Mark Fuhrman's racist monologues, the O. J. Simpson trial was a confirmation of the same police corruption and brutality and of the same racist complicity (or white conspiracy) that King was the victim of. In spite of his assimilation with the white community, Simpson became a double of black motorist Rodney King, similarly chased or hunted on the highway and (presumably) equally indicted and scapegoated merely for the color of his skin. From the defense's point of view, the outline of this repetition gave to see or put in evidence the real subject of the trial, which was not so much the murder of the wife as the bitter conflict between so-called white justice and a persecuted black community. For the prosecution, on the other hand, and for those who found the evidence of Simpson's guilt incontrovertible, the trial was a repetition in a different sense: what was ironically here reenacted was the *first* King trial—the Simi Valley trial—*in reverse,* since the legal process, here as there, resulted similarly (though inversely) in a verdict influenced by a race bias and which similarly chose to disregard or nullify the overwhelming evidence. Whatever is the case, the Simpson trial claimed its status as the trial of the century—a trial that, in other words, can represent or sum up the significance of an entire history—because its structure was indeed susceptible to such a repetition.

I would suggest, moreover, that what distinguishes historic trials is, perhaps, in general, this tendency or this propensity to repetition or to legal duplication. In much the same way as Freud theorizes that great historical events (especially events related to a murder) tend to repeat themselves and are inherently *dual* in nature, because their impact—as a consequence of trauma—takes effect and truly registers in history only through the gap of their traumatic repetition (or through their posttraumatic reenactment),[7] great trials equally make history, I would suggest,

7. See Sigmund Freud, *Moses and Monotheism,* trans. Katherine Jones (1939; New York, 1967).

in being not merely *about* a trauma but in constituting traumas in their own right; as such, they too are open to traumatic repetition; they too are often structured by *historical dualities,* in which a trial (or a major courtroom drama) unexpectedly reveals itself to be the posttraumatic legal reenactment, or the deliberate historical reopening, of a previous case or of a different, finished, previous trial.[8]

The O. J. Simpson trial, then, is structured like a trauma not simply in itself (in its own failure to provide a healing to the trauma it was meant to remedy) but *in its historical relation to other trials (and to other traumas)* on whose legal pathos it picks up and whose different claims to justice it repeats and, as it were, accumulates. What is traumatically conjured by the trial is, therefore, a (mostly unconscious) legal memory, the covered but unhealed wounds of a legal history. The trial inadvertently partakes of a trauma that is now not simply individual but is inscribed in the history of trials and whose individual complaint or grievance has now gained historical, collective, *cumulative legal meaning.* Hence, the enigmatic force, the impact of the trial; hence, the enigmatic historical momentum gained by a relatively simple (or reductive) legal argument.

The legal system, in such cases, is *cross-legally* traumatic, or is traumatic across different periods, across different legal situations, sometimes even across different legal cultures. I would suggest that the tremendous impact of the trial of the century comes not just from its immediate, conscious evocation of the Rodney King case (and of its relatively recent legal trauma) but, even more profoundly, from the way in which both Rodney King and O. J. Simpson, in their similar dramatic circumstances, may have conjured up a still less conscious echo of the Dred Scott case (1857), a case whose legal trauma, from a more remote past, still haunts Ameri-

8. Compare, for instance, the way in which the criminal trial of Emile Zola in France (in 1898, following the publication of his pamphlet "J'accuse"—criminal proceedings instituted as the French government's response to this pamphlet's printed trial of the army and the state) reopened the closed case of the Dreyfus affair (reopened, that is, the first trial and conviction of Dreyfus, 1894, and the second trial and acquittal of Esterhazy, 1898, for an additional hearing, and for a redeliberation and a reexamination of the evidence) and eventually enabled a rejudgement and a rehabilitation of Dreyfus (1906). In a similar way, I would view the Eichmann trial in Israel (1961) not just as a simple repetition or continuation of the international Nuremberg trials (1945–46) but more specifically as a traumatic reenactment of (the legal trauma of) the previous Kastner trial in Israel (1956).

In these series of historic repetitions (or of historical dualities), there is something that is legally specific, or that is specific to the legal structure. Because the social function of legal institutions is to close disputes and not to open them, the legal system cannot, in principle, accept the reopening of a case (as distinguished from the reconsideration of a precedent) except as a scandal and a shock. A case therefore requires another trial to repeat itself in order either to reverse its verdict or to change the understanding or the reading of its evidence. Judicial re-vision must take place through another trial. I believe that such an analytical perspective on historical dualities and on traumatic legal repetition can be productive in itself and illuminating, in particular, for an understanding of some critical, strategic moments in the history of trials.

can history and its history of trials, or its (changing) legal culture. As a possible unconscious echo of the Dred Scott case in its hauntingly inflammatory memory, the Simpson-King historical duality (or dual road hunt) may have unconsciously played out, replayed, issues belonging to a different period and to a slightly different legal culture, reopening old wounds of forced recaptures of alleged fugitives by a biased and committedly proslavery legal order. What the trial does, therefore, is to repeat and to awaken, to *reopen* a traumatic history of trials.

3. The Trial's Excess of Its Legal Definitions

The last feature, which accounts for the privileged historical position of the trial of the century, and which defines its philosophical dimension, is related to the way in which the trial situates itself precisely at the juncture—at the very critical convergence—of the legal and of the political.

Can the political as such be analyzed, defined, or circumscribed in legal terms? The German philosopher Karl Jaspers thought that it could not because the two domains (legal, political) are qualitatively heterogenous to each other and can by no means overlap with one another. Jaspers argued this opinion in a letter that he wrote in 1960 to his ex-student Hannah Arendt, on the occasion of her undertaking to review for *The New Yorker* the forthcoming Eichmann trial in Jerusalem: "The political realm," Jaspers insisted, "is of an importance that cannot be captured in legal terms (*the attempt to do so is Anglo-Saxon* and a self-deception that masks a basic fact in the functionings of political existence). . . . *A dimension that in being 'political' has, as it were, dignity, is larger than law, and is woven into the fabric of fate.*"[9]

Larger Than Law

It could certainly be claimed that this argument could equally apply to the O. J. Simpson case: both the fight of race (against racial prejudice) and the fight of gender (against domestic violence) involve, each in its turn, a political dimension that has "dignity." This double political dimension is, indeed, inherently "larger than law" and "is woven into the fabric of fate." This is where the trial's pathos comes from. But could the realm of the struggle for this dignity—this larger political dimension—be addressed in legal terms?

On this question, Arendt takes a different stand than Jaspers. In her answer to his letter, Arendt, who was to become herself a leading political

9. Karl Jaspers, letter to Hannah Arendt, 16 Dec. 1960, in Arendt and Jaspers, *Correspondence, 1926–1969,* trans. Robert and Rita Kimber, ed. Lotte Kohler and Hans Saner (New York, 1992), p. 413. In all cited texts, emphasis is mine unless otherwise indicated.

theorist and thinker in America, takes issue with her former teacher's criticism of the "Anglo-Saxon" inclination and redefines in her own terms the way in which the Eichmann trial illustrates, indeed, the gap, the difference and the tension, but also, paradoxically, the juncture, the indispensable critical convergence, between the realm of the legal and the realm of the political:

> All this may strike you as though I too was attempting to circumscribe the political with legal concepts. And I even admit that as far as the role of the law is concerned, I have been infected by the Anglo-Saxon influence. But quite apart from that, it seems to me to be *in the nature of this case* that *we have no tools to hand except the legal ones* with which we have to judge and pass sentence on *something that cannot even be adequately represented either in legal terms or in political terms.* That is precisely what makes the process itself, namely, the trial, so exciting.[10]

This reflection holds and could equally account for the trial of the century: the O. J. Simpson case has gained both its unique position and its paradoxical symbolic representativity because it deals, profoundly and obscurely, with *"something that cannot even be adequately represented either in legal terms or in political terms."* It is, in other words, precisely the trial's irreducibility to the legal concepts that define it that has made it the trial of the century.

This final philosophical and analytic feature of the O. J. Simpson case could in its turn illustrate, perhaps, a general characteristic of important trials. It would be safe to say that every major trial essentially involves "something larger than law." In every major trial, and certainly in every trial of political or of historical significance, something other than law is addressed in legal terms and is submitted to the narrowness of legal definitions. And "that is precisely what makes the process itself, namely, the trial, so exciting."

2

The Murders of the Century (Which Century? or, from America to Russia)

What can be, therefore, the relevance of literature to such an archetypal legal drama? Could a work of art offer a valid commentary on the real intricacies of a criminal hard case and on the real (philosophical and

10. Arendt, letter to Jaspers, 23 Dec. 1960, *Correspondence*, p. 417.

referential) understanding of the legal controversy of the century?

Since the O. J. Simpson case has been, indeed, collectively discussed and collectively experienced (lived) as a defining trial of our times, is it not surprising, in effect, to find the same case—or its duplicate (a wife's murder followed by the husband's trial)—in a literary text entitled *The Kreutzer Sonata* and written not by an American contemporary but by a Russian writer of the *nineteenth century?* If Tolstoy, the author of this text, seems to know so much about the O. J. Simpson case, could the trial of the century, after all, also paradoxically belong to the nineteenth century?[11]

Indeed, not only does Tolstoy, a century before us, write the story of the trial of the century; then as now, the writing and the publication of the story—(way before the media could be held responsible for its inflation)—wins publicity that seems to be out of proportion to the value or to the importance of the case. Then as now, the drama of the case provokes the same excitement and the same heated division of opinions, the same intensity of controversy and of passionate debate.

The link between the trial and the times, moreover, is also at the center of Tolstoy's text. Having read the manuscript to one of his friends (Prince Urusov), Tolstoy records, in March 1889, the friend's responsiveness as proof of the subject's topicality: "He liked it very much. It is true that it is something new and powerful."[12] Tolstoy is interested, indeed, not just in the contemporary sensitivity of his new topic, but in its impact, in its practical effect: he knows that writing, in this case, writing *this* case, is making an effective *intervention* in the world—committing a didactically political act. "I almost finished *The Kreutzer Sonata* or *How a Husband Killed His Wife*," he writes to his disciple and prospective publisher, Chertkov, in September 1889: "I am glad I wrote it. *I know that people need to be told what is written there.*"[13]

Censorship and Fame

Like the O. J. Simpson case, the story of *The Kreutzer Sonata* distinguishes itself, in its own century, by a particular relation to the law. In

11. Would this coincidence of cases mean, then, that Tolstoy is *our contemporary* (implicitly *ahead of his own time*)? Or could it rather mean that we ourselves, in some major respects, are still quite retrograde, that we *have not yet truly come out of the nineteenth century?*

12. Quoted in Henri Troyat, *Tolstoy,* trans. Nancy Amphoux (1965; New York, 1987), pp. 502–3.

13. Quoted in David Magarshack, afterword to Leo Tolstoy, *"The Death of Ivan Ilych" and Other Stories* (New York, 1960), p. 297.

spite of the fictional character of this innovative literary case of the murder of a wife, the publication of the text immediately provokes a scandal and becomes itself a legal case: the censor bans the text, the Russian church decries its immorality, the minister of the interior outlaws it and officially forbids its publication both as a separate volume and in Tolstoy's complete works. Ironically, it is only thanks to Tolstoy's wife—who, in a personal interview with the tsar, obtains permission partially to lift the ban (exclusively from the edition of Tolstoy's complete works)—that the text can be published at all.

But even before its publication, the case of *The Kreutzer Sonata* becomes a compulsive topic of discussion in Russia's living rooms and in the streets—very like the O. J. Simpson trial in America.

> As soon as it had been copied, the book was taken to Moscow . . . ; during the night, unpaid scribes made copies of the text and in less than a week nearly eight hundred lithographed copies were circulating in Saint Petersburg; their numbers doubled, tripled, invaded the provinces. Before the book was even printed, before the censor had given its decision, the case was being hotly debated all over Russia. According to Strakhov, people no longer greeted each other in the street with "How are you?" but with "Have you read *The Kreutzer Sonata?*"[14]

Tolstoy's daughter, Alexandra, writes in her memoirs:

> It is hard to convey now what took place when, for example, *The Kreutzer Sonata* . . . first appeared. Before [it] had been even passed for the press hundreds, even thousands of copies of [it] were made, which went from hand to hand, were translated into every language and were read everywhere with incredible passion; it sometimes seemed that the public had forgotten all its personal concerns and was living exclusively for the sake of the works of Count Tolstoy . . . The most important political events were seldom the object of such overwhelming and universal attention.[15]

As in the O. J. Simpson case, what is particularly striking in the case of *The Kreutzer Sonata* is the outstanding contradiction between the seeming triviality of the private story and the impressive magnitude and scope of the community's emotional (and economical) investment in it, the utter political importance that the audience's response confers to the drama of the crime and of the judgement, unaccountably magnified into a symbol of the times, and into a collective trial of the century.

14. Troyat, *Tolstoy,* p. 499.

15. Quoted in David Mcduff, translator's introduction to Tolstoy, *"The Kreutzer Sonata" and Other Stories* (Harmondsworth, 1985), pp. 16–17.

What, then, does Tolstoy have to tell us, not merely about *The Kreutzer Sonata,* but about the O. J. Simpson case? What can the literary text teach us that can shed light on the trial of the century?

3

Marriage and Violence

The Kreutzer Sonata is the story of a husband who has killed his wife, was tried for murder, and was legally acquitted and set free. The story—about jealousy, hostility, sex, quarrels, murder, trial, and acquittal—is narrated to a stranger on a train by the now converted husband-murderer, as an unsolicited autobiographical confession.

The confession, or the husband's retrospective testimony, is at the same time an *avowal* of his guilt and a *lesson* that he feels compelled to share about a retrospective insight he has gained—too late—into his tragedy: an insight into what he now believes to be a constitutional *relation between marriage and (domestic) violence.* Having thought about his case, he has come to be convinced that his outrageous, monstrous drama is in fact banal, ubiquitous; that violence, in other words, inhabits marriage as a rule and not as an exception or an accident (although everyone denies it). It is this unseen point about marriage, this blind spot of society, of men and women and of culture, that his confession—his example—at the same time illustrates and puts on trial.[16] "'They asked me in court how I killed her, what I used to do it with. Imbeciles! They thought I killed her that day, the fifth of October, with a knife. It wasn't that day I killed her, it was much earlier. *Exactly in the same way as they're killing their wives now, all of them. . . .*'"[17]

16. It is the universalizing, threateningly generalizing nature of this proposition, I would argue (and not the public's simple prurient interest in Tolstoy's private life and into what might be, presumably, his own unique confession), that accounts for the scandal, for the heat and for the controversy caused by *The Kreutzer Sonata* (by the daring literary treatment of the legal case). It is, in other words, not the singularity or the exceptional nature of the case of the murder of the wife but, on the contrary, its general and unexceptional validity that Tolstoy precisely emphasizes in *his* trial of the century: the general and unexceptional (though generally invisible) relation between marriage and abuse (marriage and violence) that the case merely reveals in bringing it to its concretely visible extremes.

This unsettling emphasis is central to my reading and is in any case constitutive of my own understanding of the story; it accounts for the scandalous boldness of the text and, in particular, for its provocative and paradoxical "didacticism," that is, its *collective* lesson.

17. Tolstoy, *The Kreutzer Sonata,* in *"The Kreutzer Sonata" and Other Stories,* p. 60; hereafter abbreviated *KS.*

Addictions

The speaker and the story's hero, an aristocrat named Pozdnyshev, had led a promiscuous sexual life until his marriage at age thirty. This promiscuity—characteristic of most men in his social circle—evolved into what he himself now diagnoses as a genuine *sexual addiction:*

> "I had become what is known as a fornicator. Being a fornicator is a physical condition similar to that of a morphine addict, an alcoholic or a smoker of opium. Just as a morphine addict, an alcoholic or a smoker of opium is no longer a normal individual, so a man who has had several women for the sake of his pleasure is no longer a normal person but one who has been spoiled for all time—a fornicator. And just as an alcoholic or a morphine addict can immediately be recognized by his features and physical mannerisms, so can a fornicator. A fornicator may restrain himself, struggle for self-control, but never again will his relation to women be simple, clear. . . . I, too, became a fornicator and remained one, and that was my undoing." [*KS*, p. 41]

Looking back at his own life before the marriage, he thus sees himself, along with all his male friends, as "'debauchees in our thirties with hundreds of the most varied and abominable crimes against women on our consciences'" (*KS*, p. 41). These crimes against women do not derive from the physical act or from the sexual addiction in itself, but from the *moral attitude* that goes along with it:

> "Debauchery isn't something physical. Not even the most outrageous physicality can be equated with debauchery. Debauchery—real debauchery—takes place when you free yourself from any moral regard for the woman you enter into physical relations with. But you see, I made the acquisition of that freedom into a matter of personal honour." [*KS*, p. 37]

This attitude, however, coexists in Pozdnyshev with the "'intention of getting married and building for myself the most elevated and purest of family lives,'" and with this plan in mind he looks out for "'a girl who might fill the bill'" (*KS*, p. 42). He finds her, falls in love with her, gets married.

But from the start the marital intimacy turns into an abyss of estrangement, quarrels, jealousy, hostility, followed each time by a loving reconciliation. The sole common ground of the husband and the wife is sex—sex, pregnancies, breast-feeding, and five children in eight years, who, themselves, are a source of further disagreements, further worries, quarrels, and disgust.

Between Love and Rage

At first, Pozdnyshev believes that the quarrels are pure accidents and that his misery is an exception:

> "I was tortured . . . by the dreadful thought that I was alone in having such a wretched relationship with my wife, and that everything was quite different in other people's marriages. At that stage I was still unaware that this is the common experience, that everyone believes, as I did, that theirs is an exceptional misfortune, and that everyone hides their shameful and exceptional misfortune not only from the eyes of others but also from themselves, and that they refuse to admit its existence." [*KS*, p. 58]

But, later, he perceives a real pattern in the alternation of his married life between love and hate:

> "I didn't notice it then, but I was regularly affected by bouts of animosity that used to correspond to the bouts of what we called 'love'. A bout of 'love' would be followed by one of animosity; a vigorous bout of 'love' would be followed by a long bout of animosity, while a less intense bout of 'love' would be followed by a correspondingly shorter bout of animosity. We didn't realize it then, but this 'love' and animosity were just two sides of the same coin." [*KS*, p. 74]

(Whose portrait, in effect, does Tolstoy describe? Could not O. J. Simpson's life equally be understood, accounted for, by this analysis? Would not the O. J. Simpson case in turn answer to, and quite precisely fit into, such a *Portrait of a Marriage?*)

> "We were two convicts serving life sentences of hard labor welded to the same chain, we hated each other, we were making each other's lives hell, and trying all the time not to see it. At that time I had not yet learned that this hell is the fate of ninety-nine per cent of all couples." [*KS*, p. 75][18]

After the birth of the couple's fifth child, the doctors, for health reasons, advise the wife not to get pregnant any more, and she obeys them. Pozdnyshev, who was a jealous husband from the start, becomes even more jealous now, since his thirty-year-old wife—relieved from pregnancies and from childbearing—becomes more beautiful and more "coquettish."

"'Yes, and then this man appeared,'" says Pozdnyshev (*KS*, p. 79).

18. This last paragraph is rendered in Troyat's translation, not in Penguin's English version; see Troyat, *Tolstoy*, p. 501.

The Triangle

One day, a violinist by the name of Trukhachevsky visits the couple, and the wife plays music with him at the piano. Pozdnyshev is immediately convinced that this common playing is the expression of a mutual attraction and a mutual seduction between the players. Yet instead of dismissing his guest, he extends an invitation to him to come again, to bring along his violin and give a true concert with his wife. The concert, in which Trukhachevsky and the wife—violin and piano—play together Beethoven's *The Kreutzer Sonata,* takes place. In his obsessive jealousy, Pozdnyshev listens to the music like a voyeur; listening in on the musical harmony and the dramatic tension between the instruments, he furtively spies on the excitement of this common musical performance, as one would have spied on an actual intercourse or sexual performance between the two musicians.

But Trukhachevsky soon leaves with the declared intention of not coming back, and Pozdnyshev himself goes away on a business trip, apparently calmed down. Yet on the train his jealousy, no longer a response to a real situation but only to potential ones, becomes a truly maddening obsession:

> "As soon as I got into the railway coach [Pozdnyshev narrates] I lost all control over my imagination: it began to paint for me, in the most lurid fashion, a rapid sequence of pictures which inflamed my jealousy. . . . They were all of the same thing—of what was happening there, in my absence, of her being unfaithful to me. I was consumed with rage, indignation and a kind of strange, drunken enjoyment of my own hurt pride as I contemplated these pictures, and I couldn't tear myself away from them. I couldn't help looking at them, I couldn't erase them from my mind, and I couldn't stop myself dreaming them up. But that wasn't all: the more I contemplated these imaginary pictures, the more I believed they were real. The luridness with which they appeared before me seemed proof that what I was imagining was in fact reality." [*KS*, p. 103]

The Murder

Literally intoxicated with his own projected visual hallucinations of his wife's sexual betrayal, Pozdnyshev breaks off his trip and goes back home, unexpected, to surprise his wife and spy on her, with frenzied thoughts of punishing her guilt—which he no longer doubts—on the slightest (so-called) evidence. His fears are not dispelled upon arrival, since he finds the violinist, once again, at his own home.

> "For an instant I froze there in the doorway, clutching the poniard behind my back. At the same moment he smiled and started to say, . . . 'Oh, we were just playing a little music together. . .'
> 'Goodness, I wasn't expecting . . . ' she began simultaneously. . . .
> But neither of them managed to get to the end of their sentences. The same rabid frenzy I had experienced a week previously once more took possession of me. Once again I felt that compulsion to destroy, to subjugate by force, to rejoice in the ecstasy of my furious rage, and I abandoned myself to it.
> Neither of them managed to finish what they were saying. . . . I rushed at her, still keeping the poniard hidden in case he tried to stop me plunging it into her side, under the breast. That was the spot I'd chosen right from the outset. In the very moment I attacked her, he saw what I was doing, and seized my arm—something I'd never expected he'd do. . . .
> I wrenched my arm free and went for him without a word. . . .—he ducked under the piano and was out of the room in a flash. . . . I was in a rabid frenzy, and I knew I must be a fearful sight, and was glad of it. I swung my left arm round as hard as I could, and my elbow struck her full in the face. She screamed and let go of my arm. . . . Then, without letting go of the poniard, I gripped her throat in my left hand, threw her back and started to strangle her. How hard her neck was. . . . She seized my hands in hers, trying to tear them free of her throat, and as if this were the signal for which I'd been waiting, I struck her with the poniard as hard as I could in her left side, beneath the ribs." [*KS*, pp. 111–13]

The wife lies butchered in her blood. She agonizes. As the husband contemplates this bloody sight and absorbs the image of his wife, he is stunned and shocked by her bruised face; the swollen and unrecognizably disfigured face confronts him, as though from a picture.

> "The first thing that leapt to my gaze was her light-grey dress . . .; the dress was stained black all over with blood. . . . What struck me most forcibly was her face: it was swollen, and along part of her nose and under one eye it was blue with bruises. This was the result of the blow I'd given her with my elbow when she'd been trying to hold me back. She had no beauty at all now, and I felt there was something repulsive about her." [*KS*, p. 116]

The Battered Face

It is here, when the intensity of the whole narrative translates itself into one striking visual image; here, when the story reaches its dramatic (visual) peak through this horrifying, graphic, cinematographic image of the battered face, that the narrative becomes dramatically evocative—feature by feature reminiscent—of the similarly horrifying picture of the battered face of Nicole Brown Simpson: an equally bruised, swollen, and distorted face whose photographic image was projected, during the proceedings of the trial of the century, both on the courtroom monitor and on our television screens. Let me, thus, go back for a brief moment from the dying wife of Pozdnyshev to the murdered wife of O. J. Simpson, whose swollen and disfigured face we have all seen, eternalized precisely in those photographs kept in her safe and that have reached us, through the courtroom monitor, like an uncanny visual *communication* from beyond the grave, like an unsettling, voiceless testimony of a battered, murdered woman—the wordless and suppressed appeal of a mute body—now forever silenced. Like Pozdnyshev, we have eyewitnessed this disfigured face. Like Pozdnyshev, we can bear witness to its horrifying, haunting visual legacy.

But such a face is always seen (and recognized) too late. "We know now," writes John Gregory Dunne in the *New York Review of Books,*

> We know now, as we always do in the aftermath of bloodshed, that the marriage of Nicole and O. J. Simpson prior to their 1992 divorce had been volatile, and occasionally violent. There were frequent 911 calls to settle domestic disputes, and in 1989 the Los Angeles city attorney filed a spousal battery complaint against Simpson after a fight on New Year's Eve. "He's going to kill me, he's going to kill me," she wept to the officers who answered her 911 call early that New Year's morning. They had found her hiding in the bushes outside her . . . house . . . wearing only sweatpants and a bra; her eye was blackened, her lips cut and swollen, there were scratches on her neck, and bruises on her cheek and forehead. Simpson shouted angrily at the police that it was a "family matter . . . why do you want to make a big deal out of it," and sped away in his Bentley. Cooling down . . . Nicole refused to press charges. . . . O. J. Simpson pleaded no contest to spousal battery and received the same light sentence that most first-time wife-beaters receive—a small fine, community service, and mandatory counseling. After sentence was imposed, the couple issued a joint statement: "Our marriage is as strong today as the day we were married."[19]

Let me return, now, to Pozdnyshev's own wife and to the husband's final contemplation of the image of her battered face.

> "What struck me most forcibly was her face: it was swollen, and along part of her nose and under one eye it was blue with bruises. This was

19. John Gregory Dunne, "The Simpsons," *New York Review of Books,* 22 Sept. 1995, p. 36.

the result of the blow I'd given her with my elbow when she'd been trying to hold me back. She had no beauty at all now, and I felt there was something repulsive about her."

"She looked up at me with difficulty—she had a black eye—and she said, haltingly: 'You've got what you wanted, you've killed me. . . .'

I looked at the children, at her battered face with its bruises, and for the first time I forgot about myself, about my marital rights and my injured pride; for the first time I saw her as a human being. And so insignificant did all that had hurt me and made me jealous appear, and so significant what I'd done, that I wanted to press my face to her hand and say: 'Forgive me!'—but I didn't dare to." [*KS*, pp. 116–17]

The Trial

The wife dies a few hours later. Pozdnyshev is arrested and is put on trial. He is acquitted because his crime is deemed to be a crime of passion caused by the betrayal of his wife. His attempt to explain to the court that his wife may not have been unfaithful after all, that the murder was not truly motivated by the wife's betrayal, fails. He thinks the court has not truly understood his case.

"At my trial the whole thing was made to look as though it had been caused by jealousy. Nothing could have been further from the truth. I'm not saying jealousy didn't play any part at all, mind—it did, but it wasn't the most important thing. At my trial they decided I was a wronged husband who'd killed his wife in order to defend his outraged honour (that's the way they put it in their language). So I was acquitted. During the court hearings I tried to explain what was really at the bottom of it all, but they just thought I was trying to rehabilitate my wife's honour." [*KS*, pp. 80–81]

In prison, while awaiting trial, Pozdnyshev has grasped a truth that has revolutionized his world. "'My eyes,'" he tells us, "'have been opened, and I've seen everything in a completely new light. Everything's been turned inside out, it's all inside out!'" (*KS*, p. 38).

It is this obscure truth which he could not articulate during the trial (this truth that he could not bring to the knowledge of the court) that he is now trying to communicate in his confession.

4

Portrait of a Case, or the Profile of a Murderer

Let me, now, sum up and analyze the common points between this story and the O. J. Simpson case. We know already that both cases become vehicles for an enlarged political debate and for a broader cultural trial of the times—or of the century (although the times have changed and the century moves toward us with the O. J. Simpson case). Both cases are composed of an identical chain of events consisting in two basic and defining episodes: (1) the murder of the wife; (2) the trial of the husband. I will distinguish, now, the analytical perspective of the murder from the analytical perspective of the trial and will examine separately the areas of overlap and intersection of the cases, first, in the story of the murder, then, in the story of the trial.

1. The Story of the Murder

Both murders are of an "unfaithful" wife. Both stories, therefore, are about a wife's unfaithfulness—and punishment. Whether the punishment should be attributed to a divine or human justice, to mere coincidence or to a marital revenge, the punishment is death. Both stories are stories of jealousy, and their main character is a possessive husband. Both husbands practice stalking as a means of ascertaining the behavior of their wife. Both cases implicate a triangle in that the crime scene implicates the unexpected presence or intrusion of a third participant—another man. Both stories dramatize a beating of the wife. Both are, thus, stories of domestic violence. Both cases sketch out the same portrait of a marriage in their repeated and compulsive switches between love and hate, desire and enraged hostility. The psychological make-up of the case is, thus, essentially the same. The husband in both cases is a sexual addict. Indeed, domestic violence could be itself another form of addiction—of sex addiction, since in both cases violence is sexual. After her 911 call, Nicole is found dressed only in a bra and sweatpants, and the stabbing is explicitly described in *The Kreutzer Sonata* as a destructive sexual act, a forced erotic penetration with a knife. The penetration of the knife is common to both stories; both murders are accomplished through a stabbing.

2. The Story of the Trial

If we consider, now, the functions and procedures of the trial, as distinct from the mere logic of the crime, the analogies between Tolstoy's case and the legal case are even more surprising, and quite significantly systematic.

Indictments and Acquittals

a) In both cases, the husband points an accusing finger toward the social order and the social institutions; the husband's case is argued, in both stories, not so much as a defense against the murder but as *a prosecution (and indictment) of society.*

b) The *verdict,* in both cases, is the same: *acquittal.* This verdict is, however, rather enigmatic in the context of the literary text because it stands in explicit contradiction to the husband's own confession that he did in fact commit the murder and is therefore unambiguously guilty. The question thus arises, Why does the literary text need to include at all a legal trial that acquits the husband in contradistinction to the facts? How is the acquittal necessary to the story? How does it partake of the writer's *literary* understanding (or interpretation) of the case? It seems to me that Tolstoy wants to suggest, precisely, by the introduction of the verdict a certain *complicity between the murder and the trial,* between the law and the transgression of the law—a secret but significant complicity between the crime and the society that judges it and puts the criminal on trial. Criminal proceedings are always instituted, in effect, not in the victim's name but in the name of the community whose law is broken. But the community, here, through the symbolism of a verdict that will not convict as its representative communal utterance, speaks in a voice that gives the husband's criminal offense a certain sanction of quasi-legitimacy. The murderer, in Tolstoy's text, implicitly acquires (or is legally granted by the court) a certain sort of communal amnesty, in resonance, indeed, with the communal absolution O. J. Simpson has received from his own community and with the communal sanction of legitimacy he has been granted, as a man and as a husband, by the court's pronouncement in the trial of the century.

Messages

c) A third common denominator between Tolstoy's case and the O. J. Simpson case is that both cases illustrate what I would call *a pedagogical use of the trial.* By his own explicit definition and avowed intention, Tolstoy is, at this point in life, a didactic writer, and his art is a didactic art. *The Kreutzer Sonata* is thus, paradoxically and quite provocatively, a *didactic* story about murder (the murder of a wife). A didactic story is, indeed, a narrative that is subordinated to a lesson, to a message it purports to illustrate or to exemplify.

Now, in the O. J. Simpson case the story of the trial has been equally transformed into the medium of a message. In his closing argument, defense attorney Johnny Cochran thematized explicitly this function or didactic purpose of the trial, in conjuring the jurors to acquit so as to (in his terms) "send a message" to society—about its racism, its corruption, and the fundamental unreliability both of its justice system and its police department. Since the jury has indeed acquitted Simpson, the trial *has* been used to register and to convey this message.

But, in the literary case as in the legal one, I wish to underscore the fact that it is not only the trial but the very murder of the wife that has become *a tool* for the transmission of the message. Cochran's proposition—or his message—in effect ignores, actively forgets, that the trial is not simply about Simpson but about a murder. What does it mean, however, that a message about racism *must be given through this trial* rather than through other channels? To the extent that the verdict in effect *erases* Simpson's murdered wife, or makes the murder—and the murdered woman—totally *irrelevant,* precisely, to the message, the trial in effect *repeats* the murder. The decision inadvertently reenacts the crime in killing once again the victims.

The lesson that the trial in the end incorporates, the pedagogical use of the proceedings, raises, therefore, serious questions about the moral value (the ethical significance) of murder as ideological tool. Since the body of the message is a corpse; since the message must use a dead body to promote and to legitimate itself, to what extent is such a usage—such an abstraction of the body—in itself legitimate? This question can be asked both of Tolstoy's text and of the O. J. Simpson trial. Should the wife's corpse be the vehicle, moreover, of someone else's message?

The Failure of the Trial

d) A fourth and final point of resemblance between Tolstoy's case and the O. J. Simpson case is that what is at the center of both stories is not just a trial but a *failure of the trial.* This failure of the legal framework, of the process, is what I take to be the most significant and most important common point. In Tolstoy's text, the confessing hero talks about this failure, this misfire of the trial, when he says to the narrator (his interlocutor on board the train) that the court has not really understood his case. He was acquitted on the understanding that the murder was a crime of passion, a case of jealousy and "outraged honour." But he himself has understood about the case something altogether different.[20] What precisely he has figured out remains obscure and is subject to the reader's own interpretation. But whatever it might be, the court has failed to understand it, in concluding—wrongly—that his protestations at the trial (his insistence that his wife may *not* have been unfaithful after all), his stuttering testimony or his failed attempts at testifying to a different truth,

20. "'If jealousy wasn't the pretext, some other one would have been found'" (*KS*, p. 81).

were mere words of courtesy to his wife's memory, a charitable cover-up or a rhetorical attempt to rehabilitate her name: "'During the court hearings I *tried to explain what was really at the bottom of it all,* but they just thought I was trying to rehabilitate my wife's honour'" (*KS,* p. 81). The court has failed, thus, both to understand and to translate into a legal language the hero's stuttering search for the truth.

I will argue that the O. J. Simpson case is similarly marked by a *failure of the trial* and that this failure is, in turn, equally essential to an understanding of the case. Indeed, the verdict that set free O. J. Simpson (like the one that acquitted Pozdnyshev) similarly did not *close* the case, or did not give the *sense of closure* that a verdict is designed precisely to provide. The verdict's effect was not that of an intellectual or an emotional catharsis, but that of an anticlimax that has left large portions of the trial's audience with a sort of emptiness.

I would suggest that, as in Tolstoy's case, this failure of the trial had to do with something that, within the legal framework, could not be seen. *Something that could not be seen and that in fact was not seen by the court was at the center of the trial;* something that the trial could not see was at the story's heart. What is it, therefore, that was not seen or could not be seen in the trial of the century?

"Critical Episodes of Married Life"

I would suggest that part of what could not be seen in Simpson's trial has to do with what Tolstoy precisely points to as culture's *blind spot,* namely, the invisible relation between marriage and domestic violence. In a television interview given a day after the verdict, Brenda Moran, one of the jurors in the Simpson trial, referred to her juridical experience of looking at the evidence of the domestic violence as a sheer "waste of time."[21] As a key witness to the trial, she therefore testified to the recalcitrant *invisibility of the domestic violence,* as well as to the jury's legal and judicial act of *looking through the beaten body* (of looking through and past the pictures of the battered face), in spite of the lawyers' endeavor to expose the evidence—the visual traces of the husband's blows—precisely to the jurors' *eyes* and thus to give the battered face a legal visibility. But in their verdict and, especially, in the absence of deliberation that preceded it, the jury did not so much nullify the evidence as it *nullified its visibility* and, in so doing, nullified the visibility of the face. The jury used, in other words, the court's authority to ratify, indeed, the inherent cultural *invisibility* of the battered face.

The jury, therefore, *did not see the domestic violence.* And, in line with Cochran's claim that Simpson had a normal marriage subject to "domes-

21. Quoted in Andrea Dworkin, "Trying to Flee," *Los Angeles Times,* 8 Oct. 1995, p. M6.

tic discord," which merely proved that his client was "not perfect," juror Moran even insisted, in that interview, that Simpson was not even an abusive husband; all the trial proved, she said, was *"one episode"* of violence (or maybe two). One or two "episodes" of violence do not make an abuser out of someone.

Curiously enough, *The Kreutzer Sonata,* in its turn, opens with a conversation with a *lawyer,* who (like Cochran, like Moran) talks about *"the critical episodes"* of *"married life"* in defending marriage against Pozdnyshev's denunciations of it. This polemical debate on the benign or nonbenign significance of marriage (which spontaneously evolves among passengers aboard a train) precedes (and frames) the story proper (the narrative of the confession). To Pozdnyshev's argument that "'marriage nowadays is just a deception'" that "'usually ends either in infidelity or violence'" (*KS,* p. 35), the lawyer replies: "'Yes, there's no doubt that married life has its critical episodes,' said the lawyer, endeavouring to bring to an end a conversation that had grown more heated than was seemly" (*KS,* p. 35). But rather than bringing an end to the conversation, this reference to "critical episodes" gives Pozdnyshev the opportunity to introduce himself by name (and introduce his story of the murder of the wife) both to the lawyer and to us. He introduces, thus, the fact or the reality of murder *into its cultural invisibility* and *into its legal denial.*

> "Yes, there's no doubt that married life has its critical episodes," said the lawyer. . . .
>
> "I can see you've recognized me," said the grey-haired man quietly, trying to appear unruffled.
>
> "No, I don't think I have the pleasure. . ."
>
> "It's not much of a pleasure. Pozdnyshev's the name. I'm the fellow who had one of those critical episodes you were talking about. So critical was it, in fact, that I ended up murdering my wife." [*KS,* pp. 35–36]

To go back now to O. J. Simpson in his relation to Tolstoy's text, it is quite interesting that in both cases the "critical episodes"—the story of the violence and the event of murder—are linked to something that essentially (in culture and in discourse) cannot be seen and that indeed fails to be seen within the framework of the trial.

Blind Justice (Seeing and Judging)

Could justice in effect be blind—in ways other than the ones in which it is normally expected to be? Is not seeing crucial to the very practice and the very execution of the law, because, as the saying has it, "justice must not only be done, but must be *seen* to be done"? A trial is, indeed, in its origin and in its essence, a theatrical event in that, by definition, it takes place upon a stage before an audience. The trial of the century has been only more exemplary in that respect, since it has been from the beginning a *show trial,* a spectacularized case whose evolving courtroom drama has been reproduced throughout the world, magnified and multiplied by millions of television screens. But any criminal proceedings implicate "the people" in whose name they are initiated as a community of viewers, a communal circle of social observers or of political (historical) spectators. Any court decision, in a way, is a historical decision about the significance the community derives from its spectatorial stance with respect to various happenings and, more generally, from its spectatorship of history. The rules of evidence, moreover, are in turn based on seeing. The strongest proof admitted by the court is proof corroborated by the eye: the most authoritative testimony in the courtroom is that of an eyewitness. Every trial, therefore, by its very nature as a trial, is contingent on the act of seeing.

Yet, in the case of the people versus O. J. Simpson, the jurors look but do not see. They do not see the beaten body. They look at pictures of Nicole's bruised countenance but declare they cannot see either the husband's blows or the wife's (the victim's) battered face. The jurors, in the O. J. Simpson case, are thus themselves *the trial's failed eyewitnesses.* This failure of the court to see evokes, indeed, once more, Pozdnyshev's frustration with the court's shortsightedness or blindness and the parallel philosophical and legal failure of the trial in Tolstoy's case.

But in this sense, precisely, of the failure of the court to see (or of the *failure of the trial* to *eyewitness* its own evidence), the O. J. Simpson case repeats, indeed, with an ironic symmetry, the history, the trauma, and the structure of the Rodney King case or of the Simi Valley trial, which, in its turn, was precisely about *beating*—and about an *unseen* beating, about an inexplicable, recalcitrant relation between beating and blindness, beating and invisibility, an invisibility that cannot be dispelled in spite of the most probatory visual evidence. Indeed, quite similarly to the way in which Simpson's domestic violence was visually corroborated by the photos of Nicole's bruised face, Rodney King's beating by police was documented by a videotape. And, yet, the jurors in the Simi Valley trial (all white) *did not see the beating* (of the black man). The jury watched the film but claimed it *did not see* police abuse and acquitted the four white policemen. Both decisions hinge, thus, on a failure to see beating. In both cases, what the jury *cannot see,* in other words, is (paradoxically) *the very blows that inflict trauma.* Both verdicts are in turn traumatic in that they *deny, in fact, the very trauma that the trial was supposed to remedy.* It is by virtue of this legal and historical resemblance of their basic structure in relation to the trauma (and the consequent trauma of the trial) that the Rodney King case and the O. J. Simpson case narrate at once the story—and the trial—of the century.

Beating and Invisibility, or Hatred's Prohibited Sight

If the decision, in both cases, registers a legal failure to see trauma, this inherent failure is in turn reinforced, compounded, by an equal cultural failure to acknowledge hate. It is significant, indeed, that, in both cases, what the jury fails to see—what cannot be seen precisely by the law—is *hate* (hate for women, hate for blacks) and that this secret, mute, insidious hate—this hate prohibited to sight—finds its expression, in both cases, in the graphic image—and in the physical translation—of a beating.

Beating is, indeed, a quintessential figure of *abuse of power* (physical and moral). As an emblem of oppression and humiliation, as a symbol of transgression of the other's property and of invasion of the other's body, beating is not just physiological but is inherently political. A radically offensive act, it is, I would suggest, the most rudimentary political offense and has the impact (physical and moral) of a political act par excellence.

But seeing—as the essence of the cognitive activity and as the foundation of both consciousness and memory—is in turn an act that is not simply physiological; it can in turn be inherently, unwittingly political. Louis Althusser explains how seeing and not seeing are contingent on the limits (the ideological exclusions) of a frame of reference. "It is the whole field of a problematic," writes Althusser,

> that defines and structures the invisible as its definite outside—*excluded* from the domain of visibility and *defined* as excluded by the existence and the structure of the problematic field itself. . . . The invisible is defined by the visible as *its* invisible, its prohibited sight. . . . To see this invisible . . . requires something quite different from a sharp or attentive eye, it takes an *educated eye,* a revised, renewed way of looking, itself produced by the effect of a "change of terrain" reflected back upon the act of seeing.[22]

I would argue, in my turn, that the limitations of the possibilities of seeing, the structural exclusions from our factual frames of reference, are determined not only by (conscious or unconscious) *ideology* but by a built-in cultural *failure to see trauma.* As is evident from both the Rodney King case and the O. J. Simpson case, *the abuse of power* (beating) is *inscribed in culture as a trauma.* But, as we know from psychoanalytic studies[23] and as both cases demonstrate, trauma is precisely what cannot be seen; it is

22. Louis Althusser, "Du *Capital* à la philosophie de Marx," in Althusser, Jacques Rancière, and Pierre Macherey, *Lire "Le Capital"* (Paris, 1965), pp. 28, 29, 30–31; my translation.

23. Compare the pathbreaking collection, *Trauma: Explorations in Memory,* ed. Cathy Caruth (Baltimore, 1995). Compare also the remarkable philosophical and literary analyses of traumatic structures in Caruth, *Unclaimed Experience: Trauma, Narrative, and History* (Baltimore, 1996).

something that inherently, politically and psychoanalytically, defeats sight, even when it comes in contact with the rules of evidence and with the trial's legal search for visibility. The political is thus essentially tied up with the structure of the trauma. It is to the structure of the trauma, therefore (and not simply to a different ideology), that our "eyes" should be precisely *educated*.

To return, now, to the beatings that remain persistently unseen in both the Rodney King case and the O. J. Simpson case, to return, thus, to both juries' failure to eyewitness the (physical and moral) violence whose literal invisibility cannot be dispelled in court, in spite of the most probatory visual evidence, in both cases, in effect, the photographic image (photos or videotape) turns out to be incapable of lifting out or of cancelling the cultural blind spot, or the political prescription not to see.[24] The century might well be, in Walter Benjamin's acute terms, "the age of mechanical reproduction" or the legal century of videotapes. But in spite of the advances in the technological methods of recording or of memorizing visual evidence, the trial of the century remains *a story of the century's blind spots*.

As Tolstoy's text shows, however, concerning gender, the legal story of the century is essentially the same as that of the preceding one. As regards marriage and violence, it seems we have made little progress and have not truly come out of the nineteenth century. In any case, we have not yet entirely emerged from a traumatic story (or from a trauma) whose very pattern is characteristic of the previous century. As the coincidence between the literary text and the contemporary trial shows, as far as women are concerned as targets of abusive or appropriative violence, we seem to have inherited, quite strictly and specifically, the nineteenth century's blind spots. The murders and acquittals of the nineteenth century are still with us as our tragically intact inheritance.

Law and History: Inheritance of Trauma

What have we done, thus, in a hundred years ? Has history not taken place to register at least a legal difference? Or is it law itself that is responsible not just for the recording but for the censorship of history? Could

24. Andrea Dworkin, writing in the *Los Angeles Times*, cites another stupefying case concerning the recalcitrant invisibility of beating (a case, however, whose political invisibility seems to relate to gender, rather than to race):

> On the same day the police who beat Rodney King were acquitted in Simi Valley, a white husband who had raped, beaten and tortured his wife, also white, was acquitted of marital rape in South Carolina. He had kept her tied to a bed for hours, her mouth gagged with adhesive tape. He videotaped a half-hour of her ordeal, during which he cut her breasts with a knife. The jury, which saw the videotape, had eight women on it. Asked why they acquitted, they said, he needed help. *They looked right through the victim.* [Dworkin, "Trying to Flee," p. M6; italics mine]

the voluminous *legal recording* of the O. J. Simpson trial be itself merely the witness of the way in which history is paradoxically deprived of memory? How do verdicts (the acquittal in the O. J. Simpson case) mark at once what history *remembers* and what history *forgets,* at once what is pragmatically included in and what is programmatically excluded from collective memory?

In their arbitrating function between contradictory facts and between conflicting versions of the truth, verdicts are decisions about what to admit into and what to transmit of collective memory. Law is, in this way, an organizing force of the significance of history.[25] But law relates to history through trauma.[26] What should have been historically remembered, in effect, is not only the trial but the trauma that has made the trial necessary, the individual and social trauma that the trial was supposed to remedy, to solve, or to resolve. Yet, a trauma cannot simply be remembered when, in the first place, it cannot be grasped, when, as these trials show, it cannot even be seen. Rather than memory, it compels a traumatic reenactment.

I would argue, therefore, that a legal case truly becomes a locus of embodied history, a "site of memory" or a material, literal "lieu de mémoire" in Pierre Nora's sense,[27] only when it is spontaneously endowed with what Freud calls a historical duality,[28] when it reverberates, in other

25. Law takes up, thus, indirectly and unwittingly (implicitly), the traditional tasks of historiography. Historiography, however, is inherently a cognitive or constative endeavor, whereas law is, and remains, inherently performative; it inadvertently competes with historiography (or duplicates its organizing or interpretive functions) only through the radical difference of its performative endeavor, in its essence as performativity.

26. Law relates to trauma through the social function of the trial as a structural (procedural and institutional) remedy to trauma. In a different, larger philosophical sense, Walter Benjamin has inaugurated (in the wake of Marx, but with a different kind of insight and of emphasis) an innovative tradition of historiography, whose goal is to articulate the past historically (always against the version of official or established "history"), not from the perspective of "the victors" but from the perspective of "the tradition of the oppressed," in which Benjamin underscores precisely the centrality of the experience of trauma. "To articulate the past historically," writes Benjamin,

> does not mean to recognize [the past] "the way it really was." . . . It means to seize hold of a memory as it flashes up at a moment of danger. . . . The tradition of the oppressed teaches us that the "state of emergency" in which we live is not the exception but the rule. We must attain to a conception of history that is in keeping with this insight. Then we shall clearly realize that it is our task to bring about a real state of emergency. . . . Where we perceive a chain of events, [the angel of history] sees one single catastrophe which keeps piling wreckage upon wreckage. [Walter Benjamin, "Theses on the Philosophy of History," *Illuminations,* trans. Harry Zohn, ed. Arendt (New York, 1968), pp. 255, 257]

27. Compare Pierre Nora, "Entre Mémoire et Histoire," *Les Lieux de mémoire,* vol. 1 of *La République,* ed. Nora (Paris, 1984). An English version of excerpts of Nora's introduction ("Between Memory and History: *Les Lieux de mémoire,*" trans. Mark Roudebush) was published in *Representations,* no. 26 (Spring 1989): 7–25.

28. Freud, *Moses and Monotheism,* p. 64, and see pt. 2, chap. 7 throughout.

words, with what I have defined as a *cross-legal* resonance, or triggers inadvertently the movement of a repetition or the dynamics of a *legal recall*. In its simultaneous gesture of commemoration and of forgetfulness of what it in effect repeats, the O. J. Simpson trial constitutes precisely such a "site of memory" ("lieu de mémoire") because it constitutes a "site" (a locus, a location, an abyss) of traumatic repetition.[29]

The O. J. Simpson case unwittingly repeats, thus, both the twentieth-century traumatic legal narrative of Rodney King and the nineteenth-century traumatic legal story of Tolstoy. But Tolstoy's own literary, legal case consists already in a repetition, since its very starting point is the hero's *reenactment of the legal trial* (his reopening of the criminal proceedings' failed search for the truth) through the narrative of *the confession* that, in turn, undertakes to repeat or to narrate again (to recapitulate, once more) the story that could not be heard in the proceedings and that failed to be communicated, or transmitted, to the court. The trial of the century repeats, then, all these repetitions—legal, literary, psychoanalytical, historical—by which the trial tries, and retries, to resolve the trauma and by which the trauma inadvertently repeats itself as an unconscious

29. What has acquitted Simpson is, thus, history: a repetitive historical pattern of abuse of African Americans by agents of the law. Those who voted or who would have voted for acquittal (and they are not limited to blacks) wanted to exonerate black trauma, to vindicate, to exculpate, and to empower the historical defenselessness of African Americans before the law. It is an entire history of trauma that has here weighed on the decision. What has acquitted Simpson is the way in which his confrontation with the law allowed him (irrespective of his guilt or innocence) to play an inadvertent role he did not seek and did not in effect desire: that of a physical custodian—a keeper in his very body—of collective memory. This legal and symbolic mythic role begins unwittingly when Simpson chooses to attempt to earn freedom by a physical escape or by a run in the face of the law. The dramatic televised pursuit—the mute scenario of the slow-speed chase and Simpson's ultimate surrender and return as state property—enacts or reenacts in the collective memory at once the recent drama of the high-speed chase of Rodney King (ironically pursued for speeding) and a more ancient primal scene of running slaves pursued so as to be returned to their proper, *legal* owners. Not only in the case of gender, therefore, but in the case of race as well, the traumatic legal story of the twentieth century has not entirely emerged from a traumatic story of the nineteenth century (Dred Scott, 1857).

In his embodied posture as a captured runaway and in the need to be or to become now *a survivor of the law* (or of the legal system), Simpson symbolically recovers a collective cultural past he has been trying to forget and to deny, and a shared history he has been trying, all his life, to run away from. In running from the law, he runs back toward the past. In Simpson's very body (and in his bodily presence in the court), "blackness" historically returns as erased (forgotten) memory; it returns therefore as unconscious or repressed: repressed, erased by Simpson's own assimilation. This (in part at least) accounts for the emotional explosion at the verdict. The intensity of the triumphant identification of the black community with Simpson's *survival of the law* derives precisely from the force of this *historical return of the repressed*, all the more forceful for symbolically returning an *erased* collective and traumatic memory.

From this perspective, the legal drama of the century becomes a *legal narrative of black survival*, and of the survival and *resuscitation* of black memory.

legal memory under the conscious legal process. The O. J. Simpson case, in summary, is the defining trial of our times because it recapitulates, precisely, all these repetitions. It is the trial of the century because it reenacts the Rodney King case; but this defining trial of the twentieth century turns out to be itself a repetition of the trial (of the trauma) of the nineteenth century.

I would suggest, indeed, that the main difference in this century's trials and acquittals is that history enables us, today, at least to catch up with Tolstoy—at least *to see that we do not see*—and, thus, historically to raise these questions, to ask about the meaning of the repetition. If history, indeed, repeats itself, and if events must happen at least twice to be perceived, might the repetition in itself, some day, help bring about (help train) "an educated eye"?

Eyes and Education, or Beating and Seeing

All three cases, therefore—Pozdnyshev's or Tolstoy's case, the Rodney King case, and the O. J. Simpson case—resonate with one another in similarly dramatizing, in the courtroom, a striking and misunderstood *relation between seeing and beating*, between *a violence that harms* or that seeks to hurt or kill and *a violence that blinds* or seeks to prohibit sight. In the literary scene as in the legal one, in their fictions and in their realities, all three cases (Simpson, Rodney King, Tolstoy) similarly concretize a failure of the trial through the story of the legal implications, on the one hand, of hatred as prohibited to sight and, on the other hand, of suffering or of trauma as *the structure of a blow* (or of an injury) *that cannot be seen*. All the trial can prove, therefore, is the trauma's *unlocatability*, the injury's constitutive invisibility, the blow's traumatic *non-justiciability*. All the trial does is, therefore, to *repeat the trauma* in enacting, once more, its recalcitrant invisibility and in showing how *the trauma's power to defeat sight* infiltrates the very workings of the legal process and insidiously takes over the very structure of the trial. It is precisely this complex political and epistemological *relation of the beating to the seeing*, and this profound human and political enigma of a trauma that cannot be seen and cannot be located, or translated into seeing (into seeability) even at the level of the trial, that seems to be at the center of Tolstoy's text and at the center of the story Pozdnyshev *cannot quite bring to the knowledge of the court*. But this is what, for him and for Tolstoy, the trial—and the story—are really all about.

5

The Abyss

What is it, then, that Pozdnyshev has failed to articulate and to transmit about his story (or about the real nature of his case) during the trial? What is this insight he tries desperately to articulate, but which remains deprived of legal language, this speechless, inarticulate, unheard, excessive truth that remains outside the hearing of the court, that exceeds both what is said and what is heard in the proceedings, and that is defined, in Tolstoy's text, precisely—only—as *an excess of the narrative (of literature) over the trial?* What legal event is defined—and can only be accounted for—by an excessive literary truth?

This question can be asked from two opposed perspectives: (1) What sort of paradoxical event creates a crisis that exceeds what can be legally articulated, but that nonetheless *necessitates a trial for its very definition?* (2) What is, on the other hand, this crisis or this paradoxical event that cannot do without a legal process, but that, literarily and philosophically, can only be transmitted *through a failure of the trial*—through an explosion of the legal framework? Such is the murder of the wife in Tolstoy's text (in its relation to the trial). And such, I would propose, is, similarly, the paradoxical relation of the murder of Nicole Brown Simpson to the O. J. Simpson trial, for which Tolstoy might be, indeed, a literary *key.* Philosophically, Tolstoy seems to be asking, not by chance, perhaps, a question that applies both to his fiction and to the intricate legal reality of the contemporary trial: what is the story that can be told only through an *unpaid debt* of the *decision* to the *truth,* or of the verdict to the facts? *What is this* (literary, psychological, political, historical) *debt* that the decision, the acquittal, still holds with respect to the full legal truth, but that a conviction (as we see from the reactions to the outcome of the civil case) could not in its turn possibly reduce, resolve, or fully pay?

What is it we can therefore understand, with Tolstoy's help, about the real nature of the (fictional and real) murder case? What can we ultimately understand or learn from the text—from the *confession*—of *The Kreutzer Sonata?* And how can *what* we understand illuminate the riddle of the legal case? How can the perspective of the literary text (and of a literary understanding) shed light on the overall historic lesson and on the overall historical performance of the trial of the century? What is it that Tolstoy is struggling, in conclusion, to communicate?

Let us listen, one last time, to Pozdnyshev's testimony, in its effort to convey the story which the court has missed:

> "At my trial the whole thing was made to look as though it had been caused by jealousy. Nothing could have been further from the truth.

> I'm not saying jealousy didn't play any part at all, mind—it did, but it wasn't the most important thing. At my trial they decided I was a wronged husband who'd killed his wife in order to defend his outraged honour (that's the way they put it in their language). So I was acquitted. During the court hearings I tried to explain what was really at the bottom of it all, but they just thought I was trying to rehabilitate my wife's honour." [*KS*, pp. 80–81]

Jealousy was just a pretext, Pozdnyshev insists, almost an indifferent pretext: "'If it hadn't been him, it would have been some other man. If jealousy wasn't the *pretext,* some other one would have been found'" (*KS,* p. 81).

> "Whatever her relationship with that musician was, it wasn't important to me, any more than it was to her. What was important was what I've been telling you about—my pigsty existence. *It all happened because of that terrible abyss there was between us,* the one I've been talking about, the terrible stress of our mutual hatred for each other that made the first *pretext* that came along sufficient to cause a *crisis.*" [*KS,* p. 81]

Chasm

The case, then, is about the relation of the (private, sexual, trivial) "*pretext*" to the (social, legal) "*crisis*" of the violence and of the murder: "It all happened because of that terrible *abyss* there was between us." The real motivation of the story derives, thus, neither from the wife's (real or fantasized) unfaithfulness nor from the jealousy that this presumed unfaithfulness provokes, but from the very existence of "that terrible abyss." The story, then, is not the story that we thought; it is not the banal case of adultery (of jealousy) we had at first believed, rather predictably, that we were reading. What is it, then? I would argue that what we discover in Tolstoy's text is, far less predictably, the narrative of an abyss, a case, precisely, of the unexpected revelation of a hidden and profound chasm.

The metaphor of the abyss repeats itself throughout the text of *The Kreutzer Sonata.* Although Tolstoy's Russian uses several different words to concretize and to nuance this image of a precipice *(propast, puchina, bezdna),* all these words depict the same experience of a break (a loss) of contact and of ground; all these figures point to the same insistent image of a fissure, a dividing gulf, a bottomless ocean, or a terrifying, gaping wound in the ground:

> "*It all happened because of that terrible abyss there was between us,* the one I've been talking about, the terrible stress of our mutual hatred for

each other that made the first pretext that came along sufficient to cause a crisis." [*KS*, p. 81]

"It's horrible, horrible, horrible. . . . the *abyss of error* [misunderstanding] we live in regarding women and our relations with them." [*KS*, p. 38]

"And so we continued to live, in a perpetual fog, without ever becoming aware of the situation we were in. If what finally happened hadn't happened, and I'd go on living like that until my old age, I think that even when I was dying I'd have thought I had a good life . . .; *I would never have come to perceive the abyss of unhappiness,* the loathsome falsehood in which I was wallowing." [*KS*, p. 75]

"That first quarrel had a terrible effect on me. I call it a quarrel, but it wasn't really a quarrel; it was just the *revelation of the abyss that actually separated us.*" [*KS*, p. 57]

An Abyss of Sexuality: An Abyss of Difference

What is this precipice, which Tolstoy so insistently returns to?

In its most obvious significance, the metaphor of the abyss in *The Kreutzer Sonata* seems to be linked to the space of sexuality as a frightening enigma. But what is sexuality, precisely? Sexuality is, first and foremost, in this story (as it is, indeed, in O. J. Simpson's story) an *abyss between the sexes*. And this gulf between the sexes, this ill-understood abyss that so radically and so incurably separates the woman from the man and estranges the husband from the wife, refers in turn not just to the unfathomable abyss of sexuality and sexual desire (as the story's obscure origin) but, more specifically, to a fissure or a split *within* sexuality itself, to an inner schism or a chasm not just *between the narrator and his wife* but *within the narrator's own sexual desire;* there is an abyss, precisely, that inhabits human sexuality, like an internal hollowness at the bottom of a whirling chaos of attractions and repulsions, of rivalries and of conflicting, secret sexual ambiguities. This abyss of difference (internal and external) cannot but become an abyss of conflict. The relative positions in the story of the jealousy—in the triangle of the sexual competition—can change dynamically and secretly: desire for the wife and jealousy toward the male rival; attraction for (or fascination with) the rival and a secret sexual competition with the wife;[30] love-hate for the wife; love-hate for the would-be

30. Compare *The Kreutzer Sonata:*

> "Yes, he was a musician, a violinist. . . . He had moist eyes, like almonds, smiling red lips, and a little moustache. . . . He was slight of physique, . . . and he had a particularly well-developed posterior, as women have. . . . He and his music were the real cause of it all. At my trial the whole thing was made to look as though it had been caused by jealousy. Nothing could have been further from the truth." [*KS*, p. 80]

lover; jealousy, respectively, of both; a maze of attractions and repulsions; an abyss that inhabits sexuality like a chaotic whirlpool or an internal hollowness that constantly sucks it, splits it from inside itself; an abyss that fatally and radically divides sexuality from itself, makes it different from itself.

But what is even more important than the sexual significance of the abyss, what is even more significant than its (split) sexual nature, is the relation of the split—the precipice—to its *obscure depth* or to its *abyssal, enigmatic core of darkness*. This concrete obscurity (of the abyss) is recapitulated by a metaphor of darkness that runs throughout the text[31] and that, in resonance with that of the abyss, dramatizes (concretizes) *a resistance from inside the story to what can be seen* (or to what can pierce into awareness).[32] "It all happened because of that terrible abyss there was between us." Resisting awareness, the radical darkness inside the abyss, the (literal and metaphorical) obscurity inside the story, functions, therefore, like a *black hole* that is the story's center. This narrative black hole (the dark abyss inside the story) dynamically resists the trial's search for legal visibility and undercuts the story's constant effort to obtain both light and sight.

31. Like the crime scene in the O. J. Simpson case, the scene of *The Kreutzer Sonata* (the confession) takes place in a literal obscurity outlined only by shadows and by shades. It is nighttime, dark both outside and inside the train; the story is surrounded (governed) by a darkness, in which (metaphorically and literally) nothing is entirely or simply readable: "It was too dark to read, so I closed my eyes and pretended I wanted to go to sleep," says the narrator (*KS*, p. 36). Pozdnyshev confesses in this total darkness, which protects him; his voice is heard, but his face, symbolically and literally, is never clearly seen. Like O. J. Simpson, he remains "a shadowy figure." The story never entirely emerges from the darkness in which it is plunged:

> It was *so dark* that I *could not see his face*, only hear his forceful, pleasant voice. [*KS*, p. 38]
>
> His face kept altering strangely in the *semi-darkness* where we sat. [*KS*, p. 42]
>
> "The light's getting in my eyes—do you mind if we pull the shade over it?" he said, pointing to the lamp. [*KS*, p. 53]
>
> I started to get a sinister feeling, lying there in the dark, and I struck a match. . . . He continued his story. . . . and all that could be heard in the *semi-darkness* was the rattling of the windows. . . . In the half-light of the dawn, *I could no longer make out Pozdnyshev's features*. All I could hear was his voice. [*KS*, pp. 101–2]

32. "'And so we continued to live, in a perpetual fog, without ever becoming aware of the situation we were in. If what finally happened hadn't happened. . . . I would never have come to perceive the abyss of unhappiness, the loathsome falsehood in which I was wallowing'" (*KS*, p. 75).

The Trial's Central Darkness, or the Narrative Black Hole

Like the trauma, like the narrative black hole that is the story's center, the abyss, indeed, is something normally hidden from sight, something whose obscure depth (or whose end) cannot be fathomed and whose *bottom* (or whose starting point) *cannot be seen.* But when the bottom is touched through the murder, when the abyss can suddenly and unexpectedly be glimpsed, what can be seen is nothing but an emptiness and an obscurity. At the story's end (at the conclusion of the trial, and at the horizon of the text), what is dramatically revealed is not depth, but the unsuspected bottomlessness of a terrifying chasm.

And so it is, I would propose, precisely in the O. J. Simpson case. The performance of the trial of the century was nothing if not a historical encounter with the unexpected bottomlessness of a chasm. What was finally revealed at the trial's end was, similarly, not the curtain's fall, not the closure of the case or a catharsis finally obtained by a legal resolution, but here again only the terrifying opening, only the emptiness[33] of an ungraspable abyss: an *abyss between the sexes;* an *abyss between the races;* an abyss between legality and justice; a gap in perception between blacks and whites; an abyss between contradictory experiences of the significance of law enforcement and between conflicting views of the use or the abuse of the power yielded to the justice system and to the agents of the law; an abyss between conflicting views of the significance or of the insignificance of domestic violence; an abyss between the rich who can buy justice and the poor who cannot afford to pay its price; an abyss between conflicting views or contradictory emotional perceptions of the verdict as a victory or as an absolute defeat. "Yet there was no real victory, no real defeat," writes Robert A. Jordan, "for blacks and whites who are on opposite sides of this verdict. Rather, there is the fresh realization that . . . the divide between blacks and whites, is still *very deep* in this country."[34] But the impact of the trial, and the schism suddenly uncovered by the shock of the verdict of the century, has to do with something *deeper* still and not quite so definable, something that escapes definition at the very heart of the abyss revealed by the conclusion of the trial. As in Tolstoy,

33. Compare Lisa Kennedy: "The karmic payback of this verdict [O. J. Simpson] for that injustice [Rodney King] has an *empty* quality" (Lisa Kennedy, "Neverending Story," *Village Voice,* 17 Oct. 1995, p. 25); and Henry Louis Gates: "It is a discourse . . . in which everyone speaks of payback and nobody is paid. . . . And so an *empty* vessel like O. J. Simpson becomes filled with meaning, and more meaning—more meaning than any of us can bear" (Henry Louis Gates, Jr., "Thirteen Ways of Looking at a Black Man," *The New Yorker,* 23 Oct. 1995, p. 65; rpt. in Gates, *Thirteen Ways of Looking at a Black Man* [New York, 1997], pp. 121–22).

34. Robert A. Jordan, "No Victory, No Defeat, Only an Angry Racial Divide," *Boston Globe,* 8 Oct. 1995, p. A35.

the sudden opening of the abyss is linked to the emergence of a split in the very integrity of legal justice.

An Abyss of Trauma

"But will Americans even bother to wonder how racially cleft . . . the criminal justice system must have been long before this case?" asks Francis X. Clines. "Will whites—so shocked at the television scenes of some blacks triumphant at the verdict announcement—now be ready to believe blacks' first-hand tales of negative contacts with police?"[35] "The verdict," writes Isabel Wilkerson, "exposed a chasm in place for generations."[36] I would argue that this broken integrity (the schism in society, the split in the integrity of justice) is tied up with a splitting that, itself, is (and *repeats,* precisely) the effect of a traumatic shock. The chasm between blacks and whites becomes, ironically, a dialogue of shocks. The shock is specifically related to the "accidented" space of culture as a *cultural gap,* or to the "accidented" and inherently dissociated space of the cultural trauma, insofar as trauma (individual as well as social) is precisely constituted by a gap in consciousness.

What should have been perceived, at the conclusion of the O. J. Simpson trial, is, thus, the concrete reality of the traumatic gap—or the concreteness of the trauma. What is perceived, instead, is the abyss—the gap—between two traumas: that of race and that of gender. But race and gender differ, mainly, in this trial, in their relation to a third trauma: that of law itself.

In its prosecution of a husband's murderous abuse, the law has been appealed to, here, by gender as a guardian of the victim's rights and thus as a necessary ally and, possibly, as the only *vehicle of correction of the abuse.* But in the argument of the defense (and in the collective memory of race), law is invoked as part and parcel of the trauma, and its *enforcement* is remembered and historically commemorated (litigated) as *the very source, the very vehicle of the abuse.* Race and gender differ, thus, in their thematized relation to the law and in their consequent legal perception of the trial as itself part of the problem (part of the abuse), or as its possible redress, its cure. "The verdict exposed a chasm in place for generations. . . . And nowhere was that divide more stark than it was between black women and white women," writes Wilkerson: "Pressed to choose between the men with whom they share race experience . . . and the white women with whom they share the experience of sexism," black

35. Francis X. Clines, "And Now, the Audience Rests," *New York Times,* 8 Oct. 1995, p. 4.

36. Isabel Wilkerson, "Whose Side to Take: Women, Outrage, and the Verdict on O. J. Simpson," *New York Times,* 8 Oct. 1995, p. D4; hereafter abbreviated "W."

women jurors had no choice but to "break ranks" ("W," pp. D4, D1). In choosing race solidarity with men over (and against) gender solidarity with female victims of abuse, the women jurors could not but create a cleavage within the integrity (the unity) of gender itself and have in effect revealed an abyss inside the community of women—a schism concretized in the televised images, after the acquittal, of "black women smiling to the heavens, thanking Jesus," and of "white women, sobbing, unable to speak" ("W," p. D1).

Philosophically, indeed, the abyss revealed by the trial of the century has compromised not only the integrity of gender, and not only the integrity of the legal process, but the integrity of truth itself. Or, rather, the conclusion of the trial has shown truth as an abyss between incommensurate realities, a schism between different ways of seeing, between incommensurable ways of looking at the very same facts. "Nothing that happened in the O. J. Simpson trial was as awful as the way it ended," comments *The Economist:*

> Was the jury wrong? One cannot know. . . . The distressing part was not the verdict itself; it was the proof thus confirmed that black and white America have been watching different trials. . . . This verdict makes plain what so many Americans—and so many of their friends abroad—had not wanted to believe. Thirty-odd years after the civil-rights revolution, America is two countries, not one. And they are growing apart, not together.[37]

"'It all happened,'" says Tolstoy, "'because of that terrible abyss there was between us.'" "'It wasn't really a quarrel; it was just the revelation of the abyss that actually separated us.'" "'It's horrible, horrible, horrible! . . . the abyss of error [misunderstanding] we live in regarding women and our relations to them.'"

> "To live like that would have been insufferable if we'd understood the situation we were in, but we didn't understand it—we weren't even aware of it. It's the salvation as well as the punishment of human beings that when they're living irregular lives, they're able to wrap themselves in a blanket of fog so that they can't see the wretchedness of their situation. . . .
>
> And so we continued to live, in a perpetual fog, without ever

37. "Two Nations, Divisible: The Intolerable Lesson of the O. J. Simpson Trial," *The Economist*, 7 Oct. 1995, p. 18. The degree of the amazement at the depth of the race cleavage is itself, however, yet another symptom of how history is inherently deprived of memory: forgetful of the still not so remote legal enforcement of "two countries"—two Americas—through racist segregation laws.

> becoming aware of the situation we were in. If what finally happened hadn't happened, and I'd gone on living like that until my old age, I think that even when I was dying I'd have thought I had a good life . . .; *I would never have come to perceive the abyss of unhappiness,* the *loathsome falsehood* in which I was wallowing." [*KS*, pp. 74–75]

Seeing the Gap

Could *The Kreutzer Sonata* be the narrative of what it takes (in tragedy and in destruction) to make one *see* precisely the abyss? Is the O. J. Simpson case the story of the price to pay, in turn, for the revelation of this chasm that had been there all along but that, like the protagonists of *The Kreutzer Sonata,* we in turn *could not see* or *did not want to see?* Could the trial of the century be, in other words, the legal drama or the case of law that historically sums up the century as a century that, blindly, has lived on the brink of an ungrasped historical abyss, a century that needs, thus, a defining trial to *discover* (suddenly to see) *its own history (its memory) as an abyss*—an essentially ungraspable, and still essentially *invisible* "abyss of unhappiness" and "loathsome falsehood"? And if the trial of the century is indeed the cultural story of our blindness, could this legal story of our blindness turn, like Tolstoy's, into the story of a revolutionary seeing?

> "It's no good, I just can't talk calmly about it. It's not merely because of that episode, as the other gentleman called it, but because ever since I went through it *my eyes have been opened* and I've seen everything in a completely new light. Everything's been turned inside out, *it's all inside out*!" [*KS*, p. 38]

In the O. J. Simpson trial as in Tolstoy's text, the abyss is *inside out.*

I will argue, to conclude, that the O. J. Simpson trial *was* the trial of the century *because* it has revealed precisely an abyss or told the legal story of the century's severance in consciousness. The abyss might well be "inside out": insofar as it is not just an abyss of cultural hypocrisy, but an abyss of cultural trauma, it remains the trial's secret. I argue that the case, in other words, has claimed its unique status as the trial of the century *because we still cannot decide*—and do not completely understand—*what the trial was about,* because we still do not know or cannot decide where exactly to locate the trauma, or what was really at the bottom of this (legal, cultural, and historical) abyss.

Between Law and Literature: Comparative Epistemologies

Thus it is that the comparison between the O. J. Simpson case and Tolstoy's text has helped us to review and to rethink the implications—and the impact—of the contemporary trial.

I have examined factual and interpretive legal uncertainties in the instructively imaginative and dramatically suggestive light of literary facts whose narrative logic (whose own dramatic legal tale of murder and of trial) decisively resembled the contemporary case and whose intuitive, imaginative insight into criminal (human) behavior and into the enigma of the structure of the case and of the structure of the murder (as well as of the murder's paradoxical relation to the trial) turned out to be at once compelling and inspiring.

Thus it is that the comparison between the trial and the literary text, between the intricate legal reality and the imaginative literary vision of the case of the murder of the wife (and of the trial of the husband) has cued us into the significance—and into the suggestive literary resonance—of the abyss.

I have proposed that the abyss was at the center—at the heart—both of the literary story and of the contemporary trial; and that both the trial and the text consisted in the unexpected revelation of the image—and of the ungraspable significance—of the abyss, both as an obscure original causality ("'It all happened because of that terrible abyss there was between us'") and as the fatal repetition, the unexpected and yet unavoidable return of a form of radical dispute ("'I call it a quarrel, but it wasn't really a quarrel; it was just the revelation of the abyss that actually separated us'").

Between Law and Literature (An Abyss)

But the comparison between the legal drama and the literary drama has also shown that law and literature have radically different philosophies (different approaches) with respect to the abyss. Governed by their different goals, the legal practice and the literary practice embody, in effect, two different ways of *addressing* the abyss and two ways of *relating the significance of the abyss,* specifically, *to the significance and to the functions of the trial.*

As we have seen, in both the trial and the literary text, the abyss—an abyss of difference, hatred, racism, sexuality, "unhappiness," and trauma—a "quarrel" that "is not really a quarrel" but the "revelation" of a radically divisive inner breakdown, is above all something terrifying. But it is also what we cannot grasp and do not understand. It is something we can see only from outside. It is therefore what, essentially, *cannot be totalized,* what a *closing argument* will of necessity fail to contain, to *close* or to *enclose*. *By definition, an abyss is what escapes legal summation, what eludes reflective or conceptual totalization.*

What, then, can a trial do with an abyss? The trial of the century has sought (as the law always attempts to do) *to throw a bridge over the abyss,* to stand in, or to step into, the breach by precisely *filling in the gap,* by closing the abyss or by enclosing it within the rationality of its legal categorizations (gender, race) in an attempt to cover or to *cover up its bottomlessness,* to integrate or to assimilate the gap within known categories of the social or political or legal order. In its pragmatic role as guardian of society against irregularity, derangement, disorganization, unpredictability or any form of irrational or uncontrollable disorder, the law, indeed, has no choice but to guard against equivocations, ambiguities, obscurities, confusions, and loose ends. All these the abyss embodies, in the image of a danger the law fears above all: that of a failure of accountability (or of a breakdown in foundation and in foundational stability); that of a *loss,* of a *collapse* (absence) *of grounds.* Under the practical constraints of having to insure accountability and to bring justice, the law tries to *make sense of the abyss* or to reduce its threat (its senselessness, its unintelligible chaos) by giving it a name, by codifying it or by subsuming its reality (which is inherently nameless and unclassifiable) into the classifying logic and into the technical, procedural coherence of the trial. But in so doing, the law (the trial or the litigation) inadvertently denies the abyssal nature of the abyss in pretending or in misguidedly assuming the abyss is something else, something that can be assimilated to known rules or precedents, something that can be enclosed, contained within the recognizability of known (stereotypical) legal agendas.

But the purpose of the literary text is, on the contrary, to show or to expose again the severance and the schism, to reveal once more the opening, the hollowness of the abyss, *to wrench apart what was precisely covered over, closed or covered up by the legal trial.* The literary text casts open the abyss so as to let us look, once more, into its depth, and see its bottomlessness.

And in so doing, in *reopening the case* and in revealing, once more, the obscurity, the empty opening of the abyss, the literary text enacts (or carries out through its own narrative, through its confession) a *repetition of the story* that the court has missed or has misunderstood, and which the trial could not tell. Literature enacts, thus, an artistic recapitulation of the dynamics of the trial and of the trial's search (and re-search) for the truth. By its own specific means, by its literary power or by the acuteness of its own search (struggle) for expression, the artistic trial strives to *transmit the force of the story that could not be told* (or that failed to be transmitted or articulated) in the legal trial.

What Tolstoy's text, in this way, inquires into is not just the meaning of the case, nor even simply the enigma of the case's force, but *the general significance of failed attempts (in law, in history) to close abysses,* the meaning of repeated yet impossible historical attempts to use the vehicles of law to cover over great collective traumas by the rationality and by the technicality of legal trials, by accounts of the law and by the settlements of courts.

In repeating, thus, both the story of the trauma and the dynamics of the trial, literature explains why and how the trial (like the trauma) is not closed but partakes of a traumatic memory and of an unfinished business that is bound to receive a future legal sequence. Literature explains, in other words, why the trial, like the trauma, will (historically, traumatically) repeat itself.

The most important question of the trial of the century is the question of the final opening of the abyss as a future destiny of repetition of the trial that was supposed to close or to enclose it. But what, precisely, is the meaning of this *legal, social gap* and of the *gap in understanding* that confronts it and that is bewildered, puzzled, taken by surprise by it? What lies hidden from the eye inside the gap, what is *at the bottom* of this legal, cultural, or historical abyss, or what was *left in abeyance* by the trial and what, precisely, will repeat itself again is, I would suggest, a question whose significance we should have to reflect upon, to ponder, for the next few hundred years. It encapsulates already the historical significance, the ungrasped legal meaning of the trial of the twenty-first century.

6

Postscript: The Authority of Literature

"Literature," writes Paul Celan, "often shoots ahead of us."[38] Literature is ahead of us. I have suggested elsewhere that literature can be defined (accounted for and understood) as a specific mode of testimony; and that writers often feel compelled to testify through literary or artistic channels precisely when they know, or feel intuitively that, in the court of history (and, I will now add, in a court of law) *evidence will fail* or will *fall short;* when they know that other sorts of testimonies will, for different reasons, not come through or that events have taken place that will, for different reasons, not be evidenced.[39] Writers testify not simply when they know that knowledge cannot be obtained through other channels but, more profoundly, when they know or feel that knowledge, though available, cannot become eloquent, that *information cannot become consequen-*

38. Paul Celan, "The Meridian," trans. Jerry Glenn, *Chicago Review* 29 (Winter 1978): 34.

39. See Shoshana Felman and Dori Laub, *Testimony: Crises of Witnessing in Literature, Psychoanalysis, and History* (New York, 1992).

tial.[40] I have argued that such writers can be understood (defined) as *precocious witnesses*[41] ("literature often shoots ahead of us") and that their art, their narrative, their literary style, or their artistic rhetoric is a precocious mode of bearing witness and of accessing reality when all other modes of knowledge are precluded or are rendered ineffectual. I am suggesting here that Tolstoy's literary text is, in effect, such a *precocious testimony* in (and to) the O. J. Simpson trial.

"I almost finished *The Kreutzer Sonata* or *How a Husband Killed His Wife,*" Tolstoy announced in September 1889; "I am glad I wrote it: *I know that people need to be told what is written there.*" A century later, they still do (as the obsession with the murder story of the century has once more shown). "'I've only got one thing,'" says Pozdnyshev: "'It's *what I know.* Yes, *I know something it will take other people quite a while to find out about. . . .* No, people aren't going to find out what I know for quite a while to come'" (*KS,* p. 68). What knowledge (what secret knowledge about murder, what secret knowledge about death, what secret knowledge about life) does the confessant feel he has and that, unless he shares it, people are not likely to find out about? What does the husband-murderer know? And what does Tolstoy know? How does he know, why does he know? *For whom has Tolstoy confessed?*

And why was this confession of the husband—a confession which the O. J. Simpson trial could not get—in turn censored by the law? Why was there a conflict, in Tolstoy's day, between the confession and the law? Why did the Russian law try to reduce to silence the confession? What does Tolstoy know that can be confessed only *outside the law?* And why did the confessant, even in the fiction, in the literary story of *The Kreutzer Sonata,* feel that his confession could not be transformed into evidence in court, inside a trial? What sort of knowledge guided both Tolstoy and Pozdnyshev precisely as excluded from the trial? What sort of confession was it that had to be confessed not *to* the law, but *despite* the law? And why does the master writer treat the law itself as yet another subterfuge, another misrepresentation with respect to the truth of the confession?

40. Compare, for instance, the way in which, during the Second World War, messengers (such as the underground Polish courier Ian Karski) or escapees from Nazi concentration camps failed to inform the world about the Nazis' final aims. Information was forthcoming, but it could not reach its destination; knowledge existed, but it could not be effectively *transmitted* either to the Allied governments or to the endangered victims. "Most Jews in Europe . . . had at the very least heard rumors about some horrible events in Western Europe. . . . But they were either not believed or it was assumed that 'it cannot happen here.'" The bearers of the rumors were stigmatized as unreliable or mad (Felman and Laub, *Testimony,* p. 104 and chaps. 3–4, 6–7, esp. pp. 103–5, 231–39).

41. See *Testimony,* pp. xx, 12–40, 52.

The Confession and the Law (Between Violence and Speech)

While Simpson goes to Oxford to complain about the prejudices of the legal system and about the inequities of American justice,[42] Tolstoy writes a confession that declares the law incompetent to truly comprehend the crime or to address the real nature of the case. But the legal flaws do not become his alibi. He speaks not to evade responsibility but to testify: he speaks to *plead responsible.* While Simpson feels accomplished for the fact that he has been "convicted," as he says, "of nothing,"[43] and, within the trial, denies guilt and denies his presence at the crime scene irrespective of the evidence, Tolstoy pleads guilty irrespective of the verdict. Outside the trial, inside the confession, inside literature, he assumes the burden of a crime that is not literally his own but which he nonetheless profoundly acknowledges as his, and for which he assumes an exemplary personal (and cultural) responsibility. The confession does not ask, How can the law prevail? The confession asks, *What does speech mean in relation to an act of violence?* How can we recognize, how can we *expiate* a violence that is inscribed in culture as invisible and that cannot be rendered visible in court? How can speech *make visible* a violence whose very nature is to blind? How can we *see* this blinding violence? How can we use speech to *see hate,* to look at our own hatred, when hatred (and especially our own) is normally prohibited to sight?

The confession wishes to confer on speech the highest moral value and the highest epistemological responsibility: that of *accessing the truth;* that of truly *looking* at what has been accessed, no matter how unbearable or how incriminating; that of sacrificing alibis and of *acknowledging reality,* for whatever price.

The discourse of the alibi speaks, on the other hand, precisely *not to know* and especially *not to acknowledge.* "On the night of the murder, I was asleep." You will understand that, asleep, I was not a witness to myself. How can I know where I was? Even were I a somnambulist, I wouldn't know. Has there been a murder? Who was murdered? I cannot be cross-examined, since I have no answers. But I can be interviewed—I love to be interviewed—since I do have lots and lots of replies. "At the night of the murder, I was playing golf"; I was playing games with myself. The discourse of the alibi speaks to continue to play games with itself, to maintain both consciousness and conscience in a state of numbness, to remain asleep. The confession speaks to wake up.

Inside literature, outside the trial and despite the law, the confession speaks to turn away from subterfuge. Ordinary people—like Simpson, like ourselves—do not speak to turn away from subterfuge. We speak to

42. Compare Joanna Coles, "My Dinner with O. J.," *The Guardian,* 16 May 1996, sec. 2, pp. 1–3.

43. Ibid., p. 3.

avoid guilt. We speak to avoid pain. We use speech to protect ourselves. Profoundly, we speak to hope. "White America is still with me," insists Simpson to his British hosts.[44] "I'm more popular with women now than I was before."[45] "Our marriage," said Nicole and O. J. Simpson after the police had intervened on the issue of domestic violence, "our marriage is as strong today as it was on the day we married." Only master writers are prepared to say, like Kafka, "there is hope, but not for us." Only a Camus can write, "hope is not our business. Our business is to turn away from subterfuge."[46] Only a Tolstoy can have, indeed, the strength, the courage, the integrity, the moral readiness to pay the price of this confession (a price of guilt, of cruelty, of suffering, of loneliness, of death; a legal price: a price of censorship, of legal prohibition, of exclusion from the law), to dispossess himself (and us) of all emotional illusions, to sacrifice all self-deceptions so as to unmask lies at all costs and, at all costs, to destroy—to take apart—all social, all emotional, all cultural alibis. What does Tolstoy know, to feel so compelled to give life to this brutal legal case and publically to bare the husband's guilt? What moves the master writer, in thus assuming responsibility for a crime he did not in fact commit, to shock the world, to shake up his readership, to challenge and to tease the public's incredulity and scandalized amazement, to provoke the censor's ban, to defy the rage, the outrage of the church and of the state (not to speak of that, more private, of his own wife), all the while declaring (implying by the story) that no court of law can bring this case to justice, that the law is not equipped to understand the nature of the crime or to address the nature of the case. Could Tolstoy be right?

In the twentieth century, the law attempts, but fails, to solve or to resolve the case—to bring the murderer to justice—or to a confession. In the nineteenth century, the law attempts, but fails, to silence the confession's truth. It tries to outlaw the confession's publication, but it cannot arrest the case. Even censored, the text spreads. The handwritten manuscript is secretly read and, swiftly copied by thousands of hands, is reproduced, handwritten, by the thousands and, despite the censor, is made public and immediately distributed throughout the world, translated into many languages. "According to Strakhov, people no longer greeted each other in the street with 'How are you?' but with 'Have you read *The Kreutzer Sonata*?'" A century later, it is the same kind of obsession that propels the eager public toward the murder story of the O. J. Simpson case. "This has been a walking Rorschach test," says Medria Williams, a Los Angeles

44. Quoted in Stuart Jeffries, "O. J. Survives Ten-Minute Trial by Television," *The International Guardian*, 14 May 1996, p. 2.

45. Quoted in Coles, "My Dinner with O. J.," sec. 2, p. 3.

46. Albert Camus, "L'Espoir et l'absurde dans l'oeuvre de Franz Kafka," *Le Mythe de Sisyphe: Essai sur l'absurde* (Paris, 1942), p. 189; my translation.

psychologist, of the fascination with the O. J. Simpson trial: "People are reacting as if it's O. J. when it's really about themselves" (quoted in "W," p. 4). To whom, then, has Tolstoy confessed? Why have people been so *interested* at once in the *confession* and in the *absence of confession* that has marked the trial of the century? Why have people been so drawn both to the fiction and to the reality of this case? For whom has Tolstoy confessed? "'I'd been taken to the local police station and from there to prison. And there I remained for eleven months awaiting trial. During that time I thought a great deal about myself and my past life, and I grasped what it had all been about. . . .'"

The Secrets of the Case

> "I only began to grasp it when I saw her in her coffin. . . ." He gave a sob, but continued hastily, at once: "It was only when I saw her dead face that I realized what I'd done. I realized that I'd killed her, that it was all my doing and that from a warm, moving, living creature she'd been transformed into a cold, immobile, waxen one, and that there was no way of setting this to rights, not ever, not anywhere, not by any means. If you've never experienced that, you can't possibly understand." [*KS,* p. 118]

"'There was no way of setting this to rights, not ever, not anywhere, not by any means.'" Does Pozdnyshev narrate the out-of-court truth of the O. J. Simpson trial? Can literature be viewed precisely as the *record* of what has remained *out of the legal records?* What does Tolstoy know? And, having read Tolstoy, having watched the trial of the century, what do we in our turn know?

Of course, we cannot say we know—we do not know—whether Simpson did or did not in effect murder his wife. We *do* know that, like Pozdnyshev, he treated her with cruelty and brutal violence. We *do* know, therefore, that the nature of his love was murderous. And this he probably in turn did not grasp and did not realize until it had become too late. Whether or not he killed Nicole, the overwhelming terror of his own brutality Simpson must have faced only when, like Pozdnyshev, he suddenly saw his ex-wife dead.

We also do know that, whereas Tolstoy confesses to a murder he did not empirically commit, the brutal double murderer, whoever he might be, walks free and has not confessed to a crime he did most certainly commit.

Pozdnyshev was tried and acquitted, but the acquittal has not managed to redeem, to fix, or to restore his shattered life. The havoc that the murder has caused in his soul does not cease with the execution of the crime, nor do its repercussions in his life stop with the resolution of the trial. Having been pronounced not guilty, freed, he nonetheless remains chained to the bloody murder that no washing will erase, eradicate, or cleanse out of his life. He thus becomes the haunted captive of the bloody saga of which he has become the bearer and whose guilty secrets he will try, but will remain inherently unable, to divulge.

His destiny henceforth is to remain a hostage to the story of his violence: a (willing or unwilling) medium to the transformation of his case into a legend.

Pozdnyshev is willing. But he cannot acquit himself from this Sisyphean, endless task that goes against the grain of culture. He convicts himself. Culture acquits him. He cannot, in confessing, completely overcome the cultural taboos. But this is also his Sisyphean punishment—the testimonial or discursive punishment he takes upon himself. A haunted captive of a guilt which culture will not recognize, he will remain forever the life prisoner of a confession that he still (as in the trial) feels he cannot quite *transmit* (pass to the other's comprehension, *transform into evidence* on which a consensus can be reached) and that he therefore cannot quite unload and cannot fully *terminate*.

A Confession without End

He can only close the narrative of the confession with the outside interruption of the train's (interminable) arrest. The narrator quits confessing since he has to get off, go outside the train. Tolstoy himself will die in a train station, in the middle of the route and of a life itinerary that was not as yet exhausted, terminated.

But Pozdnyshev has not quite finished. He will certainly repeat again the story to some other passenger aboard some other train, on his way to a final destination that has not yet been—perhaps cannot be—reached. In the meantime, as the writer takes a (temporary) leave by bringing the last sentence to a close and by repeating (with a difference, with a double meaning) a last word that signals a departure and an ending ("*proschayte*, goodbye"), the confessant punctuates his exit from the train—and the story's open-endedness—only with the stated knowledge that his confession has not reached (or will not reach) its end, that it is bound to remain misunderstood:

> "There was no way of setting this to rights, not ever, not anywhere, not by any means. *If you've never experienced that, you can't possibly understand.*"

(In Tolstoy's own terms, Simpson might be the one reader who will understand Tolstoy; but of course, if only for this very reason, he wouldn't read.) The confession thus remains, despite all the publicity that the confessant gives it and despite himself, his secret, a secret he cannot communicate. And this guilty secret that the court will never understand remains, at the same time, the case's and the trial's secret.

> "They asked me in court how I killed her, what I used to do it with. Imbeciles! They thought I killed her that day, the fifth of October, with a knife. It wasn't that day I killed her, it was much earlier. Exactly in the same way as they're killing their wives now, all of them."

Recapitulations

It is because what they have asked in court cannot receive a simple answer—cannot be answered, in effect, except by *recapitulating* the whole story from the start; because the knife (the murder weapon or the signifier of the trauma) is unlocatable (unfindable) except in the life story as a whole, and in the marriage story as a whole—that the confession has to renarrate not just the murder but the failure of the marriage of which it reiterates again the violence, in showing how this unseen violence, of which the unseen knife was just the final signifier, inhabited the marriage from the start: a figure in the carpet.

Trying to make visible this figure in the carpet; trying to narrate again the story that could not be told in court, the confession in its turn cannot but *repeat* the trial and once more *relive* (retell) the horror of the crime. But it cannot divulge the trial's secret. It cannot *locate* the starting point of the trauma or fully translate the trauma's origin into articulateness, into evidence or into seeability. And it cannot convert the blindness of the court and the misunderstanding of the trial into a transparent meaning or into a fully formulated and exhausted intelligibility. The confession, therefore, cannot end. It is a discourse and a speech act that go on and that will continue to go on, for as long as Pozdnyshev lives, for as long as Tolstoy lives. It is a speech performance—a confession—whose assumed responsibility of renunciation of all alibis, whose cultural insight into the ungraspability of gender traumas, and whose burden of traumatic understanding, will continue to reverberate forever, beyond the end of Tolstoy's text and beyond the confessant's—and the author's—life or death.

> "I only began to grasp it when I saw her in her coffin. . . ." "It was only when I saw her dead face that I realized what I'd done. I realized that I'd killed her. . ., and that there was no way of setting this

to rights, not ever, not anywhere, not by any means. If you've never experienced that, you can't possibly understand."

"Prostite," or Justice and Mercy

Like Pozdnyshev, O. J. Simpson has (purportedly) shared with the public his life story, under the teasingly confessional title, *I Want to Tell You.* Like Tolstoy, he has published this life story as a book and has made a celebrated publication of a celebrated autobiography. Unlike Pozdnyshev, O. J. Simpson has claimed he is innocent and has no murder story to confess to. Unlike Tolstoy, he has chosen (by virtue of his right as a criminal defendant) *not to testify.*[47]

It is, however, for a different kind of court and for a different kind of justice that Tolstoy has testified, and has left a confession that has, perhaps, confessed for many others and that speaks, perhaps, for all of us: a confession that may well include, in Camus's terms, "a portrait of no one and of everyone";[48] a confession that (not by coincidence) no censor could stop, yet that no trial could contain; a confession that no legal argument could summarize, that no court could translate into coherent legal language, that no jury could hear, yet that no legal prohibition could reduce to silence; a confession that has spoken, and still speaks, outside the trial and despite the law to turn away from subterfuge; a confession that in fact has never ended and still does not end but begins again the endless trial; a confession that continues endlessly into the night of our culture, of our history.

> "Well, *prostite,* forgive me. . ."
>
> He turned away from me. . . . I went over to him in order to say goodbye. . . .
>
> "*Proschayte,* goodbye," I said, offering my hand. . . .
>
> "Yes, *prostite,* forgive me . . . " he said, repeating the word with which he had brought his story to an end. [*KS,* p. 118]

"By nightfall on judgement day," writes Francis X. Clines,

> the national throng of juror-voyeurs was discovering that justice can be tempered with mercy, for it looked, at long last, as if the end of

47. The main difference, in effect, between the criminal trial and its legal repetition in the civil trial derived from the fact that in the civil trial Simpson was *compelled to testify.* But his testimony, in its absolute denial of reality against all evidence ("I never owned such shoes—absolutely not"; "I never hit my wife—absolutely not"), still essentially continued to maintain his choice of legal silence (even in his courtroom speech) through his absolute *refusal to become a witness;* a witness not just to the crime but *to the trial;* a witness to himself—and to the evidence.

48. Camus, *La Chute* (Paris, 1956), p. 148; my translation.

> the O. J. spectacle was in sight. . . . Such mercy was to be hoped for as the white minivan [in which O. J. Simpson was released from jail after the acquittal] returned the football star free and clear to his home, and *dragged an old image back* across the national memoryscape. In fleet *recapitulation* of the white Bronco's via doloroso crawl, the van speeding along the L.A. freeways was *as inarticulate an attempt at closing a story cycle* as might have been scripted in the film factories beyond the California hills.[49]

Stories like the O. J. Simpson trial, or the story of the murder of the wife of *The Kreutzer Sonata,* do not end. Their not ending is, perhaps, in some way, part of their poetic justice. They survive as narratives the life and death of their narrators and the convictions or acquittals of their perpetrators.

The questions that Tolstoy's confession poses to our culture have outlived Tolstoy, as they will outlive the murderer of Nicole Brown Simpson and of Ronald Goldman. The significance of the confession will survive the repercussions of the known and unknown stories of the double murder and its transformation into the spectacular court version of the trial of the century. "The verdict has exposed a chasm in place for generations . . . . People are reacting as if it's O. J. when it's really about themselves." "People no longer greeted each other in the street with 'How are you?' but with 'Have you read *The Kreutzer Sonata?*'"

"The definition of a writer," says Kafka, "of such a writer, and the explanation of his effectiveness, to the extent that he has any: He is the scapegoat of mankind. He makes it possible for men to enjoy sin without guilt, *almost without guilt.*"[50]

Have you read *The Kreutzer Sonata?*

In a situation in which justice is impossible, in a culture that does not forgive, a literary story puts the century on trial and begs for mercy that it cannot receive.

"I looked at the children, at her battered face with its bruises, and

49. Clines, "And Now, the Audience Rests," p. 4.

50. Franz Kafka, letter to Max Brod, 5 July 1922, *The Basic Kafka,* ed. Michael Kowal (New York, 1979), p. 295.

for the first time I forgot about myself, about my marital rights and my injured pride; for the first time I saw her as a human being. And so insignificant did all that had hurt me and made me jealous appear, and so significant what I'd done, that I wanted to press my face to her hand and say: 'Forgive me!'—but I didn't dare to."

"Well, *prostite,* forgive me . . ."

He turned away from me. . . . I went over to him in order to say goodbye. . . .

"*Proschayte,* goodbye," I said, offering my hand. . . .

"Yes," *prostite,* forgive me . . ." he said, repeating the word with which he had brought his story to an end.

This article constitutes the second chapter of Shoshana Felman's book, The Juridical Unconscious: Trials and Traumas in the Twentieth Century (Cambridge, MA: Harvard University Press, 2002), pp.54–105; first published in Critical Inquiry, 23:4 (Summer 1997): 738–788.

Name Index